HOLT Handbook

Grammar • Usage • Mechanics • Sentences

Sixth Course

ANNOTATED TEACHER'S EDITION

Instructional Framework by

John E. Warriner

HOLT, RINEHART AND WINSTON

A Harcourt Education Company

Austin • Orlando • Chicago • New York • Toronto • London • San Diego

AUTHOR **JOHN E. WARRINER** taught for thirty-two years in junior and senior high schools and in college. He was a high school English teacher when he developed the original organizational structure for his classic *English Grammar and Composition* series. The approach pioneered by Mr. Warriner was distinctive, and the editorial staff of Holt, Rinehart and Winston have worked diligently to retain the unique qualities of his pedagogy in the *Holt Handbook*. John Warriner also co-authored the *English Workshop* series and edited *Short Stories: Characters in Conflict*.

STAFF CREDITS

EDITORIAL

Executive Editor
Robert R. Hoyt

Program Editor
Marcia L. Kelley

Project Editors
Eileen Joyce, Kathryn Rogers

Writing and Editing
David Bradford, Thomas Browne, Gail Coupland, Gabrielle Field, Scott Hall, Suzi Hunn, Karen Kolar, Sondra Maze, Theresa Reding, Jennifer Schwan

Copyediting
Michael Neibergall, *Copyediting Manager;* Mary Malone, *Copyediting Supervisor;* Elizabeth Dickson, *Senior Copyeditor;* Christine Altgelt, Joel Bourgeois, Emily Force, Julie A. Hill, Julia Thomas Hu, Jennifer Kirkland, Millicent Ondras, Dennis Scharnberg, *Copyeditors*

Project Administration
Marie Price, *Managing Editor;* Lori De La Garza, *Editorial Finance Manager;* Jennifer Renteria, Janet Riley, *Project Administration;* Margaret Sanchez, *Word Processing Supervisor;* Casey Kelly, Joie Pickett, *Word Processing*

Editorial Permissions
Janet Harrington, *Permissions Editor*

ART, DESIGN, AND PHOTO

Book Design
Diane Motz, *Senior Design Director;* Sally Bess, *Designer*

Graphic Services
Kristen Darby, *Manager*

Image Acquisitions
Joe London, *Director;* Jeannie Taylor, *Photo Research Supervisor;* Sarah Hudgens, *Assistant Photo Researcher;* Michelle Rumpf, *Art Buyer Supervisor;* Gillian Brody, *Art Buyer*

Cover Design
Bruce Bond, *Design Director*

PRODUCTION

Belinda Barbosa Lopez, *Senior Production Coordinator*
Carol Trammel, *Production Supervisor*
Beth Prevelige, *Senior Production Manager*

MANUFACTURING/ INVENTORY

Shirley Cantrell, *Manufacturing Supervisor*
Mark McDonald, *Inventory Planner*

ISBN 0-03-066141-2

1 2 3 4 5 6 7 8 9 048 05 04 03 02

CONTENTS IN BRIEF

CONTENTS

Part 1

Grammar, Usage, and Mechanics 1

Parts of Speech Overview
Identification and Function 2

CHAPTER 1

The Parts of a Sentence

CHAPTER

2

The Phrase

Kinds of Phrases and Their Functions. **58**

The Clause

Independent and Subordinate Clauses, Sentence Structure. . . . **80**

Agreement

CHAPTER 5

Subject and Verb, Pronoun and Antecedent **104**

Using Pronouns Correctly

CHAPTER 6

Case Forms of Pronouns; Special Pronoun Problems **136**

CHAPTER 7

Clear Reference

Pronouns and Antecedents **160**

Using Verbs Correctly

CHAPTER

8

Principal Parts, Tense, Voice, Mood **174**

Using Modifiers Correctly

CHAPTER

9

Forms and Uses of Adjectives and Adverbs; Comparison . . . **226**

Laura Gilpin, *Georgia O'Keeffe* (1953). Saf. neg. (P1979.230.4297). © 1981, Laura Gilpin Collection, Amon Carter Museum, Fort Worth, Texas.

Placement of Modifiers

CHAPTER

Misplaced and Dangling Modifiers **248**

A Glossary of Usage

Capitalization

Punctuation

End Marks and Commas **324**

Punctuation
Other Marks of Punctuation **354**

Spelling
Improving Your Spelling **394**

Song-Yuan Dynasties (13th century). Tray, brown and red lacquer with gilt background. Height, 1 in.; diameter, 9 in. #B83M9. The Avery Brundage Collection. Asian Art Museum of San Francisco.

Correcting Common Errors
Key Language Skills Review **426**

Contents   **T15**

CHAPTER

19   Improving Sentence Style 512

CHAPTER

20   Sentence Diagramming 530

John Warriner: In His Own Words

The name of John Warriner has long been associated with a rather formal style of teaching traditional school grammar. Interestingly, however, John Warriner did not consider himself primarily a grammarian but rather an English teacher. Also, he did not consider his books primarily grammar textbooks but rather reference handbooks for students and teachers of composition.

In his prefaces to *Handbook of English: Book One* and *Handbook of English: Book Two* (published in 1948 and 1951, respectively), Warriner articulated his vision of what his textbooks were intended to do and how they might best be used. What he had to say might surprise you.

First, Warriner's goal in preparing these books was to create "a completely flexible teaching tool adaptable to . . . any individual classroom." He did *not* design his books to be teaching texts in which the class moves sequentially from chapter to chapter, every student doing all the exercises along the way. In fact, he asserted just the opposite: "[A] book of this kind is not intended for methodical coverage from cover to cover. The book contains more material than any one class can handle in a single year. Teachers will teach those chapters that a particular class needs and will assign exercises in proportion to the need."

John Warriner: In His Own Words

In the 1940s and '50s, John Warriner (1907–1987) published his first grammar and composition textbooks. Mr. Warriner's goal as a teacher and as a writer was to help students learn to use English effectively in order to be successful in school and in life. Throughout the years that followed, Mr. Warriner revised his original books and wrote others, creating the series on which this textbook is based. Included in Mr. Warriner's books were a number of short essays to his students. In these essays, Mr. Warriner explored the role of language in human life, the importance of studying English, and the value of mastering the conventions of standard English.

We could tell you what John Warriner thought about the study of English, but we'd rather let you read what he himself had to say.

Language Is Human

"Have you ever thought about how important language is? Can you imagine what living would be like without it?

"Of all creatures on earth, human beings alone have a fully developed language, which enables them to communicate their thoughts to others in words, and which they can record in writing for others to read. Other creatures, dogs, for example, have ways of communicating their feelings, but they are very simple ways and very simple feelings. Without words, they must resort to mere noises, like barking, and to physical actions, like tail wagging. The point is that one very important difference between human beings and other creatures is the way human beings can communicate with

Warriner's first grammar and composition textbooks, published in the 1940s and '50s.

one another by means of this remarkable thing called language. When you stop to think about it, you realize that language is involved to some extent in almost everything you do. ”

(from *English Grammar and Composition: First Course*, 1986)

Warriner's English Grammar and Composition: Fourth Course, 1977

Why Study English?

“ The reason English is a required subject in almost all schools is that nothing in your education is more important than learning how to express yourself well. You may know a vast amount about a subject, but if you are unable to communicate what you know, you are severely handicapped. No matter how valuable your ideas may be, they will not be very useful if you cannot express them clearly and convincingly. Language is the means by which people communicate. By learning how your language functions and by practicing language skills, you can acquire the competence necessary to express adequately what you know and what you think. ”

(from *English Grammar and Composition: Fourth Course*, 1977)

Why Study Grammar?

“ Grammar is a description of the way a language works. It explains many things. For example, grammar tells us the order in which sentence parts must be arranged. It explains the work done by the various kinds of words—the work done by a noun is different from the work done by a verb. It explains how words change their form according to the way they are used. Grammar is useful because it enables us to make statements about how to use our language. These statements we usually call rules.

“The grammar rule that the normal order of an English sentence is subject-verb-object may not seem very important to us, because English is our native tongue and we naturally use this order without thinking. But the rule would be very helpful to people who are learning English as a second language. However, the rule that subjects and verbs 'agree' (when the subject is plural, the verb is plural), and the rule that some pronouns (*I, he, she, we, they*) are used as subjects while others (*me, him, her, us,*

Warriner's English Grammar and Composition: Third Course, 1982

John Warriner xix

Warriner was also attuned to the needs of individual students within a class, acknowledging that "students arrive with greatly varying degrees of mastery of language essentials. One student may be weak in sentence sense, another in pronoun usage. But each student requires for his [or her] special weakness a full text explanation, a wealth of examples, and practice material," which Warriner endeavored to provide.

To organize his material, Warriner separated language instruction into sections, choosing to present grammar before usage. His rationale for doing so was that a working understanding of grammar terms and concepts would provide students and teachers a common vocabulary for discussing usage concepts. However, Warriner was not comfortable with the implications of such a separation: "This is not to imply that grammar can be separated from usage in practice. *The only valid reason for teaching grammar at all is to apply it to specific usage problems* [emphasis added]."

Finally, in spite of his reputation as a grammar curmudgeon, John Warriner had some rather modern ideas about language. He believed that English was an evolving language and that appropriate usage varied according to the situation. In fact, Warriner was adamant that a language arts textbook "must make clear to students that correctness in English is not fixed, but variable, that there are levels of usage, and that any living language suffers change."

them) are used as objects—these are helpful rules even for native speakers of English.

"Such rules could not be understood—in fact, they could not be formed—without the vocabulary of grammar. Grammar, then, helps us to state how English is used and how we should use it. "

(from *English Grammar and Composition: Third Course*, 1982)

Why Is Punctuation Important?

"The sole purpose of punctuation is to make clear the meaning of what you write. When you speak, the actual sound of your voice, the rhythmic rise and fall of your inflections, your pauses and hesitations, your stops to take breath—all supply a kind of 'punctuation' that serves to group your words and to indicate to your listener precisely what you mean. Indeed, even the body takes part in this unwritten punctuation. A raised eyebrow may express interrogation more eloquently than any question mark, and a knuckle rapped on the table shows stronger feeling than an exclamation point.

"In written English, however, where there are none of these hints to meaning, simple courtesy requires the writer to make up for the lack by careful punctuation. "

(from *English Grammar and Composition: Fourth Course*, 1973)

English Grammar and Composition: Fourth Course, 1973

John Warriner

XX

Why Learn Standard English?

"Consider the following pair of sentences:
1. George don't know the answer.
2. George doesn't know the answer.

"Is one sentence clearer or more meaningful than the other? It's hard to see how. The speaker of sentence 1 and the speaker of sentence 2 both convey the same message about George and his lack of knowledge. If language only conveyed information about the people and events that a speaker is discussing, we would have to say that one sentence is just as good as the other. However, language often carries messages the speaker does not intend. The words he uses to tell us about events often tell us something about the speaker himself. The extra, unintended message conveyed by 'George don't know the answer' is that the speaker does not know or does not use one verb form that is universally preferred by educated users of English.

"Perhaps it is not fair to judge people by how they say things rather than by what they say, but to some extent everyone does it. It's hard to know what is in a person's head, but the language he uses is always open to inspection, and people draw conclusions from it. The people who give marks and recommendations, who hire employees or judge college applications, these and others who may be important in your life are speakers of educated English. You may not be able to impress them merely by speaking their language, but you are likely to impress them unfavorably if you don't. The language you use tells a lot about you. It is worth the trouble to make sure that it tells the story you want people to hear. "

(from *English Grammar and Composition: Fourth Course*, 1973)

TO OUR STUDENTS

What is grammar?

That seems like a simple question, doesn't it? Most of us have a sense of what grammar is even though we are seldom asked to define the term. Many people use the term *grammar* to mean "the rules of language." In this book, however, *grammar* has a more specific meaning. Here, *grammar* refers to the structure of language—to the words, phrases, and clauses that are the building blocks of sentences. Grammar gives us the labels we use to talk about language.

What about the rules that govern how language is used in various social situations? In this book, these rules are called usage. Unlike grammar, **usage** determines what is considered standard ("isn't") or nonstandard ("ain't") and what is considered formal ("why") or informal ("how come"). Usage is a social convention, a behavior or rule customary for members of a group. As a result, what is considered acceptable usage can vary from group to group and from situation to situation.

To speak standard English requires a knowledge of grammar and of standard usage. To write standard English requires something more—a knowledge of mechanics. *Mechanics* refers to the rules for written, rather than spoken, language. Spelling, capitalization, and punctuation are concepts we don't even think about when we are speaking, but they are vital to effective written communication.

Why should I study grammar, usage, and mechanics?

Many people would say that you should study grammar to learn to root out errors in your speech and writing. Certainly, the *Holt Handbook* can help you learn to avoid making errors and to correct the errors you do make. More importantly, though, studying grammar, usage, and mechanics gives you the skills you need to take

To Our Students   xxi

sentences and passages apart and to put them together, to learn which parts go together and which don't. Instead of writing sentences and passages that you hope sound good, you can craft your sentences to create just the meaning and style you want.

Knowing grammar, usage, and mechanics gives you the tools to understand and discuss your own language, to communicate clearly the things you want to communicate, and to develop your own communication style. Further, mastery of language skills can help you succeed in your other classes, in future classes, on standardized tests, and in the larger world—including, eventually, the workplace.

How do I use the *Holt Handbook*?

The skills taught in the *Holt Handbook* are important to your success in reading, writing, speaking, and listening.

Not only can you use this book as a complete grammar, usage, and mechanics textbook, but you can also use it as a reference guide when you work on any piece of writing. Whatever you are writing, you can use the *Holt Handbook* to answer your questions about grammar, usage, capitalization, punctuation, and spelling.

How is the *Holt Handbook* organized?

The *Holt Handbook* is divided into three main parts:

● **PART 1** The **Grammar, Usage, and Mechanics** chapters provide instruction on and practice using the building blocks of language—words, phrases, clauses, capitalization, punctuation, and spelling. Use these chapters to discover how to take sentences apart and analyze them. The last chapter, **Correcting Common Errors,** provides additional practice on key language skills as well as standardized test practice in grammar, usage, and mechanics.

● **PART 2** The **Sentences** chapters include **Writing Clear Sentences, Combining Sentences, Improving Sentence Style,** and **Sentence Diagramming.** The first three of these provide instruction on and practice with writing correct, clear, and interesting sentences. **Sentence Diagramming** teaches you to analyze and diagram sentences so you can see how the parts of a sentence relate to each other.

PART 3 The **Resources** section includes **Manuscript Form,** a guide to presenting your ideas in the best form possible; **The History of English,** a concise history of the English language; **Test Smarts,** a handy guide to taking standardized tests in grammar, usage, and mechanics; and **Grammar at a Glance,** a glossary of grammatical terms.

How are the chapters organized?

Each chapter begins with a Diagnostic Preview, a short test that covers the whole chapter and alerts you to skills that need improvement, and ends with a Chapter Review, another short test that tells you how well you have mastered that chapter. In between, you'll see rules, which are basic statements of grammar, usage, and mechanics principles. The rules are illustrated with examples and followed by exercises and reviews that help you practice what you have learned.

What are some other features of this textbook?

- **Oral Practice**—spoken practice and reinforcement of rules and concepts
- **Writing Applications**—activities that let you apply grammar, usage, and mechanics concepts in your writing
- **Tips & Tricks**—easy-to-use hints about grammar, usage, and mechanics
- **Meeting the Challenge**—questions or short activities that ask you to approach a concept from a new angle
- **Style Tips**—information about formal and informal uses of language
- **Help**—pointers to help you understand either key rules and concepts or exercise directions

Holt Handbook on the Internet

As you work through the *Holt Handbook,* you will find the best online resources at **go.hrw.com.**

To Our Students   xxiii

Teaching Strands

Connecting Grammar and Writing

This teaching-strand chart shows you some ways to connect grammar instruction and writing instruction.

The *Holt Handbook* is designed to be a flexible teaching tool that accommodates many teaching philosophies and styles. For example, some teachers will prefer to use the handbook as a reference source, having students refer to it only as the need for explicit grammar instruction arises. Others will use the handbook as a teaching text, having their classes work through the instruction, examples, and exercises in a more methodical fashion. Your personal teaching style and the needs of your students will determine the best way for you to teach this material.

 GO TO: go.hrw.com

Writing Assignments	Rationale
DESCRIPTIVE ESSAY	Good descriptive writing relies on the precise images created by modifiers, including vivid single-word adjectives, adverbs, and well-chosen prepositional and verbal phrases.
LITERARY RESEARCH PAPER	A formal, academic paper exploring literature requires varying sentence structure. Using exact language, an objective tone, and correct citation of support establishes credibility.
LITERARY ANALYSIS	A literary analysis uses literary present tense and requires correct use of italics, quotation marks, and commas in citations. Supporting quotations, which may contain clauses, may need ellipses.
LITERARY ESSAY	Literary essays need correctly capitalized and punctuated support. Literary present tense, specific nouns, and correct subject-verb agreement are useful for plot summaries.
REFLECTIVE ESSAY	Reflective essays require careful choice of pronouns, verb tense and mood, and modifiers. Correct usage of dialogue, including contractions, is vital.
COMPARISON-CONTRAST ESSAY	Comparing and contrasting calls for comparative forms of adjectives and adverbs. Coordinating and correlative conjunctions show relationships of ideas.
PERSUASIVE ESSAY	Using active-voice verbs reinforces supporting opinions in persuasive essays. Careful word selection and the absence of double negatives produce clear support. Questions and exclamations can add emotional punch.
NONFICTION ANALYSIS	Carefully chosen words can capture a work's essence. Citations of titles, details, and direct quotations must be properly capitalized and punctuated. Using adjective clauses eliminates short, choppy sentences.
SHORT STORY	Action and conflict may develop through correctly punctuated dialogue, which may contain informal contractions and dialects. Similes and metaphors may use prepositions and predicate nominatives.
MEDIA ANALYSIS	Comparing and contrasting media may use words such as *however* and *therefore* as well as adjectives and adverbs. Parallel structure may involve using correlative conjunctions, verbal phrases, and relative clauses.

Links to Grammar	Links to Usage	Links to Mechanics
adjectives, adverbs (Ch. 1)	comparison of modifiers (Ch. 9)	punctuation of items in a series (Ch. 13)
phrases (Ch. 3)	placement of phrase modifiers (Ch. 10)	punctuation of introductory and nonessential phrases (Ch. 13)
sentences, clauses (Ch. 4)	placement of modifiers (Ch. 10)	semicolons, citing references (Ch. 14)
parts of a sentence (Ch. 2)	clear reference (Ch. 7)	words often confused (Ch. 15)
verbs, pronouns (Ch. 1)	verb tense and sequence (Ch. 8); double subjects (Ch. 11)	spelling with suffixes, prefixes (Ch. 15)
clauses, sentence types (Ch. 4)	placement of modifiers (Ch. 10)	ellipses, colons, italics, commas, quotation marks (Ch. 14)
nouns (Ch. 1)	literary present tense (Ch. 8)	ellipses, colons, italics, quotation marks (Ch. 14)
verbs (Ch. 1)	subject-verb agreement (Ch. 5)	
pronouns, adjectives, action verbs (Ch. 1)	comparisons of modifiers (Ch. 9); tense, mood (Ch. 8)	capitalization of I (Ch. 12); possessives (Ch.14)
clauses, sentence types (Ch. 4)		quotation marks, semicolons, contractions (Ch. 14)
adjectives, adverbs (Ch. 1)	form and use of modifiers (Ch. 9)	spelling with suffixes (Ch. 15)
conjunctions (Ch. 1); compound sentences (Ch. 4)	subject-verb agreement with compound subjects (Ch. 5)	punctuating compound sentences (Ch. 13 & Ch. 14)
linking, action verbs (Ch. 1)	active, passive voice (Ch. 8)	end marks (Ch. 13)
parts of speech (Ch. 1)	double negatives, formal English (Ch. 11)	words often confused (Ch. 15)
adjective clauses, relative pronouns (Ch. 4)	pronoun case (Ch. 6)	punctuating clauses (Ch. 13)
sentence types and structure (Ch. 4)		capitalizing and punctuating titles and quotations (Ch. 12 & Ch. 14)
pronouns, prepositions (Ch. 1)	pronoun-antecedent agreement (Ch. 5); like, as (Ch. 11)	capitalization and punctuation of dialogue, contractions (Ch. 14)
predicate nominatives (Ch. 2)	pronoun case (Ch. 6)	
adjectives, adverbs, conjunctions (Ch. 1)	comparative and superlative modifiers (Ch. 9)	semicolons, italics, quotation marks for titles (Ch. 14)
phrases (Ch. 3); relative clauses (Ch. 4)	intervening phrases (Ch. 5); who, which, that (Ch. 11)	commas for nonrestrictive phrases, clauses (Ch. 13)

By Amy Benjamin

Dispelling the Myths about Grammar Instruction

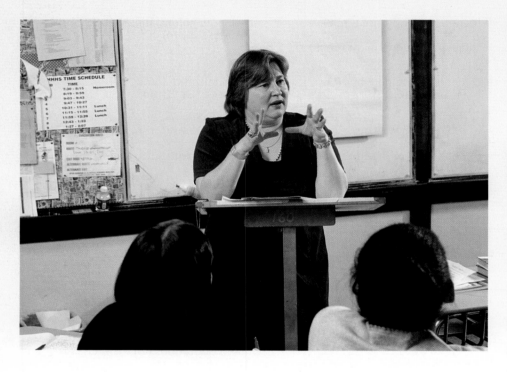

because those lessons in syntax, placement, word classification, and the subtleties of style helped them to be better writers, more efficient readers, clearer thinkers.

It is not uncommon for English teachers as well as their trainers and supervisors to hold that the teaching of grammar is quaint and unnecessary at best, prejudicial and exclusionary at worst.

I know an excellent English teacher whose students, many years after graduation, remember her for her grammar lessons. Unfortunately, instead of being proud of this, she is chagrined. . . . "*Grammar*!? Of all things in my class to remember! Why *grammar*? Why can't they remember me for all the wonderful literature I taught them? for what I taught them about composition? expression? creativity? Why just *grammar*? I don't even teach *grammar* anymore. I teach the *writing* process."

Perhaps these students remembered their grammar lessons because of the usefulness of those lessons or because of the satisfaction that they derived from learning challenging material. Perhaps they remembered

How lamentable it is that teaching writing through a process approach has become an orthodoxy in which the grammatical strand of English language arts is pitted against the literary strand, as if the two are not intertwined. Who set up this false dichotomy? The notion that grammar instruction is antithetical to the writing process is specious. My purpose in this essay is to debunk some of the myths about grammar instruction and to refurbish its tarnished reputation.

It is not uncommon for English teachers as well as their trainers and supervisors to hold that the teaching of grammar is quaint and unnecessary at best, prejudicial and exclusionary at worst. The problem begins with muddy terminology. Some people conflate the terms *grammar, usage,* and *mechanics,* as well as the terms *correct/incorrect* and *standard/non-standard.* Before I turn my fire extinguisher on the grammar myths, let me clarify my terms: By *grammar,* I refer to the rules which govern how words function in a sentence to make meaning. That *man bites dog* means something different from *dog bites man* is a function of grammar. By *usage,* I refer to the social conventions that determine what is considered standard. By *standard,* I do not mean *correct.* I mean that style of the English language which most educated people accept in formal circumstances. By *mechanics,* I refer to physical manifestations of language such as spelling, punctuation, capitalization and other conventions. In the case of *mechanics,* the terms *correct* and *incorrect* are more appropriate than they are when we are talking about matters of usage, but even spelling is not without gray areas.

Reasonable people can disagree over matters of content and methodology in teaching. However, I think everyone would agree that to under-stand a complicated system we need to know the names of its parts, their forms and functions, how the parts relate to the whole, and where these parts belong if the system is to operate at maximum efficiency. That said, here's what some people say about grammar instruction, and why I dis-agree with them.

Myth #1:

The explicit teaching of grammar does not improve writing ability, so time spent on grammar is time not spent on more worthy pursuits in the English classroom.

Think about it. Suppose my car is making a funny noise. Suppose I have no better understanding of what is going on under the hood than that. I take it to my mechanic, trusting his knowledge, integrity, and skill. He'll figure out what's wrong with my car and fix the problem. I'll pay the bill, and if all is not well, I'll get either another mechanic or another car. That is how many car owners (myself included) operate. We don't have the time or the inclination to learn the taxonomy, nomenclature, and anato-my of our cars.

When we don't speak explicitly to students about grammar, syntax, dic-tion, and coherence, we have to resort to the "funny noise" method: We have to say "This part just doesn't sound right here," or "You're not saying this clearly." We may be able to help writers fix the sentence, but we haven't given them the generality that will allow them to apply what they've learned to similar circumstances.

On the other hand, I can know the names of all the tools in my toolbox, what each is for, and how they relate to one another; but if I don't use them to facilitate an actual job in progress, then my knowledge does not fulfill its intended purpose. For many of us, the grammar lessons that we learned in school were about "picking out." We'd "pick out" all kinds of structures: the parts of speech, subjects and predicates, simple subjects, helping verbs. Later, we'd hunt down adverbial clauses, sub-ject complements, infinitives. We'd underline and double underline. We'd diagram. The trouble with our instruction was not that it was misguided, but that it was unfinished. Having learned to spot prepositional phrases, we may not have learned why doing so could improve our discourse.

How can we *use* our ability to iden-tify grammatical structures such as prepositional phrases in our own reading and writing? We may have learned that the object of a preposi-tion must be in the objective case, and that the object of a preposition is never the subject of the sentence. This knowledge helps us solve some usage problems, but that is not its main value. Knowing how to discern the subject and verb can help us read dense prose. When reading dense prose, the reader needs strategies. One such strategy is to reduce the sentence to its subject and verb. That done, the reader sees prepositional phrases for what they are: details. Beyond that, knowing about prepositions helps writers add sentence variety, as they learn not to begin sentence after sentence with the subject. Beginning a sentence with a prepositional phrase can set the stage for the action, but we have to be judicious: Sometimes, that prepositional phrase can be distracting or redundant. As modifiers, prepositional phrases can be movable, and their placement affects meaning, rhythm, and emphasis. Prepositional phrases, "time and place words," add detail and dimension. The novice writer who has difficulty fleshing out a topic can do well to consciously add more prepositional phrases. It is knowing what prepositional phrases can and can't do for you that makes being able to identify them worthwhile. Selecting standard pronoun case, creating purposeful variety in sentence structure, adding detail and dimension, and eliminating redundancy are some good reasons for being able to recognize prepositional phrases.

It is knowing what prepositional phrases can and can't do for you that makes being able to identify them worthwhile.

Recognition of a grammatical structure is only the beginning. If we think of grammar instruction as building an awareness of language choices available to the careful writer, then we view such instruction in two phases: recognition and application. Too often, the application phase does not happen. When it does not, the recognition phase seems to lack practicality. Thus does grammar instruction fall out of favor.

Myth #2:
Grammar instruction applies only to the editing phase of the writing process.

When people operate under this myth, they are confusing grammar with usage and mechanics. Usage and mechanics may be seen as "touch-ups," part of the finishing-off of a written piece. As such, they are not essential to the real intellectual work of the process, although no one should minimize their importance. Usage and mechanics can determine the first and last impressions that the reader gets of the writer's work. The point is that we should not limit our understanding of grammar to the surface features of usage and mechanics.

Along with diction and rhetoric, grammar (unlike usage and mechanics) is *organic* to the crafting of sentences and text. Writers with an awareness of grammar can make informed choices about how word order affects meaning. Picture a carpenter. He doesn't just blindly reach into his toolbox, pull out a screwdriver, try to make it do the work of a wrench, and figure he'll just sand down the rough spots later. We can make our students better writers if we teach them to use grammatical knowledge consciously as they match their syntax to their intentions.

We understand the power of graphic organizers in both reading and writing for many learners. We teach students to map their ideas as a prewriting strategy. We teach them to make Venn diagrams to show similarities and differences, and flowcharts to express sequence. Sentence structures are patterns. We can think in terms of certain grammatical templates, containers, that work well for certain types of ideas. Parallel structure and compound sentences or simple sentences with compound constituents are good containers for *like* elements bearing equal importance. Complex sentences are good containers to use when we need to show the backgrounding and foregrounding of elements that do not bear equal importance. Sentence structure selections occur in the drafting and revision stages of the writing process, as the writer searches for the clearest, most efficient way to express thoughts.

Many writers have an intuitive sense of what kinds of containers work best with what kinds of ideas. When we bring this underlying awareness of grammar to the conscious level, we help students manage inchoate ideas in the same way that a graphic organizer, such as a Venn diagram, might. Indeed, there is much to be said for using one of the many versions of graphic organizers *along with* sentence structure templates. The writer can then look at a branch diagram or a cluster, decide how the ideas are related, and then consider an array of syntactical containers to suit them.

What I've described is a way of understanding the role of grammar in the writing process that is deeper than what is commonly thought, i.e., that grammatical thinking enters the picture only as the cleanup man. In fact, we already make intuitive grammatical choices as we compose our thoughts. Those intuitive choices may or may not be the best ones for the purpose. By building awareness of sentence and textual structure, we can increase our chances that our message is clear, efficient, and graceful.

Myth #3:
Grammar is boring.

There are many ways to make our classrooms boring. We can "cover material" in a perfunctory way, "going over" the exercises done for homework or as seatwork. We can convey to students that their language is "wrong" and ours is "right." We can be language prudes, fainting and blanching at every double negative or misplaced modifier that dares to show its face in our presence. We can insist that the answer key is always the authority and that grammar is a "no discussion" subject. We can isolate the study of grammar, treat it as something we "have to get through" before moving on to literature. We can fail to make any connection between grammar and journalism, grammar and advertising, grammar and novels, grammar and drama, grammar and music, grammar and poetry. These are ways to make grammar boring.

I've heard teachers claim that grammar instruction interferes with creativity.

I've heard teachers claim that grammar instruction interferes with creativity. "Grammar is boring," they say. "And writing should be fun and interesting." This is a misguided notion, because creativity thrives within structure. The sonneteer works within a strictly prescribed structure, choosing that structure because it is the best container for particular ideas. The sonnet form is not constraining but liberating: The format frees the writer from decisions about rhythm and rhyme scheme. Because of the structure, half the work is done. I can't think of any creative pursuit—music, fine arts, dance, photography, drama, writing—that does not demand mastery of technique. I can't think of any creative pursuit in which there is no terminology, no anatomy, no structure, no tradition, no rules. Why would learning any kind of writing, much less creative writing, be detached from the fundamentals? Knowledge of structure is not a hindrance, but a guide that enables, rather than impedes, creativity.

Sometimes, grammar instruction is thought of as "drill and kill." This pejorative implies that the instruction will consist of lower level thinking skills, mindless repetition, and lack of application to authentic language. We picture fill-in-the-blank workbook-type questions in which there is one right answer. The book that you have in your hands is an extremely useful, in fact indispensable, tool for the teaching of language. However, any grammar text is most effective when used *along with*, not in place of, literature and student writing. It might seem that students would naturally make the crossover from what they learn in grammar exercises to their own language use, but such is not necessarily the case. As teachers, we have to make that crossover happen very deliberately, pointing out structures that students have learned and how those structures are used to make meaning in authentic contexts. Thus does grammar instruction transcend the practice exercises that illustrate targeted concepts.

Everybody loves language; children and teenagers love it especially, because they are in the process of defining their own culture by laying claim to words and expressions all their own. When we invite students to analyze their own neologisms, grammatical idiosyncrasies, and dialectical styles, we enliven grammar lessons immeasurably. As English teachers, we embrace all forms of the English language even while we recognize that mastery of standard English is essential for success in certain precincts of society.

Another way to make grammar instruction interesting is to let students discover how language changes right before our eyes. Movies and novels set in various pockets of the English-speaking world are museums of linguistic anthropology. Compare the idioms of *To Kill A Mockingbird* to those of *The Color Purple*. Analyze the language of a movie set in New Orleans and compare it to the language of a movie set in Los Angeles.

There are many ways to make our classrooms interesting. Our love of the subject is contagious. Grammar is exciting and rewarding to learn not because we get the answers right, but because we've applied logic and found patterns, and because there may be more than one answer, depending on the circumstances, audience, and purpose. Contrary to myth, a good grammar lesson can invite a lively discussion about ambiguities in meaning and the best way to express thought in a particular context. It can even ignite a discussion about social power structures, prejudices, and immigration. This is not boring stuff.

Myth #4:

Grammar applies only to English classes.

For lack of a better term, we refer to subjects other than English as "content areas." Aside from the obvious expectation that we use standard English in school, how can students apply grammar to their content area classes?

Every teacher wants students to be better readers. A law student told me recently that she was glad that she knew something about grammar, because she needed it to read complex materials in her courses. She found that by mentally pulling out the subject and verb, she could follow the lines of technical text.

Needless to say, grammatical knowledge of the English language is essential for learning another language. Just as grammar has fallen out of favor in many English classes, it has suffered a similar blow in the pedagogy of learning other languages as well, where grammar instruction has been supplanted by "conversation." The predictable consequence has been much confusion and frustration for both teachers, who feel that their hands are tied, and students, many of whom are bewildered by the gymnastics of the French verb when they don't even know how English verbs behave.

What about science, math, social studies, the arts? All teachers love words. The biology teacher is fussy about the difference between *osmosis* and *diffusion*. Getting students to make fine distinctions is an important part of teaching students to think like scientists. Teachers want to give away the words of their subject areas the way grandmothers want to give away food. We want to invite our students into the professional conversation of our subject areas.

> # Teachers want to give away the words of their subject areas the way grandmothers want to give away food.

As English teachers, we love words about words, language about language. To us, there is a vast difference between an action verb and a linking verb, a predicate nominative and a direct object, a transitive verb and an intransitive verb. In teaching students to talk the talk, we turn them into licensed operators, not just amateurs. A licensed operator can make the machinery run more efficiently, can anticipate potential problems, and can fix what is wrong. An amateur *hopes* that the sentence "sounds good."

Grammar should be the permeable membrane that allows knowledge learned in English class to transform into skill in the content area classes. Active voice may be preferable in English classes where the subject is often *people doing things* (S-V-O). In composing a lab report, however, passive voice may be the better choice. *The difference in pressure was recorded* might sound more scientific than *I recorded the difference in pressure*. In the language of lab reports, the fact that the technician did the action is irrelevant. A radiologist writes her report in the passive voice: *No abnormalities were found*, rather than *I found no abnormalities*. In English class, we show students the difference in tone between active and passive voice.

It is important to learn to think in action verbs in all subject areas. A student who is writing about the Reformation needs to focus on who did what: *Martin Luther <u>translated</u> the Bible into the German vernacular. His translation <u>enabled</u> more people to read the Bible*. The action verbs tell the story. They give students a starting point when writing and a focus when reading. All subject areas use this concept; it is we English teachers who actually teach it in our grammar lessons.

The social studies teacher and the science teacher may not know it, but the benefits of grammar instruction are carried through the student's entire day.

Myth #5:
Grammar instruction is ethnocentric and prejudicial.

As English teachers, we need to avoid giving the impression that we are the designated Keepers of the Language. We can teach the etiquette of standard English without denying a student the right to his or her own dialect.

An educated person has that social thermostat that linguists call code-switching. The metaphor of table manners is apt: What we are expected to do at an outdoor barbecue differs from what we're expected to do at Thanksgiving dinner. Those of us who can't tell the difference, who can't code-switch, are socially awkward. This is not to say that standard English is better than any particular dialect. Standard English is not more expressive, more poetic, or even more accurate. It is simply the expected currency of mainstream society in formal situations. We don't have to use it all of the time, but if we *can't* use it when it is expected, then we are at a cultural disadvantage that our education should remedy.

We are constantly making impressions that indicate our understanding of our social context. Those who are successful in their chosen fields,

indeed, those for whom a chosen field is an option in the first place, know how to control the impression that others have of them. People judge our status and education levels not only through language, but also through dress, manners, and gesture.

Once we acknowledge that standard English is just another form of English that is appropriate for certain situations but not for all, then we are free to enjoy the dialects of English that we find in authentic literature, regional speech, song lyrics, and casual conversation. We can look at new coinages, popular metaphors, slang, and jargon with the interest of a linguist rather than the arrogance of a pedant.

We can teach the etiquette of Standard English without denying a student the right to his or her own dialect.

That language is a changing social contract is evidenced by grammar books of yore. Even in one generation, the *who/whom* distinction has attenuated, as has the use of the past perfect tense of verbs. Certain usages, such as the nominative case after a linking verb, sound stuffy. We have yet to solve the problem that exists because we lack a generic singular pronoun: *He*, once preferred, is thought to be sexist; *one* sounds stilted and British; *they* is a grammatical mismatch. That leaves *he or she*, which can seem awfully conspicuous. It's interesting to have students compare the style guides of various publications on sensitive points such as this.

Myth #6:

As native speakers, we don't have to learn grammar.

It is true that we already know grammar intuitively. Native speakers learn, quite naturally, how to put words together to make meaning. What we don't learn naturally is the metalanguage, that is, the language of language. Absent that, we can't explain what we mean about what we are trying to say, and others are at a loss to help us.

Terminology is powerful.

Recently, I worked with a group of elementary school teachers who were looking for teaching strategies that would improve their students' writing skills. When I suggested that they develop a scope and sequence in grammar skills, they were skeptical. "They already know how to use adjectives, nouns, and verbs," one teacher said. "Why do they have to know the *names* of these things?" "That just isn't the way we teach anymore," said another with a wave of her hand. "We don't want to interfere with the children's creativity. Teaching them grammar would interrupt their flow." A fourth-grade teacher added, "But that isn't on the state test, and we really don't have time for anything that doesn't get the scores up." Here's what I would answer:

Terminology is powerful. We can't improve our sentences until we understand the crucial role played by verbs. We certainly can't understand that role until we know how to identify verbs in context and that verbs come in various flavors: finite verbs, infinitives, participles, gerunds.

Further, creativity and "flow" are enhanced, not impeded, by knowledge of language structure and what certain kinds of phrases and sentences can and can't do. When the reader has to stumble over and re-read awkward, redundant, convoluted, or misplaced structures within sentences, does it matter how creative the writer was? Doesn't the logic of grammar *improve* the flow of prose?

To answer the last objection, the statewide tests may or may not have explicit questions regarding grammar. Some do; some don't, and the nature of those tests can and will change. What will not change is that a writer who knows where commas belong makes the job easier on the reader, as does the writer who understands subordination, agreement, and overall sentence management. If we acknowledge that the whole purpose of writing is to communicate, and that communication is accomplished by writing clearly, then we can see the application of grammar to writing. Of course, if grammar instruction never makes the leap from identification of a structure to its effective application, then these teachers are right to reject it as largely irrelevant.

What Knowing Grammar Can Do for Writers

Finally, here is a list of what you can do when you know a few things about grammar:

- If you know how to use parallel structure, you can make your message smoother, clearer, easier on the reader, more logical, and more memorable.

- If you know when to use active voice and when to use passive voice, you can control the directness or indirectness of your message. You control the power and impact of your words. You can also avoid the trouble that comes from being too direct or accusatory.

- If you know how to use verb tense consistently, you can guide your reader through the tangle of time in your narrative.

- If you know how to vary the grammatical constructs in your sentence

structure, you can make your flow of sentences more musical, more nuanced, less choppy.

- If you know the difference between a phrase, a clause, and a sentence, you can guide your reader by using well-placed punctuation.

Like poetry, grammar is about the beauty of expressing exactly what we mean by placing the words just right.

Understanding how grammar works puts the writer on the right path. When writers begin a definition by saying "Osmosis is *when* . . ." they are failing to apply the concept that a subject complement, not an adverbial clause, must follow a linking verb. The "*is when* . . ." definition is going to fall on its face because the key term has not been handled properly in the sentence. Definitions call for classification. First, we must place the term in its proper realm: "Osmosis is a . . . process? means? phenomenon?" The writer must stop and think about what *kind* of thing osmosis is. Such categorical thinking is absolutely essential to the scientist, but it does not happen with the ungrammatical ". . . *is when*" structure. This example demonstrates the relation-

ship between grammar and the logical progression of ideas.

Knowing grammar is useful, but even if it weren't, learning it would still be worthwhile because it is interesting. Like chess, grammar is about how power and proximity govern relationships and possibilities. Like engineering, grammar is about structure, balance, efficiency and strength. Like mathematics, grammar is about patterns and forms. Like geology, grammar is at once eternal and dynamic. Like poetry, grammar is about the beauty of expressing exactly what we mean by placing the words just right. ■

Amy Benjamin is an English teacher at Hendrick Hudson High School in Montrose, New York. In addition, she is a consultant to teachers, administrators, staff developers, and people in the business world. Amy specializes in showing people how to use clear, concise language. She has written several books about teaching literacy skills in all subject areas, as well as two plays (Romeo and Juliet Will Not Be Performed Tonight *and* Romeo and Juliet: Still Not Dead) *and a young adult novel* (Russell Kim: My Real Name). *Amy lives in Fishkill, New York, with her husband Howard and son Mitch.*

By Brock Haussamen

Grammar: Why Teach It?

Why should students learn—and teachers teach—grammar? Simply memorizing the parts of speech doesn't, by itself, make students better writers. Worrying about errors can quickly dampen student enthusiasm for a writing project. Over the past three decades, grammar's reputation has suffered. Is grammar useful? Why teach it?

I believe the central reason for teaching and learning grammar is that it gives all of us a language for talking about language, and certainly the ability to talk about language is a fundamental educational goal. It is difficult to discuss sentences without knowing basic grammar in the same way that it is difficult to talk about a sport or a science or politics without knowing the names of its elements and how they are organized. Knowing basic grammar is what enables students to discuss the sentences in a book they are reading or in a paper they are writing, and to discuss their native language or a second language.

Think of grammar as having two faces. One is its public face, which can be quite formal. The other face is private and more friendly.

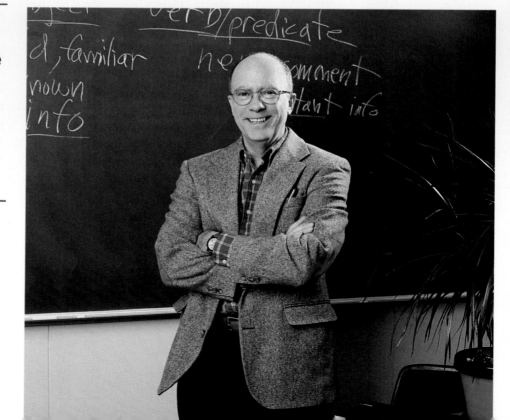

The Two Faces of Grammar

To teach grammar effectively, we need to show students how to put it to use. The language of grammar—the names for the parts of speech and other sentence components that appear in the grammar section of this textbook—has two distinct kinds of uses. Think of grammar as having two faces. One is its public face, which can be quite formal. The other face is private and more friendly.

Public Grammar

The public face of grammar consists of all the rules we teach students to follow in their writing and all the errors we tell them to avoid making. In this textbook it is the material in the sections on usage and mechanics. I call usage and mechanics "public grammar" because they identify the conventions of the standard American dialect in which our society carries on its formal writing and speaking. There are many good reasons to teach these conventions. Such a standard dialect helps people from different places and different backgrounds to communicate clearly. The conventions of public grammar help sustain the uniformity of our writing system, on which our society depends utterly. Finally, they reflect the language of economic power. In general, people who can write and speak according to the standard conventions have a better chance at participating in the influential core of our society. People who do not master those conventions will likely face obstacles at every turn.

It is important for us to remember and to remind our students that public grammar is different from, not inherently better than, the language students normally use. The do's and don'ts of public grammar create an illusion that they are rigorously logical, like the rules of mathematics, and that they are permanent. Neither of these claims is true. The do's and don'ts are sometimes illogical, and they change. Just a few decades ago, grammar textbooks like this one would have insisted on the distinction between *will* and *shall*; today that distinction is all but gone. A few decades into the future, a book such as this will probably simplify and may even omit the distinction between *who* and *whom*, which is already fading in informal English.

The "right" clothes, like the "right" grammar, depend on what is appropriate or expected in a given situation.

Try explaining to your students that their grammar is like the clothes they wear. The "right" clothes, like the "right" grammar, depend on what is appropriate or expected in a given situation. Around their friends, students talk and dress in particular ways. At formal occasions or in the workplace, they will be required to dress, to talk, and to write in other ways. This approach will less likely demean those students who do not routinely hear and use standard English. It also gives grammatical correctness a practical value and encourages your students to see language differences as an example of social diversity and opportunity.

Private Grammar

The other face of grammar is much more personal. By "private grammar," I mean the language structure that all of us already carry around in our heads and put to use when we communicate or think. In contrast to the study of public grammar, which has evolved over centuries, the description of our inherent language ability has grown from the work of linguists over the last several decades. Such grammar is private in the sense that it operates inside our heads, so quickly we are not even conscious of it. You won't find questions about private grammar on standardized tests; it is what students possess in order to read the tests in the first place.

If using public grammar can be compared to wearing socially acceptable formal clothes, private grammar can be compared to doing what comes naturally, to physical skills such as walking or running or throwing. Ask students to take a statement and turn it into a question in their native language. They can do it easily. They can fit new slang words into sentences fluidly. They know quickly when the language they hear or read sounds confusing or clear, choppy or smooth. They do all this with their private grammar.

Private grammar can be compared to doing what comes naturally, to physical skills such as walking or running or throwing.

If they can do all this already, how will studying grammar help them do more? The answer is that any skill that already comes somewhat naturally, like throwing a ball or making music, will improve if we learn about it and practice it. Students will be using the language of grammar to some degree when they revise and combine sentences in the section on "Writing Effective Sentences" in this textbook. They will do so to a greater degree whenever you show them how to improve the style of their writing by finding active verbs or expanding sentences with participles or prepositional phrases.

Putting Grammar to Use

As you can see from these descriptions of public and private faces, the language of basic grammar has many uses. Nonetheless, it is a difficult language for students to grow comfortable with; its vocabulary looks large and forbidding; many of the terms combine with each other in ways that seem strange to students ("adjective clause"); and because it is a language about language, it strains the verbal skills of many of its students, both children and adults. So, like any language it must be practiced often and put to use in a variety of contexts. Here are some general suggestions.

Use Private Grammar to Teach Public Grammar

As language users, we all have an intuitive sense that sentences are made up of sections. Give students a sentence and ask them to divide it into chunks and to group the words that go together. This approach can remain basic or can become more refined as students divide and cluster clauses and phrases.

This sort of activity easily leads to sentence diagramming. If you are not familiar with diagramming, see Chapter 20. I teach students not the whole of it but just the basic components; even elementary diagrams help many students see the subject-predicate core of a sentence more clearly. If you choose to teach diagramming more thoroughly, students will be able to analyze difficult sentences that they encounter in reading and will build their comprehension. Many students enjoy constructing the diagrams; the activity taps students' visual and spatial skills in addition to their verbal ones.

Another way to draw on students' private grammatical ability is to provide them with practical shortcuts for getting at the essential points of grammar. Grammarians over the years have assembled a number of these simple methods, and your students will love you for telling them about these methods. One good book on the subject is Rei Noguchi's *Grammar and the Teaching of Writing: Limits and Possibilities* (NCTE). Students find the shortcuts practical, and they also appreciate the positive reinforcement of their grammatical instincts.

Use Grammar for Reading

Although grammar is most closely associated with writing, students can put grammar to use when they read.

Knowing grammatical terminology gives students the tools they need to discuss a difficult sentence in a story or a poem. Ask students to pick out the main verb and then the simple subject; finding these can help them figure out the rest of the sentence. Poets bend sentences around a good deal, but most poetry consists of recognizable sentences and sentence parts. Often you can help students move beyond their perplexity about a poem by reminding them to look for the sentences and their basic parts.

In discussing with students what they enjoy or don't enjoy about a writer's style, look for the grammatical characteristics of the writer's sentences. What parts of speech stand out in the sentences? Some writers specialize in strong, active verbs, with few forms of the verb *be*. In other writers' texts, *is* and *are* abound, but the nouns stand out. In still others', the adjectives and adverbs catch the reader's attention.

Another approach is to ask students how long a writer's sentences are, on average. What characteristic sentence lengths do students notice among types of writers, or the writers of different periods? This approach can lead to a discussion of the different structures that make up a writer's sentences. Some writers like to add modifiers, phrases, and clauses; other writers keep sentences short to highlight the main nouns and verbs. Some start a sentence with long introductory word groups; others go right to the subject.

Bring grammar into the reading of advertisements, political language, and the World Wide Web. Advertisements provide good examples of sentence fragments, imperative verbs, and words that look like nouns but act like adjectives ("a Labor Day sofa sale"). Political speeches and slogans make interesting use of *we* and other personal pronouns. E-mail seems to encourage sentences that are variously clipped, casual, funny, skillful, and careless. Ask students to bring in examples for discussion.

Use Grammar for Revision

When students write, help them use grammar not just in the final editing stage, when they hunt out their violations of public grammar, but in the revising stage as well, when they can experiment with private grammar to develop their style as writers.

This textbook shows students how to combine sentences by inserting words or using conjunctions. Students can use some of the same methods to build a single sentence. They can build their sentences by adding participles (especially *–ing* participles that function half as an active verb, half as an adjective) and also by adding appositives. "A spider, **a repulsive, hairy creature, no bigger than a tarantula,** crawled into the room. . . . **Hands trembling, sweat dripping from his face,** he flung the magazine left and right, **trying to kill the spiders,** but there were too many." That example of an eighth-grader's work is from Harry Noden's *Image Grammar: Using Grammatical Structures to Teach Writing,* an excellent source for these and other techniques. Students can also add phrases, especially prepositional phrases, and clauses to a sentence, expanding the information about their main point, giving more details in order to paint a picture, building, and penetrating further into their topic. (The sentence that you just read is one example; you can find more—and better ones—in the work of most accomplished writers.) Students may think at first that they are merely making sentences longer, but they will quickly find that they are also saying more.

Conclusion

The suggestions in this essay are only a sample of the good ideas for using the language of grammar to help students become better readers and writers. The books I have mentioned will lead you to other ideas. And your colleagues in language arts can provide you with many other suggestions for using grammar in the classroom. If you think of grammar as a language for talking about language and you keep in mind the differences between public and private grammar, you can make grammar a valuable part of your students' language education.

For Further Reading

Assembly for the Teaching of English Grammar. www.ateg.org.

Berk, Lynn M. *English Syntax: From Word to Discourse*. New York: Oxford UP, 1999.

Haussamen, Brock. *Revising the Rules: Traditional Grammar and Modern Linguistics*. 2nd ed. Dubuque: Kendall/Hunt, 2000.

Kolln, Martha. *Rhetorical Grammar: Grammatical Choices, Rhetorical Effect*. 3rd ed. Boston: Allyn and Bacon, 1998.

Kolln, Martha, and Robert Funk (contributor). *Understanding English Grammar*. 5th ed. Needham: Allyn and Bacon, 1998.

Noden, Harry R. *Image Grammar: Using Grammatical Structures to Teach Writing*. Portsmouth: Heinemann/Boynton Cook, 1999.

Noguchi, Rei. *Grammar and the Teaching of Writing: Limits and Possibilities*. Urbana: NCTE, 1991.

Weaver, Constance. *Teaching Grammar in Context*. Portsmouth: Boynton/Cook, 1996.

William, Joseph M. Style: *The Lessons in Clarity and Grace*. 6th ed. New York: Longman, 2000. ∎

Brock Haussamen has taught at Raritan Valley Community College in New Jersey since 1968. He is the author of Revising the Rules: Traditional Grammar and Modern Linguistics *(Kendall/Hunt) and also of a book on the history of the local New Jersey railroads. He began serving as president of the Assembly for the Teaching of English Grammar in 2000. His hobby and passion recently is playing ragtime piano.*

By Rei R. Noguchi

Getting Down to Basics:
Using What Students Already Know

Like sentences, subjects and verbs are among the most basic elements of grammar and writing instruction.

Too often we struggle in teaching basic grammar to our students. Yet what really are the basics and how should we teach them? The most basic—the rock-bottom minimum—are sentence, verb, and subject. Surprisingly, we can teach these three basic elements by taking advantage of the unconscious linguistic knowledge that students already possess, their private grammar, so to speak. By tapping this unconscious knowledge, we can help students identify more easily the three basic elements, and, more important, help them better understand subsequent instruction in grammar, usage, and mechanics.

Why are the sentence, verb, and subject the very basics of grammar instruction? Take the notion of sentence. The sentence constitutes the most important unit in written texts, particularly in writing for school. A shaky grasp of what counts as a written sentence inevitably and unintentionally leads to distracting sentence fragments, fused sentences, and comma splices. Clearly, to master formal written English, students need to differentiate between a genuine sentence and an inappropriate nonsentence. Like sentences, subjects and verbs are among the most basic elements of grammar and writing instruction. Besides helping to define a sentence, subjects and verbs constitute elements on which a great deal of grammar and writing instruction builds. Without a reliable way of identifying subject and verb, students can almost certainly expect rough going.

How can we teach the concepts of subject, verb, and sentence so that students can identify them easily? I would suggest that, rather than relying solely on semantic definitions, we take fuller advantage of what we often ignore or downplay in our teaching of grammar, namely, the tremendous unconscious knowledge that all fluent or near-fluent speakers of English bring to the classroom every day. Put more bluntly, our students know a great deal more about grammar than many of us think. This grammar is not school grammar but their "private grammar," the system of rules unconsciously learned and unconsciously used by all fluent speakers of English in everyday conversation. We cannot teach this personal underlying grammar for the simple reason that our students already know it. All we can do is bring this knowledge to the surface and exploit it to the fullest.

Identifying the Sentence

Exploiting the unconscious linguistic knowledge of students is the key to teaching the very basics of grammar. For students unaccustomed or resistant to working with abstract definitions, identifying sentences and fragments may prove difficult. To identify fragments, students must, at minimum, understand that a fragment is an "incomplete sentence"; to apply this definition, however, students must understand what a sentence is. To understand what a

sentence is, students must understand such terms as subject, predicate, and independent clause. Each of these terms may require further definitions yet.

Exploiting the unconscious linguistic knowledge of students is the key to teaching the very basics of grammar.

To avoid the chain of seemingly endless definitions to identify sentences and fragments, teachers can take advantage of their students' unconscious knowledge of what constitutes a complete sentence. Teachers can, for example, use the following frame to help students tap what they already know.

> Sentence Frame:
> They liked the idea that
>
> _____.

Many word groups will fit in the frame, but whatever they are, they will all be genuine declarative sentences. Students can try out fragments you provide, such as *Thinking of joining the team* or *Because he joined the team,* as well as any suspicious word groups they themselves may write. If students discover a fragment, they can add or delete words to make it fit into the frame and thereby change the fragment into a genuine sentence. There is no need to define a sentence formally

at this stage. If students can perform the simple test given here, they already unconsciously know what a sentence is, and with that knowledge they can easily identify fragments, which are just parts of sentences. With a bit of guidance and exploration, students will discover that fused sentences and comma splices won't fit in the empty slot either.

Identifying Verbs

If we tap the private grammar of our students, we can also help them identify specific and important parts of the sentence. Below are two frames that will help students identify words that can serve as main verbs.

> Main-Verb Frame 1:
> They might _____ (it) now.

> Main-Verb Frame 2:
> They aren't _____-ing (it) now.

Any word that fits in the empty slots above will be the base form (infinitive) of the main verb, the form listed in the dictionary (e.g., *eat, collect, finish, sleep*). There is no need here to define *main verb*. If the word fits in the empty slot, it's a word that English speakers and writers can and do use as a main verb in sentences.

Because verbs don't always occur in the base form in actual sentences, students need other strategies to identify verbs, especially in the sentences they compose. Here again, we can take advantage of the unconscious linguistic knowledge of students, this time their uncanny ability to produce negative sentences and yes-no questions, to assist students in identifying helping verbs.

If we examine the following sentences, we see that a helping verb is a word that immediately precedes the negative element (*–n't* or *not*) in negated sentences or the word that gets fronted in yes-no questions.

EXAMPLES

1. Jim should go to the football game.
   [*Transform this into a negative sentence or a question.*]

   Jim **should**n't go to the football game.

   Should Jim go to the football game?

2. Jim went to the football game.

   Jim **did**n't go to the football game.

   Did Jim go to the football game?

If we have students transform declarative sentences into either negative sentences or yes-no questions, we can help them identify helping verbs. Again, there is no need to define *helping verb* formally. Though students may have never heard of the term *helping verb* (or *auxiliary verb*) before, they already unconsciously know what it is if they can produce a corresponding negative sentence or a corresponding yes-no question from a declarative sentence. Making such transformations requires complex linguistic knowledge. Yet, remarkably, we don't have to teach students how to do this. If students are fluent or near-fluent in spoken English, they already know it, as amply demonstrated in their daily speech. What we need to do, however, is to

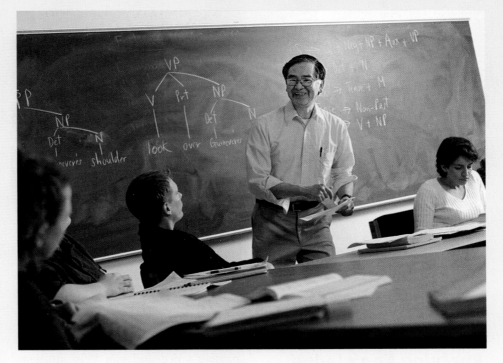

take advantage of this knowledge in teaching the basics of grammar.

Main Verb *Be*

The main verb *be* (as in *They were friends*) is especially tricky because, unlike other main verbs, it moves to the front in yes-no questions (*Were they friends?*). It also takes the negative element in negative sentences (*They weren't friends*). The main verb *be* can thus masquerade as the helping verb *be* (compare *They were friends* to *They were running*). To make matters worse, the main verb *be* appears frequently in student writing. Indeed, when we complain that our students write with too many *be* verbs, we really mean the main verb *be*, not the helping verb *be*. This gives all the more reason for students to be able to identify the

main verb *be*. Teaching students to use the main-verb frames and the helping-verb transformations can reduce confusion over the function of *be* in a sentence. Further, having students memorize the main-verb forms of *be* can reduce the confusion even more.

Identifying Subjects

Once students have identified the verb of a sentence, they can easily identify the subject. To identify the latter, they can insert the verb in the question frame below and then answer the question.

Simple-Subject Frame:
Who or what _____?

In most cases, the answer to the question will be the subject of the sentence.

Applying Knowledge of Subjects and Verbs

Being able to identify subjects and verbs brings considerable payoffs. It will help students understand *clause*, which, in turn, will help them understand *independent* (or *main*) *clause* and *subordinate* (or *dependent*) *clause*. Understanding these terms will help them better understand the notion of *sentence*, which, in turn, will help them better understand and correct any unintentional fragment or run-on sentence. (Think also of all the punctuation rules that directly or indirectly refer to these structures.) Being able to identify subjects and verbs will certainly help students identify errors in subject-verb agreement, errors in verb-tense consistency, and even the overuse of main verb *be*. This skill can also help students identify verbs in the passive voice and can help students choose the correct case of personal pronouns. In short, knowing how to identify subjects and verbs leads to an understanding of a host of other concepts.

Conclusion

For many language arts teachers, teaching grammar is both a labor of love and a love of labor. Many of us like the notion of grammar as a system, the wholes and parts fitting into place. Yet too often we struggle with difficult concepts and often with indifferent students. We can make the labor of teaching grammar less—and, hopefully, the love of grammar more for both teacher and student—if we take advantage of the prodigious private linguistic knowledge that all fluent speakers of English, native and non-native, bring to the language arts classroom every day.

Further References

DeBeaugrande, Robert. "Forward to the Basics: Getting Down to Grammar." *College Composition and Communication* 35 (1984): 358–67.

Noguchi, Rei R. *Grammar and the Teaching of Writing: Limits and Possibilities*. Urbana, IL: National Council of Teachers of English. 1991. ∎

Rei R. Noguchi, Professor of English and Linguistics at California State University, Northridge, has taught courses in linguistics to practicing and prospective language arts teachers for over seventeen years. He is the author of Grammar and the Teaching of Writing: Limits and Possibilities *(NCTE). When not teaching or writing, he enjoys reading, bicycling, and following various kinds of sports, particularly baseball.*

By Billy T. Boyar, Ph.D.

Raising Expectations:
The Importance of Teaching Grammar to ESL Students

In the sixth grade, my class was taught sentence diagramming. Trying to superimpose our simple schoolbook diagrams on the infinity of language felt mysterious. Studying grammar in such a systematic way was like mapping the stars: We named unidentified words and charted their relationships. Words and phrases depended on other words like moons held to planets by gravity, and verbs sparkled like stars. I was not surprised, years later, to learn that the word *grammar* is etymologically related to *glamour* and *gramarye*,

Studying grammar in such a systematic way was like mapping the stars: We named unidentified words and charted their relationships.

suggesting magic. To me, the study of grammar has always been interesting and provocative in its own right. There are, however, important practical reasons for studying grammar and even more important practical reasons for ESL students to study it.

In the past, some people have disparaged the formal, systematic teaching of grammar to the ESL student. When people emphasize the importance of the natural way of learning language, beginning with hearing and mimicking, I agree with them. When they stress the necessity of creating a relaxed noncritical environment in which the ESL student feels free to practice speaking his or her new language, I agree with them. I agree that the study of literature and written composition is crucial. I even agree that grammar, if taught to young children or to ESL beginners of any age, should be fun and games, or should not be taught at all. However, when people advocate such approaches to the exclusion of a formal program of grammar for ESL students who are at least on an intermediate level and at least in the sixth grade, their argument is extreme, and I disagree with them.

Why is the study of grammar, usage, and mechanics important for appropriately mature and advanced ESL students?

Avoiding False Analogies

A study of English grammar, usage, and mechanics helps ESL students to avoid developing English language habits based on false analogies with the rules for their primary language. A comparative study of different languages shows that the basic patterns of grammar, conventions such as punctuation and capitalization, and the special uses of words can be vastly different. For example, a Spanish sentence doesn't necessarily need a subject (the subject can be implied by the verb); Spanish uses the present tense where English would sometimes use the past tense; question marks and exclamation points are placed both at the beginning and at the end of sentences; and a double negative is considered standard usage. English is even further from the grammatical expectations of Chinese and other non-Western ESL students.

In the past, some people have disparaged the formal, systematic teaching of grammar to the ESL student.

In my composition class, a Mexican American student submitted an essay that contained this sentence: "The Christmas party resulted well." The cognates *to result* (English) and *resultar* (Spanish) have confusingly similar meanings, yet their usage is distinctly different. Here, *resultar* could be translated *to turn out*. My student meant that the party turned out well, but she was basing her English usage on a false analogy with Spanish usage.

Not only does the ESL student tend to base English grammar rules on such false analogies, but also he or she often hears nonstandard usage repeated by friends and family. Being continually reinforced, the false analogy becomes an ingrained habit. Without the formal, systematic study of English grammar, usage, and mechanics, the ESL student may always have difficulty with standard English.

Promoting Academic Success

Teaching grammar to ESL students will help them succeed academically, especially if they plan to attend college. I have taught ESL and English at both high school and college. In composition classes, which also often contain ESL students, I frequently need to explain a point of grammar in order to help students understand why I am asking them to revise their papers. I want them to understand the principle so that they can avoid committing the same error over and over in future essays. For example, I ask them not to separate the subject and verb with only one comma (as in *Sara, who lives nearby is on my soccer team.*). This comment inevitably requires a further explanation: "Here you have inserted a nonessential clause between the subject and verb."

"But Mister," asks one ESL student, "what do you mean . . . *nonessential?*"

"A nonessential clause is a clause that can be removed. . . ."

"But what's a clause?"

"A clause contains a subject and a verb—it can be independent or subordinate. There are three kinds of subordinate . . ."

"What do you mean *subordinate?*"

"I mean that they have a subject and verb but that they cannot stand . . ."

"So what's a subject?"

"A subject is the noun or pronoun doing the . . ."

"Noun?"

The problem is that trying to teach a little bit of grammar is like trying to paint a little bit of a wall: It doesn't work.

I encounter situations like this all the time—and of course, ESL students aren't the only ones who don't know formal English grammar. The problem is that trying to teach a little bit of grammar is like trying to paint a little bit of a wall: It doesn't work. In a college composition class, instructors typically explain points of grammar, usage, and mechanics as they are related to essays submitted by students. However, it would not be appropriate

to stop the composition class in order to devote the rest of the course to the basics of grammar. The result is that the ESL student who knows no formal English grammar is poorly served because he or she cannot take full advantage of the instructor's explanations.

Like many a native English speaker's, the ESL student's grammar and usage may never be perfect. Rather than perfection, the goal is a workable compromise. If students can communicate effectively in English, does it matter that they speak with an accent? The lives of ESL students will not be destroyed, for example, if they do not master the subjunctive mood. As teachers, we must demand excellence, but at the same time, we should carefully consider what exactly we want students to master.

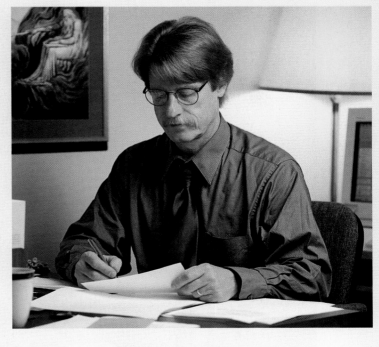

Supporting Career Success

Studying grammar will help ESL students succeed professionally. Recently, a city employee asked me to tutor him in English. He had started out as a garbage collector, but after a few years his bosses recognized his ability and promoted him, then promoted him again. He suddenly found himself having to write memos and job descriptions. Now, in order to keep

the job, he was required to improve his English grammar, usage, and mechanics.

The reality is that proficiency in standard English is a badge required for acceptance in many careers and professions in the United States. Teachers, lawyers, doctors, and so forth may not be given the respect and trust they deserve if their use of language departs too far from the standard. Beyond this country, English has become the foremost international language. The dialect of the neighborhood, rightly cherished, will not succeed very well in commerce on the World Wide Web. The formal, systematic study of grammar, usage, and mechanics helps the ESL student separate neighborhood dialect from public language, in order to develop that public language in a clear and conscious way. Being truly bilingual, of

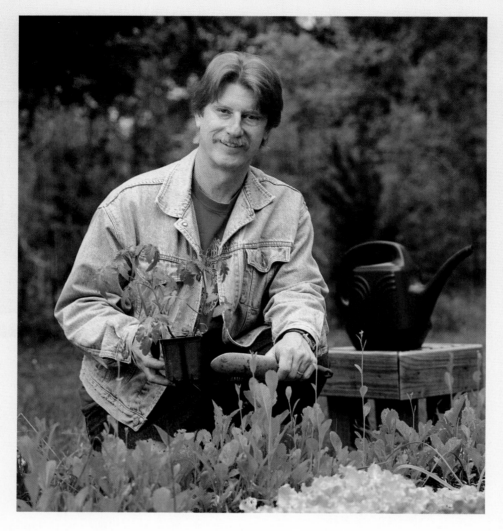

countless others, a refined bilingualism can open doors to wider possibilities.

Increasing Language Ownership

ESL students will benefit from the formal study of English because a better understanding of language patterns, a confidence in punctuation, and a command of the special uses of words will help them internalize English as a language of their own. Language ownership is an important topic. Language is a huge part of personal identity. It is a major reference point in our understanding of who we are. However, it should be emphasized that we can own more than one language; we can have two or more languages and dialects as expressions of our identity. It is helpful, healing, and sane for ESL students whose home is the United States to adopt English and care for it as their own. The problem is that immigrants have not always been welcomed with open arms, which is ironic in a land of immigrants. Our ESL students may therefore feel somewhat alien and sense that the English language is the language of others. One category of ESL students speaks English most of the time. They speak English in school; they speak it in their after-school jobs; and they even speak it most of the time at home: with brothers and sisters nearly all of the time, with parents some of the time, but with grandparents not at all. Even though these students speak English

The reality is that proficiency in standard English is a badge required for acceptance in many careers and professions in the United States.

course, is more than merely owning a badge. Coupling a career or professional training with authentic bilingualism will broaden opportunities in ways that are numerous and unforeseen: as a police officer, nurse, doctor, lawyer, salesperson, diplomat, translator, flight attendant, psychotherapist, teacher, construction supervisor, municipal work supervisor, governor, or president. In any of these careers and professions and most of the time, they paradoxically still consider English their second language. In addition, since they use their "primary" (home) language less and less, it does not grow.

The knowledge of grammar, usage, and mechanics is one tool in many, but we should not underestimate its importance.

These ESL students can be left in a world of little language indeed. A systematic study of grammar, usage, and mechanics in a friendly environment will tend to cut through the cycle of alienation. In the same way that we may feel better about our own cars when we learn how they work and can repair them ourselves, ESL students can learn how English works and can feel the pride of ownership.

Conclusion

Finally, ESL students are in the advantageous position of having a head start on bilingualism. If they continue to grow in their first language and if we give them the tools that they need for their second language, they will become truly bilingual. They need many tools in their language tool kits: the training to hear English phonemes, so that they can be good listeners; the skill of pronunciation, so that they can speak clearly; the knowledge of literature, so that they can contemplate the values of English-language cultures and the cultures of the rest of the world; and the art of writing compositions, so that they can express their own truths. The knowledge of grammar, usage, and mechanics is one tool in many, but we should not underestimate its importance. For ESL students, grammatical knowledge is a *sine qua non* of becoming bilingual on a professional level. On this level of bilingualism, the advantages are many, but it seems we and our students sometimes set our sights too low. Perhaps we have been guilty of not expecting our ESL students to accomplish as much as other students. They can aspire to the same—or better—careers and professions and can partake richly of the larger culture. Beyond these avenues, however, from the point of view of those of us who love language, ESL students will be able to look at language from a higher vantage point. From this aerial view, perhaps some will even rediscover the old meaning of grammar: magic. ■

Billy Boyar has taught composition, literature, and ESL in high schools and community colleges for twenty years. Billy lives in Austin, Texas, where he teaches at Austin Community College. He has worked with juvenile offenders, volunteered with Hospice, and mediated as an ombudsman in nursing homes. In his free time, he enjoys studying Spanish and reading philosophy and finds his garden rewarding and a great way to unwind. He believes that a formal, systematic study of grammar is an important part of an ESL program.

Holt Handbook

Your **Road Map** to Grammar, Usage, and Mechanics Mastery

Now more than ever before, there is a demand for students at all grade levels to develop competence in the language arts and facility with the English language. Students need to be able to access information with ease, to appreciate the literary arts, and perhaps most importantly, to apply their language skills at levels demanded in the twenty-first century.

GIVING ALL STUDENTS ACCESS TO LANGUAGE SKILLS

Students in each classroom—including those at grade level, special education students, students with learning difficulties, advanced learners, and English-language learners—are at varying levels of preparation and have different strengths and needs. Giving these students all the tools they need to succeed is no easy task. That's where the *Holt Handbook* comes in.

The motivating force behind this program's organization and instructional delivery is the desire to offer teachers and students a method of focusing on written and oral language conventions and to provide a compelling and effective way to teach and learn grammar, usage, and mechanics skills. Based on John Warriner's time-tested model for instruction, the *Holt Handbook* can be an integral part of any balanced language arts program, or it can stand alone as a powerful tool for giving students access to the language skills they need most.

Covering All Your Students Need to Know About **Grammar, Usage,** and **Mechanics**

THREE MAIN PARTS COVER THE BASICS

PART I: GRAMMAR, USAGE, AND MECHANICS chapters help students use and practice using the building blocks of language—words, phrases, clauses, capitalization, punctuation, and spelling. The last chapter, **Correcting Common Errors,** gives students more practice building key language skills and taking tests in standardized formats.

PART II: The **SENTENCES** section covers the building blocks of constructing sentences, such as writing complete sentences, writing effective sentences, diagramming sentences, and improving sentence style.

PART III: The **RESOURCES** chapters include **The History of English,** a concise history of the English language; **Test Smarts,** a guide to taking standardized tests in grammar, usage, and mechanics; and **Grammar at a Glance,** a glossary of grammatical terms. In addition, grades 9–12 include **Manuscript Form,** a section that covers basic guidelines for preparing and presenting manuscripts and offers a sample research paper as a model.

PART 1 — Grammar, Usage, and Mechanics

PART 2 — Sentences

PART 3 — Resources

Instructional Delivery
That Keeps Students on Track

Each chapter in the **Holt Handbook** is carefully sequenced so that students are introduced to and taught new rules and skills at the right time. Each chapter includes an entry-level diagnostic preview; direct instruction of the rules followed immediately by examples and exercises; ongoing assessment; and application of new knowledge through writing. This direct and practical instructional approach allows you to keep track of your students' pace and progress.

CHAPTER

2

Parts of Speech Overview
Noun, Pronoun, Adjective

Diagnostic Preview

A. Identifying Nouns, Pronouns, and Ad

Tell whether each italicized word or word group in sentences is used as a *noun*, a *pronoun*, or an *adjecti*

EXAMPLE   **1.** *Each* student is required to take a forei
language.

1. *Each—adjective; language—noun*

1. *That* drummer is the *best* performer.
2. That *German shepherd* puppy is a sweet-natured rascal.
3. *Everybody* says that *high school* will be more work but more fun, too.
4. *This* is the greatest year the junior varsity volleyball *team* has ever had.
5. *Who* can tell me whose bicycle *this* is?
6. Jenna prepared a special breakfast for her parents and *herself* this *morning*.
7. This is their fault because *they* ignored all the *danger* signals.
8. *We* received word that they aren't in *danger*.
9. *Each* of these clubs decorated a float for the Cinco de Mayo *parade*.
10. The runner *Carl Lewis* won several Olympic *medals*.

DIAGNOSTIC PREVIEW
offers a short test that covers the whole chapter and lets you pretest for the most essential knowledge and skills.

The Independent Clause

6b. An *independent* (or *main*) *clause* expresses a complete thought and can stand by itself as a complete sentence.

EXAMPLES
   S   V
The sun set an hour ago. [This entire sentence is an independent clause.]

   S   V
Jean Merrill wrote *The Pushcart War*, and

   S   V
Ronni Solbert illustrated the book. [This sentence contains two independent clauses.]

   S   V
After I finish studying, **I will go to the**
sentence contains one subordinate clau
independent clause.]

RULE, EXAMPLE, EXERCISE sequence
introduces a new rule and follows it immediately with examples and exercises.

Exercise 1   **Identifying Subjects and Verbs in Independent Clauses**

Identify the subject and verb in each italicized independent clause in the following sentences.

EXAMPLE   **1.** Before she left for college, *my sister read the comics in the newspaper every day.*

1. *sister—subject; read—verb*

1. *She told me* that Jump Start was her favorite.
2. Since she liked it so much, *I made a point of reading it, too.*
3. *The comic strip was created by this young man, Robb Armstrong,* who lives and works in Philadelphia.
4. *Jump Start features a police officer named Joe and his wife, Marcy,* who is a nurse.

Review B Proofreading for Words Often Confused

Identify and correct each error in words often confused in the following sentences.

EXAMPLE   1. Anne Shirley, here portrayed by actress Megan
              Follows, found a pieceful life and a loving family
              on Prince Edward Island.

           1. pieceful—peaceful

1. Does the scenery shone in the picture on this page appeal to you?
2. My family enjoyed the green hillsides and rugged seashore during our two-weak vacation there last summer.
3. Prince Edward Island is quite a beautiful spot, and its Canada's smallest province.
4. Everyone who lives there calls the island PEI, and now I do, to.
5. During our visit, the weather was quite pleasant, so I lead my parents all over PEI on foot.
6. We walked to several places of interest in Charlottetown, the capitol.
7. I got to chose our first stop, and I selected the farmhouse that's the setting for the novel *Anne of Green Gables*.
8. That novel's main character, Anne Shirley, is someone who's ideas I admire.
9. Walking around "The Garden Province," we passed many farms; the principle crop is potatoes.
10. Take my advise and visit Prince Edward Island if you get the chance.

REVIEW EXERCISES offer both reinforcement of newly learned concepts and cumulative assessment.

Chapter Review

A. Using Irregular Verbs

Write the correct past or past participle form of the italicized irregular verb provided before each sentence.

1. *break*   The thunder _____ the silence.
2. *ring*   Who _____ the fire alarm so quickly?
3. *shrink*   This shirt must have _____ in the dryer.
4. *throw*   You've _____ the ball out of bounds!
5. *lead*   Julio _____ the parade last year, so now it's my turn.
6. *rise*   The sun _____ over the pyramids of Giza in Egypt.
7. *swim*   We have _____ only three laps.
8. *choose*   Vera was _____ as captain of the volleyball team.
9. *go*   I have _____ to visit the Grand Canyon twice.
10. *sit*   The tiny tree frog _____ motionless.
11. *write*   Joan has _____ a story about aliens fro Andromeda galaxy.
12. *do*   During class, Jorge _____ the first five homework assignment.
13. *steal*   Three runners _____ bases during the
14. *break*   This summer's heat wave has _____ al
15. *drink*   Have you _____ all of the tomato juic
16. *sink*   The log had slowly _____ into the qui
17. *lie*   The old postcards have _____ in the b
18. *drive*   Have you ever _____ across the state o
19. *begin*   Our local PBS station _____ its fund-r
20. *set*   Have you _____ the paper plates and picnic table?
21. *throw*   Who _____ the ball to first base?
22. *know*   I have _____ some of my classmates fo
23. *take*   Kadeem _____ the role of Frederick D
24. *tear*   My mother _____ the paper to make
25. *come*   We _____ close to winning the tourna

CHAPTER REVIEWS provide additional practice and opportunities for ongoing assessment.

Writing Application
Using Verbs in a Story

Verb Forms and Tenses   A local writers' club is sponsoring a contest for the best "cliffhanger" opening of an adventure story. Write an exciting paragraph to enter in the contest. Your paragraph should leave readers wondering "What happens next?" In your paragraph, use at least five verbs from the lists of Common Irregular Verbs in this chapter.

Prewriting   First, you will need to imagine a suspenseful situation to describe. Jot down several ideas for your story opening. Then, choose the one you like best. With that situation in mind, scan the lists of irregular verbs. Note at least ten verbs you can use. Include some lively action verbs like *burst, swing,* and *throw.*

Writing   As you write your rough draft, think of your readers. Choose words that create a suspenseful, believable scene. Remember that you have only one paragraph to catch your readers' interest.

Revising   Ask a friend to read your paragraph. Does your friend find it interesting? Can he or she picture the scene clearly? If not, you may want to add, delete, or revise some details.

Publishing   Check your spelling, usage, punctuation, and grammar. Check to make sure the forms of verbs are correct and the tenses are consistent. You may want to exchange your cliffhanger with a partner, and complete each other's stories. With your teacher's permission, you can then read the completed stories aloud to the class.

WRITING APPLICATIONS guide students in applying grammar, usage, and mechanics skills with end-of-chapter writing activities.

Pupil's Edition

Instruction Based on Warriner's Model

An English teacher for thirty-two years, John Warriner developed the original instructional approach used throughout the grammar, usage, and mechanics chapters in the **Holt Handbook Pupil's Edition.** His logical model of instruction is based on a three-step process: Teach students the rule, show examples of the rule in writing, and provide immediate practice to reinforce the skill or concept. This model has been the authoritative standard for teaching grammar, usage, and mechanics skills for over fifty years.

RULE is always clearly stated and presented in red.

EXAMPLES illustrate the language skill or concept being taught in various student-friendly sentences.

┌─ H E L P ─

Most regular verbs that end in e drop the e before adding –*ing.* Some regular verbs double the final consonant before adding –*ing* or –*ed.*

EXAMPLES
shake—shak**ing**
hug—hu**gged**

USAGE

Reference Note
For more about **spelling rules,** see Chapter 16. For information on **standard and nonstandard English,** see page 245.

Regular Verbs

9b. A *regular verb* forms its past and past participle by adding –*d* or –*ed* to the base form.

Base Form	Present Participle	Past	Past Participle
clean	[is] cleaning	cleaned	[have] cleaned
hope	[is] hoping	hoped	[have] hoped
inspect	[is] inspecting	inspected	[have] inspected
slip	[is] slipping	slipped	[have] slipped

One common error in forming the past or the past participle of a regular verb is to leave off the –*d* or –*ed* ending.

NONSTANDARD Our street use to be quieter.
STANDARD Our street **used** to be quieter.

Another common error is to add unnecessary letters.

NONSTANDARD The swimmer almost drownded in the riptide.
STANDARD The swimmer almost **drowned** in the riptide.

NONSTANDARD The kitten attackted that paper bag.
STANDARD The kitten **attacked** that paper bag.

Oral Practice 1 Using Regular Verbs

Read each of the following sentences aloud, stressing the italicized verbs.

1. We are *supposed* to meet at the track after school.
2. The twins *happened* to buy the same shirt.
3. They have already *called* me about the party.
4. Do you know who *used* to live in this house?
5. I had *hoped* they could go to the concert with us.

© 1992 by Sidney Harris.

9 b

6. The chairs have been *moved* into the hall for the dance.
7. That salesclerk has *helped* my mother before.
8. Eli may not have *looked* under the table for the cat.

Exercise 1 **Writing the Forms of Regular Verbs**

Write the correct present participle, past, or past participle form of the italicized verb given before each of the following sentences.

EXAMPLES **1.** *learn*   Many people today are _____ folk dances from a variety of countries.

1. learning

2. *hope*   Dad and I had _____ to take lessons in folk dancing this summer.

2. hoped

1. *practice*   These Spanish folk dancers must have _____ for a long time.

2. *perform*   Notice that they are _____ in their colorful native costumes.

3. *wish*   Have you ever _____ that you knew how to do any folk dances?

4. *use*   Virginia reels _____ to be popular dances in the United States.

5. *promise*   Mrs. Stamos, who is from Greece, _____ to teach her daughter the Greek chain dance.

6. *lean*   The young Jamaican dancer _____ backward before he went under the pole during the limbo dance competition.

7. *start*   The group from Estonia is _____ a dance about a spinning wheel.

8. *request*   Someone in the audience has _____ an Irish square dance called "Sweets of May."

9. *dance*   During the Mexican hat dance, the woman _____ around the brim of the sombrero.

10. *fill*   The Jewish wedding dance _____ the room with both music and movement.

USAGE

EXERCISE
gives immediate practice applying the rule.

Pupil's Edition

Features That Help Students Along the Way

Oral Practice 5 Using Forms of *Rise* and *Raise* Correctly

Read the following sentences aloud, stressing the italicized verbs.

1. Mount Everest *rises* over 29,000 feet.
2. He *raises* the flag at sunrise.
3. The TV reporter *raised* her voice to be heard.
4. She *rose* from her seat and looked out the window.
5. The constellation Orion had not yet *risen* in the southern sky.
6. They had *raised* the piñata high in the tree.
7. I hope the bread is *rising*.
8. He will be *raising* the bucket from the well.

ORAL PRACTICE reinforces rules and concepts with spoken practice exercises.

TIPS & TRICKS

Sometimes a fragment is really a part of a nearby sentence. You can correct the fragment by attaching it to the sentence that comes before or after it.

SENTENCE WITH FRAGMENT
Mark is practicing his hook shot. Because he wants to try out for the basketball team.

SENTENCE
Mark is practicing his
h

W
me
to
fo
ca

TIPS & TRICKS offer easy-to-use hints that help students master language skills.

MEETING THE CHALLENGE

Write a poem, correctly using each of the six troublesome verbs, *sit, set, rise, raise, lie,* and *lay*. Be sure to check your poem for correct usage of the troublesome verbs.

MEETING THE CHALLENGE provides questions and short activities that ask students to approach a concept from a new angle.

STYLE TIP

To avoid the awkward use of *his or her*, try to rephrase the sentence.

AWKWARD
Each of the actors had memorized **his or her** lines.

REVISED
All of the actors had memorized **their** lines.

STYLE TIPS guide students in making sound decisions about style and usage.

HELP

Some of the subjects and verbs in Review B are compound.

HELP gives pointers that help students understand key rules or exercise directions.

Extend Grammar, Usage, and Mechanics Learning via the **Internet**!

GO.HRW.COM

Internet references throughout the *Pupil's Edition* direct students to **go.hrw.com**, a Web site that links students to resources related to concepts, rules, and assignments in the *Holt Handbook.*

HOW IT WORKS

When students see the **go.hrw.com** logo in the textbook, they can go to the **go.hrw.com** site to find resources that support the grammatical concept or rule they are studying.

INTERACTIVE EXERCISES IN GRAMMAR, USAGE, AND MECHANICS

Among the resources available to students on the *Holt Handbook* site are interactive exercises in grammar, usage, and mechanics. Students can practice skills with interactive exercises and then complete a chapter test that is scored immediately, giving students instant feedback on their progress.

Annotated Teacher's Edition

Unique Strategies That Make **Planning Lessons** Easy

The **Holt Handbook Annotated Teacher's Edition** helps you organize your lessons into manageable segments—preteaching, direct teaching, and reteaching, for example—so that students build skills in a systematic way. Suggestions for differentiating instruction are integrated with lessons to help you support students with special learning needs, including advanced learners, students with learning difficulties, and English-language learners. Features that direct you to program resources for each chapter and lesson are also there to help you along the way.

PRETEACHING

Lesson Starter

Prior Knowledge. Ask students to supply words that describe the similarities and differences between an orange and a baseball. Students might begin by saying that both objects are round. You might want to draw a Venn diagram on the chalkboard and ask students to suggest words that describe both items and words that

PRETEACHING offers strategies that help you identify prerequisite skills and build on the prior knowledge of your students.

DIRECT TEACHING

Modeling and Demonstration

Identifying Nouns. Model how to identify nouns by using the example *self-esteem.* First, ask whether the word names a person, place, thing, or idea. [*idea*] *Self-esteem* names an idea; therefore, *self-esteem* is a noun. Now, have a volunteer use another example from this chapter to demonstrate how to identify a noun.

DIRECT TEACHING helps you present content with strategies that include modeling and demonstrating new concepts.

RETEACHING

Pronouns

Activity. Ask students to write five descriptive sentences about a celebrity without ever mentioning the celebrity's name. Have two or three volunteers read their sentences, and let classmates try to guess the celebrity. Then, lead students to see that a common word in many of the sentences is *he* or *she*. Point out that pronouns like *he* and *she* are used in place of a noun, common or proper.

RETEACHING provides techniques to help you present material from a fresh perspective.

EXTENSION

Critical Thinking

Metacognition. Point out to students that there are probably too many pronouns to memorize all of them by type. Ask students what their strategies are for remembering the different types of pronouns. Have students describe and rate the effectiveness of their strategies. Students having trouble with pronouns should develop new strategies. Have students meet in groups to share and compare their ideas.

EXTENSION activities and strategies ask students to make new connections between what they are learning and what they already know.

DIFFERENTIATING INSTRUCTION

Advanced Learners

Have students read and discuss John Gardner's "Dragon, Dragon" or another folk tale that uses common nouns rather than proper names for its characters. Ask students to consider why the author uses common nouns rather than proper ones for the characters in the story. [*Students may say that there are so many characters in the story that it is easier for the reader to remember them with descriptive common nouns than with proper ones. Common nouns may also make the characters seem more universal.*]

DIFFERENTIATING INSTRUCTION helps you reinforce language skills with the wide variety of learners in your classroom, including advanced learners, on-level learners, learners having difficulty, special education students, and English-language learners.

CHAPTER RESOURCES

Internet

- Web resources: go.hrw.com

go. hrw .com

Practice & Review

- *Language & Sentence Skills Practice,* pp. 2–16; 17–20
- *Language & Sentence Skills Practice Answer Key,* pp. 1–7, 7–9

Application & Enrichment

- *Language & Sentence Skills Practice,* pp. 1, 21–22, 23
- *Language & Sentence Skills Practice Answer Key,* pp. 1, 9–10

CHAPTER RESOURCES BOXES list all materials that support each chapter lesson.

Teaching Suggestions and Resources

Teaching Suggestions That Help Students Make Connections

Because language arts skills are so interconnected, the **Annotated Teacher's Edition** provides a variety of extension and application strategies that help students make connections between the grammar, usage, and mechanics skills you're teaching them and the writing, science, and social studies skills they need to succeed in other classes. In addition, the **Annotated Teacher's Edition** gives you suggestions for facilitating an invaluable element of your students' learning experience—their families and communities.

MINI-LESSON Mechanics Conti

Punctuating Adjectives in a Series. Often two or more adjectives are used before a noun to make its meaning more specific. Remind students of the rules regarding comma usage with series of adjectives.

MINI-LESSON helps students link various grammar, usage, and mechanics skills to one another through a variety of practical lessons.

CONTENT-AREA CONNECTIONS

Social Studies
Places and Names. To give students practice in naming proper nouns, have students complete a team race on a social studies topic that they are studying. Divide the class into groups of four. Give each group a social studies category, and have the groups write as many proper nouns as they can in five minutes. All group members are responsible for generating answers. (Possible categories include states and their capitals, continents, oceans, rivers, countries, presidents, and

CONTENT-AREA CONNECTIONS suggest a variety of extension activities that reinforce the relevance of language arts skills to other disciplines, such as science and social studies.

Learning for Life

Writing a Personal Profile. For various reasons, adults are sometimes asked to write personal profiles, which require careful attention to verb tense. Ask your students to write profiles of themselves, including only material they are comfort-

LEARNING FOR LIFE offers real-world suggestions that help students relate grammar, usage, and mechanics skills to their own lives and to workplace skills they'll need in the future.

FAMILY/COMMUNITY ACTIVITY

Introductions. Most students have had or will have opportunities to introduce people to each other. In doing so, students will use complements. Provide the following examples:

1. Hi! I'm Ms. King. I teach language arts at Carson Middle School.
2. Maria, this is Tom Jones. Tom is new to our school. Tom, this is Maria Gomez. Maria is my best friend.

FAMILY/COMMUNITY ACTIVITY provides a real-world forum for students' language arts skills.

Additional **Practice** and **Strategies** to Help Students Succeed

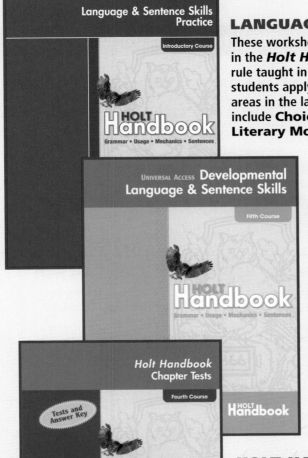

LANGUAGE & SENTENCE SKILLS PRACTICE

These worksheets provide practice, reinforcement, and extension for topics covered in the *Holt Handbook*. Traditional worksheets offer additional practice for every rule taught in the *Pupil's Edition*. **Language in Context** worksheets let students apply and extend their study of grammar, usage, and mechanics to other areas in the language arts and to content in other disciplines. These worksheets include **Choices** worksheets, **Proofreading Application** worksheets, **Literary Model** worksheets, and **Writing Application** worksheets.

DEVELOPMENTAL LANGUAGE & SENTENCE SKILLS: GUIDED PRACTICE

These worksheets provide developmental learners with instruction, practice, and reinforcement to supplement lessons in the *Holt Handbook* and in *Language & Sentence Skills Practice.* Targeted to those students who have not yet mastered specific concepts taught in the *Holt Handbook*, special features of this workbook include **Tips** that help students grasp abstract concepts with mnemonic devices, identification tests, and recognition strategies; **Points of Instruction** that explain how the rule applies to the examples provided; and **Guided Practice** that helps students with the first items of each exercise by asking guiding questions.

HOLT HANDBOOK CHAPTER TESTS

This booklet contains chapter tests in standardized test format for the grammar, usage, mechanics, and sentences chapters in the *Holt Handbook*. Presented in multiple-choice format, each test offers a sound means of assessing your students' grasp of key English-language conventions and, at the same time, offers students opportunities to practice their test-taking skills. The answer key provides useful references to specific rules that tie the answers to relevant instruction in the *Holt Handbook.* It also helps you pinpoint those skills and concepts students have mastered and those that need further attention.

Instructional Resources: Chapter by Chapter

This chart outlines the chapters of the *Holt Handbook* and the resources available to help you teach these chapters. The chart lists materials appropriate for use with on-level students, advanced students, learners having difficulty, special education students, and English-language learners. Many of the resources listed are available at go.hrw.com.

Holt Handbook Chapter	Differentiating Instruction	
	Advanced Learners	**On-Level Learners**
1 **Parts of Speech Overview**	• Teacher's Edition, pp. 17, 21, 28 • Language and Sentence Skills Practice, pp. 25–26, 27 • Language and Sentence Skills Practice Answer Key, pp. 9–10	• Teacher's Edition, pp. 2–33 • Language and Sentence Skills Practice, pp. 1–27 • Language and Sentence Skills Practice Answer Key, pp. 1–10
2 **The Parts of a Sentence**	• Teacher's Edition, p. 41 • Language and Sentence Skills Practice, pp. 50–51, 52 • Language and Sentence Skills Practice Answer Key, pp. 22–23	• Teacher's Edition, pp. 34–57 • Language and Sentence Skills Practice, pp. 28–52 • Language and Sentence Skills Practice Answer Key, pp. 11–23
3 **The Phrase**	• Teacher's Edition, pp. 64, 67, 68 • Language and Sentence Skills Practice, pp. 76–77, 78 • Language and Sentence Skills Practice Answer Key, pp. 33–34	• Teacher's Edition, pp. 58–79 • Language and Sentence Skills Practice, pp. 53–78 • Language and Sentence Skills Practice Answer Key, pp. 24–34

Differentiating Instruction		Assessment
Learners Having Difficulty	**English-Language Learners & Special Education Students**	
• Teacher's Edition, pp. 6, 26 • Developmental Language Skills Guided Practice, pp. 1–22 • Developmental Language Skills Guided Practice Teacher's Notes and Answer Key, pp. 1–5	• Teacher's Edition, pp. 5, 6, 8, 12, 16, 17, 25	• Holt Handbook Chapter Tests with Answer Key, pp. 1–2, 54
• Teacher's Edition, pp. 46, 50, 57 • Developmental Language Skills Guided Practice, pp. 23–34 • Developmental Language Skills Guided Practice Teacher's Notes and Answer Key, pp. 6–9	• Teacher's Edition, pp. 38, 45, 49, 52	• Holt Handbook Chapter Tests with Answer Key, pp. 3–4, 54
• Teacher's Edition, pp. 61, 65, 72 • Developmental Language Skills Guided Practice, pp. 35–44 • Developmental Language Skills Guided Practice Teacher's Notes and Answer Key, pp. 10–12	• Teacher's Edition, pp. 61, 65, 71	• Holt Handbook Chapter Tests with Answer Key, pp. 5–6, 54

(continued on next page)

Holt Handbook Chapter	Differentiating Instruction	
	Advanced Learners	**On-Level Learners**
4 The Clause	• Teacher's Edition, pp. 84, 85 • Language and Sentence Skills Practice, pp. 100–101, 102 • Language and Sentence Skills Practice Answer Key, pp. 42–43	• Teacher's Edition, pp. 80–103 • Language and Sentence Skills Practice, pp. 79–102 • Language and Sentence Skills Practice Answer Key, pp. 35–43
5 Agreement	• Teacher's Edition, pp. 115, 125 • Language and Sentence Skills Practice, pp. 128, 129–130, 131 • Language and Sentence Skills Practice Answer Key, pp. 53–54	• Teacher's Edition, pp. 104–135 • Language and Sentence Skills Practice, pp. 103–131 • Language and Sentence Skills Practice Answer Key, pp. 44–54
6 Using Pronouns Correctly	• Teacher's Edition, p. 143 • Language and Sentence Skills Practice, pp. 151, 152–153, 154 • Language and Sentence Skills Practice Answer Key, pp. 59–61	• Teacher's Edition, pp. 136–159 • Language and Sentence Skills Practice, pp. 132–154 • Language and Sentence Skills Practice Answer Key, pp. 55–61
7 Clear Reference	• Language and Sentence Skills Practice, pp. 166, 167–168, 169 • Language and Sentence Skills Practice Answer Key, pp. 66–67	• Teacher's Edition, pp. 160–173 • Language and Sentence Skills Practice, pp. 155–169 • Language and Sentence Skills Practice Answer Key, pp. 62–67
8 Using Verbs Correctly	• Teacher's Edition, pp. 181, 196, 211, 217 • Language and Sentence Skills Practice, pp. 196, 197–198, 199 • Language and Sentence Skills Practice Answer Key, pp. 75–76	• Teacher's Edition, pp. 174–225 • Language and Sentence Skills Practice, pp. 170–199 • Language and Sentence Skills Practice Answer Key, pp. 68–76

Differentiating Instruction		Assessment
Learners Having Difficulty	**English-Language Learners & Special Education Students**	**Assessment**
• Teacher's Edition, pp. 82, 86 • Developmental Language Skills Guided Practice, pp. 45–54 • Developmental Language Skills Guided Practice Teacher's Notes and Answer Key, pp. 13–15	• Teacher's Edition, pp. 85, 86, 88, 91, 94, 96, 98	• Holt Handbook Chapter Tests with Answer Key, pp. 7–8, 54
• Teacher's Edition, pp. 111, 112, 116, 124, 133 • Developmental Language Skills Guided Practice, pp. 55–66 • Developmental Language Skills Guided Practice Teacher's Notes and Answer Key, pp. 16–18	• Teacher's Edition, pp. 107, 111, 112, 116, 126	• Holt Handbook Chapter Tests with Answer Key, pp. 9–10, 54
• Teacher's Edition, pp. 139, 142, 145, 150 • Developmental Language Skills Guided Practice, pp. 67–72 • Developmental Language Skills Guided Practice Teacher's Notes and Answer Key, p. 19	• Teacher's Edition, pp. 138, 139, 142, 143, 144, 149, 153, 157	• Holt Handbook Chapter Tests with Answer Key, pp. 11–12, 54
• Developmental Language Skills Guided Practice, pp. 73–76 • Developmental Language Skills Guided Practice Teacher's Notes and Answer Key, p. 20	• Teacher's Edition, p. 164	• Holt Handbook Chapter Tests with Answer Key, pp. 13–14, 54
• Teacher's Edition, pp. 178, 179, 181, 196, 197, 218 • Developmental Language Skills Guided Practice, pp. 77–92 • Developmental Language Skills Guided Practice Teacher's Notes and Answer Key, pp. 21–23	• Teacher's Edition, pp. 177, 178, 179, 182, 183, 184, 198, 200, 210, 211, 212, 217	• Holt Handbook Chapter Tests with Answer Key, pp. 15–16, 54

(continued on next page)

Holt Handbook Chapter	Differentiating Instruction	
	Advanced Learners	**On-Level Learners**
9 **Using Modifiers Correctly**	• Teacher's Edition, pp. 237, 241 • Language and Sentence Skills Practice, pp. 221, 222–223, 224 • Language and Sentence Skills Practice Answer Key, pp. 85–87	• Teacher's Edition, pp. 226–247 • Language and Sentence Skills Practice, pp. 200–224 • Language and Sentence Skills Practice Answer Key, pp. 77–87
10 **Placement of Modifiers**	• Teacher's Edition, p. 255 • Language and Sentence Skills Practice, pp. 235, 236–237, 238 • Language and Sentence Skills Practice Answer Key, pp. 90–92	• Teacher's Edition, pp. 248–259 • Language and Sentence Skills Practice, pp. 225–238 • Language and Sentence Skills Practice Answer Key, pp. 88–92
11 **A Glossary of Usage**	• Teacher's Edition, pp. 264, 267, 273, 275, 278 • Language and Sentence Skills Practice, pp. 250, 251–252, 253 • Language and Sentence Skills Practice Answer Key, pp. 98–99	• Teacher's Edition, pp. 260–293 • Language and Sentence Skills Practice, pp. 239–253 • Language and Sentence Skills Practice Answer Key, pp. 93–99
12 **Capitalization**	• Teacher's Edition, pp. 299, 305 • Language and Sentence Skills Practice, pp. 272, 273–274, 275 • Language and Sentence Skills Practice Answer Key, pp. 106–108	• Teacher's Edition, pp. 294–323 • Language and Sentence Skills Practice, pp. 254–275 • Language and Sentence Skills Practice Answer Key, pp. 100–108

Differentiating Instruction		Assessment
Learners Having Difficulty	**English-Language Learners & Special Education Students**	
• Teacher's Edition, pp. 230, 231, 243 • Developmental Language Skills Guided Practice, pp. 93–100 • Developmental Language Skills Guided Practice Teacher's Notes and Answer Key, pp. 24–25	• Teacher's Edition, pp. 229, 233, 236	• Holt Handbook Chapter Tests with Answer Key, pp. 17–18, 54
• Teacher's Edition, p. 251 • Developmental Language Skills Guided Practice, pp. 101–104 • Developmental Language Skills Guided Practice Teacher's Notes and Answer Key, p. 26		• Holt Handbook Chapter Tests with Answer Key, pp. 19–20, 54
• Teacher's Edition, pp. 269, 276, 279 • Developmental Language Skills Guided Practice, pp. 105–112 • Developmental Language Skills Guided Practice Teacher's Notes and Answer Key, pp. 27–28	• Teacher's Edition, pp. 263, 265, 268, 272, 274, 281, 286	• Holt Handbook Chapter Tests with Answer Key, pp. 21–22, 54
• Teacher's Edition, pp. 296, 301, 306, 308, 315 • Developmental Language Skills Guided Practice, pp. 113–126 • Developmental Language Skills Guided Practice Teacher's Notes and Answer Key, pp. 29–32	• Teacher's Edition, pp. 304, 310	• Holt Handbook Chapter Tests with Answer Key, pp. 23–24, 54

(continued on next page)

Holt Handbook Chapter	Differentiating Instruction	
	Advanced Learners	**On-Level Learners**
13 Punctuation: End Marks and Commas	• Teacher's Edition, pp. 327, 329, 330, 341 • Language and Sentence Skills Practice, pp. 294, 295–296, 297 • Language and Sentence Skills Practice Answer Key, pp. 115–116	• Teacher's Edition, pp. 324–353 • Language and Sentence Skills Practice, pp. 276–297 • Language and Sentence Skills Practice Answer Key, pp. 109–116
14 Punctuation: Other Marks of Punctuation	• Teacher's Edition, pp. 367, 373 • Language and Sentence Skills Practice, pp. 332, 333–334, 335 • Language and Sentence Skills Practice Answer Key, pp. 126–127	• Teacher's Edition, pp. 354–393 • Language and Sentence Skills Practice, pp. 298–335 • Language and Sentence Skills Practice Answer Key, pp. 117–127
15 Spelling	• Teacher's Edition, pp. 404, 405, 413, 416, 418, 424, 425 • Language and Sentence Skills Practice, pp. 364, 365–366, 367 • Language and Sentence Skills Practice Answer Key, pp. 138–139	• Teacher's Edition, pp. 394–425 • Language and Sentence Skills Practice, pp. 336–367 • Language and Sentence Skills Practice Answer Key, pp. 128–139
16 Correcting Common Errors	• Language and Sentence Skills Practice, pp. 406, 407–408, 409 • Language and Sentence Skills Practice Answer Key, pp. 156–157	• Teacher's Edition, pp. 426–461 • Language and Sentence Skills Practice, pp. 368–409 • Language and Sentence Skills Practice Answer Key, pp. 140–157

Differentiating Instruction		Assessment
Learners Having Difficulty	**English-Language Learners & Special Education Students**	**Assessment**
• Teacher's Edition, pp. 328, 349 • Developmental Language Skills Guided Practice, pp. 127–144 • Developmental Language Skills Guided Practice Teacher's Notes and Answer Key, pp. 33–36	• Teacher's Edition, pp. 326, 336	• Holt Handbook Chapter Tests with Answer Key, pp. 25–26, 54
• Teacher's Edition, pp. 363, 385, 389 • Developmental Language Skills Guided Practice, pp. 145–166 • Developmental Language Skills Guided Practice Teacher's Notes and Answer Key, pp. 37–41	• Teacher's Edition, pp. 357, 360, 361, 362, 366, 371, 375, 380, 385, 389	• Holt Handbook Chapter Tests with Answer Key, pp. 27–28, 54
• Teacher's Edition, pp. 397, 400, 413, 416, 425 • Developmental Language Skills Guided Practice, pp. 167–182 • Developmental Language Skills Guided Practice Teacher's Notes and Answer Key, pp. 42–44	• Teacher's Edition, pp. 401, 408, 411	• Holt Handbook Chapter Tests with Answer Key, pp. 29–30, 54
• Teacher's Edition, pp. 430, 437, 451, 452 • Developmental Language Skills Guided Practice, pp. 183–184 • Developmental Language Skills Guided Practice Teacher's Notes and Answer Key, p. 45	• Teacher's Edition, pp. 445, 450	• Holt Handbook Chapter Tests with Answer Key, pp. 31–32, 55

(continued on next page)

Holt Handbook Chapter	Differentiating Instruction	
	Advanced Learners	**On-Level Learners**
17 Writing Clear Sentences		• Teacher's Edition, pp. 464–491 • Language and Sentence Skills Practice, pp. 411–432 • Language and Sentence Skills Practice Answer Key, pp. 158–165
18 Combining Sentences	• Teacher's Edition, p. 500	• Teacher's Edition, pp. 492–511 • Language and Sentence Skills Practice, pp. 433–448 • Language and Sentence Skills Practice Answer Key, pp. 166–172
19 Improving Sentence Style	• Teacher's Edition, p. 515	• Teacher's Edition, pp. 512–529 • Language and Sentence Skills Practice, pp. 449–462 • Language and Sentence Skills Practice Answer Key, pp. 173–177
20 Sentence Diagramming	• Teacher's Edition, pp. 530–543	• Teacher's Edition, pp. 530–543
Resources Manuscript Form		• Language and Sentence Skills Practice, pp. 463–464 • Language and Sentence Skills Practice Answer Key, p. 178

Differentiating Instruction		Assessment
Learners Having Difficulty	**English-Language Learners & Special Education Students**	**Assessment**
• Teacher's Edition, pp. 481, 483 • Developmental Language Skills Guided Practice, pp. 185–190 • Developmental Language Skills Guided Practice Teacher's Notes and Answer Key, p. 46	• Teacher's Edition, pp. 470, 476	• Holt Handbook Chapter Tests with Answer Key, pp. 33–36, 54
• Teacher's Edition, p. 505 • Developmental Language Skills Guided Practice, pp. 191–196 • Developmental Language Skills Guided Practice Teacher's Notes and Answer Key, p. 47		• Holt Handbook Chapter Tests with Answer Key, pp. 37–41, 54
• Developmental Language Skills Guided Practice, pp. 197–202 • Developmental Language Skills Guided Practice Teacher's Notes and Answer Key, p. 48	• Teacher's Edition, p. 515	• Holt Handbook Chapter Tests with Answer Key, pp. 42–46, 54
• Teacher's Edition, pp. 530–543	• Teacher's Edition, pp. 530–543	
• Developmental Language Skills Guided Practice, pp. 203–204 • Developmental Language Skills Guided Practice Teacher's Notes and Answer Key, p. 49		

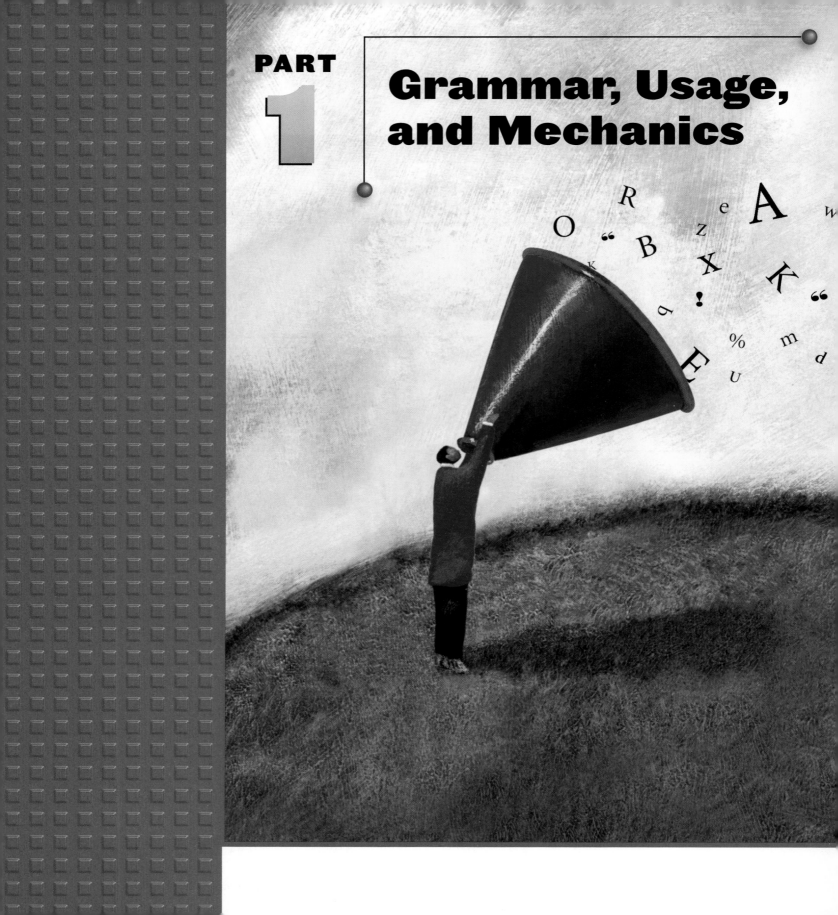

PART 1

Grammar, Usage, and Mechanics

GO TO: go.hrw.com

Grammar, Usage, and Mechanics   1

Parts of Speech Overview

Identification and Function

CHAPTER

1

INTRODUCING THE CHAPTER

- This chapter reviews the eight parts of speech. Each part of speech is defined, and subcategories of each are discussed. The chapter also provides exercises and activities for reinforcing students' understanding of this material as well as for reinforcing their critical-thinking skills.

- The chapter closes with a **Chapter Review** including a **Writing Application** feature that asks students to write a complete dictionary entry, including the word's derivation, use, meaning, pronunciation, and part of speech.

- For help in integrating this chapter with writing assignments, see the **Teaching Strands** chart on pp. T24–T25.

┌ H E L P ─

When you are identifying adjectives, do not include the articles (*a*, *an*, and *the*).

Numerals in brackets refer to rules tested by the items in the Diagnostic Preview.

1. [1b, i]
2. [1a, i]
3. [1g]
4. [1e, i]
5. [1f, i]
6. [1c, i]
7. [1d]

Diagnostic Preview

A. Identifying Parts of Speech

For each of the following sentences, identify every word or word group that is the part of speech indicated in parentheses.

EXAMPLE   **1.** On September 8, 1998, Mark McGwire hit his sixty-second home run for the season, breaking Roger Maris's record. (*noun*)

     1. *September 8, 1998; Mark McGwire; home run; season; Roger Maris's; record*

1. If anyone calls me while I am out, will you please give whoever it is one of these two numbers? (*pronoun*)

2. Although she lost her sight and hearing during childhood, Helen Keller learned to communicate with other people. (*noun*)

3. As much as we all had wanted to eat at the new French restaurant, we could not afford the prices. (*conjunction*)

4. Inca artisans were quite expert; among the works they left behind are elaborate jewelry and colorful tapestries. (*adverb*)

5. The cat came screaming around the corner, scooted under the car, and seemed almost to fly up the tree. (*preposition*)

6. This clock chimes a delicate melody on the half-hour. (*adjective*)

7. Do you think that the weather will finally turn cool once this low-pressure system moves through the area? (*verb*)

CHAPTER RESOURCES

Internet
- Web resources: go.hrw.com

go.
hrw
.com

Practice & Review
- *Language & Sentence Skills Practice,* pp. 2–24
- *Language & Sentence Skills Practice Answer Key,* pp. 1–9

Application & Enrichment
- *Language & Sentence Skills Practice,* pp. 1, 25–27
- *Language & Sentence Skills Practice Answer Key,* pp. 1, 9–10

8. I developed <u>extremely</u> painful shin splints when I jogged <u>much</u> <u>farther</u> than I <u>usually</u> do. (*adverb*)

9. <u>Oh</u>, how beautifully Kathleen Battle and Jessye Norman sang in their concert at Carnegie Hall! (*interjection*)

10. <u>Neither</u> the coach <u>nor</u> the team members offered excuses for the loss, <u>for</u> they had done their best. (*conjunction*)

B. Identifying Parts of Speech

Identify the part of speech of each italicized word in the following sentences.

EXAMPLE 1. *Although* I don't consider *myself* a chronic television viewer or an avid radio listener, I have *certainly* enjoyed my visit to the Museum of Television and Radio.

1. *Although*—conjunction; *myself*—pronoun; *certainly*— adverb

11. When *it* opened in 1991, the Museum of Television and Radio became New York City's first new major museum *since* 1966.

12. The late William Paley, the *founder* of CBS, *established* the museum with contributions from the broadcasting industry.

13. The museum doesn't contain *everything* ever heard on radio or seen on TV, *for* many early programs were never copied, and some of those that were copied are missing or unplayable.

14. *Its* collection, however, is *quite* extensive: approximately twenty-five thousand TV programs, fifteen thousand radio shows, and ten thousand commercials.

15. *Whether* you want to hear Jack Benny in a comedy sketch from the 1930s *or* you wish to watch Billie Holiday in a live performance from the 1950s, you'll find the recording *here*.

16. In fact, the earliest material *dates* to 1920, when the nation's *first* radio station, KDKA in Pittsburgh, went on the air.

17. Modern *technology* provides *easy* access to most of the collection.

18. Simply answer a *few* questions and press a button *on* one of the computers that store the catalog.

19. *Instantly*, a museum worker, using the computer, signals special machines in the basement, *which* automatically load the tapes.

20. Often by the time you've made *yourself* comfortable in one of the console rooms, the tape is *ready* for you to enjoy.

8. [1e]
9. [1h]
10. [1g]

11. pronoun/preposition [1b, f, i]
12. noun/verb [1a, d]
13. pronoun/conjunction [1b, g]
14. pronoun/adverb [1b, e, i]
15. conjunction/adverb [1g, e]
16. verb/adjective [1d, c]
17. noun/adjective [1a, c]
18. adjective/preposition [1c, f, i]
19. adverb/pronoun [1e, b]
20. pronoun/adjective [1b, c]

ASSESSING

Entry-Level Assessment

Diagnostic Preview. This **Diagnostic Preview** can be used to indicate the amount of reteaching needed. If only a few students are unable to demonstrate mastery of the parts of speech, you could have them read the definitions and work on the exercises together. You will probably want to check students' answers periodically to determine progress.

PRETEACHING

Lesson Starter

Motivating. Divide the class into groups of three or four, and have each group list the eight parts of speech, giving an example of each. Tell students to copy the following sentences and to place words from their lists in the blanks.

When [*pronoun*] was/were walking home [*adverb*], a car slammed [*preposition*] a pile of [*noun—plural*]. A(n) [*adjective*] young girl [*conjunction*] her dog [*verb—past tense*] hesitantly, and then looked up and said, "[*interjection*]!"

Ask volunteers to read sentences aloud. You could reinforce the concept of parts of speech by making eight lists (one for each category) of student examples on the board.

Differentiating Instruction

- *Developmental Language & Sentence Skills Guided Practice,* pp. 1–22
- *Developmental Language & Sentence Skills Guided Practice Teacher's Notes and Answer Key,* pp. 1–5

Assessment

- *Holt Handbook Chapter Tests with Answer Key,* pp. 1–2, 54

The Noun, the Pronoun, and the Adjective

Rules 1a–c (pp. 4–15)

OBJECTIVES

- To identify nouns in sentences and to classify the nouns as proper or common and as concrete or abstract

- To identify compound and collective nouns in sentences and to classify the nouns as common or proper and as concrete or abstract

- To identify pronouns in sentences

- To identify adjectives and the words they modify in sentences

DIRECT TEACHING

Modeling and Demonstration

Identifying Nouns. Model how to identify nouns by using the example *courage*. First, ask whether the word names a person, place, thing, or idea. [*idea*] *Courage* names an idea; therefore, *courage* is a noun. Now, have a volunteer use another example from this chapter to demonstrate how to identify a noun.

HELP

Nouns can be classified as (1) common or proper, (2) concrete or abstract, (3) collective, and (4) compound.

Reference Note

For more information about **capitalizing proper nouns**, see page 298.

MEETING THE CHALLENGE

List five proper nouns that come from common nouns, and give the origin of each proper noun—for instance, was someone or something named for a location, profession, or characteristic? Books and Web pages on the origins and meanings of names may be useful resources. Share your findings with the class in a short presentation or on a poster.

ANSWER

Responses will vary but should include explanations of five common nouns that have become proper nouns. Possible answers may point out that names come from common nouns describing locations or people's physical features, personalities, or professions.

The Noun

1a. A *noun* names a person, a place, a thing, or an idea.

Persons	carpenter, tourists, team, cousins, Faith Ringgold
Places	cities, theater, forest, neighborhood, Santa Fe
Things	merry-go-round, bricks, birds, horseshoe, Liberty Bell
Ideas	justice, creativity, self-control, opinions, Buddhism

Common Nouns and Proper Nouns

A *common noun* names any one of a group of persons, places, things, or ideas. A *proper noun* names a particular person, place, thing, or idea. A common noun is not capitalized (except when it begins a sentence or is part of a title); a proper noun, however, is capitalized.

Common Nouns	Proper Nouns
woman	Queen Isabella, Wilma Mankiller, Judith Baca
nation	Egypt, Mexico, Vietnam, New Zealand
event	Pan American Games, French Revolution, Academy Awards, Boston Tea Party
holiday	Patriot's Day; Fourth of July; Martin Luther King, Jr., Day; Mardi Gras
language	Hebrew, Spanish, Bantu, Thai, Latin

Concrete Nouns and Abstract Nouns

A *concrete noun* names a person, place, or thing that can be perceived by one or more of the senses (sight, hearing, taste, touch, and smell). An *abstract noun* names an idea, a feeling, a quality, or a characteristic.

Concrete Nouns	sneeze, star, gravel, cinnamon, jack-o'-lantern, Beijing, Leaning Tower of Pisa, Sammy Sosa
Abstract Nouns	peace, civilization, honor, courage, citizenship, Victorianism, Manifest Destiny

---

RESOURCES

The Noun, the Pronoun, and the Adjective

Practice

- *Language & Sentence Skills Practice,* pp. 2–10

Differentiating Instruction

- *Developmental Language & Sentence Skills,* pp. 1–10

Collective Nouns

The singular form of a *collective noun* names a group.

Collective Nouns	jury, band, family, class, flock, committee

Compound Nouns

A *compound noun* consists of two or more words that together name a person, a place, a thing, or an idea. The parts of a compound noun may be written as one word, as separate words, or as a hyphenated word.

One Word	stairway, bookcase, toenail, Newfoundland
Separate Words	lieutenant governor, ceiling fan, blue jay, Golden Gate Bridge
Hyphenated Word	sister-in-law, jack-of-all-trades, great-uncle, stick-in-the-mud

Exercise 1 **Identifying and Classifying Nouns**

Identify the nouns in each of the following sentences, and classify each noun as [*proper*] or *common* and as *concrete* or *abstract*.

EXAMPLE
1. In his report on the importance of religion in ancient Egypt, Joaquin wrote about the Great Sphinx and the Great Pyramid at Giza.

1. *report—common, concrete; importance—common, abstract; religion—common, abstract; Egypt—proper, concrete; Joaquin—proper, concrete; Great Sphinx—proper, concrete; Great Pyramid—proper, concrete; Giza—proper, concrete*

1. The objective was met when the crew repaired ten helicopters.
2. [Amalia Mesa-Bains] and [Michael Ríos] are among the many Hispanic artists who launched their careers in [San Francisco.]
3. In [Japan] many homes have a place of honor in which the family displays a favorite scroll or a vase of flowers.
4. We purchased tomatoes, lettuce, and corn grown by local farmers.
5. [Congress] debated the merits of the bill but could not reach a consensus.
6. My goal is to visit every state in the [United States.]

Reference Note

For information about **using verbs and pronouns that agree with collective nouns,** see pages 116 and 128.

—HELP—

If you are not sure how to write a compound noun, look it up in an up-to-date dictionary.

TEACHING (TIP)

Exercise 1 The distinction between abstract and concrete nouns is sometimes ambiguous. Student responses will vary. You might want to have students discuss their answers and explain their classifications.

DIFFERENTIATING INSTRUCTION

English-Language Learners

Spanish. In Spanish, nouns are almost always preceded by articles. For example, *She likes fruit* would be "She likes *the* fruit." In English, however, the addition of the definite article changes the meaning of the sentence from "She likes all fruit" to "She likes this particular fruit." Explain to students the difference in meaning caused by the definite article. Then, have students compose sentences using nouns with and without the definite article *the*. They could supply nouns to complete the following sentences:

I like . . .
I respect . . .
I enjoy listening to . . .
I appreciate . . . in my friends.

CONTENT-AREA CONNECTIONS

Humanities
Concrete and Abstract Nouns. Students might be interested in exploring, from a philosophical point of view, the sometimes ambiguous nature of the distinction between concrete and abstract nouns. Students could investigate the writings of Plato, Descartes, Hume, or Emerson, among others, for discussion of what is real (concrete) and what is a product of the human mind (abstract). Have students present oral reports on their findings.

7. Our family drove from our home in Kansas City to Chicago in our new van.
8. Her excellent record as treasurer convinced a majority of the students to vote for her for president.
9. Blunt honesty, quick wit, and fierce loyalty all characterize the protagonist of The Adventures of Huckleberry Finn.
10. The crowd roared as Chip sank the winning basket for the Falcons just before time ran out.

┌HELP─

Not every sentence in Exercise 2 contains both compound nouns and collective nouns.

Exercise 2 **Identifying and Classifying Nouns**

Identify the compound nouns and collective nouns in the following sentences. Then, classify each as *common* or *proper* and as *concrete* or *abstract.*

EXAMPLE

1. After her class had viewed a filmstrip about some of the ancient Egyptians' engineering feats, which included the construction of the Great Pyramid, the teacher, Ms. Ng, displayed this snapshot.

1. *compound: filmstrip—common, concrete; Great Pyramid—proper, concrete; Ms. Ng—proper, concrete; snapshot—common, concrete*

   collective: class—common, concrete

1. Did you do a double take when you saw this picture?

2. The juxtaposition of Egyptian landmarks with a seashore and a sign in Japanese writing is certainly an eye-opener.
3. Actually, the Sphinx and the pyramid are sand sculptures that a team of students from a high school in Japan built for the Kamakura Beach Carnival at Zaimokuza Beach.
4. Do you suppose the committee that judged the sculptures awarded the students' undertakings a prize?
5. The sightseers in front of the pyramid took a number of snapshots as keepsakes of the carnival.
6. Unlike the original Sphinx and Great Pyramid, which have stood for 4500 years, these sculptures will disappear with the first heavy rainstorm.
7. While the artists may use a variety of tools to carve and shape their creations, the final artwork consists of only two ingredients—sand and water.
8. Artists from around the world meet on beaches to see who can sculpt the most intricate and entertaining artwork made of sand.
9. Often, these sculptures illustrate stories or books, such as "Jack and the Beanstalk" and *Gulliver's Travels*.
10. One group built a sand castle that was over fifty-six feet tall.

The Pronoun

1b. A *pronoun* takes the place of one or more nouns or pronouns.

The word or word group that a pronoun stands for is called the *antecedent* of the pronoun.

EXAMPLES   Jay enjoys hiking and camping; in fact, **they** are his two favorite pastimes. [The nouns *hiking* and *camping* are the antecedents of the pronoun *they*.]

One of the film projectors is broken. **It** is being repaired. [The pronoun *One* is the antecedent of the pronoun *It*.]

The students complained to the principal about the dress code. **They** wished **he** had consulted **them** about **it**. [The noun *students* is the antecedent of the pronouns *They* and *them*; the noun *principal* is the antecedent of the pronoun *he*; and the compound noun *dress code* is the antecedent of the pronoun *it*.]

Reference Note

For more information on **pronouns and their antecedents,** see pages 124 and 162.

HELP

Pronouns can be classified as (1) personal, (2) reflexive or intensive, (3) demonstrative, (4) interrogative, (5) relative, or (6) indefinite.

Exercise 2 Identifying and Classifying Nouns

ANSWERS continued

2. landmarks—compound, common, concrete; seashore—compound, common, concrete; eye-opener—compound, common, concrete
3. team—collective, common, concrete; high school—compound, common, concrete; Kamakura Beach Carnival—compound, proper, concrete; Zaimokuza Beach—compound, proper, concrete
4. committee—collective, common, concrete; undertakings—compound, common, concrete
5. sightseers—compound, common, concrete; number—collective, common, concrete; snapshots—compound, common, concrete; keepsakes—compound, common, concrete
6. Great Pyramid—compound, proper, concrete; rainstorm—compound, common, concrete
7. variety—collective, common, concrete; artwork—compound, common, concrete
8. artwork—compound, common, concrete
9. "Jack and the Beanstalk"—compound, proper, concrete; *Gulliver's Travels*—compound, proper, concrete
10. group—collective, common, concrete; sand castle—compound, common, concrete

MINI-LESSON **Usage**

Agreement and Clear Reference. The beginning of the study of pronouns offers a good opportunity to remind students that pronouns should clearly agree with their antecedents in number and in gender. For more information on pronoun-antecedent agreement and clear reference, refer students to **Chapter 5: Agreement** and **Chapter 7: Clear Reference.**

DIRECT TEACHING

Modeling and Demonstration

Identifying Antecedents. Model how to identify the antecedent of a pronoun by using the example *Bill loaned Tina his book.* First, ask students to identify the pronoun. [*his*] Then, list the information the pronoun provides. [*The pronoun refers to one person. The person is male.*] Next, find the word to which the pronoun logically refers. [*The one male person in the sentence is Bill.*] *Bill* is the antecedent of *his.* Now, have a volunteer use an example from this chapter to demonstrate how to identify the antecedent of a pronoun.

DIFFERENTIATING INSTRUCTION

English-Language Learners

Spanish. Because Spanish uses more reflexive forms than English, Spanish-speaking students may overuse reflexive pronouns and may think that certain English verbs use reflexive forms because their Spanish counterparts do. For example, the Spanish equivalent of *repent* is *arrepentirse,* which translates literally as "to repent oneself." (The ending *se* makes the verb reflexive.)

Spanish. The English pronouns *your, his, her, its,* and *their* can all be rendered formally in Spanish as *su* (or *sus* if more than one thing is possessed). *Your* can be expressed as *tu* (singular) or *tus* (plural) familiarly, among family and close friends. *Yourself, himself, herself, itself,* and *themselves* can all be translated as *se.* Watch for any difficulties Spanish-speaking students may have distinguishing among pronouns in their written work.

Reference Note

For more about the various forms of **personal pronouns,** see **Chapter 6: Using Pronouns Correctly.**

┌HELP─

Do not use the nonstandard forms *hisself, theirself,* and *theirselves.* Use *himself* and *themselves* instead.

Personal Pronouns

A *personal pronoun* refers to the one(s) speaking (*first person*), the one(s) spoken to (*second person*), or the one(s) spoken about (*third person*).

	Singular	Plural
First Person	I, me, my, mine	we, us, our, ours
Second Person	you, your, yours	you, your, yours
Third Person	he, him, his, she, her, hers, it, its	they, them, their, theirs

EXAMPLES   If **I** give **you my** address, will **you** write to **me**?

We told **them** that **they** could go with **us**.

NOTE This textbook refers to the words *my, your, his, her, its, our,* and *their* as possessive pronouns. However, because they come before nouns and tell *which one* or *whose,* some authorities prefer to call these words adjectives. Follow your teacher's instructions regarding these possessive forms.

Reflexive and Intensive Pronouns

	Singular	Plural
First Person	myself	ourselves
Second Person	yourself	yourselves
Third Person	himself, herself, itself	themselves

A *reflexive pronoun* refers to the subject of a verb and functions as a complement or as the object of a preposition.

EXAMPLES   Mary excused **herself** from the table. [*Herself* is the direct object of *excused.*]

He said the mastermind was, in fact, **himself.** [*Himself* is a predicate nominative referring to the subject, *He.*]

They took extra biscuits for **themselves.** [*Themselves* is the object of the preposition *for.*]

MINI-LESSON   Usage

Case of *Who* and *Whom*. You may want to remind students that the case of a relative pronoun is determined by the pronoun's use in a clause. Give students the following steps to determine whether to use *who* or *whom* in a subordinate clause.

1. Isolate the subordinate clause.

2. Determine how the pronoun is used in the clause.

3. If the pronoun is used as a subject or a predicate nominative, it should be in the

An *intensive pronoun* emphasizes its antecedent—a noun or another pronoun.

EXAMPLES Joseph Vásquez **himself** wrote the script. [*Himself* emphasizes the subject, *Joseph Vásquez*, but has no grammatical function in the sentence.]

The final speech was given by Maya Angelou **herself.** [*Herself* emphasizes the object, *Maya Angelou,* but has no grammatical function in the sentence.]

Demonstrative Pronouns

A *demonstrative pronoun* points out a noun or another pronoun.

| this | that | these | those |

EXAMPLES Is **this** the one you want?

That may be the only reasonable solution.

These or **those** are the pictures from our vacation.

Interrogative Pronouns

An *interrogative pronoun* introduces a question.

| who | whom | whose | which | what |

EXAMPLES **What** is the capital of the Hawaiian Islands?

Whose is this red sweater?

To **whom** should I direct your call?

Relative Pronouns

A *relative pronoun* introduces an adjective clause.

| that | which | who | whom | whose |

EXAMPLES The college **that** I chose is in Texas.

The woman **who** chairs the committee is my aunt.

The birds, **which** usually have flown south by this time of the year, were still congregating in our backyard.

┌─ TIPS & TRICKS ─┐

If you are not sure whether a pronoun is reflexive or intensive, use this test: Read the sentence aloud, omitting the pronoun. If the basic meaning of the sentence stays the same, the pronoun is intensive. If the meaning changes, the pronoun is reflexive.

EXAMPLES
Mark repaired the car **himself.** [Without *himself,* the meaning stays the same. The pronoun is intensive.]

The children enjoyed **themselves** all morning. [Without *themselves,* the sentence doesn't make sense. The pronoun is reflexive.]

Reference Note

For more about **relative pronouns** and **adjective clauses,** see page 85. For information on when to use ***who*** or ***whom,*** see page 152.

---

nominative case (*who*). If the pronoun is used as an object of a verb or of a preposition, it should be in the objective case (*whom*).

4. For a "sound" check, replace the relative pronoun with *he* or *him.* If *he* sounds right, use *who.* If *him* sounds right, use *whom.*

For more information on pronoun case, refer students to **Chapter 6: Using Pronouns Correctly.**

Indefinite Pronouns

An *indefinite pronoun* refers to a person, a place, a thing, or an idea that may or may not be specifically named. In other words, the pronoun may not have a specific antecedent.

Reference Note

For more information about **indefinite pronouns,** see pages 109 and 125.

EXAMPLES   **All** of the members have voted. [*All* refers to *members.*]

Does **everyone** favor a weekly meeting? [*Everyone* has no specific antecedent.]

The fallen tree provided homes for **several** of the creatures of the woods. [*Several* refers to *creatures.*]

Common Indefinite Pronouns				
all	both	few	nobody	several
another	each	many	none	some
any	either	more	no one	somebody
anybody	everybody	most	nothing	someone
anyone	everyone	much	one	something
anything	everything	neither	other	such

Pronoun or Adjective?

Many of the words that can be used as pronouns can also be used as adjectives.

EXAMPLES   **This** is the best baklava I have ever tasted. [*This* is a pronoun referring to *baklava,* the predicate nominative.]
This baklava is delicious. [*This* is an adjective modifying *baklava.*]

Which of the rooms is yours? [*Which* is a pronoun referring to *rooms,* the object of the preposition *of.*]
Which room is yours? [*Which* is an adjective modifying *room.*]

Exercise 3 Identifying Pronouns

Identify the pronouns in the following sentences.

EXAMPLE   1. Most of those who took the photography class learned a great deal about how they perceive their environment.
1. *Most, those, who, they, their*

1. Last year <u>my</u> school gave two photography courses, <u>neither</u> of <u>which</u> had been offered before.
2. The course <u>that</u> I took dealt with the ways in <u>which</u> people perceive their environment.
3. <u>Many</u> of <u>us</u> block out <u>much</u> in <u>our</u> everyday surroundings.
4. You can demonstrate to <u>yourselves</u> how unaware of <u>our</u> surroundings nearly <u>all</u> of <u>us</u> are.
5. <u>Which</u> of <u>you</u>, on returning home from a trip, hasn't noticed how different <u>all</u> of the rooms look to <u>you</u>?
6. <u>Some</u> of <u>your</u> possessions may seem unfamiliar to <u>you</u>, and a <u>few</u> of <u>them</u> may appear quite peculiar.
7. Eventually the sensation fades, and <u>your</u> surroundings assume <u>their</u> usual background role.
8. <u>Each</u> of <u>us</u> can regain the ability to see freshly if <u>we</u> learn to make full use of <u>our</u> sense of sight.
9. <u>We</u> can train <u>ourselves</u> to perceive the objects as shapes instead of thinking about <u>their</u> functions.
10. As the French Impressionist painter Claude Monet remarked, <u>we</u> must forget the names of the things <u>that</u> <u>we</u> observe.

The Adjective

1c. An *adjective* modifies a noun or a pronoun.

To modify means "to describe" or "to make more definite." An adjective modifies a noun or a pronoun by telling *what kind, which one, how many,* or *how much.*

What Kind?	**ripening** apples	**happy** child
	Asian country	**up-to-date** look
Which One?	**this** book	**last** straw
	those girls	**next** step
How Many?	**two** students	**both** answers
	several choices	**many** people
How Much?	**one-half** cup	**enough** time
	more money	**less** trouble

—HELP—
To keep your readers from getting confused, always try to place pronouns near their antecedents—generally within the same sentence or in the next sentence.

CONFUSING
Please hand me the brushes. I also need some linseed oil. They are on the top shelf. [Does *They* refer to the brushes or to both the brushes and the linseed oil?]

CLEAR
Please hand me the **brushes. They** are on the top shelf. I also need some linseed oil. [Only the brushes are on the top shelf.]

TIPS & TRICKS

The phrase "these five interesting books" can help you remember the questions an adjective can answer: Which books? **These** books. How many books? **Five** books. What kind of books? **Interesting** books.

Exercise 3

DISTRIBUTED REVIEW
To reinforce what students have learned about nouns, have them list all the nouns in sentence 2. [*course, ways, people, environment*]

DIRECT TEACHING

Modeling and Demonstration
Words That Adjectives Modify.
Model how to identify the word an adjective modifies by using the example *The sky, blue and clear, stretched above us.* First, have students identify the adjectives. [*The, blue, clear*] Then, ask *what* stretched. [*sky*] Ask what is blue and clear. [*sky*] The adjectives *The, blue,* and *clear* modify the noun *sky.* Now, have a volunteer use another example from this chapter to demonstrate how to identify what word an adjective modifies.

Relating to Writing

Give students several examples of descriptions from mail-order clothing catalogs, and discuss and analyze with the class the use of adjectives in the descriptions.

Then, give students catalog pictures without descriptions and ask each student to pick one article of clothing and to write a description of it in the style of a catalog. Emphasize that students should use adjectives that are positive, humorous, and flowery, even to the point of ridiculousness. Collect and display pictures students have used to write their descriptions. Then, gather the descriptions, shuffle them, and read them, letting students guess which article of clothing pictured is being described.

English-Language Learners

Japanese. There are no definite or indefinite articles in Japanese. Consequently, students might omit *a, an,* and *the* from their speech and writing. If students omit articles, review the chapter material on articles thoroughly with students. Then, give them paragraphs from which articles have been deleted and have the students insert the appropriate articles.

Vietnamese. Because Vietnamese adjectives follow nouns and pronouns, Vietnamese-speaking students may produce sentences with a word order that is unusual for English. For example, a student may write "Mark saw birds beautiful" instead of "Mark saw beautiful birds." Remind students that in English single-word modifiers should precede the words they modify.

Reference Note

For more about **predicate adjectives,** see page 50. For guidelines on **using adjectives,** see Chapter 9.

┌─HELP─
Remember that the sound, not the spelling, of a word determines which indefinite article to use before that word.

┌─HELP─
In this book the words *my, your, his, her, its, our,* and *their,* which take the place of possessive nouns, are called possessive pronouns. Since they precede nouns and tell *which one* or *whose,* some teachers prefer to call these words possessive adjectives.

EXAMPLES
my job, **your** essay,

their plans

Follow your teacher's instructions in labeling these words.

An adjective usually precedes the word it modifies.

EXAMPLE   The **tired** and **hungry** hikers straggled into camp.

Sometimes, for emphasis, an adjective follows the word it modifies.

EXAMPLE   The hikers, **tired** and **hungry,** straggled into camp.

An adjective that modifies the subject may appear in the predicate. Such an adjective is called a *predicate adjective.*

EXAMPLES   The hikers felt **tired** and **hungry.**

Tired and **hungry** were the hikers.

Articles

The most frequently used adjectives are *a, an,* and *the.* These words are called *articles.*

A and *an* are called *indefinite articles* because they refer to any member of a general group. *A* is used before words beginning with a consonant sound; *an* is used before words beginning with a vowel sound.

EXAMPLES   Felipe added **a** tomato and **an** avocado to the salad.

A European said, "It is **an** honor to be here with you." [*A* is used before *European* because *European* begins with a consonant sound. *An* is used before *honor* because the *h* in *honor* is not pronounced; *honor* is pronounced as though it began with a vowel.]

The is called the *definite article* because it refers to a specific person, place, thing, or idea.

EXAMPLE   We spent **the** hour discussing **the** revolution that began in 1791 in Haiti.

Adjective or Pronoun?

In different contexts, a word may be used as different parts of speech. For example, the following words may be used as adjectives and as pronouns.

all	either	much	some	those
another	few	neither	such	what
any	many	one	that	which
both	more	other	these	whose
each	most	several	this	

Remember that an adjective *modifies* a noun or a pronoun and that a pronoun *takes the place of* a noun or another pronoun.

ADJECTIVE   Ntozake Shange wrote **both** poems. [*Both* modifies the noun *poems.*]

PRONOUN   Ntozake Shange wrote **both**. [*Both* takes the place of the noun *poems.*]

ADJECTIVE   **These** books are overdue. [*These* modifies the noun *books.*]

PRONOUN   **These** are overdue. [*These* takes the place of the noun *books.*]

ADJECTIVE   **Several** ducks had dark green heads. [*Several* modifies the noun *ducks.*]

PRONOUN   **Several** had dark green heads. [*Several* takes the place of the noun *ducks.*]

NOTE   The words *this, that, these,* and *those* are called **demonstrative pronouns** when they take the place of nouns or other pronouns and are called **demonstrative adjectives** when they modify nouns or pronouns.

Reference Note
For more about **demonstrative pronouns,** see page 9.

HELP
Possessive forms of nouns, like possessive pronouns, are sometimes referred to as adjectives. Follow your teacher's instructions regarding these forms.

EXAMPLES
Jim's desk, **Mrs. Cho's** book

Adjective or Noun?

Most words that are used as nouns can also be used as adjectives.

Nouns	Adjectives
sofa	**sofa** cushion
hotel	**hotel** lobby
taco	**taco** salad
high school	**high school** senior
Marine Corps	**Marine Corps** cadet

An adjective that is formed from a proper noun, such as *Marine Corps* in the last example above, is called a **proper adjective.** Proper adjectives, like proper nouns, are capitalized.

NOTE   Do not mistake part of a compound noun for an adjective. The entire word group is considered a noun.

COMPOUND NOUNS   paper clips, cable TV, time capsule, United States

HELP
If you are not sure if a word group is considered a compound noun or an adjective with a noun, consult a dictionary.

Exercise 4 In sentence 1 some students may mark the compound nouns *Blue Highways* and *United States* as adjectives and the nouns they modify.

TEACHING **TIP**

Review A You may want to remind students to check a dictionary to distinguish between compound nouns and word groups consisting of an adjective and a noun.

STYLE **TIP**

Using adjectives, especially those that appeal to the five senses—sight, hearing, touch, smell, and taste—can help you create vivid images. When describing nouns or pronouns, be as specific in your choices of adjectives as you can. For example, instead of using the adjective *red,* you might use an adjective that specifies a shade of red, such as *crimson, coral, magenta, maroon,* or *terra cotta.*

HELP

Two good sources to use to find precise adjectives and other parts of speech (adverbs, nouns, and verbs) are a thesaurus and a dictionary. First, check a thesaurus for possible choices to use. Then, look up the words in a dictionary and compare their meanings so that you can decide which choice will convey the precise meaning you intend.

Exercise 4 **Identifying Adjectives and the Words They Modify**

Identify the adjectives and the words they modify in the following sentences. Do not include articles (*a, an,* and *the*).

EXAMPLE   **1.** I have read two fascinating books by the talented writer William Least Heat-Moon.

 1. two—books; fascinating—books; talented—writer

 1. His first book, *Blue Highways,* chronicled a journey across the United States in 1978.
 2. That book attracted many readers and made the national bestseller lists.
 3. In *PrairyErth,* Heat-Moon narrows his focus to a single Kansas county.
 4. The unusual title comes from the shorthand term scientists use for the unique soils of the central states.
 5. Chase County lies in east-central Kansas.
 6. It is, as Heat-Moon says, "the most easterly piece" of the West.
 7. A county with a population of 3,013 may seem an unlikely location for an examination of the role humanity plays on this planet.
 8. After all, the county has only two towns and a few villages.
 9. In many ways, though, Kansas is a microcosm of America.
 10. In this masterful prose, Chase County in turn reveals itself to be a microcosm of Kansas.

Review A **Identifying Nouns, Pronouns, and Adjectives**

Tell whether each italicized word or word group in the following sentences is used as a *noun,* a *pronoun,* or an *adjective.* If a word or word group is used as an adjective, give the word it modifies.

EXAMPLE   **1.** *Everyone* in class is writing a poem about an *American* pioneer.

 1. Everyone—pronoun; American—adjective—pioneer

 1. Several students are writing *theirs* about people whose names are familiar to *many;* others have chosen people who they believe merit wider recognition.
 2. After *much* thought, I have finally narrowed my choices to two *African American* women whom I admire.

3. Both of these women broke new ground in their fields—one in the performing arts and the other in the visual arts.

4. The fieldwork [that] Katherine Dunham (right) did as an anthropology student in the West Indies inspired her to incorporate elements of African and Caribbean folk culture into *modern dance.*

5. After touring the world for several decades, the dancer-choreographer founded the Katherine Dunham Children's Workshop, which she still directs, in *East St. Louis,* Illinois.

6. Tributes to Dunham continue to pour in, for [she] is considered a true dance innovator.

7. My other potential choice is Barbara Brandon, who in 1991 became the first African American woman cartoonist to achieve syndication in the mainstream press.

8. As you can see below, Brandon's *comic strip* depicts life from the *perspective* of an African American woman.

9. Brandon pictures only the heads and, occasionally, the hands of her characters, [all] of whom are women, because she believes that women's bodies are displayed enough in the *media.*

10. As [you] might guess, my final choice of a subject will not be an easy [one].

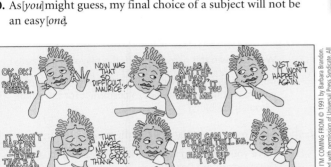

The Verb

1d. A *verb* expresses action or a state of being.

Main Verbs and Helping Verbs

A *main verb* and one or more *helping verbs* (also called *auxiliary verbs*) make up a *verb phrase.*

┌─HELP─

In this book, verbs are classified (1) as helping or main verbs, (2) as action or linking verbs, and (3) as transitive or intransitive verbs.

The Verb
Rule 1d *(pp. 15–20)*

OBJECTIVE

■ To identify verbs and verb phrases and to classify them as linking or action and as transitive or intransitive

The Verb **15**

The Verb

Practice

■ *Language & Sentence Skills Practice,* pp. 11–14

Differentiating Instruction

■ *Developmental Language & Sentence Skills,* pp. 11–16

DIRECT TEACHING

Modeling and Demonstration

Identifying Verbs and Helping Verbs. Model how to identify main verbs and helping verbs by using the examples *I do wash the dishes* and *I will do the dishes.* First, ask which word in *do wash* expresses most of the verb's meaning—which word tells you what action is being performed. [*wash*] Ask which word "helps" the word *wash.* [*do*] Then, ask students which word in *will do* expresses most of the verb's meaning [*do*] and which word helps *do.* [*will*] Point out that some words can be a helping verb in some sentences and a main verb in others. Now, have a volunteer use other examples from this chapter to demonstrate how to identify a main verb and a helping verb.

DIFFERENTIATING INSTRUCTION

English-Language Learners

Hmong. In Hmong, the verb *be* is implied by rather than used with predicate adjectives; therefore, Hmong speakers may see the verb as being redundant when it's used with a predicate adjective. Students may sometimes omit the verb entirely, writing "I happy," "she tall," or "he busy," rather than "I am happy," "she is tall," or "he is busy." Remind English-language learners that verbs are necessary in complete sentences in English, and offer practice with the use of *be,* stressing the verb's presence in posed questions and answers: ***Are*** *you happy? I* ***am*** *happy.* ***Is*** *she tall? She* ***is*** *tall.* ***Is*** *he busy? He* ***is*** *busy.*

Reference Note

For more about **modals,** see page 218.

HELP

The word *not* and its contraction, *–n't,* are adverbs telling *to what extent;* neither is part of a verb phrase.

EXAMPLES   Daniel **has played.** [*Has* is the helping verb; *played* is the main verb.]

Simon **will be going.** [*Will* and *be* are the helping verbs; *going* is the main verb.]

Lynn **should have been working.** [*Should, have,* and *been* are the helping verbs; *working* is the main verb.]

Common Helping Verbs			
Forms of *Be*	am	been	was
	are	being	were
	be	is	
Forms of *Have*	had	has	have
Forms of *Do*	do	does	did
Modals	can	might	should
	could	must	will
	may	shall	would

A ***modal*** (or ***modal auxilliary***) is a helping verb that is joined with a main verb to express an attitude such as necessity or possibility.

EXAMPLES   We **must** win this game to reach the playoffs. [necessity]

Mr. Garza said that if we work hard enough on the play we are writing, we **may** get to perform it for the whole school. [possibility]

A helping verb may be separated from the main verb.

EXAMPLES   **Have** you **seen** Tom Stoppard's play *Rosencrantz and Guildenstern Are Dead*?

You **should** not **miss** it.

Action Verbs

An ***action verb*** expresses either physical or mental activity.

Physical	speak	sleep	carry	throw
Mental	think	imagine	dream	know

EXAMPLES   The horse **galloped** across the field.

The Colorado River **runs** through the Grand Canyon.

If the ball **touched** the line, the umpire **made** the right call.

Do you ever **wonder** what dogs **dream**?

Linking Verbs

A *linking verb* connects the subject to a word or word group that identifies or describes the subject. Such a word or word group is called a *subject complement.*

EXAMPLES   Wovoka **was** an influential Paiute prophet. [The subject complement *prophet* identifies the subject *Wovoka.*]

Marcy **looks** serious. [The subject complement *serious* describes the subject *Marcy.*]

Computers **were** once so large that they could fill a room but **are** now small enough, in some cases, to fit in a pocket. [The subject complements *large* and *small* describe the subject *Computers.*]

Common Linking Verbs			
Forms of *Be*			
am	be	will be	had been
is	can be	could be	shall have been
are	may be	should be	will have been
was	might be	would be	could have been
were	must be	has been	should have been
being	shall be	have been	would have been
Others			
appear	grow	seem	stay
become	look	smell	taste
feel	remain	sound	turn

Some of the verbs listed as *Others* in the chart above can be used as either linking verbs or action verbs, depending on the context of the sentence.

LINKING   The alarm **sounded** shrill.
ACTION   I **sounded** the alarm.

Reference Note

For more about **subject complements,** see page 49.

TIPS & TRICKS

To determine whether a verb is a linking verb or an action verb, substitute a form of *be* or *seem.* If the sentence still makes sense, the verb is a linking verb.

LINKING
The fabric **felt** soft. [*The fabric was soft* makes sense.]

ACTION
I **felt** the fabric. [*I was the fabric* doesn't make sense.]

DIFFERENTIATING INSTRUCTION

Advanced Learners

If "Do Not Go Gentle into That Good Night" by Dylan Thomas is available in students' literature books, have them read the selection. Ask them to identify the action and linking verbs in the poem and to label them as *action verbs* or *linking verbs.* [*There are sixteen different action verbs and two linking verbs.*] Ask students why they think Thomas chose to include so many action verbs in the poem. Does Thomas's choice of verbs support the theme of the poem? [*The vibrant action verbs help convey Thomas's message—that the dying man should struggle with all his energy against the inevitability of death.*]

English-Language Learners

Cantonese. Because Cantonese does not use helping verbs for questions or negatives, the use of *do* as a helping verb may be particularly puzzling for Cantonese speakers. Students may use regular verb forms and avoid inserting a helping verb: *How much money you have?*

Since the helping verb is unstressed in English sentences, students may have difficulty perceiving its use. Emphasizing the use of *do* and other helping verbs when speaking to students may focus their attention on and assist them in using helping verbs.

The Verb   **17**

DIRECT TEACHING

Correcting Misconceptions

Students may mistakenly believe that every verb is either always transitive or always intransitive. Have students use the words *burst, sing, melt,* and *try* in sentences as both transitive and intransitive verbs. For sentences in which transitive verbs are used, tell students to circle the verbs and to draw arrows from the verbs to the words that receive the action.

RETEACHING

Transitive or Intransitive?

Activity. If students have difficulty differentiating between transitive and intransitive verbs, try another approach. Draw one set of three boxes arranged horizontally on the board. Under these boxes, draw a set of two boxes also horizontally arranged. Explain that each box in the first set of boxes corresponds to a major sentence part: subject, verb, or complement. Each box in the second set of boxes also corresponds to a major sentence part: subject or verb. Ask students which set should be labeled transitive and which intransitive. If students have trouble, write the verb *eat* in the second box in both rows. Ask students to use *eat* as a transitive verb by adding two words to the first row and to use *eat* as an intransitive verb by adding one word to the second row. [*Birds eat worms. Birds eat.*] Challenge students to think of five verbs that can be used both transitively and intransitively. [*Possible answers:* fly, chew, drive, paint, grow, lose, remember]

Reference Note

For more about **objects of verbs,** see page 45.

⌐HELP⌐

Most dictionaries group the definitions of verbs according to whether the verbs are used transitively (*v.t.*) or intransitively (*v.i.*). If you use a dictionary to determine whether a verb is transitive or intransitive, be sure to check all of the definitions.

NOTE The forms of *be* are not always used as linking verbs. That is, they are sometimes used as state-of-being verbs but are not used to connect subjects to subject complements. In such cases, words that tell *where* or *when* are generally used to complete the meanings of the verb forms.

EXAMPLE   You **should have been** here yesterday. [*Here* tells *where,* and *yesterday* tells *when.*]

Transitive and Intransitive Verbs

A *transitive verb* has an *object*—a word or word group that tells who or what receives the action of the verb.

EXAMPLES   The rain **lashed** the windows. [The object *windows* receives the action of the verb *lashed.*]

We **closed** and **bolted** the shutters. [The object *shutters* receives the action of the verbs *closed* and *bolted.*]

An *intransitive verb* does not have an object.

EXAMPLES   The rain **fell.**

My cousin **arrived** yesterday.

Many English verbs can be either transitive or intransitive, depending on how they are used.

TRANSITIVE   The chorus **sang** patriotic songs. [The object *songs* receives the action of the verb *sang.*]

INTRANSITIVE   The chorus **sang** beautifully. [no object]

Like a one-word verb, a verb phrase may be classified as action or linking and as transitive or intransitive.

EXAMPLES   The actors **are practicing** their lines. [action, transitive]

The director **is meeting** with the stage crew. [action, intransitive]

Preparation for the opening night **has been** hectic! [linking, intransitive]

NOTE While action verbs may be transitive or intransitive, linking verbs and state-of-being verbs are always intransitive.

Exercise 5 · Identifying and Classifying Verbs and Verb Phrases

Identify the verbs and verb phrases in the following sentences. Then, classify each verb or verb phrase as *linking* or *action*, and as *transitive* or *intransitive*.

EXAMPLE **1.** The dark clouds did not make the day more pleasant.

   1. did make—action, transitive

1. When will Halley's Comet next appear?
2. A creosote bush in the Mojave Desert has lived for approximately twelve thousand years.
3. How many decimal places of pi can you name?
4. What is the purpose of the Electoral College?
5. You can remove chewing gum from clothing more easily if you first harden it with ice.
6. Mark Twain used a typewriter when he wrote *The Adventures of Tom Sawyer.*
7. You should be more careful, young man!
8. In 1997, Tiger Woods became the youngest winner of the Masters Tournament.
9. Have you been listening to the Shostakovich CD that I lent you?
10. The first Super Bowl was very exciting; the Green Bay Packers defeated the Kansas City Chiefs, 35 to 10.

—HELP—

Some sentences in Exercise 5 have more than one verb or verb phrase.

1. act., int.
2. act., int.

3. act., tr.
4. link., int.
5. act., tr./act., tr.

6. act., tr./act.,tr.

7. link., int.
8. link., int.

9. act., int./act., tr.
10. link., int./act., tr.

Exercise 6 · Identifying and Classifying Verbs and Verb Phrases

Identify the verbs and verb phrases in the following sentences. Then, classify each verb or verb phrase as *linking* or *action*, and as *transitive* or *intransitive*.

EXAMPLES **1.** I have never visited the Statue of Liberty.

   1. have visited—action, transitive

2. It must be a truly amazing sight.

   2. must be—linking, intransitive

1. link., int./link., int.

1. The Statue of Liberty, which has become a major American landmark, may be the most famous structure in the world.
2. It possesses a twofold appeal: It symbolizes human liberty, and it unfailingly awes the visitor by its colossal size.

   2. act., tr./act., tr./act., tr.

—HELP—

Some sentences in Exercise 6 have more than one verb or verb phrase.

PRACTICE

Guided and Independent

Exercises You may wish to use **Exercise 5** as guided practice and have students complete **Exercise 6** as independent practice.

HOMEWORK

EXTENSION

Relating to Writing

Have students bring to class compositions they are writing for this or another class. Then, have students identify all of the verbs in their writing. Tell students to evaluate each verb and to replace overused and dull verbs with interesting, specific ones.

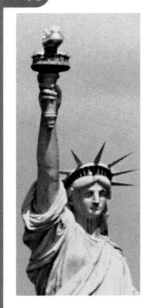

The Adverb
Rule 1e *(pp. 20–23)*

OBJECTIVE

- To identify adverbs and the words they modify in sentences

DIRECT TEACHING

Modeling and Demonstration

Identifying Adverbs. Model how to identify an adverb by writing on the chalkboard the example *The squirrel ran swiftly,* along with the questions *Where? When? How? How often?* and *To what extent?* Next, ask students if any words in the sentence answer any of those questions. [*swiftly—how*] Tell students that *swiftly* is an adverb. Now, have a volunteer use another example from this chapter to demonstrate how to identify an adverb.

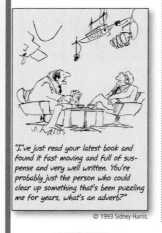

"I've just read your latest book and found it fast moving and full of suspense and very well written. You're probably just the person who could clear up something that's been puzzling me for years, what's an adverb?"

© 1993 Sidney Harris.

---

3. Moreover, it has <u>withstood</u> the continuous assaults of time and weather.   **3.** act., tr.

4. Frédéric Auguste Bartholdi <u>designed</u> the statue, and plans for the supporting framework <u>came</u> from the drawing board of Alexandre Gustave Eiffel.   **4.** act., tr./act., int.

5. The copper-plated statue <u>has</u> an intricate and strong iron framework that <u>supports</u> Liberty's familiar pose.   **5.** act., tr./act., tr.

6. The statue <u>was</u> a gift from the people of France, but Americans <u>paid</u> the construction costs for the pedestal.   **6.** link., int./act., tr.

7. In newspaper editorials, Joseph Pulitzer <u>persuaded</u> the American people that they <u>needed</u> the statue.   **7.** act., tr./act., tr.

8. The people <u>agreed</u>, and in 1886, the nation <u>celebrated</u> the dedication of the Statue of Liberty on what <u>was</u> at that time Bedloe's Island in Upper New York Bay. **8.** act., int./act., tr./link., int.

9. Bartholdi <u>modeled</u> Liberty's face after his mother's features. **9.** act., tr.

10. Those features <u>have remained</u> symbols of quiet determination.   **10.** link., int.

The Adverb

1e. An **adverb** modifies a verb, an adjective, or another adverb.

An adverb tells *where, when, how,* or *to what extent* (*how much, how often,* or *how long*). Adverbs are most commonly used to modify verbs and verb phrases.

Adverbs may modify verbs.

EXAMPLES   Teresa spoke **eloquently**. [The adverb *eloquently* modifies the verb *spoke,* telling *how.*]

Have you heard this melody **before**? [The adverb *before* modifies the verb phrase *Have heard,* telling *when.*]

They searched **everywhere**. [The adverb *everywhere* modifies the verb *searched,* telling *where.*]

He had **not** read the contract **thoroughly**. [The adverbs *not* and *thoroughly* modify the verb phrase *had read,* telling *to what extent.*]

NOTE   The word *not* and its contraction, *–n't,* are adverbs telling *to what extent.*

RESOURCES

The Adverb
Practice
- *Language & Sentence Skills Practice,* pp. 15–16

Differentiating Instruction
- *Developmental Language & Sentence Skills,* pp. 17–18

Adverbs may modify adjectives.

EXAMPLES   Phuong Vu is **quite** creative. [The adverb *quite* modifies the adjective *creative*, telling *to what extent*.]

This species is found on an **extremely** remote island. [The adverb *extremely* modifies the adjective *remote*, telling *to what extent*.]

Adverbs may modify other adverbs.

EXAMPLES   Jackie Joyner-Kersee runs **remarkably** swiftly. [The adverb *remarkably* modifies the adverb *swiftly*, telling *to what extent*.]

It's **too** soon to know the results. [The adverb *too* modifies the adverb *soon*, telling *to what extent*.]

Noun or Adverb?

Some words that are often used as nouns may also be used as adverbs.

EXAMPLES   My parents left **yesterday.** [The noun *yesterday* is used as an adverb telling *when*.]

They will return **home Saturday.** [The noun *home* is used as an adverb telling *where*. The noun *Saturday* is used as an adverb telling *when*.]

Exercise 7 **Identifying Adverbs and the Words They Modify**

Identify the adverbs and the words they modify in the following sentences.

EXAMPLE   1. I recently read an article about the American physicist Rosalyn Yalow.

1. *recently—read*

1. Yalow helped develop an extremely sensitive biological technique.
2. Radioimmunoassay, which is now used in laboratories around the world, readily detects antibodies and hormones.
3. Yalow realized that anyone who proposes a distinctly new idea must always anticipate that it will not be widely accepted at first.
4. Most scientists do not leap excitedly from the bath crying "Eureka!" as people say Archimedes did.
5. Yalow and her colleague accidentally discovered radioimmunoassay while observing two patients.

STYLE   TIP

The most frequently used adverbs are *too, so, really,* and *very.* In fact, these words are often overused. To make your speaking and writing more interesting, you can replace these adverbs with less common ones, such as *completely, especially,* or *quite.*

Reference Note

For more about **using adverbs,** see Chapter 9.

HELP

Some sentences in Exercise 7 contain more than one adverb.

The Adverb   **21**

GRAMMAR

Exercise 7 Identifying Adverbs and the Words They Modify

ANSWERS continued

6. carefully—interpreted

7. undeniably—prestigious

8. ultimately—became
   very—different

9. ordinarily—resist
   not—quickly
   quickly—was accepted

10. not—can be impeded
    forever—can be impeded
    eventually—are accepted

TEACHING TIP

Review B Some students may label *his* in number 7 as an adjective.

Reference Note

For information about **adverbs used to join words or word groups,** see **relative adverbs** (page 85) and **conjunctive adverbs** (page 95).

6. After they carefully interpreted their observations, they arrived at their exciting discovery.

7. In 1977, although Yalow's collaborator had died, the Nobel Prize Committee awarded Yalow and two other researchers the undeniably prestigious Nobel Prize for medicine.

8. Radioimmunoassay ultimately became a basic diagnostic tool in very different areas of medicine.

9. According to Yalow, because people ordinarily resist change, the technique was not quickly accepted.

10. She believes that progress cannot be impeded forever and that good ideas are eventually accepted.

Review B Identifying Parts of Speech

Identify the part of speech of each italicized word in the following sentences. If the word is used as an adjective or an adverb, tell what word or words it modifies. n.=noun; pro.=pronoun; adj.=adjective; v.=verb; adv.=adverb

EXAMPLE
1. The *Mexican* artist Diego Rivera was a *remarkably* talented *muralist.*

1. *Mexican—adjective—artist*
   remarkably—adverb—talented
   muralist—noun

1. adv./v.
1. Diego Rivera is *chiefly* <u>famous</u> for his murals, but he was a prolific artist who *worked* in a wide variety of styles.

2. adj./pro.
2. *This* <u>landscape</u> is an example of his early work; *it* was painted in 1904.

3. Rivera, *who* was born in Guanajuato, Mexico, in 1886, entered the San Carlos Academy of Fine Arts in Mexico City when he was *only* <u>eleven</u>.

3. pro./adv.
4. adj./n.
4. In 1907, with the proceeds from his first *art* <u>show</u>, he made the *first* of several lengthy visits to Europe.

5. adv./pro.
5. *There* he <u>experimented</u> with different approaches until he realized it was the fresco process, the art of painting on wet plaster, *that* best suited his artistic vision.

6. n./v.
6. *Two* of Rivera's lifelong interests *were* machinery and Mexican history.

7. n./n.
7. His murals in the former palace of *Hernán Cortés* in Cuernavaca, in the state of Morelos, depict the history of Morelos from before the *conquest* by Spain until after the Mexican Revolution of 1910.

8. *One of the works that* Rivera created in the United States was a series of twenty-seven murals that the Detroit Arts Commission asked him to paint on subjects related to Detroit and the general theme of industrialization.   8. pro./pro.

9. <u>Rivera</u> was *controversial* in the United States because he included *political* <u>themes</u> in his work.   9. adj./adj.

10. Ironically, capitalists sometimes attacked *him* for his affiliation with Communists, and Communists sometimes attacked him for accepting *commissions* from capitalists.   10. pro./n.

Diego Rivera, *La Era* (1910). Oil on canvas (100 cm x 114.6 cm). Reproduction authorized por el Instituto Nacional de Bellas Artes y Literatura, Marte R. Gomez Collection (INBA)/The Detroit Museum of Art.

The Preposition

1f. A *preposition* shows the relationship of a noun or pronoun, called the *object of the preposition,* to another word.

Notice how changing the preposition in the following examples changes the relationship between the verb *swam* and the noun *raft.*

EXAMPLES
   I swam **to** the raft.
   I swam **from** the raft.
   I swam **around** the raft.
   I swam **past** the raft.
   I swam **under** the raft.

Object of a Preposition

The *object of a preposition* is a noun, a pronoun, or a word group that functions as a noun; in most cases it follows a preposition. Together, the preposition, its object, and any modifiers of the object make a *prepositional phrase.*

EXAMPLES
   Did you see Juanita **at the last game**?

   The line starts **behind him.**

   They played a new song **by Hootie and the Blowfish.**

---HELP---

As a preposition, the word *to* usually precedes a noun or a pronoun to form a prepositional phrase. Do not confuse a prepositional phrase with an *infinitive*—a verb form preceded by *to.*

PREPOSITIONAL PHRASES
   to the lake   to them
INFINITIVES
   to consider   to choose

Reference Note

For more information about **prepositional phrases,** see page 60. For more information about **infinitives,** see page 70.

The Preposition   **23**

EXTENSION

Viewing the Art
Students might be interested in the fact that Rivera was only eighteen when he painted the work shown here. Challenge the class to describe the scene depicted in the painting. Students should write an informative descriptive paragraph containing vivid verbs, adjectives, and adverbs to convey the mood evoked by the painting.

The Preposition, the Conjunction, the Interjection, and Determining Parts of Speech
Rules 1f–i *(pp. 23–30)*

OBJECTIVES

■ **To add prepositional phrases to sentences**

■ **To identify and classify conjunctions in sentences**

■ **To complete sentences by adding interjections**

■ **To identify the parts of speech of words used in sentences**

DIRECT TEACHING

Prepositions

Activity. Ask students to compose a sentence containing a blank to be filled with a preposition. The sentence should make sense with as many of the prepositions listed on this page as possible. Students might work in groups to see which group can create the most "adaptable" sentence.

EXTENSION

Critical Thinking

Analysis. After students complete the activity above, have each group list the prepositions that do not fit in their sentence. Ask groups to share these prepositions. Then, have students decide which prepositions are the hardest to fit in the student-composed sentences. Ask students how these prepositions differ from the ones that do fit. Refer students to the definition of a preposition on p. 23. [*The prepositions that are least likely to fit the student sentences are those that indicate relations of time* (during, as of), *exclusion* (except, without, but, instead of), *cause* (because of, on account of), *use* (by means of), *source* (according to), *and subject* (concerning). *Most prepositions indicate a relation of position.*]

STYLE TIP

Sometimes a preposition comes after its object. In formal writing and speaking situations, it is usually best to avoid using a preposition at the end of a sentence.

INFORMAL
The frescoes on the ceiling of the Sistine Chapel are perhaps the works that Michelangelo is most famous for.

FORMAL
The frescoes on the ceiling of the Sistine Chapel are perhaps the works **for which** Michelangelo is most famous.

Commonly Used Prepositions			
about	beside	in	through
above	besides	inside	throughout
across	between	into	to
after	beyond	like	toward
against	but (meaning	near	under
along	"except")	of	underneath
among	by	off	until
around	concerning	on	unto
at	down	out	up
before	during	outside	upon
behind	except	over	with
below	for	past	within
beneath	from	since	without

A preposition that consists of two or more words is called a *compound preposition.*

EXAMPLES Alexandra has been accepted by several private colleges **in addition to** both state universities.

As of today, she hasn't made her final choice.

Commonly Used Compound Prepositions		
according to	because of	in spite of
along with	by means of	instead of
apart from	in addition to	next to
aside from	in front of	on account of
as of	in place of	out of

Adverb or Preposition?

Some of the words that are commonly used as prepositions may also be used as adverbs. Keep in mind that an adverb is a modifier and that it does not have an object. Prepositions always have objects.

ADVERB Jerry will meet you **outside** at noon. [*Outside* modifies *will meet.*]

PREPOSITION I will meet you **outside** the library. [*Outside* introduces a prepositional phrase and has an object, *library.*]

Exercise 8   Completing Sentences by Adding Prepositional Phrases

Complete the following sentences by replacing each blank with a prepositional phrase.   *Answers will vary.*

EXAMPLE   1. I found this information _____.

1. *I found this information on the Internet.*

1. Rob collects postcards _____.
2. _____ we fixed lunch.
3. We first heard the rumor _____.
4. _____ people had gathered to hear the concert.
5. I tiptoed _____ and listened quietly.
6. The deer darted quickly _____ and raced _____.
7. Everyone _____ applauded Branford Marsalis's solo.
8. Exhausted _____, the explorers pitched their tents _____ and planned the next day's work.
9. _____ the city council has voted to renovate the abandoned building _____ and turn it _____.
10. _____ I thought that something might have gone wrong _____.

1. from foreign countries
2. After our shopping expedition
3. at the recreation center
4. In the park
5. across the living room
6. across the road/out of sight
7. in the audience
8. by the long trek/near a stream
9. During the meeting/next to the firehouse/into a storage facility
10. In spite of his reassurances/because of the storm

The Conjunction

1g. A *conjunction* joins words or word groups.

Coordinating Conjunctions

A *coordinating conjunction* joins words or word groups that are used in the same way.

Coordinating Conjunctions						
and	but	for	nor	or	so	yet

EXAMPLES   In A.D. 711, the Berbers invaded **and** conquered Spain. [*And* joins two verbs.]

We missed the opening scene, **but** we enjoyed the rest of the play. [*But* joins two clauses.]

TIPS & TRICKS

You can remember the coordinating conjunctions as FANBOYS:

For
And
Nor
But
Or
Yet
So

The Conjunction   **25**

Learners Having Difficulty

Some students may need practice to understand the relationships that coordinating and subordinating conjunctions can show. Write the following pairs of sentences on the chalkboard, and ask students to combine each pair by using conjunctions that show the relationship of the two sentences.

1. Harry planned a day of shopping. He forgot his money. [*until*]

2. The two dogs barked loudly. A man was walking down the alley. [*because*]

3. Latoya goes fishing most Sundays. She doesn't go fishing when it is raining. [*although* or *but*]

4. The contractor promised that the house would be ready by March 1. We didn't move in until April 15. [*Although*]

Reference Note

For more information about **subordinate clauses,** see page 83.

Correlative Conjunctions

Correlative conjunctions are pairs of conjunctions that join words or word groups that are used in the same way.

Correlative Conjunctions		
both . . . and	either . . . or	whether . . . or
not only . . . but also	neither . . . nor	

EXAMPLES   **Either** Fred **or** Manuela will bring music for the party. [*Either . . . or* joins two nouns.]

Not only did Garrett Morgan patent the first gas mask, **but** he **also** invented the automatic traffic signal. [*Not only . . . but also* joins two clauses.]

Subordinating Conjunctions

A *subordinating conjunction* begins a subordinate clause and connects it to an independent clause.

Commonly Used Subordinating Conjunctions			
after	because	since	until
although	before	so that	when
as	how	than	whenever
as if	if	that	where
as much as	in order that	though	wherever
as though	provided	unless	while

EXAMPLES   Many American Indians are reluctant to reveal their traditional names for some places **because** the names have spiritual meanings.

I gasped **when** I saw the headline.

A subordinating conjunction may come at the beginning of a sentence instead of between the clauses it joins.

EXAMPLE   **When** I saw the headline, I gasped.

26   **Chapter 1**   Parts of Speech Overview

Punctuating Compound Sentences. Remind students that a coordinating conjunction that joins the two parts of a compound sentence is preceded by a comma. Write ", and, but, or" on the chalkboard, emphasizing the commas preceding the conjunctions. Tell students to pronounce the punctuation by saying aloud the word *comma*: "comma and," "comma but," "comma or." Remind them that *for, nor, so,*

NOTE Some words can be used either as prepositions or as subordinating conjunctions.

PREPOSITION **After** the election, we celebrated.
SUBORDINATING **After** we won the election, we celebrated.
CONJUNCTION

Exercise 9 **Identifying and Classifying Conjunctions**

Identify the conjunctions in the following sentences, and tell whether each is a *coordinating conjunction*, a *correlative conjunction*, or a *subordinating conjunction*.

EXAMPLE 1. To avoid the traffic, Arturo and I left the stadium a few minutes before the game ended.

1. *and—coordinating conjunction; before—subordinating conjunction*

1. Our old car needs either a valve job or a new engine. | 1. corr.
2. Can you tell me whether the express train will stop here or on the far platform? | 2. corr.
3. Before you write your paper, you must submit an outline. | 3. sub.
4. Would you prefer to go to Greece or Machu Picchu for the senior trip? | 4. coor.
5. Workers here pay city, state, and federal taxes. | 5. coor.
6. The exhibit of jade Olmec carvings is in either the main gallery or the museum's annex. | 6. corr.
7. During the Tang dynasty (A.D. 618–906), China experienced not only a revival of Confucianism but also the development of Chinese schools of Buddhism. | 7. corr.
8. Mi Kyung enjoyed the movie as much as Sarah did. | 8. sub.
9. Have you decided whether you will take physics or economics? | 9. corr.
10. While we are in Kwangju, Korea, we will visit a traditional celadon pottery studio. | 10. sub.
11. Thomas Hardy found a publisher for his poetry only after he had published more than a dozen novels. | 11. sub.
12. Dad said we can go mountain biking if we promise to be careful. | 12. sub.
13. Not only did the movie feature scenes of the streets of Vienna, but it also included dialogue from a popular Austrian play. | 13. corr.
14. I would like to be able to travel in time, for I want to see live dinosaurs. | 14. coor.
15. José Martí, a hero of the Cuban rebellion against Spain, was both a revolutionary leader and a great poet. | 15. corr.

The Conjunction 27

and *yet* can join independent clauses, forming a compound sentence. Then, have students each write four compound sentences that require commas before the conjunctions. Have volunteers share their sentences with the class.

For more information on punctuating compound sentences, refer students to **Chapter 13: Punctuation: End Marks and Commas.**

16. sub.
17. coor.
18. corr.
19. sub.

20. sub.

16. Give these documents to the official <u>so that</u> he can process your passport application.
17. They say the prince is angry, <u>yet</u> he is smiling.
18. We can <u>neither</u> relax at home <u>nor</u> go ouside during the storm.
19. <u>When</u> Liberia was founded in 1821, thousands of free African Americans moved there.
20. Please turn down the stereo <u>so that</u> I can concentrate on my homework.

Reference Note

For information about **punctuating interjections,** see page 327.

The Interjection

1h. An *interjection* expresses emotion and has no grammatical relation to the rest of the sentence.

ah	oh	well	whew
yahoo	whoa	yeah	hooray
aha	alas	aw	oops
ow	hey	ouch	wow

An interjection is often set off from the rest of the sentence by an exclamation point or one or more commas. Exclamation points indicate strong emotion. Commas indicate mild emotion.

EXAMPLES Hey! I think I know the answer!

Well, I thought I knew the answer.

I think that, aw, you two are the greatest.

Oral Practice **Completing Sentences by Adding Interjections** Answers will vary.

Read the following conversation aloud, replacing each blank with an appropriate interjection from the list above. Do not use any interjection more than twice.

EXAMPLE **[1]** "_____ , Mom, please don't use the telephone now!" pleaded Mariana.

    1. Oh

1. Well

"[1] _____ , Mariana, why are you so edgy tonight?" Mrs. Montero asked her eighteen-year-old daughter.

2. Aw

"[2] _____ , Mom, don't you remember? Tonight's the night KHOP announces who won the drawing for a free car."

Differentiating Instruction

Advanced Learners

Etymology. You may want to share with students the interesting origin of the interjection *Eureka!*

More than two thousand years ago, between 200 and 300 B.C.E., the king of Syracuse supposedly asked Archimedes, the Greek mathematician and inventor, to determine the percentage of gold and silver in the king's crown. At first Archimedes was unable to do so. Then one day, as Archimedes was stepping into his bath, he shouted "Eureka!" (*Eureka* means "I have found it" in Greek.) He had realized that he could determine the percentage of gold in the crown by placing it in water and comparing the amount of water displaced to that displaced by an equal weight of gold.

Today, some people still exclaim "Eureka!" when they have found or discovered something.

Learning for Life   *Continued on pp. 29–30*

Description. Tell students to think about being in one of the following situations in which accurate description is essential.

- A witness describing a car that left the scene of an accident

- A witness describing a robbery

- A car owner who has a car problem of unknown origin describing the problems to a mechanic

- A person describing stomach pain to a doctor

"[3] _____ , yes, how could I forget? You've been talking about it for months."

"[4] _____ , Mom, it's only been two weeks, and—wait, that's the phone; I'll get it. Hello? This is Mariana Montero. What?

[5] _____ , are you kidding me? I did? Really?! [6] _____ , you're serious!

[7] _____ ! That's incredible! When can I pick it up? Tonight?

[8] _____ , that's great! I'll be there in twenty minutes! 'Bye—and thanks! [9] _____ , Mom, will you drive me? [10] _____ , just think: That's the last time you'll ever hear me say those words!"

3. Ah
4. Oh
5. Wow
6. Hey
7. Yahoo
8. Yeah
9. Well
10. Whew

Determining Parts of Speech

1i. The way a word is used in a sentence determines what part of speech the word is.

EXAMPLES   This **plant** is native to North America. [noun]
We **plant** tomatoes every year. [verb]
Bacteria cause many **plant** diseases. [adjective]

Marisa led, and we followed **after.** [adverb]
We congratulated Marisa **after** the race. [preposition]
We crossed the finish line **after** all the other runners did, too.
[conjunction]

This pillow is filled with **down** from geese. [noun]
I've always wanted a **down** pillow. [adjective]
Put it **down;** it's too expensive. [adverb]
We can find cheaper pillows at the store **down** the street.
[preposition]

Review C   **Identifying Parts of Speech**

Identify the part of speech of each italicized word in the following sentences.
n.=noun; pro.=pronoun; adj.=adjective; v.=verb; adv.=adverb; prep.=preposition; conj.=conjunction; int.=interjection

EXAMPLE   **1.** The first day *after* Christmas marks the *beginning* of the week-long *cultural* festival called Kwanzaa.

     1. after—preposition; beginning—noun; cultural—adjective

1. Did you know that millions of African Americans celebrate a *uniquely* American holiday *that* has its roots in ancient Africa?

1. adv./pro.

RETEACHING

Parts of Speech

Activity. To offer another approach to understanding parts of speech, write the following familiar sayings on the chalkboard:

1. A stitch in time saves nine.

2. A penny saved is a penny earned.

3. What goes around comes around.

4. A rolling stone gathers no moss.

Give each student (or group of students) the following four-part patterns without the answers in brackets:

    n adj v adj [*penny saved is a*]
    pro v adv v [*what goes around
        comes*]
    adj n prep n [*a stitch in time*]
    n v adj n [*stone gathers no moss*]

Tell students to match the four-part patterns with a four-word sequence in one of the sayings above. Remind students that participles (like *saved*) function as adjectives. Have groups of students think of four sayings (or titles) and create four-part patterns to correspond to the sayings. Have them exchange their work with other groups.

2. int./prep.

3. conj./n.

4. v./adj.

5. v./n.

6. prep./adj.

7. adj./pro.

8. adv./pro.

9. conj./adv.

10. adj./adj.

2. *Well,* they do; called Kwanzaa, which in Swahili means "the first fruits of the harvest," the holiday is observed *during* the week between Christmas and New Year's Day.

3. Kwanzaa isn't a religious holiday *or* a substitute for Christmas but a celebration of black Americans' rich cultural *heritage.*

4. The holiday, which was created in 1966 by Maulana Karenga of California State University in Long Beach, *synthesizes* elements from a variety of *African* harvest festivals.

5. Kwanzaa *focuses* on seven basic principles: unity, collective work and responsibility, self-determination, cooperative economics, purpose, *creativity,* and faith.

6. *Among* the symbols of the holiday are *a* straw mat for respect for tradition; an ear of corn for each child in the family; and a candle-holder with seven green, red, and black candles for the continent of Africa.

7. *Each* day during the week, family members light *one* of the candles and discuss one of the principles.

8. They *also* exchange simple gifts *that* reflect their heritage and eat foods from Africa and from the lands to which their ancestors traveled, such as the Caribbean and South America.

9. Some families strictly follow Karenga's original program for the holiday, *while* others *freely* adapt it.

10. In *some* communities families gather for concerts and *dance* performances.

Learning for Life

Continued from p. 29

of the questioners should ask at least four questions.

After the skits have been performed, discuss what it is like to actually be in one of these situations. Ask volunteers who have had such experiences to recount how accurate they were and what problems they had with giving accurate descriptions. Lead the class to see that asking adjective and adverb questions can help add details to their descriptions.

Chapter Review

A. Identifying Parts of Speech

For each of the following sentences, identify each word that is the part of speech indicated in parentheses.

1. Whenever Anna started a new sculpture, she was usually not thinking of the time it would take to finish. (adverb)

2. Ms. Garcia decided to buy or lease a new computer because the speed and memory capacity of her old one were no longer satisfactory. (conjunction)

3. The film might be available on videotape, on a videodisc, or in some other form. (noun)

4. My mother's book of short stories, written when she was in college, was titled *New Yorkers* because of the stories' similarity in subject matter to James Joyce's stories in *Dubliners*. (preposition)

5. Only recently has my youngest sister, Jorena, been riding her bicycle outside the yard. (verb)

6. In modern times, poets have usually used the term *elegy* to mean "a poem of lamentation for the dead." (noun)

7. This is just the book I wanted. (pronoun)

8. The word *atom* was first used by the ancient Greeks. (adverb)

9. In literature, a novel is not distinguished from other genres by its subject matter but is distinguished by its form and length. (conjunction)

10. Some Irish songs are comic songs, but others are patriotic songs, love songs, or laments. (adjective)

11. The mountain climber plants his flag in the snowbank on top of the mountain. (verb)

12. Will the plants in your garden survive the frost tonight? (noun)

13. As Anita walked along the river, a light rain was falling steadily. (preposition)

14. The dog trotted along with us as we jogged toward the light. (adverb)

15. After every issue had gone to press, the editor of the school paper gave a weekly party. (conjunction)

HELP

In the Chapter Review, do not identify articles as adjectives.

Numerals in brackets refer to rules tested by the items in the Chapter Review.

1. [1e]
2. [1g]
3. [1a]
4. [1f]
5. [1d]
6. [1a]
7. [1b, i]
8. [1e]
9. [1g]
10. [1c, i]
11. [1d, i]
12. [1a, i]
13. [1f, i]
14. [1e, i]
15. [1g, i]

ASSESSING

Monitoring Progress
Chapter Review. To assess student progress, you may want to compare the types of items missed on the **Diagnostic Preview** to those missed on the **Chapter Review.** If students have not made significant progress, you may want to work out specific goals with individual students who are still having difficulty mastering essential information.

GRAMMAR

RESOURCES

Parts of Speech Overview

Review
■ *Language & Sentence Skills Practice,* pp. 22–24

Assessment
■ *Holt Handbook Chapter Tests with Answer Key,* pp. 1–2, 54

16. [1e]
17. [1h, i]
18. [1a, i]
19. [1g, i]
20. [1c]

16. The coach and the football team reviewed the game videotapes <u>weekly</u>, on the day after each game. (adverb)

17. "<u>Well</u>!" exclaimed Ollie. "This is another fine mess!" (interjection)

18. Do you think this old <u>pump</u> will draw any <u>water</u> from the <u>well</u>? (noun)

19. <u>Before</u> he answered the question, he tried to remember just how high a falcon could fly. (conjunction)

20. Take the oregano from the <u>high</u> shelf above the stove, and sprinkle some in the stew before adding the thyme. (adjective)

21. conj. [1g]
22. pro. [1b]
23. adj. [1c]
24. v. [1d]
25. prep. [1f, i]
26. adj. [1c]
27. conj. [1g, i]
28. adv. [1e]
29. adj. [1c, i]
30. pro.[1b]
31. n. [1a, i]
32. adv. [1e, i]
33. adj. [1c]
34. adj. [1c, i]
35. v. [1d]
36. conj. [1g]
37. pro. [1b]
38. pro. [1b]
39. adv. [1e]
40. conj. [1g]
41. int. [1h]
42. n. [1a]
43. pro. [1b]
44. prep. [1f]
45. v. [1d]

B. Identifying Parts of Speech

Identify each italicized word in the following paragraphs as a *noun*, a *pronoun*, an *adjective*, a *verb*, an *adverb*, a *conjunction*, a *preposition*, or an *interjection*.

For less **[21]** *than* what you might pay to see a movie, **[22]** *you* can get to know yourself better. Simply purchase a **[23]** *blank* notebook and begin to keep a personal journal. You'll be amazed to see what you **[24]** *learn* **[25]** *about* yourself in just a short time.

Keeping a journal is **[26]** *easy,* **[27]** *for* there's only one rule: Date all of the entries. Writing four or five entries a week is a realistic goal; **[28]** *usually* your mood will determine the length of each entry. One type of entry is the **[29]** *daily* log, in which you record **[30]** *what* you did and how you felt on a particular day. Another is a **[31]** *list* of your favorite songs, movies, and poetry. **[32]** *Most* **[33]** *important* are **[34]** *those* entries that have nothing to do with your exterior life and, instead, **[35]** *reveal* your inner life: your dreams, your thoughts, your questions, your goals, and your feelings. **[36]** *Because* the journal is a personal book, which **[37]** *no one* else reads, it becomes a place where you're free to say **[38]** *anything* you want. Re-reading your entries **[39]** *later* will show you how you've changed.

If you're wondering **[40]** *whether* keeping a journal is worth the effort, **[41]** *yes,* it certainly is. According to one girl in **[42]** *Connecticut,* her journal is "the closest I've ever come to knowing **[43]** *myself.*" The journal is an adventure **[44]** *in* self-awareness. **[45]** *Try* keeping one yourself.

Writing Application
Creating a Dictionary of New Words

The Parts of Speech   For a school project, you and your classmates have decided to create a dictionary of words that should exist but do not. What, for instance, do you call your former best friend or the feeling you have when a word is on the tip of your tongue but you can't quite remember it? Write a complete dictionary entry proposing a name for something that doesn't have a name or that you think could be more aptly named. Give the new word's derivation, use, meaning, and pronunciation.

Prewriting   Use observation, brainstorming, or freewriting to come up with situations, things, places, thoughts, feelings, and qualities that could benefit from a new word. Then, choose the one that appeals to you the most, and create a word for it. Next, think of the information you will need for your dictionary entry. How is your new word spelled and pronounced? What is its part of speech, and what other forms does it have? What is the word's derivation? definition(s)?

Writing   Refer to your prewriting notes often as you write your first draft. Do not be concerned about using complete sentences. Include an example sentence that gives the word in context.

Revising   As you re-read your dictionary entry, check to make sure that your organization and tone are appropriate for a dictionary entry. Make any changes that you think will improve your entry.

Publishing   Proofread your dictionary entry carefully. You and your classmates may want to gather all of your dictionary entries into a new-word dictionary, which could be photocopied for the entire class.

Writing Application

Writing Tip. Tell students that although the English language involves a large vocabulary, it does not have a word for everything. For example, there is no English equivalent for the Italian word *culacino,* which refers to the ring left on a table by a glass, or for the German word *schadenfreude,* which means "taking delight in the misfortune of others." If you have English-language learners in your class, ask them if they know of any words in their languages for which there are no equivalents in English.

Scoring Rubric. While you will want to pay particular attention to students' use of parts of speech, you will also want to evaluate overall writing performance. You may want to give a split score to indicate development and clarity of the composition as well as grammar skills.

The Parts of a Sentence
Subject, Predicate, Complement

Diagnostic Preview

Numerals in brackets refer to rules tested by the items in the Diagnostic Preview.

1. p.n. [2k(1)]
2. s. [2b, c]
3. v. [2b, d]
4. d.o. [2h]
5. s. [2b, c]
6. i.o. [2i]

A. Identifying Subjects, Verbs, and Complements

Identify the italicized word or word group in each of the following sentences as a *subject*, a *verb*, a *direct object*, an *indirect object*, an *objective complement*, a *predicate nominative*, or a *predicate adjective*.

EXAMPLE   1. We *took* the shortest route.
           1. *verb*

1. Since she won the Pulitzer Prize in 1983, Alice Walker has become a famous *writer*.
2. In 1928, *Carlos Chávez* established the well-known Symphony Orchestra of Mexico.
3. The antique dresser *was* carefully *moved* to a protected corner of the showroom.
4. Margaret wants a *set* of leather luggage as a graduation present.
5. On Fajada Butte in northwestern New Mexico is an ancient Anasazi solar *calendar*.
6. The director gave my *grandfather* an interesting part in a play at the community theater.

7. Please *call* me at work immediately after you get home from school; it's urgent.
8. Exercising regularly and eating well keep me *energetic* despite my busy schedule.
9. My mother is much *taller* than any of her four sisters but not as tall as her brother.
10. Yesterday the girls' gymnastics team unanimously elected Ming Chin their *captain*.

B. Identifying Subjects, Verbs, and Complements

Identify each italicized word or word group in the following sentences as a *subject*, a *verb*, a *direct object*, an *indirect object*, an *objective complement*, a *predicate nominative*, or a *predicate adjective*.

EXAMPLE
1. In 1675, the Spanish friar Juan Paiva recorded the *rules* of a major sports contest between the Apalachee and the Timucuan peoples of North Florida.

1. *direct object*

11. The arrival of a messenger in a raccoon costume was a *challenge* to a ballgame from the loser of the last game.
12. On acceptance of the challenge, *all* of the villagers traveled to meet their opponents.
13. In an all-night vigil before the game, elders of the host village interpreted their dreams and told the home *team* their predictions of the game's outcome.
14. Meanwhile, the visitors *made* a stew with rancid food, *mixed* it with decorative clays, and *painted* their bodies with the foul mixture to repel the other players.
15. On game day, a village leader started *play* by tossing out a small, hard ball to teams of forty to fifty players on each side.
16. Suddenly, eighty to one hundred men *were scrambling* for a ball only about an inch in diameter!
17. The goal post in the center of an empty field was a ten- to fifteen-foot *pole* with an eagle's nest on top.
18. Teams scored one *point* for each throw of the ball against the pole and two *points* for each basket.
19. When one team had scored eleven points, the game was *over*.
20. According to historians, these rules probably made the average game a one- to two-hour *contest*.

ASSESSING

Entry-Level Assessment
Diagnostic Preview. Both **Part A** and **Part B** of the **Diagnostic Preview** ask students to identify either a word or a group of words in each sentence as a subject, a verb, or a specific type of complement. You may want to use the results to determine which lessons require special emphasis.

PRETEACHING

Lesson Starter
Motivating. Divide the class into groups of three, and set a time limit in which each group must compose the longest complete sentence they can that does not have a compound subject or compound verb. Tell students they can add modifiers and phrases, but can include only one subject and one verb.

When time is up, have a volunteer from each group write the group's sentence on the chalkboard. Have other members of the class identify the simple subject and the verb.

Differentiating Instruction
- *Developmental Language & Sentence Skills Guided Practice,* pp. 23–34
- *Developmental Language & Sentence Skills Guided Practice Teacher's Notes and Answer Key,* pp. 6–9

Assessment
- *Holt Handbook Chapter Tests with Answer Key,* pp. 3–4, 54

The Sentence

Rule 2a (pp. 36–37)

OBJECTIVE

- To identify and revise sentences and sentence fragments

DIRECT TEACHING

Modeling and Demonstration

What Is a Sentence? Model how to identify sentences and sentence fragments with the example *When the judges announced the winner.* First, ask if the word group has a subject and a verb. [*yes;* judges, announced] Then, ask if this example expresses a complete thought. [*no*] Next, ask whether this is a sentence or a sentence fragment. [*sentence fragment*] Explain that since the subordinating conjunction *when* introduces this word group, it is a dependent clause and cannot stand alone. Then, ask how this sentence fragment can be corrected. [*When the judges announced the winner, everyone applauded.*] Point out that this fragment can be corrected either by adding the independent clause *everyone applauded* to complete the thought or by eliminating the subordinating conjunction *When.* [*The judges announced the winner.*] Now, have a volunteer use another example from this chapter to demonstrate how to identify sentences and sentence fragments.

Reference Note

For more about the **understood subject,** see page 41. For more about the **purposes of sentences,** see page 97. For more about **end marks,** see page 326.

Reference Note

For information about **correcting sentence fragments,** see page 480.

The Sentence

2a. A *sentence* is a word group that contains a subject and a verb and that expresses a complete thought.

A thought is complete when it makes sense by itself.

EXAMPLES   In many ways, the development of the microprocessor has revolutionized technology.

When did Mexico achieve independence from Spain?

How quickly this year has passed!

Stop! [The understood subject is *you.*]

A sentence should begin with a capital letter. The punctuation mark that follows a sentence depends on the purpose of the sentence.

Do not mistake a sentence fragment for a sentence. A ***sentence fragment*** is a group of words that is capitalized and punctuated as a sentence but that does not contain both a subject and a verb or does not express a complete thought.

SENTENCE FRAGMENT	Sponsors election-year debates. [This group of words does not contain a subject or express a complete thought.]
SENTENCE	The League of Women Voters sponsors election-year debates.
SENTENCE FRAGMENT	Students representing sixty-one historically black universities and colleges. [This group of words does not contain a verb or express a complete thought.]
SENTENCE	Students representing sixty-one historically black universities and colleges competed.
SENTENCE FRAGMENT	Because the graduation ceremony was rescheduled for June 20. [This group of words contains a subject and a verb but does not express a complete thought.]
SENTENCE	Because the graduation ceremony was rescheduled for June 20, my cousin Larry could attend after all.

Exercise 1 **Identifying and Revising Sentences and Sentence Fragments**

Decide which of the following word groups are sentences and which are sentence fragments. If a word group is a sentence, add appropriate

RESOURCES

The Sentence

Practice

- *Language & Sentence Skills Practice,* p. 29

capitalization and punctuation. If a word group is a sentence fragment, revise the fragment by adding or deleting words to make it a sentence. Then, add appropriate capitalization and punctuation.

EXAMPLE 1. such as the Sioux, Cheyenne, and Comanche

1. *American Indians, such as the Sioux, Cheyenne, and Comanche, were expert equestrians.*

1. here in the basement of the library lay stacks and stacks of dusty magazines, each a collector's prize
2. stretching in a seemingly endless blue expanse from the coast of Peru to the Great Barrier Reef
3. have you changed the drill bit
4. to estimate expenses accurately for the next three quarters of this fiscal year
5. when they swam under the boat and checked the hull
6. one of the only buildings from this period still in use today
7. an event held but once a year and eagerly anticipated by the population of this small rural county
8. take this as an example
9. covering the portrait's face with a few diagonal pink pastel strokes was the bold act of a creative genius
10. how surprised we all were at the news

The Subject and the Predicate

2b. Sentences consist of two basic parts: *subjects* and *predicates*. The **subject** is a word or word group that tells whom or what the sentence is about. The **predicate** is a word or word group that tells something about the subject.

Notice in the following examples that the subject may appear before or after the predicate or between parts of the predicate.

EXAMPLES

SUBJECT	PREDICATE
Rain	pelted the sailors.

SUBJECT	PREDICATE
Each of the amateur mimes	performed.

PREDICATE	SUBJECT
Away on the breeze sailed	the dry leaves.

PREDICATE	SUBJECT	PREDICATE
When did	Alex Haley	write *Roots*?

The Subject and the Predicate   **37**

| STYLE   TIP |

Sentence fragments are commonly used in casual conversation, in written dialogue, and in advertisements. In these situations, the context usually clarifies any confusion caused by the sentence fragment. In formal speaking and writing, however, it is best to use complete sentences for greater clarity.

Exercise 1 Identifying and Revising Sentences and Sentence Fragments

ANSWERS
Answers for sentences 2, 4, 5, 6, and 7 will vary.

1. Here in the basement of the library lay stacks and stacks of dusty magazines, each a collector's prize.

2. Stretching in a seemingly endless blue expanse from the coast of Peru to the Great Barrier Reef, the Pacific Ocean is immense.

3. Have you changed the drill bit?

4. To estimate expenses accurately for the next three quarters of this fiscal year, we need the figures from the accountant.

5. They found problems when they swam under the boat and checked the hull.

6. We will see the play at the Paramount Theater, one of the only buildings from this period still in use today.

7. The Garlic Festival is an event held but once a year and eagerly anticipated by the population of this small rural county.

8. Take this as an example.

9. Covering the portrait's face with a few diagonal pink pastel strokes was the bold act of a creative genius.

10. How surprised we all were at the news!

The Subject and the Predicate
Rules 2b–f *(pp. 37–44)*

OBJECTIVES

■ To identify complete and simple subjects in sentences

■ To identify complete predicates and verbs in sentences

English-Language Learners

Asian Languages. In some Asian languages, the verb always appears at the end of a sentence. As a result, speakers of such languages may have difficulty in identifying subjects and verbs in English sentences.

Make sure students are aware that verbs in English can appear at the beginning, in the middle, or at the end of a sentence. Give students examples of the various possibilities.

┌HELP┐
In this book, the term *subject* generally refers to the simple subject unless otherwise indicated.

Reference Note
├ For more information about **compound nouns,** see page 5.

The Simple Subject and the Complete Subject

2c. The *simple subject* is the main word or word group that tells whom or what the sentence is about.

The simple subject may be a noun, a pronoun, or a word group that functions as a noun. The *complete subject* consists of the simple subject and any word or word groups used to modify the simple subject.

SIMPLE SUBJECT	The **view** from the observatory on the top floor of the building is extraordinary.
COMPLETE SUBJECT	**The view from the observatory on the top floor of the building** is extraordinary.
SIMPLE SUBJECT	Lasting for eight days, **Hanukkah** celebrates the rededication of the temple in Jerusalem in 165 B.C.
COMPLETE SUBJECT	**Lasting for eight days, Hanukkah** celebrates the rededication of the temple in Jerusalem in 165 B.C.
SIMPLE SUBJECT	Was the **Memorial Coliseum** in Los Angeles filled to capacity?
COMPLETE SUBJECT	Was **the Memorial Coliseum in Los Angeles** filled to capacity?
SIMPLE SUBJECT	**Everyone** was very impatient for the feature to begin.
COMPLETE SUBJECT	**Everyone** was very impatient for the feature to begin. [The complete subject and the simple subject may be the same if no words modify the simple subject.]

NOTE A compound noun, such as *Memorial Coliseum,* may serve as a simple subject because it is considered a single name.

Exercise 2 **Identifying Complete Subjects and Simple Subjects**

Identify each complete subject in the following sentences. Then, underline each simple subject.

EXAMPLE　　**1.** The population of Abu Dhabi is one of the richest in the world.

　　　　　　1. The population of Abu Dhabi

1. Ravi Shankar was instrumental in popularizing Indian music in the West.

Learning for Life　　　**Continued on pp. 39–40**

Résumé. Many career counselors now recommend writing a résumé using active verbs that describe the type of experience involved in a position. For this type of résumé, instead of writing "Clerk in department store," you would write "Dealt with inventory, sales, and customer service in the housewares department"; instead of writing "Baby sitter," you would write "Supervised children's activities, prepared lunches, and was responsible for transportation to and from soccer practice three days a week."

2. That dachshund was the only dog in the world with a taste for asparagus in hollandaise sauce.
3. Did he shoot, develop, print, and frame all these photographs?
4. Walking is a cheap, reliable, and healthful form of exercise.
5. A long line of ants was heading directly toward my lunch.
6. Few of the sailors aboard the *Caroline B* could claim a clear view of the strange sea creature.
7. Unfortunately, "Turkey in the Straw" occupied the sole slot on this young harmonica player's playlist.
8. I think of the remote control as my own personal property.
9. What a day the children in Ms. Gage's class had!
10. At the top of a very long flight of stairs and almost touching the roof were our seats.

The Simple Predicate and the Complete Predicate

2d. The *simple predicate*, or verb, is the main word or word group that tells something about the subject.

The simple predicate may be a one-word verb or a *verb phrase* (a main verb with one or more helping verbs). The *complete predicate* consists of the simple predicate and all of the words used to modify the simple predicate and to complete its meaning.

Reference Note

For more about **verbs** and **verb phrases,** see page 15.

SIMPLE PREDICATE (VERB)	The victorious athletes **were surrounded** by admirers.
COMPLETE PREDICATE	The victorious athletes **were surrounded by admirers.**
SIMPLE PREDICATE (VERB)	In an hour-long press conference, the players graciously **answered** reporters' questions.
COMPLETE PREDICATE	**In an hour-long press conference,** the players **graciously answered reporters' questions.**
SIMPLE PREDICATE (VERB)	The crowd **surged.**
COMPLETE PREDICATE	The crowd **surged.** [The complete predicate and the simple predicate may be the same if no words modify or complete the meaning of the simple predicate.]

NOTE In this book, the term *verb* generally refers to the simple predicate (a one-word verb or a verb phrase) unless otherwise indicated.

DIRECT TEACHING

Inverted Word Order
Challenge students to revise sentences by inverting the order of subjects and verbs. Suggest that each student examine various types of writing—novels, poetry, newspapers, and magazines—to find examples of sentences suitable for inversion. Remind students that occasionally reversing the order of the subject and verb is a good way to add variety to their writing. Have volunteers share their revised sentences with the class.

EXTENSION

Critical Thinking
Analysis. Have a volunteer give the definition of *predicate*. [*A predicate tells something about the subject.*] Ask students to work in small groups to create lists of the kinds of things predicates can tell about subjects. [*A predicate can tell what something does; what it looks like, tastes like, smells like; to whom it belongs; where it is; and so forth.*] After groups have completed their lists, have them share their lists with the class and generate a composite list for the whole class. To extend the activity, you could ask students to choose three items from the list and to write sentences with predicates that give the specified type of information about the subject.

Education	Attended Lincoln High School; studied a college preparatory curriculum, including computer and art courses. Maintained a grade-point average of 3.5 (B+).	Work Experience	Summer 2003—Assisted a professional designer by copying plans, organizing files, and receiving calls.

> **Exercise 3** **Identifying Complete Predicates and Verbs**
>
> Identify each complete predicate in the following sentences. Then, underline each verb.
>
> EXAMPLE   **1.** Will you be joining us for dinner tonight?
>
>   *1. Will be joining us for dinner tonight*

1. This new theory certainly does deserve consideration among the scientific community.
2. Debate about the voting district boundaries will be headline news.
3. Should the statistician have included these figures in the tally?
4. On the boardwalk, a glass blower was demonstrating her craft.
5. I will report to the registrar on July 22 at 8:00 A.M.
6. In the lower left-hand corner, a legend lists the symbols used on the map and their meanings.
7. When will the armadillo cross the solid white line?
8. The Ubangi River meanders through almost fifteen hundred miles of magnificent African country.
9. Under the circumstances, a pair of cutoffs and sandals would not be in the best of taste.
10. Among the pine tree's dark and shining branches waited one very hungry owl.

The Compound Subject and the Compound Verb

2e. A *compound subject* consists of two or more subjects that are joined by a conjunction and that have the same verb.

The parts of a compound subject are usually joined by the conjunction *and* or *or*.

EXAMPLES   **Michelle** or **Chondra** will lead the petition drive.

           Hokkaidō, Honshū, Shikoku, and **Kyūshū** are the four main islands of Japan.

           When were **East Germany** and **West Germany** reunited?

2f. A *compound verb* consists of two or more verbs that are joined by a conjunction and that have the same subject.

The parts of a compound verb are usually joined by the conjunction *and, but,* or *or*.

┌─────────────────────┐
│ TIPS **&** TRICKS │
└─────────────────────┘

When you are identifying compound verbs, be sure to include all parts of any verb phrases.

EXAMPLE
Should we **wait** for Alex or **leave** a note for him?

Learning for Life   ***Continued from p. 39***

Point out that sentence fragments are acceptable in a résumé but that complete sentences should be used in cover letters. Have students gather information (education, work experience, hobbies and interests, awards and honors, travel, and references) they need in order to write a résumé. Tell them to express as much of this information as possible with verbs rather than nouns. Have students keep their résumés on computer disks so that revisions and additions can be made easily.

EXAMPLES   Mary McLeod Bethune **founded** Bethune-Cookman College and twice **served** as its president.

Gabrielle and Margaret **read** the book but **missed** the movie.

Would you rather **wash** the dishes or **dry** them?

NOTE Do not mistake a simple sentence containing a compound subject or a compound verb, or both, for a compound sentence. In a compound sentence, the conjunction joins independent clauses.

EXAMPLES   **Anna** and **Lyle will sing** in the talent show. [simple sentence with a compound subject]

Anna and **Lyle will sing** and **dance** in the talent show. [simple sentence with a compound subject and compound verb]

Anna will sing, and **Lyle will dance** in the talent show. [compound sentence containing two independent clauses]

How to Find the Subject of a Sentence

To find the subject of a sentence, ask *Who?* or *What?* before the verb.

EXAMPLES   In the auditorium, friends and relatives of the graduates awaited the ceremony. [Who awaited? *Friends* and *relatives* awaited.]

Sharing the island of Hispaniola with Haiti is the Dominican Republic. [What is sharing? *Dominican Republic* is sharing.]

Here is the last history assignment for the week. [What is? *Assignment* is.]

There will be a meeting in the cafeteria immediately after school. [What will be? *Meeting* will be.]

Keep the following four guidelines in mind whenever you are trying to find the subject of a sentence.

• The subject in a sentence expressing a command or a request is always understood to be *you*, even if the word *you* does not appear in the sentence.

COMMAND   Always document the source of a direct quotation. [Who documents? *You* document.]

REQUEST   Please write soon. [Who writes? *You* write.]

Reference Note

For more about **simple sentences** and **compound sentences**, see page 94.

DIFFERENTIATING INSTRUCTION

Advanced Learners

Ask each student to write three sentences with compound subjects, using *and, or,* and *but* to join the compound subjects. If students have trouble coming up with a compound subject joined by *but,* write this sentence on the chalkboard: *Not Raoul, but Phyllis went on the trip.*

Lead students in a discussion of when each of the three primary coordinating conjunctions is appropriate for linking parts of a compound subject. [*And* indicates a conjunction of things, *or* indicates a disjunction or alternative, and *but* indicates an opposition. *But* can be used to join parts of a compound subject only when one part of the subject is negated.] Next, have students try again to write a sentence with a compound subject joined by *but.*

EXTENSION

Relating to Literature

Consider giving students different examples of subject-verb order from literature. For example, if Shakespeare's "When Icicles Hang by the Wall" from *Love's Labour's Lost* is available, have the class read and discuss it. The first five lines of each stanza follow a common subject-verb order, but the sixth line reverses the pattern.

Other examples of poetry with unusual syntax include Lord Byron's "The Destruction of Sennacherib" and Percy Shelley's "Ode to the West Wind." Discuss with students the effect that inverted word order has. [*It adds rhythm and variety, and it shifts the emphasis to different words.*]

RETEACHING

Finding the Subject

Activity. For another approach to finding the simple subjects of sentences, hand out short news articles, and have students work with partners to identify the subjects in the first five sentences of an article. Tell them to bracket prepositional phrases, turn questions into statements, and cross out *here* or *there* used as adverbs or expletives. Finally, they should underline the simple subject in each sentence.

Reference Note

For more information about **prepositional phrases,** see pages 23 and 60.

TIPS & TRICKS

Turning a question into a statement will often help you find the subject of the question.

QUESTION
Have you tasted sushi?

STATEMENT
You have tasted sushi.
[Who has tasted? *You* have tasted.]

STYLE TIP

Expletives add no information to a sentence and can cause confusion about subject-verb agreement. You can improve your style by revising your sentences to eliminate unnecessary expletives.

ORIGINAL
There will be a special broadcast at 11:30 P.M.

REVISED
A special broadcast will air at 11:30 P.M.

If a command or a request contains a **noun of direct address**—a word naming the one or ones spoken to—the subject is still understood to be *you.*

EXAMPLES   Frances, [you] walk the dog.

[You] Come here, Bill.

- The subject of a sentence is never the object of a prepositional phrase.

EXAMPLES   A committee of students investigated the allegations. [Who investigated? *Committee* investigated. *Students* is the object of the preposition *of.*]

One of the parks in Austin, Texas, is named for the Mexican general Ignacio Seguín Zaragoza. [What is named? *One* is named. *Parks* is the object of the preposition *of. Austin, Texas* is the object of the preposition *in.*]

From the alley came the wail of a siren. [What came? *Wail* came. *Alley* is the object of the preposition *From. Siren* is the object of the preposition *of.*]

- The subject in a sentence expressing a question usually follows the verb or comes between the parts of a verb phrase.

EXAMPLES   Are these jeans on sale? [What are on sale? *Jeans* are.]

What year did Thurgood Marshall retire from the United States Supreme Court? [Who did retire? *Thurgood Marshall* did retire.]

Where are the children playing after school? [Who are playing? *Children* are playing.]

- The word *there* or *here* is almost never the subject of a sentence.

In the following examples, *there* and *here* are adverbs telling *where.*

EXAMPLES   There goes Rebecca. [Who goes? *Rebecca* goes.]

Here is your receipt. [What is? *Receipt* is.]

NOTE The word *there* is not always an adverb. It may be used as an **expletive**—a word that fills out the structure of a sentence but does not add to the meaning.

EXAMPLE   There will be a special **broadcast** tonight at 11:30 P.M. [What will be? *Broadcast* will be.]

MINI-LESSON Grammar

Types of Sentence Structure. While students are studying the parts of a sentence, you may want to review with the class the types of sentence structure. Remind students of the following definitions:

1. A simple sentence has one independent clause and no subordinate clauses.
2. A compound sentence has two or more independent clauses and no subordinate clauses.

Exercise 4 **Identifying Subjects and Verbs**

Identify each <u>simple subject</u> and <u>verb</u> in the following sentences.
Include all parts of any compound subjects and compound verbs and
all words in any verb phrases.

EXAMPLE   **1.** The miniature Japanese sculptures shown on this page
            are called *netsuke*.

    1. subject—sculptures; verb—are called

1. These exquisite <u>pieces</u> <u>originated</u> as a practical solution to an
   everyday problem.
2. During Japan's Tokugawa period (1603–1868), an integral <u>part</u> of
   the traditional costume of the new merchant class <u>was</u> a set of
   lacquerware boxes for medicines and spices.

3. The <u>boxes</u> <u>were threaded</u> onto the sash of the kimono and <u>served</u>
   as pockets for the otherwise pocketless garment.
4. Originally just small, plain toggles of lightweight ivory or wood,
   the *<u>netsuke</u>* <u>held</u> the boxes in place along the sash.
5. Under the feudal system then in effect, there <u>were</u> strict <u>laws</u> against
   any display of wealth by persons below the rank of *samurai*.
6. However, many wealthy <u>merchants</u> <u>wanted</u> some obvious symbol
   of their prosperity.
7. Over time, increasingly elaborate *<u>netsuke</u>* from the nation's finest
   artisans <u>became</u> that symbol.

3. A complex sentence has one independent
clause and one or more subordinate
clauses.

4. A compound-complex sentence has two
or more independent clauses and one or
more subordinate clauses.

For more information on classification
of sentences according to structure, refer
students to **Chapter 4: The Clause.**

Complements

Rules 2g–k *(pp. 44–54)*

OBJECTIVE

■ To identify direct objects, indirect objects, objective complements, and subject complements in sentences

DIRECT TEACHING

Modeling and Demonstration

Direct Objects and Indirect Objects. Model how to identify direct objects and indirect objects by using the example *Jonathan gave David some help.* First, identify the subject and verb. [*Jonathan—subject; gave—verb*] Next, ask whether the subject and verb express a complete thought by themselves. [*no*] Then, ask what he gave. [*help*] Explain that *help* is the direct object of the verb. Finally, ask to whom the help was given. [*David*] *David* is the indirect object of the verb. Now, have a volunteer use another example from this chapter to demonstrate how to identify direct and indirect objects.

┌ TIPS & TRICKS ┐

You can remember the difference in spelling between *complement* (the grammar term) and *compliment* (an expression of affection or respect) by remembering that a compl**e**ment compl**e**tes a sentence.

┌ TIPS & TRICKS ┐

Both independent and subordinate clauses contain subjects, verbs, and, sometimes, complements.

EXAMPLE
When **we attend** hockey **games,** my **sister** and **I cheer** loudly for our home team.

8. Eventually, the Japanese adopted Western clothing, with pockets.
9. As a result, both the small boxes and the *netsuke* became obsolete.
10. Today, collectors all over the world gladly pay large sums for specimens of these beautiful objects with humble origins.

Complements

2g. A *complement* is a word or word group that completes the meaning of a verb.

Some verbs do not need a complement to complete their meanings. Together, the subject and the verb express a complete thought.

EXAMPLES
    S **V**
    She won.

    V
    Look! [The understood subject is *you*.]

Often, however, a sentence requires one or more complements for the meaning of the verb to be complete.

              S   **V**
INCOMPLETE   Judith Baca created

             S   **V**   **C**
COMPLETE   Judith Baca created the **mural.**

             S **V**
INCOMPLETE   They mailed

             S   **V**   **C**   **C**
COMPLETE   They mailed **me** the **information.**

             S   **V**
INCOMPLETE   The republics declared

             S   **V**   **C**   **C**
COMPLETE   The republics declared **themselves independent.**

             S   **V**
INCOMPLETE   Who in the world named

             S   **V**   **C**   **C**
COMPLETE   Who in the world named the **puppy Cerberus**?

RESOURCES

Complements

Practice

■ *Language & Sentence Skills Practice,* pp. 37–45

Differentiating Instruction

■ *Developmental Language & Sentence Skills,* pp. 27–34

```
                        S        V
INCOMPLETE    Seiji Ozawa became

                        S        V                      C
COMPLETE      Seiji Ozawa became a successful conductor.

                        S        V
INCOMPLETE    The horse seems

                        S        V        C
COMPLETE      The horse seems skittish.
```

Nouns, pronouns, and adjectives may be complements. Be careful not to mistake an adverb for a complement.

ADVERB   Hatshepsut ruled **ably.** [The adverb *ably* modifies the verb *ruled,* telling *how* Hatshepsut ruled. The sentence does not contain a complement.]

COMPLEMENT   Hatshepsut ruled **Egypt** during the early fifteenth century B.C. [The noun *Egypt* completes the meaning of the verb *ruled.*]

Reference Note

For more about **adverbs,** see page 20.

The object of a prepositional phrase is not a complement.

OBJECT OF PREPOSITION   At first Hatshepsut ruled with her husband. [The noun *husband* is the object of the preposition *with.* The sentence does not contain a complement.]

Reference Note

For more information on **prepositional phrases,** see pages 23 and 60.

Direct Objects and Indirect Objects

2h. A *direct object* is a complement that tells who or what receives the action of a verb or shows the result of the action.

A direct object may be a noun, a pronoun, or a word group that functions as a noun. To find a direct object, ask *Whom?* or *What?* after a transitive verb.

Reference Note

For more about **transitive verbs,** see page 18.

EXAMPLES   The employer interviewed several **applicants** for the job. [Interviewed whom? Applicants.]

Does a virus cause a common **cold**? [Cause what? Cold.]

I miss **you.** [Miss whom? You.]

They usually buy **whatever is on sale.** [Buy what? Whatever is on sale.]

| STYLE   TIP |

For emphasis, a writer may place the direct object before the subject and the verb.

EXAMPLE
What an eerie **sound** we heard! [Heard what? Sound.]

Complements   **45**

![MINI-LESSON] **Mechanics**   *Continued on p. 46*

Homonyms. Remind students that homonyms are words that sound the same but have different meanings. Write on the chalkboard the words *complement* and *compliment.* Have students consult a dictionary to check the meaning and etymology of both words. [*The two etymologies differ in their more recent developments, but both words originate from the Latin* complere, *meaning "to*

DIFFERENTIATING INSTRUCTION

English-Language Learners

General Strategies. The English language commonly uses a subject-verb-object sentence structure. Other languages use subject-object-verb or verb-subject-object structures. For example, if you ask native speakers of Japanese, Korean, or Persian "Whom did Ann call?" and they answer, "Her friend called" or "Her friend did," they are saying that Ann called her friend. Consequently, these students may need extra practice in using the English subject-verb-object sentence structure.

DIFFERENTIATING INSTRUCTION

Learners Having Difficulty

Ask students to act out several sentences that have both direct and indirect objects. For example, they could act out sample sentences given in this lesson or write original sentences to present to the class. For each sentence, you could reinforce the distinction between the direct and indirect objects.

RETEACHING

Complements

Activity. To illustrate for students the way parts of a sentence fit together and the relationship between complements and other sentence parts, you may want to ask students to diagram sentences like this one, illustrating direct and indirect objects.

EXAMPLE

We sold that **lady** our **car.**

┌HELP┐
Some transitive verbs that commonly take indirect objects are *ask, get, give, grant, hand, lend, offer, pay, send, teach, tell,* and *write.*

Reference Note
For more information about **prepositional phrases,** see pages 23 and 60.

┌ TIPS & TRICKS ┐
Remember that a sentence cannot have an indirect object unless the sentence has a direct object. Indirect objects usually come between the verb and the direct object.

┌HELP┐
Not every sentence in Exercise 5 has an indirect object.

A direct object may be compound.

EXAMPLES   The team included **Bob** and **Ray.**

         Did the car need **brakes, belts,** and a **battery**?

2i. An ***indirect object*** is a complement that often appears in sentences containing direct objects and that tells *to whom* or *to what* or *for whom* or *for what* the action of a transitive verb is done.

An indirect object may be a noun, a pronoun, or a word group that functions as a noun. To find an indirect object, ask *To whom?* or *To what?* or *For whom?* or *For what?* after a transitive verb.

EXAMPLES   The Swedish Academy awarded **Octavio Paz** the 1990 Nobel Prize in literature. [Awarded the prize to whom? Octavio Paz.]

         Julie's part-time work experience earned **her** a full-time position. [Earned the position for whom? Her.]

         The teacher gives **whoever turns in the earliest paper** a bonus. [Gives a bonus to whom? Whoever turns in the earliest paper.]

NOTE   Do not mistake an object of the preposition *to* or *for* for an indirect object.

| OBJECT OF PREPOSITION | Clarice wrote a letter to **me.** [The pronoun *me* is the object of the preposition *to.*] |
| INDIRECT OBJECT | Clarice wrote **me** a letter. |

An indirect object may be compound.

EXAMPLES   Did the travel agent give **Aaron, Todd,** and **Steve** their itinerary?

         That incident earned my **sister-in-law** and **me** our nicknames.

Exercise 5   Identifying Direct and Indirect Objects

Identify each <u>direct object</u> and <u>indirect object</u> in the following sentences.

EXAMPLE   **1.** An assistant showed the visitors the laser's interior design.

         1. visitors—indirect object; design—direct object

1. The Rhind papyrus and the Golonishev papyrus provide <u>proof</u> that the decimal system was used by the ancient Egyptians.

 Mechanics   *Continued from p. 45*

complete." A complement is "something that fills or completes something," and a compliment is "an act or expression of courtesy, respect, praise, or flattery."]

Discuss with the class how the words are related, and then ask students to name other homonyms. (The **Words Often Confused** section of **Chapter 15: Spelling** consists largely of homonyms.)

2. Make me a graph of the results of your experiment.
3. Perhaps a neighbor would write you a recommendation.
4. That one small grapefruit tree gave us over ten bushels of fruit.
5. Some extinct dragonfly species had wingspans as long as 30 inches.
6. Tell Greg, Wesley, and Carol the story about your first day aboard the submarine.
7. A bland food, tofu quickly absorbs other flavors.
8. By the clear and bountiful waters of the Columbia River, thousands of Chinook Indians lived prosperous lives.
9. In fact, chefs will be serving ground gourmet worms in the near future.
10. Technology has always brought some people new opportunities and others an end to their way of life.

Objective Complements

2j. An *objective complement* is a complement that helps complete the meaning of a transitive verb by identifying or modifying the direct object.

An objective complement may be a noun, a pronoun, an adjective, or a word group that functions as a noun or an adjective.

EXAMPLES   France made Miles Davis a **knight** in the Legion of Honor. [The noun *knight* identifies the direct object *Miles Davis.*]

Mayor Thompson named Felicia **"Mayor for a Day."** [The word group *"Mayor for a Day"* identifies the direct object *Felicia.*]

Garfield considers the refrigerator **his.** [The possessive pronoun *his* modifies the direct object *refrigerator.*]

We have painted the new house **blue.** [The adjective *blue* modifies the direct object *house.*]

NOTE Only a few verbs take objective complements. These verbs are *consider, make,* and any verbs that can be replaced by *consider* or *make,* such as *appoint, believe, call, choose, color, cut, dye, elect, find, keep, name, paint, render,* and *sweep.*

EXAMPLES   The referee **called** [or *considered*] the line drive foul. [*Foul* is the objective complement.]

The Supreme Court's 1954 decision **rendered** [or *made*] the segregation of public schools unlawful. [*Unlawful* is the objective complement.]

TIPS & TRICKS

Remember that a sentence cannot have an objective complement unless the sentence has a direct object.

CONTENT-AREA CONNECTIONS

Social Sciences
Indirect Objects. Ask students to work in groups of three to write a sentence that has both a direct object and an indirect object and describes a concept or a fact learned in a social science course. Tell them that since social science is largely the study of effects on groups or institutions, their sentences will describe these effects. Groups could read their sentences to the class and explain the effect of the subject on the indirect object. [*Example: The Bill of Rights guarantees the citizens of the United States freedom of speech.*]

STYLE TIP

Objective complements generally come after the direct object, near the end of a clause. For emphasis, a writer may place the objective complement before the subject, verb, and direct object.

EXAMPLE
How **interesting** and **pleasant** the tour guide made our visit to the cliff dwellings! [The adjectives *interesting* and *pleasant* modify the direct object *visit.*]

An objective complement may be compound.

EXAMPLES   Did the stockholders elect Sara Gardner **president** and **chief executive officer**?

Lack of ventilation made the workroom **hot, stuffy,** and **uncomfortable.**

Exercise 6 **Identifying Direct Objects, Indirect Objects, and Objective Complements**

Identify each direct object, indirect object, and objective complement in the following sentences.

EXAMPLE   1. The photograph below shows an interactive television system.

    1. *system—direct object*

1. Recent advances in technology have made interactive television systems a reality.
2. The system shown below includes a remote-control converter box with a computer inside.
3. The computer gives viewers several on-screen options for the content of a program.

4. During a football game, for example, viewers can order different camera <u>angles</u>, alternative <u>views</u>, instant <u>replays</u>, or the <u>scores</u> of other games.

5. The computer records each <u>response</u> made by the viewer.

6. Viewers can also select exercise <u>workouts</u> suited to their needs and can tailor <u>news</u> and comedy <u>shows</u> to their interests.

7. Most viewers have found the new <u>technology</u> quite ⟨enjoyable⟩.

8. In addition, advertisers consider it a ⟨boon⟩ to their business.

9. Viewers' responses give the <u>advertisers</u> valuable demographic <u>data</u>.

10. With that data, they can create <u>commercials</u> that target highly specific <u>audiences</u>.

Subject Complements

2k. A *subject complement* is a complement that identifies or modifies the subject of a linking verb.

Like other kinds of complements, the two kinds of subject complements—the *predicate nominative* and the *predicate adjective*—appear in the predicate.

(1) A *predicate nominative* identifies or refers to the subject of a linking verb.

A predicate nominative may be a noun, a pronoun, or a word group that functions as a noun.

EXAMPLES   Robert Hayden is my favorite **poet.** [The noun *poet* identifies the subject *Robert Hayden.*]

               Who are the people over there? [The pronoun *Who* refers to the subject *people.*]

               The object of the game is **to trap your opponent in a corner.** [The infinitive phrase *to trap your opponent in a corner* identifies the subject *object.*]

    A predicate nominative may be compound.

EXAMPLES   The four most populous states are **California, New York, Texas,** and **Florida.**

               The last people off the bus were **Julie** and **I.**

Reference Note
For more about **linking verbs,** see page 17.

STYLE TIP

For emphasis, a writer may place the subject complement before the subject and the verb.

PREDICATE NOMINATIVE
What a truly amazing **coincidence** that is! [The noun *coincidence* identifies the subject *that.*]

PREDICATE ADJECTIVES
Hungry and **weary** were the refugees. [The adjectives *Hungry* and *weary* modify the subject *refugees.*]

English-Language Learners
Spanish. Because Spanish has two verbs, *estar* and *ser,* that function as the one English verb *be,* Spanish-speaking students may have trouble understanding certain sentences.

Before students begin the exercises requiring them to find subject complements, have students work in pairs to develop sentences about themselves or their families by using forms of *be* with predicate nominatives and predicate adjectives.

Complements   **49**

Learners Having Difficulty

Have students work in pairs to interview each other and then write—about their partners—two sentences that end in predicate nominatives and two that end in predicate adjectives.

After each person has written four sentences about his or her partner, have students read the sentences aloud, introducing their partners to the class. Alternatively, students could hand in their papers, and you could read the sentence sets to see if other class members know who is being described.

Remind students not to share any information that they do not want the class to know.

PRACTICE

Guided and Independent

Exercise 7 You may want to use the first ten sentences in **Exercise 7** as guided practice and assign the last ten sentences as independent practice.

HOMEWORK

┌ H E L P ──

When identifying kinds of complements, check first to see whether the verbs in the sentences are action or linking. Remember that only action verbs can take direct objects, indirect objects, and objective complements and that only linking verbs can take subject complements (predicate nominatives and predicate adjectives).

(2) A *predicate adjective* is an adjective that is in the predicate and that modifies the subject of a linking verb.

EXAMPLES   Your lotus-blossom necklace is **lovely.** [The adjective *lovely* modifies the subject *necklace.*]

Does the cottage cheese smell **sour**? [The adjective *sour* modifies the subject *cottage cheese.*]

That small wood flute is **South American.** [The adjective *South American* modifies the subject *flute.*]

A predicate adjective may be compound.

EXAMPLES   Freedom is **precious** and **costly.**

Has the weather turned **cold, wet,** and **foggy**?

NOTE   Do not assume that every adjective in the predicate is a predicate adjective. Keep in mind that a predicate adjective modifies the subject of a linking verb.

EXAMPLES   The epic hero Beowulf was **bold** and **courageous.** [The adjectives *bold* and *courageous* are predicate adjectives because they modify the subject *Beowulf.*]

The epic hero Beowulf was a bold and courageous warrior. [The adjectives *bold* and *courageous* are not predicate adjectives; they modify the predicate nominative *warrior,* not the subject *Beowulf.*]

Exercise 7   **Identifying Predicate Nominatives and Predicate Adjectives**

Identify the subject complement in each of the following sentences. Indicate whether the complement is a *predicate nominative* or a *predicate adjective.*

EXAMPLE   1. In Latvian mythology, Meness is the god of the moon and the protector of travelers and soldiers.

   1. *god—predicate nominative; protector—predicate nominative*

1. Do the strawberries on this vine look ripe to you?
2. The candidate's speech at last night's rally was brief but effective.
3. The villainous warrior became more ruthless and dictatorial.
4. On that day, thirteen colonies became one nation.
5. The dog grew restless and quiet just before the storm hit.

6. Pablo Casals was not only a brilliant <u>cellist</u> but also a sensitive <u>conductor</u> of orchestras.

7. The sea spray tasted extremely <u>salty</u> as it whipped over the bow and into my face.

8. How <u>musty</u> the rooms in this empty house smell!

9. Mark Russell is a popular political <u>humorist</u>.

10. Kicking Bear was a Sioux <u>warrior</u>, <u>artist</u>, and <u>prophet</u>.

11. In order to survive, young mountain goats must be <u>quick</u> and <u>sure-footed</u>.

12. He would remain a practicing <u>physician</u> and <u>author</u> for the rest of his life.

13. At that time, shiny chrome was the prime <u>requirement</u> on a brand-new automobile.

14. The capital of Colombia is the <u>city</u> of Bogotá.

15. Brushed by a careless visitor, a porcelain statue tilted dangerously but remained <u>intact</u>.

16. In one stroke, she would become the <u>owner</u> and <u>president</u> of her company's chief competitor.

17. Our Korean friends became avid <u>fans</u> of Italian food.

18. Can one be <u>wealthy</u> and <u>free</u> at the same time?

19. Wouldn't three days in Hawaii be <u>magical</u> and <u>exciting</u>?

20. Very <u>sleek</u>, very <u>red</u>, and incredibly <u>powerful</u> is Eric's dream car.

Oral Practice **Writing Complements**

Read each item aloud, filling the blank with an appropriate complement.

EXAMPLE   1. All of a sudden, my dreams seemed _____.
     1. *possible* Answers will vary. Suggested answers are provided.

1. On the last warm day of the season, a group of first-graders played _____ on the sunny playground.

2. After years of small plays in small towns, the young actress became _____.

3. Why on earth did you paint your room _____?

4. The jungles of South America are _____ and _____.

5. Could we cook a _____ for dinner tonight?

6. However, the experience taught _____ a great deal about people.

7. My favorite book is _____.

8. Jamal, on a sudden inspiration, named his limestone sculpture _____, after his grandfather.

1. baseball
2. famous

3. yellow
4. lush/green
5. pizza
6. me
7. *Leaves of Grass*
8. Tom

Complements   **51**

9. him

10. hard

11. prize
12. the tomb

13. energetic
14. Sarah
15. *Old Yeller*

16. me
17. the winner

18. goals
19. treasurer
20. diamonds

9. Strangely enough, her casual remark gave _____ a wonderful idea for an invention.

10. Back in those days, life in the Australian outback must have been _____.

11. To whom will the judges award the _____ at the banquet?
12. After decades of futile searching, the diligent archaeologist finally discovered _____, and all his theories were confirmed.

13. That painting by van Gogh is incredibly _____.
14. The pitcher threw _____ a nasty curveball.
15. I have finally made a decision; my least favorite movie of all time is _____.

16. Why do you never show _____ your poems?
17. Despite the wonderful performances by many of the others, the committee named Aaron _____.

18. How many _____ did Jarret score in last night's game?
19. Did the class really elect Janice _____?
20. Under intense heat and pressure, carbon can become _____.

DIFFERENTIATING INSTRUCTION

Special Education Students

Some students may have difficulty reading lengthy blocks of material. You could simplify **Review A** by having a helper double-space each line of the copy on individual sheets on which students can write. Then, students can concentrate on the task of identifying subjects, verbs, and complements.

┌HELP──

Not every sentence in Review B has a complement.

Review A **Identifying Subjects, Verbs, and Complements**

Identify each subject, verb, and complement in the sentences in the following paragraphs. Indicate whether each complement is a *direct object*, an *indirect object*, an *objective complement*, a *predicate nominative*, or a *predicate adjective*.

EXAMPLE **[1]** Arabesques are complex, elaborate designs of flowers, foliage, calligraphy, and geometric patterns.

1. *subject—Arabesques; verb—are; predicate nominative—designs*

1. d.o.
2. d.o.
3. i.o./d.o.

4. d.o./o.c.
5. d.o./o.c.

6. p.a.

[1] The arabesques from the fortress-palace of the Alhambra in Granada, Spain, and the ones from the king's palace in Fez, Morocco, illustrate a historic link between two cultures. [2] In A.D. 711, Arabs and Muslim Berbers from North Africa invaded and occupied Spain. [3] The Spanish gave them a name: the Moors.

[4] The Moors' encouragement of commerce made Spain's major cities wealthy. [5] Meanwhile, the Moors' patronage of art, literature, and science rendered the cities centers of learning for Christian, Jewish, and Muslim scholars.

[6] Through reconquest, parts of Spain became Christian again as early as 1085. [7] At the end of the fifteenth century, Granada remained

the Moors' last (stronghold). **[8]** In 1492, it too fell to the forces of Ferdinand V and Isabella I. **[9]** Spain expelled (most) of the Moors from the country. **[10]** Still, traces of their rich culture survive in the architecture, poetry, and music of Spain.

7. p.n.
9. d.o.

Review B | **Writing Sentences with Complements**

Write your own sentences according to the following guidelines. In your sentences, underline the words you use as the italicized sentence parts. Use a variety of subjects, verbs, and complements in your sentences.

EXAMPLE **1.** Write a sentence with an *indirect object* and a *direct object.*

1. *The Lady of the Lake gave* Arthur *the* sword *known as Excalibur.*

1. Write a sentence with a *compound subject.*
2. Write a sentence with a *compound verb.*
3. Write a sentence with a *direct object.*
4. Write a sentence with a *compound direct object.*
5. Write a sentence with an *indirect object* and a *direct object.*
6. Write a sentence with a *compound indirect object* and a *compound direct object.*

Review B | **Writing Sentences with Complements**

POSSIBLE ANSWERS

1. Was King Arthur or Sir Galahad the hero of the poem Dad read us?

2. Dad read and memorized many passages of the Arthurian legends.

3. Aunt Leona gave my brother Lance a video of a cartoon version of an Arthurian legend.

4. Lance wrote her a thank-you note and a poem.

5. She then gave him a call to show her appreciation.

6. Readers of Arthurian legends have given Lancelot and Arthur attention and admiration for centuries.

Complements **53**

Sentences with Complements

POSSIBLE ANSWERS
continued

7. King Arthur is Lance's hero.

8. Was Queen Guinevere, King Arthur's wife, beautiful and charming?

9. Many subjects called Arthur king.

10. Dad considers much of the Arthurian legend a moral tale as well as beautiful poetry.

---

7. Write a sentence with a *predicate nominative.*

8. Write a sentence with a *compound predicate adjective.*

9. Write a sentence with a *direct object* and an *objective complement.*

10. Write a sentence with a *direct object* and a *compound objective complement.*

Seven Common Sentence Patterns

The subject and the verb produce one sentence pattern. The subject, the verb, and the various complements produce six other common sentence patterns.

```
S      V
Velma painted.

S      V       DO
Velma painted a landscape.

      S    V   IO       DO
The judges gave Velma an award.

    S     V       DO        OC (Noun)
They considered her landscape a masterpiece.

    S    V        DO      OC (Adjective)
They called the painting brilliant.

      S      V      PN
Velma has become a celebrity.

 S  V   PA
She is famous.
```

Numerals in brackets refer to rules tested by the items in the Chapter Review.

1. s. [2a]
2. s.f. [2a]
3. s.f. [2a]
4. s. [2a]
5. s.f. [2a]

Chapter Review

A. Identifying Sentences and Sentence Fragments

Identify each of the following word groups as a *sentence* or a *sentence fragment*.

1. Aren't the first ten amendments to the Constitution called the Bill of Rights?
2. Guaranteeing the people four basic freedoms.
3. Besides freedom of religion and freedom of the press, freedom of speech and of public assembly.
4. Most of the other amendments in the Bill of Rights are less sweeping than the First Amendment.
5. If the Third Amendment pertains specifically to the quartering of soldiers in private homes.

B. Identifying the Simple Subject and the Simple Predicate

Identify each <u>simple subject</u> and each <u>simple predicate</u> in the following sentences. Be sure to include all parts of a verb phrase and all parts of a compound subject or verb.

6. [2b, c, d]
7. [2b, c, d]
8. [2b, c, d]
9. [2b, c, d, e]
10. [2b, c, d, e]
11. [2b, c, d, f]
12. [2b, c, d]
13. [2b, c, d]
14. [2b, c, d]
15. [2b, c, d, f]

6. <u>Garrett</u> <u>had become</u> fluent in several languages.
7. <u>Will</u> <u>you</u> <u>lend</u> me some change for the telephone, please?
8. <u>Leilani</u> <u>was</u> unquestionably the best player on the team.
9. Down into the cave <u>went</u> the <u>guide</u> and the <u>tourists</u>.
10. The restaurant <u>manager</u> and his <u>staff</u> <u>have</u> never <u>refused</u> service to anyone.
11. Every <u>student</u> <u>must complete</u> his or her immunization card and <u>return</u> it to the office.
12. <u>Is</u> the elderly <u>lady</u> with the green hat Mrs. Daly?
13. This tiny <u>room</u> <u>would be</u> extremely uncomfortable to most people.
14. The National League <u>playoff</u> between the Philadelphia team and the Houston team <u>was</u> one of the most exciting in recent years.
15. <u>Mimi</u> <u>has picked</u> a kitten from the litter and <u>will call</u> him Mr. Alp.

Chapter Review **55**

GRAMMAR

C. Identifying Complements

Identify each <u>complement</u> in the following sentences as a *direct object,* an *indirect object,* a *predicate nominative,* or a *predicate adjective.*

16. i.o./d.o. [2g, i, h]
17. p.a./p.a. [2g, k(2)]
18. i.o./d.o. [2g, i, h]
19. p.n. [2g, k(1)]
20. p.a. [2g, k(2)]
21. d.o. [2g, h]
22. p.a. [2g, k(2)]
23. i.o./d.o. [2g, i, h]
24. p.n. [2g, k(1)]
25. d.o. [2g, h]
26. i.o./d.o. [2g, i, h]
27. d.o./d.o. [2g, h]
28. i.o./d.o. [2g, i, h]
29. p.n. [2g, k(1)]
30. p.a. [2g, k(2)]

16. They will send <u>you</u> an <u>application</u> if you write for one.
17. Is your dog <u>male</u> or <u>female</u>?
18. The doctor brought <u>each</u> of the nurses a <u>cup</u> of tea.
19. Roald Amundsen was the first <u>man</u> to reach the South Pole.
20. Does this photograph look <u>old</u> to you?
21. Many fugitive slaves found <u>shelter</u> with the Seminoles of Florida.
22. The water in the bay feels quite <u>cold</u>.
23. Cheryl gave <u>me</u> her <u>paper</u> to read.
24. The Great Wall of China is <u>one</u> of that nation's oldest structures.
25. Mr. Nickles divided the <u>class</u> into smaller sections.
26. The coach tossed <u>Yolanda</u> the soccer <u>ball</u>.
27. Please rinse your <u>dishes</u> and put <u>them</u> into the dishwasher.
28. Yesterday the mail carrier left <u>me</u> this <u>letter</u> from a bookstore.
29. Is Harrison Ford a more popular movie <u>star</u> than Mel Gibson?
30. The carrot bread smelled <u>wonderful</u> just after it came out of the oven.

D. Identifying Subjects, Verbs, and Complements

Identify the <u>subject</u> and <u>verb</u> in each sentence in the following paragraph. If a sentence has any (complements), identify them as well, and indicate whether each is a *direct object,* an *indirect object,* an *objective complement,* a *predicate nominative,* or a *predicate adjective.*

31. [2b, c, d]
32. p.n. [2b, c, d, g, k(1)]
33. i.o./d.o. [2b, c, d, e, g, i, h]
34. d.o./o.c. [2b, c, d, g, h, j]
35. p.a./p.a. [2b, c, d, f, g, k(2)]
36. [2b, c, d, e]
37. p.n. [2b, c, d, g, k(1)]

[31] Along the coast of the Atlantic Ocean in Brooklyn, New York, <u>lies</u> Coney <u>Island</u>, a world-famous amusement park. [32] Until 1654, the <u>island</u> (now a peninsula) <u>was</u> the summer (campground) of the Canarsie and the Nyack peoples. [33] In that year, the <u>Canarsie</u> and the <u>Nyack</u> <u>sold</u> a (group) of Dutch settlers the (island). [34] The <u>Dutch</u> <u>named</u> the (island) (Konynen Eyland) (Dutch for "rabbit island") because of the abundance of wild rabbits in the area. [35] In the 1820s, the <u>island</u> <u>became</u> (popular) as an ocean resort and throughout the nineteenth and early twentieth centuries <u>grew</u> increasingly (lavish). [36] Among its many attractions <u>were</u> the mechanical <u>horses</u> and the 250-foot <u>Parachute Jump</u> of Steeplechase Park and the onion <u>domes</u>, <u>minarets</u>, and Japanese tea <u>gardens</u> of Luna Park. [37] Today, after years of neglect and a series of fires, the amusement <u>area</u> of this once-grand resort <u>is</u>

only a five-block (strip) between Surf Avenue and the eighty-foot-wide boardwalk along the ocean. **[38]** However, ten million people still visit (Coney Island) each year. **[39]** Now the founder of a restaurant chain is planning a major (face lift) for the area. **[40]** He holds the (rights) to the former site of Steeplechase Park and envisions the (park) spectacularly (beautiful) once again.

38. d.o. [2b, c, d, g, h]
39. d.o. [2b, c, d, g, h]
40. d.o./d.o./o.c. [2b, c, d, f, g, h, j]

Writing Application

Using Sentence Variety in an Essay

Improving Sentence Style   You have been looking through a number of college brochures. At last, you have found a school that seems right for you and have decided to apply for admission. The admissions essay instructions are as follows: "In a short essay, tell about something that is important to you." Be sure to use a variety of subjects, verbs, and complements in your essay.

Prewriting   First, you'll need to decide on a topic for your essay. Brainstorm a list of issues, ideas, and activities that are important to you. Is playing music, writing fiction, or doing volunteer work a significant part of your life? Choose the most engaging topic from your list. Decide whether the tone of your essay will be serious or lighthearted. Jot down facts, details, and examples to help develop your topic.

Writing   You might start with a brief anecdote, a thoughtful question, or a surprising statement. Then, develop your topic with supporting examples, facts, and details. Sum up your ideas in a clincher paragraph.

Revising   Fine-tune the content, organization, and style of your essay. First, make sure that your thesis statement gives a clear focus to your essay. Then, make sure the body of your essay supports that thesis. Do your supporting paragraphs follow a clear, logical sequence? Next, evaluate the tone of your essay. Finally, check your sentence style. Have you varied the elements of your sentences to avoid a monotonous rhythm? Ask a friend to read your essay and give you suggestions.

Publishing   Check your writing carefully for errors in usage, spelling, and punctuation. Be sure that you've used only complete sentences. You may want to use the essay that you write for this assignment as part of an actual application packet.

APPLICATION

Writing Application

Writing Tip. You may want to display sample essay questions from a variety of college application forms and have students discuss how the essay requirements compare with the requirements of this assignment.

Scoring Rubric. While you will want to pay particular attention to students' use of subjects, predicates, and complements, you will also want to evaluate overall writing performance. You may want to give a split score to indicate development and clarity of the composition as well as grammar skills.

DIFFERENTIATING INSTRUCTION

Learners Having Difficulty

For students who are not interested in college, you may want to present an alternative to the college essay. You could have them write cover letters stating their employment goals or short personal essays to be submitted with an application to join an organization.

CHAPTER

The Phrase
Kinds of Phrases and Their Functions

INTRODUCING THE CHAPTER

- This chapter begins with a definition of phrases, then defines prepositional phrases and describes how they are used as either adjective or adverb phrases. Then, verbals and verbal phrases, including participles, participial phrases, gerunds, gerund phrases, infinitives, and infinitive phrases, are presented. The final lesson discusses appositives and appositive phrases.

- The chapter closes with a **Chapter Review** including a **Writing Application** feature that asks students to write a letter using at least three infinitive phrases and two appositive phrases.

- For help in integrating this chapter with writing assignments, see the **Teaching Strands** chart, pp. T24–T25.

Diagnostic Preview

A. Identifying Prepositional, Verbal, and Appositive Phrases

Identify the italicized phrase in each of the following sentences as a *prepositional phrase*, a *participial phrase*, a *gerund phrase*, an *infinitive phrase*, or an *appositive phrase*.

┌HELP┐

In the Diagnostic Preview, you do not need to identify separately a prepositional phrase or a verbal phrase that is part of a larger phrase.

Numerals in brackets refer to the rules tested by the items in the Diagnostic Preview.

1. inf. [3j]
2. part. [3f]
3. part. [3f]
4. ger. [3h]
5. app. [3l]
6. part. [3f]
7. inf. [3j]
8. prep. [3b]
9. prep. [3b]
10. inf. [3j]

EXAMPLES
1. The sunlight shimmering *on the lake* was beautiful.
   1. prepositional phrase

2. *Stretched out in a patch of sunlight,* the cat seemed to be grinning.
   2. participial phrase

1. Juanita likes *to draw caricatures of her friends.*
2. *Arriving late at school,* Bill went to the office to get a pass.
3. *Made in Ireland,* this kind of crystal is admired and collected throughout the world.
4. By *inventing the telephone,* Alexander Graham Bell assured himself a place in history.
5. Luciano Pavarotti, *the great Italian tenor,* received a hearty standing ovation at the end of his concert.
6. After the concert, we saw them *looking in vain for a taxi.*
7. Raúl has the talent *to sculpt and design beautiful objects.*
8. "It is a pleasure to be here with you today," remarked the mayor *at the beginning* of her talk.
9. A number of pioneer women kept diaries and journals *of their experiences* settling the American wilderness.
10. *To speak freely on almost any issue* is a right guaranteed to all U.S. citizens.

CHAPTER RESOURCES

Internet
- Web resources: go.hrw.com

go. hrw .com

Practice & Review
- *Language & Sentence Skills Practice,* pp. 54–75
- *Language & Sentence Skills Practice Answer Key,* pp. 24–33

Application & Enrichment
- *Language & Sentence Skills Practice,* pp. 53, 76–78
- *Language & Sentence Skills Practice Answer Key,* pp. 24, 33–34

B. Identifying Prepositional, Verbal, and Appositive Phrases

Identify each underlined italicized phrase in the following paragraph as a *prepositional phrase*, a *participial phrase*, a *gerund phrase*, an *infinitive phrase*, or an *appositive phrase*.

EXAMPLES   **[1]** *For more than fifty years,* Thurgood Marshall worked
                 [2] *to protect the rights of all people in the United States.*

            1. prepositional phrase
            2. infinitive phrase

[11] *Ranked at the top of his law school class,* Thurgood Marshall began law practice in Baltimore; and in 1936, he was selected [12] *to be a counsel for the National Association for the Advancement of Colored People.* From the start of his career, he believed strongly in [13] *using the U.S. Constitution to fight injustice.* [14] *Risking his life at times,* Marshall, [15] *the son of a schoolteacher,* won many civil rights cases [16] *before federal and state courts.* His arguments played an important role in [17] *convincing the Supreme Court that "separate but equal" educational facilities were unconstitutional.* [18] *During the Kennedy administration,* Marshall became a federal judge. [19] *After a two-year term* as U.S. solicitor general, he was nominated to the Supreme Court by President Lyndon Johnson. Marshall was the first African American [20] *to serve on the nation's highest court.*

11. part. [3f]
12. inf. [3j]
13. ger. [3h]
14. part. [3f]
15. app. [3l]
16. prep. [3b]
17. ger. [3h]
18. prep. [3b]
19. prep. [3b]
20. inf. [3j]

What Is a Phrase?

3a. A ***phrase*** is a group of related words that is used as a single part of speech and that does not contain both a verb and its subject.

VERB PHRASE	have been waiting [no subject]
PREPOSITIONAL PHRASE	during the storm [no subject or verb]
INFINITIVE PHRASE	to run swiftly [no subject or verb]

NOTE A group of words that has both a subject and a verb is called a ***clause.***

Reference Note

For more about **clauses,** see Chapter 4.

Differentiating Instruction

- *Developmental Language & Sentence Skills Guided Practice,* pp. 35–44
- *Developmental Language & Sentence Skills Guided Practice Teacher's Notes and Answer Key,* pp. 10–12

Assessment

- *Holt Handbook Chapter Tests with Answer Key,* pp. 5–6, 54

ASSESSING

Entry-Level Assessment

Diagnostic Preview. The **Diagnostic Preview** contains two parts. **Part A** focuses on identifying prepositional, participial, gerund, infinitive, and appositive phrases in sentences. **Part B** asks students to identify these types of phrases in a paragraph.

You may want to use the results of this preview to determine whether students need to study some or all of the related material in this chapter.

PRETEACHING

Lesson Starter

Motivating. Challenge students to write poems whose texts are made up entirely of prepositional phrases. Read them this example:

Fishing
Beside the water
Onto the hook
Below the water
Into action
Against the boat
Into the net
Off the hook
On the way home

Tell students they can refer to the list of prepositions on p. 24. Students may work in small groups to check each other's poems.

Prepositional Phrases

Rules 3a–d *(pp. 60–64)*

OBJECTIVES

- To identify adjective phrases and the words they modify
- To identify adverb phrases and the words they modify

DIRECT TEACHING

Modeling and Demonstration

Prepositional Phrases. Model how to identify adjective phrases and the words they modify by using the example *The members of the club want sweatshirts with the club emblem.* First, ask if the sentence contains any prepositional phrases. [*yes; of the club, with the club emblem*] Next, ask what word or words *of the club* modifies. [*members*] Ask what part of speech *members* is. [*noun*] Explain that *of the club* is an adjective phrase because it modifies the noun *members*. Then, ask what *with the club emblem* modifies. [*sweatshirts*] Next, ask what part of speech *sweatshirts* is. [*noun*] Ask what kind of prepositional phrase *with the club emblem* is. [*adjective phrase*] Now, have a volunteer use another example from this chapter to demonstrate how to identify adjective phrases.

Reference Note

For more about **prepositions,** see page 23.

MEETING THE CHALLENGE

If you stand in front of a bookshelf for a few minutes, chances are you'll encounter a prepositional phrase or two. The titles of many books contain prepositional phrases, and the titles of some books actually *are* prepositional phrases. By yourself or in a small group, find out just how many prepositional phrases you can find in book titles. Head to the school library for a short period—fifteen to twenty minutes should be plenty of time—and write down as many titles as you can that contain prepositional phrases. When you are finished, share your list with your class.

ANSWER

Lists will vary, but students should be able to come up with a sufficient number of titles.

Reference Note

For more about **infinitives,** see page 70.

Prepositional Phrases

3b. A *prepositional phrase* includes a preposition, the object of the preposition, and any modifiers of that object.

EXAMPLES   Did officials **of the Smithsonian Institution** recently unveil plans **for a new museum**? [The compound noun *Smithsonian Institution* is the object of the preposition *of.* The noun *museum* is the object of the preposition *for.*]

     According to them, the National African-American Museum opened **in 1995.** [The pronoun *them* is the object of the compound preposition *According to.* The noun *1995* is the object of the preposition *in.*]

The object of a preposition may be compound.

EXAMPLE   Do you know the Greek myth about **Daedalus** and **Icarus**?

HI & LOIS reprinted with special permission of King Features Syndicate, Inc.

NOTE   Be careful not to confuse a prepositional phrase beginning with *to* with an infinitive or infinitive phrase beginning with *to* (*to swim, to know, to see*). Remember, a preposition always has a noun or pronoun as an object.

The Adjective Phrase

3c. A prepositional phrase that modifies a noun or a pronoun is called an *adjective phrase.*

An adjective phrase tells *what kind* or *which one.*

EXAMPLE   One **of my friends** is making a film **about school.** [*Of my friends* modifies the pronoun *One,* telling *which one. About school* modifies the noun *film,* telling *what kind.*]

An adjective phrase almost always follows the word it modifies.
That word may be the object of another preposition.

EXAMPLE   The film won't include all **of the students in our class.** [*Of the students* modifies the pronoun *all*. *In our class* modifies the noun *students*, which is the object of the preposition *of*.]

More than one adjective phrase may modify the same word.

EXAMPLE   Instead, it will relate the adventures **of five students at school** and **in their neighborhood.** [The three phrases *of five students*, *at school*, and *in their neighborhood* modify the noun *adventures*.]

NOTE   Sometimes an adjective phrase is combined with a noun to form a compound noun.

EXAMPLES   Helen of Troy   Meals on Wheels

tug-of-war   jack-in-the-box

Exercise 1   **Identifying Adjective Phrases and the Words They Modify**

The following sentences contain adjective phrases. Identify each adjective phrase and the word it modifies.

EXAMPLE   1. If you are a rafting enthusiast, you might enjoy a trip to New Guinea, a large island in the East Indies.

1. to New Guinea—trip; in the East Indies—island

1. New Guinea rivers like the one shown are popular areas for rafting enthusiasts.
2. As you can see, a series of nearly continuous rapids crisscrosses jungles of primeval beauty.
3. The twenty-eight major rapids on the Tua River make it a course for rafters with experience and courage.
4. Brilliantly colored butterflies brighten the riverbanks, and the metallic whine of cicadas almost completely covers the roar of the river.
5. The banks are a chaos of tumbled boulders and uprooted trees.
6. Beautiful tropical forests along the way blanket the mountains above the river.

Prepositional Phrases   **61**

EXTENSION

Relating to Literature

If your literature textbook contains "Sonnet 43" from *Sonnets from the Portuguese* by Elizabeth Barrett Browning, have students read and discuss the poem. Direct students' attention to the kinds of words and phrases the speaker uses to explain how she loves [*adverbs and adverb prepositional phrases*]. Have students identify the prepositional phrases and explain why—with the repetition of so many similar constructions—the poem does not seem repetitious. [*Browning uses different prepositions and both adjective and adverb phrases in her sentences; and in lines 7 and 8, in the exact middle of the poem, she varies the pattern by using two adverbs instead of adverb phrases.*]

S T Y L E   T I P

Prepositional phrases are handy for adding descriptive information to writing. Used excessively, however, these phrases can make writing wordy and stilted. Whenever possible, replace prepositional phrases with more concise expressions.

WORDY
Both of the debaters in an eloquent manner presented arguments with persuasiveness and with emotion.

REVISED
Both debaters eloquently presented emotionally persuasive arguments.

COMPUTER TIP

Do you use too many prepositional phrases in your writing? If you use a computer and have access to style-checking software, there is an easy way to find out. Use a program that highlights prepositional phrases. Then, check each highlighted phrase in a piece of your writing to be sure that you have expressed yourself as concisely as possible.

7. However, rafters don't have much <u>chance</u> for sightseeing.
8. They can't pay much <u>attention</u> to anything except the swirling water around their rafts.
9. Do you enjoy <u>moments</u> of high adventure?
10. Wouldn't you love a <u>trip</u> down this wild river in the South Pacific?

The Adverb Phrase

3d. A prepositional phrase that modifies a verb, an adjective, or an adverb is called an *adverb phrase*.

An adverb phrase tells *how, when, where, why,* or *to what extent* (*how much, how long,* or *how far*).

An adverb phrase may modify a verb.

EXAMPLE   **After the early 800s,** the Fujiwara family ruled **as regents in Japan for more than three hundred years.** [Each phrase modifies the verb *ruled. After the early 800s* tells *when, as regents* tells *how, in Japan* tells *where,* and *for more than three hundred years* tells *how long.*]

As the preceding example shows, more than one adverb phrase can modify the same word, and an adverb phrase, unlike an adjective phrase, often precedes the word it modifies.

An adverb phrase may modify an adjective.

EXAMPLE   Then the Minamoto, another family active **in court intrigues,** gained power. [*In court intrigues* modifies the adjective *active,* telling *how.*]

An adverb phrase may modify an adverb.

EXAMPLE   The Fujiwara had ruled too complacently **for their own good.** [*For their own good* modifies the adverb *complacently,* telling *how.*]

Exercise 2   **Identifying Adverb Phrases and the Words They Modify**

Each of the following sentences contains at least one adverb phrase. Identify each <u>adverb phrase</u> and the <u>word or words it modifies</u>.

EXAMPLE   1. From the map at right, you can clearly tell the function of the Panama Canal.
            1. *From the map at right—can tell*

1. The canal, which is fifty-one miles long, links the Pacific Ocean to the Atlantic Ocean.
2. On the canal's elaborate series of locks, which raise and lower the water levels, ships can travel from ocean to ocean.
3. Construction of the canal, an engineering marvel, began in 1904 and continued until 1914.
4. Naturally, the builders faced many obstacles during the canal's construction.
5. Mosquitoes posed a major health risk throughout the area and had to be eliminated.
6. For the duration of the canal project, Dr. William C. Gorgas, an army surgeon, fought the mosquitoes.
7. With great efficiency, he drained swamps, fumigated buildings, and installed a pure water supply.
8. After the resignation of two chief engineers, President Theodore Roosevelt in 1907 appointed Army Lieutenant Colonel George W. Goethals chief engineer.
9. Goethals, active in all phases of canal construction, quickly gained the respect of workers.
10. This photograph shows some of the workers who dug through the mountains along the Isthmus of Panama.

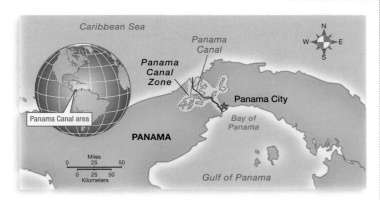

PRACTICE

Guided and Independent
You may wish to use **Exercise 2** as guided practice and **Review A** as independent practice.

HOMEWORK

GRAMMAR

Prepositional Phrases   **63**

DIFFERENTIATING INSTRUCTION

Advanced Learners

Looking at Language. Write the following expressions on the chalkboard: *verbal protest, verbal aptitude.* Then, ask the class if anyone can explain what *verbal* means in these contexts. [*relating to or consisting of words; in* verbal contract, *oral rather than written*]

Explain to students that usually an adjective ending in the suffix *–al* takes its meaning directly from the root word preceding the suffix. Therefore, *verbal* would mean "of, relating to, or formed from a verb." *Verbal* can also refer to words in general; however, this meaning derives from the origin of *verb*, the Latin *verbum*, meaning "word."

Ask students to look up *verbal* and *word* in dictionaries and to study the words' etymologies. To extend the lesson, you could ask each student to write two sentences demonstrating the two meanings of *verbal* (*of a verb* and *of a word*).

The Participle and the Participial Phrase

Rules 3e, f *(pp. 64–68)*

OBJECTIVE

■ To identify participial phrases and the words they modify

Identify each prepositional phrase in the following sentences. Then, tell whether it is an *adjective phrase* or an *adverb phrase*.

EXAMPLE
1. The clay in bone china has actually been blended with bone ash.

1. *in bone china—adjective phrase; with bone ash—adverb phrase*

1. Tito, jump off and coil a line around that piling.
2. A large mirror reflected the light from the window.
3. Men in that part of the world commonly wear turbans, which protect their hair from sand.
4. Without a password, you cannot access the network.
5. Why do such small differences between people sometimes seem so large to the people themselves?
6. According to this source, the merger will take place later this week.
7. Hot corn bread muffins in the shape of fish tumbled out of the cast-iron pan.
8. Dozens of small framed photographs stood on the mantel over the fireplace.
9. Between the radiator and the engine, a large boa constrictor was taking a nap.
10. In England, the rear storage compartment of a car is called the "boot," not the "trunk."

Verbals and Verbal Phrases

A **verbal** is a verb form that is used as a noun, an adjective, or an adverb. The three kinds of verbals are the *participle*, the *gerund*, and the *infinitive*. A **verbal phrase** consists of a verbal and its modifiers and complements. The three kinds of verbal phrases are the *participial phrase*, the *gerund phrase*, and the *infinitive phrase*.

The Participle

3e. A *participle* is a verb form that can be used as an adjective.

Two kinds of participles are the *present participle* and the *past participle*.

RESOURCES

The Participle and the Participial Phrase

Practice
■ *Language & Sentence Skills Practice,* pp. 59–61

Differentiating Instruction
■ *Developmental Language & Sentence Skills,* pp. 37–38

(1) Present participles end in *–ing.*

EXAMPLES   The **freezing** rain made the road slick. [*Freezing* modifies the noun *rain.*]

Bowing, the performers acknowledged the applause. [*Bowing* modifies the noun *performers.*]

Did I hear someone **knocking** on the door? [*Knocking* modifies the pronoun *someone.*]

(2) Most past participles end in *–d* or *–ed.* Others are irregularly formed.

EXAMPLES   First prize was an **engraved** trophy. [*Engraved* modifies the noun *trophy.*]

The lab tested samples of water **taken** from wells in the area. [*Taken* modifies the noun *water.*]

Rested and **relaxed,** we returned to work. [Both *Rested* and *relaxed* modify the pronoun *we.*]

NOTE In addition to their present and past forms, participles have a *present perfect* form. This form adds *having* or *having been* to the past participle of a verb and indicates a completed action.

EXAMPLES   **Having completed** his chores, Brian decided to join his friends playing soccer in the park.

Having been declared the winner, she called a press conference to thank her supporters.

The Participial Phrase

3f. A *participial phrase* consists of a participle and its modifiers and complements. The entire phrase is used as an adjective.

EXAMPLES   **Grinning broadly,** Whoopi Goldberg accepted the award. [The participial phrase modifies the compound noun *Whoopi Goldberg.* The adverb *broadly* modifies the present participle *Grinning.*]

Proclaiming his innocence, the candidate vehemently denied the charges. [The participial phrase modifies the noun *candidate.* The noun *innocence* is the direct object of the present participle *Proclaiming.*]

Reference Note

For lists of verbs that have **irregular past participles,** see page 180.

Reference Note

For more about **present perfect participles,** see page 209.

┌─ H E L P ─

Do not confuse a participle used as an adjective with a participle used as part of a verb phrase.

ADJECTIVE
The Hispanic Association of Colleges and Universities, **founded** in 1986, is based in San Antonio, Texas.

VERB PHRASE
The Hispanic Association of Colleges and Universities, which **was founded** in 1986, is based in San Antonio, Texas.

DIRECT TEACHING

Modeling and Demonstration

The Participle and the Participial Phrase. Model how to identify participles and the words they modify by using the example *The barking dog ran toward the stopped car.* First, ask which word is the main verb here. [*ran*] Next, ask which words in this sentence are verbals. [*barking, stopped*] Next, ask what *barking* does in this sentence. [*describes dog*] Explain that *barking* is a participle because it is a verbal that acts as an adjective modifying the noun *dog.* Point out that *stopped* is also a participle because it is a verbal modifying the noun *car.* Now, have a volunteer use another example from this chapter to demonstrate how to identify participles and the words they modify.

DIFFERENTIATING INSTRUCTION

Learners Having Difficulty

To give students extra practice with participles, hand out pages from a newspaper and have students highlight the participles on the pages in one color and the words that the participles modify in a second color.

English-Language Learners

General Strategies. Because some languages do not have participles, students might have difficulty identifying and using participles. To help clarify the concept, list the verbs *sleep, laugh, yawn, cook, crack,* and *honor* on the chalkboard. Ask students to add *ing* to the first three verbs and *ed* to the last three verbs and to modify a noun with these newly formed participles. [*sleeping baby, laughing hyena, yawning worker, cooked carrots, cracked egg, honored guest*]

RETEACHING

Participial Phrases

Activity. If students have difficulty understanding participles from a direct teaching approach, use a hands-on method. Write on the chalkboard the following sentences:

1. The sun, which was shining brightly, made the water sparkle.

2. The dog, which was barking furiously, pulled against his chain.

3. The man, who was miraculously not injured, struggled out of the wrecked car.

Have students identify which words in each sentence are participles used with a helping verb [*shining, barking, injured*]. Ask students to rewrite the sentences so that these participles used as a part of a verb are used as adjectives. Students will have to delete the relative pronoun and the verb *was*. [*Possible answers: The sun, shining brightly, made the water sparkle. The dog, barking furiously, pulled against his chain. The man, miraculously not injured, struggled out of the wrecked car.*]

TEACHING TIP

Exercise 3 Some students may mistake main verbs for participles, especially in items 1 and 7. You may wish to have students first find the subject and verb for each sentence and then find the participle and the noun or pronoun it modifies. It may be helpful to color-code words.

S T Y L E T I P

To prevent confusion, place participial phrases as close as possible to the words they modify.

MISPLACED
Stalking the squirrel, I saw the cat in the yard.

IMPROVED
I saw the cat **stalking the squirrel** in the yard.

Reference Note

For more about **misplaced participial phrases,** see page 250.

Puzzled by their behavior, I asked for an explanation. [The participial phrase modifies the pronoun *I*. The adverb phrase *by their behavior* modifies the past participle *Puzzled*.]

Zimbabwe, **formerly known as Rhodesia,** is in southern Africa. [The participial phrase modifies the noun *Zimbabwe*. The adverb *formerly* modifies the past participle *known*. The prepositional phrase *as Rhodesia* modifies the past participle *known*.]

Exercise 3 Identifying Participial Phrases and the Words They Modify

Each of the following sentences contains at least one participial phrase. Identify each participial phrase and the word or words it modifies.

EXAMPLE   1. Living far from the city, I developed an interest in nature at an early age.
1. *Living far from the city—I*

1. All of the students trying out for the soccer team have heard from the coach or her assistant.
2. Thanking us several times, the piano teacher returned the chairs borrowed for the recital.
3. Today's newspaper, printed last night, made no mention of the president's announcement.
4. Annoyed by the high prices, Mr. Sims has decided not to shop at that store anymore.
5. Addressing the senior class, the principal praised all of the students for their work on the cleanup campaign.
6. Having studied hard, Karen did well on both the Spanish test and the calculus quiz.
7. The movies showing at that theater are ones released before 1940.
8. Cheered by the crowd, our school's Special Olympics team rushed onto the field.
9. Looking through the catalog, Earl found a Cajun cookbook.
10. Smiling shyly, Lynn showed us the pictures she had taken.

The Absolute Phrase

An *absolute phrase* consists of (1) a participle or a participial phrase, (2) a noun or a pronoun that the participle or participial phrase modifies, and (3) any other modifiers of that noun or pronoun. The entire word group is used as an adverb to modify a clause in a sentence.

MINI-LESSON Mechanics

Punctuating Participial Phrases. To help students punctuate sentences that contain interior participial phrases, write the following sentences on the chalkboard, underlining the participial phrases:

1. The groceries packed in the crate are for the local food bank.

2. The twins, laughing loudly, raced to the car.

An absolute phrase has no grammatical connection to any word in the clause it modifies. Rather, the phrase, which tells *when, why,* or *how,* modifies the whole clause.

EXAMPLES   **Their car having been repaired,** the Pfeiffers continued their road trip. [The absolute phrase modifies the independent clause, telling *when* the Pfeiffers continued their road trip. The present perfect participle *having been repaired* modifies the noun *car.*]

            Chris said that, **the weather being so fine,** he would prefer to go for a hike. [The absolute phrase modifies the subordinate clause, telling *why* Chris would prefer to go for a hike. The participial phrase *being so fine* modifies the noun *weather.*]

            Wearily, the explorer trudged onward through the snow, **his loyal Alaskan malamute keeping pace at his side.** [The absolute phrase modifies the independent clause by telling *how* the explorer trudged onward through the snow. The participial phrase *keeping pace at his side* modifies the noun *Alaskan malamute.*]

Review B   **Identifying Prepositional and Participial Phrases and the Words They Modify**

Identify each italicized phrase in the following sentences as a *prepositional phrase* or a *participial phrase.* Then, give the word or words each phrase modifies. If a participial phrase is part of an absolute phrase, write *absolute.*

EXAMPLE   **[1]** *Visiting friends in Los Angeles last year,* I became interested *in low-riders.*

        1. *participial—I; prepositional—interested*

[1] My friend Jorge told me that this unique form *of folk art* has been popular *for forty years or more.* **[2]** He said the term "low-rider" refers *to the automobile, its driver, and any passengers.* **[3]** *Making artistic statements with their automobiles,* many young men *in the Southwest* spend both time and money on their cars. **[4]** First, a car is lowered *by several methods* so that its chassis just skims the pavement. **[5]** *After the height adjustment,* the car is embellished *with exterior paint and trim work.* **[6]** *Decorated elaborately,* Jorge's car, *shown on the next page,* is a good example *of a low-rider.* **[7]** *Their cars finished and spotlessly clean,* riders drive slowly *through their communities.* **[8]** *Relaxing behind the*

┌HELP┐
In Review B, you do not need to identify separately a prepositional phrase that is part of a participial phrase.

7. absolute—modifies entire clause

Verbals and Verbal Phrases   **67**

steering wheel of his car, *Jorge* is proud when people admire the *results* *of his hard work.* **[9]** *On sunny days,* long caravans of low-riders *may* *drive* for hours *through the neighborhood.* **[10]** Low-riders in some cities have even formed clubs that *work* *with charitable organizations.*

GRAMMAR

The Gerund and the Gerund Phrase

Rules 3g, h *(pp. 68–70)*

OBJECTIVE

■ To identify gerund phrases and their functions

DIFFERENTIATING INSTRUCTION

Advanced Learners

Diagram on the chalkboard the main sentence parts and gerunds in the example sentences following **Rule 3g** to illustrate the grammatical functions of gerunds and gerund phrases.

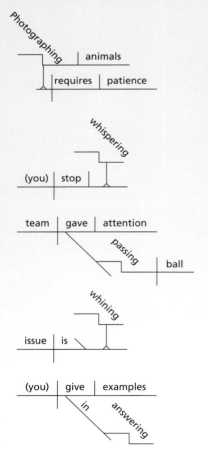

Reference Note

For more about **subjects,** see page 37. For more about **direct and indirect objects,** see page 45. For more about **predicate nominatives,** see page 49. For more about **objects of a preposition,** see page 23.

The Gerund

3g. A *gerund* is a verb form ending in *–ing* that is used as a noun.

SUBJECT	**Photographing** animals requires great patience.
DIRECT OBJECT	Please stop **whispering.**
INDIRECT OBJECT	The team gave **passing** the ball their full attention.
PREDICATE NOMINATIVE	The issue is his **whining.**
OBJECT OF PREPOSITION	In **answering,** give specific examples.

Do not confuse a gerund with a present participle used as an adjective or as part of a verb phrase.

GERUND	I remember **driving** from Florida to Texas last fall. [direct object of the verb *remember*]
PRESENT PARTICIPLE	**Driving** on long road trips, we usually take turns behind the wheel. [adjective modifying the pronoun *we*]
PRESENT PARTICIPLE	We heard mostly country music on the radio while we were **driving.** [main verb in the verb phrase *were driving*]

RESOURCES

The Gerund and the Gerund Phrase

Practice

■ *Language & Sentence Skills Practice,* pp. 62–65

Differentiating Instruction

■ *Developmental Language & Sentence Skills,* pp. 39–40

NOTE Generally, a noun or a pronoun directly before a gerund should be in the possessive case.

EXAMPLES   **Lee's** pitching won the game.

What did the teacher say about **your** missing the test yesterday?

The Gerund Phrase

3h. A *gerund phrase* consists of a gerund and its modifiers and complements. The entire phrase is used as a noun.

EXAMPLES   **Managing the restaurant efficiently** required much hard work. [The gerund phrase is the subject of the verb *required*. The noun *restaurant* is the direct object of the gerund *Managing*. The adverb *efficiently* modifies *Managing*.]

My cousin enjoys **working as a lifeguard.** [The gerund phrase is the direct object of the verb *enjoys*. The adverb phrase *as a lifeguard* modifies the gerund *working*.]

Her greatest achievement was **winning three gold medals.** [The gerund phrase is a predicate nominative identifying the subject *achievement*. The noun *medals* is the direct object of the gerund *winning*.]

We were fined for **parking there.** [The gerund phrase is the object of the preposition *for*. The adverb *there* modifies the gerund *parking*.]

> ┌ TIPS & TRICKS ┐
>
> If you're not sure whether an *–ing* word is a gerund or a participle, try this test. Substitute a pronoun for the *–ing* word. If the sentence still makes sense, the word is a gerund.
>
> EXAMPLES
> Swimming is good exercise. [It is good exercise. *It* makes sense in the sentence. *Swimming* is a gerund.]
>
> We watched the dolphins swimming in circles. [We watched the dolphins it in circles. *It* does not make sense here. *Swimming* is a participle.]

Exercise 4   Identifying Gerund Phrases and Their Functions

Identify the gerund phrase in each of the following sentences, and tell whether it is used as a *subject*, a *predicate nominative*, a *direct object*, an *indirect object*, or an *object of a preposition*.

EXAMPLE   **1.** Learning to type has been one of my most practical accomplishments.

1. Learning to type—subject

1. Give traveling by rail a try.
2. Sylvia's method of making decisions reveals a great deal about her.
3. My grandparents enjoy practicing their square-dance routines.
4. Before making changes, please notify our secretary, Ms. Erikson.
5. Ms. Sanapaw finished writing her paper.

1. i.o.
2. o.p.
3. d.o.
4. o.p.
5. d.o.

DIRECT TEACHING

Correcting Misconceptions

Gerunds and Participles. Students may mistakenly identify all *–ing* forms as participles. To help students learn to identify gerunds, tell the class that if a pronoun can be substituted for the word or phrase in question, the word is a gerund or the phrase is a gerund phrase. Write the following sentences on the chalkboard to illustrate the technique:

1. Hiking is an adventuresome way to exercise.

2. Mercedes excels at playing the oboe.

3. Snoring loudly, Hal continued to sleep.

[*Pronouns can be substituted in the first two sentences; therefore, they contain gerunds. 1. It is an adventuresome way to exercise; 2. Mercedes excels at it. A pronoun cannot be substituted for* Snoring loudly, *which is a participial phrase.*]

RETEACHING

Gerunds

Activity. If students are having trouble identifying gerunds, allow them to see a representation of the action of a gerund. Find five large pictures or slides showing activities. Ask students to identify the activity in each picture using the formula "A picture of _____." Show the first picture, and ask students what part of speech the word that fits in the blank should be. [*Students should recognize that the word that will fill the blank is the object of the preposition of and will therefore be a noun or something that functions as a noun.*] As you show the pictures, ask students to supply gerunds to fill in the blanks and to write their suggestions on the chalkboard.

Ask students to write two characteristics of gerunds in their notebooks. [*Gerunds are used as nouns; gerunds end in –ing.*]

The Infinitive and the Infinitive Phrase
Rules 3i, j *(pp. 70–73)*

OBJECTIVE

■ To identify infinitive phrases, their functions, and the words they modify

---

6. s.

7. p.n.

8. s.

9. o.p.

10. s.

6. <u>Producing a movie for Mr. Matsuyama's cinematography course</u> requires organization and communication.
7. One habit that is very bad for teeth is <u>chewing ice</u>.
8. <u>Dropping two cannonballs of different sizes from the Leaning Tower of Pisa</u> may have proven to Galileo that falling objects travel at the same speed, whatever their masses.
9. Hector earns money on the weekends by <u>giving guitar lessons</u>.
10. My brother's <u>singing in the shower early in the morning</u> annoys me.

Review C **Identifying Gerunds and Participles**

For each of the following sentences, identify the italicized word as either a *gerund* or a *participle*.

EXAMPLE   **1.** Isn't *shopping* becoming boring?
            1. gerund

1. The pilot leaned forward and lowered the flaps to twenty degrees in preparation for a *landing*.
2. Wait until proper weather conditions before *burning* leaves.
3. *Confusing* some listeners, the president's press secretary called the reporter by the wrong name.
4. The package was flown across the ocean, *arriving* at its destination in only a few hours.
5. *Saving* should be an important part of your budget.
6. Her favorite pastime was *diving* for Spanish doubloons.
7. What an *exhausting* day that was!
8. *Deciphering* the hieroglyphics, the professor realized that they were a fragment of a story.
9. We finished *gathering* firewood and returned to camp.
10. Carefully *following* instructions increases the likelihood of getting good results.

The Infinitive

3i. An *infinitive* is a verb form that can be used as a noun, an adjective, or an adverb. Most infinitives begin with *to*.

NOUNS   **To leave** now would be rude. [subject of *would be*]

          No one wants **to stay.** [direct object of *wants*]

          Her goal is **to win.** [predicate nominative identifying the subject *goal*]

RESOURCES

The Infinitive and the Infinitive Phrase
Practice
■ *Language & Sentence Skills Practice,* pp. 66–69
Differentiating Instruction
■ *Developmental Language & Sentence Skills,* pp. 41–42

ADJECTIVES She is the candidate **to watch.** [adjective modifying
the noun *candidate*]

The one **to see** is the class president. [adjective modifying
the pronoun *one*]

ADVERBS We came **to cheer.** [adverb modifying the verb *came*]

Is everybody ready **to go**? [adverb modifying the adjective
ready]

NOTE In addition to the present form, infinitives have a ***present
perfect*** form. This form adds *to have* to the past participle and *to have
been* to the present or past participle and indicates completed action.

EXAMPLES **To have seen** him would have pleased Jerome.

Elsa was known **to have been chosen.**

The word *to*, the sign of the infinitive, is sometimes omitted.

EXAMPLES Let's [to] **wait** here.

The clowns made us [to] **laugh.**

Help me [to] **wash** the car.

The Infinitive Phrase

3j. An ***infinitive phrase*** consists of an infinitive and its modifiers
and complements. The entire phrase can be used as a noun, an
adjective, or an adverb.

NOUNS **To get a medical degree** is her goal. [The infinitive phrase is
the subject of the verb *is*. The noun *degree* is the direct
object of the infinitive *To get*.]

They promised **to return soon.** [The infinitive phrase is the
direct object of the verb *promised*. The adverb *soon* modifies
the infinitive *to return*.]

ADJECTIVE We have time **to walk to the concert.** [The infinitive phrase
modifies the noun *time*. The adverb phrase *to the concert*
modifies the infinitive *to walk*.]

ADVERB He is eager **to give Chris the award.** [The infinitive phrase
modifies the adjective *eager*. The noun *Chris* is the indirect
object of the infinitive *to give*, and the noun *award* is the
direct object of *to give*.]

Reference Note

For more about **present
perfect infinitives,** see
page 208.

┌─HELP─┐

Do not confuse
an infinitive with a
prepositional phrase beginning with *to*. Remember
that a preposition has a
noun or a pronoun as an
object.

INFINITIVES
  to go
  to forget
  to graduate

PREPOSITIONAL PHRASES
  to them
  to the loud party
  to everyone

DIFFERENTIATING INSTRUCTION

Learners Having Difficulty

Tell students that a good test to help them distinguish infinitives from prepositional phrases beginning with *to* is to put the words *to try* in front of *to*. If the sentence makes sense with *to try* before *to*, *to* is part of an infinitive. If not, *to* is part of a prepositional phrase. Write the following sentences on the chalkboard:

1. The bad lights make it hard for me to work.

2. My dog brings the newspaper to me every morning.

Have students insert *to try* before *to* in each of the sentences, and ask them which sentence contains an infinitive. [*sentence 1*] Then, ask students to apply the *to try* test to the *to* phrases in sentence 3 of **Exercise 5**. [*To Italy* is a prepositional phrase; *to see our grandparents* is an infinitive phrase.]

TEACHING TIP

Exercise 5 You may want to point out to students that *me [to] learn about photography* in item 10 is an infinitive clause with *me* as its subject.

STYLE TIP

Placing words between the sign of the infinitive, *to*, and the verb results in a ***split infinitive.*** Generally, you should avoid using split infinitives in formal writing and speaking situations.

SPLIT
   Most people should try to regularly have their blood pressure checked.

REVISED
   Most people should try **to have** their blood pressure checked regularly.

Sometimes, however, you may need to use a split infinitive so that the meaning of the sentence is clear.

UNCLEAR
   She expects her investment more than to triple by the year 2010.

CLEAR
   She expects her investment **to more than triple** by the year 2010.

NOTE An infinitive may have a subject. An infinitive or infinitive phrase with a subject is called an ***infinitive clause.***

EXAMPLES Everyone expects **Guadalupe to win the election.**
[*Guadalupe* is the subject of the infinitive *to win*. The entire infinitive clause is the direct object of the verb *expects*.]

We wanted **her to lead the discussion.** [*Her* is the subject of the infinitive *to lead*. The entire infinitive clause is the direct object of the verb *wanted*.]

I believe **them to be trustworthy.** [*Them* is the subject of the infinitive *to be*. The entire infinitive clause is the direct object of the verb *believe*.]

Notice in the examples above that the subjects of the verbs are in the nominative case and that the subjects of the infinitives are in the objective case.

Exercise 5 Identifying Infinitive Phrases and Their Functions

Identify each infinitive phrase or infinitive clause in the following sentences as a *noun*, an *adjective*, or an *adverb*. If a phrase is used as a noun, tell whether it is the *subject*, the *direct object*, or the *predicate nominative*. If the phrase is used as a modifier, give the word it modifies.

EXAMPLE   1. I like to compose music for the guitar.

   1. *to compose music for the guitar*—noun, direct object

1. To win an Olympic medal is the dream of every member of the women's ski team.   **1.** n.—sub.   **2.** adj.—courage
2. The candidate had the courage to speak on a controversial issue.
3. We went to Italy to see our grandparents.   **3.** adv.—went   **4.** n.—d.o.
4. The Latin and French clubs try to work together on projects.
5. Dr. Martin Luther King, Jr., believed that all U.S. citizens should be free to exercise their civil rights.   **5.** adv.—free
6. Louis Pasteur experimented for many years to discover a method for preventing rabies.   **6.** adv.—experimented   **7.** adj.—ability
7. The ability to speak distinctly is an advantage in job interviews.
8. To open the box required a hammer and a crowbar.   **8.** n.—sub.
9. Alana's hobby is to spend hours each day developing original computer programs.   **9.** n.—p.n.
10. Marvella, please help me learn about photography.   **10.** n.—d.o.

Review D Identifying Prepositional, Participial, Gerund, and Infinitive Phrases

Identify each numbered italicized word group in the following paragraph as a *prepositional phrase*, a *participial phrase*, a *gerund phrase*, or an *infinitive phrase*.

EXAMPLES   Vijay Amritraj first gained international attention for
[1] *playing a world-class game of tennis,* and it almost
seems that he has made a second career **[2]** *of taking
on new challenges.*

1. gerund phrase
2. prepositional phrase

[1] *Being a famous tennis player* was not enough for Vijay Amritraj. For almost twenty years, Amritraj, [2] *born in Madras, India,* was a tennis superstar. [3] *Playing in the Wimbledon tournament for seventeen consecutive years,* he also led India to the Davis Cup finals in 1974 and 1987. Ranked the number-one player in Asia for fourteen years, he decided [4] *to branch out.* [5] *Along with his proficiency on the tennis court,* Amritraj added credits as a film actor by [6] *appearing in several TV and studio films,* including the fourth Star Trek movie. [7] *In recent years,* Amritraj, [8] *now living in California,* has become a movie producer, and he is still a leading tennis commentator for U.S. and Asian TV networks. [9] *To help U.S. media corporations enter the Indian marketplace,* he founded California-based First Serve Entertainment, which has become one of the leading multimedia companies [10] *working in Asia.*

┌ H E L P ───
In Review D, you do not need to identify separately a prepositional phrase, a verbal, or a verbal phrase that is part of a larger phrase.

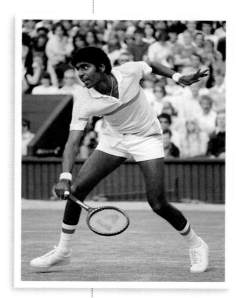

Review D Identifying Prepositional, Participial, Gerund and Infinitive Phrases

ANSWERS
1. gerund phrase
2. participial phrase
3. participial phrase
4. infinitive phrase
5. prepositional phrase
6. gerund phrase
7. prepositional phrase
8. participial phrase
9. infinitive phrase
10. participial phrase

Appositives and Appositive Phrases

3k. An **appositive** is a noun or a pronoun placed beside another noun or pronoun to identify or describe it.

An appositive usually follows the word it identifies or describes.

EXAMPLES   My cousin **María** is an accomplished violinist.

Riboflavin, a **vitamin,** is found in leafy vegetables.

Appositives and Appositive Phrases   73

Appositives and Appositive Phrases
Rules 3k, l *(pp. 73–74)*

OBJECTIVE

■ To identify appositives and appositive phrases in sentences

RESOURCES

Appositives and Appositive Phrases
Practice
■ *Language & Sentence Skills Practice,* pp. 70–72
Differentiating Instruction
■ *Developmental Language & Sentence Skills,* pp. 43–44

GRAMMAR

DIRECT TEACHING

Appositives

Activity. Explain to the class that the word *appositive* has nothing to do with *positive,* as in "positive and negative"; rather, it has to do with *position,* because an appositive is literally "placed near to" the noun or pronoun it identifies or explains. Tell students that the appositive and the noun or pronoun it modifies are like the two parts of a two-sided name tag.

To reinforce this idea, make a name tag with your name on one side and "the teacher for senior English" on the back. Make a sentence containing just your name, and ask students to add the appositive from the other side of the name tag. [*Ms. Smith drives a truck. Ms. Smith, the teacher for senior English, drives a truck.*]

Have students work in groups of three to create for each member of the group three name tags with a name on one side and an appositive phrase on the other. Then, they should create a sentence for each name tag. After they have finished, groups could exchange sentences to check each other's appositives, and volunteers could share some of their sentences with the rest of the class.

Reference Note

For information on **how to punctuate appositives,** see page 344. For more about **the use of appositives,** see pages 500 and 148.

For emphasis, however, an appositive may come at the beginning of a sentence.

EXAMPLE　　**Mollusks,** both snails and clams have shells.

3l. An *appositive phrase* consists of an appositive and its modifiers.

EXAMPLES　　My brother's car, **a sporty red hatchback with bucket seats,** has over 100,000 miles on it.

Mr. Hudson, **a member of the jury,** asked the judge a question.

An appositive phrase usually follows the word it describes or identifies but may precede it.

EXAMPLE　　**Once a pagan feast,** Valentine's Day is now celebrated as a day of love.

Exercise 6　Identifying Appositives and Appositive Phrases

Identify the appositive or appositive phrase in each of the following sentences.

EXAMPLE　　1. The sapling, a variety of oak, will grow rather slowly.

　　　　　　1. a variety of oak

1. The design, a complex pattern of interlocking knots, ran all the way around the door.
2. Look out; their cat, a Siamese, hates visitors.
3. Elsa is visiting her oldest brother, Joseph, in Ohio.
4. Dan's dog, a border collie, came running up to greet him.
5. A small animal, a hare, had been carved in the lid of the wooden chest over there.
6. One of only three in existence today, this folio remains in the possession of the British Museum.
7. "Have you ever read the poem 'Ozymandias'?" Sergio asked.
8. A gift from his grandfather, the silver-and-turquoise ring was never off his finger.
9. She wore a long, flowing gown tied with an *obi,* the traditional Japanese sash.
10. What I need is a job, an entry-level position with a good chance of advancement.

Learning for Life

Continued on pp. 75–76

Thank-you note. Explain to students that verbal phrases—participial, gerund, and infinitive—can add variety and interest to any kind of writing. In this activity, they will write thank-you notes using several verbal phrases. If any students have received gifts recently, this activity will be especially useful. Tell students first to think of a gift they have received or would like to receive. Next, tell students to brainstorm and write

Review E Identifying Prepositional, Verbal, and Appositive Phrases

Identify each italicized phrase in the following paragraph as a *prepositional phrase*, a *participial phrase*, a *gerund phrase*, an *infinitive phrase*, or an *appositive phrase*.

EXAMPLES   Altamont Pass, **[1]** *located in northern California,* has become the topic of discussion **[2]** *among many energy entrepreneurs.*

1. participial phrase
2. prepositional phrase

Altamont Pass, **[1]** *an area of grassy hills* **[2]** *surrounding San Francisco Bay,* is producing a new cash crop. Energy entrepreneurs are hurrying **[3]** *to lease wind rights on acreage* **[4]** *throughout the Altamont.* One rancher owns several hundred acres **[5]** *dotted with tall white wind machines like the ones shown here.* **[6]** *Standing in rows on the wind-swept hills,* these machines work almost nonstop at **[7]** *producing electricity.* **[8]** *With any luck,* the wind-power industry may soon spread **[9]** *to other parts* of the country. The temperature differences **[10]** *between the cool coast and the hot valley* can create air surges **[11]** *funneling inland through natural gaps* **[12]** *like the Altamont.*

┌HELP─
In Review E, you do not need to identify separately a prepositional or verbal phrase that is part of a larger phrase.

1. app.
2. part.
3. inf.
4. prep.
5. part.
6. part.
7. ger.
8. prep.
9. prep.
10. prep.
11. part.
12. prep.

DISTRIBUTED REVIEW

Review E   To reinforce what students have learned about adjectives, ask them to identify all the adjectives (excluding articles) and the words they modify in the first two sentences of **Review E**. [*grassy—hills; new—crop; cash—crop; Energy—entrepreneurs; wind—rights*]

---

five sentences starting with *I* and using the gift in the complete predicate, such as "I enjoy writing poems with my new pen." Then, have them write five sentences with the gift as the subject, such as "The pen

feels comfortable when I hold it."
    Ask students to check their sentences for verbal phrases and to circle any they find. Then, have them look for word groups that can be converted to verbal phrases. (For

ANSWERS

Sentences will vary. Here are some possibilities:

1. We stayed inside because of the rain.
2. My aunt from Puerto Rico is a doctor.
3. The children shouted in surprise, running toward us.
4. Seen from a distance, the city looked majestic.
5. We tried to help our neighbor by building a fence.
6. Writing résumés is an important part of finding jobs.
7. Every night, she likes to dream of moving away.
8. In the summer, air conditioners are easy to sell to overheated customers.
9. His dream is to study music.
10. *The Gazette,* our local newspaper, has many subscribers.

13. prep.
14. inf.
15. part.
16. inf.
17. part.
18. app.
19. part.
20. prep.

In 1997, wind energy [13] *from areas like this in California* produced enough electricity [14] *to light a city the size of San Francisco.* Electricity [15] *produced by these turbines* has the potential [16] *to provide 20 percent of the energy* [17] *needed by the world.* With developing countries, [18] *India and China, for example,* [19] *rapidly expanding their wind resources,* wind could produce over 18,000 megawatts more in the near future than it does today. Modern wind turbines may someday become as numerous [20] *in the United States* as windmills once were in the Netherlands.

Oral Practice   **Using Phrases in Sentences**

Create sentences according to the guidelines given, and say each aloud.

EXAMPLE   1. Use *into the wind* as an adverb phrase.
　　　　　1. *The plane took off into the wind to get more lift.*

1. Use *because of the rain* as an adverb phrase.
2. Use *from Puerto Rico* as an adjective phrase.
3. Use *running toward us* as a participial phrase.
4. Use *seen from a distance* as a participial phrase.
5. Use *building a fence* as a gerund phrase that is the object of a preposition.
6. Use *writing résumés* as a gerund phrase that is the subject of a verb.
7. Use *to dream* in an infinitive phrase that is the direct object of a verb.
8. Use *to sell* in an infinitive phrase that is a modifier.
9. Use *to study music* as an infinitive phrase that is a predicate nominative.
10. Use *our local newspaper* as an appositive phrase.

Learning for Life   *Continued from p. 75*

example, from the last sentence in the previous paragraph, they could create "writing comfortably when I hold it.")

Tell students they are each to compose a thank-you note containing three of the phrases they wrote. If appropriate, students could copy their notes on stationery and mail them.

Chapter Review

A. Identifying Phrases

Identify the italicized phrase in each of the following sentences as a *prepositional phrase*, a *participial phrase*, a *gerund phrase*, an *infinitive phrase*, or an *appositive phrase*.

1. *Rolling up his shirt sleeves*, Tam prepared to chop wood for his fireplace.
2. Before we called in the others, we had decided *to discuss the matter thoroughly*.
3. *Seeing that opera* was an unforgettable experience.
4. The sentence *for the crime* was suspended.
5. Laura thought about *going away to college*.
6. The problem, *considered from this angle*, seems simple.
7. My suggestion was *to leave the baby with us*.
8. Her endurance was of great help to her in the marathon, *a twenty-six mile footrace*.
9. *In spite of its forbidding expression*, the bulldog is gentle with children.
10. I thought I saw a friend *in the audience*.

B. Identifying Phrases in a Paragraph

Identify each italicized phrase in the following paragraph as a *prepositional phrase*, a *participial phrase*, a *gerund phrase*, an *infinitive phrase*, or an *appositive phrase*.

[11] *Until the early years* of the twentieth century, the blacksmith's shop, or smithy, was a familiar part of the American scene. [12] The blacksmith's work included not only shoeing horses but also *making iron parts for wagons and carriages*. [13] A blacksmith was often expected *to repair a broken plow* or mend a broken frying pan. [14] Many blacksmiths provided a bench outside the front door of the smithy *for the convenience of the customers*. [15] A person waiting *to have a horse shod or a wagon fixed* could relax on the bench and chat with passersby. [16] In some communities, the blacksmith's bench came to serve as a center for the exchange of news, *a kind of substitute for a local newspaper*. [17] The

ASSESSING

Monitoring Progress
Chapter Review. To assess student progress, you may want to compare the types of items missed on the **Diagnostic Preview** to those missed on the **Chapter Review.** If students have not made significant progress, you may want to work out specific goals with individual students who are still having difficulty mastering essential information.

GRAMMAR

RESOURCES

The Phrase
Review
■ *Language & Sentence Skills Practice,* pp. 73–75
Assessment
■ *Holt Handbook Chapter Tests with Answer Key,* pp. 5–6, 54

reason that most smithies went out of business in the early years of the twentieth century was not that the work *done by blacksmiths* had ceased to be important. **[18]** On the contrary, work with iron and steel became so important and so technical that a job often had to be given *to a specialist within the field*. **[19]** *Manufacturing a car* was a far more complicated task than making new metal parts for a wooden wagon. **[20]** Many men *trained in blacksmithing* decided to concentrate on the specialized aspect of the business that appealed to them most, some by opening hardware stores, others by going into the auto service industry.

18. prep. [3b]
19. ger. [3h]
20. part. [3f]

C. Identifying Participial, Gerund, and Infinitive Phrases

Identify the participial, gerund, and infinitive phrases in the following sentences. For each participial phrase, give the word it modifies. For each gerund phrase, tell whether it is the *subject*, the *direct object*, or the *object of a preposition*. For each infinitive phrase, indicate whether it functions as a *noun*, an *adjective*, or an *adverb*.

21. d.o. [3h]
22. o.p. [3h]
23. adv. [3j]
24. n. [3j]
25. all [3f]

21. My friend Alecca considered sending me a postcard from Rome.

22. My cousin, who is deaf, gives his full attention to ensuring that more television programs are close-captioned.

23. To learn about car repair, Herb is taking vocational courses.

24. To hurry home was my immediate goal.

25. Moving to the right, all of the drivers let the ambulance pass.

D. Identifying Phrases in a Paragraph

For each sentence in the following paragraph, identify the italicized phrase as an *adjective phrase*, an *adverb phrase*, a *participial phrase*, a *gerund phrase*, an *infinitive phrase*, or an *appositive phrase*.

┌─ HELP ─
In Part D of the Chapter Review, you do not need to identify separately a prepositional phrase that is part of a larger phrase.

26. inf. [3j]
27. adj. [3c]
28. app. [3l]
29. adv. [3d]
30. part. [3f]
31. app. [3l]

[26] After a lively discussion in home economics class, Marcie wanted *to learn more about the history of fabrics, clothes, and clothing parts*. **[27]** One material *of special interest* to the entire class was Velcro. **[28]** In her research, Marcie discovered that the idea for Velcro is attributed to Georges de Mestral, *a Swiss hiker and engineer*. **[29]** *During an outing in the 1940s*, de Mestral started thinking about the burrs that stuck to his socks. **[30]** *Adapting the idea from nature*, de Mestral developed a pair of nylon tapes that fastened together. **[31]** The new material was called "Velcro," *a name that combines the French words for* velvet (velours) *and* hook (crochet). **[32]** *Patented in 1955,* Velcro is widely used today instead of other fasteners, such as zippers. **[33]** However, zippers were once considered high-tech in the fashion industry, and *learning about these devices* was Marcie's next goal. **[34]** The zipper, she found out, was patented in 1893 *by Whitcomb Judson* of Chicago. **[35]** The public was reluctant to try the new fasteners until the United States military decided *to use zippers on some uniforms during World War I.*

32. part. [3f]
33. ger. [3h]
34. adv. [3d]
35. inf. [3j]

Writing Application

Using Phrases in a Business Letter

Infinitive and Appositive Phrases Every year your school holds a raffle to raise funds for special equipment and activities. As secretary of the student council, you have been asked to contact owners of local businesses and ask them to donate prizes for the raffle. Write a letter explaining the purpose of the raffle and persuading the business owners to donate their products or services. Include at least three infinitive phrases and two appositive phrases in your letter.

Prewriting Invent specific information about the upcoming raffle, including when and where it is being held. Think about how you can convince business owners that they should donate prizes.

Writing Begin your letter by clearly stating your purpose for writing. Then, give specific information about the raffle. Conclude by restating your request. Also, tell your reader whom to contact to make a donation.

Revising Make sure that the form and the tone of your letter are appropriate for business correspondence. Be sure that you include at least three infinitive phrases and two appositive phrases.

Publishing Errors in grammar, usage, spelling, and punctuation will not help your cause, so be sure to proofread carefully. Show your letter to two or three business owners in your area. Ask them if they find the letter effective. What changes would they suggest to make the letter more persuasive?

Writing Application

Prewriting Tip. Remind students to analyze the intended audience when writing their letters—to consider the audience's desire for promotion and need for advertising at a low cost. The suggestions students make about donating products should be planned both to enhance the fund-raising potential of the raffle and to serve the business community's goals.

Writing Tip. Because infinitive phrases and appositive phrases can be added to a piece of writing in the revision stage, you may want to suggest that students write their rough drafts without being overly concerned about whether all five assigned phrases are included. Tell students that they can combine sentences to create the phrases or add required phrases in the revision stage.

Scoring Rubric. While you will want to pay particular attention to students' use of phrases, you will also want to evaluate overall writing performance. You may want to give a split score to indicate development and clarity of the composition as well as grammar skills.

The Clause

Independent and Subordinate Clauses, Sentence Structure

INTRODUCING THE CHAPTER

■ This chapter defines and discusses the independent clause and the types of subordinate clauses. Subordinate clauses are classified as adjective, noun, or adverb clauses according to their use in sentences. Sentences are then classified according to structure and purpose.

■ The chapter closes with a **Chapter Review,** which includes a **Writing Application** feature that asks students to write the results of an interview, using end marks to reflect tone and attitude.

■ For information on how to integrate the material in this chapter with writing assignments, see the **Teaching Strands** chart, pp. T24–T25.

Diagnostic Preview

A. Identifying and Classifying Clauses

Identify the italicized clause in each of the following sentences as an *independent clause* or a *subordinate clause*. If a clause is subordinate, tell whether it is an *adjective clause*, an *adverb clause*, or a *noun clause*.

Numerals in brackets refer to the rules tested by the items in the Diagnostic Preview.

EXAMPLE   1. *While I was at the orthodontist's office,* Dr. Liu adjusted my retainer.

1. subordinate clause—adverb clause

1. ind. [4b]
2. sub./n. [4c, e]
3. ind. [4b]
4. sub./adj. [4c, d]
5. sub./adv. [4c, f]
6. sub./n. [4c, e]
7. ind. [4b]
8. ind. [4b]
9. sub./adv. [4c, f]

1. *Tamara applied for the job last Monday,* and each day since then she has been waiting for a call from the company.
2. Serious hikers know *that a topographical map is often useful in unfamiliar territory.*
3. *The band played calypso and reggae music from the West Indies.*
4. Amelia Earhart, *who was the first woman to fly solo over both the Atlantic Ocean and the Pacific Ocean,* had great courage.
5. Mr. Benoit was the best coach at Northeast High School *even though he had been there only a year.*
6. As you wait, concentrate on *what you have to do to win.*
7. Since last year Erin and Jim have been rotating household tasks; *as a result, each of them has become more understanding.*
8. *Renowned underwater explorer Jacques-Yves Cousteau was ten years old* when he made his first dive.
9. How was I ever going to get the parts of the engine put back together *before my father got home?*

CHAPTER RESOURCES

Internet

■ Web resources: go.hrw.com

go.
hrw
.com

Practice & Review

■ *Language & Sentence Skills Practice,* pp. 80–99

■ *Language & Sentence Skills Practice Answer Key,* pp. 35–42

Application & Enrichment

■ *Language & Sentence Skills Practice,* pp. 79, 100–102

■ *Language & Sentence Skills Practice Answer Key,* pp. 35, 42–43

10. The Vietnam Veterans Memorial, a black granite wall engraved with the names of those Americans *who died in the war in Vietnam,* was designed by Maya Ying Lin.

11. Tired after a long day in the summer sun, the lifeguard reported *that there had been no accidents.*

12. In high school, Lori Garcia set an all-city scoring record in basketball, and *she later went to college on a scholarship.*

13. Can you tell me *why there is still famine in parts of the world?*

14. After World War II, President Harry Truman authorized the Marshall Plan, *which was a program designed to speed economic recovery in Europe.*

15. Lawrence, who transferred to our school last month, is taller *than the other boys on the team.*

10. sub./adj. [4c, d]
11. sub./n. [4c, e]
12. ind. [4b]
13. sub./n. [4c, e]
14. sub./adj. [4c, d]
15. sub./adv. [4c, f, g]

B. Classifying Sentences

Classify each of the following sentences first according to its structure (simple, compound, complex, or compound-complex) and then according to its purpose (declarative, interrogative, imperative, or exclamatory).

EXAMPLE   1. Did you know that some of the best-preserved Anasazi dwellings are in Mesa Verde National Park in Colorado?
           1. *complex—interrogative*

16. *Anasazi* means "ancient ones," and that term accurately describes these cliff dwellers.

17. The Anasazi had a thriving culture around A.D. 1100.

18. They lived primarily in an area now called the Four Corners, where the states of New Mexico, Colorado, Utah, and Arizona converge.

19. These remarkable people built dwellings, some of which were several stories high, in the cliffs.

20. What unusual villages they created, and what views they had!

21. Don't assume, however, that this fascinating civilization lasted as long as the Mayan and Aztec civilizations did.

22. The Anasazi disappeared around A.D. 1300.

23. Do you know why they disappeared?

24. Nobody knows for sure, but anthropologists have several theories that may explain the disappearance.

25. A drought that lasted many years is one possibility, but the Anasazi may have been driven from their villages by enemies or by changes in climate.

16. compound—declarative [4h(2), i(1)]
17. simple—declarative [4h(1), 4i(1)]
18. complex—declarative [4h(3), 4i(1)]
19. complex—declarative [4h(3), 4i(1)]
20. compound—exclamatory [4h(2), 4i(4)]
21. complex—imperative [4h(3), 4i(2)]
22. simple—declarative [4h(1), 4i(1)]
23. complex—interrogative [4h(3), 4i(3)]
24. compound-complex—declarative [4h(4), 4i(1)]
25. compound-complex—declarative [4h(4), 4i(1)]

Diagnostic Preview   **81**

Differentiating Instruction

■ *Developmental Language & Sentence Skills Guided Practice,* pp. 45–54

■ *Developmental Language & Sentence Skills Guided Practice Teacher's Notes and Answer Key,* pp. 13–15

Assessment

■ *Holt Handbook Chapter Tests with Answer Key,* pp. 7–8, 54

ASSESSING

Entry-Level Assessment
Diagnostic Preview. To prevent needless reteaching, you could analyze the results of students' preview and divide students into groups based on the areas in which they need instruction and review.

PRETEACHING

Lesson Starter
Motivating. To introduce the study of clauses, have students work in pairs to find clauses in a page of comics from a daily newspaper. Challenge pairs to find and bracket or highlight four independent clauses and four subordinate clauses. Students will probably find that independent clauses outnumber subordinate clauses. Ask students why there are so few subordinate clauses in the comics. [*Most of the dialogue in comic strips is written simply and briefly because of space considerations and so that the comics will be easy to read.*]

The Independent Clause and the Subordinate Clause

Rules 4a–c *(pp. 82–84)*

OBJECTIVE

- To identify clauses in sentences as independent or subordinate

DIRECT TEACHING

Modeling and Demonstration

What Is a Clause? Model how to identify independent and subordinate clauses by using the example *As we were singing, we joined hands and formed a circle.* First, ask which words make up the first clause. [*As we were singing*] Then, ask if this clause expresses a complete thought and can stand alone as a sentence. [*no*] Explain that this is a subordinate clause and becomes part of a complete thought only when it is combined with an independent clause. Next, ask if there is another clause in the example. [*yes:* we joined hands and formed a circle] Ask if this clause expresses a complete thought and can stand alone as a sentence. [*yes*] Then, ask what kind of clause this is. [*independent*] Now, have a volunteer use another example from this chapter to identify independent and subordinate clauses.

DIFFERENTIATING INSTRUCTION

Learners Having Difficulty

You may want to read aloud the examples in this lesson and also the italicized clauses in **Exercise 1**. It will be easier for some students to hear the differences between complete and incomplete thoughts than to see the differences.

┌HELP─

By itself, an independent clause is called a sentence. It is generally called an independent clause only when it is combined with at least one other clause (independent or subordinate) to form a sentence.

What Is a Clause?

4a. A *clause* is a word group that contains a verb and its subject and that is used as a sentence or as part of a sentence.

EXAMPLES

$$\overset{V\ \ S}{\text{where are you now}}$$

$$\overset{S\quad V}{\text{after we won the game}}$$

Every clause has both a subject and a verb. Not every clause expresses a complete thought, however.

SENTENCE   A sitar is a stringed instrument that resembles a lute.

CLAUSE $\overset{S\quad\ V}{\text{A sitar is a stringed instrument.}}$ [complete thought]

CLAUSE $\overset{S\qquad V}{\text{that resembles a lute}}$ [incomplete thought]

There are two basic kinds of clauses: the ***independent clause*** and the ***subordinate clause.*** Standing alone, an independent clause is a complete sentence. A subordinate clause, like a word or a phrase, acts as a single part of speech and by itself is not a complete sentence.

The Independent Clause

4b. An ***independent*** (or ***main***) ***clause*** expresses a complete thought and can stand by itself as a sentence.

EXAMPLES

$$\overset{S\qquad\qquad\qquad\qquad\qquad V}{\textbf{The Mexican artist José Guadalupe Posada opposed}}$$
the dictatorship of Porfirio Díaz. [one independent clause]

$$\overset{\qquad\qquad\qquad S\qquad\ \ V}{\textbf{In his paintings, Posada attacked the Díaz regime,}}\text{ and}$$

$$\overset{S\ \ \ V}{\textbf{he made thousands of inexpensive prints of his work.}}$$
[two independent clauses joined by *and*]

$$\overset{S\qquad V}{\textbf{Posada's art helped to stir the social unrest}}\overset{S\ \ V}{\text{that led}}$$
to the overthrow of Díaz in the revolution of 1910. [an independent clause combined with a subordinate clause]

RESOURCES

The Independent Clause and the Subordinate Clause

Practice

- *Language & Sentence Skills Practice,* pp. 80–83

The Subordinate Clause

4c. A *subordinate* (or *dependent*) *clause* does not express a complete thought and cannot stand by itself as a sentence.

EXAMPLES   whoever knows the song

which always pleases my mother

as we were singing

The meaning of a subordinate clause becomes clear only when the clause is combined with an independent clause.

        S   **V**

Whoever knows the song may join in.

                S   **V**

We sang "We Shall Overcome," **which always pleases my mother.**

      S   **V**

As we were singing, we joined hands and formed a circle.

Exercise 1 **Identifying Independent and Subordinate Clauses**

Identify the italicized word group in each of the following sentences as an *independent clause* or a *subordinate clause.*

EXAMPLE   **1.** *The inscriptions on the Rosetta stone,* which was found in 1799, *helped scholars learn more about ancient Egyptian hieroglyphics.*

               1. independent clause

1. Egyptology is the branch of learning *that is concerned with the language and culture of ancient Egypt.*   **1.** sub.
2. *Until the Rosetta stone was discovered in 1799,* the ancient Egyptian language was an enigma to scholars.   **2.** sub.
3. A man named Bouchard, *who was a captain under Napoleon,* and some of Bouchard's men found the stone near Rosetta, a city near the mouth of the Nile.   **3.** sub.
4. As you can see in the following photograph of the Rosetta stone, *it has three different kinds of writing inscribed on it.*   **4.** ind.
5. Because the same message was written on the stone in two kinds of Egyptian writing and in Greek script, *the stone provided the needed key for deciphering ancient Egyptian writings.*   **5.** ind.

| STYLE | ✏ | TIP |

Subordinate clauses are often used by themselves in informal conversation when the speaker and the listener both understand the context. If the listener does not understand, he or she may interrupt and ask for clarification. However, in formal writing and speaking, the reader or listener does not have an opportunity to ask for clarification. Using complete sentences helps ensure that the reader or listener will understand your meaning.

┌HELP

Notice in the example for Exercise 1 that an independent clause may be divided by one or more subordinate clauses.

RETEACHING

Subordinate Clauses

Activity. If students have difficulty understanding subordinate clauses, try another approach. Divide the class into groups of four or five. Write on the chalkboard the following word groups. Have students create complete sentences by providing the types of clauses indicated. Have a volunteer write the sentences.

1. I spent the summer working . . . (subordinate).

2. Because I was so young, . . . (independent).

3. I had a lot of fun that summer, mainly . . . (subordinate).

4. I learned a lot . . . (conjunction and independent).

After they have finished, groups can exchange papers to determine if the correct clause types have been used. To help students avoid using phrases instead of clauses, ask each group to decide upon the subject and the verb in each clause they create and to appoint one group member to circle both the subject and the verb.

GRAMMAR

DIFFERENTIATING INSTRUCTION

Advanced Learners

To give students more background in Egyptology, explain that the writing of the ancient Egyptian priesthood is a picture script. Each pictorial character, or hieroglyph, represents a word, syllable, or sound.

Have students consult a dictionary to find the etymology of *hieroglyphic.* [*The word* hieroglyphic *comes from the French* hiéroglyphique, *which is from the late Latin,* hieroglyphicus, *from the Greek* hieroglyphikos, *combining* hieros, *meaning "sacred" and* glyphein, *meaning "to carve."*] Discuss this etymology with the class, pointing out that the priests' "writing" was originally carving.

The Adjective Clause

Rule 4d *(pp. 84–87)*

OBJECTIVE

- To identify adjective clauses and the words they modify and to label the uses of relative pronouns and relative adverbs in sentences

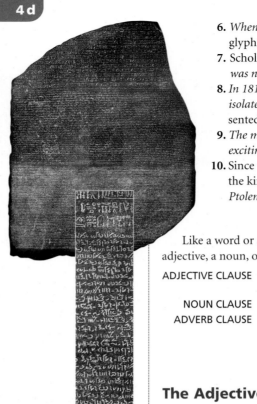

6. *When the Rosetta stone was found,* part of the hiero-glyphic portion was missing.   6. sub.
7. Scholars could easily read the Greek inscription, *which was nearly complete.*   7. sub.
8. *In 1816, Jean François Champollion and Thomas Young isolated several hieroglyphics* that they believed represented names.   8. ind.
9. *The message* that was inscribed on the stone *was not very exciting.*   9. ind.
10. Since the priests of Egypt were grateful for benefits from the king, *they were commemorating the crowning of Ptolemy V.*   10. ind.

Like a word or a phrase, a subordinate clause can be used as an adjective, a noun, or an adverb.

ADJECTIVE CLAUSE	We sang "We Shall Overcome," **which always pleases my mother.**
NOUN CLAUSE	**Whoever knows the song** may join in.
ADVERB CLAUSE	**As we were singing,** we joined hands and formed a circle.

The Adjective Clause

4d. An *adjective clause* is a subordinate clause that modifies a noun or a pronoun.

An adjective clause usually follows the word or words it modifies and tells *what kind* or *which one.*

EXAMPLES

The report **that Diego wrote** was on the Battle of the Little Bighorn. [The adjective clause modifies the noun *report.*]

The Cuban Cultural Heritage Walk, **which is located in Hialeah, Florida,** honors Cuban artists in exile. [The adjective clause modifies the compound noun *Cuban Cultural Heritage Walk.*]

Amanda is someone **whom I admire.** [The adjective clause modifies the pronoun *someone.*]

Mark Twain is the writer **whose books I have enjoyed the most.** [The adjective clause modifies the noun *writer.*]

84   Chapter 4   The Clause

RESOURCES

The Adjective Clause

Practice

- *Language & Sentence Skills Practice,* pp. 84–86

Differentiating Instruction

- *Developmental Language & Sentence Skills,* pp. 45–46

Relative Pronouns

An adjective clause is usually introduced by a *relative pronoun*—a word that relates the clause to the word or words the clause modifies.

Common Relative Pronouns				
that	which	who	whom	whose

A relative pronoun has three functions.

(1) It refers to a preceding noun or pronoun—the antecedent.

(2) It connects the adjective clause with the rest of the sentence.

(3) It performs a function within its own clause by serving as a subject, a direct object, an indirect object, an object of a preposition, or a modifier in the adjective clause.

EXAMPLES Mr. Mendoza is a good counselor **who never betrays a confidence.** [The relative pronoun *who* relates the adjective clause to the noun antecedent, *counselor,* and serves as the subject of the verb *betrays.*]

Have you practiced the speech **that you will give on Friday**? [The relative pronoun *that* relates the adjective clause to the noun antecedent, *speech,* and serves as the direct object of the verb *will give.*]

The mariachi band **in which I play** once performed for Governor Tommy Thompson. [The relative pronoun *which* relates the adjective clause to the noun antecedent, *band,* and serves as the object of the preposition *in.*]

Han-Ling is the one **whose essay took first place.** [The relative pronoun *whose* relates the adjective clause to the pronoun antecedent, *one,* and modifies the noun *essay* by showing possession.]

To modify a time or place, an adjective clause may be introduced by a relative adverb, such as *when* or *where.*

EXAMPLES Dr. Martin Luther King, Jr., dreamed of the day **when freedom and justice would reign in the United States.** [The relative adverb *when* relates the adjective clause to the noun antecedent, *day,* and modifies *would reign.*]

The site **where Dr. King delivered his great "I Have a Dream" speech in 1963** is the Lincoln Memorial. [The relative adverb *where* relates the adjective clause to the noun antecedent, *site,* and modifies *delivered.*]

Reference Note

For information about **using *who* and *whom* correctly,** see page 152. For information about **using *who, that,* and *which* correctly,** see page 283.

The Subordinate Clause **85**

DIFFERENTIATING INSTRUCTION

English-Language Learners

Spanish. Some students may have difficulty with adjective clauses that end with verbs, as in *I like the book that Maria is reading.* In Spanish, it is considered awkward to end a clause with a verb. Spanish-speakers will invert the subject and the verb in the adjective clause to produce the following sentence: *Me gusta el libro que lee Maria.* Inverting the word order in this manner may occur when students write in English.

Advanced Learners

Explain to students that an adjective clause may not be needed where a single adjective will do. Ask students to examine paragraphs from their writing and revise them for wordiness by substituting precise adjectives for adjective clauses where possible.

 MINI-LESSON Usage

Who, Which, That. While discussing relative pronouns, you may want to remind students that *who* refers to persons only, *which* refers to things only, and *that* may refer to either persons or things. For more information on standard usage of *who, which,* and *that,* refer students to **Chapter 11: A Glossary of Usage.**

DIFFERENTIATING INSTRUCTION

Learners Having Difficulty

Activity. Give groups of students the following four sentences. Challenge students to make as many complex sentences as possible by converting sentences to adjective clauses and using the five relative pronouns listed on page 85.

My dog chased the squirrel.
My dog is courageous.
The squirrel scolded my dog.
The squirrel is a real pest.

[*Sample answers: My dog, whom the squirrel scolded, chased the squirrel. My dog, who is courageous, chased the squirrel. My dog chased the squirrel that is a real pest.*]

English-Language Learners

General Strategies. The use of relative pronouns varies with languages; for example, in Vietnamese, a relative pronoun is placed before an essential clause but after a nonessential clause. Some languages do not even use relative pronouns. Because usage differs so widely, you may want to reinforce the concept that in English, a relative pronoun introduces an adjective clause and refers to a noun or pronoun in the main clause.

Learners Having Difficulty

Students may need practice in determining which words are modified by adjective clauses. To help students more readily see the function of adjective clauses, work with them to draw arrows from the adjective clauses in **Exercise 2** to the nouns or pronouns that are being modified.

Reference Note

For more about **punctuating nonessential clauses,** see page 338.

┌HELP─

In the example for Exercise 2, the relative pronoun *that* is used as a direct object in the adjective clause.

Sometimes the relative pronoun or relative adverb is not expressed but is understood.

EXAMPLES   The vase **[that] my family brought from the Philippines** was made by my great-grandmother.

Do you remember the first time **[when] we met each other**?

Depending on how it is used, an adjective clause is either essential or nonessential. An ***essential clause*** provides information that is necessary to the meaning of a sentence. A ***nonessential clause*** provides additional information that can be omitted without changing the basic meaning of a sentence. A nonessential clause is set off by commas.

ESSENTIAL   Students **who are auditioning for the school play** should meet in the auditorium at 4:15 P.M. [Omitting the adjective clause would change the basic meaning of the sentence.]

NONESSENTIAL   Liza Minnelli, **whose mother, Judy Garland, was best known for starring in *The Wizard of Oz*,** earned her own fame as a singer and actress. [The adjective clause gives extra information. Omitting the clause would not affect the basic meaning of the sentence.]

Exercise 2 Identifying Adjective Clauses and the Words They Modify

Each of the following sentences contains at least one adjective clause. Identify each adjective clause, and give the noun or pronoun that the adjective clause modifies. Be prepared to tell whether the relative pronoun or relative adverb is used as the *subject*, the *direct object*, the *object of a preposition*, or a *modifier* in the adjective clause.

EXAMPLE   1. Has the scientific information that the *Mariner* and *Pathfinder* space missions gathered about Mars increased readers' interest in science fiction books about the planet?

1. *that the* Mariner *and* Pathfinder *space missions gathered about Mars—information*

1. The Mars of the nonscientist is a planet of the imagination, where an ancient civilization has left its mark and where maps blossom with romantic place names like Utopia and Elysium. **1.** mod./mod.
2. "Earthlings," who were awed by the planet's red glow in the evening sky, looked on Mars as a home for creatures who might someday cross cosmic barriers and visit planet Earth. **2.** sub./sub.

3. Such thinking was encouraged by an Italian astronomer, Giovanni V. Schiaparelli, (who) observed the planet through a telescope and saw a series of fine lines (that) crisscrossed its surface. **3.** sub./sub.

4. He called the lines *canali*, (which) is Italian for "channels"; this word was erroneously translated into English as "canals." **4.** sub.

5. A planet (where) there are such canals would, of course, be inhabited by people (who) are capable of building not only canals but also cities (that) presumably sprang up at their intersections. **5.** mod./sub./sub.

6. Percival Lowell, the astronomer (who) founded the Lowell Observatory in Flagstaff, Arizona, brought new life to old myths about life on Mars with nonscientific observations most astronomers disputed.

7. Lowell reported a total of more than four hundred Martian canals, of (which) a considerable number were discovered by his own team of astronomers. **7.** o.p.

8. One writer (whose) interest was drawn to Mars was Edgar Rice Burroughs, (whom) many people know as the creator of the Tarzan books. **8.** mod./d.o.   **9.** sub.

9. In his Martian books, Burroughs recounts the adventures of John Carter, (who) could get to Mars by standing in a field and wishing.

10. Burroughs's best-known literary successor is Ray Bradbury, (who) wrote *The Martian Chronicles*, (which) was published in 1950.
                        10. sub./sub.

The Noun Clause

4e. A *noun clause* is a subordinate clause that is used as a noun.

A noun clause may be used as a subject, a predicate nominative, a direct object, an indirect object, an object of a preposition, or an appositive.

SUBJECT	**How students can apply for college loans** was the speaker's topic.
PREDICATE NOMINATIVE	My suggestion is **that we all meet again tomorrow.**
DIRECT OBJECT	I wonder **whether Columbus was truly the first European to explore the Americas.**
INDIRECT OBJECT	Mrs. Romero offers **whoever completes additional assignments** extra credit.

6. sub./In the second adjective clause, *that* is understood and functions as the direct object.

Reference Note

For more about **subjects,** see page 37. For more about **predicate nominatives,** see page 49. For more about **direct objects** and **indirect objects,** see page 45. For more about **appositives,** see page 73.

The Subordinate Clause   **87**

RESOURCES

The Noun Clause
Practice
■ *Language & Sentence Skills Practice,* p. 87
Differentiating Instruction
■ *Developmental Language & Sentence Skills,* pp. 47–48

The Noun Clause
Rule 4e *(pp. 87–90)*

OBJECTIVE

■ **To identify noun clauses and their functions in sentences**

DIRECT TEACHING

Modeling and Demonstration

The Noun Clause. Model how to identify noun clauses by using the example *My suggestion is that we all meet again tomorrow.* First, explain that a noun clause is a subordinate clause that is used as a noun. Then, ask what the subordinate clause is in this example. [*that we all meet again tomorrow*] Next, ask how this clause is used in the sentence. [*as the predicate nominative identifying the subject,* suggestion] Ask what kind of subordinate clause this is. [*noun clause*] Point out that a noun clause may be used as a subject, a predicate nominative, a direct object, or the object of a preposition. Now, have a volunteer use another example from this chapter to demonstrate how to identify noun clauses.

Do not mistake an adjective clause for a noun clause used as an appositive. An adjective clause *modifies* a noun or a pronoun. A noun clause used as an appositive *identifies* or *explains* the noun or pronoun beside it and can take the place of that noun or pronoun.

ADJECTIVE CLAUSE
The theory **that Copernicus proposed** was rejected by most other astronomers at the time. [The clause modifies the noun *theory*.]

NOUN CLAUSE
The theory **that the sun is the center of our solar system** was proposed by Copernicus. [The clause identifies the noun *theory*.]

Reference Note
For more about **introductory words in subordinate clauses,** see pages 85 and 91.

Reference Note
For more about **infinitive clauses,** see page 72.

OBJECT OF A PREPOSITION	Write your research paper about **whomever you admire most.**
APPOSITIVE	Copernicus's theory **that the sun, not the earth, is the center of our solar system** was rejected at the time.

Common Introductory Words for Noun Clauses		
how	whenever	who
if	where	whoever
that	wherever	whom
what	whether	whomever
whatever	which	whose
when	whichever	why

The word that introduces a noun clause may or may not serve a grammatical function in the noun clause.

EXAMPLES Tawana will do well at **whatever she attempts.** [The word *whatever* introduces the noun clause and serves as the direct object of the verb *attempts.*]

Does Luís think **that Puerto Rico will become a state someday?** [The word *that* introduces the noun clause but does not serve a grammatical function in the clause.]

Sometimes the word that introduces a noun clause is not expressed but is understood.

EXAMPLES I think **[that] I. M. Pei is one of the judges of the design contest.**

Did you know **[that] the actor James Earl Jones was once a pre-med student?**

NOTE Another type of noun clause is the infinitive clause. An ***infinitive clause*** consists of an infinitive with a subject, along with any modifiers and complements the infinitive has. The entire infinitive clause can function as the direct object of a verb.

EXAMPLE Judy's father expected **her to finish her homework.** [The entire infinitive clause is the direct object of the verb *expected. Her* is the subject of the infinitive *to finish.* The infinitive *to finish* has a direct object, *homework.*]

Notice that the subject of an infinitive clause is in the objective case and that the infinitive takes the place of a main verb in the infinitive clause.

DIFFERENTIATING INSTRUCTION

English-Language Learners

General Strategies. Some students might have difficulty with the omission of the introductory word *that* in noun clauses. You may want to write the following sentences on the chalkboard and have students read the sentences aloud. Tell the students to omit the word *that* in parentheses.

1. I wish (that) I could be an astronaut.

2. I understand (that) you are building a go-cart.

3. The firefighter said (that) she rescued a baby yesterday.

4. The mayor told us (that) he would be happy to review our petition.

MINI-LESSON **Grammar**

Infinitives and Infinitive Clauses.
Remind students that infinitives and infinitive phrases do not have subjects—only when an infinitive is part of an infinitive clause does it have a subject. Write the following sentences on the chalkboard, and ask students to identify the infinitive constructions as phrases or clauses.

I wanted him to leave. [him to leave–*infinitive clause*]

Exercise 3 Identifying Noun Clauses and Their Functions

Identify each underlined noun clause in the following sentences, and tell whether it is a *subject*, a *direct object*, an *indirect object*, a *predicate nominative*, or an *object of a preposition*.

EXAMPLE
1. Do you know what the word *serendipity* means?
1. *what the word* serendipity *means—direct object*

1. My finances don't quite allow me to live in style; in fact, I'm completely broke!
2. Do you know what the referee says to the opponents at the start of a boxing match?
3. Through scientific research, psychologists have learned that everyone dreams during sleep.
4. Scientists disagree about why dinosaurs died out.
5. Sometimes I am amused and sometimes I am amazed by what I read in the newspaper's advice column.
6. What I like most about Harriet is that she never complains.
7. What the dancers Agnes de Mille and Martha Graham created was a new form of American dance.
8. Can you please tell me where the Museum of African Art is located and when it opens?
9. The radio station will give whoever can answer the next question one hundred dollars.
10. I don't know how they decided who would be the leader.

Review A Distinguishing Between Adjective and Noun Clauses

Identify the subordinate clause or clauses in each of the following sentences. Tell whether each subordinate clause is used as an *adjective* or a *noun*. Be prepared to tell what word each adjective clause modifies and whether each noun clause is a *subject*, a *predicate nominative*, a *direct object*, an *indirect object*, or an *object of a preposition*.

EXAMPLES
1. According to Dr. Athelstan Spilhaus, children are not the only ones who enjoy playing with toys.
1. *who enjoy playing with toys—adjective*

2. Did you think that only children enjoy playing with toys?
2. *that only children enjoy playing with toys—noun*

HELP
Some sentences in Exercise 3 contain more than one noun clause.

1. d.o.

2. d.o.

3. d.o.

4. o.p.
5. o.p.

6. sub./p.n.
7. sub.

8. d.o./d.o.

9. i.o.

10. d.o./d.o. [The second noun clause is the direct object of the verb in the first noun clause.]

HELP
In the first example in Review A, the adjective clause modifies the pronoun *ones*. In the second example, the noun clause is the direct object of the verb *Did think*.

The Subordinate Clause **89**

PRACTICE

Guided and Independent

Exercise You may wish to use **Exercise 3** as guided practice. Then, have students complete **Review A** as independent practice.

HOMEWORK

I was ready for someone to leave. [someone to leave–*infinitive clause*]

I expect to leave soon. [to leave soon–*infinitive phrase*]

For more information on infinitives, refer students to **Chapter 3: The Phrase.**

Review A Distinguishing Between Adjective and Noun Clauses

ANSWERS

1. n.—d.o.
2. adj.; adj.
3. adj.; adj.
4. n.—d.o.; adj.
5. n.—d.o.
6. adj.; adj.
7. adj.; n.—d.o.
8. adj.; n.—d.o.
9. n.—sub.; n.—p.n.
10. n.—d.o.

The Adverb Clause

Rules 4f, g *(pp. 90–93)*

OBJECTIVE

■ To identify adverb clauses, the words they modify, and the question each adverb clause answers

1. Dr. Spilhaus found that toys are not meant only for children.
2. Some of the toys that he collects are simply to be admired; his favorites are those that can be put into action.
3. Some of his collectibles are put into "intensive care," where he skillfully replaces parts that have been damaged or lost.
4. Dr. Spilhaus says that a toy is anything that gives us a chance to stop and refresh ourselves during our hectic lives.
5. I have read that many mechanical principles were first applied to playthings.
6. For example, the toy monkey shown here is activated by squeezing a rubber bulb that uses the same basic principle as the jackhammer that digs up our streets.
7. Only those who have lost touch with childhood question what a toy can be worth to a young boy or girl.
8. Ask someone who knows toys what their enchantment is worth.
9. What is appealing about some toys is that they can make us laugh.
10. Dr. Spilhaus, an oceanographer, admits he has sometimes been unable to distinguish between his work and his play.

The Adverb Clause

4f. An *adverb clause* is a subordinate clause that modifies a verb, an adjective, or an adverb.

An adverb clause tells *how, how much, when, where, why, to what extent,* or *under what conditions.*

EXAMPLES   The squirrel ran **as though it were being chased by a cat.** [The adverb clause modifies the verb *ran*, telling *how* it ran.]

Many Western artists were influenced by the Asian art they saw **while they were studying in Paris.** [The adverb clause modifies the verb *saw*, telling *when* the artists saw the art.]

Miriam Makeba attracts huge audiences **wherever she performs.** [The adverb clause modifies the verb *attracts*, telling *where* Miriam Makeba attracts huge audiences.]

Spain considered the conquest of Cuba essential **because the island is strategically located at the entrance to the Gulf of Mexico.** [The adverb clause modifies the verb *considered*, telling *why* Spain considered the conquest of Cuba essential.]

Davita likes instrumental music more **than she likes opera.** [The adverb clause modifies the adverb *more*, telling *to what extent* Davita likes instrumental music.]

If you want to gain an understanding of American Indian culture, read *Voices of Our Ancestors* by Dhyani Ywahoo. [The adverb clause modifies the verb *read*, telling *under what conditions* you should read Ywahoo's book.]

NOTE An adverb clause that begins a sentence is followed by a comma.

EXAMPLE   When the weather starts getting cold, many animals grow heavier fur.

Reference Note

For more information about **punctuating adverb clauses,** see page 343.

Subordinating Conjunctions

An adverb clause is introduced by a *subordinating conjunction*—a word or word group that shows the relationship between the adverb clause and the word or words that the clause modifies.

Common Subordinating Conjunctions			
after	as though	since	when
although	because	so that	whenever
as	before	than	where
as if	if	though	wherever
as long as	in order that	unless	whether
as soon as	provided that	until	while

NOTE The words *after, as, before, since, until,* and *while* may also be used as prepositions.

CONJUNCTION   You must clean your room **before** you go to play basketball.

PREPOSITION   You must clean your room **before** dinner.

Reference Note

For more about **prepositions,** see page 23.

The Elliptical Clause

4g. Part of a clause may be left out when its meaning can be clearly understood in the context of the sentence. Such a clause is called an *elliptical clause.*

Most elliptical clauses are adverb clauses. In the examples on the following page, the words in brackets may be omitted because their meanings can be understood from the context.

EXTENSION

Relating to Literature

If the Keats sonnet "When I Have Fears" is available in students' literature books, have them read the selection. Tell students that the poem is one long sentence, and ask them to find the subject and verb of the independent clause. ["*I stand . . . think. . . ."*] Next, ask them to count the number of *when* clauses. [*three*] Then, ask students how the *when* clauses function in the sentence/poem. [*They are all adverb clauses modifying the compound verbs* stand *and* think.] Finally, ask students to tell what effect the poet achieves by using three long *when* clauses in a row. [*Students may say that the repetition adds to the rhythmic feel of the poem. Some students may feel that the repeated use of* when *makes the long clauses easier to follow.*]

DIFFERENTIATING INSTRUCTION

English-Language Learners

General Strategies. Most languages have adverb clauses; however, the order of the subject and the verb in the clauses is often inverted. You may want to have students practice saying and writing sentences with adverb clauses that contain subordinating conjunctions from the **Common Subordinating Conjunctions** list. Emphasize the subject-verb pattern that is most common in English by having students label the subject and the verb of each clause they write.

Learning for Life

Continued on pp. 92–93

Senior Will. Tell students that they are going to prepare a senior will, bequeathing possessions or attributes to members of succeeding classes. The will can be placed in a school publication.
    Read students the following examples:

I, Sherise, will to my best friend, Miguel, whom I always helped out of jams, my sense of humor, because it might help him laugh at his predicaments.

EXAMPLES   Australia is smaller **than the other continents** [are small].

When [you are] **taking notes,** use your own words.

NOTE) Often the meaning of an elliptical clause depends on the form of the pronoun in it.

EXAMPLES   I like Anne as much as **she** [likes Anne].

I like Anne as much as [I like] **her.**

To be certain that you have expressed your meaning clearly, be sure to use the correct pronoun case when you write an elliptical clause.

Reference Note

For more about using the **correct forms of pronouns in elliptical clauses,** see page 149.

Exercise 4 **Identifying Adverb Clauses and the Words They Modify**

Identify the adverb clause in each of the following sentences. Give the word or words that the clause modifies. Be prepared to state whether the clause tells *how, how much, when, where, why, to what extent,* or *under what conditions.*

EXAMPLE   1. After they had invited their friends to dinner, Lola Gómez and her father began preparing the meal.

1. *After they had invited their friends to dinner—began*

1. Because it's one of their specialties, Lola and her father prepared a special treat of Cuban-style black beans.   **1.** why
2. After Lola had soaked a pound of black beans overnight, she drained them and covered them with fresh water to make the beans easier to digest.   **2.** when
3. Before she lit the stove, she added some chopped onion and green pepper, a bay leaf, cilantro leaves, oregano, and salt pork to the beans.   **3.** when   **4.** when
4. While the beans were simmering, Mr. Gómez prepared the *sofrito,* which is a characteristic ingredient in many Latin American dishes.
5. Whenever a recipe calls for *sofrito,* the cook finely chops some onion, green pepper, and garlic.   **5.** under what conditions [*or* when]
6. Then these vegetables are fried in a little oil until they are tender, and herbs and spices such as basil, cilantro, cumin, and black and white pepper are added.   **6.** to what extent
7. As soon as the *sofrito* was ready, Mr. Gómez added it to the bean mixture.   **7.** when

┌HELP─

The adverb clause in the example for Exercise 4 tells *when* they began.

Learning for Life   *Continued from p. 91*

To the driver of bus 14, who put up with my repeated last-minute dashes to catch the bus, I will a relaxation tape so that he can endure other students like me in the years to come.

Tell students that each bequest (act of willing someone something) is only one sentence long. Subordination will make their sentences sound like legal documents and will allow them to say many things

8. He then crushed some of the beans against the side of the pot so that the bean mixture would thicken.   **8.** why

9. When the mixture had thickened, Lola put in a blend of vinegar and sugar, which gives the beans that extra "tang."   **9.** when

10. No one at the dinner table was happier than I to enjoy a large helping of the Gómezes' special black beans.   **10.** to what extent

Review B **Identifying and Classifying Subordinate Clauses**

Identify the subordinate clause or clauses in each of the following sentences. Then, tell whether each subordinate clause is used as an *adjective*, a *noun*, or an *adverb*.

EXAMPLE   **1.** Many scholars were skeptical when their colleagues began applying computer science to the study of literature.

1. *when their colleagues began applying computer science to the study of literature—adverb*

1. When a group of scholars first applied computer science to the study of literature, their colleagues expressed what can only be described as polite disbelief.   **1.** adv./n.

2. They asked what the computer could do.   **2.** n.

3. Some scornful scholars argued that measuring the length of Hemingway's sentences was dreary enough when it was done without computers.   **3.** n./adv.

4. Would precise mathematical analyses of style determine whether the Earl of Oxford wrote Shakespeare's plays?   **4.** n.

5. Initial studies made along these lines fueled controversy that raged for years.   **5.** adj.   **6.** adv.

6. Researchers now use computers whenever their projects involve such mechanical tasks as compiling an index or a bibliography.

7. Since ancient languages are now stored on computers, scholars can make analyses that shed light on etymology.   **7.** adv./adj.

8. There are some features of literary works that computers can identify faster than human readers can.   **8.** adj./adv.

9. Of course, today many students take advantage of computer technology when writing research papers about literature.   **9.** adv.

10. After they have written their first drafts, students may then revise their papers by using software programs that check spelling, grammar, and style.   **10.** adv./adj.

TIPS & TRICKS

Some of the words that introduce adverb clauses may also introduce adjective clauses and noun clauses. To determine what type of clause the introductory word begins, look at how the clause is used in the sentence.

ADJECTIVE CLAUSE
The day **when we got our puppy** was a Friday. [The clause modifies the noun *day*.]

NOUN CLAUSE
Does Jimmy remember **when we got our puppy**? [The clause is the direct object of the verb *remember*.]

ADVERB CLAUSE
Our older dog sulked a little **when we got our puppy**. [The clause modifies the verb *sulked*.]

RETEACHING

Subordinate Clauses

Activity. If students have trouble doing exercises with adverb clauses, offer the following approach. On strips of poster board, write the following word groups:

| after she had already sent the letter |

| Judith realized |

| that she had not enclosed the check |

| which was necessary to pay the debt |

Have four students come to the front of the room, and ask each of them to hold up one of the strips and to arrange themselves in a sequence that will make a grammatically correct sentence.

Ask students if any of the parts of the sentence could be moved to a different position. [*The adverb clause can be moved to follow the verb. Often an adverb clause can be placed at the end of the sentence.*] Have the student holding this card actually make these moves.

Ask the class which of the three clauses is most essential to the meaning of the sentence. [*The noun clause cannot be omitted.*] Have the student holding the noun clause card move out of the sentence to demonstrate that the noun clause is essential. Finally, ask the class to identify the three subordinate clauses.

without simply stringing them together with coordinating conjunctions. Then, ask each student to compose three bequests containing at least one subordinate clause each.

When students have finished, have them work in small groups to check their bequests for clarity and correctness. Have them identify at least one subordinate clause in each bequest.

Sentences Classified According to Structure

Rule 4h *(pp. 94–97)*

O B J E C T I V E

■ To classify sentences according to structure

DIFFERENTIATING INSTRUCTION

English-Language Learners

General Strategies. You may wish to remind students that in English a clause has to contain both a subject and a verb. (In some languages, clauses do not always require expressed subjects.) You could have students identify the subject and verb in independent and subordinate clauses in some of the example sentences on pp. 94–96.

DIRECT TEACHING

Modeling and Demonstration

Identifying Compound-Complex Sentences. Model how to identify a compound-complex sentence by using the example *When Gary left, he closed the door, but he forgot to lock it.* First, ask students how many independent clauses the sentence has. [*two,* He closed the door; He forgot to lock it.] Then, ask students whether the sentence has any subordinate clauses. [*yes;* When Gary left] Explain to students that because there are at least two independent clauses and at least one subordinate clause, the sentence is a compound-complex sentence. Now, have a volunteer use another example from this chapter to demonstrate how to identify a compound-complex sentence.

COMPUTER TIP

Because an adverb clause usually does not have a fixed location in a sentence, the writer must choose where to place the clause. The best place for it is usually a matter of personal taste and style, but often the placement is determined by the context.

If you use a computer, you can easily experiment with the placement of adverb clauses in sentences. Print out different versions of the sentence containing the adverb clause, along with the sentences that immediately precede and follow it. Read each version aloud to see how the placement of the clause affects the flow, rhythm, and overall meaning of the passage.

HELP

A colon or a dash may be used between two independent clauses when the second clause explains or restates the idea of the first clause.

EXAMPLES

The aardvark discovered that the old saying was true: The early bird does get the worm.

It was a difficult decision—one job included benefits, while the other offered flexible hours.

Sentences Classified According to Structure

4h. Depending on its structure, a sentence can be classified as simple, compound, complex, or compound-complex.

(1) A *simple sentence* contains one independent clause and no subordinate clauses.

A simple sentence may contain a compound subject, a compound verb, or both, and any number of phrases.

EXAMPLES   Great literature stirs the imagination.

Located on an island in Lake Texcoco, Tenochtitlán was the capital of the Aztec empire and may have had more than 100,000 inhabitants in the 1500s.

(2) A *compound sentence* contains two or more independent clauses and no subordinate clauses.

Independent clauses may be joined by a comma and a coordinating conjunction (*and, but, for, nor, or, so,* or *yet*), by a semicolon, or by a semicolon and a conjunctive adverb or transitional expression.

EXAMPLES   In 1528, the Spanish explored the area near present-day Tampa, **but** Europeans did not begin settling there until 1823. [two independent clauses joined by a comma and the coordinating conjunction *but*]

We could drive to San Antonio on the freeway, **or** we could take back roads to get there. [two independent clauses joined by a comma and the coordinating conjunction *or*]

The Aswan High Dam is on the Nile River in Egypt; it is one of the world's largest dams. [two independent clauses joined by a semicolon]

We should leave early; **otherwise,** we will miss our bus. [two independent clauses joined by a semicolon, the conjunctive adverb *otherwise,* and a comma]

Not all birds fly south for the winter; **for instance,** cardinals live in the northern states throughout the year. [two independent clauses joined by a semicolon, the transitional expression *for instance,* and a comma]

RESOURCES

Sentences Classified According to Structure

Practice

■ *Language & Sentence Skills Practice,* p. 94

Differentiating Instruction

■ *Developmental Language & Sentence Skills,* pp. 51–54

Common Conjunctive Adverbs		
also	incidentally	next
anyway	indeed	nonetheless
besides	instead	otherwise
consequently	likewise	still
finally	meanwhile	then
furthermore	moreover	therefore
however	nevertheless	thus

Common Transitional Expressions		
after all	even so	in fact
as a result	for example	in other words
at any rate	for instance	on the contrary
by the way	in addition	on the other hand

Reference Note

For more about **semicolons,** see page 356. For more about **dashes,** see page 384.

NOTE Do not confuse a simple sentence that has a compound subject, a compound verb, or both, with a compound sentence.

SIMPLE SENTENCE The 1991 eruption of Mount Pinatubo destroyed many homes and led to the closing of Clark Air Base. [This sentence contains a compound verb.]

COMPOUND SENTENCE The 1991 eruption of Mount Pinatubo destroyed many homes, and it led to the closing of Clark Air Base. [This sentence contains two independent clauses.]

Reference Note

For more information about **compound subjects** and **compound verbs,** see page 40.

(3) A *complex sentence* contains one independent clause and at least one subordinate clause.

EXAMPLES Yiddish, which is a Germanic language, is now spoken by millions of people all over the world. [The independent clause is *Yiddish is now spoken by millions of people all over the world.* The subordinate clause is the adjective clause *which is a Germanic language.*]

After Napoleon Bonaparte was defeated at Waterloo, he was exiled to Saint Helena, where he died. [The independent clause is *he was exiled to Saint Helena.* One subordinate clause is the adverb clause *After Napoleon Bonaparte was defeated at Waterloo.* The adjective clause *where he died* is another subordinate clause.]

Special Education Students

Because of the number of lines in **Exercise 5,** some students might lose their places. You could adapt the activity by providing index cards or rulers for students to use as horizontal guides. The guides will help students concentrate on one line at a time.

┌─ S T Y L E T I P ─┐

Although the use of short sentences is effective at times, overusing them will result in choppy writing. One way to avoid choppy sentences is to change some sentences into subordinate clauses. Furthermore, by using subordinate clauses, you can avoid the unnecessary repetition of words, such as *The blue whale* in the following example.

CHOPPY
The blue whale is the largest animal that has ever lived. The blue whale can grow up to one hundred feet long and weigh over two hundred metric tons.

SMOOTH
The blue whale, which can grow up to one hundred feet long and weigh over two hundred metric tons, is the largest animal that has ever lived.

Whatever you can give will be very much appreciated. [The independent clause is *Whatever will be very much appreciated.* The subordinate clause is the noun clause *Whatever you can give.*]

(4) A *compound-complex sentence* contains two or more independent clauses and at least one subordinate clause.

EXAMPLES   The interest that you pay on a car loan will increase the cost of the car, so be sure to shop for the lowest interest rate. [The two independent clauses are *The interest will increase the cost of the car* and *be sure to shop for the lowest interest rate.* The subordinate clause is the adjective clause *that you pay on a car loan.*]

Hong Kong had been a crown colony of Britain since 1898; however, as my teacher explained, it reverted to China when the treaty expired in 1997. [The two independent clauses are *Hong Kong had been a crown colony of Britain since 1898* and *it reverted to China.* One subordinate clause is the adverb clause *as my teacher explained.* The adverb clause *when the treaty expired in 1997* is another subordinate clause.]

Exercise 5   **Classifying Sentences According to Structure**

Classify each of the following sentences as *simple, compound, complex,* or *compound-complex.*

EXAMPLE   1. H. J. (Henry Jackson) Lewis is generally regarded as the first African American political cartoonist.
            1. simple

1. During the late 1800s, H. J. Lewis drew political cartoons for *The Freeman,* which was the first illustrated African American newspaper.   **1.** cx
2. Through his cartoons Lewis frequently criticized the U.S. government's racial policies; however, he also produced nonpolitical ink drawings, sketches, and chalk plates.   **2.** cd
3. If you examine the following self-portrait of Lewis, you can see evidence of his artistic versatility, and you can get a sense of the atmosphere in which he worked.   **3.** cd-cx
4. Lewis had to overcome many difficulties to achieve success as an artist, and parts of his life are shrouded in mystery.   **4.** cd

5. Lewis was born into slavery in Mississippi, and he was blinded in one eye and badly burned when he was a toddler. **5.** cd-cx

6. As a young man he worked at various menial jobs until a Little Rock newspaper artist taught him how to draw. **6.** cx

7. Lewis made sketches for archaeological studies in Arkansas, Mississippi, Tennessee, and Louisiana in 1882 and 1883. **7.** s

8. The Smithsonian Institution now has most of these sketches; they include drawings of pre-historic Native American burial mounds. **8.** cd

9. Throughout his life, Lewis produced drawings for various publications. **9.** s

10. Upon Lewis's death in 1891, *The Freeman*, the newspaper that had made him famous, praised his talent and mourned his loss. **10.** cx

Henry Jackson Lewis, *Self Portrait.* Courtesy of the DuSable Museum of African American History, Chicago, Illinois.

Sentences Classified According to Purpose

4i. Depending on its purpose, a sentence can be classified as declarative, imperative, interrogative, or exclamatory.

(1) A *declarative sentence* makes a statement and ends with a period.

EXAMPLE   Many homes are being made more accessible for people who have disabilities.

(2) An *imperative sentence* gives a command or makes a request. Most imperative sentences end with a period. A strong command ends with an exclamation point.

Exercise 5

DISTRIBUTED REVIEW

To provide students with a review of identifying and classifying nouns, ask students to list all the nouns in sentences 3 and 8 of **Exercise 5** and to tell whether each noun is common or proper, abstract or concrete. Ask them also to note any compound nouns. (Students may differ on the classification of nouns as concrete or abstract. Accept reasonable responses, and ask students to explain their reasoning.)

3. self-portrait—common, concrete, compound
   Lewis—proper, concrete
   evidence—common, concrete
   versatility—common, abstract
   sense—common, abstract
   atmosphere—common, abstract

8. Smithsonian Institution—proper, concrete, compound
   sketches—common, concrete
   drawings—common, concrete
   mounds—common, concrete

Sentences Classified According to Purpose
Rule 4i *(pp. 97–100)*

OBJECTIVE

■ **To classify sentences according to purpose**

Sentences Classified According to Purpose

Practice

■ *Language & Sentence Skills Practice*, p. 95

DIFFERENTIATING INSTRUCTION

English-Language Learners

General Strategies. You may want to review the punctuation of the four sentence types. Because not all languages use the same marks of punctuation or punctuate exclusively at the end of sentences, students may benefit from additional instruction.

EXTENSION

Relating to Vocabulary Skills

Have students work in pairs to find other English words that are derived etymologically from the same roots as the words *declarative, imperative, interrogative,* and *exclamatory.* Tell students to look up the roots in dictionaries, to take some guesses about words that might be related, and then to look up those additional words to check their hunches. For example, it would be fairly easy to tell that *declare* and *declaration* are related to *declarative,* but the fact that *clear, claret,* and *clarify* also come from the same root will take a bit more research. Tell students that the etymologies will usually give them some clues to follow. After the groups have finished, compile a composite class list of words related to each of the four original words.

PRACTICE

Guided and Independent

Exercise You may wish to use **Oral Practice** as guided practice. Then, have students complete **Review C** as independent practice.

HOMEWORK

Reference Note

For more about the **understood subject,** see page 41.

STYLE   TIP

In dialogue and informal writing, statements may be used as questions and questions may be used to show strong emotion. In such cases, use the punctuation that indicates the tone you would use if you were speaking.

EXAMPLES

Rex came back yesterday**?** [declarative sentence structure with interrogative tone]

Ask Robin**?** [imperative sentence structure with interrogative tone]

How do you expect me to react**?!** [interrogative sentence structure with exclamatory tone]

In formal writing, however, you should use traditional sentence structure and punctuation to express your emotions and ideas clearly.

EXAMPLES   Please pay attention to the guest speaker**.** [request]

Listen to me**.** [command]

Stop what you're doing and listen**!** [strong command]

NOTE Imperative sentences always have the understood *you* as the subject.

(3) An *interrogative sentence* asks a question and ends with a question mark.

EXAMPLES   What is the name of the song you were singing**?**

Have you seen Alma at all today**?**

(4) An *exclamatory sentence* shows excitement or expresses strong feeling and ends with an exclamation point.

EXAMPLES   How happy you look**!**

What a surprise it is to see you here**!**

Oral Practice **Classifying Sentences According to Purpose**

Read each of the following sentences aloud. Then, identify each as *declarative, imperative, interrogative,* or *exclamatory.* Next, tell which end mark should complete the sentence.

EXAMPLE   **1.** Is soprano the highest range for a singing voice

1. interrogative— ?

1. In Greek mythology, Pygmalion was a sculptor who fell in love with a statue; it was then transformed into a real woman**.** **1. dec.**
2. Will any baseball player ever surpass Hank Aaron's record of 755 career home runs**?** **2. int.**
3. Write your report on Clara Barton, the nurse who founded the American Red Cross**.** **3. imp.**
4. Why, that's preposterous**.** *or* **!** **4. dec. *or* exc.**
5. Do you believe the claim that Archimedes shouted "Eureka!" when he realized that volume could be measured by the displacement of water**?** **5. int.**
6. What beautiful designs these are**!** **6. exc.**

7. Stephen, please explain to the class the concept of a sonic boom. **7. imp.**

8. Vulcanization, the process that strengthens natural rubber, is named after the Roman god of fire, Vulcan. **8. dec.**

9. Why is an unlikely political candidate called a "dark horse"? **9. int.**

10. The United States Constitution, written in 1787 and often considered the model of protection of individual rights, may have been based largely on the Magna Carta, which was signed by King John of England in 1215. **10. dec.**

Review C   Classifying Sentences According to Structure and Purpose

Classify each of the following sentences first as *simple*, *compound*, *complex*, or *compound-complex* and then as *declarative*, *interrogative*, *imperative*, or *exclamatory*.

EXAMPLE   **1.** Please read this article, which is about butterflies.

       1. *complex—imperative*

1. Are you aware that there is a huge worldwide demand for butterflies?

2. Millions are caught and sold each year to entomologists, museums, private collectors, and factories.

3. The plastic-encased butterflies that are used to decorate ornamental objects such as trays, tabletops, and screens are usually common varieties, many of which come from Taiwan, Korea, and Malaysia.

4. There is a difference, though, between collection practices in those countries and those used in Papua New Guinea.

5. Papua New Guinea, which was administered by Australia until 1975, has taken advantage of a growing interest in tropical butterflies.

6. Butterfly ranchers gather, raise, and market high-quality specimens, which are accompanied by scientific data.

7. Since biologists have not yet determined the life cycles of all of these butterflies, local villagers, because of their experience, have become the experts; as a result, butterfly ranching has improved the country's economy.

8. Some butterfly specimens are quite small, but others are larger than an adult human hand.

9. Look at the photograph, and you will see a butterfly emerging from a cocoon.

10. What rich, vibrant colors butterflies have!

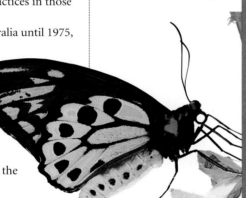

MEETING THE CHALLENGE

No matter what career path you eventually take, chances are you will use all four types of sentences as a natural part of your job. As you picture yourself in your dream career, think of a work situation that would require you to use each of the four sentence types—declarative, imperative, interrogative, and exclamatory. Then, piece these situations together and create a dialogue that shows what your future job might be like. You may show your future job any way you like, but make sure to include all four sentence types.

ANSWER
Job depictions will vary.

Review C   Classifying Sentences According to Structure and Purpose

ANSWERS

1. complex—interrogative
2. simple—declarative
3. complex—declarative
4. simple—declarative
5. complex—declarative
6. complex—declarative
7. compound-complex—declarative
8. compound—declarative
9. compound—imperative
10. simple—exclamatory

EXTENSION

Critical Thinking

Analysis. Divide the class into five groups to investigate the use of sentence types in different kinds of writing. Distribute the following items, one for each group: a recipe, an editorial, a letter to the editor, an advertisement with several sentences of copy, and the words to a love song or poem. Have students classify sentences as imperative, indicative, exclamatory, and interrogative, and then tabulate the number of each type of sentence in the texts. Tell them to work out the percentage of each type out of the total number of sentences. Have each group list their results on the chalkboard, and then discuss the following questions with the class:

1. Is there an obvious reason why certain sentence types predominate in certain types of texts? [*Recipes tell how to do something, so they are likely to contain imperatives. An editorial will probably be explanatory and will contain declarative sentences. Letters to the editor, if in the form of inquiry, would contain interrogative sentences. Advertising appeals to emotion and attempts to rouse enthusiasm, so it is likely to contain exclamations. A poem or love song might contain sentences of all four types.*]

2. Which sentence type is most frequent? Why? [*Probably declaratives are, because most writing states information.*]

3. Which sentence type is least frequent? Why? [*Probably exclamations are, because emotional response is personal, and public forms of writing tend to be impersonal.*]

COMPUTER TIP

Computers can help you get a better sense of your own sentence style. If you have access to style-checking software, run a style check on a few paragraphs of your writing.

The style checker will analyze your writing and will provide information such as the number of sentences per paragraph, the kinds of sentences, the average number of words per sentence, and the lengths of the longest and shortest sentences. If, for example, you discover that you tend to use only one or two sentence structures and that your sentences tend to be of similar length, you can focus your attention on revising sentences for greater variety.

Review D **Classifying Sentences**

Classify each of the following sentences first as *simple, compound, complex,* or *compound-complex* and then as *declarative, interrogative, imperative,* or *exclamatory.*

EXAMPLE   1. I have taken many interesting courses in high school, and one of my favorites is a course that Ms. Klein taught last year.

    1. *compound-complex—declarative*

1. Have you discovered that imaginative teachers who are enthusiastic about their work can make school more enjoyable for their students?
2. Last year, when I took a social studies elective, Law and Order, I found myself looking forward to fourth period each day.
3. Our teacher, Ms. Klein, made our course more interesting by bringing the outside world into the classroom.
4. She had us watch the TV news and read the local newspaper, and she invited guest speakers who shared their experiences with us.
5. By the end of three months, the class had heard from a defense attorney, a prosecutor, and several local police officers; and we had interviewed an FBI agent.
6. Ms. Klein also invited four state representatives, and they talked to us about writing laws.
7. How hard it must be to write clear laws!
8. Ms. Klein set up a schedule of field trips, and she then took the classroom out into the world.
9. For example, on one of our trips, we visited the local jail; on another, when we observed a jury trial, we spoke personally with the judge.
10. I am glad that I was in Ms. Klein's Law and Order class, and I was very pleased when she was voted "Outstanding Educator of the Year."

  1. cx.—int.   6. cd.—dec.
  2. cx.—dec.   7. s.—exc.
  3. s.—dec.   8. cd.—dec.
  4. cd-cx.—dec.   9. cd-cx.—dec.
  5. cd.—dec.   10. cd-cx.—dec.

1. sub. [4c]
2. ind. [4b]
3. ind. [4b]
4. ind. [4b]
5. sub. [4c]

6. sub.—adj. [4c, d]
7. sub.—adv. [4c, f]
8. ind. [4b]
9. sub.—n. [4c, e]
10. sub.—adv. [4c, f]
11. sub.—adj. [4c, d]
12. sub.—adv. [4c, f]
13. ind. [4b]
14. sub.—adj. [4c, d]

Chapter Review

A. Identifying Independent and Subordinate Clauses

Identify the underlined word group in each of the following sentences as an *independent clause* or a *subordinate clause.*

1. Most film critics agree that the most important member of a film crew is the director.
2. One director who is known for his distinctive style is the Japanese filmmaker Akira Kurosawa.
3. Although he made contemporary dramas and gangster stories, Kurosawa is perhaps best known for his epic action films about medieval Japan.
4. One such film is the action-packed *Seven Samurai,* which may very well be Kurosawa's most popular film.
5. His other epics include *Throne of Blood* and *Ran,* which are based on Shakespeare's plays *Macbeth* and *King Lear,* respectively.

B. Identifying and Classifying Clauses

Identify the italicized word group in each of the following sentences as an *independent clause* or a *subordinate clause.* Then classify each subordinate clause as an *adjective clause,* an *adverb clause,* or a *noun clause.*

6. The violinist *whom I most enjoy hearing* is Itzhak Perlman.
7. Patricia put a pet flap in her back door *so that her cat, Tiger, could come in and go out by himself.*
8. *The pitcher read the catcher's signals,* and then she struck out the hitter with a fastball.
9. *Where the city will build the bridge* has still not been decided.
10. *When champion golfer Juan Rodríguez was a boy,* he worked on a sugar-cane plantation in Puerto Rico.
11. Here is the savings bond *that Dad gave me for graduation.*
12. *Because his artwork received wide recognition during his lifetime,* Pablo Picasso became famous and wealthy.
13. As we walked along the road, *we saw the wheat waving in the wind.*
14. The Kimbell Art Museum, *which was designed by architect Louis Kahn,* is one of the leading attractions in Fort Worth, Texas.

Chapter Review   **101**

ASSESSING

Monitoring Progress
Chapter Review. To assess student progress, you could compare the types of items missed on the **Diagnostic Preview** to those missed on the **Chapter Review.** If individual students are still having difficulty, you may want to set specific goals with them for mastering essential information.

GRAMMAR

RESOURCES

The Clause
Review
■ *Language & Sentence Skills Practice,* pp. 96–99
Assessment
■ *Holt Handbook Chapter Tests with Answer Key,* pp. 7–8, 54

15. sub.—n. [4c, e]
16. ind. [4b]
17. sub.—adv. [4c, f]
18. sub.—adv. [4c, f]
19. sub.—adv. [4c, f]
20. sub.—n. [4c, e]
21. ind. [4b]
22. sub.—adj. [4c, d]
23. sub.—adv. [4c, f, g]
24. sub.—n. [4c, e]
25. sub.—adj. [4c, d]

15. During the quiz bowl, *whoever rings the buzzer first* gets to answer the question.

16. After you put all the dishes in the dishwasher, *wipe off the kitchen counter with a clean sponge.*

17. *Ever since Jacob traveled to Chile*, he has been fascinated by the history of Latin America.

18. Tell me *if you see another raccoon in the backyard.*

19. *If you're interested in computers*, you ought to take Mr. Stefano's class.

20. Petra hopes *that the snow will be deep and solid enough for sledding.*

21. After we planted the tulip bulbs, *we had to wait through the winter for the tulips to appear.*

22. Mr. Chulski, *who served in the army thirty-five years ago,* can tell you what Vietnam was like in the 1960s.

23. This car is more fuel efficient *than the other ones.*

24. The playwright decided *that she preferred not to attend her play.*

25. Isn't that the writer *whose books are so popular?*

C. Classifying Sentences According to Structure and Purpose

Classify each sentence of the following paragraph as *simple, compound, complex,* or *compound-complex* and then as *declarative, interrogative, imperative,* or *exclamatory.*

26. s.—exc. [4h(1), i(4)]
27. s.—imp. [4h(1), i(2)]
28. cx.—dec. [4h(3), i(1)]
29. cd-cx.—dec. [4h(4), i(1)]
30. cx.—exc. [4h(3), i(4)]
31. cx.—int. [4h(3), i(3)]
32. cd.—dec. [4h(2), i(1)]
33. cx.—exc. [4h(3), i(4)]
34. cd-cx.—dec. [4h(4), i(1)]
35. cx.—int. [4h(3), i(3)]

[26] What simple beginnings great men and women often have! [27] Consider the life of the famed animator Walt Disney, for example. [28] Although he was born in Chicago in 1901, Disney grew up on a farm in Missouri. [29] Disney loved farm life, and he paid particular attention to the animals, which he sketched constantly. [30] Surely you're not surprised that his early drawings were of farm animals! [31] Where do you think he got his ideas for Mickey Mouse, Donald Duck, and the other Disney-animated animals that are now household names? [32] During his school years, Disney and a friend enjoyed acting; indeed, they even performed a short-lived comedy routine together. [33] How fortunate it is that Disney's main interest remained art! [34] He continued to doodle, and later he attended several art institutes where he learned not only about drawing anatomical figures but also about drawing cartoons. [35] Is it any wonder that one of Disney's first jobs was to draw farm animals for an advertising company?

Writing Application

Using a Variety of Sentences in an Interview

Sentence Purpose   For a class project, you are to interview someone employed in a field that interests you. Find out what kind of training the person needed for his or her job and what a typical day on the job is like. If possible, arrange to visit the person's workplace. When you write your interview, use end marks to reflect accurately your interviewee's tone and attitude.

Prewriting   First, brainstorm a list of interesting jobs. Choose the one that most appeals to you, and find someone to interview who works in that field. Next, write down a number of questions that you might ask about the person's job. If you are planning to use a tape recorder, be sure to get the person's permission before you begin recording.

Writing   Begin with a brief paragraph introducing your interviewee and telling the date and location of the interview. In writing the interview itself, you will need to record the interviewee's responses exactly. As you write, use types of sentences that accurately reflect the speaker's questions, exclamations, and tone.

Revising   Evaluate the written version of your interview for accuracy and clarity. Keep in mind the purpose of the interview—to gather information about an interesting job. If you are lacking needed information, you may have to call your interviewee and conduct a brief follow-up interview.

Publishing   Be sure that you have quoted the person exactly and that your punctuation accurately reflects contractions, pauses, questions, and exclamations. Proofread your interview for any errors in grammar, usage, and mechanics. You and your classmates may want to collect the interviews in a booklet. Work together to write a brief introduction explaining the nature and purpose of the interviews. Also include an acknowledgment page thanking each of the contributors.

APPLICATION

Writing Application

Prewriting Tip. Asking good questions can require background research. Lead an analytical discussion focusing on what types of information about a profession would help interviewers ask good questions. Students might suggest that knowledge of production processes, managerial structure, daily schedules, and so forth would provide background that could lead to good questions. As a follow-up, have students find some background information that is applicable to their topics—they might even ask their interviewees for some materials to read, if such materials are available.

Writing Tip. It is important not to record speech peculiarities in a way that the subject of the interview would find offensive. Point out that people may feel trivialized by a style of reporting that they feel is critical of their ability to use standard English. Discuss how students can show sensitivity in making decisions about how they record their interviews.

Scoring Rubric. While you will want to pay particular attention to students' use of clauses, you also will want to evaluate overall writing performance. You may want to give a split score to indicate development and clarity of the composition as well as usage skills.

CHAPTER

Agreement
Subject and Verb, Pronoun and Antecedent

Diagnostic Preview

A. Proofreading for Subject-Verb Agreement and Pronoun-Antecedent Agreement

Most of the following sentences contain an error in agreement. If a sentence contains an error, identify the incorrect verb or pronoun and supply the correct form. If a sentence is already correct, write *C*.

EXAMPLE   **1.** Do you know where my binoculars is? I would like to take it with me on the nature hike.

   1. is—are; it—them

1. One of the South's most precious ecological treasures‸are the flatlands and estuary of Galveston Bay.

2. In September, the new teacher was delighted because her class‸were enthusiastic and cooperative.

3. One junior, as well as four seniors,‸have been invited to attend the Milford Youth Council next month.

4. The number of investors in companies that manufacture robots is large, and‸they are increasing daily.

5. Twenty miles‸are quite far for someone to walk without stopping and resting.

6. Neither Charlotte nor Tyrone answers the telephone on Saturdays.

7. Anyone earning such a small salary will occasionally have difficulty paying‸their bills.

8. You may be surprised to know that many a city dweller grows vegetables in a backyard garden.

9. A completed application, in addition to a full financial statement, are required of all students seeking college scholarships.

10. Every file cabinet, bookcase, and desk drawer have been stuffed with books and papers.

11. Don't the employees get bonuses for his or her work?

12. Where there's people and excitement, you're sure to find Kazuo and Yori.

13. Public relations and advertising is exciting but often stressful work.

14. Do you know whether the Netherlands are closer to Germany or to France?

15. Did you know that the city of Savannah, Georgia, has their own spectacular parade on Saint Patrick's Day?

B. Correcting Errors in Subject-Verb and Pronoun-Antecedent Agreement

Most of the sentences in the following paragraph contain errors in agreement. Identify each incorrect verb or pronoun, and give the correct form. If a sentence is already correct, write *C*.

EXAMPLE   **[1]** Many a species are either endangered or threatened.
    1. *are—is*

[16] There's a number of people and programs making life safer for endangered and threatened animals. [17] For example, many a preservation effort have been directed at saving eagles. [18] What, you may ask, is the biggest threats to eagles? [19] Most of the danger comes from poachers and expanding civilization. [20] Fortunately, eagles are one of the world's most admired animals; in fact, it may be one of the most common symbols of freedom. [21] As a result, many governments have passed laws to protect eagles and their habitats. [22] The United States, for example, have created sanctuaries for bald eagles and golden eagles. [23] The Philippine eagle, which are the rarest of these magnificent birds, receives special protection on the Philippine island of Mindanao. [24] Ethiopia, as well as some other countries, has planted trees for their eagles to use as nesting places. [25] Anybody who wants to know more about these and other preservation programs for eagles should consult their local library or conservation club.

8. C [5o]
9. is [5c]
10. has [5o]
11. their [5q]
12. there are [5i]
13. are [5e, n]
14. is [5m]
15. its [5q]

16. There are [5i]
17. has [5o]
18. are [5i]
19. C [5d(3)]
20. they [5q]
21. C [5b, q]
22. has [5m]
23. is [5p]
24. its [5c, q]
25. his or her local library *or* the local library [5r(1)]

Differentiating Instruction

■ *Developmental Language & Sentence Skills,* pp. 55–66

■ *Developmental Language & Sentence Skills Guided Practice Teacher's Notes and Answer Key,* pp. 16–18

Assessment

■ *Holt Handbook Chapter Tests with Answer Key,* pp. 9–10, 54

ASSESSING

Entry-Level Assessment

Diagnostic Preview. If students are having problems with subject-verb or pronoun-antecedent agreement in their compositions, you can use the **Diagnostic Preview** to pinpoint specific strengths and weaknesses.

PRETEACHING

Lesson Starter

Motivating. To impress on students that form and placement help indicate parts of speech, write these two nonsense sentences on the chalkboard.

1. The shink (*grimp* or *grimps*) the vork.

2. The shinks (*grimp* or *grimps*) the vork.

Ask students to select the correct verbs. [1. *grimps*; 2. *grimp*]

Have students write three more nonsense sentences and then trade sentences with another student to check each other's subject-verb agreement.

Agreement of Subject and Verb

Rules 5b–g (pp. 106–114)

OBJECTIVES

- To identify subjects and verbs that agree in number
- To revise subject-verb agreement in sentences
- To identify verbs that agree with compound subjects

DIRECT TEACHING

Modeling and Demonstration

Agreement of Subject and Verb.
Model how to identify verbs that agree in number with their subjects by using the example *A boy in my class has written a report on reptiles.* First, ask students to identify the subject. [*boy*] Next, ask if this subject is singular or plural. [*singular*] Then, ask which word or word groups function as the verb. [*has written*] Ask whether this verb phrase is singular or plural. [*singular*] Point out that singular subjects take singular verbs and plural subjects take plural verbs. Also, point out that in a verb phrase, the first helping verb—in this case, *has*—agrees with the subject in number. Now, have a volunteer use another example from this chapter to demonstrate how to determine subject-verb agreement.

─HELP─

Present-tense verbs, except *be* and *have*, add –*s* or –*es* when the subject is third-person singular. Present-tense verbs do not add –*s* or –*es* when the subject is a first-person pronoun (*I, we*), a second-person pronoun (*you*), or a third-person plural pronoun (*they*).

Reference Note

For more about **gerund phrases** and **infinitive phrases,** see page 69 and page 71. For information on **finding the subject,** see page 41.

Number

Number is the form a word takes to indicate whether the word is singular or plural.

5a. A word that refers to one person, place, thing, or idea is *singular* in number. A word that refers to more than one is *plural* in number.

Singular	employer	theory	woman	that	either	it
Plural	employers	theories	women	those	both	they

Agreement of Subject and Verb

5b. A verb should agree in number with its subject.

(1) Singular subjects take singular verbs.

EXAMPLES   In her spare time, the art **student restores** old paintings.

He illustrates books for young readers.

Is the next lunar **eclipse** a full eclipse?

(2) Plural subjects take plural verbs.

EXAMPLES   In their spare time, the art **students restore** old paintings.

They illustrate books for young readers.

Are the next lunar **eclipses** full eclipses?

NOTE   A gerund phrase or an infinitive phrase used as a complete subject usually takes a singular verb. Do not be misled by any particular noun or pronoun in the phrase. The gerund or infinitive serves as a singular simple subject.

EXAMPLES   **Restoring old paintings occupies** much of her spare time. [The singular verb *occupies* is used because the gerund *Restoring*, not the noun *paintings,* is the subject of the verb.]

To illustrate books for young readers requires a vivid imagination. [The singular verb *requires* is used because the infinitive *To illustrate*, not the noun *books* or *readers,* is the subject of the verb.]

Agreement of Subject and Verb
Practice
- *Language & Sentence Skills Practice,* pp. 104–110
Differentiating Instruction
- *Developmental Language & Sentence Skills,* pp. 55–58

In a verb phrase, the first helping verb agrees in number with the subject.

EXAMPLES   The **Vietnam Veterans Memorial was designed** by Maya Lin. [singular subject and singular verb phrase]

The **Vietnam Veterans Memorial** and the **Civil Rights Memorial were designed** by Maya Lin. [plural subject and plural verb phrase]

Has he been studying since noon? [singular subject and singular verb phrase]

Have they been studying since noon? [plural subject and plural verb phrase]

Intervening Phrases and Clauses

5c. The number of a subject is not changed by a word in a phrase or a clause following the subject.

EXAMPLES   The **short stories are** by various contemporary American Indian writers.

The **short stories** in this anthology **are** by various contemporary American Indian writers. [*Are* agrees with the subject *short stories,* not *anthology,* which is part of the prepositional phrase *in this anthology.*]

Edmonia Lewis was the first African American woman to achieve renown for her sculpture.

Edmonia Lewis, whose subjects included John Brown and Abraham Lincoln, **was** the first African American woman to achieve renown for her sculpture. [*Was* agrees with the subject *Edmonia Lewis,* not with any of the nouns in the adjective clause *whose subjects included John Brown and Abraham Lincoln.*]

NOTE   Do not be misled by a phrase that begins with a compound preposition such as *along with, as well as, in addition to,* or *together with.* Such a phrase does not affect the number of a subject.

EXAMPLES   The **man** in the next apartment, as well as the people across the hall, **has lived** in the building since the mid-1980s. [singular subject and singular verb]

The **people** across the hall, as well as the man in the next apartment, **have lived** in the building since the mid-1980s. [plural subject and plural verb]

Reference Note

For more about **verb phrases,** see page 15.

COMPUTER TIP

Some word-processing programs can find problems in subject-verb or pronoun-antecedent agreement. You can use such a program to search for errors when you proofread your writing. If you are not sure that an error found by the program is truly an error, check the rules in this textbook.

MINI-LESSON   Mechanics

Spelling. Some students might be confused by nouns whose singular and plural forms are spelled the same. Some of these nouns are *sheep, moose,* and *Sioux.* Students can get more information about these kinds of nouns in **Chapter 15: Spelling.** Have students suggest other nouns that have the same singular and plural spellings.

EXTENSION

Critical Thinking

Have students use the following questions to analyze how they chose the correct verbs in the sentences in the **Preteaching** activity on page 105.

• Was it obvious to you which verb was correct?

• If so, how did you know? If not, what steps did you take to identify the correct verb?

• Was the presence or absence of an *s* on the end of the verb a clue?

USAGE

DIFFERENTIATING INSTRUCTION

English-Language Learners

General Strategies. Some languages do not show number in nouns or verbs. Students should be reminded that in standard English, proper agreement is essential in every sentence.

General Strategies. Some English-language learners might think that *agreement* means that when the subject ends in *–s,* the verb must also end in *–s.* Emphasize that for agreement, a singular subject requires a singular verb, one ending in *–s* in the present tense.

Japanese and Korean. In these languages, objects often appear before their verbs. For example, the English sentence "Mary sees the boys" might be worded as "The boys Mary sees" or "Mary the boys sees." To help students avoid lapsing into these patterns and trying to make the verb agree with the object, you might stress that those just becoming comfortable with English write sentences in subject-verb-object order.

Exercise 1 **Identifying Subjects and Verbs That Agree in Number**

For each of the following sentences, identify the subject of the verb in parentheses. Then, choose the verb form that agrees in number with the subject.

EXAMPLE   1. The scientist, along with her two assistants, (*is, are*) working on a computer simulation of earthquake activity.

1. *scientist; is*

1. The theory of plate tectonics (*has, have*) explained causes of earthquake activity throughout the world.
2. Enormous plates of rock (*is, are*) shifting constantly far beneath the earth's surface.
3. These movements, in addition to the pressure of molten rock, (*causes, cause*) the plates to collide.
4. The pressure of colliding plates (*forces, force*) the rock to bend until it breaks.
5. A ridge of these breaks (*is, are*) called a fault.
6. The cause of most earthquakes (*is, are*) the sudden release of stress along a fault.
7. The Richter scale, as well as other measurements, (*has, have*) been used to record the magnitude of earthquakes.
8. The tremors of the great San Francisco earthquake that occurred in 1906 (*was, were*) estimated to have measured 8.3 on the Richter scale.
9. California, with two major fault lines, (*has, have*) about ten times the world average of earthquake activity.
10. A map of the earth's plates, such as the one shown here, (*gives, give*) you a pretty good idea of why California has so many quakes.

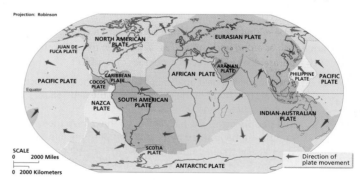

CONTENT-AREA CONNECTIONS

Mathematics
Agreement. Tell students that the concept of agreement also occurs in mathematics. For example, in adding or subtracting fractions, it is necessary to find a common denominator, or denominators that agree. For example, in $\frac{1}{2} + \frac{1}{10}$, $\frac{1}{2}$ must be written as $\frac{5}{10}$ so that the denominators agree. Ask volunteers to explain other concepts of agreement in math, such as balance on either side of the

Indefinite Pronouns

5d. Some indefinite pronouns are singular, some are plural, and some can be singular or plural depending on how they are used.

(1) The following indefinite pronouns are singular: *anybody, anyone, anything, each, either, everybody, everyone, everything, neither, nobody, no one, nothing, one, somebody, someone,* and *something.*

EXAMPLES **Is anyone** in the audience a medical doctor?

Each of the boys **does** his own cooking.

Either of these videos **is** suitable for a four-year-old.

(2) The following indefinite pronouns are plural: *both, few, many,* and *several.*

EXAMPLES **Both** of the universities **offer** degrees in forestry.

Few on the committee ever **miss** a meeting.

Several of the students **have transferred.**

(3) The indefinite pronouns *all, any, more, most, none,* and *some* may be singular or plural, depending on their meaning in a sentence.

These pronouns are singular when they refer to singular words. They are plural when they refer to plural words.

EXAMPLES **All** of the workout **seems** simple. [*All* refers to the singular noun *workout.*]

All of the exercises **seem** simple. [*All* refers to the plural noun *exercises.*]

Is any of the salad left? [*Any* refers to the singular noun *salad.*]

Are any of the vegetables left? [*Any* refers to the plural noun *vegetables.*]

More of the Senate **was** in favor of the highway funding bill than **was** against it. [*More* refers to the singular noun *Senate.*]

More of the senators **were** in favor of the highway funding bill than **were** against it. [*More* refers to the plural noun *senators.*]

HELP

Some words that can be used as indefinite pronouns, such as *both, each,* and *some,* can also be used as adjectives. When such a word comes before the subject of a sentence, the verb agrees with the subject as it normally would.

EXAMPLE
An **astronaut dreams** of walking on Mars.

Each **astronaut dreams** of walking on Mars.

COMPUTER TIP

If you use a computer when you write, you may want to create a help file containing lists of indefinite pronouns and their rules for agreement. Fill this file with information that will help you determine whether an indefinite pronoun is used correctly. Then, as you proofread your work, you can access the file whenever you have a question about the agreement between an indefinite pronoun and a verb or another pronoun.

Agreement of Subject and Verb **109**

RETEACHING

Indefinite Pronouns

Activity. To help students learn when the pronouns mentioned in **Rule 5d (3)** are singular and when they are plural, divide the class into groups of three and have each group come up with six prepositional phrases beginning with *of.* Then, ask groups to trade phrases and to make complete sentences using the pronouns *some, all, more, most, any,* and *none* as subjects, each modified by one of the prepositional phrases. Have groups trade sentences to check for proper subject-verb agreement.

Mnemonic. If students have difficulty distinguishing between singular and plural indefinite pronouns, offer another approach. The following rhyme may be useful in helping students remember which of the indefinite pronouns can be either singular or plural (**Rule 5d [3]**).

One or two,
Two or one,
All, any, more
Most, some, none

equal sign in an equation [*if 5 is added on one side of the equal sign, 5 must be added on the other side*] and the necessity of agreement in units of measure [*minutes and hours cannot be added until the units of measure agree*]. A student interested in science may wish to demonstrate in a simple chemical formula how coefficient and valence achieve balance similar to agreement.

DIRECT TEACHING

Correcting Misconceptions

False Singulars. Students may mistakenly believe that words such as *media, data, criteria, phenomena,* and other similar words of Latin and Greek origin are singular. Ask students to look in a dictionary to find the singular forms of these words [medium, datum, criterion, *and* phenomenon]. Remind students to use plural verbs with plural subjects.

PRACTICE

Guided and Independent

Exercises Since **Oral Practice** and **Exercise 2** both deal with indefinite pronouns as subjects, you may want to have students complete **Exercise 2** as independent practice.

HOMEWORK

None of the deck **is** missing. [*None* refers to the singular noun *deck.*]

None of the cards **are** missing. [*None* refers to the plural noun *cards.*]

Oral Practice **Identifying Subjects and Verbs That Agree in Number**

Read each of the following sentences aloud. Then, identify the <u>subject</u> of each. Next, say <u>which</u> <u>verb form agrees in number with the subject.</u>

EXAMPLE 1. One of the most entertaining animated films I have seen (*is, are*) Kiki's Delivery Service, a movie crafted by the Japanese animator Hayao Miyazaki.

1. One; is

1. <u>Each</u> of the pictures (*was, were*) in a silver frame.
2. <u>One</u> of my friends (*play, plays*) the tuba.
3. <u>All</u> of our belongings (*is, are*) carefully unpacked.
4. <u>Some</u> of these rare books (*has, have*) leather covers.
5. <u>None</u> of the people in the theater (*was, were*) sitting in the first two rows.
6. More band <u>members</u> (*arrive, arrives*) early now that the bus schedules have changed.
7. A <u>few</u> in my class (*help, helps*) the coach set up the bleachers.
8. <u>Both</u> of the fund-raisers (*was, were*) successful.
9. <u>Everybody</u> living in Lewis Heights (*go, goes*) to George Washington Carver High School.
10. Each <u>one</u> of these computer games (*is, are*) on sale.

Exercise 2 **Revising Subject-Verb Agreement in Sentences**

Rewrite the following sentences according to the instructions in brackets after each sentence. Make any needed changes in the form of each verb.

EXAMPLE 1. Each of the contestants was confused by the question. [Change *Each* to *Several.*]

1. *Several of the contestants were confused by the question.*

1. oranges have
2. Many of us were

1. All of the fruit has been picked. [Change *fruit* to *oranges.*]
2. Each of us was angry about the election. [Change *Each* to *Many.*]

3. Has anybody joined the choir lately? [Change *anybody* to *any of the new students.*]

4. The committee leaves today for Washington, D.C. [Add *representing the farmers* after *committee.*]

5. Our team is going to Austin for the debate tournament. [Add *Three members of* before *Our team.*]

6. Most of the classrooms were equipped with new microcomputers. [Change *Most* to *None.*]

7. The pitcher was disappointed by the head coach's decision. [Add *as well as the other players* after *pitcher.* Put a comma after *pitcher* and after *players.*]

8. Each one of the smoke detectors works well. [Change *Each one* to *All but two.*]

9. Both of them usually hope that things will turn out for the best. [Change *Both of them* to *Everyone.*]

10. Some of her plan has been adopted. [Change *plan* to *ideas.*]

3. Have any of the new students

4. representing the farmers

5. Three members of/are

6. None

7. as well as the other players

8. All but two/work

9. Everyone/hopes

10. ideas have

Review A **Proofreading Sentences for Subject-Verb Agreement**

Most of the following sentences contain errors in subject-verb agreement. Identify each verb that does not agree with its subject, and give the correct form. If a sentence is already correct, write *C.*

EXAMPLE   1. The history of the Hawaiian Islands tell of some interesting rulers.

　　　　　1. *tell—tells*

1. One of the royal rulers of the Hawaiian Islands were Queen Liliuokalani, pictured here.

2. Of course, none of these rulers is more amazing than King Kamehameha I.

3. This powerful leader, together with his followers, are credited with uniting the numerous islands into a kingdom in 1795.

4. Kamehameha I, whose family ruled the islands until 1872, was sometimes called the Napoleon of the Pacific.

1. was
2. are
3. is
4. C

DIFFERENTIATING INSTRUCTION

Learners Having Difficulty
Some students may benefit from doing **Review A** in a small group. Encourage students to work in groups of three, reading the sentences aloud and evaluating their ability to identify problems in subject-verb agreement. You may want to walk about the room to listen to conversations and to verify that the information is being explained adequately.

English-Language Learners
General Strategies. You can help English-language learners with **Review A** by having the class identify the verbs in the sentences before starting to work on the exercise. Once the verbs have been identified, students can concentrate on analyzing the sentences for agreement.

Exercise 3 Identifying Verbs That Agree with Compound Subjects

Choose the verb form in parentheses that correctly completes each of the following sentences.

EXAMPLE   1. A world atlas and an almanac (*is, are*) good sources of geographical information.

    1. *are*

1. Del Rio and San Antonio (*is, are*) two Texas cities that have names of Spanish origin.
2. My books and tennis racket barely (*fit, fits*) in the locker.
3. Either my cat or the raccoons always (*eat, eats*) all the food on the back steps by morning.
4. Together, that white blouse and this blue scarf (*makes, make*) a good combination.
5. Neither Mariah Carey nor Gloria Estefan, I believe, (*sing, sings*) that song.
6. Rhythm and blues (*have, has*) pockets of popularity all over the world today.
7. Either regular 3.5-inch disks or one of those high-density disks (*work, works*) on this new computer.
8. Cindy and her brother (*do, does*) yard work for many people in our neighborhood.
9. If you want a good, inexpensive car, both that sedan over there and this compact here (*run, runs*) well.
10. The owner and president of Clowns for Our Towns (*were, was*) a woman with a great sense of humor.

Review B Correcting Errors in Subject-Verb Agreement

Most of the following sentences contain verbs that do not agree with their subjects. If a verb does not agree with its subject, give the correct form of the verb. If a sentence is already correct, write *C*.

EXAMPLE   1. Either surface water or underground water are the source of a region's water supply.

    1. *are—is*

1. One of the most precious resources in the nation is water.
2. The abundance and the use of water varies greatly among the regions of the United States.

Compound Subjects

Activity. Tell students that they will be placed in small groups to create expressive paragraphs collectively. (If you choose to have students create sentences orally, have them tape-record their work.) Have one student in each group offer a topic sentence with a compound subject. If students have trouble getting started, suggest topics such as music, sports, or fashion. As each group member finishes a sentence, a second group member will add a sentence with another compound subject. When all students have finished contributing, have groups share their sentences either by reading what they have written or by playing their tape.

Review B Correcting Errors in Subject-Verb Agreement

ANSWERS

1. C
2. varies—vary

Review B Correcting Errors in Subject-Verb Agreement

ANSWERS continued

3. come—comes
4. C
5. continue—continues
6. have—has
7. sparkle—sparkles
8. C
9. is—are
10. is—are
11. come—comes
12. has—have
13. C
14. cause—causes
15. contaminates—contaminate
16. C
17. are—is
18. C
19. are—is
20. have—has

3. The water supply in every region come from either surface water or underground water.
4. Unfortunately, neither overuse nor contamination of our water supplies has stopped completely.
5. After years of study, the pollution of lakes, rivers, and streams continue to be a serious problem.
6. Lake Erie, as well as the Potomac River and the Cuyahoga River, have been saved by cleanup efforts.
7. As you can see in the picture on this page, Lake Erie, which is bounded by several large industrial cities, sparkle again.
8. Many in the government, in addition to environmentalists, are worried about the quality and abundance of ground water.
9. Aquifers, a source of ground water, is layers of rock, sand, and soil that hold water.
10. Billions of gallons of water is pumped out of the ground each day.
11. In some regions, drinking water for thousands of people come from aquifers.
12. Several recent studies of aquifers has revealed contamination to some degree.
13. The causes of contamination are varied.
14. Salt for melting ice on city streets cause pollution.
15. The chemicals that sometimes leak out of a sewer system or waste dump contaminates aquifers.
16. Some fertilizers and pesticides that are used widely all over the country also add pollutants to the water.
17. The extent of the damages from pollution are not known.
18. Another problem, according to scientists, is the uncontrolled use of water sources.
19. Ground water in some areas are being used faster than the supply can be renewed.
20. Each one of the fifty states have a stake in preserving sources of fresh water.

Special Problems in Subject-Verb Agreement

5h. The contractions *don't* and *doesn't* should agree with their subjects.

Use *don't*, the contraction of *do not*, with all plural subjects and with the pronouns *I* and *you*. Use *doesn't*, the contraction of *does not*, with all singular subjects except the pronouns *I* and *you*. Avoid the common error of using *don't* for *doesn't*.

| NONSTANDARD | He don't [do not] live here anymore. |
| STANDARD | **He doesn't** [does not] live here anymore. |

| NONSTANDARD | It don't [do not] look like rain. |
| STANDARD | **It doesn't** [does not] look like rain. |

| NONSTANDARD | Ruth don't [do not] know about the surprise party. |
| STANDARD | **Ruth doesn't** [does not] know about the surprise party. |

5i. When the subject follows the verb, find the subject and make sure that the verb agrees with it.

The subject generally follows the verb in sentences that begin with *Here* or *There* and in questions.

EXAMPLES Here **is** the **book** you reserved.
Here **are** the **books** you reserved.

There **was** a **detour** on the interstate.
There **were** no **detours** on the interstate.

When **is Passover** this year?
When **are Passover** and **Easter** this year?

NOTE The contractions *here's, there's, when's,* and *where's* incorporate the verb *is.* Use such contractions only with subjects that are singular in meaning.

| NONSTANDARD | When's your finals? |
| STANDARD | **When are** your **finals**? |

NONSTANDARD	Here's your gloves.
STANDARD	**Here are** your **gloves.**
STANDARD	Here**'s** your **pair** of gloves.

Reference Note
For more information about **contractions,** see page 378.

TIPS & TRICKS

To find the subject when it follows the verb, rearrange the sentence to put the subject first.

EXAMPLE
The **book** you reserved **is** here.

STYLE TIP

Many people consider contractions informal. Therefore, it is generally best to avoid using contractions in formal speech and writing.

USAGE

Special Problems in Subject-Verb Agreement
Rules 5h–p *(pp. 115–123)*

OBJECTIVE

■ To identify subjects and verbs that agree in number

DIFFERENTIATING INSTRUCTION

Advanced Learners
Changes in English. Tell students that the use of *do* as a helping verb in yes-or-no questions and negation is relatively new in the English language. In Shakespeare's time, the usual way to ask a yes-or-no question was to put the verb first in the sentence, as in "Want you some salad?" Negative statements were formed by adding *not* after the verb, as in "I want not any salad." Write those two examples of sixteenth-century usage on the chalkboard, and have students copy them and write the modern usage next to them. Tell students there is a general belief that changes in language always simplify grammar. Ask students if they think the modern form is simpler or more complicated. [*Some will say that* "Do you want some salad?" *is more complicated than* "Want you some salad?" *and that* "I don't want any salad" *is more complicated than* "I want not any salad."]

RESOURCES

Special Problems in Subject-Verb Agreement
Practice
■ *Language & Sentence Skills Practice,* pp. 111–116
Differentiating Instruction
■ *Developmental Language & Sentence Skills,* pp. 59–62

Special Education Students

A helpful strategy for some students is for them to hear the material, then to say it, then to see it, and finally to involve the motor processes. Have a helper say a collective noun from the chart (for example, *army*), and have students repeat the word while pointing to it in the book. Then, have students write or dictate a sentence using the word and draw a stick-figure illustration of the sentence.

Learners Having Difficulty

Because the rules in this section (Rules 5h–p) each address a different aspect of agreement, you may want to discuss the rules individually during the school year as each one applies to the class's writing or speech activities. The fact that titles of books, poems, and stories are treated as singular, for instance, could be addressed when students are preparing literary analysis assignments.

Reference Note

For more about **collective nouns,** see page 5.

CROCK reprinted with special permission of North America Syndicate, Inc.

5j. A collective noun may be either singular or plural, depending on its meaning in a sentence.

The singular form of a ***collective noun*** names a group of persons or things.

Common Collective Nouns			
army	club	flock	squadron
assembly	committee	group	staff
audience	crowd	herd	swarm
band	family	jury	team
class	fleet	public	troop

A collective noun is

- singular when it refers to the group as a unit
- plural when it refers to the individual members or parts of the group

SINGULAR   The **class meets** Monday, Wednesday, and Friday. [The class meets as a unit.]

PLURAL   The **class** usually **bring** their calculators with them. [The members of the class bring separate calculators.]

SINGULAR   The **team has won** the semifinals. [The team won as a unit.]

PLURAL   The **team have voted** twenty-one to three to buy new uniforms. [The members of the team voted individually.]

SINGULAR   A **herd was stranded** by the flood. [The herd was stranded as a unit.]

PLURAL   The **herd were separated** by the rising waters. [The herd is thought of in terms of its individuals.]

5k. An expression of an amount (a measurement, a percentage, or a fraction, for example) may be singular or plural, depending on how it is used.

An expression of an amount is

- singular when the amount is thought of as a unit
- plural when the amount is thought of as separate parts

EXAMPLES   **Twenty-seven dollars is** all we have raised so far. [The amount refers to one unit.]

Twenty-seven dollars were lying crumpled on the floor. [The amount refers to separate dollars.]

Eight hours is now the standard workday throughout the United States. [one unit]

Eight hours were set aside for that week-long miniseries about the Civil War. [separate hours]

A fraction or a percentage is

• singular when it refers to a singular word

• plural when it refers to a plural word

EXAMPLES   **Two thirds** of my works-cited page **has been typed.** [The fraction refers to the singular noun *page*.]

Two thirds of my citations **have been typed.** [The fraction refers to the plural noun *citations*.]

Forty-two percent of the senior class **is planning** to go to college. [The percentage refers to the singular noun *class*.]

Forty-two percent of the seniors **are planning** to go to college. [The percentage refers to the plural noun *seniors*.]

Expressions of measurement such as length, weight, capacity, and area are usually singular.

EXAMPLES   **Two and fifty-four hundredths centimeters equals** one inch.

Seven pounds was the baby's weight at birth.

Ninety miles is the distance between Florida and Cuba.

Reference Note

For information about when to **spell out numbers** and when to **use numerals,** see page 407.

Exercise 4   **Identifying Verbs That Agree in Number with Their Subjects**

Choose the word or word group in parentheses that correctly completes each of the following sentences.

EXAMPLE   **1.** (*Is, Are*) 2.2 pounds equivalent to 1 kilogram?

   1. *Is*

1. Forty dollars (*is, are*) too much to pay for those jeans.
2. (*Where's, Where are*) my coat and boots?
3. There (*seems, seem*) to be something for everyone.

RETEACHING

Expressions of Amounts

Activity. If students have difficulty in determining whether to use singular or plural verbs with fractions, help them visualize the meaning of the sentence. Ask students to use the materials on their desks in sentences with subjects that are fractions and percentages. Then, divide the class into pairs and have students say the sentences to partners, holding up objects from their desks to demonstrate the sentences. Use the following sentences as examples to demonstrate the process.

1. Half of my notebook is in order.

2. Fifty percent of this pencil is used up.

3. Two thirds of these pens are blue.

USAGE

---

4. The newspaper staff (*has, have*) turned in all their stories for the next edition.

5. One half of the receipts that we were looking for (*was, were*) found in a shoe box.

6. (*Here's, Here are*) the notes you took about the history and symbolism of Japanese pagodas.

7. Two thirds of the students (*intend, intends*) to go to trade school or college.

8. The orchestra (*specialize, specializes*) in the Big Band music of Count Basie and Duke Ellington.

9. Ninety percent of us (*think, thinks*) the college placement test was hard.

10. Fifty miles (*is, are*) a long way to drive to work every day.

11. (*When's, When are*) the moving truck coming?

12. Three quarters of the film (*takes, take*) place in India.

13. It just (*don't, doesn't*) matter, as far as I can tell.

14. In those days, thirty cents (*was, were*) good pay for an hour's work, young lady.

15. To our horror, we discovered that a swarm of wasps (*was, were*) nesting in the mulch.

16. Mom says that Reginald (*don't, doesn't*) have a blue backpack.

17. Yes, our family (*do, does*) spend Wednesday evening together whenever possible.

18. Three yards of fabric (*was, were*) all we needed for that futuristic costume, Mrs. Winter.

19. Surely 70 percent of the population (*knows, know*) that tune.

20. Dad, (*where's, where are*) the keys to the car?

5l. **Some nouns that are plural in form take singular verbs.**

The following nouns take singular verbs.

┌HELP┐

If you do not
know whether a noun that
is plural in form is singular
or plural in meaning, look
it up in a dictionary.

civics	gymnastics	news
economics	linguistics	physics
electronics	mathematics	summons
genetics	molasses	

EXAMPLES   The **news is** good.

Economics was my mother's major in college.

However, some nouns that refer to single items take plural verbs.

binoculars	pliers	shears
eyeglasses	scissors	trousers

EXAMPLES   The **binoculars are** on the screened porch.

Have these **shears** ever **been sharpened**?

NOTE   Many nouns ending in *–ics,* such as *acoustics, athletics, ethics, politics,* and *tactics,* may be either singular or plural in meaning. Generally, such a noun takes a singular verb when it names a science, a system, or a skill. It takes a plural verb when it names qualities, operations, or activities.

EXAMPLES   Who said, **"Politics is** the art of the possible"?

Are your **politics** like those of your parents?

5m. Even when plural in form, the titles of creative works (such as books, songs, movies, or paintings) and the names of countries, cities, and organizations generally take singular verbs.

EXAMPLES   ***Dust Tracks on a Road* is** Zora Neale Hurston's autobiography.

***Vermilion Lotuses* was** among the paintings by the Chinese artist Chang Dai-chien exhibited at the Smithsonian Institution.

The **Netherlands borders** the North Sea and **exports** various chemical products.

Is Las Cruces where you spent your vacation?

The **Boy Scouts was founded** in 1908 in England.

NOTE   The names of some organizations may take either singular or plural verbs, depending on how the names are used. When the name refers to the organization as a unit, it takes a singular verb. When the name refers to the members of the organization, it takes a plural verb.

EXAMPLES   The **Veterans of Foreign Wars was founded** in 1899.
[The organization was founded in 1899.]

The **Veterans of Foreign Wars are leading** the parade.
[The members of the organization are leading the parade.]

TIPS & TRICKS

Some nouns that name games are singular if they refer to the game itself and plural if they refer to the pieces used in the game.

EXAMPLES

Checkers is an easy game to learn but hard to master.

Your **checkers are** going to get lost if you don't pick them up after the game.

HELP

Generally, geographical names (other than names of countries and cities) that are plural in form take plural verbs.

EXAMPLE

The **Rocky Mountains extend** from the central part of New Mexico to the northern part of Alaska.

Reference Note

For more information on **predicate nominatives,** see page 49.

USAGE

5n. A verb agrees with its subject but not necessarily with a predicate nominative.

EXAMPLES   Quick **reflexes are** one requirement for becoming an astronaut.

One **requirement** for becoming an astronaut **is** quick reflexes.

The **highlight** of the evening **was** the compositions by Quincy Jones.

The **compositions** by Quincy Jones **were** the highlight of the evening.

5o. Subjects preceded by *every* or *many a(n)* take singular verbs.

EXAMPLES   **Every takeoff** and **landing is cleared** with the tower.

Many a runner finishes a marathon long after the winner.

5p. When the relative pronoun *that, which,* or *who* is the subject of an adjective clause, the verb in the clause agrees with the word to which the relative pronoun refers.

EXAMPLES   San Juan, **which is** the capital of Puerto Rico, is a major tourist destination. [*Which* refers to the singular noun *San Juan.*]

I know some people **who own** a Christmas-tree farm. [*Who* refers to the plural noun *people.*]

┌HELP┐

In the expression *the number of,* *number* takes a singular verb. In the expression *a number of, number* takes a plural verb.

EXAMPLES

The number of volunteers **is** surprising.

A number of volunteers **are** signing up now.

NOTE   When the relative pronoun is preceded by *one of* + a plural word, it takes a plural verb. When it is preceded by *the only one of* + a plural word, it takes a singular verb.

EXAMPLES   Egypt is **one of the nations that border** the Red Sea. [The relative pronoun *that* takes the plural verb *border* because it refers to the plural noun *nations.*]

Quebec is **the only one of the Canadian provinces that has** a majority of French-speaking citizens. [The relative pronoun *that* takes the singular verb *has* because it refers to the singular pronoun *one.*]

Exercise 5   **Identifying Subjects and Verbs That Agree in Number with Their Subjects**

Choose the verb form in parentheses that correctly completes each of the following sentences.

MINI-LESSON **Usage**

Who, Which, That. Some students have a hard time deciding when to use *who, which,* or *that* in adjective clauses. Explain that the antecedent determines which relative pronoun to use. In general, writers use *who* to refer to people, *which* to refer to places or things, and *that* to refer to persons or things. Examples of correct usage are "Any student *who* (or *that*) wants to pass the test had better study hard"; "The nuts *that*

1. Mark Russell was one of the political humorists who (*was, were*) interviewed about the recent developments in Washington, D.C.

   1. *were*

1. Many a gymnast (*dreams, dream*) of winning a medal.
2. A number of unusual phenomena (*indicates, indicate*) a shift in the microclimate.
3. *Franny and Zooey* (*is, are*) my favorite book.
4. The Chicago Cubs is a team that (*rallies, rally*) in the late innings.
5. Civics (*is, are*) supposed to be his best subject.
6. The Society of Procrastinators (*has, have*) postponed its meeting.
7. The kitchen scissors (*was, were*) not on the counter when I looked there this morning.
8. That was one of those jokes that (*offends, offend*) everyone.
9. Every volunteer in the regional hospitals (*is, are*) being honored.
10. My favorite part of the movie (*was, were*) scenes in New York's Adirondack Mountains.
11. The tactics he used (*were, was*) very effective.
12. Roseanne's new eyeglasses (*looks, look*) nice.
13. They must be the children who (*were, was*) selling greeting cards.
14. When we walked into the American Legion Hall, "Sixteen Tons" (*were, was*) playing on the jukebox.
15. The only one of us who (*don't, doesn't*) plan to apply is Marcy.
16. (*Isn't, Aren't*) Barbados located just north of South America?
17. Allison's Imports (*trades, trade*) mostly in home accessories.
18. Every boy or girl (*needs, need*) a place to think and dream.
19. Ella Fitzgerald's songs (*was, were*) the best part of the show.
20. Ever since he dismantled a toaster in third grade, electronics (*have, has*) fascinated him.

Review C Correcting Errors in Subject-Verb Agreement

Most of the sentences in the following paragraph contain verbs that do not agree with their subjects. Give the correct form of each verb that does not agree with its subject. If a sentence is already correct, write *C*.

EXAMPLE **[1]** Every year, many a tourist visit the White House.

   1. *visit—visits*

[1] The White House, which has been home to all U.S. presidents

---

Exercise 5

DISTRIBUTED REVIEW
To review the ways the *–ing* form of a verb can be used, ask students to identify the *–ing* forms in sentences 1, 9, and 14, and to tell how the forms are used in the sentences.

 1. winning—gerund
 9. being—verb
14. playing—verb

USAGE

---

work best in this recipe are pecans"; "This paper, *which* is thicker, will work better in your project." For more on using *who, which,* and *that,* refer students to **Chapter 11: A Glossary of Usage.**

Review C — Correcting Errors in Subject-Verb Agreement

ANSWERS

1. C
2. likes—like
3. tours—tour
4. are—is
5. There's—There are
6. don't—doesn't
7. is—are
8. have—has
9. works—work
10. C

Review D — Proofreading Sentences for Subject-Verb Agreement

ANSWERS

1. differs—differ
2. are—is
3. discover—discovers
4. requires—require

since John Adams, is a national treasure. [2] The public, as you can see in this picture, likes to view the White House and grounds when visiting Washington, D.C. [3] How many people actually tours the White House each year? [4] One million are a conservative estimate. [5] There's more than 130 rooms in the White House.

[6] Of course, a tourist don't get to see all the rooms. [7] In fact, only seven rooms, including the State Dining Room, is open to the public on the official tour. [8] Many a party have been given in the East Room, another large reception area. [9] The White House chefs, who works in two kitchens, sometimes prepare food for more than one hundred people in a single day. [10] The presence of recreational facilities, such as a movie theater and a bowling alley, in the White House surprises some visitors.

Review D — Proofreading Sentences for Subject-Verb Agreement

Most of the following sentences contain errors in subject-verb agreement. Identify each verb that does not agree with its subject. Then, supply the correct form of the verb. If a sentence is already correct, write *C*.

EXAMPLE 1. This great book, called *Games of the World,* not only describe all kinds of games but also explain how to make and to play them.

    1. *describe—describes; explain—explains*

1. Although customs and languages differs across continents, people worldwide enjoy playing games.
2. The game of dominoes are a popular pastime throughout Europe and Latin America.
3. Many a player discover that winning a game of dominoes takes skill and strategy rather than luck.
4. One of the games that requires even more strategy than dominoes is chess.

5. Scholars believe that the earliest version of chess originated in India during the seventh century.

6. As chess became popular throughout Asia and Europe, its rules and appearance was transformed.

7. There's a number of skills a good chess player needs; among these are imagination, concentration, and foresight.

8. Like many other games, marbles require physical skills in addition to strategy and concentration.

9. Children all over the world, from the schoolyards of Israel to the sidewalks of Tahiti, enjoys "knuckling down outside the circle."

10. Don't the number of different games that can be played with marbles seem limitless?

Review D Proofreading Sentences for Subject-Verb Agreement

A N S W E R S continued

5. C
6. was—were
7. There's—There are
8. require—requires
9. enjoys—enjoy
10. Don't—Doesn't

USAGE

Review E Revising Subject-Verb Agreement in Sentences

Rewrite each of the following sentences according to the directions given in brackets after each one. Make any needed changes in the forms of verbs.

EXAMPLE
1. A number of famous sports stars have made television commercials. [Change *A number of famous sports stars* to *Many a famous sports star.*]

1. *Many a famous sports star has made television commercials.*

1. The band holds its annual banquet in the school cafeteria. [Add *as well as many of the school's other organizations* after *band.* Put a comma after *band* and after *organizations.*]

2. Where is my book? [Add *and my pen* after *book.*]

3. Both of the candidates have promised to cut taxes. [Change *Both* to *Neither.*]

4. She writes neatly. [Add *is the only person in our group who* after *She.*]

5. Our basketball team has won the city championship. [Add *Neither our soccer team nor* at the beginning of the sentence.]

6. Nearly all people need at least one friend who is a good listener. [Change *all people* to *everyone.*]

1. , as well as many of the school's other organizations,
2. are/and my pen
3. Neither/has
4. is the only person in the group who
5. Neither our soccer team nor
6. everyone needs

7. , together with a completed application form and an autobiographical essay,

8. Either the lion or

9. The captions on/are

10. Two days

7. A complete copy of your high school transcript₍is required by the state university. [After *transcript*, add *together with a completed application form and an autobiographical essay.* Put a comma after *transcript* and after *essay.*]

8. ₍The tigers are growling ferociously. [At the beginning of the sentence, add *Either the lion or.*]

9. ₍The movie screen ₍is hard to see. [At the beginning of the sentence, add *The captions on.*]

10. A day in the library is all the time I will need to finish my research. [Change *A day* to *Two days.*]

Agreement of Pronoun and Antecedent

A pronoun usually refers to a noun or another pronoun. The word to which a pronoun refers is called its **antecedent.**

5q. A pronoun should agree in number, gender, and person with its antecedent.

(1) Singular pronouns refer to singular antecedents. Plural pronouns refer to plural antecedents.

EXAMPLES   **Arthur Mitchell** founded **his** own ballet company.

           Raccoons often dunk **their** food in water before eating.

(2) Some singular pronouns indicate gender.

The pronouns *he, him, his,* and *himself* refer to masculine antecedents. The pronouns *she, her, hers,* and *herself* refer to feminine antecedents. The pronouns *it, its,* and *itself* refer to antecedents that are neuter (neither masculine nor feminine).

EXAMPLES   **Rudolfo** stated **his** position clearly. [masculine]

           Maxine has already prepared **her** acceptance speech. [feminine]

           The **river** overflowed **its** banks. [neuter]

(3) *Person* indicates whether a pronoun refers to the one(s) speaking (*first person*), the one(s) spoken to (*second person*), or the one(s) spoken of (*third person*).

Reference Note

For more about **antecedents,** see page 7.

Agreement of Pronoun and Antecedent

Rules 5q–t *(pp. 124–128)*

OBJECTIVE

■ To correct errors in pronoun-antecedent agreement in sentences

DIFFERENTIATING INSTRUCTION

Learners Having Difficulty

Ask your students to find *antecedent* in a dictionary and to read its etymology. The word consists of two parts, both from Latin. *Ante–* means "before," while *cedent,* derived from *cedere,* means "going." Ask students how the etymology of the word can help them remember how its meaning is applied in grammar. [*An antecedent usually comes before the pronoun that refers to it.*]

RESOURCES

Agreement of Pronoun and Antecedent

Practice

■ *Language & Sentence Skills Practice,* pp. 117–119

Differentiating Instruction

■ *Developmental Language & Sentence Skills,* pp. 63–64

FIRST PERSON	**I** promised **myself** yesterday that **I** would clean **my** room today.
SECOND PERSON	Do **you** have **your** library card with **you**?
THIRD PERSON	**They** built **their** new house **themselves**.

5r. Some indefinite pronouns are singular, some are plural, and some can be either singular or plural, depending on how they are used in the sentence.

(1) Use a singular pronoun to refer to any of the following antecedents: *anybody, anyone, anything, each, either, everybody, everyone, everything, neither, nobody, no one, nothing, one, somebody, someone,* or *something.*

EXAMPLES   **Each** of the birds had staked out **its** own territory.

                Someone left a pair of shoes on the boys' locker room floor, and **he** had better pick them up before the coach sees them.

Indefinite pronouns do not indicate gender. Often a word in a phrase following such a pronoun indicates the gender of the pronoun.

EXAMPLES   **Each** of these **women** runs **her** own business.

                One of the **men** in the audience forgot **his** coat.

If the antecedent may be either masculine or feminine, use both the masculine and feminine pronouns to refer to it.

EXAMPLES   **Everyone** here knows how **he or she** can get help.

                Each of the participants in the contest paid **his or her** own entry fee.

In informal situations, plural pronouns are often used to refer to singular antecedents that can be either masculine or feminine.

INFORMAL   **Everybody** stayed late at the dance because **they** were enjoying **themselves.**

Such usage is becoming increasingly popular in writing. In fact, using a singular pronoun to refer to a singular antecedent that is clearly plural in meaning may be misleading in some cases.

MISLEADING   **Everybody** stayed late at the dance because **he or she** was enjoying **himself or herself.** [Since *Everybody* is clearly plural in meaning, the singular constructions *he or she* and *himself or herself,* though grammatically correct, are confusing.]

STYLE TIP

You can often avoid the awkward *his or her* construction by substituting an article (*a, an,* or *the*) for the construction or by using the plural forms of both the pronoun and its antecedent.

EXAMPLES
  Each of the participants in the contest paid **an** entry fee.

  All of the participants in the contest paid **their** own entry fees.

DIFFERENTIATING INSTRUCTION

Advanced Learners

Nonsexist Language. You may wish to point out that use of the expressions *his or her* and *he or she* when the antecedent may be either masculine or feminine has arisen in fairly recent times. Parents of some students may recall that the masculine singular pronouns *he, him,* or *his* were used when the antecedent referred to both males and females. After the 1970s, greater effort was made to avoid gender bias in everyday language. Over time, changes such as the adoption of *Ms.,* as opposed to *Mrs.* or *Miss,* and the more inclusive reference *his or her* gained fairly widespread acceptance, but gender-specific language is still quite common.

Agreement of Pronoun and Antecedent   **125**

DIFFERENTIATING INSTRUCTION

English-Language Learners

General Strategies. English-language learners whose native languages do not use pronouns in the same way that English does may have difficulty with this lesson. For example, in Korean, pronouns are not differentiated by gender. The Japanese and Turkish languages have no number agreement. In the languages of Vietnam and Laos, there are no neuter pronouns. To prevent any confusion, you can explain which personal pronouns refer to which sorts of antecedents, with special emphasis on the use of *he, she,* and *it.* If someone mentions that in Spanish it is possible to identify the gender of a group—as in *ellos hablan* (they [masculine] speak), *ellas hablan* (they [feminine] speak)—note that English uses the third-person plural pronoun *they* for males, females, and mixed-gender groups.

┌ **HELP** ─

Some words that can be used as indefinite pronouns, such as *both, each,* and *some,* can also be used as adjectives. When such a word modifies a pronoun's antecedent, that pronoun and its antecedent should agree as they normally would.

EXAMPLE

Golfers dream of making **their** first hole in one.

Some **golfers** dream of making **their** first hole in one. [In both sentences, the pronoun *their* agrees with the antecedent *golfers.*]

In formal situations, revise such sentences to make them both clear and grammatically correct.

EXAMPLE **All** of the students stayed late at the dance because **they** were enjoying **themselves.**

(2) Use a plural pronoun to refer to any of the following indefinite pronouns: *both, few, many,* or *several.*

EXAMPLES **Several** of the seniors discussed with the principal **their** ideas about forming another service club.

The judge met with **both** of the attorneys and **their** clients.

(3) Use a singular or a plural pronoun, depending on the meaning of the sentence, to refer to any of the following indefinite pronouns: *all, any, more, most, none,* or *some.*

SINGULAR I accidentally deleted **some** of the document. Is there a way that I can retrieve **it**? [*It* is used because *some* refers to the singular noun *document.*]

PLURAL I accidentally deleted **some** of the files. Is there a way that I can retrieve **them**? [*Them* is used because *some* refers to the plural noun *files.*]

5s. Use a plural pronoun to refer to two or more antecedents joined by *and.*

EXAMPLES **Hilda and Lupe** presented **their** reports.

After **Ethel, Jared, and Cam** ate lunch together, **they** went to **their** next class.

NOTE Antecedents joined by *and* that name only one person, place, thing, or idea take a singular pronoun.

EXAMPLE For my birthday dinner, Dad made **chicken and yellow rice.** He knows **it** is my favorite dish. [*Chicken and yellow rice* is a single dish.]

5t. Use a singular pronoun to refer to two or more singular antecedents joined by *or* or *nor.*

EXAMPLES Either **Paul or Diego** is willing to drive **his** car to the retreat in September.

Neither **Sue nor María** remembered to bring **her** vacation photos with **her.**

Using a pronoun to refer to antecedents of different number may create an unclear or awkward sentence.

UNCLEAR   Neither the puppies nor our full-grown dog likes its new toys. [*Its* agrees with the nearest antecedent, *dog*. However, it is unclear whether all the animals were dissatisfied with their toys or all the animals were dissatisfied only with the full-grown dog's toys.]

UNCLEAR   Neither our full-grown dog nor the puppies like their new toys. [*Their* agrees with the nearest antecedent, *puppies*. However, it is unclear whether all the animals were dissatisfied with all of the new toys or all the animals were dissatisfied only with the puppies' toys.]

AWKWARD   Neither our full-grown dog nor the puppies like its or their new toys.

You should revise sentences to avoid unclear and awkward constructions like the ones above.

REVISED   Neither our full-grown dog nor the puppies like **the** new toys.

Our full-grown **dog** doesn't like **its** new toys, and the **puppies** do not like **theirs.**

None of the dogs like **their** new toys.

Exercise 6 **Correcting Errors in Pronoun-Antecedent Agreement**

Most of the following sentences contain pronouns that do not agree with their antecedents. If a pronoun does not agree with its antecedent, rewrite the sentence to correct the error. If a sentence is already correct, write *C*.

EXAMPLE   1. Each of the skiers waxed their skis every morning.

1. *Each of the skiers waxed his or her skis every morning.*

or

The skiers waxed their skis every morning.

1. Neither Elena nor Barbara made any errors on their test.
2. All of the senior citizens enjoyed their trip to Boston, where they walked the Freedom Trail.
3. Several of the reporters at the press conference asked her questions too quickly.
4. I believe that anybody should be free to express their opinion.
5. No one brought their camera to the party.

STYLE   **TIP**

Sentences with singular antecedents joined by *or* or *nor* can be misleading or can sound awkward when the antecedents are of different genders. Avoid using such sentences in your writing.

AWKWARD
Either Anthony or Dolores is bringing his or her guitar.

REVISED
Either Anthony or Dolores is bringing **a** guitar.

HELP

Although two answers are given for the example in Exercise 6, you need to give only one answer for each item.

1. her
2. C
3. their
4. his or her opinion *or* an opinion
5. his or her camera *or* a camera

Agreement of Pronoun and Antecedent   **127**

6. their
7. their
8. he or she

9. their

10. C

6. Both of the male soloists pronounced his words clearly.
7. Did any of the newborn kittens seem steady on its feet?
8. If anyone becomes lost while exploring Salt Lake City, they should use the street maps available from the tour guide.
9. As far as I could see, Ned and Dennis made a mistake while presenting his arguments during the debate.
10. Neither President Gerald Ford nor Vice President Nelson Rockefeller was elected to his high office.

USAGE

Special Problems in Pronoun-Antecedent Agreement

Rules 5u–x *(pp. 128–132)*

OBJECTIVE

■ To proofread sentences for errors in pronoun-antecedent agreement

DIRECT TEACHING

Modeling and Demonstration

Special Problems in Pronoun-Antecedent Agreement. Model how to identify correct pronoun-antecedent agreement by using the examples *The committee concluded its meeting* and *The committee discussed their different ideas.* First, ask what the subject of the first sentence is. [*committee*] Then, ask whether *committee* is singular or plural. [*singular*] Explain that although a committee has more than one member, the collective noun *committee* takes a singular pronoun—in this case, *its*—when it refers to the group as a single unit. Next, ask whether the subject of the second sentence is singular or plural. [*plural*] Point out that *different ideas* highlights the individuals in the committee, so *committee* takes the plural pronoun *their.* Now, have a volunteer use another example from this chapter to demonstrate how to identify correct pronoun-antecedent agreement.

Reference Note

For a list of **commonly used collective nouns,** see page 5.

MEETING THE CHALLENGE

Rules 5k and 5v, which refer to measurements, percentages, and fractions, are two of the most complex agreement rules in this textbook. Combine your math skills and your English skills by writing two word problems that use Rules 5k and 5v. Let a partner check your subject-verb and pronoun-antecedent agreement, and be sure your partner can solve the problem, too.

ANSWER
Word problems will vary.

Reference Note

For information about when to **spell out numbers** and when to **use numerals,** see page 407.

Special Problems in Pronoun-Antecedent Agreement

5u. A collective noun may be either singular or plural, depending on how it is used.

A collective noun takes

• a singular pronoun when the noun refers to the group as a unit
• a plural pronoun when the noun refers to the individual members or parts of the group

SINGULAR   The tour **group** surprised **its** guide by presenting her with a lovely thank-you gift. [*Its* is used because the tour group as a unit surprised the guide.]

PLURAL   The guide surprised the tour **group** by presenting **them** with lovely souvenirs. [*Them* is used because the individual members of the tour group were presented with souvenirs.]

5v. An expression of an amount (a measurement, a percentage, or a fraction, for example) may take a singular or a plural pronoun, depending on how it is used.

An expression of an amount is

• singular when the amount is thought of as a unit
• plural when the amount is thought of as separate parts

EXAMPLES   That magazine costs **four dollars,** and I don't have **it.** [The amount refers to one unit.]

He had dropped **four dollars,** so I picked **them** up for him. [The amount refers to separate dollars.]

A fraction or a percentage is

• singular when it refers to a singular word
• plural when it refers to a plural word

RESOURCES

Special Problems in Pronoun-Antecedent Agreement

Practice
■ *Language & Sentence Skills Practice,* pp. 120–123

Differentiating Instruction
■ *Developmental Language & Sentence Skills,* pp. 65–66

One third of the casserole is left, but **it** will be gone soon. [*One third* refers to *casserole*.]

One third of the bagels are left, but **they** will be gone soon. [*One third* refers to *bagels*.]

5w. Some nouns that are plural in form take singular pronouns.

The following nouns take singular pronouns.

civics	gymnastics	news
economics	linguistics	physics
electronics	mathematics	summons
genetics	molasses	

EXAMPLE   I am taking **physics** this year, and **it** is a very challenging course.

NOTE   Many nouns ending in –*ics,* such as *acoustics, athletics, ethics, politics, statistics,* and *tactics,* may take either singular or plural pronouns. Generally, when such a noun names a science, a system, or a skill, the noun takes a singular pronoun. When the noun names qualities, activities, or individual items, the noun takes a plural pronoun.

SINGULAR   Today, our government class discussed **ethics** and the role **it** has played in recent political campaigns.

PLURAL   We believe that the candidate's **ethics** are beyond reproach; we have seen no evidence that would cause us to question **them.**

However, a few nouns that refer to single items take plural pronouns.

binoculars	pants	shears
eyeglasses	pliers	shorts
Olympics	scissors	slacks

EXAMPLE   The **pliers** are not in the toolbox. Have you seen **them**?

Even when plural in form, the titles of creative works (such as books, songs, movies, and paintings) and the names of countries, cities, and organizations generally take singular pronouns.

┌**HELP**─

If you are not sure whether to use a singular or a plural pronoun to refer to an antecedent ending in –*ics,* look up the word in a dictionary.

Learning for Life   **Continued on pp. 130–131**

Writing a Letter of Application.
Remind students that although informal usage is acceptable in casual conversation, they must be able to write according to the rules of standard, formal usage when they need to make a good impression in an application. To review agreement while building skills for real-life situations, have each student compose a letter of application for financial aid or a scholarship.

The names of some organizations, though plural in form, may take either singular or plural pronouns. When the name refers to the organization as a unit, use a singular pronoun. When the name refers to the members of the organization, use a plural pronoun.

SINGULAR
The **Bayview Rockets** won **its** first game of the season. [*Its* is used because the Bayview Rockets won as a unit.]

PLURAL
The **Bayview Rockets** left the field, waving **their** helmets high over **their** heads. [*Their* is used because the individual players were waving separate helmets over their heads.]

PRACTICE

Guided and Independent

Exercise You may want to have students complete **Exercise 7** as guided practice and **Review F** as independent practice.

HOMEWORK

1. their

2. them

3. it

4. its

EXAMPLES Have you ever watched *The X-Files*? I think I have seen every episode of **it.**

Sleeping Musicians was painted by Rufino Tamayo. **It** is one of his best-known works.

Situated in the Indian Ocean, **Seychelles** comprises about ninety islands; **its** three principal islands are Mahé, Praslin, and La Digue.

I don't know how many people live in **Grand Rapids,** but I do know that **it** is the second-largest city in Michigan.

Have you shopped at **Computers Unlimited**? **It** may have the software that you need.

5x. The gender and number of the relative pronoun *that, which,* or *who* are determined by the gender and number of the word to which it refers—its antecedent.

SINGULAR Wendy, **who** has already fulfilled most of **her** campaign promises, was elected president of the student council a few weeks ago. [*Who* refers to the singular, feminine noun *Wendy*. Therefore, the singular, feminine form *her* is used to agree with *who.*]

PLURAL These retainers, **which** have my name on **them,** were made for me by my orthodontist. [*That* refers to the plural, neuter noun *retainers*. Therefore, *them* is used to agree with *that.*]

Exercise 7 **Proofreading for Errors in Pronoun-Antecedent Agreement**

Most of the following sentences contain errors in pronoun-antecedent agreement. Write the incorrect pronoun and the correct form. If a sentence is already correct, write *C*.

EXAMPLE **1.** If we had seventy dollars, they would be enough for that program.

1. *they—it*

1. The students who left his or her uniforms on the bus should report to the front hall.

2. The good scissors should be back next week; the repair shop is sharpening it.

3. No, two thirds of a tablespoon of oregano will be too much; they will make the pizza taste like lawn clippings.

4. In the summer, the team made Sarasota their home.

Learning for Life *Continued from p. 129*

If students are already thinking about these types of letters in preparation for attending college, they can use this opportunity to write the letters they need to send.

Ask guidance counselors for samples of application letters and entrance requirements. Then, suggest that students brainstorm in small groups about what to include in their letters. For example, they

5. "The Stars and Stripes Forever" has been popular for decades, and they will probably continue to be a favorite.

6. *Drovers* will be on display in the library until Saturday, when they will join the sculpture exhibit at the university.

7. The news should be on in a few minutes; the game's overtime delayed them.

8. Does the band post its rehearsal schedule on the bulletin board?

9. Valencia Industries may provide wiring if they can meet our schedule.

10. Did you ask anyone who has finished their college applications to look over your personal essay?

5. it

6. it

7. it

8. C

9. it

10. his or her

Review F **Proofreading Sentences for Pronoun-Antecedent Agreement**

Most of the following sentences contain errors in pronoun-antecedent agreement. If a sentence contains an error in agreement, rewrite the sentence to correct the error. If a sentence is already correct, write *C*.

EXAMPLE
1. The band is practicing the selections that they will perform in the statewide competition.

1. *The band is practicing the selections that it will perform in the statewide competition.*

1. Each of the men says that they will help deliver the gift packages to the families.

2. One of those cars has their own factory-installed stereo.

3. That factory has robots working on its assembly line.

4. Either Mrs. Wilson or Mrs. Kim will bring their camera.

5. Has either of the new students been assigned his or her locker?

6. Anyone who speaks a foreign language increases their chance for a high-paying job.

7. After you locate the Netherlands on the map, write the name of its capital.

8. No one in the crowd had noticed the pickpocket stealing their wallet.

9. Neither Jason nor Maggie bought their shoes until they went on sale.

10. Brenda and Charlene read her report about Rosa Parks and the civil rights movement.

11. The study of economics and their practical applications can last a lifetime.

12. Do you know someone who could lend me their community college catalog?

1. he

2. its

3. C

4. her *or a*

5. C

6. his or her

7. C

8. his or her [*or* The people in the crowd had not . . . their wallets.]

9. his or her

10. their

11. its

12. his or her *or a*

might begin by introducing themselves and then outlining the reasons they believe they need and qualify for a scholarship or other financial aid.

After students have written their letters, pair them to work on identifying subjects, verbs, pronouns, and antecedents and to edit their letters for correct agreement. If possible, have students store their letters on computer diskettes for future use and reference.

13. its
14. its
15. their
16. its
17. it
18. C
19. their
20. their

13. The jury will receive ~~their~~ instructions from the judge.

14. Red Feather Enterprises may award ~~their~~ million-dollar advertising campaign to us.

15. Three saxophone players and two trumpet players are waiting for ~~his or her~~ auditions.

16. Whom did the Confederate States of America make ~~their~~ president?

17. It was around then that the album *Rumours* soared through the airwaves as ~~they~~ became part of our pop history.

18. Nothing in the room was out of its place.

19. Awestruck by the final number, the audience remained in ~~its~~ seats, silent for a full minute.

20. Both of the artists had shown ~~his or her~~ work at the new gallery.

Numerals and terms in brackets refer to rules and concepts tested by the items in the Chapter Review.

1. [5m]
2. [5f]
3. [5d(1), i]
4. [5i, *a number of*]
5. [5f]
6. [5f]
7. [5i]
8. [5l]
9. [5p]
10. [5k]
11. [5g]
12. [5j, n]
13. [5o]
14. [5e, h]
15. [5e, n]

Chapter Review

A. Choosing Verbs That Agree in Number with Their Subjects

Choose the correct verb form in parentheses in each of the following sentences.

1. *The Pickwick Papers* (*was*, *were*) Dickens's first published novel.
2. Neither Francisco nor Joe (*has*, *have*) called to order tickets yet.
3. (*Are*, *Is*) either one of them participating in the play?
4. There (*was*, *were*) a number of students in the hall.
5. Theodore or William always (*has*, *have*) a pocket calculator.
6. Either the guidance counselor or the principal (*is*, *are*) certain to know the answer to this question.
7. Here (*are*, *is*) the attendance figures for the current week.
8. Mathematics (*seem*, *seems*) more difficult than any of my other subjects.
9. Shelley is one of those poets who (*are*, *is*) almost certain to be represented in any anthology of English verse.
10. Nine dollars and fifty cents (*is*, *are*) too much to spend on lunch.
11. Either Carl or his parents (*was*, *were*) willing to leave early.
12. The Chess Club (*is*, *are*) Margaret Doyle, Robert Viapiano, Victor Mothersbaugh, and Judy Cheng-Cochran.
13. Every student and teacher in the school (*are*, *is*) contributing to the fund-raiser for the new library.
14. Jeremy and Chad (*don't*, *doesn't*) know the words to the song.
15. Ray, his brother Dave, Chrissy, and her brother Arthur (*is*, *are*) the Village Green Preservation Society.

B. Proofreading for Pronoun-Antecedent Errors

Each of the following sentences contains an error in pronoun-antecedent agreement. Identify each error, and then write the correct pronoun form.

16. her [5r(1)]
17. he or she [5r(1)]

16. One of the girls left their coat in my locker.
17. If anyone does not understand the directions, they should feel free to ask questions.

Chapter Review **133**

USAGE

18. his or her [5q]
19. their [5u]
20. her [5t]
21. it [5q]
22. his [5r(1)]
23. their [5q]
24. their [5s]
25. her [5r(1)]
26. them [5s]
27. she [5t]
28. them [5w]
29. its [5r(1)]
30. it [5w]

18. Did each person sign their name on the get-well card that we are sending to Frieda?

19. The band have been measured for its new uniforms.

20. Either Elena or Carla is driving their car to the picnic tomorrow.

21. Rock-and-roll is my father's favorite music; he has listened to them since he was a boy.

22. One of the repairmen left their toolbox in our kitchen.

23. Several actors in the play forgot his lines during the dress rehearsal.

24. The books and magazines had smiling faces on its covers.

25. One of the girls fell down and cut their knee.

26. When Jamal and Dustin get through the snowstorm to the gas station, ask him to call us.

27. Neither Mimi nor Miriam believes that they will lose the spelling bee to the other.

28. After Jim used the scissors, he put it back in the kitchen drawer.

29. Each of the horses in the pasture had a white mark on their face.

30. Tanya is studying physics this semester, and she says she might major in them.

C. Proofreading a Paragraph for Subject-Verb Agreement and Pronoun-Antecedent Agreement

Each of the sentences in the following paragraph contains an error in agreement between subject and verb or between pronoun and antecedent. Identify each error, and then write the correct form.

31. have [5d(3)]
32. are [5n]
33. their [5q]
34. takes [5o]
35. include [5c]
36. his or her [5r(1)]
37. their [5r(2)]
38. enjoy [5b]
39. are [5i]

[**31**] Most of us has some knowledge of the periods in European history known as the Middle Ages and the Renaissance. [**32**] Those times is the special interest of the Society for Creative Anachronism. [**33**] Members of this society take his or her pleasure in the study of the Middle Ages and the Renaissance. [**34**] Every member take a name and becomes a character appropriate to the society's historical period (A.D. 500 to A.D. 1500). [**35**] Popular characters in the society includes princes, princesses, lords, and ladies. [**36**] After joining, everyone is free to choose a new name and to re-create their favorite aspect of medieval or Renaissance life. [**37**] Many of the members pursue his or her own interests. [**38**] For example, some people enjoys costuming, armor making, calligraphy, and woodworking. [**39**] There is also some members who compete in tournaments to become monarchs of the

society's kingdoms. **[40]** If you want to learn more about such histori-cal activities in your area, remember that the society usually displays their brochures at Renaissance festivals.

Writing Application
Using Correct Agreement in a Letter

Subject-Verb Agreement   A friend of yours is applying for a summer job as a camp counselor and has asked you to write a letter of recommendation. Write the letter of recommendation that you will send to the director of the summer camp. In your letter, follow the rules of formal, standard English and pay particular attention to subject-verb agreement.

Prewriting   Take a few minutes to write down a list of your friend's positive qualities and outstanding abilities. Focus on traits that you think would make your friend a good camp counselor. Think of specific exam-ples that illustrate the qualities you have listed.

Writing   Begin your letter by introducing yourself and stating your purpose. Tell how long you have known the person you are recommend-ing. Then, express your positive opinion of the person and his or her abil-ities. Be specific. You may want to give two or three brief examples to illustrate your friend's qualities, or you may want to tell one interesting anecdote that achieves the same result.

Revising   Read through your letter once before you begin to revise it. Does it have the effect you want? Will it help your friend get the job? On a second reading, identify specific parts of the letter that need revising. Check to be sure you have followed the standard form for a business letter.

Publishing   Be sure to proofread your letter carefully. When you check for errors in subject-verb agreement, take extra care with collective nouns, plural nouns, expressions of an amount, and relative pronouns. In pairs, conduct mock interviews with your classmates. The students play-ing the employer should ask questions about the letter of reference.

40. its [5j]

USAGE

CHAPTER

6

Using Pronouns Correctly

Case Forms of Pronouns; Special Pronoun Problems

INTRODUCING THE CHAPTER

- You might want to concentrate on helping learners having difficulty and English-language learners with the nominative and objective case pronouns. Advanced students who make few errors in pronoun usage in written work might focus on the section titled **Special Pronoun Problems.** The conventions taught in this section challenge even accomplished writers.

- The chapter closes with a **Chapter Review** including a **Writing Application** in which students use pronouns preceding gerunds and participles in an article giving tips to students studying for exams.

- For help in integrating this chapter with writing assignments, see the **Teaching Strands** chart, pp. T24–T25.

Diagnostic Preview

A. Selecting Correct Forms of Pronouns

Terms and numerals in brackets refer to concepts and rules tested by items in the Diagnostic Preview.

1. [6a]
2. [6i]
3. [who, whom]
4. [6h]
5. [6j]
6. [6a]

Choose the underlined correct pronoun form in parentheses in each of the following sentences.

EXAMPLE
1. After a pause, I heard Mr. Karas say into the phone, "Yes, this is (*he, him*)."

   1. *he*

1. Last summer, my friend Megan and (*I, me*) worked in a factory that produces microchips for computers.
2. Before we began, we made a pact that (*we, us*) teenagers would show the adults that we were responsible workers.
3. For the first two weeks, everything ran smoothly because our supervisor, Mr. Karas, was a person (*who, whom*) we admired for being firm and just.
4. In fact, we were surprised by (*him, his*) showing interest in our progress and going out of his way to train us.
5. When Mr. Karas went on vacation, we doubted that his assistant, Ms. Sullivan, would be as firm as (*he, him*).
6. Our first mistake was in thinking that Mr. Karas and (*she, her*) would have different sets of standards.

CHAPTER RESOURCES

Internet
- Web resources: go.hrw.com

go.hrw.com

Practice & Review
- *Language & Sentence Skills Practice,* pp. 133–150
- *Language & Sentence Skills Practice Answer Key,* pp. 55–59

Application & Enrichment
- *Language & Sentence Skills Practice,* pp. 132, 151–154
- *Language & Sentence Skills Practice Answer Key,* pp. 55, 59–61

7. We started giving (*us*, *ourselves*) ten extra minutes at lunch.

8. One afternoon, Ms. Sullivan walked up to us at our job stations and said, "Megan and Rick, until recently I had thought you were employees (*who*, *whom*) took pride in your work."

9. "If you continue to come back late," she said calmly, "we, Mr. Karas and (*I*, *me*), will be looking for two new trainees."

10. The experience has really taught (*we*, *us*) some valuable lessons.

11. First, (*us*, *our*) deliberately taking extra time at the break was wrong.

12. Second, we had let Mr. Karas down because it was (*he*, *him*) who had hired us, trained us, and trusted us.

13. Third, we had mistakenly presumed that Ms. Sullivan would not do her job as well as (*he*, *him*).

14. Fourth, we had let (*us*, *ourselves*) down by failing to do our best.

15. (*Who*, *Whom*) do you think became model employees?

B. Proofreading a Paragraph for Correct Pronoun Usage

Most of the sentences in the following paragraph contain errors in pronoun usage. Identify each error, and then give the correct pronoun form. If a sentence is already correct, write *C*.

EXAMPLE   **[1]** Gaius Caesar Germanicus, whom perhaps is better known as Caligula, was emperor of Rome from A.D. 37 to A.D. 41.

    1. whom—who

[16] Do you know whom Tiberius Claudius Drusus Nero Germanicus was? [17] Such a long, elegant name certainly seems fitting for a Roman emperor, and that is exactly what he was. [18] Us modern readers and television watchers, as well as historians, know him simply as Claudius. [19] Robert Graves wrote about he in the popular novel *I, Claudius*. [20] Claudius, whom had a severe speech impediment, lived from 10 B.C. to A.D. 54. [21] Him becoming emperor in A.D. 41 troubled many Romans because they thought that he was a fool and would be a weak ruler. [22] He had not been an important government figure during the reigns of emperors Tiberius and Caligula, but he outlived both of they. [23] Claudius was a more stable ruler than Caligula and accomplished more than him. [24] Claudius, who historians now generally praise, initiated many building programs, such as the huge Claudian Aqueduct. [25] In addition, many Roman civil and military accomplishments of the time are credited to himself.

7. [reflexive pronouns]
8. [*who, whom*]
9. [6i]
10. [6d]
11. [6h]
12. [6b]
13. [6j]
14. [reflexive pronouns]
15. [*who, whom*]

16. who [*who, whom*]
17. C [6a]
18. We [6i]
19. him [6e]
20. who [*who, whom*]
21. His [6h]
22. them [6e]
23. he [6j]
24. whom [*who, whom*]
25. him [6k]

Lesson Starter

Prior Knowledge. Read students a paragraph or a brief excerpt from an article or a composition after you have changed some of the pronouns in the excerpt to incorrect forms. Students should listen and write down any incorrectly used pronoun forms that they hear. Then, you can read through the selection again to discuss and correct each incorrect pronoun usage. Tell students that in this lesson they will expand their knowledge of pronoun usage.

DIFFERENTIATING INSTRUCTION

English-Language Learners

General Strategies. Although English pronouns have three cases, other languages vary in their number of cases. Students who speak languages that use several cases may wonder what cases to use in English. Those who speak languages that do not indicate case may have trouble understanding what case is and why it is important. You may wish to hold individual or small-group sessions with students to answer any questions they might have.

Hmong. The objective and nominative cases of Hmong pronouns depend upon their placement within the sentence rather than on the forms of the pronouns themselves, while the possessive case relies upon the use of a possessive classifier. Remind Hmong speakers that English pronouns change form in order to indicate their functions within a sentence, and offer additional review and practice using pronouns in their different cases.

Reference Note

For more about **forming possessive nouns,** see page 375.

STYLE TIP

As a matter of courtesy, first-person pronouns are placed at the end of compound constructions.

EXAMPLES
Nan and **I** went to the opera.

My uncle Evander met Nan and **me** outside the theater.

Uncle Evander paid for Nan's ticket and **mine.**

Case

Case is the form that a noun or a pronoun takes to show its relationship to other words in a sentence. In English, there are three cases: *nominative, objective,* and *possessive.*

The form of a noun is the same in both the nominative case and the objective case. For example, a noun used as a subject (nominative case) will have the same form if used as an object (objective case).

NOMINATIVE CASE   The **ghost** of Banquo suddenly appeared. [subject]

OBJECTIVE CASE   Only Macbeth saw the **ghost.** [direct object]

A noun changes its form for the possessive case, usually by adding an apostrophe and an *s.*

POSSESSIVE CASE   What effect did the **ghost's** appearance have on Macbeth?

NOTE   Some authorities prefer the term *subjective case* to *nominative case.* Follow your teacher's directions when labeling words in this case.

Case Forms of Personal Pronouns

Unlike nouns, most personal pronouns have three different forms, one for each case. The form a pronoun takes depends on its function in a sentence.

NOMINATIVE CASE   **We** enjoyed reading *Macbeth.* [subject]

OBJECTIVE CASE   Some of **us** had seen a performance of the play on PBS. [object of the preposition *of*]

POSSESSIVE CASE   **Our** next assignment is to read *Othello.*

Within each case, the forms of the personal pronouns indicate *number, person,* and *gender.*

- Number tells you whether the pronoun is singular or plural.
- Person tells you whether the pronoun refers to the one(s) speaking (**first person**), the one(s) spoken to (**second person**), or the one(s) spoken of (**third person**).
- Gender tells you whether the pronoun is masculine, feminine, or neuter (neither masculine nor feminine).

RESOURCES

Case Forms of Personal Pronouns

Practice

- *Language & Sentence Skills Practice,* p. 133

Personal Pronouns			
	Nominative Case	Objective Case	Possessive Case
Singular			
First Person	I	me	my, mine
Second Person	you	you	your, yours
Third Person	he, she, it	him, her, it	his, her, hers, its
	Nominative Case	Objective Case	Possessive Case
Plural			
First Person	we	us	our, ours
Second Person	you	you	your, yours
Third Person	they	them	their, theirs

Notice that *you* and *it* have the same forms for the nominative and objective cases and that *her* has the same form for the objective and possessive cases. All other personal pronouns have different forms for each case. Notice also that only the third-person singular pronouns indicate gender.

MOTHER GOOSE & GRIMM © Tribune Media Services, Inc. All rights reserved. Reprinted with permission.

The Nominative Case

The personal pronouns in the nominative case—*I, you, he, she, it, we,* and *they*—are used as subjects of verbs and as predicate nominatives.

6a. The subject of a verb should be in the nominative case.

EXAMPLES   **They** are playing backgammon.

We think that **she** deserves the Most Valuable Player award.

Case Forms of Personal Pronouns   **139**

STYLE   TIP

Use the neuter pronoun *it* when referring to an animal unless the gender of the animal is made clear by another word in the sentence.

EXAMPLES

The dog was barking because **its** food dish was empty. [The sentence does not indicate the dog's gender.]

The lioness watched the film crew warily from **her** resting spot in the shade of a tree. [The word *lioness* indicates that the animal is female.]

Josie's cat, Max, froze in **his** tracks when **he** heard the phone ring. [The name *Max* indicates that the animal is male.]

Reference Note

The personal pronouns in the nominative case may also be used as appositives. For more about **appositives,** see page 73.

Reference Note

For more about **subjects of verbs,** see page 37.

DIFFERENTIATING INSTRUCTION

Learners Having Difficulty

Some students may benefit from rearranging the information on pronoun case presented in the chart on the left. Ask them to make two columns labeled *Singular* and *Plural* and to add information in the following manner, creating a chart for each case.

NOMINATIVE CASE	
SINGULAR	PLURAL
I	we
you	you
he, she, it	they

English-Language Learners

General Strategies. Emphasize that the English subject pronoun is an essential part of the sentence. In some languages (Spanish, for example) the subject pronoun is not necessary—it is used for stress or clarification. The verb ending alone implies the subject.

The Nominative Case

Rules 6a, b *(pp. 139–141)*

OBJECTIVE

- To supply nominative case pronouns in sentences

PRACTICE

Guided and Independent

Exercise 1 You may want to use the first ten sentences in **Exercise 1** as guided practice and have students complete sentences 11–20 as independent practice.

HOMEWORK

Exercise 1 **Using Pronouns in the Nominative Case**

ANSWERS

1. he
2. She
3. We
4. they
5. she
6. you
7. We
8. she
9. I

A compound subject may include a pronoun in combination with a noun or another pronoun.

EXAMPLES The twins and **they** will be giving a concert tonight.

You and **I** are in the same math class.

6b. **A predicate nominative should be in the nominative case.**

A ***predicate nominative*** is a word or word group in the predicate that refers to or identifies the subject. A pronoun used as a predicate nominative usually completes the meaning of a form of the linking verb *be: am, is, are, was, were, be, being,* or *been.*

EXAMPLES The first speaker will be **I.** [*I* completes the meaning of *will be* by identifying the subject *speaker.*]

The most polite person in class is **he.** [*He* completes the meaning of *is* by identifying the subject *person.*]

Like a subject, a predicate nominative may be compound, with a pronoun appearing in combination with a noun or another pronoun.

EXAMPLES The only seniors who volunteered were **Elia** and **I.** [*Elia* and *I* complete the meaning of *were* by identifying the subject *seniors.*]

The managers of the new Thai restaurant are **she** and **he.** [*She* and *he* complete the meaning of *are* by identifying the subject *managers.*]

Exercise 1 **Using Pronouns in the Nominative Case**

For each of the following sentences, give a personal pronoun that can be substituted for the word or words in brackets.

EXAMPLE **1.** Carl and [*Sue Ann*] always seem to be happy.
        1. she

1. Jorge and [*Mike*] are tied for third place.
2. [*Donna*] and her parents have moved to San Antonio.
3. [*First-person plural*] will take the exam on Friday.
4. Can it be [*those choir members*] in that picture?
5. Either Ellen or [*Sally*] will be in charge.
6. Jennifer and [*second-person singular*] will represent the class.
7. [*First-person plural*] earned our trophies.
8. Neither [*Carolyn*] nor Michele has change for the bus.
9. Did you know that Greg and [*first-person singular*] are leaving?

CONTENT-AREA CONNECTIONS

Mathematics

Equivalence. Tell students a sentence containing both a form of the verb *be* and a predicate nominative functions in a similar way to the math equation *if A=B, then B=A.* Similarly, the sentence *They are the students* is equivalent to the sentence *The students are they.* Explain to the class that, since subject pronouns are in the nominative case, this analogy can help them to remember to use nominative case pronouns as predicate nominatives.

10. I am sure the ones on the dance floor were you and [*Ed*].
11. The designers of the set were Philip and [*first-person plural*].
12. One good practitioner of this laboratory technique is [*Marcus*].
13. Will our new team teachers be Mrs. Niari and [*Mr. Howard*]?
14. Believe it or not, [*those boys*] in the van over there are all my brothers.
15. In the whole school, the only students with pet iguanas are Betsy and [*first-person singular*].
16. With a little luck, the winners will be [*second-person plural*].
17. As usual, the first people in line for tickets were Terri and [*Paula*].
18. Kirara and [*first-person singular*] went to see the exhibit of Pakistani art.
19. The only volunteers are Aidan and [*third-person plural*].
20. Are Max and [*the Wilson twins*] on the list?

The Objective Case

The personal pronouns in the objective case—*me, you, him, her, it, us,* and *them*—are used as direct objects, as indirect objects, and as objects of prepositions.

6c. A direct object should be in the objective case.

A **direct object** completes the meaning of a transitive verb by telling *who* or *what* receives the action of the verb.

EXAMPLES   Carmen has invited **me**. [*Me* tells *whom* Carmen has invited.]

The kittens were asleep until the sudden noise woke **them**. [*Them* tells *what* the noise woke.]

A direct object may be compound.

EXAMPLES   My father drove my **friends** and **me** to the game.

Mr. Pascoe chose **him** and **her** for the leading roles.

6d. An indirect object should be in the objective case.

Indirect objects appear sometimes in sentences containing direct objects and tell *to whom* or *to what* or *for whom* or *for what* the action of a transitive verb is done.

EXAMPLES   His uncle bought **him** a poncho in Mexico. [*Him* tells *for whom* his uncle bought a poncho.]

Because the engine was running poorly, Uncle Theo gave **it** a tune-up. [*It* tells *to what* Uncle Theo gave a tune-up.]

| STYLE 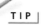 TIP |

Expressions such as *It's me, This is her,* and *It was them* are examples of informal usage. Though common in everyday situations, such expressions should be avoided in formal speaking and writing.

Reference Note

The personal pronouns in the objective case may also be used as appositives. For more about **appositives,** see page 73.

Reference Note

For more about **direct objects,** see page 45.

Reference Note

For more about **indirect objects,** see page 46.

Case Forms of Personal Pronouns   **141**

RESOURCES

The Objective Case
Practice
- *Language & Sentence Skills Practice,* pp. 136–138
Differentiating Instruction
- *Developmental Language & Sentence Skills,* pp. 69–70

Exercise 1 Using Pronouns in the Nominative Case

ANSWERS continued

10. he
11. we
12. he
13. he
14. they
15. I
16. you
17. she
18. I
19. they
20. they

The Objective Case
Rules 6c–e *(pp. 141–146)*

OBJECTIVES

- To supply pronouns in the objective case to complete sentences
- To select correct pronouns as objects of prepositions in sentences

DIRECT TEACHING

Modeling and Demonstration

The Objective Case. Model how a pronoun takes the objective case when it is the direct object of a verb by using the example *Carmen has invited me.* First, ask which word or words in this sentence are pronouns. [*me*] Then, ask how this pronoun is used in the sentence. [*as the direct object of the verb*] The forms of the pronoun *I* include the subject forms: *I, we;* the object forms: *me, us;* and the possessive forms: *my/mine* and *our/ours.* Ask which form is used in the sentence. [*object form*] Now, have a volunteer demonstrate how to identify the objective case of a pronoun, using another example from this chapter.

DIFFERENTIATING INSTRUCTION

English-Language Learners

In **Exercise 2** and other exercises in this chapter, some students may have difficulty recognizing whether the names used are male or female. You may wish to identify male and female names prior to assigning the exercise so that the students can focus on using the correct pronouns.

Learners Having Difficulty

As an alternative to one of the exercises or as a supplementary activity, have students bring articles from their favorite magazines or newspapers to class. Then, ask students to identify the nominative and objective case pronouns used in the articles. (If the articles are long, assign smaller portions.)

PRACTICE

Guided and Independent

Exercise 2 You may want to use the first ten items in **Exercise 2** as guided practice. Then, have students complete the exercise as independent practice. **HOMEWORK**

┌─HELP─
Do not mistake the object of a preposition for an indirect object.

INDIRECT OBJECT
Dad bought me a sandwich.

OBJECT OF A PREPOSITION
Dad bought a sandwich for me. [*Me* is the object of the preposition *for*.]

┌ TIPS & TRICKS ┐

To help you choose the correct pronoun form in a compound direct object or indirect object, try each form separately with the verb.

CHOICES
Celia showed (*he, him*) and (*I, me*) photographs of her vacation in Hawaii. [*Showed he* or *showed him*? *Showed I* or *showed me*?]

ANSWER
Celia showed **him** and **me** photographs of her vacation in Hawaii.

An indirect object may be compound.

EXAMPLES Aunt Marion sent my **brother** and **me** a letter from Portugal.

Did you give **her** and **him** the message?

Exercise 2 **Using Pronouns in the Objective Case**

For each of the following sentences, write a personal pronoun that can be substituted for the word or words in brackets.

EXAMPLES **1.** I helped [*Rod*] and her with their projects.
1. him

2. Sonia and Molly sent [*first-person singular*] a get-well card last week.
2. me

1. Did you tell the superintendent or [*Ms. Marshall*]? **1.** her
2. Mrs. Hanks gave Josh and [*first-person plural*] the motivation we needed. **2.** us
3. Leave [*first-person plural*] alone for a while. **3.** us
4. Carmen will be inviting both you and [*first-person singular*] to the recital. **4.** me
5. Did you see Lois or [*Andy*] today? **5.** him
6. I sent the admissions director and [*her assistants*] a letter. **6.** them
7. The coach chose Joan and [*Michelle and me*]. **7.** us
8. The principal should have notified [*Stephen*] and Gail. **8.** him
9. Ron just passed Tina and [*first-person singular*] in the hall. **9.** me
10. Please don't ask [*the athletes*] about today's game. **10.** them
11. As during similar roundups, the old mustang easily evaded [*third-person plural*]. **11.** them   **12.** her
12. Will you make [*Brenda*] a necklace out of those Chinese beads?
13. Georgia is giving Ted and [*first-person plural*] a ride to the Renaissance Festival. **13.** us
14. A sampan carried [*the spies*] across the busy river. **14.** them
15. Did they mention Anthony or [*first-person singular*]? **15.** me
16. Why did Mrs. Johnson assign Ricky and [*first-person singular*] an extra report? **16.** me
17. Tell [*Dad*] about your plan. **17.** him   **18.** them
18. Who taught [*those paramedics*] the new emergency procedures?
19. Show Karen and [*Uncle Joseph*] the new trophy. **19.** him
20. [*Carla*] and [*second-person singular*] I would never doubt.
20. Her/you

Review A Choosing Correct Forms of Personal Pronouns

Choose the correct pronoun form in parentheses in each of the following sentences.

EXAMPLE   **1.** Paulo and (*her, she*) are my lab partners.

    1. she

1. The guests thanked Rita and (*she, her*).
2. Gloria and (*I, me*) are giving a report on the relationship between the Shoshone people and the Mormon settlers in the 1800s.
3. (*We, Us*) are learning about Hendrick Arnold, a scout who helped Texas win independence from Mexico.
4. What were you telling Chuck and (*we, us*) earlier?
5. Of course, I remember Monica and (*she, her*).
6. We knew the first guests to arrive would be (*they, them*).
7. Give (*we, us*) the message as soon as possible.
8. Jana and (*she, her*) are active members.
9. It is either you or (*he, him*) in the runoff against Jamie.
10. That's (*he, him*) standing on the corner.

Review B Proofreading a Paragraph for Correct Pronoun Usage

Most sentences in the following paragraph contain errors in pronoun usage. Identify each error, and then give the correct pronoun form. If a sentence is already correct, write *C*.

EXAMPLE   **[1]** Sarah and me are on the track team.

    1. me—I

    [1] At the start of track season, our coach told Sarah and I the story of the famous sprinter Evelyn Ashford. **[2]** During high school, Ashford had started running races against the boys at lunchtime, and eventually she beat they. **[3]** The champion coach Pat Connolly recognized the young runner as a great talent when she saw Ashford race at the University of California at Los Angeles in 1976. **[4]** In 1983 and 1984, Ashford set records in the women's 100-meter dash, and her became the fastest woman in the world. **[5]** Our coach said that Ashford's speed—10.76 seconds for the 100-meter dash in 1984—amazed even he. **[6]** At the 1988 Olympic games, Ashford hoped that she could better her record time. **[7]** The other competitors knew that the runner to beat that year was her. **[8]** Ashford's talent, hard work,

1. me
2. them
3. C
4. she
5. him
6. C
7. she

DIFFERENTIATING INSTRUCTION

English-Language Learners

Spanish. Some Spanish personal pronouns have the same form when they are used as objects of prepositions as they do when they are used in the nominative case, as in *Ella habla a ella,* which translates as "She spoke to she," or *Ellos hablan a ellos,* which translates as "They spoke to they." Therefore, Spanish speakers may be unaccustomed to making a distinction between some nominative and objective case personal pronouns. Have students read aloud the sentences in the exercises to hear how nominative and objective case pronouns are used.

PRACTICE

Guided and Independent

Exercise 3 You may want to use the first ten items in **Exercise 3** as guided practice. Then, have students complete the exercise as independent practice. **HOMEWORK**

EXTENSION

Critical Thinking

Analysis. Ask students who speak or study foreign languages to comment on how the complexity of pronoun case in English compares with that in other languages. While some may say pronoun choice is more complex in English, those studying French or German may say that pronoun case or noun case is simpler in English, in which the objective case covers three distinct uses. Point out that in Latin there are six cases for nouns as well as pronouns: nominative, genitive, dative, accusative, vocative, and ablative.

---

8. her
9. she

10. C

TIPS & TRICKS

An object of a preposition may be compound, as in the phrase *between you and me.* To help you determine the pronoun form to use in such a construction, try each form separately with the preposition.

CHOICES
Dwayne sat behind Norman and (*I, me*) at the jazz concert. [*Behind I* or *behind me*?]

ANSWER
Dwayne sat behind Norman and **me** at the jazz concert.

Reference Note

For more information about **prepositions,** see page 23. For more about **prepositional phrases,** see page 60.

---

and determination earned she a gold and a silver medal, but she set no new records at those games. [9] The athlete in the picture on the previous page is her running for the American team at the 1988 Olympics. [10] Don't you think she looks like a winner?

6e. An object of a preposition should be in the objective case.

A noun or pronoun (or a word group functioning as a noun) that follows a preposition is called the ***object of a preposition.*** Together with any modifiers of the object, the preposition and its object make a ***prepositional phrase.***

EXAMPLES	with **Joe**	before **her**	against **them**
	above **him**	for **talking** too much	along with **you** and **me**

Exercise 3 Choosing Pronouns Used as Objects of Prepositions

Choose the correct pronoun form in parentheses in each of the following sentences.

EXAMPLE   1. This letter is addressed to you and (*I, me*).
1. *me*

1. The chess team sent a challenge to Don and (*him, he*).
2. The two of (*we, us*) must discuss the schedule.
3. John went to the movie with Alice and (*them, they*).
4. I dedicated my poem to both Marcia and (*she, her*).
5. After Juanita and (*I, me*) come the twins.
6. The responsibility has fallen upon (*we, us*).
7. Were you sitting near Tony and (*she, her*)?
8. The matter is strictly between Ms. James and (*them, they*).
9. Consuelo has been asking about you and (*she, her*).
10. Will you draw a cartoon of (*we, us*) for me?
11. A fax from (*him, he*) just arrived.
12. Between you and (*I, me*), those hamburgers are the best I've ever had.
13. Did you make that coat for (*she, her*) or for yourself?
14. The hostess circulated among (*them, they*) and made introductions.
15. Don't you sit in front of Dave and (*him, he*) in chemistry?
16. Owners know that, at a show, dogs must stand quietly beside (*them, they*).
17. Everyone except Brandon and (*we, us*) had ridden on the subway.

MINI-LESSON Grammar

Prepositions. A review of prepositions and prepositional phrases may be a useful addition to **Rule 6e.** Remind students of the following rules: (1) A preposition is used to show how a noun or pronoun is related to some other word in the sentence, and (2) prepositional phrases are usually used as adjectives or adverbs. Write the following sentences on the chalkboard. Ask students to identify the prepositions, to identify the object of each preposition, to identify the prepositional phrases as adjectival or

18. We aren't arguing against (*him*, *he*); we're arguing against his statements.

19. I've never met anyone like Rachel or (*she*, *her*) before.

20. Why does that macaw keep flying over and landing near Manny and (*I*, *me*)?

Review C **Choosing Correct Forms of Personal Pronouns**

For each of the following sentences, choose the <u>correct pronoun form</u> in parentheses. Then, tell how it is used in the sentence—as a *subject*, *predicate nominative*, *direct object*, *indirect object*, or *object of a preposition*.

EXAMPLE **1.** Leave the pamphlets with Kim and (*he*, *him*).

 1. *him—object of a preposition*

1. The coach chose Darrell and (*he*, *him*).
2. Luckily, the Smiths and (*we*, *us*) got tickets to the concert.
3. I have not heard from Mark and (*she*, *her*) in ages.
4. It could be (*they*, *them*) across the street.
5. Ms. Grant, the Dodges, and (*she*, *her*) went to the Palos Verdes Peninsula for the day.
6. The mayor granted (*they*, *them*) an interview.
7. (*She*, *Her*) and Heather always sit in the last row.
8. Would you please leave Simon and (*I*, *me*) alone?
9. Adele painted a picture for (*they*, *them*) and (*we*, *us*).
10. Jim Bob visited (*she*, *her*) and (*I*, *me*) in the hospital.

1. d.o.
2. s.
3. o.p.
4. p.n.
5. s.

6. i.o.
7. s.
8. d.o.
9. o.p./o.p.
10. d.o./d.o.

Review D **Proofreading a Paragraph for Correct Pronoun Usage**

Most of the sentences in the following paragraph contain errors in pronoun usage. Identify each error, and then give the correct pronoun form. If a sentence is already correct, write *C*.

EXAMPLE **[1]** Mom showed Larry and I an old history book that she had found in the attic.

 1. *I—me*

[1] Looking through the book, Larry and me found a fascinating picture of four famous men. [2] Look at the next page: Do you recognize any of they? [3] Of course, most of we are familiar with Thomas Edison and his inventions. [4] The man standing on the left is him. [5] Beside him on the old mill wheel are John Burroughs, Henry Ford, and Harvey Firestone. [6] Burroughs was an American naturalist and author; such

1. I
2. them
3. us
4. he
5. C

DIFFERENTIATING INSTRUCTION

Learners Having Difficulty
Students may be able to choose the correct pronouns in sentences, but they may have difficulty identifying grammatical function. You may want to limit the focus of **Review C** by asking students only to choose the correct form of the personal pronoun.

EXTENSION

Relating to Writing
Point out to students that a common mistake in writing is to inappropriately use the indefinite *you*. Sometimes this mistake is made in an effort to avoid using the pronoun *I*. Tell the class that second-person pronouns should be used primarily when a writer directly addresses the reader or uses dialogue. Have students revise these sentences:

1. The book makes you feel happy and hopeful. [*The book makes me feel happy and hopeful. The tone of the book is happy and hopeful.*]

2. My English teacher always wants you to type your homework. [*My English teacher always wants us to type our homework. My English teacher requires typed homework.*]

---

adverbial, and to tell what words the phrases modify.

1. Norman ran to the track. [to *shows how the object* track *is related to* ran. *The phrase* to the track *is an adverb phrase modifying* ran.]

2. The puppy in the cage is hungry. [in *shows how the object* cage *is related to* puppy. *The phrase* in the cage *is an adjective phrase modifying* puppy.]

6. him
7. C
8. him
9. me
10. them

books as *Birds and Poets* and *Field and Study* were written by he. [7] Ford, as you probably know, gave us the Model T in 1908 and helped usher in the age of the automobile. [8] Standing next to he is Firestone, who was head of the world's largest rubber company. [9] It surprised Larry and I to see these four noted Americans together. [10] Wouldn't it have been great to meet and talk with they at the old mill?

Pictured above from left to right are Thomas Edison, John Burroughs, Henry Ford, and Harvey Firestone.

The Possessive Case

Rules 6f–h *(pp. 146–148)*

OBJECTIVE

■ To complete sentences by supplying possessive case pronouns

---

DIRECT TEACHING

Modeling and Demonstration

The Possessive Case. Model how to identify a pronoun in the possessive case by using the examples *That is her computer* and *The computer is hers.* First, ask which pronoun in the first sentence shows ownership. [*her*] Point out that the possessive pronoun *her* modifies the noun *computer.* Next, ask which pronoun in the second sentence shows ownership. [*hers*] Then, ask if *hers* modifies a noun or pronoun here. [*no*] Ask how *hers* is used in this sentence. [*as the predicate nominative*] Explain that the possessive pronouns *mine, yours, hers, ours,* and *theirs* can be used like personal pronouns in the nominative and objective cases, while the possessive pronouns *my, your, her, our,* and *their* are used to modify nouns and pronouns.

His and *its* can be used in all three cases. Now, have a volunteer demonstrate how to identify a pronoun in the possessive case, using another example from this chapter.

The Possessive Case

The personal pronouns in the possessive case—*my, mine, your, yours, his, her, hers, its, our, ours, their,* and *theirs*—are used to show ownership or possession.

6f. The possessive pronouns *mine, yours, his, hers, its, ours,* and *theirs* are used in the same ways that the pronouns in the nominative and objective cases are.

SUBJECT	**Mine** has a flat tire.
PREDICATE NOMINATIVE	This floppy disk is **hers.**
DIRECT OBJECT	We haven't received **ours** yet.
INDIRECT OBJECT	Do they give **theirs** a weekly allowance?
OBJECT OF PREPOSITION	My mother wants to talk to **yours.**

RESOURCES

The Possessive Case

Practice

■ *Language & Sentence Skills Practice,* pp. 139–141

Differentiating Instruction

■ *Developmental Language & Sentence Skills,* pp. 67–70

6g. The possessive pronouns *my, our, your, his, her, its,* and *their* are used to modify nouns and pronouns.

EXAMPLES   The subject of **my** report is the Inuit of Canada.

Her first novel was published in 1960.

Do you have **their** telephone number?

NOTE In this book the words *my, our, your, his, her, its,* and *their* are called possessive pronouns. Some authorities prefer to call these words possessive adjectives because they are used to modify nouns or pronouns. Follow your teacher's instructions when labeling these words.

6h. A noun or a pronoun preceding a gerund should be in the possessive case.

A *gerund* is a verb form that ends in *–ing* and functions as a noun. Since a gerund acts as a noun, the noun or pronoun that comes before it must be in the possessive case in order to modify the gerund.

EXAMPLES   John objected to his **sister's** using his new computer. [*Sister's,* not *sister,* is used because John objected to the using, not to his sister.]

Their winning the Stanley Cup surprised us ice hockey fans. [*Their,* instead of *them* or *they,* is used because the winning, not they, surprised us.]

NOTE Do not confuse a gerund with a present participle, which also ends in *–ing.* A gerund serves as a noun, whereas a present participle serves as an adjective or as part of a verb phrase. A noun or a pronoun that is modified by a present participle does not need to be in the possessive case.

EXAMPLES   Suddenly, her Chihuahua started chasing a **boy** riding on a skateboard. [*Riding* is a participle that modifies the noun *boy.*]

All of the other children were impressed with the **boy's** riding. [*Riding* is a gerund modified by the possessive noun *boy's.*]

We heard **them** talking in the hallway. [*Talking* is a participle that modifies the pronoun *them.*]

Their talking in the hallway disturbed the class. [*Talking* is a gerund modified by the possessive pronoun *Their.*]

STYLE TIP

The form of a noun or a pronoun before an *–ing* word often depends on the meaning you want to express. If you want to emphasize the *–ing* word, use the possessive form. If you want to emphasize the noun or pronoun preceding the *–ing* word, do not use the possessive form.

EXAMPLES
Can you imagine **my** singing? [emphasis on *singing*]

Can you imagine **me** singing? [emphasis on *me*]

Reference Note
For more about **gerunds,** see page 68. For more about **present participles,** see page 176.

Possessive Pronouns
Mnemonic. If students have trouble distinguishing possessive pronouns and contractions, they may find the following sentences helpful as a memory aid for possessives and uses of the apostrophe:

Is the book Amy's?

If its cover's torn, it is.

If it's anyone's, it's hers.

USAGE

MINI-LESSON   **Mechanics**

Spelling. Tell students that it is common to confuse the possessive form *its* with the contraction *it's.* Similarly, the possessive form *whose* is often confused with the contraction *who's.* For more information on these and other troublesome pairs, refer students to **Chapter 15: Spelling.**

USAGE

Special Pronoun Problems
Rules 6i–k *(pp. 148–156)*

OBJECTIVES

- To select pronouns to use as appositives in sentences

- To select pronouns to complete elliptical constructions and to add words to make the meaning of the clauses clear

- To complete sentences by supplying reflexive and intensive pronouns

- To select standard forms of *who* and *whom* in sentences

DIRECT TEACHING

Modeling and Demonstration

Special Pronoun Problems. Model how to identify pronouns used as appositives with the example *Both teachers, Mr. Petrakis and she, have agreed to coach the academic team.* First, explain that an appositive is a noun or pronoun placed beside another noun or pronoun to identify or describe it. Then, ask if there is an appositive that identifies the noun *teachers* in the example. [*yes;* Mr. Petrakis *and* she] Next, ask what case *teachers* is in. [*nominative*] Ask what case *Mr. Petrakis* and *she* are in. [*nominative*] Point out that a pronoun used as an appositive should be in the same case as the word to which it refers. Now, have a volunteer use another example from this chapter to demonstrate how to identify pronouns used as appositives.

Exercise 4	Using Possessive Pronouns

Complete each of the following sentences with an appropriate possessive pronoun. Answers may vary.

EXAMPLE   **1.** _____ postponing the concert disappointed us fans.

     1. Their

1. her
2. mine
3. his
4. yours
5. Their
6. its
7. my
8. your
9. her
10. Her

1. I admire the work of Edmonia Lewis; _____ sculptures of famous people are outstanding.
2. His car looks great, but _____ is in better running condition.
3. Nathan is a dedicated student, but _____ winning the science contest was a surprise.
4. If you don't mind, I'd like to borrow _____.
5. _____ rescuing the kitten certainly was a humane act.
6. "Tell me about _____ rigging," the boat buyer asked the dealer.
7. "I hope _____ practicing drums isn't bothering you," I said.
8. "Thank you, _____ singing cheered us up," the residents of the hostel told the first-graders.
9. The skeptical executive asked, "Is this _____ recording?"
10. _____ playing the piano at such an early age astonished both her family and her teachers.

Special Pronoun Problems

Appositives

An **appositive** is a noun or a pronoun placed next to another noun or pronoun to identify or describe it.

6i. A pronoun used as an appositive should be in the same case as the word to which it refers.

EXAMPLES   Both teachers, Mr. Petrakis and **she,** have agreed to coach the academic team. [*Mr. Petrakis* and *she* identify the subject *teachers.* Since a subject of a verb is in the nominative case, an appositive identifying the subject is also in the nominative case.]

           For two of the major roles in *Purlie Victorious,* the director chose us, Joel and **me.** [*Joel* and *me* identify the direct object *us.* Since the direct object is in the objective case, an appositive identifying *us* is also in the objective case.]

Reference Note
For more information about **appositives,** see page 73.

RESOURCES

Special Pronoun Problems
Practice
- *Language & Sentence Skills Practice,* pp. 142–146
Differentiating Instruction
- *Developmental Language & Sentence Skills,* pp. 71–72

Exercise 5 **Selecting Pronouns to Use as Appositives**

For each of the following sentences, choose the correct pronoun form in parentheses.

EXAMPLE   **1.** Many of (*we, us*) seniors have part-time jobs.

      1. us

1. On the first day of school, the bus driver greeted (*we, us*) students with a smile.
2. Owen said that, for the first time, the basketball team had elected co-captains, Mario and (*he, him*).
3. Two students, Angela and (*she, her*), toured the Frederick Douglass National Historic Site in Washington, D.C.
4. Should (*we, us*) members of the fitness club sponsor the next walk-a-thon?
5. The new mural in the cafeteria was painted by two seniors, Chad and (*he, him*).
6. The audience gave the comedians, Ken and (*she, her*), a standing ovation.
7. Mr. Webster awarded a special prize to his four best students, Tim and (*we, us*).
8. Who could have guessed that the winners would be our friends, Ms. Stein and (*he, him*)?
9. However, Grandma hadn't taught her two granddaughters, Lisa and (*I, me*), everything about candle making yet.
10. After the match, the reigning doubles champions remained the same team, Robin and (*I, me*).

Elliptical Constructions

An ***elliptical construction*** is a clause from which words have been omitted. The word *than* or *as* often begins an elliptical construction.

6j. A pronoun following *than* or *as* in an elliptical construction should be in the same case as it would be if the construction were completed.

ELLIPTICAL	The tenor sang louder **than he.**
COMPLETED	The tenor sang louder **than he sang.**
ELLIPTICAL	The accident hurt Tim as much **as her.**
COMPLETED	The accident hurt Tim as much **as the accident hurt her.**

┌HELP─

Sometimes the pronoun *we* or *us* is followed by a noun appositive. To determine which pronoun form to use, try each form without the noun appositive.

CHOICES
(*We, Us*) seniors are in charge of the paper drive. [*We are* or *Us are* in charge?]

ANSWER
We seniors are in charge of the paper drive.

CHOICES
Coach Klein talked to (*we, us*) players about the regionals. [*To we* or *to us*?]

ANSWER
Coach Klein talked to **us** players about the regionals.

EXTENSION

Relating to Library Skills
You may wish to integrate the study of appositives with learning how to use the library. Have students familiarize themselves with biographies by locating in the library the biography/autobiography section and any biographical dictionaries or encyclopedias.

Have each student select a famous person to research. Each student should then write a short informative paragraph about his or her chosen subject. The paragraph should contain at least three sentences with appositives. Pair students and have them exchange paragraphs for evaluation.

DIFFERENTIATING INSTRUCTION

Special Education Students
Oral practice can be useful when teaching students to develop an ear for recognizing correct and incorrect usage. Recording the corrected exercises provides a set of model sentences for students to hear repeatedly without having to struggle with reading.

USAGE

┌─HELP─

In several sentences in Exercise 6, either pronoun form may be correct, depending on how the elliptical clause is completed. In such cases, give both correct forms.

1. they have lived in this area
2. he has been working there
3. I am
4. they blame us *or* we blame Taylor
5. it will benefit me
6. I am old
7. she understands him *or* I understand her
8. we play handball
9. he does
10. I can tutor Paula *or* she can tutor me

In an elliptical construction, the pronoun form determines the meaning of the construction. Therefore, you should be sure to use the pronoun form that expresses the meaning you intend. Notice how the meaning of each of the following sentences depends on the form of the pronoun in the elliptical construction.

EXAMPLES   I think I helped Macaulay more **than she.** [I think I helped Macaulay more *than she helped Macaulay.*]

I think I helped Macaulay more **than her.** [I think I helped Macaulay more *than I helped her.*]

Exercise 6   Selecting Pronouns for Elliptical Constructions

For each of the following sentences, add words to the elliptical clause to make its meaning clear. Include in the clause the correct pronoun form. Answers may vary.

EXAMPLE   1. I don't know Brenda as well as (*she, her*).

1. *as well as she knows Brenda*

   or

   as well as I know her

1. Have you and the rest of your family lived in this area as long as (*they, them*)?
2. Nolan has been working at that grocery store longer than (*he, him*).
3. I'm certain that Eva is shorter than (*I, me*) by at least four inches.
4. Surely they don't blame Taylor as much as (*we, us*).
5. The field trip next week will probably benefit Roger more than (*I, me*).
6. Can she really be six months older than (*I, me*)?
7. I understand him better than (*she, her*).
8. Do they play handball as often as (*we, us*)?
9. The results show that I do better on essay tests than (*he, him*).
10. Can Ms. Edwards tutor Paula as well as (*I, me*)?

Reflexive and Intensive Pronouns

Reflexive and intensive pronouns (sometimes called *compound personal pronouns*) have the same forms.

Reflexive and Intensive Pronouns		
	Singular	**Plural**
First Person	myself	ourselves
Second Person	yourself	yourselves
Third Person	himself	themselves
	herself	
	itself	

A reflexive pronoun ends in *–self* or *–selves* and refers to the subject of the sentence or clause. A reflexive pronoun may serve as a direct object, an indirect object, an object of a preposition, or a predicate nominative.

DIRECT OBJECT	I can't believe I hurt **myself** laughing.
INDIRECT OBJECT	With part of the money from his first paycheck, Daniel bought **himself** a new CD.
OBJECT OF A PREPOSITION	Clarice and Sarah Jane should be proud of **themselves** for completing the project early.
PREDICATE NOMINATIVE	Sharon is not **herself** today.

An *intensive pronoun* emphasizes its antecedent and has no grammatical function in the sentence.

EXAMPLES Simon **himself** developed both rolls of film. [*Himself* emphasizes *Simon.*]

Jorge and Kim installed the tape player **themselves.** [*Themselves* emphasizes *Jorge* and *Kim.*]

NOTE The words *hisself, theirself,* and *theirselves* are nonstandard.

6k. A pronoun ending in *–self* or *–selves* should not be used in place of a personal pronoun.

Avoid using a pronoun ending in *–self* or *–selves* when there is no word that it can refer to or emphasize.

NONSTANDARD	Mariah and myself went to the rodeo.
STANDARD	Mariah and **I** went to the rodeo.

NONSTANDARD	I know I can depend on Katrina and yourself.
STANDARD	I know I can depend on Katrina and **you.**

TIPS & TRICKS

Unlike a reflexive pronoun, an intensive pronoun may be omitted from a sentence without significantly changing the sentence's meaning. To determine whether a pronoun is intensive or reflexive, try removing it from the sentence.

INTENSIVE
Tamisha **herself** washed and waxed the car. [The sentence makes sense without the pronoun, so the pronoun is intensive.]

REFLEXIVE
Tamisha washed and waxed the car by **herself.** [The sentence does not make sense without the pronoun, so the pronoun is reflexive.]

Do not be misled, however, by a reflexive pronoun used as an indirect object, which may be omitted from a sentence without a significant change in meaning.

EXAMPLE
The children built **themselves** a treehouse. [The sentence still makes sense without the reflexive pronoun.]

DIRECT TEACHING

Correcting Misconceptions
Reflexive and Intensive Pronouns. Students may not realize that the *–self* form always refers to another noun or pronoun in the sentence. Tell students to find the word to which the *–self* form refers. If they cannot find such a word, remind them to replace the form *–self* with the appropriate case, person, and number form of a personal pronoun.

USAGE

Review E Using Reflexive and Intensive Pronouns

POSSIBLE ANSWERS

1. herself—intensive
2. myself—reflexive
3. myself—reflexive
4. themselves—reflexive
5. herself—intensive
6. himself—intensive
7. yourself—reflexive
8. myself—reflexive
9. ourselves—intensive
10. himself—reflexive

EXTENSION

Relating to Writing

Divide the class into groups of three or four. Tell each group to think of a famous person about whom the group can write questions using *who* and *whom*. For example, a group that chooses Stephen King might ask, "Who has been called the 'master of horror'?" Each group member should write and initial at least one question using *who* and another using *whom*.

When the questions have been formulated, ask a representative from each group to read the group's questions to the class. Students should try to guess the names of the other groups' subjects.

Reference Note

For more about **reflexive and intensive pronouns,** see page 150. For more about *hisself* and *theirselves,* see page 274.

Reference Note

For more information about **subordinate clauses,** see page 83.

Review E Using Reflexive and Intensive Pronouns

Complete each of the following sentences with an appropriate pronoun. Identify each pronoun you use as *reflexive* or *intensive.*

EXAMPLE
1. Diners at this restaurant serve _____ from a buffet.
1. *themselves—reflexive*

1. Will the principal _____ preside at the academic awards ceremony?
2. After I ace the test, I will give _____ a pat on the back.
3. I bought _____ a Scottish kilt at the import store.
4. Mark and Ginger should be ashamed of _____ for forgetting your birthday.
5. Evelyn _____ raked the leaves in the front yard.
6. Probably, the person who was most surprised was Bill _____.
7. If you are hungry, you can fix _____ a sandwich.
8. "Can I do the experiment by _____ instead of with a partner?" she asked.
9. We promised that we would do all the carpentry work for the gazebo _____.
10. He remained true to _____ and his own values.

Who and *Whom*

Like most personal pronouns, the pronoun *who* (*whoever*) has three case forms.

Nominative	who	whoever
Objective	whom	whomever
Possessive	whose	whoever

These pronouns may be used to form questions and to introduce subordinate clauses.

NOTE When *who,* *whom,* and *whose* are used to introduce adjective clauses, they are called **relative pronouns.**

In questions, *who* is used as a subject of a verb or as a predicate nominative. *Whom* is used as a direct object, an indirect object, or an object of a preposition.

Learning for Life

Continued on pp. 153–155

Writing a Police Report. Tell students that correct pronoun usage is especially important in situations where accuracy is absolutely necessary. Have each student imagine that he or she has witnessed an auto accident and has to write for a police report a detailed account of what happened.

On the chalkboard, copy the diagram and the list of details shown at right, and have each student write a report for the police based on this information.

NOMINATIVE	**Who** plays the part of Jack in the film *Titanic*? [*Who* is the subject of the verb *plays*.]
	Who could it be? [*Who* is a predicate nominative identifying the subject *it*.]
OBJECTIVE	**Whom** did Ella choose? [*Whom* is the direct object of the verb *did choose*.]
	With **whom** did Aaron Neville sing that ballad? [*Whom* is the object of the preposition *With*.]
	Whom did you ask the question? [*Whom* is the indirect object of the verb *did ask*.]

When choosing between *who* and *whom* in a subordinate clause, follow the steps shown in the following examples.

EXAMPLE	Nadine Gordimer, (*who, whom*) is famous for writing novels and short stories set in South Africa, won the Nobel Prize in literature in 1991.
STEP 1	Find the subordinate clause. In the sentence above, the subordinate clause is (*who, whom*) *is famous for writing novels and short stories set in South Africa.*
STEP 2	Decide how the pronoun is used in the clause—*subject, predicate nominative, direct object, indirect object,* or *object of a preposition*. In the example sentence, the pronoun serves as the subject of the verb *is*.
STEP 3	Determine the case for this use of the pronoun. A subject of a verb is in the nominative case.
STEP 4	Select the correct case form of the pronoun. The nominative form of the pronoun is *who*.
ANSWER	Nadine Gordimer, **who** is famous for writing novels and short stories set in South Africa, won the Nobel Prize in literature in 1991.

EXAMPLE	Harry Houdini, (*who, whom*) audiences adored, performed daring escape tricks.
STEP 1	The subordinate clause is (*who, whom*) *audiences adored.*
STEP 2	The pronoun serves as the direct object of the verb *adored*.
STEP 3	A direct object is in the objective case.
STEP 4	The objective form of the pronoun is *whom*.
ANSWER	Harry Houdini, **whom** audiences adored, performed daring escape tricks.

Remember that the case of a pronoun beginning a subordinate clause is not affected by any word outside the subordinate clause.

STYLE TIP

In informal situations, *who* is often used in place of *whom* to begin a question. In formal speaking and writing, however, the distinction between *who* and *whom* should be observed.

INFORMAL
Who did Jan call?

FORMAL
Whom did Jan call?
[direct object]

TIPS & TRICKS

If you have trouble choosing between *who* and *whom* in a question, turn the question into a statement. What you end up with may not be a good sentence, but it may help you decide how the pronoun functions and which case form to use.

QUESTION
(*Who, Whom*) did Jan call?

STATEMENT
Jan did call (*who, whom*). [The pronoun is the direct object and should be in the objective case.]

CORRECT
Whom did Jan call?

Special Pronoun Problems **153**

- Auto A is a red sport utility vehicle driven by a young man.

- Auto B is a blue pickup driven by a middle-aged woman.

RETEACHING

Who and Whom

Activity. If students have difficulty distinguishing between nominative and objective case, have them work in pairs to compose sentences containing *who* and *whom* clauses. Put the following clauses on the chalkboard:

1. whom we admire

2. who trusted us

3. who trotted past

4. who asked directions

5. whom we comforted

Have each pair of students write two sentences with each of the clauses. After they have finished, have pairs exchange sentences to check each other's work.

EXAMPLE	A plaque will be given to (*whoever, whomever*) catches the most fish.
STEP 1	The subordinate clause is (*whoever, whomever*) *catches the most fish.*
STEP 2	The pronoun serves as the subject of the verb *catches,* not as the object of the preposition *to.* (The entire subordinate clause is the object of *to.*)
STEP 3	A subject of a verb is in the nominative case.
STEP 4	The nominative form of the pronoun is *whoever.*
ANSWER	A plaque will be given to **whoever** catches the most fish.

When choosing between *who* and *whom* to begin a question or a subordinate clause, do not be misled by an expression consisting of a subject and a verb, such as *I think, he feels,* or *they believe.* Select the pronoun form you would use if the expression were not in the sentence.

EXAMPLES	**Who** do you suppose will win the election? [*Who* is the subject of the clause *Who will win the election.*]
	Roberta is the student **who** Mr. Hines thinks should be a chemist. [*Who* is the subject of the clause *who should be a chemist.*]

Exercise 7 Using *Who* and *Whom* Correctly

For each of the following sentences, choose the correct pronoun from the pair in parentheses. Then, tell how it is used in the subordinate clause—as a *subject, predicate nominative, direct object, indirect object,* or *object of a preposition.*

EXAMPLE	**1.** Can you tell me (*who, whom*) wrote *Bury My Heart at Wounded Knee*?
	1. who—subject

1. d.o.   **1.** The two people (*who, whom*) I like most are Will and Rosa.

2. p.n.   **2.** Someone called, but I don't know (*who, whom*) she was.

3. d.o.   **3.** Be sure to talk to (*whoever, whomever*) she interviewed.

4. s.   **4.** Several of the women (*who, whom*) had served on other committees were considered for the position.

5. i.o.   **5.** I can't remember (*who, whom*) I asked that question.

6. s.   **6.** Allen is the only person in school (*who, whom*) I think deserves the honor.

154   Chapter 6   Using Pronouns Correctly

Learning for Life   *Continued from p. 153*

- Auto C is a sports car driven by a young woman.

- Auto A ran a stop sign at First and Main streets and was hit by Auto B on Auto A's passenger side.

- Auto C stopped abruptly, denting Auto A's rear bumper.

Instruct students to use nominative, objective, and possessive case pronouns; pronouns as appositives and in elliptical

7. I never found out (*who*, *whom*) the driver was.
8. Was he the person to (*who*, *whom*) this package belongs?
9. It does not matter (*who*, *whom*) wins, as long as you do your best.
10. Ralph Bunche was a man (*who*, *whom*) many people respected for helping to found the United Nations.

7. p.n.
8. o.p.
9. s.
10. d.o.

Review F **Proofreading a Paragraph for Correct Pronoun Usage**

Each sentence in the following paragraph contains an error in pronoun usage. Identify each error, and then give the pronoun form that is correct according to the rules of formal, standard usage.

EXAMPLE **[1]** Satoshi Yabuuchi is the artist whom created the sculptures shown below.

  1. *whom—who*

[1] Satoshi Yabuuchi is a modern Japanese sculptor ~~whom~~ works with wood. [2] Critics generally agree that few sculptors today are as inventive as ~~him~~. [3] For example, look at some works by ~~he~~, which are on this page. [4] ~~Them~~ are figures of children's heads representing the seven days of the week. [5] Working with simple tools, Yabuuchi created ~~they~~ out of cypress. [6] ~~Whom~~ do you think could resist these engaging faces? [7] As you can see, Yabuuchi's imagination and sense of humor are important to ~~himself~~. [8] Other modern Japanese wood sculptors and ~~him~~ use techniques that date back more than 1,500 years. [9] Yabuuchi, ~~whom~~ was born in 1953, first studied European art but then became interested in wood carving and sculpture. [10] A number of works by ~~himself~~ also incorporate elements of American pop art.

1. who
2. he
3. him
4. They
5. them
6. Who
7. him
8. he
9. who

10. him

Satoshi Yabuuchi. Courtesy of Gallery Kitano, Tokyo, Japan.

Review F

DISTRIBUTED REVIEW
Have students review nouns and adjectives by identifying and labeling the nouns and adjectives (excluding the articles *a*, *an*, and *the*) in the first two sentences.

1. *Satoshi Yabuuchi—noun; modern—adjective; Japanese—adjective; sculptor—noun; wood—noun*

2. *Critics—noun; few—adjective; sculptors—noun; inventive—adjective*

PRACTICE

Guided and Independent

Reviews You may want to use **Review F** as independent practice after students have completed the **Oral Practice** on p. 156.

HOMEWORK

USAGE

constructions; reflexive and intensive pronouns; and *who* and *whom*. When students have completed their statements, have them exchange papers with a partner to check for correct pronoun usage.

Proofreading Sentences for Correct Pronoun Usage

Each of the following sentences has an error in pronoun usage. Read each sentence aloud. Identify the error, and then read the sentence aloud again, giving the pronoun form that is correct according to the rules of formal, standard usage.

EXAMPLE   1. Do you know whom won the women's 100-meter dash at the 2000 summer Olympic games?

       1. whom—who

1. "We sprinters are better than the ones on Central High's team," Phillip said, "so why aren't we doing better than them?"   **1. they**
2. Oscar, whom I believe is the most adventurous member of our family, is backpacking in the Appalachians.   **2. who**
3. Do you know who they gave the blue ribbon?   **3. whom**
4. When Anna and I were young, us children loved to ride on the tractor with my father.   **4. we**
5. John and myself wish we could excel in both baseball and football, as Deion Sanders does.   **5. I**
6. Who did the teacher choose to give the first speech?   **6. Whom**
7. When Andrew and I study together, nobody else in our class does better than us.   **7. we**
8. Kyle was here looking for Josh and yourself.   **8. you**
9. When we heard that Ms. Cohen was going to retire, all three of we seniors felt sad.   **9. us**
10. The two people who you can always rely on are Dave and she.
       10. whom

| STYLE | TIP |

Do not make the mistake of trying to sound formal by using *whom* in all cases. In formal speech and writing, determine the function of the pronoun and use the correct form—*who* for nominative case, *whom* for objective case.

"Whom shall I say is calling, sir?"

© 1999; reprinted courtesy of Bunny Hoest and Parade magazine.

Terms and numerals in brackets refer to concepts and rules tested by the items in the Chapter Review.

1. [6k]
2. [who, whom]
3. [6e]
4. [6i]
5. [6b]
6. [6j]
7. [who, whom]
8. [6d]
9. [or my] [6c, h]
10. [6h]

Chapter Review

A. Selecting Correct Forms of Pronouns

For each of the following sentences, choose the <u>correct pronoun form</u> in parentheses.

1. Greg and (*I*, *myself*) both got our driver's licenses on the same day.

2. My uncle Bill, after (*who*, <u>*whom*</u>) I am named, worked in the Peace Corps for two years after he had finished college.

3. As we waited at the starting line, I knew in my heart that the race was really going to be between Ted and (*I*, <u>*me*</u>).

4. At the town meeting, Ellen McCarthy asked, "If (<u>*we*</u>, *us*) citizens don't vote, how can we expect the situation to change?"

5. I thought Manuel was in Kansas City; so when he walked into the restaurant, I could hardly believe it was (<u>*he*</u>, *him*).

6. "Does anyone dance better than (<u>*she*</u>, *her*)?" I wondered, as I watched the dancer on the stage.

7. (<u>*Who*</u>, *Whom*) can describe the different shapes of the Navajo hogans?

8. The patrol officer gave her and (*I*, <u>*me*</u>) directions to the park.

9. The coach watched (<u>*me*</u>, *my*) running and decided to tap me for the marathon team.

10. Although the tenor was handsome and funny, what the crowd appreciated most was (*him*, <u>*his*</u>) singing.

B. Proofreading Sentences for Correct Pronoun Forms

For each of the following sentences that contains an incorrect pronoun form, identify the error and then give the correct form. If a sentence is already correct, write *C*.

11. he [6a]
12. Who [who, whom]
13. C [6h]
14. whom [who, whom]

11. Losing the playoff game was an experience from which you and ~~him~~ have learned a valuable lesson.

12. ~~Whom~~ do you think made this mistake?

13. We knew about his giving her a birthday present.

14. I would like to know ~~who~~ you are voting for in the next election.

ASSESSING

Monitoring Progress

Chapter Review. To assess student progress, you may want to compare the types of items missed on the **Diagnostic Preview** to those missed on the **Chapter Review**. If students have not made significant progress, you could refer them to **Chapter 16: Correcting Common Errors, Exercise 10.**

DIFFERENTIATING INSTRUCTION

Special Education Students

Students with visual-processing deficits might have trouble reading the sentences in the **Chapter Review** in a limited amount of time. To ensure that the testing situation is fair to these students, engage student helpers to read the sentences aloud. Student helpers should read the sentences slowly and pause after each sentence to allow their partners to record their answers. The helper may then re-read sentences if necessary.

USAGE

RESOURCES

Placement of Modifiers

Review
■ *Language & Sentence Skills Practice,* pp. 147–150

Assessment
■ *Holt Handbook Chapter Tests with Answer Key,* pp. 11–12, 54

EXTENSION

Relating to Literature

If D. H. Lawrence's poem "Snake" is available in your literature textbook, have students read and discuss the selection. Then, ask them to re-read it and to pay special attention to Lawrence's use of first-person pronouns. Ask students what effect the speaker's frequent use of the first person has in the poem. [*Students may suggest that it shows the speaker's self-centeredness, that it shows humankind as the center of the universe, or that it shows the separation of humans and nature.*] Explain to the students that this poem is an example of how the proper use of pronouns can convey meaning beyond that of the words themselves.

15. me [6c]
16. C [6e]
17. me [6d]
18. who [*who, whom*]
19. whoever [*who, whom*]
20. he [6j]
21. she [6a]
22. me [6c]
23. her [6c]
24. I [6k]
25. whom [*who, whom*]
26. C [6j]
27. Who [*who, whom*]
28. he [6a]
29. C [*who, whom*]
30. her [6i]

15. They watched her and I playing a game of tennis.
16. Nobody remembered to bring paper plates except him and her.
17. The reporter asked him and I a series of tough yet interesting questions.
18. Dolores is one person whom I am sure will be successful.
19. The prize will be awarded to whomever sells the most subscriptions.
20. Do you think I can play center on the basketball team even though I am shorter than him?
21. That is a matter about which you and her do not agree.
22. They respected Cornelius and I.
23. I had never met Gina and she before.
24. Sally and myself are planning to attend the weekend conference.
25. Was it Mr. Ross who they chose as their leader?
26. No one has worked harder than she.
27. Whom did you think it was on the phone?
28. We asked that Kara and him speak at the assembly.
29. No one knew who the woman in the mask could be.
30. I have already written to two of the women, she and Eva Dawson.

C. Proofreading a Paragraph for Correct Pronoun Usage

Most of the sentences in the following paragraph contain an error in pronoun usage. Identify each error, and then give the correct pronoun form. If a sentence is already correct, write *C*.

31. us [6i]
32. C [*who, whom*]
33. he [6j]
34. he [6k]
35. Who [*who, whom*]
36. we [6i]
37. he [6a]

[31] Jim Henson's gifts to all of we puppet fans were some of the most beloved characters in show business—Kermit the Frog, Miss Piggy, and the Cookie Monster, to name a few. [32] You probably know that Henson was the puppeteer who created the Muppets. [33] In the history of television, few puppeteers have been as successful as him. [34] Henson's associate Frank Oz and himself operated many of the Muppets. [35] Whom do you think spoke for Kermit on *Sesame Street* and *The Muppet Show* and in such movies as *The Muppets Take Manhattan*? [36] As you may have guessed, us Kermit fans were listening to Henson's voice. [37] Kermit and him started performing together in 1956 when Henson introduced his frog to the audience

of the late-night TV show *Sam and Friends* in Washington, D.C.
[38] Henson, ~~whom~~ originally fashioned Kermit out of an old coat
and a split Ping-Pong ball, revolutionized puppetry. **[39]** Henson's ability to give each of his puppets a life of its own earned ~~himself~~
international renown and many awards. **[40]** When Henson died in
1990, people throughout the world mourned his passing.

Writing Application

Using Pronouns in a Newspaper Article

Pronouns with Gerunds and Participles   Exam week is
approaching fast, and soon everyone will be busy studying for finals.
To help students cope with test anxiety, the editor of your school's
newspaper has decided to devote an entire issue to that subject. Write
an article to submit for publication in the paper. In your article, present some helpful tips for students studying for exams. Your article
may be humorous or serious. Use at least two pronouns preceding
gerunds and three pronouns preceding participles. Be sure to check
your writing for correct pronoun usage.

Prewriting   Brainstorm a list of strategies that have helped you
stay calm and collected through exams. If you wish, poll a number of
other students about their "survival" strategies. From your notes,
choose several of the most practical suggestions. Be sure to organize
your information in a rough outline.

Writing   Refer to your prewriting outline and notes as you write
your first draft. Begin with a lively, attention-grabbing opener.
Remember: You want to inform as well as to entertain the reader.

Revising   Ask a friend or classmate to read your article. Is it helpful
and interesting? Does it address the concerns of students preparing for
exams? If not, add, cut, and revise details. Be sure you have used at
least two gerunds and three participles preceded by pronouns.

Publishing   Read through your article once, checking for errors in
pronoun usage. Then, proofread for other errors in grammar, usage,
punctuation, and spelling. To publish your articles, you and your classmates may want to create a bulletin board display for your classroom
or for another area in your school.

38. who [*who, whom*]
39. him [6k]
40. C [6h]

APPLICATION

Writing Application
Prewriting Tip. Before students
begin this **Writing Application,** you
may want to review the information on gerunds and participles in
Chapter 3 to help clear up any confusion students may have about the
verbals and to allow them to focus
on the use of pronouns as they write
and revise.

Scoring Rubric. While you will want
to pay particular attention to students'
use of personal pronouns preceding
gerunds and participles, you will also
want to evaluate overall writing performance. You could give a split score
to separate development and clarity
of the composition from skill in usage.

CHAPTER

7

Clear Reference
Pronouns and Antecedents

INTRODUCING THE CHAPTER

- This chapter helps students become aware of four pronoun reference problems.
- The chapter concludes with a **Chapter Review** including a **Writing Application** involving writing a letter using clear pronoun reference.
- For help in integrating this chapter with writing assignments, see the **Teaching Strands** chart on pp. T24–T25.

Diagnostic Preview

A. Correcting Faulty Pronoun References

Each of the following sentences contains at least one ambiguous, general, weak, or indefinite pronoun reference. Revise the sentences to correct each faulty pronoun reference.

EXAMPLE   1. On this train, they served meals without charge.

1. *On this train, meals were served without charge.*

or

On this train, meals were included in the ticket price.

┌─HELP─┐

Although some sentences in Part A may be correctly revised in more than one way, you need to give only one revision for each.

Numerals in brackets refer to rules tested by items in the Diagnostic Preview.

1. [7d]
2. [7d]
3. [7c]
4. [7c]
5. [7c]
6. [7b]
7. [7e]
8. [7b, c]

1. Golf wouldn't cost me quite so much if I didn't lose so many in the rough.
2. The radiator was leaking badly; it ran all over the garage floor.
3. In the log cabin, Ed checked the fuel supply; in those days this might mean the difference between life and death.
4. She overcame her hip injury, which doctors had said was nearly impossible.
5. Her spelling and sentence variety are not good, but most of it is due to carelessness.
6. Ruth saw Julie when she was in town last week.
7. In yesterday's editorial, it says that the mayor has failed to live up to his campaign promises.
8. The witness testified that she had seen the accused when she was eating dinner in the dining car, which convinced the jury that she had been on the train.

CHAPTER RESOURCES

Internet
- Web resources: go.hrw.com

go.
hrw
.com

Practice & Review
- *Language & Sentence Skills Practice,* pp. 156–165
- *Language & Sentence Skills Practice Answer Key,* pp. 62–65

Application & Enrichment
- *Language & Sentence Skills Practice,* pp. 155, 166–169
- *Language & Sentence Skills Practice Answer Key,* pp. 62, 66–67

9. In Washington they are skeptical about the success of the new federal farm program.

10. The library does not have enough of the books in greatest demand by students writing research papers, which makes it difficult to find the information you need.

B. Revising Sentences to Correct Faulty Pronoun References

Revise the following sentences to correct each ambiguous, general, weak, or indefinite pronoun reference.

EXAMPLE   1. I enjoy reading science fiction; the one I am reading now, *Contact,* was written by Carl Sagan.

    1. *I enjoy reading science fiction; the novel I am reading now,* Contact, *was written by Carl Sagan.*

or

I enjoy reading science fiction novels such as the one I am reading now, Contact. *It was written by Carl Sagan.*

┌HELP─

Although some sentences in Part B may be correctly revised in more than one way, you need to give only one revision for each.

11. The scientist Carl Sagan wrote and lectured extensively about the possibility of life on other planets, which contributed to his appeal to the general public.

12. Johnny Carson liked Sagan's informal science lectures so much that he appeared many times on *The Tonight Show* after his first appearance in 1972.

13. Sagan came to be known around the world as an expert in the study of extraterrestrial life, even though he had never seen one.

14. In Daniel Cohen's book *Carl Sagan: Superstar Scientist,* it tells about Sagan's childhood in Brooklyn and about his early fascination with the stars and planets.

15. As a boy, Sagan discovered the genre of science fiction, and he read them regularly.

16. At the University of Chicago, they had a highly regarded astronomy department, so Sagan enrolled there in 1951.

17. Sagan served as a consultant for many of NASA's major programs, including the *Mariner, Viking,* and *Voyager* planetary expeditions; this resulted in such awards as the NASA Medal for Distinguished Public Service and the NASA Medal for Exceptional Scientific Achievement.

18. When my father saw Sagan on the popular television series *Cosmos,* he was greatly impressed.

9. [7e]
10. [7c, e]

11. [7c]
12. [7b]
13. [7d]
14. [7e]
15. [7d]
16. [7e]
17. [7c]
18. [7b]

Diagnostic Preview   **161**

Differentiating Instruction

■ *Developmental Language & Sentence Skills,* pp. 73–76

■ *Developmental Language & Sentence Skills Guided Practice Teacher's Notes and Answer Key,* p. 20

Assessment

■ *Holt Handbook Chapter Tests with Answer Key,* pp. 13–14, 54

USAGE

ASSESSING

Entry-Level Assessment

Diagnostic Preview. You can use the preview to pinpoint the exercises on which students should concentrate and the problems students should target in their writing.

Diagnostic Preview: Part A
Correcting Faulty Pronoun References

POSSIBLE ANSWERS

Revisions will vary.

1. Golf wouldn't cost me quite so much if I didn't lose so many balls in the rough.
2. The radiator was leaking badly; fluid ran all over the garage floor.
3. In the log cabin, Ed checked the fuel supply; in those days the amount of fuel remaining might mean the difference between life and death.
4. She overcame her hip injury, although doctors had said recovery was nearly impossible.
5. Her spelling and sentence variety are not good, but most of her errors are due to carelessness.
6. When Ruth was in town last week, she saw Julie.
7. Yesterday's editorial says that the mayor has failed to live up to his campaign promises.
8. The witness testified to having seen the accused eating dinner in the dining car. This testimony convinced the jury that the accused had been on the train.
9. In Washington, politicians are skeptical about the success of the new federal farm program.
10. Because the library does not have enough of the books in greatest demand for writing research papers, students have difficulty finding the information they need.

Diagnostic Preview   **161**

Usage

Diagnostic Preview: Part B
Revising Sentences to Correct Faulty Pronoun References

POSSIBLE ANSWERS

11. The scientist Carl Sagan's extensive writing and lecturing about the possibility of life on other planets contributed to his appeal to the general public.

12. Because Johnny Carson liked Sagan's informal science lectures so much, Sagan appeared many times on *The Tonight Show* after his first appearance in 1972.

13. Sagan came to be known around the world as an expert in the study of extraterrestrial life, even though he had never seen an extraterrestrial.

14. Daniel Cohen's book *Carl Sagan: Superstar Scientist* tells about Sagan's childhood in Brooklyn and about his early fascination with the stars and planets.

15. As a boy, Sagan discovered the genre of science fiction and read science fiction novels regularly.

16. Because the University of Chicago had a highly regarded astronomy department, Sagan enrolled there in 1951.

17. Sagan served as a consultant for many of NASA's major programs, including the *Mariner, Viking,* and *Voyager* planetary expeditions. His involvement with these expeditions resulted in such awards as the NASA Medal for Distinguished Public Service and the NASA Medal for Exceptional Scientific Achievement.

18. My father was greatly impressed when he saw Sagan on the popular television series *Cosmos.*

19. That Sagan's novel *Contact* explores a number of scientific and social issues that arise when extraterrestrial life makes contact with earthlings made me want to read some of Sagan's nonfiction books, of course.

20. Carl Sagan died on December 20, 1996, six months before the movie version of *Contact* was released.

162 Clear Reference

19. [7c]
20. [7e]

Reference Note
For more information about **pronouns and antecedents,** see page 7.

Reference Note
For more about **agreement between pronouns and their antecedents,** see page 124.

19. Sagan's novel *Contact* explores a number of scientific and social issues that arise when extraterrestrial life makes contact with earthlings; of course, this made me want to read some of his nonfiction books.

20. Carl Sagan died on December 20, 1996, and it was six months before the movie version of *Contact* was released.

Pronouns and Their Antecedents

One cause of ambiguity in writing is the use of pronouns without clear antecedents. A pronoun generally has no definite meaning in itself. Its meaning is clear only when the reader knows to which word or word group the pronoun refers. This word or word group is called the *antecedent* of the pronoun.

7a. A pronoun should refer clearly to its antecedent.

In the following examples, arrows point from the pronouns to their antecedents.

EXAMPLES
Steven wanted to visit the Museum of Modern Art, but **it** had closed for the day.

Amy promised Jim **she** would help **him** clean the kitchen.

The Sanchezes have a new sailboat on **which they** intend to cruise to the Bahamas.

Handing Shina the novel, the librarian told **her,** "**This** won the Pulitzer Prize."

Often, a pronoun reference is unclear due to a lack of agreement between a pronoun and its antecedent.

UNCLEAR Eli is always thinking about computers. It seems to be his only interest.

CLEAR Eli is always thinking about computers. **They** seem to be his only interest.

UNCLEAR You should learn how to use several different Internet search engines. It can make research much easier.

CLEAR You should learn how to use several different Internet search engines. **They** can make research much easier.

162 Chapter 7 Clear Reference

MINI-LESSON Mechanics

Punctuating Introductory Elements.
The second example under **Rule 7b** is corrected by using an introductory phrase or clause. Remind students that some kinds of introductory phrases and clauses are followed by commas. For more about punctuating introductory elements, refer students to **Chapter 13: Punctuation.**

Ambiguous Reference

7b. Avoid an *ambiguous reference,* which occurs when any one of two or more words could be a pronoun's antecedent.

A simple way to correct some ambiguous pronoun references is to replace the pronoun with an appropriate noun.

AMBIGUOUS   The partnership between Jones and Potter ended when he withdrew the firm's money from the bank and flew to Brazil. [To whom does *he* refer: *Jones* or *Potter*?]

CLEAR   The partnership between Jones and Potter ended when **Jones** withdrew the firm's money from the bank and flew to Brazil.

CLEAR   The partnership between Jones and Potter ended when **Potter** withdrew the firm's money from the bank and flew to Brazil.

If replacing the pronoun with a noun results in awkward repetition, rephrase the sentence to eliminate the ambiguous pronoun reference.

AMBIGUOUS   The mayor appointed Ms. Vásquez chairperson of the committee because she was convinced of the need for an environmental study. [To whom does *she* refer: *mayor* or *Ms. Vásquez*?]

CLEAR   Convinced of the need for an environmental study, the mayor appointed Ms. Vásquez chairperson of the committee.

CLEAR   Because Ms. Vásquez was convinced of the need for an environmental study, the mayor appointed her chairperson of the committee.

Exercise 1   **Correcting Ambiguous Pronoun References**

Revise each of the following sentences to correct the ambiguous pronoun reference.

EXAMPLE   1. As soon as Lucinda arrived with Gwen, we asked her to tell us about the trip to the Yukon.

   1. *As soon as Lucinda arrived with Gwen, we asked Lucinda to tell us about the trip to the Yukon.*

         or

   As soon as Lucinda arrived with Gwen, we asked Gwen to tell us about the trip to the Yukon.

┌─**HELP**─

As you may remember, a noun is a word that stands for a certain person, place, thing, or idea. When you write or speak, make sure that your readers or listeners can tell exactly which noun you are replacing with each pronoun you use. If you use the pronoun *it,* for example, make sure your readers or listeners can tell exactly which thing or idea the word *it* refers to.

┌─**HELP**─

Although some sentences in Exercise 1 may be correctly revised in more than one way, you need to give only one revision for each.

Ambiguous Reference   **163**

Exercise 1 Correcting Ambiguous Pronoun References

POSSIBLE ANSWERS

1. After dropping Tom off, Dad went to class.

2. One of the passengers accused the bus driver of not knowing the route very well.

3. The treasurer became very much alarmed right after the accountant sent him a report.

4. After the sergeant reported to the lieutenant, the lieutenant informed the captain of the situation.

5. We washed the jars after separating them from the bottles.

6. This lever that controls the conveyor belt is broken. I want you to get it fixed.

7. Leta offered Molly a bowl of plantain porridge, a meal that Molly thoroughly enjoyed.

8. That cord shouldn't be tangled around the leg of a chair. People can trip and break the cord and hurt themselves.

9. While the musicians were talking to some of the dancers, the dancers were called onstage.

10. Set the first reel next to the second one. Then, make sure the case of the first reel isn't cracked.

DIFFERENTIATING INSTRUCTION

English-Language Learners

General Strategies. The English pronoun *it* may seem doubly vague to native speakers of languages in which neuter gender is nonexistent or used minimally. In Romance languages, for example, masculine or feminine pronouns may be used to refer to things as well as to people.

1. Dad dropped Tom off, and then he went to class.

2. One of the passengers told the bus driver that she didn't know the route very well.

3. Right after the accountant sent in a report to the treasurer, he became very much alarmed.

4. After the sergeant reported to the lieutenant, he informed the captain of the situation.

5. We separated the jars from the bottles and washed them.

6. This lever controls the conveyor belt; it's broken, and I want you to get it fixed.

7. Leta offered Molly a bowl of plantain porridge, which she thoroughly enjoyed.

8. That cord shouldn't be tangled around the leg of a chair where people can trip and break it and hurt themselves.

9. While the musicians were talking to some of the dancers, they were called onstage.

10. Set the first reel next to the second one and make sure its case isn't cracked.

General Reference

7c. Avoid a *general reference,* which is the use of a pronoun that refers to a general idea rather than to a specific antecedent.

The pronouns that are most commonly used in general references are *it, that, this,* and *which.* To correct a general pronoun reference, either replace the pronoun with an appropriate noun or rephrase the sentence.

GENERAL   Great ships were moving slowly up the harbor; tugs and ferryboats scurried in and out among them; here and there a white cabin cruiser sliced through the blue water under the suspension bridge. It was thrilling to a young farmer. [*It* has no specific antecedent.]

CLEAR   Great ships were moving slowly up the harbor; tugs and ferryboats scurried in and out among them; here and there a white cabin cruiser sliced through the blue water under the suspension bridge. **The sight** was thrilling to a young farmer.

GENERAL   In her act Mariana told jokes, did impersonations, and sang comic songs. This amused her audience. [*This* has no specific antecedent.]

CLEAR   Mariana **amused her audience by** telling jokes, doing impersonations, and singing comic songs.

CONTENT-AREA CONNECTIONS

Life Skills. Explain to students that in applications for college, scholarships, and jobs, applicants are asked to provide references. The term *reference* in this context means people who can testify to the applicant's character and ability. The actual written testimonials attesting to a person's character and qualifications are also called *references.*

GENERAL	More than half of the elm trees along the street had to be cut down, which was unfortunate. [*Which* has no specific antecedent.]
CLEAR	That more than half of the elm trees along the street had to be cut down was unfortunate.
CLEAR	Unfortunately, more than half of the elm trees along the street had to be cut down.

Exercise 2 Revising Sentences to Correct General Pronoun References

Revise the following sentences to correct each general pronoun reference.

EXAMPLE
1. Carla was declared the winner of the debate, which didn't surprise me.

1. *That Carla was declared the winner of the debate didn't surprise me.*

or

The debate, which Carla won, didn't surprise me.

1. In the 1800s, Spanish-language newspapers sprang up throughout the Southwest. This helped many Mexican Americans maintain ties to their culture.
2. Clarissa's four-year-old sister brought a frog inside and let it loose, which made Clarissa shriek.
3. I enjoyed the author's style and the types of characters she wrote about. It made me want to read her other books.
4. Rabbi Meyer came to the house daily, from which a sturdy friendship grew.
5. A great deal of effort went into planning that expedition, hiring the right people, and anticipating every emergency, which accounts for the success of the undertaking.
6. Much songbird habitat in North America is rapidly being destroyed, and this greatly concerns ornithologists.
7. The children were asleep, all the chores were done, and the house was clean. It was almost shocking to the young parents.
8. Complex operations can be performed with a single click. Please remember that when you program your trackball buttons.
9. A sailboat with a tall mast was moving toward the bridge. That caused the bridge to open and traffic to stop.
10. Last night in the mountains, it started to snow heavily. This made a lot of skiers, including me, quite happy.

HELP

Although some sentences in Exercise 2 may be correctly revised in more than one way, you need to give only one revision for each.

Exercise 2 Revising Sentences to Correct General Pronoun References

ANSWERS
Revisions will vary.

1. In the 1800s, the emergence of Spanish-language newspapers in the Southwest helped many Mexican Americans maintain ties to their culture.
2. Clarissa shrieked when her four-year-old sister brought a frog inside and let it loose.
3. I enjoyed the author's style and the type of characters she wrote about so much that I want to read her other books.
4. A sturdy friendship grew from Rabbi Meyer's daily visits to the house.
5. The success of the undertaking resulted from the great deal of effort that went into planning the expedition, hiring the right people, and anticipating every emergency.
6. Ornithologists are greatly concerned because much songbird habitat in North America is rapidly being destroyed.
7. That the children were asleep, all the chores were done, and the house was clean was almost shocking to the young parents.
8. When you program your trackball buttons, please remember that complex operations can be performed with a single click.
9. The bridge opened and traffic stopped because a sailboat with a tall mast was moving toward the bridge.
10. Last night in the mountains, it started to snow heavily. The snowfall made a lot of skiers, including me, quite happy.

USAGE

Review A Correcting Ambiguous and General Pronoun References

POSSIBLE ANSWERS

1. Benito Pablo Juárez was a liberal reformer and president of Mexico during the 1860s and early 1870s. His help in molding Mexico into a nation established him as Mexico's foremost national hero.

2. Juárez, who was of Zapotec ancestry, was a serious, hard-working man; these qualities are suggested in this photograph.

3. A professor who obviously had researched Juárez's life kept the students' attention by describing Juárez's childhood in Oaxaca, his interest in law and social reforms, and his military successes.

4. One of the students told the professor that he hoped the professor would write a biography of Juárez someday.

5. Juárez, a state governor in 1855, opposed General Santa Anna and was exiled.

6. Juárez later returned to Mexico and joined a brave and risky endeavor—the revolution to overthrow Santa Anna, who had seized control of the government.

7. Because France installed Maximilian as emperor of Mexico in 1864, Juárez moved his capital from Mexico City. Maximilian, however, was not popular.

8. The collapse of Maximilian's government in 1867 opened the way for Juárez to be reelected president.

9. Juárez's interest in education and his help in establishing free public schools in Mexico had a major impact, of course, on Mexico's people.

10. The government of José de la Cruz Porfirio Díaz, who overthrew Juárez's successor and governed Mexico longer than any other person, was certainly a contrast to Juárez's government.

USAGE

166 Clear Reference

─HELP─

Some sentences in Review A may be revised in more than one way. You may find it helpful to read all of the sentences before you begin to revise them. Context may make it easier to identify the antecedents for some of the pronouns.

Review A Correcting Ambiguous and General Pronoun References

Revise the following sentences to correct all ambiguous and general pronoun references.

EXAMPLE
1. After Maximilian was defeated by Juárez in 1867, he was reelected president of Mexico.

1. *After Maximilian was defeated by Juárez in 1867, Juárez was reelected president of Mexico.*

1. Benito Pablo Juárez was a liberal reformer and president of Mexico during the 1860s and early 1870s, and he helped mold Mexico into a nation. That established Juárez as Mexico's foremost national hero.

2. Juárez, of Zapotec ancestry, was a serious, hard-working man, which is suggested in this photograph.

3. A professor who obviously had researched Juárez's life described his childhood in Oaxaca, his interest in law and social reforms, and his military successes. This kept the students' attention.

4. One of the students told the professor that he hoped he would write a biography of Juárez someday.

5. Juárez, a state governor in 1855, and General Santa Anna were on opposing sides, and he was exiled.

6. Juárez later returned to Mexico and joined the revolution to overthrow Santa Anna, who had seized control of the government. It was a brave and risky endeavor.

7. France installed Maximilian as emperor of Mexico in 1864, and Juárez moved his capital from Mexico City, but he was not popular.

8. Maximilian's government collapsed in 1867, which opened the way for Juárez to be reelected president.

9. Juárez was interested in education and helped to establish free public schools in Mexico. This, of course, had a major impact on Mexico's people.

10. José de la Cruz Porfirio Díaz overthrew Juárez's successor and governed Mexico longer than any other person. It was certainly a contrast to Juárez's government.

Weak Reference

7d. Avoid a *weak reference,* which occurs when a pronoun refers to an antecedent that has been suggested but not expressed.

To correct a weak pronoun reference, either replace the pronoun with an appropriate noun or give the pronoun a clear antecedent.

WEAK   The people want honest public servants, but many voters think that is not a virtue of any of the candidates. [The antecedent of *that* is not expressed.]

CLEAR   The people want honest public servants, but many voters think that **honesty** is not a virtue of any of the candidates.

WEAK   We spent the entire day on a fishing boat, but we didn't catch a single one. [The antecedent of *one* is not expressed.]

CLEAR   We spent the entire day on a fishing boat, but we didn't catch a single **fish.**

CLEAR   We spent the entire day on a fishing boat, trying to catch **some fish,** but we didn't catch a single **one.**

Exercise 3   Revising Sentences to Correct Weak Pronoun References

Revise each of the following sentences to correct the weak pronoun reference.

EXAMPLE   1. We went to the card shop but did not buy any.

    1. We went to the card shop but did not buy any cards.

or

We went shopping for cards but did not buy any.

1. I take many photographs with my camera and consider it an enjoyable hobby.
2. Being neighborly is important because you may need their help someday in an emergency.
3. Nguyen has become a virtuoso violinist, but he has never owned a valuable one.
4. Luis is highly intelligent, but he hides it from people he doesn't know well.
5. Our guide said the Pueblo village was well worth seeing, but it would take three hours.
6. Evan wanted to be like the public speakers who seem so relaxed, but he rarely got the chance to do any.

┌HELP┐

Although some sentences in Exercise 3 may be correctly revised in more than one way, you need to give only one revision for each.

USAGE

Weak Reference and Indefinite Reference

Rules 7d, e *(pp. 167–170)*

OBJECTIVES

- **To revise sentences to correct weak pronoun references**
- **To revise sentences to correct indefinite pronoun references**

DIRECT TEACHING

Modeling and Demonstration

Weak Reference. Model how to revise sentences to correct weak pronoun references by using the example *Adrian is very athletic. Two of these are soccer and track.* First, ask whether there is a pronoun in the second sentence. [*yes; these*] Then, ask whether *these* has an antecedent. [*no*] Explain that the lack of an antecedent is a problem called weak reference and must be corrected. Ask how the second sentence could be revised. [*Adrian is very athletic. Two of the sports he likes are soccer and track.*] Now, have a volunteer use another example from this chapter to demonstrate how to revise sentences to correct weak pronoun references.

Exercise 3   Revising Sentences to Correct Weak Pronoun References

ANSWERS
Revisions will vary.

1. I take many pictures with my camera and consider photography an enjoyable hobby.
2. Being neighborly is important because neighbors may someday need each other's help in an emergency.
3. Nguyen has become a virtuoso violinist, but he has never owned a valuable violin.

Exercise 3 · Revising Sentences to Correct Weak Pronoun References

ANSWERS continued

4. Luis is highly intelligent, but he hides his intelligence from people he doesn't know well.

5. Our guide said the Pueblo village was well worth seeing but that a proper tour of it would take three hours.

6. Evan wanted to be like the public speakers who seem so relaxed, but he rarely got the chance to do any public speaking.

7. The sisters traveled to their family's ancestral land, hoping to meet some of their relatives.

8. Even though the roommates spent two-and-a-half hours at the laundry room, they didn't finish all the laundry.

9. I'd love antique collecting, but I can't afford antiques.

10. Prospective students must fill out a college admission form if they want to get into a college.

Exercise 3

DISTRIBUTED REVIEW

To review classifications of sentences according to structure, students could look at sentences 1–3 to find the following kinds of sentences:

1. a complex sentence [*sentence 2*]
2. a simple sentence with a compound verb [*sentence 1*]
3. a compound sentence [*sentence 3*]

STYLE TIP

The indefinite use of *it* in familiar expressions such as *it is raining, it seems,* and *it is late* is acceptable.

COMPUTER TIP

You can use a word processor's search function to locate all occurrences of the pronoun *it* in a piece of your writing. Every time the pronoun appears, check its reference carefully. Is the reference clear, or is it general or indefinite? You can use the same procedure to check your use of the pronouns *this, that, which, such, they,* and *you.*

7. The sisters traveled to their family's ancestral land, hoping to meet some.

8. Even though the roommates spent two-and-a-half hours at the laundry room, they didn't finish it all.

9. I'd love antique collecting, but I can't afford them.

10. Prospective students must fill out a college admission form if they want to get into one.

Indefinite Reference

7e. Avoid an *indefinite reference*—the use of a pronoun that refers to no particular person or thing and that is unnecessary to the structure and meaning of a sentence.

The pronouns that commonly cause indefinite references are *you, it,* and *they.* To correct an indefinite reference, rephrase the sentence, eliminating the unnecessary pronoun.

INDEFINITE	In some countries, you do not dare express your political views openly. [*You* and *your* do not refer to any specific person.]
CLEAR	In some countries, **people** do not dare express **their** political views openly.
INDEFINITE	In the magazine article, it describes the aftermath of the eruption of Mount Pinatubo. [*It* does not refer to any specific thing.]
CLEAR	**The magazine article describes** the aftermath of the eruption of Mount Pinatubo.
INDEFINITE	Each summer in Cherokee, North Carolina, they present the historical drama *Unto These Hills* outdoors. [*They* does not clearly refer to any specific group.]
CLEAR	Each summer in Cherokee, North Carolina, **the historical drama *Unto These Hills* is presented** outdoors.

Exercise 4 · Revising Sentences to Correct Indefinite Pronoun References

Revise each of the following sentences to correct the indefinite pronoun references.

EXAMPLE
1. In the newsmagazine, it profiles each of the presidential candidates.

1. *The newsmagazine profiles each of the presidential candidates.*

Learning for Life

Writing an Ad. Remind students that in advertising, the success of an ad campaign can depend on whether potential customers associate a slogan with the advertised product. Ask students to suggest familiar slogans that include the word *it,* or suggest the following slogans. Record slogans on the chalkboard.

"Don't leave home without it."
"Try it, you'll like it."
"I'm worth it."
"It makes all the difference."

1. In many households in India, they serve a flat, pancakelike bread called a *chapati*.
2. In large cities you often don't feel comfortable calling the mayor about problems.
3. In the newspaper article, it calls this presidential election the closest race in many years.
4. Each summer in Round Top, Texas, they have an international music festival that is extremely popular.
5. In the telephone book, it lists only five music stores in the city.
6. Underneath the headline, it read, "Related story on page 12."
7. Only about six feet from shore, it drops off about twenty feet.
8. During much of the colonial period in New England, you were supposed to obey strict regulations governing Sabbath activities.
9. After the age of ten, you just don't do certain things.
10. Throughout the book, it uses expressions unique to Maine.

DRABBLE reprinted by permission of United Feature Syndicate, Inc.

Indefinite Reference   **169**

Exercise 4 **Revising Sentences to Correct Indefinite Pronoun References**

ANSWERS
Revisions will vary.

1. A flat, pancakelike bread called a *chapati* is served in many households in India.
2. People in large cities often don't feel comfortable calling the mayor about problems.
3. According to the newspaper article, this presidential election is the closest race in many years.
4. Each summer in Round Top, Texas, there is an international music festival that is extremely popular.
5. The telephone book lists only five music stores in the city.
6. Underneath the headline was the line "Related story on page 12."
7. Only about six feet from shore, the bottom drops off about twenty feet.
8. During much of the colonial period in New England, citizens were supposed to obey strict regulations governing Sabbath activities.
9. After the age of ten, people just don't do certain things.
10. Throughout the book are expressions unique to Maine.

USAGE

EXTENSION

Relating to Writing
Have each student search for unclear pronoun references in a paper he or she has written for a social studies class. The best papers for this assignment are short biographies of individuals or explanations of events or concepts in history or government. Ask students to circle each pronoun and its antecedent, decide whether each pronoun reference is clear, and revise sentences with unclear references.

Divide the class into groups of four, and have each group pick one slogan. Then, have each group write an ad to accompany the slogan. The text of the ad should make the reference to the pronoun *it* in the slogan clear. The ad could be for print, billboard, radio, or television. After groups have finished, have them exchange ads to check each other's pronoun references. Invite follow-up discussion about problems with vague language in ad campaigns.

ANSWERS

Revisions will vary.

1. The Irish author Christy Brown (1932–1981) was extremely talented, but he had to overcome great physical challenges for his talent to be recognized.

2. Brown's autobiography, *My Left Foot,* tells about his lifelong struggle with a debilitating illness.

3. Some biographies don't invite readers' emotional involvement, but Brown's autobiography is very personal.

4. Brown had cerebral palsy, which is a type of brain damage leading to lack of muscle control.

5. In most cases of cerebral palsy, the cause of the damage, which occurs before or shortly after birth, cannot be determined.

6. The book explains how Brown learned to write and type with his only functioning limb—his left foot.

7. Brown married in 1972, and his wife's help contributed to Brown's improved muscular control.

8. Brown excelled as a writer, but locating his books in libraries and bookstores in the United States is sometimes difficult.

9. Brown was acclaimed as a poet as well as a novelist, but many people have never read any of his poems.

10. The following books by Brown are listed in the card catalog: *My Left Foot, Down All the Days, A Shadow on Summer,* and *Wild Grow the Lilies.*

┌HELP┐

Although some sentences in the Oral Practice may be correctly revised in more than one way, you need to give only one revision for each.

Oral Practice | **Revising Sentences to Correct Weak and Indefinite Pronoun References**

Read each of the following sentences aloud. Then, identify each weak pronoun reference or indefinite pronoun reference. Finally, read each sentence aloud again, revising it to correct the error in pronoun reference.

EXAMPLE

1. Many writers create fictional stories about overcoming great odds, but I prefer it when they are real people.

1. *it, they—Many writers create fictional stories about overcoming great odds, but I prefer stories about real people.*

1. The Irish author Christy Brown (1932–1981) was extremely talented, but he had to overcome great physical challenges for it to be recognized.

2. In Brown's autobiography, *My Left Foot,* it tells about his lifelong struggle with a debilitating illness.

3. In some biographies, you don't become emotionally involved, but Brown's autobiography is very personal.

4. Brown had a disorder they call cerebral palsy, which is a type of brain damage leading to lack of muscle control.

5. In most cases of cerebral palsy, you cannot determine the cause of the damage, which occurs before or shortly after birth.

6. In the book, they explain how Brown learned to write and type with his only functioning limb—his left foot.

7. Brown married in 1972, and her help contributed to Brown's improved muscular control.

8. Brown excelled as a writer, but locating them in libraries and bookstores in the United States is sometimes difficult.

9. Brown was acclaimed as a poet as well as a novelist, but many people have never read one.

10. In the card catalog it lists these books by Brown: *My Left Foot, Down All the Days, A Shadow on Summer,* and *Wild Grow the Lilies.*

Numerals in brackets refer to rules tested by items in the Chapter Review.

1. [7b]
2. [7c]
3. [7a]
4. [7c]
5. [7b]
6. [7c]
7. [7a]
8. [7b]
9. [7c]
10. [7a]

Chapter Review

A. Correcting Ambiguous and General References

Most of the following sentences contain ambiguous or general references. Revise each faulty sentence. If a sentence is already correct, write *C*.

1. Margaret e-mailed Gretchen about the interesting Web pages she had seen at the Web site of the British Broadcasting Corporation (BBC).

2. The BBC had asked two British writers, Malcolm Bradbury and J. G. Ballard, each to name the ten greatest writers of the last one thousand years, which resulted in the Web page that Margaret saw.

3. Gretchen read Bradbury's list; she found it surprising.

4. Bradbury's number-one writer, for example, was not Shakespeare, but Dante, which Gretchen did not expect.

5. Ballard also had Shakespeare on his list, where he was number one.

6. Only Shakespeare and Miguel Cervantes, the author of *Don Quixote,* were on both lists, which also surprised Gretchen.

7. While Cervantes is on both lists, Gretchen noticed that Ballard ranked him higher than Bradbury did.

8. Malcolm Bradbury provides more commentary with his list than J. G. Ballard does, perhaps because he is an English professor.

9. Ballard mentions four twentieth-century writers, Franz Kafka, Joseph Heller, George Orwell, and Aldous Huxley, which is different from Bradbury, who mentions only one, James Joyce.

10. "Jane Austen is the only woman on either list," Margaret wrote to Gretchen, "and she appeared only on Bradbury's list."

B. Correcting Weak and Indefinite References

Most of the following sentences contain weak and indefinite pronoun references. Revise each faulty sentence. If a sentence is already correct, write *C*.

11. In San Antonio they have the Alamodome, one of the largest domed stadiums in the world.

12. Keith finds bird-watching most exciting when he actually sees one.

USAGE

ASSESSING

Monitoring Progress
Chapter Review. To assess student progress, you may want to compare the types of items missed on the **Diagnostic Preview** to those missed on the **Chapter Review.** If students have not made significant progress, you could refer them to **Chapter 16: Correcting Common Errors, Exercises 11** and **12** for additional practice.

Chapter Review

A. Correcting Ambiguous and General References

POSSIBLE ANSWERS

1. When Margaret saw some interesting pages at the Web site of the British Broadcasting Corporation (BBC), she e-mailed Gretchen about them.

2. The BBC had asked two British writers, Malcolm Bradbury and J.G. Ballard, each to name the ten greatest writers of the last one thousand years. These lists resulted in the Web page that Margaret saw.

3. C

4. Bradbury's number-one writer, for example, was not Shakespeare, but Dante, a choice Gretchen did not expect.

5. Ballard's list had Shakespeare as number one.

6. The fact that only Shakespeare and Miguel Cervantes, the author of *Don Quixote,* were on both lists also surprised Gretchen.

7. C

8. Malcolm Bradbury provides more commentary with his list than J.G. Ballard does, perhaps because Bradbury is an English professor.

9. Ballard's list, which mentions four twentieth-century writers, Franz Kafka, Joseph Heller, George Orwell, and Aldous Huxley, is different from Bradbury's list, which mentions only one twentieth-century writer, James Joyce.

10. C

Chapter Review

B. Correcting Weak and Indefinite References

POSSIBLE ANSWERS

11. The Alamodome, one of the largest domed stadiums in the world, is in San Antonio.

12. Keith finds bird-watching most exciting when he actually sees a bird.

13. I spent several hours at the library, but I didn't bring any books home.

14. C

15. I decided to request information on how to become a member of the Peace Corps.

16. How many meteors did you see last night? Wasn't the meteor shower spectacular?

17. The documentary on television last night told the story of Lewis and Clark's expedition.

18. The best job my father ever had was teaching for twenty-five years at a small college in Michigan.

19. We have been listening to a collection of English poetry on tape, but I haven't decided yet which poem is my favorite.

20. Ileana has read so much it is hard for her to remember all of the books.

Chapter Review

C. Revising Sentences to Correct Faulty Pronoun References

POSSIBLE ANSWERS

21. Dana is afraid of large dogs, but she doesn't let her fear show.

22. Washington, D.C., has a subway system that is modern and efficient.

23. When James was ten years old, he saw Michael Jordan play basketball.

24. After my cousins showed . . . Puerto Rico, I wanted to visit the island.

25. Beth wanted Laura to see the movie because Laura is a fan . . .

13. [7d]
14. [7a]
15. [7e]
16. [7d]
17. [7e]
18. [7d]
19. [7d]
20. [7d]

13. I spent several hours at the library, but I didn't bring any home.

14. Aunt Dee enjoys reading the works of Raymond Chandler, who is a mystery novelist.

15. I decided to request information on how you become a member of the Peace Corps.

16. How many meteors did you see last night? Wasn't it spectacular?

17. In the documentary on television last night, they told the story of Lewis and Clark's expedition.

18. My father taught at a small college in Michigan for twenty-five years, and it was the best job he ever had.

19. We have been listening to a collection of English poetry on tape, but I haven't decided yet which one is my favorite.

20. Ileana has read so much it is hard for her to remember them all.

C. Revising Sentences to Correct Faulty Pronoun References

Revise the following sentences to correct ambiguous, general, weak, and indefinite pronoun references.

21. [7d]
22. [7e]
23. [7b]
24. [7c]
25. [7b]

21. Dana is afraid of large dogs, but she doesn't let it show.

22. In Washington, D.C., they have a subway system that is modern and efficient.

23. James saw Michael Jordan play basketball when he was ten years old.

24. My cousins showed a video and several photos of their travels in Puerto Rico, which made me want to go there.

25. Beth wanted Laura to see the movie because she is a fan of Lou Diamond Phillips.

D. Revising Sentences to Correct Faulty Pronoun References

Revise the following sentences to correct ambiguous, general, weak, and indefinite pronoun references.

26. [7e]
27. [7b]

26. In the city library, they have a videotape about Martha Washington's early life and first marriage to a wealthy Virginia planter.

27. After Aaron Burr played matchmaker for Dolley Payne Todd and James Madison, he married Dolley.

USAGE

28. Abigail Adams was the first woman to be the wife of one president and mother of another, which is an interesting bit of First Lady trivia.

29. Julia Tyler supported her husband John Tyler's causes, especially the annexation of Texas, and that gave him strength.

30. In one book I read, it says that people accused Mary Todd Lincoln, who was from Kentucky, of opposing the Union, but she actually was a strong Unionist.

28. [7c]
29. [7c]
30. [7e]

Writing Application
Using Pronouns Correctly in a Letter

Clear Pronoun Reference A famous Hollywood producer wants to make British literature more accessible to high school students. As a result, he is sponsoring a "Be a Movie Director" contest. To enter, you have to write a letter explaining your idea for a movie version of a story, poem, or play that you have read in English class. Tell which actors you would cast in your movie and what music you would want for the soundtrack. Include at least ten pronouns in your sentences. Be sure that every pronoun has a clear antecedent.

Prewriting Start by choosing the work for which you want to create a movie. Then, list some ideas for three or four scenes in your movie. Next to each scene idea, list the actors you would use in that scene and describe the action.

Writing As you write, make the sequence of events clear. Make the spatial relationships clear, too, telling where the cast members should be located in each scene. Remember that the producer will need to have a clear picture of what you want, and you have only words with which to paint that picture for him. Be sure to use the proper form for a business letter.

Revising Check your rough draft to be sure that your explanation is clear. Have a classmate read your letter, looking for unclear uses of the pronouns *it, this, that,* and *which.* Revise any unclear references.

Publishing Proofread your letter for any errors in grammar, usage, and mechanics. Collect the letters written by the other members of your class, and make a chart showing which works would be made into movies, who the cast members would be, and what music would be included.

Chapter Review
D. Revising Sentences to Correct Faulty Pronoun References
POSSIBLE ANSWERS

26. In the city library there is a video-tape about Martha . . .

27. James Madison married Dolley Payne Todd after Aaron Burr played matchmaker for the two.

28. An interesting bit of First Lady trivia is that Abigail Adams was the first woman to be . . .

29. Julia Tyler's support of her husband John Tyler's causes, especially the annexation of Texas, gave . . .

30. One book I read said that people accused Mary Todd Lincoln, who was from Kentucky, of opposing the Union, but . . .

APPLICATION

Writing Application
Prewriting Tip. If screenplays or teleplays are available in the school library or a local library, you could have the class study one before they write their letters. Analyze with the class the different components of a scene and the way the screenwriter presents dialogue, directions, and settings.

Scoring Rubric. While you will want to pay particular attention to students' use of clear pronoun reference, you will also want to evaluate overall writing performance. You could give a split score to assess development and clarity of the letter separately from skill in usage.

CHAPTER

Using Verbs Correctly

Principal Parts, Tense, Voice, Mood

Reference Note

For more about **formal, standard English,** see page 262.

Terms and numerals in brackets refer to concepts and rules tested by the items in the Diagnostic Preview.

1. sitting [*sit, set*]
2. brought [8a, c]
3. had/broken [8d, e(5)]
4. her son took [8m]
5. C [8c, *lie, lay*]
6. began [8a, c]

Diagnostic Preview

A. Proofreading Sentences for Verb Usage

Most of the following sentences contain awkward, informal, or incorrect verb usage. If a sentence has an awkward, informal, or incorrect usage, revise the sentence, using the verb form that is correct according to the rules of formal, standard English. If a sentence is already correct, write *C*.

EXAMPLE   1. Oh no, I think I have broke my watch.

        1. Oh no, I think I have broken my watch.

1. They were setting on the bench and feeding the ducks.
2. She brung her brother when she came over to visit our family last Saturday evening.
3. When we saw the group perform, Julia, the lead vocalist, just broke her contract with a big recording company.
4. Mrs. Ames was pleased that when the driver's test was taken by her son, he passed easily.
5. The shoppers laid down their purchases carefully.
6. We cheered when the movie finally begun.

7. If we had the chance, we would have stopped by your house before we went to the concert.

8. They hoped to interview the astronauts.

9. On vacation they plan to ~~have gone~~ deep-sea fishing.

10. Yesterday I ~~swum~~ in the Millers' new pool.

11. The rate of inflation has ~~raised~~ steadily.

12. When they returned to the scene, they discovered that the weapon ~~was~~ taken.

13. When I enter college, my parents will ~~be~~ married thirty years.

14. We would have preferred to ~~have eaten~~ Chinese food.

15. If I ~~was~~ Anne, I would ask for a promotion and a raise.

B. Proofreading for Correct Verb Usage

Most of the sentences in the following paragraph contain awkward, informal, or incorrect verb usage. Revise the sentences, using appropriate verb forms. If a sentence is already correct, write *C*.

EXAMPLE   [1] How to use an abacus to do arithmetic problems was shown to my classmates and me by our second-grade teacher, Ms. Atchison.

1. *Our second-grade teacher, Ms. Atchison, showed my classmates and me how to use an abacus to solve arithmetic problems.*

[16] When you were a child, you might have played with an abacus as though it was a toy. [17] A teacher may have told you that the abacus was a device for counting—for adding and subtracting. [18] If you would have spent the time, you might have learned to calculate on this simple device. [19] An abacus consists of a series of bars on which beads have slid. [20] Because the abacus has been widely used for hundreds of years, many forms have been taken by it. [21] For example, on a Chinese abacus you move beads toward a crossbar to add a sum, while other types of abacuses did not even have crossbars. [22] Mastering the appropriate technique, operators calculate quickly and accurately. [23] In fact, on any number of occasions, people using abacuses have beated people using calculators in speed trials. [24] Consequently, an abacus sits beside many tradespeople all over Asia, just as it has did for centuries. [25] A century from now, the abacus will probably have remained practical, rugged, portable, fast, accurate, and comparatively inexpensive.

Diagnostic Preview   175

Reference Note

Depending on how they are used, verbs may be classified as **transitive verbs** or **intransitive verbs,** as **action verbs** or **linking verbs,** and as **main verbs** or **helping verbs.** For a discussion of these different kinds of verbs, see page 15.

7. had [8d, e(5)]
8. C [8d, e(2), h]
9. go [8h]
10. swam [8a, c]
11. risen [8c, *rise, raise*]
12. had been [8d, e(5)]
13. have been [8d, e(6)]
14. eat [8h, i]
15. were [8p(2)]

16. [8p(2)]
17. [8q(2), d, e(5, 2)]
18. [8g]
19. [8d, e(1), f(1), l]
20. [8m]
21. [8l, m, d, e(1), f(1)]
22. [8k, e(1)]
23. [8a, c]
24. [8a, c, e(4)]
25. [8d, e(3, 6)]

ASSESSING

Monitoring Progress
Diagnostic Preview. The **Diagnostic Preview** covers all aspects of verb usage. Students' performance on this preview should indicate the amount of reteaching needed and the areas in which various students need additional study and practice.

Diagnostic Preview: Part B Proofreading for Correct Verb Usage

POSSIBLE ANSWERS

[16] When you were a child, you might have played with an abacus as though it were a toy. [17] C [18] If you had spent the time, you might have learned to calculate on this simple device. [19] An abacus consists of a series of bars on which beads are slid. [20] Because the abacus has been widely used for hundreds of years, it has taken many forms. [21] For example, on a Chinese abacus, beads are moved toward a crossbar to add a sum, while other types of abacuses do not even have crossbars. [22] Having mastered the appropriate technique, operators calculate quickly and accurately. [23] In fact, on any number of occasions, people using abacuses have beaten people using calculators in speed trials. [24] Consequently, an abacus sits beside many tradespeople all over Asia, just as it has done for centuries. [25] A century from now, the abacus will probably remain practical, rugged, portable, fast, accurate, and comparatively inexpensive.

Differentiating Instruction

■ *Developmental Language & Sentence Skills,* pp. 77–92

■ *Developmental Language & Sentence Skills Guided Practice Teacher's Notes and Answer Key,* pp. 21–23

Assessment

■ *Holt Handbook Chapter Tests with Answer Key,* pp. 15–16, 54

USAGE

Diagnostic Preview. Some verbs have alternative past-tense forms such as *dived* or *dove* and *shrank* or *shrunk.* Explain that most of these alternatives are centuries old and may be used in different dialects of English and that students may encounter them on this preview and in other exercises and tests.

Regular Verbs and Irregular Verbs
Rules 8a–c *(pp. 176–193)*

OBJECTIVE

- To use the past and past participle forms of regular and irregular verbs correctly in sentences

PRETEACHING

Lesson Starter

Prior Knowledge. Ask students to consider the words *regular* and *irregular.* What can we say about something that is regular? about something that is irregular? [*Something that is regular is predictable. Something that is irregular is unpredictable.*] Next, write the following verbs on the board:

> chase, is chasing, chased, has chased
>
> write, is writing, wrote, has written
>
> fix, is fixing, fixed, has fixed

Ask students which of the three verbs seems unpredictable in the way it changes form. Tell them *write* is an irregular verb because it does not follow the standard rule for forming its parts. In this lesson students will learn the parts of regular and irregular verbs.

HELP

The words *is* and *have* are included in some charts in this chapter because the present participle and the past participle forms require helping verbs (forms of *be* and *have*) to form tenses.

TIPS & TRICKS

Sometimes the helping verb is not obvious. It may appear as part of a contraction.

EXAMPLES
He**'s** buying a new hat.

We**'ve** already finished.

Pay close attention to contractions so that you can be certain you are using the appropriate verb forms.

The Principal Parts of a Verb

8a. The *principal parts* of a verb are the *base form,* the *present participle,* the *past,* and the *past participle.* All other verb forms are derived from these principal parts.

Base Form	Present Participle	Past	Past Participle
live	[is] living	lived	[have] lived
talk	[is] talking	talked	[have] talked
run	[is] running	ran	[have] run
rise	[is] rising	rose	[have] risen
hit	[is] hitting	hit	[have] hit

All verbs form the present participle in the same way: by adding *–ing* to the base form. Not all verbs form the past and past participle in the same way, however. The way in which a verb forms its past and past participle determines whether the verb is classified as *regular* or *irregular.*

NOTE Some teachers refer to the base form as the *infinitive.* Follow your teacher's directions in labeling this verb form.

Regular Verbs

8b. A *regular verb* forms its past and past participle by adding *–d* or *–ed* to its base form.

Base Form	Present Participle	Past	Past Participle
care	[is] caring	cared	[have] cared
remove	[is] removing	removed	[have] removed
fix	[is] fixing	fixed	[have] fixed
suppose	[is] supposing	supposed	[have] supposed
match	[is] matching	matched	[have] matched
offer	[is] offering	offered	[have] offered
stay	[is] staying	stayed	[have] stayed
push	[is] pushing	pushed	[have] pushed

RESOURCES

Regular Verbs and Irregular Verbs
Practice
- *Language & Sentence Skills Practice,* pp. 171–177

Differentiating Instruction
- *Developmental Language & Sentence Skills,* pp. 77–80

NOTE Most regular verbs that end in *e* drop the *e* before adding *–ing* or *–ed.* Some regular verbs double the final consonant before adding *–ing* or *–ed.*

EXAMPLES   use   **us**ing   **us**ed

plan   **plann**ing   **plann**ed

A few regular verbs have alternative past and past participle forms ending in *–t.*

Base Form	Present Participle	Past	Past Participle
burn	[is] burning	burned *or* burnt	[have] burned *or* burnt
dream	[is] dreaming	dreamed *or* dreamt	[have] dreamed *or* dreamt
leap	[is] leaping	leaped *or* leapt	[have] leaped *or* leapt

NOTE The regular verbs *deal* and *mean* always form the past and past participle by adding *–t: dealt,* [have] *dealt; meant,* [have] *meant.*

When forming the past and past participle of regular verbs, do not make the common mistake of leaving off the *–d* or *–ed* ending. Pay particular attention to the forms of the verbs *ask, attack, drown, prejudice, risk, suppose,* and *use.*

NONSTANDARD   We use to live in Bakersfield.
STANDARD   We **used** to live in Bakersfield.

NONSTANDARD   I was suppose to be home by now.
STANDARD   I was **supposed** to be home by now.

SALLY FORTH reprinted with special permission of King Features Syndicate, Inc.

Reference Note
For information on **spelling rules,** see Chapter 15.

Reference Note
For information on **standard and non-standard English,** see page 262.

The Principal Parts of a Verb   **177**

MINI-LESSON Grammar   *Continued on p. 178*

Gerund Phrases and Participial Phrases. Tell students that a *gerund* is a verb form ending in *–ing* and used as a noun: *Running* keeps me fit. A *gerund phrase* consists of a gerund and its modifiers and complements and is used in its entirety as a noun:

Running around a track can keep a person fit. In addition, the present participle and past participle forms of verbs can be used as adjectives: *Shouting,* Luís tried to get Avery's attention. A participial phrase consists of a participle and its modifiers and

---

DIRECT TEACHING

Past and Past Participles
Activity. Many traditional writers and grammar purists frown on the use of nouns as verbs, but the practice has become quite common. [*Juan* hosts *his first party this weekend. Poor sales will* impact *the company's bottom line this year.*] Often the past and past participles of these noun-verbs require only a *–d* or an *–ed: hosted, impacted.* Suggest that before using a noun as a verb, students should check a dictionary to see if that particular usage has become commonly accepted. You might want to have the class list all the nouns they can think of that are currently used as verbs. [*access, message, conference*]

DIFFERENTIATING INSTRUCTION

English-Language Learners
General Strategies. Students may not realize that a past-tense verb form that they hear every day is spelled with a *–d* or an *–ed.* This confusion arises because native speakers of English often barely pronounce the *d* or even pronounce it as a *t.* In some dialects of English, the *–d* or *–ed* ending for the past tense is omitted entirely, as in "She miss the bus yesterday." You may want to create sentences containing regular past-tense verb forms. Ask students to underline all the present-tense endings, circle the past-tense endings, and then read the sentences aloud. Listen carefully, and model standard pronunciation when necessary.

USAGE

DIFFERENTIATING INSTRUCTION

Learners Having Difficulty

Give students the following four pairs of irregular verbs, and have students read them aloud saying "I" before each verb form.

run	ride
speak	sing
drive	write
swim	swing

Now rhythmically ask the question "What do you do on a holiday?" Go around the room and let each individual respond with one verb pair until all students have participated. You might want to keep a steady beat as the sequence gets going.

Now change your question to "What did you do on the holiday?" and proceed as before, having students use the same verb pairs they used before.

Finally, ask students the question "What have you ever done on your own?" Give them a few minutes to consult one another to verify the past participles they plan to use for completing the statement "I have _____." For the final round, you could proceed as before or have students answer chorally.

English-Language Learners

Spanish. Remind Spanish speakers that the English present participle suffix *–ing* is equivalent to the Spanish *–ando* and *–iendo* (e.g., *hablando,* "speaking," from *hablar,* "to speak," and *comiendo,* "eating," from *comer,* "to eat"), and that the English past participle suffix *–(e)d* is equivalent to the Spanish *–ado* and *–ido* (e.g., *marcado,* "marked," and *adquirido,* "acquired"). In English and in Spanish, the past participle can also be used as an adjective.

Exercise 1 **Proofreading for Errors in the Use of Regular Past and Past Participle Verbs**

Most of the following sentences contain errors in the use of past or past participle forms of verbs. If a verb form is incorrect, give the correct form. If a sentence is already correct, write *C.*

EXAMPLES
1. Weren't these parts order over two months ago?
1. *ordered*

2. Alec and Maribel are suppose to meet at the museum.
2. *supposed*

1. stretched
2. populated
3. C
4. used
5. etched
6. survived
7. popularized
8. checked
9. supposed
10. tamed

1. Before them ~~stretch~~ the great Kalahari Desert.
2. Once, centuries ago, tens of thousands of men, women, and children had ~~populate~~ this ancient city.
3. Actually, I meant to do that.
4. You ~~use~~ to work for Mr. Hall's lawn service.
5. Those magnificent examples of Native American pottery were ~~etch~~ with a traditional design.
6. Before arriving in Santa Fe, the wagon train had ~~survive~~ every sort of hardship.
7. A month-long national advertising blitz had successfully ~~popularize~~ this unlikely product.
8. Hadn't she ~~check~~ the gas gauge?
9. Oh, no, you were ~~suppose~~ to answer questions on both sides of the test!
10. After a week of constant effort and attention, Nicole finally ~~tame~~ the little parrot.

Irregular Verbs

8c. An *irregular verb* forms its past and past participle in some way other than by adding *–d* or *–ed* to its base form.

An irregular verb forms its past and past participle in one of these ways:

- changing vowels

Base Form	Past	Past Participle
sing	sang	[have] sung

MINI-LESSON **Grammar** *Continued from p. 177*

complements, and the entire phrase is used as an adjective: *Encouraged by Jerry's reaction,* Luís decided to try out for the team. Gerunds and gerund phrases are not set off by commas. Participles and participial phrases that begin a sentence are set off by commas. For more information on gerund phrases and participial phrases, refer students to **Chapter 3: The Phrase.**

- changing consonants

Base Form	Past	Past Participle
lend	lent	[have] lent

- changing vowels and consonants

Base Form	Past	Past Participle
buy	bought	[have] bought

- making no change

Base Form	Past	Past Participle
cost	cost	[have] cost

When forming the past and past participle of irregular verbs, avoid these common errors:

- Do not use the past form with a helping verb.

NONSTANDARD	I have sang in the Alexander Hamilton High School chorus for three years.
STANDARD	I **sang** in the Alexander Hamilton High School chorus for three years.

- Do not use the past participle form without a helping verb.

NONSTANDARD	I sung three solos this year.
STANDARD	I **have sung** three solos this year.

- Do not add *d*, *ed*, or *t* to the base form.

NONSTANDARD	This cassette costed only $6.95.
STANDARD	This cassette **cost** only $6.95.

NOTE If you are not sure about the principal parts of a verb, look up the verb in a dictionary. Generally, entries for irregular verbs list the principal parts. If the principal parts are not listed, the verb is a regular verb.

The Principal Parts of a Verb **179**

DIFFERENTIATING INSTRUCTION

Special Education Students

Some students may have difficulty remembering irregular verb forms. Have a helper assist each student to make a chart of verb forms. Then, have students focus on a limited number of sentences in the exercises. It may also be effective to have students highlight the verbs and work with partners to correct problems.

Learners Having Difficulty

Some students may find it easier to learn from a verb wheel, a chart form that they can manipulate. Consider making for them a pattern of two circles, one slightly smaller than the other. Cut a partial pie wedge out of the smaller circle, and attach the two circles at the center with a brad. Base-form verbs that are problematical for students can be recorded on the outside rim of the larger circle. As students turn the verb wheel, they can record the other principal parts in the exposed part of the smaller circle.

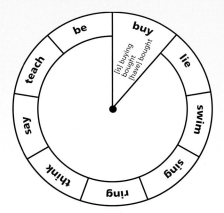

The verb wheel might be kept in the pocket of a folder or binder and consulted when necessary.

EXTENSION

Relating to Writing

To help students improve their writing, explain that they should choose precise, vibrant verbs whenever possible. Let them work in groups of three to practice replacing dull verbs. In each group, have one person write a common verb on a piece of paper. Have another group member suggest a synonymous, more interesting verb, possibly by using a thesaurus. Then, have the last group member create a sentence with the more precise verb. Finally, have students repeat the process, rotating roles each time, until they have completed this process with nine verbs. Ask volunteers to share their verbs and sentences with the class.

STYLE / TIP

Some irregular verbs have two correct past or past participle forms. However, these forms are not always interchangeable.

EXAMPLES
Judy **shone** the lantern into the woods. [*Shined* would also be correct.]

Al **shined** his shoes. [*Shone* would be incorrect in this usage.]

If you are unsure about which past or past participle form to use, look up the word in an up-to-date dictionary.

Common Irregular Verbs

Group I: Each of these irregular verbs has the same form for its past and past participle.

Base Form	Present Participle	Past	Past Participle
bind	[is] binding	bound	[have] bound
bring	[is] bringing	brought	[have] brought
build	[is] building	built	[have] built
buy	[is] buying	bought	[have] bought
catch	[is] catching	caught	[have] caught
creep	[is] creeping	crept	[have] crept
feel	[is] feeling	felt	[have] felt
fight	[is] fighting	fought	[have] fought
find	[is] finding	found	[have] found
fling	[is] flinging	flung	[have] flung
have	[is] having	had	[have] had
hear	[is] hearing	heard	[have] heard
hold	[is] holding	held	[have] held
keep	[is] keeping	kept	[have] kept
lay	[is] laying	laid	[have] laid
lead	[is] leading	led	[have] led
leave	[is] leaving	left	[have] left
lend	[is] lending	lent	[have] lent
lose	[is] losing	lost	[have] lost
make	[is] making	made	[have] made
meet	[is] meeting	met	[have] met
pay	[is] paying	paid	[have] paid
say	[is] saying	said	[have] said
seek	[is] seeking	sought	[have] sought
sell	[is] selling	sold	[have] sold
send	[is] sending	sent	[have] sent
sit	[is] sitting	sat	[have] sat
spend	[is] spending	spent	[have] spent
spin	[is] spinning	spun	[have] spun
stand	[is] standing	stood	[have] stood
sting	[is] stinging	stung	[have] stung
swing	[is] swinging	swung	[have] swung

Common Irregular Verbs

Group I: Each of these irregular verbs has the same form for its past and past participle.

Base Form	Present Participle	Past	Past Participle
teach	[is] teaching	taught	[have] taught
tell	[is] telling	told	[have] told
think	[is] thinking	thought	[have] thought
win	[is] winning	won	[have] won

Exercise 2 Using the Past and Past Participle Forms of Irregular Verbs Correctly

Most of the following sentences contain errors in the use of the past or past participle forms of irregular verbs. If a verb form is incorrect, give the correct form. If a sentence is already correct, write *C*.

EXAMPLE
1. Uncle Octavio brung all of us souvenirs of his visit to Costa Rica.
   1. *brought*

1. Before the festival last Sunday, the Conchero dancers had meet behind the church to practice.
2. By some unlucky chance, I winned the door prize—a full-grown leghorn rooster.
3. The accomplishments of Maggie Lena Walker, the first female bank president in the United States, layed a firm financial foundation for the African American community of Richmond, Virginia.
4. The macaw, happy to see its owner, standed at the door of its cage and shrieked excitedly.
5. After a few hesitant steps, we swinged into the rhythm of the fox trot.
6. For all those years, the old man had keeped the dogeared photograph of his childhood home in Hawaii.
7. While in Arizona, Uncle Arthur boughten a magnificent storm-pattern Navajo rug by Shirley Tsinnie.
8. How could you have spended all of your weekly allowance before Saturday afternoon!
9. A green velvet ribbon binded the large white box that was on the dining room table.
10. The cool skin of the chameleon feeled dry, not wet.
11. She lost her hat when a gust of wind blew it into the lake.

1. met
2. won
3. laid
4. stood
5. swung
6. kept
7. bought
8. spent
9. bound
10. felt
11. C

The Principal Parts of a Verb **181**

English-Language Learners

General Strategies. Some languages, such as Indonesian, Japanese, Korean, Turkish, and Vietnamese, have few or no irregular verbs. Give students a comprehensive list of irregular verbs. Leave blank spaces for the past-tense and past-participle forms. Tell students to fill in the blanks and to keep this list as a reference in their notebooks.

12. spun	**12.** No one said a word as the host spinned the big yellow arrow to determine who would take the first turn.
13. said	**13.** Haven't you sayed enough?
14. fought	**14.** On the front porch that very afternoon, the two second-graders had fighted furiously over the only blue crayon.
15. led	**15.** In modern China, Qiu Jin leaded the way for women's emancipation.
16. sold	**16.** Have you selled the mare with three white feet and a white mane?
17. C	**17.** My father taught me to save some money—even just a few dollars—each month.
18. sought	**18.** I seeked my fortune in a faraway country.
19. C	**19.** We should have sat in the shade of a towering oak tree on the university's front lawn.
20. lent	**20.** That colorful painting by the Haitian artist Euguerrand Gourgue lended a cheery touch to the room.

Exercise 3 **Using the Past and Past Participle Forms of Irregular Verbs Correctly**

Complete each of the following sentences, using the correct past or past participle form of the italicized verb.

EXAMPLE   **1.** *tell*   Mr. Paz _____ us about the early Spanish explorers who searched for gold in the Americas.

   1. *told*

	1. sought	**2.** found
1. *seek*	Spanish explorers had _____ gold in the Americas.	
2. *find*	The gold they _____, however, was in golden ears of corn.	
3. *leave*	Spanish ships _____ carrying the precious kernels to	
3. left	Europe.	
4. *bring*	The holds of the ships _____ a cheap, new food source into	
4. brought	a land of recurrent famine.	
5. *lead*	A diet of corn _____ many of the world's poor to suffer	
5. led	from pellagra, a disease of the stomach, mind, and skin.	
6. *build*	The peoples of Mexico and Central America, however,	
6. built	had _____ healthy bodies on a steady diet of corn.	
7. *make*	When the people of Mexico and Central America _____	
7. made	tortillas, they added some lime or ashes to the dough.	
8. *stand*	Then, after the mixture of corn, water, and lime or ashes	
8. stood	had _____ for a few hours, the tortillas were cooked.	
9. *have*	Heated, this alkali solution _____ the ability to release not	
9. had	only corn's niacin but also its protein and calcium.	
10. *lose*	In European and African methods of preparation, corn	
10. lost	had unfortunately _____ much of its nutrient value.	

Common Irregular Verbs

Group II: Most of these irregular verbs have different forms for the past and past participle.

Base Form	Present Participle	Past	Past Participle
arise	[is] arising	arose	[have] arisen
be	[is] being	was, were	[have] been
bear	[is] bearing	bore	[have] borne *or* born
beat	[is] beating	beat	[have] beaten *or* beat
become	[is] becoming	became	[have] become
begin	[is] beginning	began	[have] begun
bite	[is] biting	bit	[have] bitten *or* bit
blow	[is] blowing	blown	[have] blown
break	[is] breaking	broke	[have] broken
choose	[is] choosing	chose	[have] chosen
come	[is] coming	came	[have] come
dive	[is] diving	dove *or* dived	[have] dived
do	[is] doing	did	[have] done
draw	[is] drawing	drew	[have] drawn
drink	[is] drinking	drank	[have] drunk
drive	[is] driving	drove	[have] driven
eat	[is] eating	ate	[have] eaten
fall	[is] falling	fell	[have] fallen
fly	[is] flying	flew	[have] flown
forbid	[is] forbidding	forbade *or* forbad	[have] forbidden *or* forbid
forget	[is] forgetting	forgot	[have] forgotten *or* forgot
forgive	[is] forgiving	forgave	[have] forgiven
forsake	[is] forsaking	forsook	[have] forsaken
freeze	[is] freezing	froze	[have] frozen
get	[is] getting	got	[have] gotten *or* got
give	[is] giving	gave	[have] given

(continued)

—HELP—

Several of these verbs have alternate past or past participle forms.

DIFFERENTIATING INSTRUCTION

Special Education Students

The **Common Irregular Verbs** charts may overwhelm some students. Ask them to choose five of these verbs and to write autobiographical sentences that incorporate the past or past participle form of each of the five verbs. For example, a student might incorporate the past participle form of *dive* into the autobiographical sentence "I have dived off the highest diving board at the public pool." Because this activity allows students to work with a manageable number of verbs and to use the verbs in context, it may make the material more meaningful and less intimidating.

EXTENSION

Relating to Dictionary Skills

Point out to students that when they have questions about the principal parts of irregular verbs, they can look up the verbs in a dictionary. Explain that the entry word in a dictionary is the base form and that the past, past participle, and present participle forms are listed following the entry word. For example, if students look up *sing,* they will find *sang, sung,* and *singing* listed after *sing.* Have each student choose two or three irregular verbs to look up in a dictionary. Students should write each verb's principal parts.

USAGE

DIFFERENTIATING INSTRUCTION

English-Language Learners

General Strategies. Point out to students that mastering all irregular verb forms takes time and that many native speakers benefit from regular review and practice. You may want to pair English-language learners with responsible native speakers who will prioritize among irregular verbs listed in the **Common Irregular Verbs** charts. Have each native speaker select six to ten verb forms each week until the irregular forms seem more familiar to the English-language learner with whom he or she is working.

(continued)

Common Irregular Verbs			
Group II: Most of these irregular verbs have different forms for the past and past participle.			
Base Form	**Present Participle**	**Past**	**Past Participle**
go	[is] going	went	[have] gone
grow	[is] growing	grew	[have] grown
hide	[is] hiding	hid	[have] hidden *or* hid
know	[is] knowing	knew	[have] known
lie	[is] lying	lay	[have] lain
ride	[is] riding	rode	[have] ridden
ring	[is] ringing	rang	[have] rung
rise	[is] rising	rose	[have] risen
run	[is] running	ran	[have] run
see	[is] seeing	saw	[have] seen
shake	[is] shaking	shook	[have] shaken
show	[is] showing	showed	[have] shown or showed
shrink	[is] shrinking	shrank *or* shrunk	[have] shrunk
sing	[is] singing	sang	[have] sung
sink	[is] sinking	sank *or* sunk	[have] sunk
slay	[is] slaying	slew	[have] slain
speak	[is] speaking	spoke	[have] spoken
spring	[is] springing	sprang *or* sprung	[have] sprung
steal	[is] stealing	stole	[have] stolen
strike	[is] striking	struck	[have] struck *or* stricken
strive	[is] striving	strove *or* strived	[have] striven *or* strived
swear	[is] swearing	swore	[have] sworn
swim	[is] swimming	swam	[have] swum
take	[is] taking	took	[have] taken

184 Chapter 8 Using Verbs Correctly

MINI-LESSON **Mechanics** *Continued on pp. 185–186*

Spelling. To help students correctly form the principal parts of verbs, review with them the spelling rules that apply when adding suffixes.

1. Drop the final silent *e* before a suffix beginning with a vowel (dine + ing = dining).

2. Double the final consonant before adding a suffix that begins with a vowel if the verb ends in a single consonant preceded by a single vowel and either has only one syllable or is accented on the last syllable (drop + ed = dropped [one-syllable word

Common Irregular Verbs

Group II: Most of these irregular verbs have different forms for the past and past participle.

Base Form	Present Participle	Past	Past Participle
tear	[is] tearing	tore	[have] torn
throw	[is] throwing	threw	[have] thrown
wake	[is] waking	woke *or* waked	[have] waked *or* woken
wear	[is] wearing	wore	[have] worn
weave	[is] weaving	wove *or* weaved	[have] woven *or* weaved
write	[is] writing	wrote	[have] written

Oral Practice **Using the Past and Past Participle Forms of Irregular Verbs Correctly**

Choose the <u>correct one</u> of the two verb forms in parentheses in each of the following sentences. Then, read each sentence aloud.

EXAMPLE
1. Bantu languages, which are (*spoke, spoken*) by many Africans, have an interesting history.

1. *Bantu languages, which are spoken by many Africans, have an interesting history.*

1. Years ago in Africa, Bantu languages had no alphabet, and no one (<u>*wrote*</u>, *written*) in these languages.
2. In fact, the musical quality of many African languages (*gived*, <u>*gave*</u>) them an intricacy unsuitable for written alphabets.
3. Consequently, drums (*sung*, <u>*sang*</u>) these languages throughout equatorial and southern Africa, and the drum songs acted as a kind of musical writing.
4. According to Janheinz Jahn, the use of drums (<u>*arose*</u>, *arisen*) for communication at a distance.
5. Just as you learned to read using the alphabet, young Africans learned to "read" the different sounds of the drums and (<u>*knew*</u>, *known*) the meanings of these sounds in combinations.
6. The wide acoustic range of drums like the Yorubas' *dundun* (*gived*, <u>*gave*</u>) quick and easy access to a complex language.
7. By varying tone, pitch, and modulation, a skillful drummer (*striven*, <u>*strove*</u>) to re-create the sounds of the language.

The Principal Parts of a Verb **185**

USAGE

RETEACHING

Past Participles

Activity. Students may help themselves and their classmates who are English-language learners by creating rhyming couplets that demonstrate similarly formed past participles, such as the following examples:

"The ship hasn't *shrunk*—
It has *sunk*!"

"Can she be *forgiven*
For where she has *driven*?"

"The horse you have *ridden*
Has finally *hidden*."

"The bell had just *rung*,
But the choir had not *sung*."

ending in single consonant preceded by single vowel]; refer + ed = referred [accent on last syllable]; differ + ing = differing [accent on first syllable]; droop + ed = drooped [single consonant preceded by double vowel]).

To extend the lesson, write the following exercise on the chalkboard and have students add suffixes as indicated.

1. propel + ed [*propelled*]
2. fire + ing [*firing*]

Irregular Verbs

Activity. Ask your students to think of examples of irregular verbs that form their past tenses and past participles in one of the following ways:

1. changing a vowel [*sit, begin*]

2. changing a consonant [*send, build*]

3. changing vowels and consonants [*take, go*]

4. changing nothing [*set, bid*]

Students can use the **Common Irregular Verbs** charts if necessary.

Guided and Independent

Exercise 4 You may want to use the first ten items in the exercise as guided practice. Then, have students complete the exercise as independent practice.

HOMEWORK

8. With this meaningful music, the drummer (*wove, woven*) the news of the day into an informative report.

9. At the speed of sound, the drummer's warnings, invitations, and other messages (*flew, flown*) over miles of jungle and plain.

10. With drum scripts that had been (*beated, beaten*) for decades, the drummer sent information to interested listeners.

11. Many of the scripts eventually (*became, become*) classic epics.

12. Drummers were not just musicians; they (*been, were*) also teachers and historians.

13. Through them, generations of young Africans (*drank, drunk*) in the history of their ancestors.

14. When European missionaries came to Africa, however, they (*forbidden, forbade*) the playing of drums.

15. Their prohibitions (*struck, stricken*) severely at the hearts of many African cultures.

16. Today, through disuse, almost all of the old drum scripts have been (*forgotted, forgotten*).

17. Some scholars have (*did, done*) their best to record many of the remaining scripts.

18. Sadly, many listeners have not (*spoke, spoken*) Bantu in their whole lives; consequently, even verbal translations of the drum songs are meaningless to many Bantu people.

19. Has the power of the drums (*went, gone*)?

20. Like so much other ancient knowledge and wisdom, this marvelous system of communication has largely been (*forsaken, forsook*).

Exercise 4 **Using the Past and Past Participle Forms of Irregular Verbs Correctly**

Most of the following sentences contain incorrect past or past participle forms of irregular verbs. If a verb form is incorrect, give the correct form. If a sentence is already correct, write *C*.

EXAMPLE   **1.** By the time Beowulf arrives, the monster Grendel has slew many of King Hrothgar's warriors.

1. slain

1. drawn

1. She should not have ^drew a beard on that poster.

2. C

2. Benjamin Franklin may have gotten many of his ideas for the structure of our government from his observations of the League of the Iroquois.

3. stolen

3. Why would you think someone had ^stole your notebook?

4. run

4. Frank said, "I have ^ran too far to turn back now."

MINI-LESSON **Mechanics**   *Continued from p. 185*

3. live + ed [*lived*]

4. thunder + ed [*thundered*]

5. leap + ing [*leaping*]

For more information on adding suffixes, refer students to **Chapter 15: Spelling.**

5. Dwayne has ~~growed~~ two inches taller than his older brother, the all-state basketball player.

6. After the discoveries made in the tomb of Tutankhamen, other ancient treasures seemed to Joseph to have ~~shrank~~ in significance.

7. The noise from the party woke the neighborhood.

8. I ~~seen~~ that movie several times, but I would be happy to see it again.

9. Who in the world ~~throwed~~ out all my old baseball cards?

10. They have frozen a peck of green beans for next winter.

11. Henry ~~done~~ his best yesterday, and it was enough.

12. In the courtroom the young man ~~sworn~~ to give truthful testimony.

13. Jesse Owens's spectacular run at the 1936 Olympic games ~~shaked~~ the world.

14. Have you ever ~~dove~~ from the high board at the swimming pool?

15. As we huddled in the corner, thunder crashed and wind ~~blowed~~ the candles out.

16. I guess we should have ~~chose~~ seats closer to the stage.

17. Why have they ~~tore~~ up the newspapers?

18. The coach said, "I think we have ~~began~~ to wear them down."

19. He always ~~rid~~ the bus to school, even if his parents offered to drive him.

20. Has the bell for third period rung yet?

5. grown	
6. shrunk	
7. C	
8. saw [or have seen]	
9. threw	
10. C	
11. did	
12. swore	
13 shook	
14. dived	
15. blew	
16. chosen	
17. torn	
18. begun	
19. rode	
20. C	

> **Review A** **Proofreading for Correct Verb Forms**

Find and correct any errors in verb forms in each sentence in the following paragraphs. If a sentence is already correct, write *C*.

EXAMPLE   **[1]** Part of an Apache ceremony called Sunrise Ceremonial is shone in the photograph here.

     1. shown

[**1**] Many cultures have not ~~forsaked~~ their traditional ceremonies that mark the significant stages in a person's life. [**2**] For instance, when an Apache girl has ~~came~~ of age, she sometimes receives a Sunrise Ceremonial. [**3**] Through this ceremony, the young woman is forever separated from her girlhood and ~~lead~~ into womanhood. [**4**] Everything in the ceremony is ~~suppose~~ to remind the young woman of the deep spiritual meaning of her life. [**5**] Perhaps part of that meaning can be ~~founded~~ in the glad hearts of her many friends and family members who come to participate in the ceremony.

The Principal Parts of a Verb   **187**

> **Review A** **Proofreading for Correct Verb Forms**

ANSWERS

1. forsaken
2. come
3. led
4. supposed
5. found

PRACTICE

Guided and Independent

> **Review A**   You may want to use the first ten items in the review as guided practice. Then, have students complete the review as independent practice.

HOMEWORK

ANSWERS continued

6. sought
7. begun
8. chose
9. made
10. kept
11. C
12. sung
13. slain
14. brought
15. C
16. stood
17. wore
18. attended
19. gave
20. become

RETEACHING

Irregular Verbs

Activity. Ask students if they can think of any verbs besides the ones in, the chart on this page that have the same form for their base, past, and past participle forms [*cast, shut, thrust*]. Write the following sentences on the chalkboard, and ask students to explain how they can tell the tense of the verb.

1. My mother will let me go. [*The helping verb* will *indicates that the verb is future tense.*]

2. By that time, Arnie had already let him have the skateboard. [*The phrase* by that time, *the helping verb* had, *and the adverb* already *indicate past perfect tense.*]

Ask students to choose one of the verbs that uses the same form for the base, past, and past participle forms and to write sentences containing the chosen verb in each of the six tenses.

[6] Not long ago, Carla, the young woman in the photograph on the previous page, and her mother seeked the blessings of a traditional Sunrise Ceremonial. [7] Complex preparations had began months in advance. [8] During the winter Carla's mother choose a campsite where Carla, her family, and her friends would live for two weeks according to the ways of their ancestors. [9] The crucial choice of godparents for the young woman also had been maked by Carla's mother. [10] Not surprisingly, she chose a couple who had keeped to the traditional Apache way of life. [11] By summer Carla's mother and godparents had built enough shelters at the campsite to house at least eight families.

[12] During Carla's ceremonial, many traditional songs were sang. [13] The two cows that had been slew for the feasting were eaten. [14] In addition, Carla and her family gave the gifts they had brung to the godparents and other friends. [15] Young women used to dance all night, and Carla danced for six hours at a time. [16] Then she standed for endless hours in the burning sun. [17] Through it all, she worn a hot, heavy buckskin dress. [18] Surely, these tests of self-discipline taught Carla and everyone who attend the ceremony about the endurance and strength that a woman needs to live as a proper Apache. [19] Finally, after offering a blessing, a medicine man gived Carla a cane, a reminder that she will not always be young. [20] In her old age, when the cane has became her constant companion, it will, no doubt, remind her of the strength of her youth.

Common Irregular Verbs			
Group III: Each of these irregular verbs has the same form for its base form, past, and past participle.			
Base Form	**Present Participle**	**Past**	**Past Participle**
burst	[is] bursting	burst	[have] burst
cost	[is] costing	cost	[have] cost
cut	[is] cutting	cut	[have] cut
hit	[is] hitting	hit	[have] hit
hurt	[is] hurting	hurt	[have] hurt
let	[is] letting	let	[have] let
put	[is] putting	put	[have] put
read	[is] reading	read	[have] read
set	[is] setting	set	[have] set
spread	[is] spreading	spread	[have] spread

Exercise 5 Using the Past and Past Participle Forms of Irregular Verbs Correctly

Most of the following sentences contain incorrect past or past participle forms of irregular verbs. If a verb form is incorrect, give the correct form. If a sentence is already correct, write *C*.

EXAMPLE   **1.** In the fourteenth century a plague known as Black Death spreaded throughout Europe and Asia.

     1. *spread*

1. During the freeze last March, the water pipes at school bursted.   **1.** burst

2. My jaw hurted after the orthodontist adjusted my braces.   **2.** hurt

3. Yesterday evening, I had just putted dinner on the table when the phone rang.   **3.** put

4. Shaka Zulu led his warriors into battle, and soon news of Shaka's victory had spreaded throughout Zululand.   **4.** spread

5. Have you ever cutted out a pattern before?   **5.** cut

6. Have you read the assignment yet?   **6.** C

7. After art class, Jeremy, Mr. Fitzcarraldo, and I setted our pottery out in the sun to dry.   **7.** set

8. The drought hitted the spring crops hard.   **8.** hit

9. One chance remark costed her the election.   **9.** cost

10. Wisely, Francisca Henrique de Ribera letted the Andean people treat her malaria attack with cinchona bark, from which the medicinal ingredient quinine is extracted.   **10.** let

11. Have you ever hit a ball out of the park?   **11.** C

12. News of the new state-of-the-art computers spreaded quickly through the high school.   **12.** spread

13. Yikes, Timmy, you've cutted a hole right in the middle of the lace tablecloth!   **13.** cut

14. Shouldn't you have setted those forks on the other side of the plate?   **14.** set

15. Wow! That big house on the hill must have costed a fortune to design and build.   **15.** cost

16. Of course, Eric and I putted the slides back in the drawer, Mr. Stevens.   **16.** put

17. Have you letted those puppies out of the laundry room?   **17.** let

18. Overnight, the daffodil bulbs planted last fall had bursted into vivid bloom.   **18.** burst

19. This book by Amy Tan was so good that I readed the whole thing last night.   **19.** read

20. No, those horseshoe nails haven't hurted a horse yet.   **20.** hurt

The Principal Parts of a Verb   **189**

CONTENT-AREA CONNECTIONS

World Languages

Esperanto. Tell students that Esperanto is an invented international language developed for the purpose of easier communication among cultures speaking different languages. Ask students to research Esperanto. Have them report on what they find about the regularity of verb forms in this language. Some students may find the Internet useful for finding up-to-date information on the use of Esperanto today. Engage students in a dialogue about the benefits and drawbacks of adopting an invented language.

PRACTICE

Guided and Independent

Review B You may want to use the first ten items in the review as guided practice. Then, have students complete the review as independent practice.

HOMEWORK

DIRECT TEACHING

Archaic Verb Forms

Activity. You might point out to students that some forms of irregular verbs are rarely used today. For example, the past tense of *speak* is *spoke*. In their reading, students might encounter the archaic past-tense form *spake*. Another example is the verb *beget,* meaning "to father or to cause." The current past-tense form is *begot,* while the former past-tense form, *begat,* is archaic. You might ask students to suggest other examples or to list archaic verb forms that they encounter as they read older works in this or other classes. Explain that using such archaic verb forms might be one way to draw a reader into a scene set in a distant historical period. In most cases, however, writers today avoid using archaic verb forms.

Review B **Proofreading for Correct Verb Forms and Usage**

Most of the sentences in the following paragraphs contain errors in verb usage. If a verb form is incorrect, give the correct form. If a sentence is already correct, write *C*.

EXAMPLE [1] The early European and Asian explorers of the Americas taked home with them many foods indigenous to North and South America.

1. *took*

1. read
2. eaten
3. become

4. C

5. put
6. became
7. took

8. hit

9. found
10. used
11. lost
12. arose
13. C
14. put
15. grown

16. C
17. lay
18. fought
19. lent

[1] Now that you have readed the map shown on the next page, are you surprised by where these food products originated? [2] Perhaps you have ate some of these foods. [3] Many food products have became vital, even characteristic, parts of their adopted nations. [4] Consequently, most people have forgotten that key ingredients, such as tomato sauce on pizza, originated in the Americas.

[5] Reports from early explorers putted cooks all over Europe into a creative frenzy. [6] As soon as the explorers returned home, dozens of strange and exotic foods become available to Europeans. [7] Some of the foods that the explorers taked home included sweet potatoes, white potatoes, corn, peppers, tomatoes, avocados, vanilla, maple sugar, chocolate, peanuts, all sorts of beans (kidney, lima, snap, string, butter, pole, and navy), and a host of other welcome additions to a chef's pantry. [8] So many new spices, fruits, vegetables, meats, and grains hitted the market that this period in history can be called a "Food Revolution."

[9] In these unfamiliar foods, many peoples also founded new hope. [10] For example, the Chinese use to experience severe famine. [11] Countless people losed their lives when rice crops failed. [12] However, with the introduction of the sweet potato, an alternative to rice arisen. [13] Sweet potatoes cost little and did well in poor soil. [14] Soon, cooks had putted sweet potato flour into Chinese dumplings, noodles, and many other dishes. [15] Because of the continuing popularity of the sweet potato in China, Chinese farmers have growed more sweet potatoes than farmers in any other country.

[16] Famine often had struck Europe, too, because of poor weather conditions. [17] For Europeans, their salvation lain in the Andean potato. [18] With harvest after harvest of potatoes, Europeans fighted famine and also created a whole new menu. [19] In soups, stews, pancakes, and pies, the potato lended its substance and nutrition to a host

of European dishes. [20] Who in the time of Columbus could have dreamt of the vast variety of American food sources or of the vital roles they would play in the world's fight against famine?

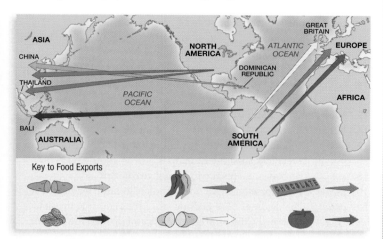

Key to Food Exports

Review C **Using the Past and Past Participle Forms of Verbs Correctly**

For each of the following sentences, write the correct past or past participle form of the given italicized verb.

EXAMPLE   **1.** *know*   A sport called baggataway was first played by North American Indians; today, the sport is _____ as lacrosse.

    1. known

1. *steal*   While the children were asleep, their father _____ into their room to kiss them good night.

2. *let*   After breakfast I _____ the cat outside.

3. *visit*   Many Cheyenne, Arapaho, Shoshone, Blackfoot, Crow, and Sioux have _____ the Bighorn Medicine Wheel in Wyoming, a ceremonial site for perhaps two thousand years.

4. *fling*   Joyfully, he _____ his cap into the air.

5. *sting*   Where had the bee _____ her?

6. *win*   The baby's trusting smile _____ our hearts.

7. *think*   At last, I had _____ of the perfect present for Amy.

8. *bear*   We _____ his rudeness for only a few minutes.

1. stole

2. let
3. visited

4. flung
5. stung
6. won
7. thought
8. bore

PRACTICE

Guided and Independent

Review C   You may want to use the first ten items in the review as guided practice. Then, have students complete the review as independent practice.

HOMEWORK

USAGE

The Principal Parts of a Verb   **191**

9. swam
10. blown

11. sunk

12. hid

13. set
14. lay

15. held
16. bit
17. led

18. cut
19. thrown
20. broke

9. *swim*   The frantic cat _____ desperately to the shore.
10. *blow*   Even before the whistle had _____, they had seen the train coming across the bridge.
11. *sink*   After the excitement, we had gratefully _____ into the plush velvet chairs to wait.
12. *hide*   Someone _____ one of my birthday presents at the back of the top shelf in a kitchen cabinet.
13. *set*   That afternoon, we hurriedly _____ the table for the party.
14. *lie*   During World War II, the success of England's military blood bank _____ in the capable hands of Dr. Charles Drew.
15. *hold*   Only that morning, I had _____ the tiny bird in my hands.
16. *bite*   Sharks _____ the whale but did not badly injure it.
17. *lead*   Boadicea, a queen in ancient Britain, _____ her people in a revolt against the Romans.
18. *cut*   He had _____ his ties to his native country.
19. *throw*   That horse has _____ everybody who has tried to ride it.
20. *break*   The death of Mao Zedong _____ the rigid rule that had governed China for many years and opened the way for somewhat greater freedom for the Chinese people.

PRACTICE

Guided and Independent

Review D You may want to use the first ten items in the review as guided practice. Then, have students complete the review as independent practice.

HOMEWORK

Review D **Proofreading for Correct Verb Forms and Usage**

Most of the sentences in the following paragraphs contain at least one error in the use of verbs. If a verb form is incorrect, give the correct form. If a sentence is already correct, write *C*.

EXAMPLE   **[1]** From my aunt I learned a great deal about the use of lacquer, a substance that is drawed from certain trees of the cashew family.

1. *drawn*

1. C
2. was

3. forbade [*or* forbad]
4. ran
5. hit
6. fell/spun
7. sat

[1] For over thirty years, my aunt has had a lacquerware plate similar to the one in the picture on the next page. [2] When I been a child, she displayed the plate on a low table in her living room in Tacoma, Washington. [3] Naturally, she forbidded me to touch her prized plate, and I respected her wish. [4] One day, however, my younger brother runned through the living room. [5] As he zoomed past the table, his foot accidentally hitted the leg. [6] In the blink of an eye, my aunt's beautiful plate falled and spinned wildly on the floor. [7] After that, the plate, which was miraculously unbroken, sitted on the top shelf of my aunt's china closet.

[8] Ever since I first expressed an interest in lacquerware, my aunt has telled me more and more about its history and production. [9] People have maked lacquerware since around 300 B.C. [10] The art begun in China and later spreaded to Japan and then to the Western world. [11] To protect their trade, the tappers of lacquer in ancient China keeped their valuable knowledge of lacquer production secret. [12] Now we know that they drew the sap from lacquer trees, filtered it, and dried it to a thick, syrupy consistency. [13] Then they selled it to artists for its beauty and for its waterproofing ability.

[14] In the finer pieces of lacquerware, like this one, an artist may have spread some two hundred coats of lacquer over the plate. [15] For each coat, a thin film of lacquer was applied and then was leaved to dry thoroughly. [16] Consequently, the whole lacquering process sometimes taked as long as a year to complete. [17] Then, when the artist had choosed a design, the carving began. [18] Would you have devote a year's work to such an intricate design? [19] What confidence these artists must have feeled! [20] My aunt bought her plate years ago for only a few dollars; now, it has brought offers of many, many times the price that she payed.

8. told

9. made
10. began/spread
11. kept

12. C
13. sold

14. C
15. left

16. took
17. chosen
18. devoted
19. felt
20. paid

Song-Yuan Dynasties (13th century). Tray, brown and red lacquer with gilt background. Height, 1 in.; diameter, 9 in. B83M9. The Avery Brundage Collection. Asian Art Museum of San Francisco.

Viewing the Art

Ideas for Writing. Students will probably be impressed with the artist's diligence in applying lacquer to the pictured plate. Ask students to think of a project they completed that, like this plate, required a lot of work. Then, have them write an informative paragraph explaining the steps they used to complete that project. You may want students to read their paragraphs aloud to the class.

The Principal Parts of a Verb **193**

Six Troublesome Verbs

(pp. 194–197)

OBJECTIVES

- To choose the correct forms of *lie* and *lay*
- To choose the correct forms of *sit* and *set*
- To choose the correct forms of *rise* and *raise*

DIRECT TEACHING

Modeling and Demonstration

Six Troublesome Verbs. Model how to read aloud and use the verbs *rise* and *raise* correctly by using the examples *One by one, the students' hands were rising* and *One by one, the students were raising their hands.* First, ask whether a word or word group in the first sentence receives the action of the verb *were rising.* [no] The verb *rise* takes no direct object; therefore, *were rising* is used correctly here because there is no direct object in the sentence. Next, ask whether a word or word phrase in the second sentence receives the action of the verb *were raising.* [yes; their hands] *Raise* does take a direct object; therefore, *were raising* is correct here. Now, have a volunteer use other examples from this chapter to demonstrate the correct use of the problem verbs *sit, set, lie,* and *lay.*

┌HELP───

The verb *lie* can also mean "to tell an untruth." Used in this way, *lie* still does not take an object. The past participle forms of this meaning of *lie* are *lied* and [*have*] *lied.*

EXAMPLE
You should never **lie** on an application.

Six Troublesome Verbs

Lie and *Lay*

The verb *lie* means "to rest," "to recline," or "to be in a certain place." *Lie* does not take a direct object. The verb *lay* means "to put [something] in a place." *Lay* generally takes a direct object.

Base Form	Present Participle	Past	Past Participle
lie	[is] lying	lay	[have] lain
lay	[is] laying	laid	[have] laid

EXAMPLES   A napkin **is lying** on each diner's plate. [no direct object]

The servers **are laying** a napkin on each diner's plate. [*Napkin* is the direct object of *are laying.*]

The seed **lay** on the ground. [no direct object]

We **laid** seed on the ground for the wild birds. [*Seed* is the direct object of *laid.*]

The issues **have lain** before the voters. [no direct object]

The state legislators **have laid** the issues before the voters. [*Issues* is the direct object of *have laid.*]

Exercise 6 Choosing the Forms of *Lie* and *Lay*

Choose the <u>correct verb form</u> in parentheses in each of the following sentences.

EXAMPLE   **1.** On your desk are (*lying, laying*) several letters that require your signature, Ms. Carmichael.

     1. lying

1. If you are sick, you should be (*lying, laying*) down.
2. They (*lay, laid*) the heavy crate on the handcart.
3. Lucia's mother has been (*lying, laying*) the canvas out to dry.
4. Amy (*lay, laid*) down for a while.
5. (*Lie, Lay*) down and rest for a minute.
6. She had just (*lain, laid*) down when the doorbell rang.
7. They (*lay, laid*) their plans before the committee.
8. The calf (*lay, laid*) on a pile of straw.
9. Kiyoshi has just (*lain, laid*) his paintbrush down.
10. Please (*lie, lay*) all of those blankets down here.

RESOURCES

Six Troublesome Verbs

Practice
- *Language & Sentence Skills Practice,* pp. 178–181

Differentiating Instruction
- *Developmental Language & Sentence Skills,* pp. 81–84

Sit and Set

The verb *sit* means "to be in a seated, upright position" or "to be in a place." *Sit* seldom takes a direct object. The verb *set* means "to put [something] in a place." *Set* generally takes a direct object.

Base Form	Present Participle	Past	Past Participle
sit	[is] sitting	sat	[have] sat
set	[is] setting	set	[have] set

EXAMPLES   Who **is sitting** next to the hearth? [no direct object]

Who **is setting** the chair next to the hearth? [*Chair* is the direct object of *is setting*.]

Where **should** we **sit**? [no direct object]

Where **should** we **set** the groceries? [*Groceries* is the direct object of *should set*.]

We **sat** near the end zone during last night's game. [no direct object]

We **set** the giant papier-mâché football near the end zone during last night's game. [*Football* is the direct object of *set*.]

Exercise 7   Choosing the Forms of *Sit* and *Set*

Choose the <u>correct verb form</u> in parentheses in each of the following sentences.

EXAMPLE   **1.** (*Sit, Set*) this box of diskettes on her computer desk, please.

    1. Set

1. After he had struck out, Pete (*sat*, *set*) on the bench.
2. Part of San Francisco's Chinatown (*sits*, *sets*) on an incline that overlooks San Francisco Bay.
3. Where were the packages (*sitting*, *setting*) this morning?
4. We had (*sat*, *set*) the new cushions on the Adirondack chairs.
5. In Japan people often (*sit*, *set*) on tatami instead of chairs.
6. They were (*sitting*, *setting*) placemats on the table.
7. Have you (*sat*, *set*) here long, Aaron?
8. We have (*sat*, *set*) down our packs and gotten out our map.
9. Mr. Carr told me to (*sit*, *set*) the equipment on his desk.
10. I may never know who (*sat*, *set*) on my glasses.

Six Troublesome Verbs   **195**

EXTENSION

Critical Thinking

Analysis. Have each student choose two television shows to view and analyze. Tell each student that he or she should watch one scene and write down the verbs that one of the characters uses. Students should repeat this activity with another scene and character from a different TV show. Then, have each student use the following questions as the basis for a summary of his or her findings.

1. Was the character's verb choice standard or nonstandard?

2. Did the character's word choice make him or her appealing? Why?

3. Describe the scenes in which these verbs were used.

4. Is there a connection between the scenes and the choice of language?

USAGE

Usage

Transitive and Intransitive Verbs.
Learning which verbs are transitive and which are intransitive might help students with the pairs of troublesome verbs. Remind students that transitive verbs take objects and intransitive verbs do not take objects. Have students identify which of the six troublesome verbs are transitive and which are intransitive. [*transitive: set, lay, and* raise; *intransitive: sit, lie, and* rise] For more information on transitive and intransitive verbs, refer students to **Chapter 1: Parts of Speech Overview.**

Six Troublesome Verbs   **195**

Advanced Learners

You may want to have students develop rules for using additional verb pairs that frequently cause problems—verbs such as *learn* and *teach* or *leave* and *let*. Ask students to write explanations of each of the verbs and to include sentences as examples of standard use.

Learners Having Difficulty

Have students make collages of pictures that illustrate the six troublesome verbs. Students could look in magazines for pictures of people performing the actions of the verbs, arrange their pictures on poster board, and write under each picture a sentence using the appropriate verb.

─HELP─

The verb *raise* has definitions other than the one given here. Another common definition is "to grow" or "to bring to maturity."

EXAMPLES
They **raise** sorghum.

She **raised** two foster children.

Notice that both of these uses take an object.

Rise and *Raise*

The verb *rise* means "to go up" or "to get up." *Rise* does not take a direct object. The verb *raise* means "to lift up" or "to cause [something] to rise." *Raise* generally takes a direct object.

Base Form	Present Participle	Past	Past Participle
rise	[is] rising	rose	[have] risen
raise	[is] raising	raised	[have] raised

EXAMPLES   One by one, the students' hands **were rising.** [no direct object]

One by one, the students were **raising** their hands. [*Hands* is the direct object of *were raising.*]

Una **rose** and then walked to the front of the classroom. [no direct object]

Una **raised** her eyebrows and then walked to the front of the classroom. [*Eyebrows* is the direct object of *raised.*]

The number of women who work outside the home **has risen** steadily during the past decade. [no direct object]
Has working outside the home **raised** their economic status? [*Status* is the direct object of *Has raised.*]

Exercise 8 **Choosing the Forms of *Rise* and *Raise***

Choose the correct verb form in parentheses in each of the following sentences.

EXAMPLE   **1.** The financial planner predicted, "In the near future, interest rates will not (*rise, raise*); they may decline."

    1. rise

1. Air bubbles have been (*rising, raising*) to the surface.
2. Increasing the import duty had (*risen, raised*) retail prices.
3. The speaker (*rose, raised*) from her chair and took the microphone.
4. The star has (*risen, raised*) in the east.
5. The rooster (*rises, raises*) early.
6. Before and during the Revolutionary War, many colonists worked hard to (*rise, raise*) public sentiment against King George III.

7. Hot-air balloons can (*rise*, *raise*) because they contain heated air, which is less dense than the surrounding air.

8. At the tribal council meeting, someone (*rose*, *raised*) the issue of land ownership within reservation boundaries.

9. Taylor is (*rising*, *raising*) the fallen child to her feet.

10. To make traditional challah, braid the bread dough after it has (*risen*, *raised*) for an hour.

Review E **Choosing the Forms of *Lie* and *Lay*, *Sit* and *Set*, and *Rise* and *Raise***

Choose the <u>correct verb form</u> in parentheses in each of the following sentences.

EXAMPLE   1. The snapshots of our trip to Kenya are (*lying*, *laying*) on top of the photo album.
　　　　　　1. *lying*

1. All week that box has (*lain*, *laid*) unopened on the desk.
2. We had (*rose*, *raised*) our hats to salute the astronauts.
3. The fawn (*lay*, *laid*) motionless in the underbrush.
4. Our applications were (*lying*, *laying*) in front of the file.
5. Would you like to (*sit*, *set*) with us at the powwow?
6. Yesterday I (*sat*, *set*) the telephone book on this table.
7. Where have you (*laid*, *lain*) your glasses?
8. Kathy sang as she (*lay*, *laid*) the baby in the crib.
9. Please (*rise*, *raise*) if you have a question.
10. Last night's victory really (*rose*, *raised*) the team's confidence.
11. Our potbellied pig, Oscar, often (*lies*, *lays*) in my lap when I watch TV.
12. Fred should (*lie*, *lay*) on his side to stop snoring.
13. After the fire, the museum curator (*sat*, *set*) on the curb and wept.
14. Tempers (*rose*, *raised*) as the debate progressed.
15. In Washington, D.C., we will (*lie*, *lay*) flowers at the Vietnam Veterans Memorial.
16. Mrs. Nasser (*sat*, *set*) the tabbouleh and the kibbe next to other traditional Lebanese foods.
17. He has (*sit*, *set*) the pie on the ledge.
18. Billows of dust had (*risen*, *raised*) from the field.
19. Haven't they (*sat*, *set*) down yet?
20. You should (*lie*, *lay*) on a padded surface to do exercises.

DIFFERENTIATING INSTRUCTION

Learners Having Difficulty

Have students work in pairs to write short paragraphs using forms of *lie* and *lay*, *sit* and *set*, or *rise* and *raise*. [*Lying under summer skies, I try to lay my troubles aside. I wish I could have laid them aside before they troubled me. Instead, though, I'll sit up, set my priorities straight, raise my spirits, and rise to the occasion.*] Then, have students exchange paragraphs with another group to check each other's work.

PRACTICE

Guided and Independent

Review E   You may want to use the first ten items in the review as guided practice. Then, have students complete the review as independent practice.   **HOMEWORK**

Tense

Rules 8d, e *(pp. 198–206)*

OBJECTIVES

- To identify verb tense and to explain differences in meaning in pairs of sentences
- To identify the tenses that correctly express given meanings in sentences

Reference Note

For information about **conjugating verbs in the passive voice,** see page 212. For more information about **active and passive voice,** see page 211.

DIFFERENTIATING INSTRUCTION

English-Language Learners

General Strategies. To help students with present perfect verb tense, you might use the following oral exercise. Give each student a question to ask the other members of the class. Have them use one of the following questions:

1. Have you ever ridden a horse?

2. Have you ever been to Canada?

3. Have you ever slept outside?

4. Have you ever seen a flamingo?

5. Have you ever had the mumps?

The repetition of a phrase is a key method of language acquisition and will help students fix this construction in their minds.

DIRECT TEACHING

Correcting Misconceptions

Tense. Because many verbs use the same form for the past tense and the past participle, some students may think all verbs follow this pattern. Remind students that many irregular verbs use a past participle form that is entirely different from the past tense form. If students have difficulty with this concept, have them proofread all of their papers with this misconception in mind. You may want to direct them to the list on pp. 183 and 184.

Tense

8d. The *tense* of a verb indicates the time of the action or of the state of being expressed by the verb.

Listing all the forms of a verb according to tense is called *conjugating* a verb. The tenses are formed from the verb's principal parts. Verbs in English have the six tenses shown on the following time line:

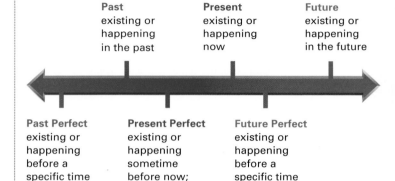

Past	**Present**	**Future**
existing or happening in the past	existing or happening now	existing or happening in the future

Past Perfect	**Present Perfect**	**Future Perfect**
existing or happening before a specific time in the past	existing or happening sometime before now; may be continuing now	existing or happening before a specific time in the future

Conjugation of the Verb *Give*	
Present Tense	
Singular	*Plural*
I give	we give
you give	you give
he, she, it gives	they give
Past Tense	
Singular	*Plural*
I gave	we gave
you gave	you gave
he, she, it gave	they gave

RESOURCES

Tense

Practice

- *Language & Sentence Skills Practice,* pp. 182–184

Differentiating Instruction

- *Developmental Language & Sentence Skills,* pp. 85–88

Conjugation of the Verb *Give*	
Future Tense	
Singular	*Plural*
I will (shall) give	we will (shall) give
you will (shall) give	you will (shall) give
he, she, it will (shall) give	they will (shall) give
Present Perfect Tense	
Singular	*Plural*
I have given	we have given
you have given	you have given
he, she, it has given	they have given
Past Perfect Tense	
Singular	*Plural*
I had given	we had given
you had given	you had given
he, she, it had given	they had given
Future Perfect Tense	
Singular	*Plural*
I will (shall) have given	we will (shall) have given
you will (shall) have given	you will (shall) have given
he, she, it will (shall) have given	they will (shall) have given

The Progressive Form

Each tense has an additional form called the ***progressive form,*** which expresses continuing action or state of being. In each tense the progressive form consists of the appropriate tense of *be* plus the present participle of a verb.

PRESENT PROGRESSIVE	am, is, are giving
PAST PROGRESSIVE	was, were giving
FUTURE PROGRESSIVE	will (shall) be giving
PRESENT PERFECT PROGRESSIVE	has been, have been giving
PAST PERFECT PROGRESSIVE	had been giving
FUTURE PERFECT PROGRESSIVE	will (shall) have been giving

STYLE   TIP

Traditionally, the helping verbs *shall* and *will* were used quite differently. Now, however, *shall* can be used almost interchangeably with *will.*

EXTENSION

Relating to Literature

Students are told to be consistent in their use of verb tense and are often confused when they read a short story that incorporates several tenses. Tell students to read a short story and to identify the various tenses it incorporates. Ask students why they think short stories often include many different verb tenses. [*A short story is a fictional narrative that relates a series of events. In order to show the sequence of events, several tenses often must be used.*]

Tense   **199**

DIFFERENTIATING INSTRUCTION

English-Language Learners

Asian Languages. Some languages, such as Chinese, Lao, Indonesian, and Vietnamese, do not use verb tenses to indicate time. Instead, a speaker will use either context or an adverb to establish the time of the events being discussed. The idea of specifying tense in every sentence might seem redundant to some students; therefore, they might use only the present tense. Emphasize that in English the correct tense must be used in every sentence if the reader is to understand what has been written.

┌─HELP─

The emphatic form is also used in questions and negative statements. These uses do not place special emphasis on the verb.

QUESTION
Do you **know** who wrote that?

NEGATIVE STATEMENT
They **do**n't **have** the answer.

┌─HELP─

The emphatic form is not a separate tense but is another form of each of the present and past tenses.

NOTE The progressive form is not a separate tense but another form of each of the six tenses.

The Emphatic Form

Only the present and the past tenses have another form, called the *emphatic form,* which shows emphasis. In the present tense the emphatic form consists of *do* or *does* plus the base form of a verb. In the past tense the emphatic form consists of *did* plus the base form of a verb.

PRESENT EMPHATIC I **do** not **intend** to give up on our team.

Although the grass is green, the front lawn **does need** watering.

PAST EMPHATIC The explorers suffered many hardships, yet they **did** finally **reach** their destination.

She **did** not **say** what they thought she had said.

The Verb *Be*

The conjugation of the verb *be* is different from that of any other verb. The progressive form of *be* is rarely used in any tenses other than the present and past tenses, and not one of the tenses of *be* has an emphatic form.

Conjugation of the Verb *Be*	
Present Tense	
Singular	*Plural*
I am	we are
you are	you are
he, she, it is	they are
Present Progressive: am, are, is being	
Past Tense	
Singular	*Plural*
I am	we were
you were	you were
he, she, it is	they were
Past Progressive: was, were being	

Conjugation of the Verb *Be*

Future Tense

Singular	*Plural*
I will (shall) be	we will (shall) be
you will (shall) be	you will (shall) be
he, she, it will (shall) be	they will (shall) be

Present Perfect Tense

Singular	*Plural*
I have been	we have been
you have been	you have been
he, she, it has been	they have been

Past Perfect Tense

Singular	*Plural*
I had been	we had been
you had been	you had been
he, she, it had been	they had been

Future Perfect Tense

Singular	*Plural*
I will (shall) have been	we will (shall) have been
you will (shall) have been	you will (shall) have been
he, she, it will (shall) have been	they will (shall) have been

The Uses of the Tenses

8e. Each of the six tenses has its own uses.

(1) The *present tense* expresses an action or a state of being that is occurring now, at the present time.

EXAMPLES   Deborah, Ashley, and Brendan **wait** patiently for the bus. [present]

Deborah, Ashley, and Brendan **are waiting** patiently for the bus. [present progressive]

Deborah, Ashley, and Brendan **do wait** patiently for the bus. [present emphatic]

RETEACHING

Tense

Activity. Have students play a writing round robin in groups of three or four. Ask one student in each group to begin a short story describing a series of events in the past tense. After five minutes, call time and have students hand their stories to another student in the group. Then, tell students to shift to the present perfect tense. Continue calling time and shifting tenses at five-minute intervals until students have written in all tenses. Encourage students to make their shifts in tense as smooth and logical as possible. You may want students to read their stories to the class. Have the class discuss the relative difficulty of each tense. While students are waiting to take a turn, you may want to have them review the tenses they will be using.

┌─HELP─

A past action or state of being may also be shown in another way.

EXAMPLE
  She **used to collect** stamps.

Used to typically expresses habitual action in the past.

The present tense is also used

- to show a customary or habitual action or state of being
- to state a general truth—something that is always true
- to summarize the plot or subject matter of a literary work (such use is called the *literary present*)
- to make a historical event seem current (such use is called the *historical present*)
- to express future time

EXAMPLES   After school I **wash** the breakfast dishes and **start** supper. [customary actions]

In the Northern Hemisphere the summer solstice **occurs** when the sun is at its northernmost position each year. [general truth]

Countee Cullen **uses** traditional verse forms such as the epigram and the sonnet to explore African American themes. [literary present]

In 1520 Ferdinand Magellan **rounds** the southern tip of South America and **names** the ocean that **lies** before him the Pacific Ocean. [historical present]

The movie that **opens** tomorrow **runs** through next week. [future time]

(2) The *past tense* expresses an action or a state of being that occurred in the past and did not continue into the present.

EXAMPLES   I **stayed** at the library until closing time. [past]

I **was researching** the life and times of Timothy Thomas Fortune, an early civil rights advocate in the 1800s. [past progressive]

My research **did provide** me with enough information for my paper on Fortune. [past emphatic]

(3) The *future tense* expresses an action or a state of being that will occur. The future tense is formed with the helping verb *will* or *shall* and the base form of a verb.

EXAMPLES   I **will attend** the Writer's Workshop at the University of Iowa in the fall. [future]

I **will be attending** the Writer's Workshop at the University of Iowa in the fall. [future progressive]

NOTE A future action or state of being may also be expressed by using

- the present tense of *be* with *going to* and the base form of a verb

EXAMPLE My aunt and uncle **are going to visit** the Philippines next year.

- the present tense of *be* with *about to* and the base form of a verb

EXAMPLE Mr. Campos **is about to open** the time capsule in front of the whole school.

- the present tense of a verb with a word or word group that expresses future time

EXAMPLE Finals **begin next Monday.**

(4) The ***present perfect tense*** expresses an action or a state of being that occurred at some indefinite time in the past. The present perfect tense is formed with the helping verb *have* or *has* and the past participle of a verb.

EXAMPLES I **have written** to the governor, but I **have** not **received** a reply. [present perfect]

Who **has been playing** my cassettes? [present perfect progressive]

NOTE Avoid the use of the present perfect tense to express a specific time in the past. Instead, use the past tense.

NONSTANDARD *Prairie Schooner* has published a new short story by Louise Erdrich last month.

STANDARD *Prairie Schooner* **published** a new short story by Louise Erdrich last month.

The present perfect tense is also used to express an action or a state of being that began in the past and that continues into the present.

EXAMPLES Over one thousand United States communities **have joined** the International Sister City program. [present perfect]

The program **has been pairing** cities in the United States with cities in other nations since 1956. [present perfect progressive]

Critical Thinking

Synthesis. Have students apply what they have learned about future and future perfect tenses by writing descriptive paragraphs about what they think school will be like two hundred years from now. After students finish their drafts, tell them to underline their verbs, to check their papers for correctness, and to write final drafts to share with the class.

Reference Note

For information about using **past perfect** in "if" clauses, see page 207, Rule 8g.

(5) The *past perfect tense* expresses an action or a state of being that ended before some other past action or state of being. The past perfect tense is formed with the helping verb *had* and the past participle of a verb.

EXAMPLES   I finally remembered where I **had seen** a copy of Rufino Tamayo's mural *Nature and the Artist.* [past perfect—The seeing occurred before the remembering.]

I **had been looking** through dozens of old magazines before I finally remembered to check the latest issue of *Smithsonian.* [past perfect progressive—The looking occurred before the remembering.]

(6) The *future perfect tense* expresses an action or a state of being that will end before some other action or state of being. The future perfect tense is formed with the helping verbs *will have* or *shall have* and the past participle of a verb.

EXAMPLES   By the time the bus arrives, we **will have waited** for an hour. [future perfect—The waiting will occur before the arrival of the bus.]

By then, we **will have been waiting** for two hours. [future perfect progressive—The waiting will occur before the time indicated by *then.*]

Exercise 9 Understanding the Uses of the Six Tenses

Identify the tenses of the verbs in each of the following pairs of sentences. Also tell whether the verbs are in the progressive or emphatic form. Be prepared to explain how these differences in tense affect the meanings of the sentences.

EXAMPLE   1. a. Why had she gone to the theater?
                  b. Why has she been going to the theater?

          1. a. *past perfect tense*
             b. *present perfect progressive tense*

1. a. Margo lived in Brazil for eight years.
   b. Margo has lived in Brazil for eight years.
2. a. How many home runs did Sammy Sosa hit this season?
   b. How many home runs has Sammy Sosa hit this season?
3. a. Have the directions been explained clearly?
   b. Had the directions been explained clearly?

HELP

In the example in Exercise 9, the past perfect is used in the first sentence to show action that was completed in the past, while the second sentence uses present perfect progressive to show action that is continuing into the present.

Exercise 9 Understanding the Uses of the Six Tenses

ANSWERS

1. past tense—indicates that Margo's stay in Brazil began and ended at a specific time; present perfect tense—indicates that Margo still lives in Brazil
2. past emphatic tense—indicates a completed action; present perfect tense—indicates that the season continues into the present
3. present perfect tense—indicates that the directions were explained at some indefinite time in the past; past perfect tense—indicates that the directions were explained in the past before some other past occurrence

4. **a.** Was she driving?

   b. Had she been driving?

5. **a.** As of June 30, they will have raised taxes twice this year.

   b. As of June 30, they will be raising taxes for the second time this year.

6. **a.** Our team is producing the whole film ourselves.

   b. Our team will be producing the whole film ourselves.

7. **a.** People do like these science fiction films.

   b. People did like these science fiction films.

8. **a.** Uncle Jed lived in Abilene for sixty years.

   b. Uncle Jed has lived in Abilene for sixty years.

9. **a.** The game has been on for an hour.

   b. The game was on for an hour.

10. **a.** His quail eggs will have hatched by Saturday.

   b. His quail eggs will be hatching by Saturday.

Exercise 10 **Understanding the Uses of the Six Tenses**

Identify which sentence in each of the following pairs of sentences most clearly expresses the meaning given. Be prepared to name the tense(s) used in each sentence and to tell whether the verbs are in the progressive or emphatic form.

EXAMPLE   **1.** *Meaning:* The Yeary family no longer lives in Anchorage.
         a. The Yeary family lived in Anchorage for years.
         b. The Yeary family has lived in Anchorage for years.

      1. *a*

1. *Meaning:* John still works for Mr. Porzio.
   a. John had worked for Mr. Porzio for a year.
   b. John has worked for Mr. Porzio for a year.

2. *Meaning:* Ann Rosine could be on her way to Worcester right now or could be going in the future.
   a. Ann Rosine is moving to Worcester, Massachusetts.
   b. Ann Rosine will be moving to Worcester, Massachusetts.

3. *Meaning:* Jaime is still studying physics.
   a. Jaime has been studying physics since last summer.
   b. Jaime studied physics last summer.

4. *Meaning:* Alison takes a bus to work on a regular basis.
   a. Alison will be taking the bus to work.
   b. Alison takes the bus to work.

—HELP—

In the example in Exercise 10, the first sentence uses the past tense, while the second sentence uses the present perfect tense.

1. a. past perf.
   b. pres. perf.

2. a. pres. prog.
   b. future prog.

3. a. pres. perf. prog.
   b. past

4. a. future prog.
   b. pres.

Tense   **205**

Exercise 9 **Understanding the Uses of the Six Tenses**

ANSWERS continued

4. past progressive tense—indicates an action that began and ended at a specific time; past perfect progressive tense—indicates that she was driving in the past before some other past occurrence

5. future perfect tense—indicates that taxes will be raised in the future before some other future occurrence; future progressive tense—indicates that the raising of taxes will be an ongoing action in the future

6. present progressive tense—indicates that the production is an ongoing process in the present; future progressive tense—indicates that producing will be an ongoing action in the future

7. present emphatic tense—indicates, with emphasis, that the liking is in the present; past emphatic tense—indicates, with emphasis, that the liking occurred in the past but did not continue into the present

8. past tense—indicated that Uncle Jed's time in Abilene began and ended in the past; present perfect tense—indicates that Uncle Jed still lives in Abilene

9. present perfect tense—indicates that the game is still on; past tense—indicates that the game began and ended in the past

10. future perfect tense—indicates that the eggs will have completed hatching before some other event in the future; future progressive tense—indicates that the hatching will be an ongoing action in the future

5. a. pres. prog.
   b. past

6. a. future
   b. future perf.

7. a. pres. prog.
   b. pres.

8. a. past emp.
   b. pres. emp.

9. a. pres. perf. prog.
   b. past perf. prog.

10. a. past/past perf.
    b. past/past

5. *Meaning:* Joe has not yet reached the school.
   (a.) Joe is riding his bike to school today.
   b. Joe rode his bike to school today.

6. *Meaning:* The opening of the shop will occur before September 8.
   a. On September 8, the shop will open.
   (b.) On September 8, the shop will have opened.

7. *Meaning:* Aunt Nell is currently photographing Alaskan wildflowers.
   (a.) Aunt Nell is photographing Alaskan wildflowers.
   b. Aunt Nell photographs Alaskan wildflowers.

8. *Meaning:* I no longer enjoy ice skating every winter.
   (a.) I did enjoy ice skating every winter.
   b. I do enjoy ice skating every winter.

9. *Meaning:* My brother is no longer practicing piano.
   a. My brother has been practicing piano all day.
   (b.) My brother had been practicing piano all day.

10. *Meaning:* Ray was a bank officer at the age of twenty-four.
    (a.) When Ray turned twenty-five, he had been promoted to the position of bank officer.
    b. When Ray turned twenty-five, he was promoted to the position of bank officer.

USAGE

Special Problems in the Use of Tenses
Rules 8f–k *(pp. 206–210)*

OBJECTIVE

■ **To identify and correct errors in the use of verb tenses in sentences**

Special Problems in the Use of Tenses

Sequence of Tenses

8f. Use tense forms correctly to show relationships between verbs in a sentence.

(1) When describing events that occur at the same time, use verbs in the same tense.

EXAMPLES The bell **rings,** and the classroom **empties.** [present tense]
The bell **rang,** and the classroom **emptied.** [past tense]

(2) When describing events that occur at different times, use verbs in different tenses to show the order of events.

EXAMPLES I **play** football now, but I **played** basketball in junior high.
[Because I am playing football now, the present tense form *play* is correct. My playing basketball occurred in the past and did not continue into the present; therefore, the past tense form *played* is correct.]

RESOURCES

Special Problems in the Use of Tenses
Practice
■ *Language & Sentence Skills Practice,* pp. 185–186
Differentiating Instruction
■ *Developmental Language & Sentence Skills,* pp. 89–90

Sabrena **mentioned** that she **had invited** some of her neighbors to the party. [Because Sabrena made the statement in the past, the past tense form *mentioned* is correct. She invited the neighbors before she made the statement; therefore, the past perfect form *had invited* is correct.]

The tense you use depends on the meaning you want to express.

EXAMPLES   I **believe** they **own** the Flamingo Cafe. [Both verbs are in the present tense to indicate both actions are occurring now.]

I **believe** they **owned** the Flamingo Cafe. [The change in the tense of the second verb implies that they no longer own the Flamingo Cafe.]

Joan **said** that she **worked** at the textile mill last year. [Both verbs are in the past tense to indicate that both actions no longer occur.]

Joan **said** that she **will work** at the textile mill next year. [The change in the tense of the second verb implies that Joan did not work at the textile mill when she made the statement but that she planned to work there.]

8g. Do not use *would have* in an "*if*" clause that expresses the earlier of two past actions. Use the past perfect tense.

NONSTANDARD   If he would have taken more time, he would have won.
STANDARD   If he **had taken** more time, he would have won.

NONSTANDARD   I would not have been late if I would have had a watch.
STANDARD   I would not have been late if I **had had** a watch.

Exercise 11 Using Tenses Correctly

Each of the following sentences contains an error in the use of tenses. Revise each sentence to correct the error.

EXAMPLE   **1.** Frida not only wrote the story but also has illustrated it.

1. Frida not only wrote the story but also illustrated it.

or

Frida not only has written the story but also has illustrated it.

1. Pam appreciated the old saying that every cloud had a silver lining.

2. By the time we graduate in June, Ms. Vargas will be teaching Spanish for twenty-four years.

3. Although Denny's skill was demonstrated during the season, he was not chosen to play in the all-star game.

MEETING THE CHALLENGE

Choose a simple activity to teach the rest of your class. Break your activity into several steps, and write out clear instructions for each step. An important part of your instructions will be correct use of verb tenses, so check over your verbs and correct any errors before presenting to the class. Try to include a correct form of one or more of the following verbs: *sit, set, lie, lay, rise,* and *raise*.

ANSWER
Demonstrations will vary, but students should use correct verb tenses throughout their presentations. All uses of *sit, set, lie, lay, rise,* and *raise* should be correct as well.

┌─**HELP**─
Although two answers are given for the example in Exercise 11, you need to give only one answer for each sentence.

1. has
2. have been

3. had been

PRACTICE

Guided and Independent

Exercise 11   You may want to use the first ten items in the exercise as guided practice. Then, have students complete the exercise as independent practice.   **HOMEWORK**

USAGE

Tense   **207**

4. had   4. If they ~~would have~~ called sooner, we would have given them a ride.

5. had   5. When Jeremy got to the dentist after school, his tooth ᴧ already stopped hurting.

6. had   6. The company hired Ms. Littmann because she ᴧ lived for many years in Japan.

7. had   7. By the time I presented my report before the special committee, the members ᴧ ~~have~~ already studied several other reports on nuclear-waste disposal.

8. had   8. Mr. Frey ᴧ already complained to the neighbors many times before he called the police.

9. have received   9. By then I will ~~receive~~ my first paycheck.

10. had forgotten   10. If she ~~forgot~~ the directions, we could have been lost.

11. had   11. Hiram R. Revels, the first African American to be elected United States senator, ᴧ ~~has~~ been a minister and teacher before he entered into politics.

12. had   12. If they had ᴧ enough money, they could have taken a taxi to the opening of that new musical.

13. had   13. As I thought about our argument, I was sure that you ᴧ lost your temper first.

14. have been   14. Next Saturday is a very important anniversary for Mai's family; they will ᴧ ~~be~~ living in the United States for exactly one year.

15. had   15. When we reviewed the videotapes of the game, we saw that the other team ᴧ committed the foul.

16. had   16. The clerk remembered that the manager ᴧ ~~has~~ ordered the new shipment last Tuesday.

17. rises   17. How could I have forgotten that the sun ᴧ ~~rose~~ in the east?

18. have been   18. We estimate that when we are in our forties, we will ᴧ ~~be~~ working more than twenty years.

19. had   19. If Gary ᴧ ~~would have~~ read the ad more carefully, he could have saved more than fifty dollars on his new camera.

20. had   20. J. D. would have done much better on the art history exam if he ᴧ reviewed the chapter on Aztec stonework.

The Present Infinitive and the Present Perfect Infinitive

Present Infinitive	Present Perfect Infinitive
to be	to have been
to discover	to have discovered

8h. The *present infinitive* expresses an action or a state of being that follows another action or state of being.

EXAMPLES   Charlotte had expected **to go** with us to the state fair. [The action expressed by *to go* follows the action expressed by *had expected*.]

Charlotte had planned **to ask** her boss for time off. [The action expressed by *to ask* follows the action expressed by *had planned*.]

8i. The *present perfect infinitive* expresses an action or a state of being that precedes another action or state of being.

EXAMPLES   My little brother pretended **to have read** my diary. [The action expressed by *to have read* precedes the action expressed by *pretended*.]

I would like **to have gone** to the new movie with you and your brother and sister. [The action expressed by *to have gone* precedes the action expressed by *would like*.]

Reference Note

For more information about **infinitives,** see page 70.

The Present Participle, the Past Participle, and the Present Perfect Participle

Present Participle	Past Participle	Present Perfect Participle
being	been	having been
discovering	discovered	having discovered

8j. When used as a verbal, the *present participle* or *past participle* expresses an action or a state of being that occurs at the same time as another action or state of being.

EXAMPLES   **Receiving** word of their freedom in June 1865, former slaves in Texas created the Juneteenth holiday. [The action expressed by *Receiving* occurs at the same time as the action expressed by *created*.]

Gathered at my grandmother's house, my family celebrated Juneteenth this year. [The state of being expressed by *Gathered* occurs at the same time as the action expressed by *celebrated*.]

Thrown at over ninety miles per hour, the baseball flew past the batter before he could swing. [The action expressed by *Thrown* occurs at the same time as the action expressed by *flew*.]

USAGE

Reference Note

For more information about **participles used as verbals,** see page 64.

8k. When used as a verbal, the ***present perfect participle*** expresses an action or a state of being that precedes another action or state of being.

EXAMPLES **Having missed** the midterm exam, I took a makeup test.
[The action expressed by *Having missed* precedes the action expressed by *took.*]

Having been accepted by several colleges, Rosa chose one.
[The action expressed by *Having been accepted* precedes the action expressed by *chose.*]

DIFFERENTIATING INSTRUCTION

English-Language Learners

General Strategies. Some students whose first language is not English might be confused by the English infinitive. English generally uses a two-word construction for infinitives (instead of one word, as in many other languages). To help such students, you might have them circle the word *to* in the sentences in **Exercise 12.** For more information on infinitives, refer students to **Chapter 3: The Phrase.**

EXTENSION

Critical Thinking

Synthesis. Ask students to work in pairs to apply the rules they have learned in this lesson. Ask one student in each pair to write an introductory participial phrase or infinitive phrase in any tense, and ask their partners to write the second half of the sentence. After students have written three sentences, ask them to switch roles.

HELP

Although some sentences in Exercise 12 can be correctly revised in more than one way, you need to give only one revision for each item.

3. [*or* To have written about Pueblo ceremonies, I would have had to do more research at the library.]

9. [*or* If you want to go shopping, I will drive you to the mall with Neil.]

Exercise 12 **Using Tenses Correctly**

Each of the following sentences contains an error in the use of verb forms. Identify the error, and then give the correct form of the verb.

EXAMPLE 1. Finishing his research, Simon began writing his report on the Seneca chief Kaiiontwa'ko.
1. *Finishing—Having finished*

1. Spending three hours on a review of chemistry, we then worked on irregular French verbs. **1.** Having spent
2. Standing in line for more than two hours, Vicky finally got tickets to the Trisha Yearwood concert. **2.** Having stood
3. To have written about Pueblo ceremonies, I would have to do more research at the library. **3.** write [See left for alternative answer.]
4. Flying from Missouri to California before, we remembered to set our watches back. **4.** Having flown
5. We wanted to have avoided any controversy about the new rules for packaging dairy products. **5.** avoid
6. Having attempted to travel across the African continent, the explorers encountered vast deserts, dense rain forests, and tall mountains. **6.** Attempting
7. Through the centuries, arctic peoples learned to have survived in a harsh environment. **7.** survive
8. They were hoping to have had a multiple-choice test in history instead of an essay exam.
9. If you want to go shopping, I would have driven you to the mall with Neil. **9.** had wanted [See left for alternative answer.]
10. Tutankhamen, Helen of Troy, and Shakespeare are the three people I would have most liked to have met. **10.** meet

Active Voice and Passive Voice

8l. *Voice* is the form a transitive verb takes to indicate whether the subject of the verb performs or receives the action.

Transitive verbs may be in the *active voice* or the *passive voice*. When the subject of a verb performs the action, the verb is in the **active voice.** When the subject receives the action, the verb is in the **passive voice.**

As the following examples show, verbs in the active voice take direct objects, and verbs in the passive voice do not.

ACTIVE VOICE   Mark Riley **anchors** the news. [*News* is the direct object.]
PASSIVE VOICE   The news **is anchored** by Mark Riley. [no direct object]

ACTIVE VOICE   The firefighters **have extinguished** the blazing fire. [*Fire* is the direct object.]
PASSIVE VOICE   The blazing fire **has been extinguished** by the firefighters. [no direct object]
PASSIVE VOICE   The fire **has been extinguished.** [no direct object]

From the preceding examples, you can see how an active construction can become a passive construction.

- The direct object of the verb in the active voice becomes the subject of the verb in the passive voice.
- The subject of the verb in the active voice may become an object of a prepositional phrase beginning with *by*. (As the last example shows, this prepositional phrase is not always included.)

The Retained Object

A verb in the active voice often has an indirect object as well as a direct object. When such a verb is put into the passive voice, either object can become the subject. The other object then serves as a complement called a *retained object.*

	S	**V**		**IO**	**DO**
ACTIVE VOICE	Mrs. Platero gives each new employee a tour of the plant.				

	S	**V**	**RO**
PASSIVE VOICE	Each new employee is given a tour of the plant by Mrs. Platero.		

	S	**V**	**RO**
PASSIVE VOICE	A tour of the plant is given each new employee by Mrs. Platero.		

Reference Note

For more about **transitive verbs,** see page 18.

USAGE

Active Voice and Passive Voice
Rules 8l, m *(pp. 211–215)*

OBJECTIVE

- To revise sentences in the passive voice

DIFFERENTIATING INSTRUCTION

Advanced Learners
Tell students that although as a general rule they should avoid overusing the passive voice, there are times when it is effective. For example, the passive voice can be used to neutralize the sense of action, to create a sense of evasiveness, or to create suspense in writing. Have students look in magazines or newspapers for examples of effective use of the passive voice. You may want to ask students to share their examples of passive voice with the class and to explain why those examples are effective.

English-Language Learners
Hmong. Hmong relies primarily upon the active voice, so the distinction in English between active and passive uses may pose both translation difficulties and writing challenges for some Hmong speakers. Remind students of the purpose of the passive voice—to stress the object of a verb's action—and offer translation assistance when necessary.

Reference Note

For the **conjugation of *give* in the active voice,** see page 198.

STYLE TIP

The progressive forms of the passive voice exist for the future, present perfect, past perfect, and future perfect tenses. However, the forms are not shown in the chart because the use of *be* or *been* with *being* is extremely awkward. *Give,* for example, in the passive future perfect progressive is *will (shall) have been being given.*

A verb in the passive voice always includes a form of *be* and the past participle of a verb. The form of *be* and the helping verb, if any, indicate the tense of the verb phrase.

Conjugation of the Verb *Give* in the Passive Voice	
Present Tense	
Singular	*Plural*
I am given	we are given
you are given	you are given
he, she, it is given	they are given
Present Progressive: am, are, is being given	
Past Tense	
Singular	*Plural*
I was given	we were given
you were given	you were given
he, she, it was given	they were given
Past Progressive: was, were being given	
Future Tense	
Singular	*Plural*
I will (shall) be given	we will (shall) be given
you will (shall) be given	you will (shall) be given
he, she, it will (shall) be given	they will (shall) be given
Present Perfect Tense	
Singular	*Plural*
I have been given	we have been given
you have been given	you have been given
he, she, it has been given	they have been given
Past Perfect Tense	
Singular	*Plural*
I had been given	we had been given
you had been given	you had been given
he, she, it had been given	they had been given

212 Chapter 8   Using Verbs Correctly

CONTENT-AREA CONNECTIONS

Conjugation of the Verb *Give* in the Passive Voice	
Future Perfect Tense	
Singular	*Plural*
I will (shall) have been given	we will (shall) have been given
you will (shall) have been given	you will (shall) have been given
he, she, it will (shall) have been given	they will (shall) have been given

The Uses of the Passive Voice

8m. Use the passive voice sparingly.

Choosing between the active voice and the passive voice is a matter of style, not correctness. In general, however, the passive voice is less direct, less forceful, and less concise than the active voice. In fact, the passive voice may produce an awkward effect.

AWKWARD PASSIVE	The event was completed when a triple somersault was done by Mario.
ACTIVE	Mario **completed** the event by doing a triple somersault.

A string of passive-voice verbs is particularly awkward.

STRING OF PASSIVES	I was invited by Ms. Long to visit her animal shelter. Rows of cages had been placed along two sides of a large storage shed. Dozens of cats, dogs, hamsters, and guinea pigs were held in the cages. In one corner of the noisy building, a scrawny brown puppy was being hand-fed by an assistant. I was told by Ms. Long that so many unwanted pets had been brought to her by people that homes could not be found for all of them. It was agreed by us that the responsibility of owning a pet should be understood by people before one is bought.
ACTIVE	Ms. Long **invited** me to visit her animal shelter. She **had placed** rows of cages along two sides of a large storage shed. The cages **held** dozens of cats, dogs, hamsters, and guinea pigs. In one corner of the noisy building, an assistant **was hand-feeding** a scrawny brown puppy. Ms. Long **told** me that people **had brought** her so many unwanted pets that she **could** not **find** homes for all of them. We **agreed** that people **should understand** the responsibility of owning a pet before they **buy** one.

Exercise 13 Revising
Sentences in the Passive Voice

ANSWERS
Answers will vary. Here are some possibilities.

1. The service representatives gave us a training session after they had installed all of the new computers.
2. C
3. The area homeowners held a meeting to discuss the landfill project that the city council had proposed.
4. C
5. While Clarence creates the decorations, Edna will prepare the buffet.
6. C
7. Estevanico, a well-known black explorer, guided the 1539 expedition of Francisco Vásquez de Coronado.

COMPUTER TIP

If you use a computer when you write, you may want to find out about the different kinds of style-checking programs that are available. At least one such program checks for use of the passive voice. Remember, though, that the program can only highlight the passive-voice verbs it finds; it cannot tell whether they are used for a particular reason.

HELP

The active voice is preferable in the example in Exercise 13 because it makes the sentence more direct and forceful.

Passive voice constructions are not always awkward. In fact, the passive voice is useful in the following situations:

- when you do not know who performed the action

EXAMPLE   All of the tickets **had been sold** weeks before the concert.

- when you do not want to reveal the performer of the action

EXAMPLE   Mistakes **were made.**

- when you want to emphasize the receiver of the action rather than the performer

EXAMPLES   Lasers **are used** in industry, communications, and medicine.

Aretha Franklin **has been emulated** by many singers.

Exercise 13 **Revising Sentences in the Passive Voice**

Revise the following sentences by changing verbs from the passive voice to the active voice wherever you think the changes are desirable. If you think the passive voice is preferable, write *C*. For each verb, be prepared to explain why you think the active or passive voice is preferable.

EXAMPLE   1. An interesting legend about the origin of the moon was told to us by one of the participants in the Hopi ceremonial dance.

1. *One of the participants in the Hopi ceremonial dance told us an interesting legend about the origin of the moon.*

1. After all of the new computers had been installed by the service representatives, a training session was given to us by them.
2. If the children had been enchanted by Mr. Wright's tales before, they would be even more enthralled by his new story of a fantasy kingdom on the moon.
3. A meeting was held by the area homeowners to discuss the landfill project that had been proposed by the city council.
4. The value of storytelling is explained in an ancient Seneca myth.
5. While the decorations are being created by Clarence, the buffet will be prepared by Edna.
6. Potatoes had been cultivated in South America for more than twenty centuries before they were grown in Europe.
7. The 1539 expedition of Francisco Vásquez de Coronado was guided by Estevanico, a well-known black explorer.

8. The chapters on constitutional amendments, which had been assigned to us last week by Mrs. Robinson, were reviewed by us before the test.

9. Shinae Chun is admired and respected by her colleagues.

10. If the practicality of home robots had been demonstrated by Mike Smith, his request for funding would not have been rejected by the review committee.

Mood

Mood is the form a verb takes to indicate the attitude of the person using the verb. Verbs may be in one of three moods: *indicative*, *imperative*, or *subjunctive*.

8n. The *indicative mood* expresses a fact, an opinion, or a question.

EXAMPLES   Heitor Villa-Lobos **was** a composer who **became** known for his use of Brazilian folk music.

Isabel Allende **is** a gifted writer.

Can you **tell** me when the United States **entered** World War I?

8o. The *imperative mood* expresses a direct command or a request.

A verb in the imperative mood has only one form. That form is the same as the verb's base form.

EXAMPLES   **Tell** me when the United States entered World War I.

Please **pass** the salsa.

8p. The *subjunctive mood* expresses a suggestion, a necessity, a condition contrary to fact, or a wish.

Only the present and past tenses have distinctive forms in the subjunctive mood.

Notice in the following partial conjugation of *be* how the present tense and the past tense in the subjunctive mood differ from those in the indicative mood.

Reference Note

For more information about **conjugating verbs**, see pages 198 and 200.

Exercise 13 Revising Sentences in the Passive Voice

ANSWERS continued

8. Before the test, we reviewed the chapters on constitutional amendments, which Mrs. Robinson had assigned to us last week.

9. C

10. If Mike Smith had demonstrated the practicality of home robots, the review committee would not have rejected his request for funding.

Mood and Modals

Rules 8n–q *(pp. 215–222)*

OBJECTIVES

- To identify moods of verbs
- To supply appropriate modals in sentences

DIRECT TEACHING

Imperative Mood

Reminder. Remind students that the imperative mood relies on an implied *you* as the subject of the sentence, as in the following examples:

1. (You) Turn off the radio immediately.

2. (You) Draw a circle around the verb phrase.

Present Indicative		Present Subjunctive	
Singular	**Plural**	**Singular**	**Plural**
I am	we are	[that] I be	[that] we be
you are	you are	[that] you be	[that] you be
he, she, it is	they are	[that] he, she, it be	[that] they be

Past Indicative		Past Subjunctive	
Singular	**Plural**	**Singular**	**Plural**
I was	we were	[if] I were	[if] we were
you were	you were	[if] you were	[if] you were
he, she, it was	they were	[if] he, she, it were	[if] they were

┌HELP──

The use of *that* and *if* in the chart is explained in Rules 8p(1) and 8p(2).

The present subjunctive form of a verb is the same as the base form of the verb. *Be* is the only verb whose past subjunctive form is different from its past indicative form.

(1) The *present subjunctive* expresses a suggestion or necessity.

The verb in a subordinate clause beginning with *that* is usually in the subjunctive mood when a word in the independent clause indicates a suggestion (such as *ask, request, suggest,* or *recommend*) or a necessity (such as *necessary* or *essential*).

EXAMPLES We recommended that Marva Collins **be invited** to speak at the assembly tomorrow.

The students have urged that John **be reinstated.**

I move that the committee **adjourn.**

It is essential that she **have** a chance to compete in the state debating finals.

│STYLE   TIP│

Although the use of the subjunctive is declining in informal situations, you should use it in formal writing and speech.

(2) The *past subjunctive* expresses a condition contrary to fact or expresses a wish.

A clause beginning with *if, as if,* or *as though* often expresses a condition contrary to fact—something that is not true. In such a clause, use the past subjunctive.

EXAMPLES   If I **were** you, I'd be pleased.

If she **were** careful, she would make fewer errors.

My friend Doris teases me as though she **were** my sister.

Similarly, use the past subjunctive to express a wish.

EXAMPLES   I wish I **were** on a Caribbean island.

Jaime wishes that his mother **weren't** feeling ill.

MISS PEACH courtesy of Mell Lazarus and Creators Syndicate. ©1991, Mell Lazarus.

Exercise 14 Identifying the Moods of Verbs

For each of the following sentences, identify the mood of the italicized verb as *indicative*, *imperative*, or *subjunctive*.

EXAMPLE   **1.** If I *were* as talented an actor as you, I would try out for the lead in the play.

1. *subjunctive*

1. Willis had insisted that every employee *be* invited.
2. Felicia, *sit* closer to the table, please.
3. Did you hear that Tanya's mother *is* the new deputy fire chief?
4. Having struck out again, Katie moaned, "I wish I *were* a better hitter!"
5. *Are* you and your brother excited about seeing your grandparents?
6. If you want to join the league, *sign* up before the end of school.
7. "I wish this book *were* a little shorter," sighed Sabrena as she turned to page 378.
8. Please *wait* here while I get the rest of my books.
9. I wish I *were* able to go to the sneak preview of the new Spike Lee movie, but I have to work.
10. "This time next year, I *will be* in college," Takala said.

1. sub.
2. imp.
3. ind.
4. sub.

5. ind.
6. imp.
7. sub.

8. imp.
9. sub.

10. ind.

Mood   **217**

USAGE

| STYLE | TIP |

Can is often used to express permission in informal situations. In formal situations, you should use *may*.

INFORMAL Can I borrow your book?
  FORMAL **May** I borrow your book?

| STYLE | TIP |

In the past, careful writers and speakers of English used the modals *shall* and *will* quite differently. Currently, however, *will* and *shall* are generally interchangeable, except in a few cases.

EXAMPLES
  Shall we **dance**? [*Shall* expresses an invitation or request.]
  We **shall** overcome the odds. [*Shall* expresses determination.]

Modals

8q. A modal is a helping (auxiliary) verb that is joined with a main verb to express an attitude toward the action or state of being of the main verb.

(1) The modals *can* and *could* are used to express ability.

EXAMPLES **Can** you **swim**?

  I **could** not **move** my computer desk.

(2) The modal *may* is used to express permission or possibility.

EXAMPLES **May** I **drive** your car? [permission]

  I **may have put** my library card in my locker before I came to class. [possibility]

(3) The modal *might*, like *may*, is used to express a possibility.

Often, the possibility expressed by *might* is less likely than the possibility expressed by *may*.

EXAMPLE I **might have put** my library card in my locker before I came to class, but I doubt it.

(4) The modal *must* is used most often to express a requirement. Sometimes *must* is used to express an explanation.

EXAMPLES First, we **must obtain** our principal's permission to hold the fund-raiser in the school cafeteria. [requirement]

  My aunt Rowena said, "You **must have** a green thumb, for all of your plants are healthy and beautiful." [explanation]

(5) The modal *ought* is used to express an obligation or a likelihood.

EXAMPLES We **ought to reserve** judgment until we have examined all of the evidence. [obligation]

  The soccer game **ought to be** over by 6:00 P.M. [likelihood]

(6) The modals *shall* and *will* are used to express future time.

EXAMPLES I **will** [or **shall**] **graduate** from high school this June.

  Where **will** the graduation ceremony **be held**?

Learning for Life

Continued on pp. 219–220

Writing a Résumé. Since many seniors will soon be looking for work, they will probably be interested in learning to write a good résumé. Explain that in some modern styles of résumé writing, in addition to listing the job title, résumé writers use active verbs to state the duties performed. This stating of duties creates a more dynamic résumé. For example, "Volunteer office worker, Boys and Girls Club: operated

(7) The modal *should* is used to express a recommendation, an obligation, or a possibility.

EXAMPLES   You **should visit** each campus again before deciding which university to attend. [recommendation]

I see now that I **should have asked** before borrowing the book. [obligation]

Should you **decide** to accept the other job offer, please let me know. [possibility]

(8) The modal *would* is used to express the conditional form of a verb.

A conditional verb form usually appears in an independent clause that is joined with an *"if"* clause. The *"if"* clause explains *under what condition(s)* the action or state of being of the conditional verb takes place.

EXAMPLE   If it had continued to rain, we **would have canceled** the outdoor concert.

Would is used also to express future time in a subordinate clause when the main verb in the independent clause is in the past tense.

EXAMPLE   Janetta wrote in her e-mail message that she **would call** me tonight at nine o'clock.

Additionally, *would* is used to express an action that was repeated in the past, a polite request, or an invitation.

EXAMPLES   I remember that each year, usually in February, our school **would hold** a winter carnival. [action repeated in the past]

Would you please **take** these letters to the post office for me? [polite request]

Would you **accompany** me to the picnic? [invitation]

Reference Note

For more about **helping (auxiliary) verbs** and **main verbs,** see page 15.

Exercise 15 **Writing Appropriate Modals**

For each of the following sentences, supply an appropriate modal.

EXAMPLE   **1.** If no one objects, I _____ tell the council what our decision is.

     1. will

                                    Answers will vary.

1. One of the amazing things about Lord Byron is the way he _____ write both romantic love poems and biting satire.   **1.** could

┌**HELP**─

Although more than one response may be possible for each item in Exercise 15, you need to give only one answer for each.

---

switchboard, entered membership data into database, and reorganized filing system" is more dynamic and gives a prospective employer much more specific information to go on than "Volunteer office worker, Boys and Girls Club."

Have students gather information they need to write résumés—education, work experience, hobbies and interests, awards or honors, employment goals, and refer-

2. may

2. Because you asked so politely, you ———— choose the subject of your report first.

3. Should

3. "———— I call you when it's over?" asked Deanna.

4. will

4. If this weather continues, we ———— have snow on the field during the finals.

5. must

5. "You really ———— read that story by Isak Dinesen!" Jerome urged.

6. Will

6. ———— you ask Ms. Gibson about the assembly on Friday?

7. should

7. While the sun is still shining, you ———— wash your parents' car.

8. might

8. Without Yoshi's help, we ———— not finish this on time.

9. will

9. If you have time, we ———— listen to the new Brandy album.

10. can

10. After using that brand of computer, I ———— highly recommend it to all my friends.

Review F

DISTRIBUTED REVIEW
For a quick review of pronouns and antecedents, have students find the personal pronouns with clearly stated antecedents in sentences 4, 10, and 18 of **Review F**. [4. *her, she, her*—Cindy; 10. *his, he*—Mr. Washington; 18. *its*—eagle]

PRACTICE

Guided and Independent

Review F You may want to use the first ten items in the review as guided practice. Then, have students complete the review as independent practice.

HOMEWORK

Review F Proofreading Sentences for Errors in the Form and Use of Verbs

Each of the following sentences contains awkward, informal, or incorrect verb usage. Revise each sentence according to the rules of formal, standard English.

EXAMPLE 1. Keisha said that if she was the President, she would veto the bill.

1. *was—were*

1. had

1. If we ~~would have~~ checked, we would have known the library was closed.

2. especially liked the movie

2. ~~The movie was especially liked by~~ Kira and her brother ˄ because of the beautiful nature photography.

3. were

3. If I ˄ ~~was~~ Luís, I wouldn't have argued with the umpire.

4. had

4. Cindy retraced her steps and found the cafe at which she ˄ left her credit card.

5. are

5. Did Kadonna realize that *hurricane* and *typhoon* ˄ ~~were~~ two names for the same phenomenon?

6. swung

6. As he slowly turned the key, the door suddenly ˄ ~~swings~~ wide open.

7. Last week, the school newspaper ~~has~~ printed Kim's story.

8. Having won

8. ~~Winning~~ the medal, she revised her practice schedule and gave herself more free time.

9. have been

9. By the time the next presidential election comes up, I will ˄ be in the United States for six years.

10. show

10. Mr. Washington wanted to ˄ ~~have shown~~ them his collection of African sculptures, but he was suddenly called away on business.

Learning for Life

Continued from p. 219

ences. Provide the class with some sample résumés from the library, the business education department, or the school guidance counselor. Analyze a few of the résumés with students, and guide them through

revising parts of any résumés that do not already contain active verbs.

Then, have students write their own résumés, working in pairs or small groups to critique each other's work each step of

11. Ladies and gentlemen of the jury, I demand that this innocent man
    is acquitted.
12. She would have volunteer for the project, but she already had too
    much to do.
13. If you are tired, why don't you lay down for a while before dinner.
14. Yes, I use to baby-sit them years ago.
15. To have celebrated the victory, the team met at a local pizza parlor.
16. Do you mean that the letter was setting right there in plain sight
    the whole time?
17. I realized suddenly that I had tore up the directions that I needed.
18. As we watched, the eagle spread its wings and raised into the sky.
19. In only an hour, he had wrote almost eight pages.
20. If you would have been watching the clock, you would have been
    on time.

11. be
12. volunteered
13. lie
14. used
15. celebrate
16. sitting

17. torn
18. rose
19. written
20. had

Review G **Proofreading Paragraphs for Errors in the Form and Use of Verbs**

Most of the sentences in the following paragraphs contain awkward,
informal, or incorrect verb usage. Revise each such sentence according
to the rules of formal, standard English. If a sentence is already correct,
write C.

EXAMPLE   **[1]** Every time I have performed this experiment, the
           outcome amazed me.

    1. *Every time I have performed this experiment, the
       outcome has amazed me.*

                              or

       *Every time I performed this experiment, the outcome
       amazed me.*

[1] Have you ever seen a band of light shimmering over a hot
road, as though a pool of water was lying just ahead? [2] Mirages have
been just one of many types of optical illusions that will fool the average observer.

[3] The simple illustration shown on the next page will allow you to
have experienced another kind of illusion. [4] In a few minutes the flying bird will be returned to its cage by you. [5] However, to do so, it is
essential that you are calm and give the experiment your full attention.
[6] Fix your stare on the bird for a minute or two, and then focus on
the white space in the center of the cage next to the bird. [7] Having
stared at the white space, you will, at the same time, see the bird

1. were
2. are

3. experience
4. you will return
5. be

6. C
7. Staring

the way so that the finished products will
be dynamic, thorough, and ready to use. If
possible, have students use word-processing
programs to create professional-looking
résumés, and suggest that they keep their
résumés on computer disks so that revisions
and additions can be made easily.

8. notice

9. are/remains

10. C

appear. **[8]** When the bird appears, you will probably ~~have noticed~~ notice something strange—its feathers will be green and purple. **[9]** Although you ~~have~~ are no longer ~~been~~ looking at the bird, its image (or, rather, its afterimage) ~~has remained~~ remains on your retina. **[10]** The afterimage is composed of colors opposite to the bird's original red and yellow colors.

Terms and numerals in brackets refer to concepts and rules tested by the items in the Chapter Review.

1. crept [8a, c]
2. caught [8a, c]
3. flung [8a, c]
4. beaten *or* beat [8a, c]
5. tore [8a, c]

6. [*sit, set*]
7. [*rise, raise*]
8. [*lie, lay*]
9. [*sit, set*]
10. [*lie, lay*]

11. have been [8d, e(6)]
12. had [8g]
13. had/seen [8d, e(5), f(2)]

Chapter Review

A. Using the Past and Past Participle Forms of Verbs Correctly

For each of the following sentences, write the correct form of the italicized verb in parentheses.

1. The lion had silently (*creep*) up behind its prey.
2. The outfielder has (*catch*) the ball in the tip of his glove.
3. She (*fling*) open the door and raced out of the house.
4. Candida has always (*beat*) me at tennis.
5. She (*tear*) her coat while she was climbing over the fence.

B. Choosing the Forms of *Lie* and *Lay*, *Sit* and *Set*, and *Rise* and *Raise*

Choose the correct verb form in parentheses in each of the following sentences.

6. What time did you (*set, sit*) down to start your report?
7. The exhausted wrestler could not (*rise, raise*) himself from the mat.
8. In a hurry to go to work, I couldn't remember where I had (*laid, lain*) my keys.
9. Malcolm (*sat, set*) his new computer on the desk.
10. Whenever Joan reads, her puppy (*lies, lays*) down at her feet.

C. Using Tenses Correctly

Each of the following sentences contains an error in the use of tenses. Identify the error, and then give the correct form of the verb.

11. By the time we get to the concert, the orchestra will be playing for half an hour.
12. If Benito would have done his homework after school, he would have been allowed to go to the play last night.
13. Sophie did not want to go to the movie because she already saw it twice.

ASSESSING

Monitoring Progress
Chapter Review. To assess student progress, you may want to compare the types of items missed on the **Diagnostic Preview** to those missed on the **Chapter Review.** If students have not made significant progress, you could refer them to **Chapter 16: Correcting Common Errors, Exercises 13–17,** for additional practice.

USAGE

RESOURCES

Using Verbs Correctly
Review
■ *Language & Sentence Skills Practice,* pp. 192–195

Assessment
■ *Holt Handbook Chaper Tests with Answer Key,* pp. 15–16, 54

Chapter Review

D. Revising Sentences in the Passive Voice

POSSIBLE ANSWERS

16. We hoped for clearer skies that spring, so that the sun would melt the snow.
17. C
18. William Faulkner wrote the novel *As I Lay Dying* when he was working as a night watchman.
19. C
20. The principal told us the results of the aptitude test.

---

14. be [8h]
15. includes [8d, e(1)]

14. Mrs. Gleason had hoped to ~~have been~~ here today.
15. Did you know that the solar system ~~included~~ asteroids and comets as well as planets and moons?

D. Revising Sentences in the Passive Voice

Revise the following sentences by changing verbs from the passive voice to the active voice wherever you think the changes are appropriate. If you think the passive voice is preferable for a sentence, write *C*.

16. [8m]
17. [8m]
18. [8m]
19. [8m]
20. [8m]

16. Clearer skies were hoped for by us that spring, so that the snow would be melted by the sun.
17. The missing painting was replaced in the middle of the night.
18. The novel *As I Lay Dying* was written by William Faulkner when he was working as a night watchman.
19. Special effects are often used to create excitement in Hollywood blockbusters.
20. The results of the aptitude test were told to us by the principal.

E. Identifying Indicative, Imperative, and Subjunctive Mood

For each of the following sentences, identify the mood of the italicized verb or verb phrase as *indicative*, *imperative*, or *subjunctive*.

21. imp. [8o]
22. sub. [8p(1)]
23. imp. [8o]
24. sub. [8p(2)]
25. ind. [8n]

21. *Send* a thank-you note to anyone who gives you a gift.
22. Tollie asked that her suggestion *be reconsidered*.
23. *Be* quiet while I'm talking.
24. Karen spoke to her brother as though she *were* his mother.
25. The brown color of the leaves showed that they *were* about to fall.

F. Revising Sentences in a Paragraph by Correcting Verb Forms

Identify each incorrect verb form in the following paragraph. Then, write the correct form.

26. have [8a, e(4)]
27. fell [8a, c]
28. used [8a, b]
29. remembered [8d, e(2)]

[26] For at least five thousand years, people been eating popcorn. [27] If you are like most of them, you probably ~~falled~~ in love with popcorn when you were a child. [28] The ancient Aztecs thought so highly of popcorn that they even ~~use~~ to wear it around their necks. [29] Centuries ago adult American Indians probably ~~remember~~

popcorn as a source of delight and excitement in their childhoods. [**30**] After all, at that time popcorn was often simply ~~throwed~~ into a fire or roasted on a stick. [**31**] What a stir there must have been among the children when the kernels began to ~~have popped~~ clear of the fire! [**32**] Like children today, they probably would not ~~be~~ too bothered by the sand or dirt that the popcorn ~~has~~ picked up. [**33**] Still, these early popcorn lovers were not plagued by duds, which can ~~have broken~~ your teeth and which were the scourge of the popcorn industry until the 1950s. [**34**] That was when Orville Redenbacher and Charles Bowman successfully ~~growed~~ a variety of corn that did not have as many duds. [**35**] When the big popcorn manufacturers rejected the new corn, Redenbacher started his own company, and as you probably know, he ~~had~~ experienced phenomenal success.

Writing Application
Using Standard Verb Forms in a Paragraph

Irregular Verbs   The editor of your school's yearbook is planning a seniors-only feature. Interested seniors may submit one-paragraph descriptions of school events that have helped to make this year memorable. Write a paragraph to submit for publication. In your paragraph, include at least five irregular verbs. Be sure to use the correct past and past participle forms of verbs.

Prewriting   Make a list of memorable events in which a number of students participated during the school year. From your list, choose the event that you remember most vividly, and note what made the event special.

Writing   Describe the event, capturing the mood it inspired in your school. Include sensory details to hold the reader's interest. Take extra care with the past and past participle forms of verbs.

Revising   Ask a classmate who took part in the event to read your paragraph. Add, cut, and revise details as necessary to improve your description. Be sure that you have used at least five irregular verbs.

Publishing   Proofread your paragraph, checking for errors in grammar, usage, spelling, and punctuation. To publish your descriptions, you and your classmates can compile them in a mini-yearbook. You may want to include photographs or drawings to accompany the descriptions.

30. thrown [8a, c]
31. pop [8h]
32. have been/had [8d, e(4), e(5)]
33. break [8d, e(1), f(2)]
34. grew [8a, c]
35. [8d, e(2), f(1)]

Reference Note
For more information about **irregular verbs,** see page 178.

Chapter Review   **225**

CHAPTER

9

Using Modifiers Correctly

Forms and Uses of Adjectives and Adverbs; Comparison

Terms and numerals in brackets refer to concepts and rules tested by items in the Diagnostic Preview.

1. wider [9f]
2. other [9g]
3. [9h]
4. badly [9b, d]
5. less [9f]
6. attractive [9a, c]

Diagnostic Preview

A. Using Modifiers Correctly

Most of the following sentences contain ~~errors in the use of modifiers and comparisons~~. Rewrite each incorrect sentence to correct the error. If a sentence is already correct, write *C.*

EXAMPLE   1. Of my three brothers and sisters, my sister Giselle has the better sense of humor.

   1. *Of my three brothers and sisters, my sister Giselle has the best sense of humor.*

1. Which is ~~widest~~, the Mississippi River or the Colorado River?
2. When the temperature reached 103 degrees in August, hotter than any day that year, the board of health warned people not to go outdoors unless they absolutely had to do so.
3. That is the ~~most~~ palest shade of blue I have ever seen.
4. Because the drummer played ~~bad~~, the band's rhythm was thrown off.
5. Pointing to the two glasses partially filled with water, the magician asked, "Which glass contains ~~the least~~ water?"
6. When you dress for job interviews, you should wear the styles and colors of clothing that look ~~attractively~~ on you.

7. If Mark keeps moving that slowly, he'll never get home before dark.
8. Has Thomas been saving money ~~regular~~ for his trip to the Yucatán this year?
9. Philadelphia and Atlantic City are the largest cities near my home, and Philadelphia is the ~~closest~~ of the two.
10. Although they can't play their guitars very ~~good~~, they sell many CDs.
11. "Nurse López, I feel remarkably well today, better than I have ever felt before," said Mr. Parker.
12. "Sharon, you have been working harder than anyone here," I said.
13. My brother William became the strongest player on the local wheelchair-basketball team.
14. You can adjust the control on the television set to make the picture a little less ~~brighter~~.
15. The cheese smells ~~badly~~ but tastes good.

B. Selecting Modifiers to Complete Sentences

For each sentence in the following paragraph, select the <u>correct modifier</u> from the pair given in parentheses.

EXAMPLE   **[1]** The skilled house movers dismantled the beautiful Victorian mansion (*careful, carefully*).

    1. carefully

[**16**] It's (*real, <u>really</u>*) amazing what house movers can accomplish! [**17**] The (*<u>most</u>, more*) interesting house-moving feat that I have ever heard of involved the Queen Anne Mansion in Eureka Springs, Arkansas. [**18**] Built in 1891, the three-story home, with a tower and wrap-around porch, was moved (*efficient, <u>efficiently</u>*) from Carthage, Missouri. [**19**] Crews worked (*speedy, <u>speedily</u>*) to dismantle the mansion. [**20**] They used special tools and worked (*careful, <u>carefully</u>*) to cut and pry the building apart. [**21**] The contractor had planned (*<u>well</u>, good*) for the move to Eureka Springs. [**22**] It was the (*bigger, <u>biggest</u>*) move ever seen in that area, requiring thirty-seven long flatbed trucks and three storage vans. [**23**] The new owners looked on (*happy, <u>happily</u>*) as workers reassembled the mansion's more than two thousand exterior stones, its wooden walls and floors, its hand-beveled windows, and its central oak staircase. [**24**] The restored Victorian mansion, which is open for tours, has a more unusual history than (*<u>any other</u>, any*) house in the city. [**25**] It now looks (*<u>impressive</u>, impressively*), set atop a hill near downtown Eureka Springs.

---

7. C [*slow, slowly*]
8. regularly [9b, d]
9. closer [9f]
10. well [*good, well*]
11. C [*good, well*]
12. else [9g]
13. C [9e(1), f]
14. bright [9e(4), h]
15. bad [*bad, badly*]

16. [*real, really*]
17. [9f]
18. [9b, d]
19. [9b, d]
20. [9b, d]
21. [*good, well*]
22. [9f]
23. [9b, d]
24. [9g]
25. [9a, c]

ASSESSING

Entry-Level Assessment
Diagnostic Preview. The **Diagnostic Preview** is designed to be used with your assessments of students' writing to detect problems students may be having with using adjectives and adverbs. Evaluation of responses to the **Diagnostic Preview** can help determine which sections of the chapter students need to study especially closely.

Differentiating Instruction
- *Developmental Language & Sentence Skills,* pp. 93–100
- *Developmental Language & Sentence Skills Guided Practice Teacher's Notes and Answer Key,* pp. 24–25

Assessment
- *Holt Handbook Chapter Tests with Answer Key,* pp. 17–18, 54

Forms and Uses of Modifiers

Rules 9a–d *(pp. 228–232)*

OBJECTIVES

- To identify adjective and adverb forms—single words, phrases, or clauses—used in sentences
- To select correct modifiers to complete sentences

PRETEACHING

Lesson Starter

Motivating. Divide the class into groups of four to compose stories. Give each student a slip of paper with three modifiers written on it. (Less common modifiers such as the following ones may help spark students' imaginations: *stark, brittle, harmonious, lucid, sumptuous, benign, vivacious, treacherous, stealthily, robustly, callously, tentatively, feverishly, pointlessly.*)

Each team is to create a story that includes as many of the modifiers as possible, with individuals incorporating at least two of their modifiers into the group story. Suggest that groups brainstorm possible words and topics. Students could contribute their sentences in a round-robin format. Have one student record the story on audiotape so that groups can make revisions after a draft of the story has been taped.

Reference Note

For more information about **adjectives,** see page 11. For more about **adverbs,** see page 20.

Forms of Modifiers

A *modifier* is a word or word group that makes the meaning of another word or word group more specific. The two kinds of modifiers are *adjectives* and *adverbs.*

One-Word Modifiers

Adjectives

9a. An *adjective* makes the meaning of a noun or a pronoun more specific.

EXAMPLES
perfect score	**eager** participant	**Irish** accent
clear water	**last** one	**falling** snow

Adverbs

9b. An *adverb* makes the meaning of a verb, an adjective, or another adverb more specific.

EXAMPLES
walks **briskly**	ran **very quickly**
completely innocent	**not** lonesome

Adjective or Adverb?

Most modifiers with an *–ly* ending are used as adverbs. Many adverbs, in fact, are formed by adding *–ly* to adjectives.

Adjectives	usual	calm	brief
	absurd	appropriate	sad
Adverbs	usual**ly**	calm**ly**	brief**ly**
	absurd**ly**	appropriate**ly**	sad**ly**

However, some modifiers ending in *–ly* are used as adjectives.

EXAMPLES   **monthly** budget   **early** indication   **likely** outcome

A few modifiers have the same form whether they are used as adjectives or as adverbs.

Adjectives	a **fast** train	a **little** sleep	an **early** start
Adverbs	moves **fast**	slept **little**	starting **early**

RESOURCES

Forms and Uses of Modifiers

Practice

- *Language & Sentence Skills Practice,* pp. 201–204

Phrases Used as Modifiers

Like one-word modifiers, phrases can also be used as adjectives and adverbs.

EXAMPLES   I prefer this time **of the year.** [The prepositional phrase *of the year* acts as an adjective that modifies the noun *time.*]

Falling from the very top of the tree, the leaf seemed to take hours to float to the ground. [The participial phrase *Falling from the very top of the tree* acts as an adjective that modifies the noun *leaf.*]

Drive especially carefully **on wet roads.** [The prepositional phrase *on wet roads* acts as an adverb that modifies the verb *Drive.*]

You will have to climb to the top of that hill **to see what is happening on the other side.** [The infinitive phrase *to see what is happening on the other side* acts as an adverb that modifies the verb *climb.*]

Reference Note

For more about **phrases,** see page 59.

Reference Note

For information about **dangling and misplaced modifiers,** see pages 250 and 252.

Clauses Used as Modifiers

Like words and phrases, clauses can also be used as modifiers.

EXAMPLES   Guglielmo Marconi helped develop wireless telegraphy, **which we now know as radio.** [The adjective clause *which we now know as radio* modifies the noun *telegraphy.*]

Before he became famous for such feats as sending a message across the Atlantic Ocean, Marconi worked in his father's attic, sending signals across the room. [The adverb clause *Before he became famous for such feats as sending a message across the Atlantic Ocean* modifies the verb *worked.*]

Reference Note

For more about **clauses,** see page 82.

Oral Practice   **Identifying Adjectives and Adverbs**

Read each of the following sentences aloud. Then, tell whether each italicized word or word group functions as an *adjective* or an *adverb.*

EXAMPLE   **1.** The girl with the *brown* hair is a new student.

     1. adjective

1. How many birds would you guess are sitting in the *tallest* tree?   **1.** adj.
2. The chipmunk quickly disappeared into a hole *in the ground.*   **2.** adj.
3. The kite soared *majestically* over the treetops.   **3.** adv.
4. Stephan always has *more* homework than his brother.   **4.** adj.

MINI-LESSON   **Grammar**

Phrases and Clauses. Remind students of the following definitions: (1) A phrase is a group of words used as a single part of speech that does not contain a verb and its subject, and (2) A clause is a group of words that contains a verb and its subject and is used as a sentence or as part of a sentence. For more on phrases and clauses, refer students to **Chapter 3: The Phrase** and **Chapter 4: The Clause.**

Learners Having Difficulty

Students sometimes have difficulty understanding that the role of adjectives is to describe. Play a guessing game in which you give five adjectives that describe the same thing and challenge students to guess what is being described. For example, you could give the five adjectives *exciting, visual, fast-paced, electronic,* and *challenging* to describe video games.

Have students work with partners to complete the following brief personality questionnaire. Let them complete the sentences below in an interview format. Each item should be completed with a single modifier. Tell students they may be sharing this information with the class.

1. When I meet new people I feel _____.

2. If I make an A on a test I feel _____.

3. My friends say I seem _____.

4. Before a crowd, I speak _____.

5. If I am late, I enter _____.

6. I try to drive _____.

Remind students that modifiers for the first three statements are adjectives, while the last three statements will be completed by adverbs.

Reference Note

For more about **predicate adjectives,** see page 50.

5. *Since he left the White House in 1981,* Jimmy Carter has stayed active internationally as an unofficial diplomat and domestically as a spokesperson for Habitat for Humanity.   **5.** adv.

6. *On quiet, moonlit nights,* Jason likes to go for long walks.   **6.** adv.

7. Sarah's paper airplane stayed in the air *longer* than anyone else's in her class.   **7.** adv.

8. Photosynthesis, *which converts carbon dioxide and water into sugar and oxygen,* is the process plants use to turn solar energy into energy they can use.   **8.** adj.   **9.** adj.

9. The *annual* wildflower blooms are later than usual this year.

10. *Although they are not as blind as some people think,* many types of bats rely more on smell or sound than on sight to find their way around.   **10.** adv.

Uses of Modifiers

9c. Use an adjective to modify the subject of a linking verb.

The most common linking verbs are the forms of *be: am, is, are, was, were, be, been,* and *being.* A linking verb often connects the subject to a **predicate adjective**—an adjective that is in the predicate and that modifies the subject.

EXAMPLES   The company's training program is **rigorous.**

The baby soon became **tired** and **cranky.**

9d. Use an adverb to modify an action verb.

An action verb is often modified by an adverb—a word that explains *how, when, where,* or *to what extent* the action is performed.

EXAMPLES   The world's population is increasing **rapidly.**

The astronaut spoke **enthusiastically** about her successful mission in space.

Some verbs may be used as linking verbs or as action verbs.

EXAMPLES   Carlos looked **happy.** [*Looked* is a linking verb. Notice that the modifier following it, *happy,* is an adjective.]

Carlos looked **happily** at his latest design. [*Looked* is an action verb. Notice that the modifier following it, *happily,* is an adverb.]

Selecting Modifiers to Complete Sentences

Select the correct modifier from the pair in parentheses in each of the following sentences.

EXAMPLE   **1.** The pizza you are baking smells (*delicious, deliciously*).

       1. *delicious*

1. The sled's runners glided (*smooth, smoothly*) over the ice and packed snow of the trail.
2. The weather outside looks (*miserable, miserably*).
3. Neka embroidered the rain-bird symbol (*perfect, perfectly*), checking each stitch as she worked.
4. Do you think the official explanation of the budget cut sounds (*incredible, incredibly*)?
5. Why was she looking (*suspicious, suspiciously*) at me?
6. This apple tastes (*peculiar, peculiarly*) to me.
7. Mike smiled (*proud, proudly*) when he told us about his West African heritage.
8. Dawn goes jogging (*regular, regularly*).
9. He disappeared (*silent, silently*) into the underbrush.
10. The conference room smelled (*stuffy, stuffily*).
11. With the proper care and conditions, these flowers will grow (*rapid, rapidly*).
12. Still, we remain (*confident, confidently*) that there will be a solution to these problems.
13. The young architect's design for the apartment complex was (*simple, simply*) and efficient.
14. His model engine ran (*rapid, rapidly*) at first but soon ran down.
15. Although we reassured Alexandra about her solo, she remained (*nervous, nervously*).
16. Doesn't this cashmere coat feel (*soft, softly*) to you?
17. An open can of paint tilted (*precarious, precariously*) at the top of the ladder.
18. The six spaniel puppies grew (*bold, boldly*) in the company of their mother.
19. She's only six, but she dances (*beautiful, beautifully*) and already has an audition for a commercial.
20. A good chemist must be (*careful, carefully*) with materials and containers used at work.

Reference Note

For more information about **linking verbs** and **action verbs,** see page 16.

TIPS & TRICKS

To determine whether to use an adjective or an adverb after a verb, replace the verb with the appropriate form of the linking verb *seem.* If the form of *seem* makes sense in the sentence, the original verb is being used as a linking verb, which calls for an adjective. If the form of *seem* is absurd in the sentence, the original verb is being used as an action verb, which calls for an adverb.

EXAMPLES

Carlos looked happy. [Since *Carlos seemed happy* makes sense, *looked* is being used as a linking verb and calls for the adjective *happy.*]

Carlos looked happily at his latest design. [Since *Carlos seemed happily at his latest design* is absurd, *looked* is being used as an action verb and calls for the adverb *happily.*]

DIFFERENTIATING INSTRUCTION

Learners Having Difficulty

You may want to have students work in pairs to complete **Exercise 1** orally. Have one student in each pair read each sentence aloud twice, first including one of the modifiers in parentheses, and then including the other. The second student in each pair should listen to decide which modifier correctly completes each sentence.

PRACTICE

Guided and Independent

Exercise 1   You may want to use the first ten items in **Exercise 1** as guided practice. Then, have students complete the exercise as independent practice.   **HOMEWORK**

EXTENSION

Relating to Writing

To give practice in using vivid modifiers, have each student select a piece of his or her writing. Then, ask students to revise the writing by replacing some of the modifiers in the pieces with more vivid adjectives and adverbs. Students can use a thesaurus or a dictionary to find colorful synonyms.

USAGE

Eight Troublesome Modifiers

(pp. 232–235)

OBJECTIVE

■ To revise sentences to correct errors in the use of *bad* and *badly, good* and *well, real* and *really,* and *slow* and *slowly*

For each sentence in the following paragraph, select the correct modifier from the pair given in parentheses.

EXAMPLE **[1]** Debbie Allen is an (*incredible, incredibly*) talented performer and choreographer.

1. *incredibly*

[1] In the picture to the left, Debbie Allen dances quite (*energetic, energetically*) in a scene from the TV series *Fame*. [2] You might say that fame itself looks (*comfortable, comfortably*) on her. [3] Allen, who grew up in Houston, Texas, has danced (*regular, regularly*) since the age of three. [4] She attended the Houston Ballet School, graduated from Howard University, and then headed (*confident, confidently*) to New York City. [5] On Broadway she was (*triumphant, triumphantly*) in revivals of the musicals *West Side Story* and *Sweet Charity*. [6] Later, she (*successful, successfully*) choreographed *Fame* and won two Emmy Awards for her work on that show. [7] Allen looks (*natural, naturally*) in a producer's chair, too, and worked with Steven Spielberg and Colin Wilson to produce the film *Amistad*. [8] Through the years, she has worked (*diligent, diligently*) and has battled racism and sexism to succeed. [9] Never one to accept second best, Allen has risen (*steady, steadily*) to the top in her profession. [10] In interviews Debbie Allen seems (*proud, proudly*) of her achievements but also ready for new challenges.

Eight Troublesome Modifiers

Bad and *Badly*

Bad is an adjective. *Badly* is an adverb. In standard English, only the adjective form should follow a sense verb, such as *feel, look, sound, taste,* or *smell,* or other linking verb.

NONSTANDARD   This leftover chicken smells badly.
STANDARD   This leftover chicken smells **bad.**

The expression *feel badly* is common in informal situations, but you should use *feel bad* in formal speaking and writing.

INFORMAL   The boys feel badly about forgetting your birthday.
FORMAL   The boys feel **bad** about forgetting your birthday.

RESOURCES

Eight Troublesome Modifiers

Practice

■ *Language & Sentence Skills Practice,* pp. 205–207

Differentiating Instruction

■ *Developmental Language & Sentence Skills,* pp. 93–96

Good and Well

Good is an adjective. *Well* may be used as an adjective or an adverb. Avoid using *good* to modify an action verb. Instead, use *well* as an adverb meaning "capably" or "satisfactorily."

NONSTANDARD   The track team did good at the meet.
STANDARD   The track team did **well** at the meet.

Feel good and *feel well* mean different things. *Feel good* means "to feel happy or pleased." *Feel well* means "to feel healthy."

EXAMPLES   Helping pick up litter in our neighborhood makes me feel **good.**

Chris had to leave because she didn't feel **well.**

Real and Really

Real is an adjective. *Really* is an adverb meaning "actually" or "truly." Although *real* is often used as an adverb meaning "very" in informal situations, avoid this use in formal speaking and writing.

INFORMAL   Your new car is real nice.
FORMAL   Your new car is **really** nice.

Slow and Slowly

Slow is used as both an adjective and an adverb. *Slowly* is used as an adverb. In most adverb uses, it is better to use *slowly* than to use *slow.*

EXAMPLES   Jorge sat at the intersection watching the **slow** progress of the train.

Jorge sat at the intersection as the train **slowly** rolled past.

> **Exercise 3** Revising Sentences to Correct Errors in the Use of Troublesome Modifiers

Most of the following sentences contain errors in the standard, formal use of modifiers. Identify each incorrect modifier, and then give the correct form. If the sentence is already correct, write *C.*

EXAMPLE   **1.** After a long rehearsal, the dance troupe performed quite good.

1.   good—well

1. After she had lost the election, Bernadette felt very bad.

2. Charlotte seemed real happy about getting an A on her history test.

1. C
2. really

STYLE TIP

Well is also used as an adjective meaning "suitable, proper, right" or "in satisfactory condition."

EXAMPLES
It is **well** you arrived when you did.

All is **well** with us.

STYLE TIP

The expressions *drive slow* and *go slow* are common in informal situations. In formal speaking and writing, however, use *drive slowly* and *go slowly.*

DIFFERENTIATING INSTRUCTION

English-Language Learners
General Strategies. When native English speakers are asked how they are doing, they often respond by saying "good" rather than "well." Because most English-language learners put a great deal of faith in the spoken forms they hear, they need to know that these forms often deviate from those in the textbook. You could tell these students that the use of *good* in response to the greeting "How are you doing?" is a casual, informal use of English and that it is acceptable in everyday speech.

EXTENSION

Relating to Vocabulary Skills
Students often overuse the modifier *really* in their speech and writing. Explain that overusing a word dulls the word in the same way that repeated washing of a shirt fades its color. Have students use a dictionary or thesaurus to generate a list of vivid adverbs that could be used in place of *really.* [*Possibilities include* genuinely, extremely, certainly, positively, *and* extraordinarily.]

PRACTICE

Guided and Independent
> **Exercise 3** You may want to use the first ten items in **Exercise 3** as guided practice. Then, have students complete the exercise as independent practice.   **HOMEWORK**

USAGE

FOX TROT ©1989 Bill Amend. Reprinted with permission of Universal Press Syndicate. All rights reserved.

3. Ms. Stein is a good teacher who prepares her lessons well. **3.** C

4. Some shades of blue and green go ~~good~~ together. **4.** well

5. "Life can't be treating you all that ~~bad~~," I told Walker as we sat down at the lunch table. **5.** badly

6. "I'm positive I did ~~good~~ on that test," Edward confidently remarked to his friends. **6.** well

7. Since the Turkish candy halvah is very sweet, it should be served in small pieces and eaten ~~slow~~. **7.** slowly

8. Everyone wondered whether the stone he had found in his backyard was a real diamond. **8.** C

9. "Remember to speak ~~slow~~ when you give your speech," Mr. Wells advised the nervous candidate. **9.** slowly

10. Chen tried to teach me to use chopsticks, but the lesson didn't go very ~~good~~. **10.** well

11. Yuck! That burnt milk smells ~~badly~~! **11.** bad

12. The plot wasn't much, but the actors were good. **12.** C

13. Wakame may be seaweed, but I am told it tastes quite ~~well~~ in many Japanese dishes. **13.** good

14. Don't worry; almost everybody plays ~~bad~~ when they start learning a new sport. **14.** badly

15. Doesn't the train seem ~~slowly~~ to you? **15.** slow

16. Actually, once you see it, the solution is ~~real~~ easy. **16.** really

17. Wow! Is that a real saber-toothed tiger jaw? **17.** C

18. No, adult raccoons certainly do not make ~~well~~ pets. **18.** good

19. Their weather reports are always ~~well~~. **19.** good

20. Go ~~slow~~ at first until you get used to the course. **20.** slowly

Review A **Determining the Correct Use of Modifiers**

Each of the following sentences contains an _italicized modifier_. First, identify the _word that each modifier describes_. If the modifier is incorrect according to the rules of standard, formal usage, give the correct form. If the modifier is already correct, write _C_.

EXAMPLE   **1.** Something sounds _strangely_ next door.
            1. something—strange

1. The players did _good_ in the fourth quarter. **1.** well

2. The bread dough rose too _rapid_. **2.** rapidly

3. We walked _slowly_ on the icy sidewalk. **3.** C

234   **Chapter 9**   Using Modifiers Correctly

USAGE

PRACTICE

Guided and Independent

Reviews Because **Reviews A** and **B** cover the same material, you could use **Review A** as guided practice and then assign **Review B** as independent practice.

HOMEWORK

4. Sam feels *badly* about forgetting to meet us.　　**4.** bad

5. <u>She</u> sounded very *angrily* on the phone.　　**5.** angry

6. These new jeans <u>do</u> not <u>fit</u> me *good* at all.　　**6.** well

7. Rita <u>answered</u> the questions *precisely*.　　**7.** C

8. Fortunately, no one <u>was hurt</u> *bad* in the accident.　　**8.** badly

9. Mr. Tate's company <u>can do</u> the job *efficiently*.　　**9.** C

10. The judge <u>rapped</u> her gavel *sharp* to restore order.　　**10.** sharply

---

Review B　**Proofreading for Correct Use of Modifiers**

Most of the sentences in the following paragraph contain errors in the standard, formal use of modifiers. Identify ~~each incorrect modifier~~, and then give the correct form. If a sentence is already correct, write *C*.

EXAMPLE:　**[1]** Country and western music is rooted firm in the traditional music of the American South.

　　1. *firm—firmly*

[1] The popularity of country and western music (C & W) has grown ~~rapid~~ in the past thirty-five years. [2] In fact, many radio stations all over the nation are playing C & W ~~exclusive~~. [3] Nowadays, country music appeals to fans of ~~near~~ all ages and occupations. [4] For example, one modern American president, George Bush, officially declared his fondness for country music when he attended the Country Music Awards ceremony. [5] Top country stars, such as Clint Black, Reba McEntire, and Garth Brooks, not only have best-selling albums but play to ~~increasing~~ large numbers of fans. [6] In the photo on the left, for example, Garth Brooks looks ~~ecstatically~~ as he acknowledges his fans' enthusiastic applause. [7] Many C & W performers, such as Brooks, are known for their ~~real~~ successful music videos. [8] Some country singers feel ~~badly~~ about the problems in the United States and have started taking stands on social issues. [9] Others do really ~~good~~ singing songs on the traditional country themes of love and heartache. [10] Veteran performer Loretta Lynn, country music's own "Coal Miner's Daughter," is shown on the right singing movingly before an admiring crowd.

© 1999 Troy Wayrynen.

Review B　**Proofreading for Correct Use of Modifiers**

ANSWERS

1. rapidly
2. exclusively
3. nearly
4. C
5. increasingly
6. ecstatic
7. really
8. bad
9. well
10. C

Comparison of Modifiers

Rules 9e–i *(pp. 236–244)*

OBJECTIVES

- ■ To write the comparative and superlative forms of modifiers
- ■ To use the comparative and superlative forms of modifiers correctly in sentences
- ■ To correct unclear and illogical comparisons in sentences

USAGE

DIRECT TEACHING

Correcting Misconceptions

Use of Comparative and Superlative Forms. Some students may think that the *–er* ending is interchangeable with *more* and that *–est* is interchangeable with *most*. Point out to students that shorter words tend to use the inflected ending, but longer words use *more* or *most* to show comparisons. Encourage students who are unsure of word forms to check dictionaries.

DIFFERENTIATING INSTRUCTION

English-Language Learners

Vietnamese. The comparison forms used in English—*more than* or adjective+*er than* and *(not) as . . . as*—are expressed differently in Vietnamese.

Comparison in Vietnamese follows the pattern noun+adjective+*more than*+noun being compared, as in *Mr. Nguyen old more than Mr. Tran.* Students may use such constructions in English and may prefer the *more*+adjective form to the adjective+*er* forms. Students need to practice making comparisons in formal and informal class situations.

┌─**HELP**─

A dictionary will tell you when a word forms its comparative or superlative form in some way other than just by adding *–er* or *–est* or *more* or *most*. Be sure to look in a dictionary if you are not sure whether a word has irregular comparative or superlative forms. A dictionary will also tell you if you need to double a final consonant (or otherwise change the spelling of a word) before adding *–er* or *–est*.

┌**STYLE** — **TIP**┐

Most two-syllable modifiers can form their comparative and their superlative forms either way. If adding *–er* or *–est* makes a word sound awkward, use *more* or *most* instead.

Comparison of Modifiers

9e. Modifiers change form to show comparison.

There are three degrees of comparison: *positive*, *comparative*, and *superlative*.

	Positive	**Comparative**	**Superlative**
Adjectives	big	bigger	biggest
	eager	more eager	most eager
	good	better	best
	late	later	latest
Adverbs	swiftly	more swiftly	most swiftly
	well	better	best

Regular Comparison

(1) Most one-syllable modifiers form the comparative degree by adding *–er* and the superlative degree by adding *–est*.

Positive	**Comparative**	**Superlative**
neat	neat**er**	neat**est**
warm	warm**er**	warm**est**
fast	fast**er**	fast**est**
strong	strong**er**	strong**est**

(2) Two-syllable modifiers may form the comparative degree by adding *–er* and the superlative degree by adding *–est*, or they may form the comparative degree by using *more* and the superlative degree by using *most*.

Positive	**Comparative**	**Superlative**
gentle	gentl**er**	gentl**est**
lively	liveli**er**	liveli**est**
agile	**more** agile	**most** agile
clearly	**more** clearly	**most** clearly

236 | Chapter 9 | Using Modifiers Correctly

RESOURCES

Comparison of Modifiers

Practice

- ■ *Language & Sentence Skills Practice*, pp. 208–216

Differentiating Instruction

- ■ *Developmental Language & Sentence Skills*, pp. 97–100

(3) Modifiers that have three or more syllables form the comparative degree by using *more* and the superlative degree by using *most*.

Positive	Comparative	Superlative
expensive	**more** expensive	**most** expensive
delightful	**more** delightful	**most** delightful
poetically	**more** poetically	**most** poetically

(4) To show a decrease in the qualities they express, modifiers form the comparative degree by using *less* and the superlative degree by using *least*.

Positive	Comparative	Superlative
weak	**less** weak	**least** weak
useful	**less** useful	**least** useful
urgently	**less** urgently	**least** urgently

Irregular Comparison

The comparative and superlative degrees of some modifiers are not formed by the usual methods.

Positive	Comparative	Superlative
bad	worse	worst
ill	worse	worst
good	better	best
well	better	best
many	more	most
much	more	most
far	farther/further	farthest/furthest
little	less	least

NOTE The word *little* also has regular comparative and superlative forms: *littler, littlest.* These forms are used to describe physical size (the **littlest** kitten). The forms *less* and *least* are used to describe an amount (**less** rain). An alternative comparative form, *lesser,* is usually used to describe importance (the **lesser** infraction).

STYLE TIP

In formal English the words *farther* and *farthest* are used to compare physical distance; the words *further* and *furthest* are used to compare amounts, degrees, and abstract concepts.

EXAMPLES
Kiyoshi walked **farther** than any other senior in the walkathon.

The defendant told his attorney, "The witness's testimony could not have been **further** from the truth."

Comparison of Modifiers **237**

Exercise 4 Writing the Comparative and Superlative Forms of Modifiers

ANSWERS

All decreasing comparisons of regular modifiers are formed by adding *less* or *least* to the base form.

1. tinier, tiniest *or* more tiny, most tiny
2. more ill, most ill
3. more wistful, most wistful
4. more modest, most modest
5. more curious, most curious
6. more proudly, most proudly
7. thinner, thinnest
8. better, best
9. more gently, most gently
10. more abruptly, most abruptly
11. more quickly, most quickly
12. easier, easiest *or* more easy, most easy
13. colder, coldest
14. more glorious, most glorious
15. more fiercely, most fiercely
16. worse, worst
17. more jealous, most jealous
18. sourer, sourest *or* more sour, most sour
19. more magnificent, most magnificent
20. more politely, most politely
21. more agile, most agile
22. more placidly, most placidly
23. more precisely, most precisely
24. mistier, mistiest *or* more misty, most misty
25. more colorful, most colorful

┌─HELP─
If you are unsure how to spell the forms of any of the words in Exercise 4, look the words up in a dictionary.

┌ STYLE   TIP ┐
In informal situations, the superlative degree is sometimes used to emphasize the comparison of only two things. Avoid such use of the superlative degree in formal speaking and writing.

INFORMAL
Which park did you enjoy most, Yellowstone or Hot Springs?

FORMAL
Which park did you enjoy **more,** Yellowstone or Hot Springs?

The superlative degree is also used to compare two things in some idiomatic expressions.

EXAMPLE
Put your best foot forward.

Exercise 4 Writing the Comparative and Superlative Forms of Modifiers

Give the comparative forms and the superlative forms of each of the following modifiers.

EXAMPLE   1. brave
          1. *braver, less brave; bravest, least brave*

1. tiny	10. abruptly	19. magnificent
2. ill	11. quickly	20. politely
3. wistful	12. easy	21. agile
4. modest	13. cold	22. placidly
5. curious	14. glorious	23. precisely
6. proudly	15. fiercely	24. misty
7. thin	16. bad	25. colorful
8. good	17. jealous	
9. gently	18. sour	

Uses of Comparative Forms and Superlative Forms

9f. Use the comparative degree when comparing two things. Use the superlative degree when comparing more than two things.

COMPARATIVE   Both Laura and Justin wrote about the development of the Swahili culture, but Laura's paper was **longer.** [comparison of two papers]

After listening to both candidates, we concluded that Ms. García was the **more highly** qualified. [comparison of two candidates]

SUPERLATIVE   Of the four major river-valley cultures that arose long ago in Africa and Asia, the Huang He was probably the **most fully** isolated from the others. [comparison of four civilizations]

I bought this model of car because it gets the **best** mileage. [comparison of many models]

9g. Include the word *other* or *else* when you are comparing one member of a group with the rest of the group.

Keep in mind that the original member is a part of the group. You must use *other* or *else* to avoid an illogical comparison of one thing with itself.

MINI-LESSON   Mechanics

Spelling. Remind students of the following rules:

1. With words ending in *y* preceded by a consonant, change *y* to *i* before adding any suffix that does not begin with *i.* (For example, *dry* becomes *drier* or *driest.*)

2. Double the final consonant before adding a suffix that begins with a vowel if the word ends in a single consonant preceded by a single vowel and has only one syllable or is accented on the last syllable. (For example, *thin* becomes *thinner* or *thinnest.*)

ILLOGICAL	Diamond, a crystalline form of carbon, is harder than any mineral in the world. [Diamond is one of the minerals of the world. Logically, the diamond cannot be harder than itself.]
LOGICAL	Diamond, a crystalline form of carbon, is harder than any **other** mineral in the world.
ILLOGICAL	Pete has won more races than anyone in his club. [Pete is a member of his club. Logically, he cannot have won more races than himself.]
LOGICAL	Pete has won more races than anyone **else** in his club.

9h. Avoid using double comparisons.

A *double comparison* is the result of using two comparative forms (usually *–er* and *more*) or using two superlative forms (usually *–est* and *most*) to modify the same word.

| NONSTANDARD | Alice is a more faster swimmer than you. |
| STANDARD | Alice is a **faster** swimmer than you. |

| NONSTANDARD | What is the name of the most brightest star in the sky? |
| STANDARD | What is the name of the **brightest** star in the sky? |

Exercise 5 **Using the Comparative and Superlative Forms of Modifiers**

Most of the following sentences contain errors in the use of comparisons and comparative and superlative forms. Rewrite each incorrect sentence to correct the ~~error~~. If a sentence is already correct, write *C*.

EXAMPLE   **1.** Is that your most highest grade?
    1. *Is that your highest grade?*

1. Colleen thought nothing could be as bad as the sleet, wind, and snow; but when the ice storm hit, she said, "This is even ~~worser~~!"
2. Both twins, Holly and Julie, have brown eyes, but Holly's are ~~darkest~~.
3. In each graduating class, the valedictorian is the student whose academic average is higher than that of any ∧ senior.
4. Thomas Jefferson is sometimes regarded as the ~~more~~ important statesman in United States history.
5. To gain a ~~more~~ better understanding of the problems in the Middle East, people should learn more about the history of that region.
6. Suzanne made the mistake of buying less paint than she needed for the small room.

MEETING THE CHALLENGE

Modifiers often make subtle comparisons between things. If someone says that a soup tastes silky, for instance, that person is comparing one sense—taste—to another, touch. Listen a few times to a piece of music that involves many instruments. Then, write a sentence for each instrument you hear, using modifiers to describe that instrument's sound. You might wish to compare instruments: Which has the mellower sound, the cello or the French horn? How does each instrument modify the whole piece of music? Be sure to use correct forms of modifiers.

ANSWER
Sentences will vary, but students should demonstrate correct use of modifiers.

1. worse
2. darker

3. other
4. most

6. C

USAGE

PRACTICE

Guided and Independent

Exercise 4   You may want to use the first ten items in **Exercise 4** as guided practice. Then, have students complete the exercise as independent practice.   **HOMEWORK**

DIRECT TEACHING

Modeling and Demonstration

Use of Comparative and Superlative Forms. Model how to identify degrees of comparison by using the examples: *Laura's report was longer than mine, but Robert's report was the longest in the class.* First, ask which words in the example are adjectives. [*longer, longest*] Then, ask how many things are compared by *longer.* [*two;* Laura's report *and* mine] Because only two things are compared, the adjective *longer* is in the comparative degree. Next, ask how many things are compared by *longest.* [*more than two;* Robert's report *and all of the other reports in the class*] Three or more things are compared here, so *longest* is in the superlative degree. Point out that the adjective *long* takes the regular forms *longer* in the comparative and *longest* in the superlative. Now, have a volunteer use other examples from this chapter to demonstrate how to identify degrees of comparison.

---

3. Drop the final silent *e* before a suffix that begins with a vowel. (For example, *safe* becomes *safer* or *safest*.)

Refer students to **Chapter 15: Spelling** for more information on adding suffixes.

DIRECT TEACHING

Modeling and Demonstration

Clear Comparisons. Model how to indicate clearly which items are being compared by using the example *The wingspread of the wandering albatross is greater than any other bird.* First, ask which items are being compared in this sentence. [*the length of the albatross's wingspread and the length of other birds*] Next, ask whether this comparison is logical or illogical. [*illogical*] Then, ask what should be compared in this sentence. [*the albatross's wingspread and the wingspread of other birds*] Ask how this sentence could be revised for clarity. [*The wingspread of the wandering albatross is greater than that of any other bird.*] Point out that the pronoun *that* refers to *the wingspread.* Now, have a volunteer use other examples from this chapter to demonstrate how to indicate clearly which items are being compared in sentences.

EXTENSION

Relating to Writing

To give students practice using comparisons, ask them to act as movie critics. They should each choose two movies and then write reviews that compare and contrast the movies. Suggest categories of evaluation for students to use, such as plot, acting, special effects, and music. Encourage students to include as many comparative and superlative forms of modifiers as possible.

---

7. other

8. better

9. larger

10. other

7. Performing better than all the gymnasts, Mary Lou Retton was the first American woman to win an Olympic gold medal in her sport.

8. Which of the two flavors do you like ~~best~~?

9. Dividing the remaining pumpkin pie in two, Felicia gave me the ~~largest~~ portion.

10. My friend Juan says that Houston, Texas, is more interesting and more exciting than any city in that state.

Clear Comparisons

9i. Be sure comparisons are clear.

When making comparisons, clearly indicate what items you are comparing.

ILLOGICAL	Deciding after the auditions that Julia's characterization of Lady Macbeth was more compelling than Rita, the director offered Julia the role. [The sentence makes an illogical comparison between a characterization and Rita.]
LOGICAL	Deciding after the auditions that Julia's characterization of Lady Macbeth was more compelling than **Rita's [characterization]**, the director offered Julia the role. [The sentence logically compares Julia's characterization with Rita's characterization.]
ILLOGICAL	The wingspread of the wandering albatross is greater than any other bird. [The sentence makes an illogical comparison between a wingspread and a bird.]
LOGICAL	The wingspread of the wandering albatross is greater than **that of** any other bird. [By including *that,* which stands for *wingspread,* the sentence logically compares the wingspread of the wandering albatross with the wingspread of any other bird. Notice that using *that* instead of *wingspread* prevents unnecessary repetition.]

Reference Note
For more about **elliptical constructions,** see page 91.

Use a complete comparison if there is any chance that an incomplete, or elliptical, one could be misunderstood.

UNCLEAR	We have known Chen a great deal longer than Anzu. [The comparison is unclear because the elliptical construction *than Anzu* may be completed in more than one way.]
CLEAR	We have known Chen a great deal longer **than we have known Anzu.**
CLEAR	We have known Chen a great deal longer **than Anzu has known her.**

240 Chapter 9 Using Modifiers Correctly

 Learning for Life

Continued on pp. 241–243

Self-analysis. Explain to students that many employers and college boards of admission ask questions that require applicants to reflect on their growth as individuals, to compare past and present attributes, to name and describe what they consider to be their best qualities, to compare themselves to their peers, and to show that they have an awareness of how others perceive them.

UNCLEAR	Ms. Vasquez offered me a better job than anyone else.
CLEAR	Ms. Vasquez offered me a better job **than she offered anyone else.**
CLEAR	Ms. Vasquez offered me a better job **than anyone else offered me.**

Include all of the words necessary to complete a *compound comparison,* which uses both the positive and the comparative degrees of a modifier. Avoid the common error of omitting the second *as* in the positive degree.

| NONSTANDARD | This year's soccer team is playing as well, if not better than, last year's team. |
| STANDARD | This year's soccer team is playing **as well as,** if not better than, last year's team. |

Absolute Adjectives

Some adjectives have no comparative or superlative forms; they do not vary in degree. Such adjectives are called *absolute adjectives.* In formal situations, avoid using absolute adjectives in comparative constructions.

Common Absolute Adjectives		
complete	eternal	round
correct	full	square
dead	impossible	true
endless	infinite	unique
equal	perfect	

INFORMAL	Smiling, Mr. Martin told me, "I have heard many excuses, but I must say that yours is more unique than most."
FORMAL	Smiling, Mr. Martin told me, "I have heard many excuses, but I must say that yours is **unique.**"
FORMAL	Smiling, Mr. Martin told me, "I have heard many excuses, but I must say that yours is **more ingenious** than most."
INFORMAL	Don't you agree that Brentwood Park is the most perfect place to have the senior-class picnic?
FORMAL	Don't you agree that Brentwood Park is the **perfect** place to have the senior-class picnic?
FORMAL	Don't you agree that Brentwood Park is the **most suitable** place to have the senior-class picnic?

┌─ TIPS & TRICKS ─┐

To make sure a sentence contains all of the words necessary for a compound comparison, try creating a sentence using each part of the comparison separately.

EXAMPLES
This year's soccer team is playing **as well as** last year's team.

This year's soccer team is playing **better than** last year's team.

RETEACHING

Clear Comparisons

Tell students they will work in groups of three to create a display to teach clear comparisons. First, they will need sentences with unclear comparisons. Have one member of each group find three unclear comparisons in books, magazines, conversations, the Internet, television, or radio; or the student could write three sentences containing unclear comparisons. Then, assign a second student to write corrections of the unclear comparisons and a third group member to illustrate both the sentences with the unclear comparisons and the corrected sentences. The illustrator may wish to use a computer graphics program to generate the artwork. Groups should create a display of their completed lesson for a bulletin board or Web site.

Encourage students to make unclear comparisons as funny as possible. Here is an example.

The Smiths enjoy catching fish even more than their neighbors. [*The Smiths enjoy catching fish even more than their neighbors do.*]

DIFFERENTIATING INSTRUCTION

Advanced Learners

Challenge students to think of as many absolute adjectives as they can or to bring in examples from newspapers and magazines. You might want to keep a list on a bulletin board and have students add to it as they think of more. [*Some possibilities are* wooden, opposite, legal, newborn, misspelled, prime, first, *and* last.]

Ask each student to choose three of the questions from the following questionnaire and to respond with a paragraph or two for each question chosen.

1. Are you more or less self-confident now than you were five years ago? Explain.

2. Are you more or less optimistic about the future today than you were five years ago? Explain.

3. How self-disciplined do you believe you are compared to other people your age? Explain.

Comparison of Modifiers **241**

USAGE

Exercise 6

DISTRIBUTED REVIEW
After students have completed **Exercise 6,** you could provide them with a review of the parts of a sentence by having them identify the complete subject and simple predicate in the main clauses of sentences 1, 4, and 5. Students could draw a single line under the subject and a double line under the predicate.

1. <u>Sarah's test scores</u> <u><u>arrived</u></u> by mail two weeks sooner than Jesse's.

4. <u>Some historians</u> <u><u>say</u></u> that Lincoln's accomplishments in such a relatively short time far exceed those of any other president.

5. <u>Shirley's design for the set of the next musical</u> <u><u>was</u></u> obviously more practical than Ruben's.

Exercise 6 Correcting Unclear and Illogical Comparisons

POSSIBLE ANSWERS

1. Sarah's test scores arrived by mail two weeks sooner than Jesse's.

2. Which one of these is more nearly complete?

3. Bryan amazed even himself by swimming as far as, if not farther than, anyone else at the school had ever swum before.

4. Some historians say that Lincoln's accomplishments in such a relatively short time far exceed those of any other president.

5. Shirley's design for the set of the next musical was obviously more practical than Ruben's.

6. Luisa sees movies much more often than her friend Sandra does.

7. C

8. Hercules had to perform twelve labors, each of which was more difficult than the previous one.

9. Katherine agrees with the literary critics who call Sonnet 18 Shakespeare's best poem.

10. C

242 **Using Modifiers Correctly**

STYLE   TIP

Throughout the years, the rules regarding absolute adjectives have changed, becoming alternately more and less strict. Current usage increasingly allows comparisons of absolute adjectives. One historical precedent for this usage occurs in the preamble to the Constitution of the United States of America.

*We the People of the United States, in order to form a **more perfect** Union, establish Justice, insure domestic Tranquility, provide for the common defense, promote the general Welfare, and secure the Blessings of Liberty to ourselves and our Posterity, do ordain and establish this Constitution for the United States of America.*

Follow your teacher's instructions regarding the use of absolute adjectives.

HELP

Some sentences in Exercise 6 may be correctly revised in more than one way. You need to give only one revision for each sentence.

An absolute adjective may be used in comparison if the adjective is accompanied by *more nearly* or *most nearly.*

NONSTANDARD	Ben's responses to survey questions were more complete than anyone else's.
STANDARD	Ben's responses to the survey questions were **more nearly complete** than anyone else's.
NONSTANDARD	Scientists said that the diamond had the most perfect crystalline structure they had ever seen.
STANDARD	Scientists said that the diamond had the **most nearly perfect** crystalline structure they had ever seen.

Exercise 6 Correcting Unclear and Illogical Comparisons

Most of the following sentences contain unclear or illogical comparisons. Rewrite each sentence, following the rules of formal, standard usage and making sure the comparisons are clear. If a sentence is already correct, write *C.*

EXAMPLE   **1.** Of all the creatures on earth, the platypus is one of the most unique.

1. *Of all the creatures on earth, the platypus is one of the most unusual.*

or

Of all the creatures on earth, the platypus is unique.

1. Sarah's test scores arrived by mail two weeks sooner than Jesse.

2. Which one of these is more complete?

3. Bryan amazed even himself by swimming as far, if not farther than, anyone at the school had ever swum before.

4. Some historians say that Lincoln's accomplishments in such a relatively short time far exceed any other president.

5. Shirley's design for the set of the next musical was obviously more practical than Ruben.

6. Luisa sees movies much more often than her friend Sandra.

7. Ernesto enjoyed the literature of the Romantic Period as much as, if not more than, the literature of the Renaissance.

8. Hercules had to perform twelve labors, each of which was more impossible than the previous one.

9. Katherine agrees with the literary critics who call Sonnet 18 Shakespeare's most perfect poem.

10. Jason's bike is even lighter than Daniel's.

Learning for Life

Continued from p. 241

4. How would other people describe you—agreeable? more agreeable than most people? a most agreeable sort of person? disagreeable? Explain.

5. How often do you achieve your personal goals—less often than most people? as often as anyone else does? most of the time? Explain.

Review C Using Modifiers Correctly

Most of the following sentences contain ~~errors in the use of comparisons and modifiers~~. Rewrite each incorrect sentence to correct the error. If a sentence is already correct, write *C*.

EXAMPLE   1. Which of the two teams has won the most games?
           1. *Which of the two teams has won more games?*

1. I am ~~least~~ prepared to take the test than you.   **1.** less   **2.** other
2. Jim speaks Portuguese more fluently than any person in his class.
3. You cheered more often than anyone at the concert.   **3.** else
4. Mr. Brown is many pounds ~~more~~ heavier than I.
5. We thought Patti was the most talented of all the actors in the community play.   **5.** C
6. The picture looks much ~~more~~ clearer on this television set than on that one.
7. I read the ~~shorter~~ of the three books for my report.   **7.** shortest
8. I have narrowed my choices to two colleges, and I want to visit them to see which I like ~~best~~.   **8.** better
9. She was less determined to win than her sister was.   **9.** C
10. Modeling her mother's silk kimono, Toshi seemed even more ~~gracefuller~~ than usual.   **10.** graceful

Review D Proofreading for Correct Use of Modifiers

Most of the sentences in the following paragraph contain errors in the standard, formal use of comparisons and modifiers. Identify ~~each error~~, and then give the correct form. If a sentence is already correct, write *C*.

EXAMPLE   **[1]** Moviegoers who have enjoyed George Lucas's *Star Wars* trilogy may also find Akira Kurosawa's samurai films real appealing, especially *The Hidden Fortress,* which inspired Lucas's trilogy.
           1. *real—really*

[1] Of all the world's movie directors, Akira Kurosawa of Japan is considered one of the ~~greater~~. [2] He is certainly better known in the United States than any Japanese director. [3] In addition to directing, the multitalented Kurosawa edited and wrote many of his films. [4] Acclaimed by critics, his films not only look ~~beautifully~~ but also contain serious moral themes. [5] Among the most popular of his dozens of films is *Ran,* which blends Shakespeare's *King Lear* with a Japanese folk tale. [6] Kurosawa made his version of the story more

1. greatest
2. other
3. C
4. beautiful
5. C

Some word-processing software packages include a thesaurus. The thesaurus can help you find precise modifiers to use in your writing. To make sure, however, that a modifier you choose from the thesaurus has exactly the meaning you intend, you should look up the word in a dictionary.

Comparison of Modifiers   **243**

---

6. What is the most positive experience you have had so far at school or at work? Describe the experience.

   Tell students to take time to verify the correctness of comparative and superlative forms in their paragraphs. Then, have students exchange papers to check each other's use of modifiers.

6. unusual

7. really

8. best

9. fierce

10. better

~~unique~~ by creating a conflict between a father and three sons instead of three daughters. [7] That conflict is ~~real~~ apparent in the scene below from *Ran*. [8] Moviegoers in the United States also enjoyed Kurosawa's film *Dersu Uzala,* which won an Academy Award for ~~bestest~~ foreign film. [9] The stark scenery in that film certainly shows how ~~fiercely~~ the Siberian wilderness can be. [10] If you have the chance to see these two films, you can decide which one you like ~~best~~.

USAGE

Terms and numerals in brackets refer to concepts and rules tested by items in the Chapter Review.

1. [9b, d]
2. [9a, c]
3. [9b, d]
4. [9a, c]
5. [9b, d]

6. badly [*bad, badly*]
7. really [*real, really*]
8. C [*good, well*]
9. slowly [*real, really; slow, slowly*]
10. really well [*real, really; good, well*]

11. larger [9f]
12. other [9g]
13. wonderful [9h]
14. [9h]
15. better [9f]

Chapter Review

A. Selecting Modifiers to Complete Sentences

For each of the following sentences, select the correct modifier from the pair given in parentheses.

1. The rainstorm hit the town (*sudden, suddenly*).
2. Cindy looked (*cheerful, cheerfully*) before beginning her solo.
3. Carry the flag (*proud, proudly*) in the parade.
4. The tabletop felt (*smooth, smoothly*) after we had sanded it.
5. Lynea wrapped the package (*careful, carefully*).

B. Revising Sentences to Correct Errors in the Use of Troublesome Modifiers

Most of the following sentences contain at least one error in the standard, formal use of modifiers. Identify ~~each incorrect modifier~~, and then give the correct form. If the sentence is already correct, write *C*.

6. Was anyone hurt ~~bad~~ in the train derailment?
7. The conductor was ~~real~~ happy with the choir's performance.
8. Larry does not play the tuba well, but he is a good drummer.
9. When you're really hungry, the lunch line always seems to move too ~~slow~~.
10. The baby behaved ~~real good~~ on the long car trip.

C. Using Modifiers Correctly

Most of the following sentences contain ~~errors in the use of comparisons and modifiers~~. Rewrite each incorrect sentence to correct the error. If a sentence is already correct, write *C*.

11. Which city is ~~largest~~, Wichita or Topeka?
12. My cat Mr. Alp is smarter than all the cats I own.
13. That was the most ~~wonderfullest~~ day of my life.
14. My mother has worked in the real estate business ~~more~~ longer than my father has.
15. Lara is obviously the ~~best~~ qualified of the two candidates.

Chapter Review **245**

ASSESSING

Monitoring Progress
Chapter Review. To assess student progress, you may want to compare the types of items missed on the **Diagnostic Preview** to those missed on the **Chapter Review.** If students have not made significant progress, you may want to refer them to **Chapter 16: Correcting Common Errors, Exercise 18,** for additional practice.

USAGE

RESOURCES

Using Modifiers Correctly
Review
■ *Language & Sentence Skills Practice,* pp. 217–220
Assessment
■ *Holt Handbook Chapter Tests with Answer Key,* pp. 17–18, 54

16. C [9g]
17. more [9f]
18. C [9f, i]
19. best [9f]
20. else [9g]

16. Stephen King has probably sold more books than any other writer of his generation.
17. Of the two themes that I wrote, this one is ~~most~~ coherent.
18. Ms. Harrington's comments were more useful than Mr. Karswell's.
19. Of the three sisters, Leora is the ~~better~~ singer.
20. My brother Roger knows more about German history than anyone in our family.

D. Correcting Unclear and Nonstandard Comparisons

Most of the following sentences contain ~~unclear or informal comparisons~~. Rewrite each sentence, following the rules of standard, formal English and making sure the comparisons are clear. If a sentence is already correct, write *C.* Some revisions may vary.

21. uncle's did [9i]
22. C [9i]
23. we have been acquainted with [9i]
24. else [9g]
25. [absolute adjectives]

21. My father's photos of our trip to the Grand Canyon arrived by mail a week before my ~~uncle.~~
22. Keith's list of the birds of Washtenaw County is more complete than Nick's list.
23. We have been acquainted with Carlyle longer than Robert.
24. I know the songs of John Lennon better than I know the songs of anyone.
25. What you are asking me to do is ~~extremely~~ impossible.

E. Proofreading a Paragraph for Correct Use of Modifiers

Most of the sentences in the following paragraph contain ~~errors in standard, formal use of modifiers~~. Rewrite the paragraph to correct the errors. If a sentence is already correct, write *C.*

26. other [9g]
27. peaceful [9a, c]
28. slowly [*slow, slowly*]
29. most [9f]
30. really [*real, really*]

[26] Making a pot on a potter's wheel, or "throwing" a pot, is more relaxing than any artistic activity I know. [27] I feel ~~peacefully~~ as the wheel spins and I shape the ball of clay with my fingers. [28] Sometimes I plan what to make, but other times a pot takes shape ~~slow,~~ almost by itself. [29] To me, kneading the clay to get rid of air bubbles is the ~~more~~ difficult of the dozen or so steps in throwing a pot. [30] The ~~real~~ exciting part is pulling up on the clay to form a cone and then pressing a hole in

the center. **[31]** To prevent the pot from becoming lopsided, I have to work ~~steady~~ and keep the wheel spinning. **[32]** I'm happiest while gently pressing the clay and forming the walls of a pot. **[33]** This stage is more pleasant than any stage because I can daydream as my fingers seem to do the work almost automatically. **[34]** Most of the time, though, I have to concentrate ~~careful~~ to try to make a perfect pot. **[35]** I usually don't feel too ~~badly~~ if a pot doesn't turn out right the first time; part of the fun is starting over.

31. steadily [9b, d]
32. C [9f]
33. other [9g]
34. carefully [9b, d]
35. bad [*bad, badly*]

Writing Application

Using Comparisons in a Consumer's Guide

Comparative and Superlative Forms   You and your classmates have decided to compile a consumer's guide to some products available in your community. Choose a product, and write a paragraph comparing at least three different choices for the product and telling which you think is best. Include at least three comparative and two superlative forms of modifiers.

Prewriting   Write down notes on at least three brands, judging the quality, effectiveness, and cost of each. Using your notes and a set of criteria, compare the brands. You may wish to look in some reliable consumer guides to see the criteria their evaluators use.

Writing   Begin by identifying the type of product you are evaluating and the brands on which you will focus. Then, write a detailed comparison of the brands, rating them on quality and cost. Give specific, objective reasons for your opinions.

Revising   Ask a classmate to read your draft. Have you evaluated each brand thoroughly? Have you stated your opinions and reasons clearly? Be sure that you have used at least three comparative and two superlative forms of modifiers.

Publishing   Check your writing for errors in grammar, usage, punctuation, and spelling. Pay special attention to modifiers, and revise any double comparisons. You and your classmates may wish to compile the evaluations into a booklet, which can serve as a handy reference.

Chapter Review   **247**

APPLICATION

Writing Application

Prewriting Tip. This assignment gives students practice in writing clear comparisons in paragraphs for a consumer's guide. Students must consider their audience (their peers) and their purpose (to inform their peers how various products compare with one another). To decide which products their classmates might be interested in learning more about, students may want to take short, informal surveys.

To evaluate the products in question, students will need to develop lists of criteria by which the products can be rated. These criteria will depend, of course, on the kinds of products being evaluated. Work with students to develop criteria by which to evaluate a specific product, such as a camera. They might want to start with a list of pros and cons and then consider criteria such as upkeep and cost.

Scoring Rubric. While you will want to pay particular attention to students' use of comparative and superlative forms of modifiers, you will also want to evaluate overall writing performance. You could give a split score to assess development and clarity of the composition separately from skill in usage.

USAGE

Placement of Modifiers
Misplaced and Dangling Modifiers

Diagnostic Preview

┌HELP─┐

Sentences in Diagnostic Preview, Part A, may be correctly revised in more than one way.

Numerals in brackets refer to rules tested by items in the Diagnostic Preview.

1. we chose [10c]
2. I found [10c]
3. [10a]
4. [10d]
5. [10a]
6. [10a]

A. Revising Sentences by Correcting Faulty Modifiers

The following sentences contain misplaced and dangling modifiers. Revise each sentence so that its meaning is clear and correct.

EXAMPLE   1. We bought a gadget from a vendor at the flea market that was guaranteed to reduce gas consumption in our car by ten percent.

1. *From a vendor at the flea market, we bought a gadget that was guaranteed to reduce gas consumption in our car by ten percent.*

Answers may vary.

1. Preferring the mountains rather than the nearby seashore, the Adirondacks were chosen as our vacation spot.
2. After working in Washington, D.C., for more than twenty years, the methods of lobbyists were familiar.
3. This bank approves car loans to qualified individuals of any size.
4. Because they were untamed, the signs warned that the animals were dangerous.
5. One can see more than a hundred lakes flying at an altitude of several thousand feet.
6. Jack bought a book of shorthand lessons along with his new word processor, which he read and studied diligently.

7. The people in line <u>only</u> had to stand out in the cold for␣a few
   minutes.

8. ␣We followed several routes that early Spanish explorers took
   on vacation last year.

9. Salvador said after the game the head referee had explained his
   unpopular decision to the two team captains␣.

10. Rounding a sharp curve on El Camino del Río on the way to
    Big Bend, ␣a detour sign␣warned of danger.

B. Revising Sentences by Correcting Faulty Modifiers

Tell whether the following sentences contain <u>misplaced</u> or <u>dangling</u>
modifiers. Then, revise each sentence so that <u>its</u> meaning is clear
and correct.

EXAMPLE
    1. We saw Agatha Christie's play *The Mousetrap* last year in
       London, which has been running since 1952.

    1. *misplaced modifier—Last year in London, we saw Agatha*
       Christie's play The Mousetrap, *which has been running*
       since 1952.

11. Among popular mystery writers, the works of Agatha Christie
    continue to lead sales.

12. Phoebe said during the summer Karl is planning to read all of
    Christie's books about the Belgian detective Hercule Poirot.

13. Famous as the world's longest running play, audiences have
    enjoyed Christie's *The Mousetrap* for over forty years.

14. Concluding the play, the audience is always told by the cast
    not to give away the surprise ending.

15. After reading all of Christie's works, our library received a
    number of requests for books by another great mystery writer,
    Dorothy L. Sayers.

16. When in junior high school, Mom bought me my first Sayers
    mystery novel.

17. Named Lord Peter Wimsey, there are few criminal investigators
    who rival Sayers' amateur detective.

18. After reading a detective story by Ngaio (pronounced Ny-o)
    Marsh, New Zealand became an interest of mine.

19. Reading Marsh's *Died in the Wool* for the third time, it is still
    one of my favorites.

20. Fond of mysteries, novels such as *Devices and Desires* by the British
    author P. D. James keep Ben spellbound.

7. [10a]
8. [10a]
9. [10b]
10. we saw/that [10c]

┌─ H E L P ─

Sentences in
Diagnostic Preview, Part B,
may be correctly revised in
more than one way.

11. m [10a]
12. m [10b]
13. m [10a]
14. d [10c]
15. d [10c]
16. d [10c]
17. m [10a]
18. d [10c]
19. d [10c]
20. d [10c]

ASSESSING

USAGE

Entry-Level Assessment

Diagnostic Preview. If students
have problems with placement of
modifiers in their writing, use the
Diagnostic Preview to identify error
patterns and specific strengths and
weaknesses and to help you determine which parts of the chapter students need to review.

Diagnostic Preview: Part B
**Revising Sentences by Correcting
Faulty Modifiers**

POSSIBLE ANSWERS

11. Among popular mystery writers,
    Agatha Christie continues to lead
    sales.

12. Phoebe said Karl is planning to
    read during the summer all of
    Christie's books about the Belgian
    detective Hercule Poirot.

13. For over forty years, audiences
    have enjoyed Christie's *The
    Mousetrap,* famous as the world's
    longest-running play.

14. Concluding the play, the cast
    always tells the audience not to
    give away the surprise ending.

15. After reading all of Christie's
    works, some students sent our
    library a number of requests for
    books by another great mystery
    writer, Dorothy L. Sayers.

16. When I was in junior high school,
    Mom bought me my first Sayers
    mystery novel.

17. Few criminal investigators rival
    Lord Peter Wimsey, Sayers' ama-
    teur detective.

18. After I read a detective story by
    Ngaio (pronounced Ny-o) Marsh, I
    became interested in New Zealand.

19. Even on the third reading, Marsh's
    Died in the Wool is still one of my
    favorites.

20. Ben, who is fond of mysteries, is
    kept spellbound by novels such as
    Devices and Desires by the British
    author P. D. James.

Misplaced Modifiers

Rules 10a, b (pp. 250–252)

OBJECTIVE

- To revise sentences by correcting misplaced modifiers

PRETEACHING

Lesson Starter

Prior Knowledge. Write the word *modifier* on the board, and ask students to define this term. [*A modifier is a word, phrase, or clause that describes a word or word group in a sentence.*] Ask several volunteers each to write a sentence containing a modifier on the board. To begin, you may wish to write the following sentence: *Wrapped in foil, the sandwich occupied a shelf in my locker.* Have additional volunteers underline the modifiers in each sentence. [In the sentence above, underline *Wrapped in foil* and *in my locker.*] Tell students that in this lesson they will revise sentences in which modifiers have been placed incorrectly.

DIRECT TEACHING

Modeling and Demonstration

Misplaced Modifiers. Model how to revise sentences to correct squinting modifiers using the example *My doctor told me before winter arrived to get a flu shot.* First, ask if the phrase *before winter arrived* could describe when my doctor spoke to me. [*yes*] Then, ask if the phrase could also describe when I should get a flu shot. [*yes*] Point out that *before winter arrived* is a squinting modifier and seems to modify either of two things. Ask how this sentence could be revised. [*My doctor told me to get a flu shot before winter arrived.*] Now, have a volunteer use another example from this chapter to demonstrate how to correct squinting modifiers.

Misplaced Modifiers

A modifying word, phrase, or clause that seems to modify the wrong word or word group in a sentence is a *misplaced modifier.*

10a. Avoid using misplaced modifiers.

To correct a misplaced modifier, place the modifying word, phrase, or clause as close as possible to the word or words you intend to modify.

MISPLACED	We plan to go to the antique auto show that we read about in the paper tomorrow. [Did we do the planning before reading the paper?]
CLEAR	**Tomorrow,** we plan to go to the antique auto show that we read about in the paper.
MISPLACED	I finished reading the book that Alice Walker wrote about Langston Hughes during spring break. [Did Alice Walker write the book about Langston Hughes during spring break?]
CLEAR	**During spring break** I finished reading the book that Alice Walker wrote about Langston Hughes.
MISPLACED	The thief tried to run away from the police officer abandoning the stolen car and dashing into the woods. [Was the police officer abandoning the stolen car and dashing into the woods?]
CLEAR	**Abandoning the stolen car and dashing into the woods,** the thief tried to run away from the police officer.
MISPLACED	Each actor needs to affect a British accent that auditions for the role of Professor Higgins. [Does a British accent audition for the role?]
CLEAR	Each actor **that auditions for the role of Professor Higgins** needs to affect a British accent.
MISPLACED	My nephew told me that he wanted to become an astronaut and fly to the moon when he was six years old. [Could my nephew become an astronaut at the age of six and fly to the moon?]
CLEAR	**When he was six years old,** my nephew told me that he wanted to become an astronaut and fly to the moon.

Squinting Modifiers

10b. Avoid misplacing a modifying word, phrase, or clause so that it seems to modify either of two words.

RESOURCES

Misplaced Modifiers

Practice

- *Language & Sentence Skills Practice,* pp. 226–229

Differentiating Instruction

- *Developmental Language & Sentence Skills,* pp. 101–102

Such a misplaced modifier is often called a *squinting,* or *two-way,* modifier.

MISPLACED   Mary said during rehearsal Lori acted nervous. [Did Mary say this about Lori during rehearsal, or did Lori act nervous during rehearsal?]

CLEAR   **During rehearsal** Mary said Lori acted nervous.

CLEAR   Mary said Lori acted nervous **during rehearsal.**

MISPLACED   Tell Marco before he goes to his karate class I want to see him. [Do I want to see him before he goes, or do I want you to tell him before he goes?]

CLEAR   **Before he goes to his karate class,** tell Marco I want to see him.

CLEAR   Tell Marco I want to see him **before he goes to his karate class.**

Exercise 1 Revising Sentences by Correcting Misplaced Modifiers

The following sentences contain misplaced modifiers. Revise each sentence so that its meaning is clear and correct.

EXAMPLE   1. Recently vetoed by the president, Congress is amending the tax bill.

1. *Congress is amending the tax bill recently vetoed by the president.*

1. Captain Andre Callioux was one of many heroic African American soldiers during the Civil War that fought in the Union Army.
2. Rolling slowly down the alley, the bowler watched the straightest ball he had ever thrown.
3. One of our observers sighted a plane through binoculars that she could not identify.
4. The causeway has a drawbridge to permit the passage of large fishing boats from which all fishing is prohibited.
5. Please tell Terry when he gets home from the mall Mom wants him to make dinner.
6. At Tuesday's meeting, the mayor discussed the enormous cost of draining Buskill Swamp with city council members.
7. According to the hieroglyphics, the mummy had nearly been buried for four thousand years.
8. Li Hua inherited that antique fan from her great-aunt that has a mother-of-pearl handle.

─HELP─

Be sure to place modifiers correctly to show clearly the meaning you intend.

EXAMPLES

Only Mr. Reyes sees the essays. [Mr. Reyes, not anybody else, sees the essays.]

Mr. Reyes **only** sees the essays. [Mr. Reyes sees the essays; he does not mark them.]

Mr. Reyes sees **only** the essays. [Mr. Reyes does not see anything else.]

─HELP─

Sentences in Exercise 1 may be correctly revised in more than one way.

DIFFERENTIATING INSTRUCTION

Learners Having Difficulty

To place a modifier correctly, a student must determine which word the modifier is intended to modify. Work with students to identify the words being modified in the example sentences in this lesson. You could write the sentences on the chalkboard, using one color to underline the modifiers and another color to underline the words modified.

Exercise 1 Revising Sentences by Correcting Misplaced Modifiers

POSSIBLE ANSWERS

1. Captain Andre Callioux was one of many heroic African American soldiers that fought in the Union Army during the Civil War.
2. The bowler watched the straightest ball he had ever thrown rolling slowly down the alley.
3. One of our observers sighted through binoculars a plane that she could not identify.
4. The causeway drawbridge, from which all fishing is prohibited, permits the passage of large fishing boats.
5. Please tell Terry that Mom wants him to make dinner when he gets home from the mall.
6. At Tuesday's meeting, the mayor discussed with city council members the enormous cost of draining Buskill Swamp.
7. According to the hieroglyphics, the mummy had been buried for nearly four thousand years.
8. Li Hua inherited from her great-aunt that antique fan that has a mother-of-pearl handle.

USAGE

9. Ms. Steinberg, the explorer, described her trips through the jungle in our social studies class.

10. Uncle Jim said after reading all the consumer guides and asking his friends for advice he would decide what kind of personal computer to buy.

Exercise 1 Revising Sentences by Correcting Misplaced Modifiers

POSSIBLE ANSWERS continued

9. In our social studies class Ms. Steinberg, the explorer, described her trips through the jungle.

10. Uncle Jim said that he would decide what kind of personal computer to buy after reading all the consumer guides and asking his friends for advice.

Dangling Modifiers

A modifying word, phrase, or clause that does not clearly and sensibly modify any word or word group in a sentence is a *dangling modifier.*

10c. Avoid using dangling modifiers.

To correct a dangling modifer, add or replace words to make the meaning of the sentence clear.

DANGLING	Foggy, we couldn't see eight feet in front of us. [Were we foggy?]
CORRECT	**In the fog,** we couldn't see eight feet in front of us.
CORRECT	We couldn't see eight feet in front of us **in the foggy weather.**
DANGLING	After reading the article "Keeping America Beautiful," a recycling program was organized in their neighborhood. [Who read the article?]
CLEAR	**After reading the article "Keeping America Beautiful," Luís and Gabrielle** organized a recycling program in their neighborhood.
CLEAR	**After Luís and Gabrielle read the article "Keeping America Beautiful,"** they organized a recycling program in their neighborhood.
DANGLING	To win the election, your support will be needed. [Is your support trying to win the election?]
CLEAR	**To win the election, I** will need your support.
CLEAR	**If I am to win the election,** your support will be needed.
DANGLING	Convicted of stealing a loaf of bread for his sister's seven starving children, Jean Valjean's sentence was five years in prison. [Was Jean Valjean's sentence convicted?]
CLEAR	**Convicted of stealing a loaf of bread for his sister's seven starving children, Jean Valjean** was sentenced to five years in prison.
CLEAR	**Jean Valjean was convicted of stealing a loaf of bread for his sister's seven starving children** and was sentenced to five years in prison.

STYLE   TIP

A few dangling modifiers have become standard idiomatic expressions.

EXAMPLES

Considering the circumstances, the pilot program is going well.

Relatively speaking, the cost of living has remained static for several years.

To be perfectly frank, the rate of inflation is still too high.

Reference Note

For more about **modifying phrases and clauses,** see Chapter 3 and Chapter 4.

Dangling Modifiers and Clear Comparisons
Rule 10c *(pp. 252–256)*

OBJECTIVES

■ To revise sentences by correcting dangling modifiers

■ To revise sentences by correcting faulty modifiers

RETEACHING

Dangling Modifiers

Students may recognize sentences with dangling modifiers but still have difficulty revising the sentences. Suggest that they divide complicated sentences into smaller units, revise the units into complete sentences, and then recombine the sentences to avoid dangling modifiers. Here is an example:

Camping in the woods, a bear stole my lunch. [Division: *I was camping in the woods. A bear stole my lunch.* Recombination: *A bear stole my lunch while I was camping in the woods.*]

Possessive nouns and pronouns act as adjectives and therefore cannot be modified by adjectives. Adjective phrases and clauses that seem to modify possessive nouns or pronouns are considered dangling modifiers. The most common way to correct such dangling modifiers is to reword the sentence to avoid using the possessive form.

DANGLING   Having chopped off the Green Knight's head, Gawain's part of the bargain must be fulfilled.

CLEAR   Having chopped off the Green Knight's head, **Gawain** must fulfill his part of the bargain.

DANGLING   Washing them repeatedly, Lady Macbeth's hands still appear bloody.

CLEAR   Washing her hands repeatedly, **Lady Macbeth** still sees blood on them.

Exercise 2 Revising Sentences by Correcting Dangling Modifiers

The following sentences contain dangling modifiers. Revise each sentence so that its meaning is clear and correct.

EXAMPLE   1. Before moving to San Angelo, Miami had been their home.

   1. Before they moved to San Angelo, Miami had been their home.

1. Listening to his grandfather's stories, it was amazing to learn that several of their ancestors had worked with the Underground Railroad.
2. Architecturally striking, everyone is quite impressed by the new building's size and elegance.
3. When selecting a college, a number of factors should be carefully considered.
4. While talking with some friends of mine, the topic of careers in dentistry came up.
5. After searching all over the bookstore, Amy Tan's novel was found in the "Bestseller" section.
6. When using a word processor, the spellchecker should not be relied on to proofread.
7. After working in the fields all day, little energy was left for social activities.
8. To understand many of the allusions in modern literature, Greek and Roman mythology is essential.

Dangling Modifiers   **253**

Reference Note

For more about **active voice** and **passive voice,** see page 211.

USAGE

Exercise 2

DISTRIBUTED REVIEW

To review prepositional phrases, ask students to find prepositional phrases in sentences 1 and 3, to identify the phrases as adjective or adverb, and to tell what words the phrases modify.

1. to his grandfather's stories—adv.—Listening; of their ancestors—adj.—several; with the Underground Railroad—adv.—had worked

3. of factors—adj.—number

Exercise 2 Revising Sentences by Correcting Dangling Modifiers

POSSIBLE ANSWERS

1. Listening to his grandfather's stories, he was amazed to learn that several of their ancestors had worked with the Underground Railroad.

2. Architecturally striking, the new building impresses everyone with its size and elegance.

3. When selecting a college, you should carefully consider a number of factors.

4. While I was talking with some of my friends, the topic of careers in dentistry came up.

5. After searching all over the bookstore, we found Amy Tan's novel in the "Bestseller" section.

6. When using a word processor, you should not rely on the spellchecker to proofread.

7. After working in the fields all day, we had little energy left for social activities.

8. A knowledge of Greek and Roman mythology is essential to understanding many of the allusions in modern literature.

MINI-LESSON Usage

Voice. To aid students in revising sentences by changing verbs from passive to active voice, you could review the definition of *voice: Voice* in grammar is the form a transitive verb takes to indicate whether the subject of the verb performs or receives the action. For more information on voice, refer students to **Chapter 8: Using Verbs Correctly.**

Dangling Modifiers   **253**

Exercise 2 **Revising Sentences by Correcting Dangling Modifiers**

POSSIBLE ANSWERS continued

9. Thirsty and weary, we found the oasis a welcome sight.

10. Riding in the glass-bottomed boat, they could see hundreds of beautiful tropical fish.

Oral Practice **Revising Sentences by Correcting Faulty Modifiers**

POSSIBLE ANSWERS

1. Having left the box cutter in the drawer under the front counter, the librarian had difficulty opening the boxes of new science fiction and fantasy books in the back room.

2. Elected to serve the people of her state in Congress for the next two years, the new representative began her term with a difficult vote about taxes.

3. To get his students ready for the coming semester, the Latin teacher asked his class to read over Christmas break the versions of Homer's *Iliad* and *Odyssey* translated by Robert Fagles.

4. Aiming the giant radio telescope at the distant star in the constellation of Cassiopeia, the astronomer hoped to quickly detect signs of extraterrestrial intelligence.

5. He wanted to be the first to see the scary new film that was advertised on television and in the newspaper.

6. After talking to a friend who knew quite a bit about automobiles and trucks, Aunt Alice told us she had decided to buy a new car with air conditioning, automatic transmission, and a sun roof.

7. An understanding of Chinese history helps the reader to enjoy ancient Chinese poetry, even in translation.

MEETING THE CHALLENGE

"When dangling, watch your modifiers." What? This humorous advice both reminds you not to make an error and makes it. Choose one of the rules in this chapter and write a rule that teaches itself by making the error. Then, rewrite the rule so that it is correct. Share your "unrules" with other students, and enjoy theirs, too.

ANSWER
Incorrect rules will vary, but corrected rules must follow their own advice.

9. Thirsty and weary, the oasis was a welcome sight.
10. Riding in the glass-bottomed boat, hundreds of beautiful tropical fish could be seen.

Oral Practice **Revising Sentences by Correcting Faulty Modifiers**

The following sentences contain misplaced and dangling modifiers. Revise each sentence so that its meaning is clear and correct. Then, read each revised sentence out loud.

EXAMPLES

1. Candace told me at the conference Leora gave a very interesting presentation about solar eclipses.

1. *At the conference, Candace told me Leora gave a very interesting presentation about solar eclipses.*

or

1. *Candace told me Leora gave a very interesting presentation about solar eclipses at the conference.*

2. After hiking across the South Downs from Eastbourne to Brighton, Jim's boots were battered and scratched.

2. *After Jim hiked across the South Downs from Eastbourne to Brighton, his boots were battered and scratched.*

1. Having left the box cutter in the drawer under the front counter, the boxes of new science fiction and fantasy books in the back room were difficult for the librarian to open.

2. Elected to serve the people of her state in Congress for the next two years, the new representative's term began with a difficult vote about taxes.

3. To get his students ready for the coming semester, the Latin teacher asked his class to read the versions of Homer's *Iliad* and *Odyssey* translated by Robert Fagles over Christmas break.

4. Aiming the giant radio telescope at the distant star in the constellation of Cassiopeia, the astronomer's hope was that it would quickly detect signs of extraterrestrial intelligence.

5. He wanted to see the scary new film that was advertised on television and in the newspaper before anybody else saw it.

6. Aunt Alice told us after talking to a friend who knew quite a bit about automobiles and trucks she had decided to buy a new car with air conditioning, automatic transmission, and a sun roof.

7. To enjoy ancient Chinese poetry, even in translation, an understanding of Chinese history is helpful.

Learning for Life

Marketing Slogans. Discuss with students the impact slogans have in advertising and marketing. Ask them to work in small groups to develop slogans for diverse products such as automobiles, hair-care products, exercise equipment, and healthful snacks.

Have students begin their slogans with modifying phrases, and remind them to avoid faulty modifiers. Students should be able to identify the problems in the following examples before they generate their own slogans:

8. The university's planetological survey team discovered a large asteroid with the enormous new reflecting telescope in the Andes that no one had ever catalogued or even seen before.

9. The champion bicyclist in the Tour de France tried to break away from the other bicyclists pedaling harder and faster than anyone else.

10. Having hidden the silver, Nostromo's reputation was made as the man who rescued the country from the rebels.

Review **Revising Sentences by Correcting Faulty Modifiers**

The sentences in the following paragraph contain misplaced and dangling modifiers. Revise each sentence so that its meaning is clear and correct.

EXAMPLE   [1] Using the map shown on the next page, it is easy to identify the homelands of many American Indians.

1. *Using the map shown on the next page, a person can easily identify the homelands of many American Indians.*

[1] I found a fascinating book at the library book sale that includes a map showing where American Indians traditionally lived. [2] You can see the homelands of the major Plains peoples looking

The Granger Collection, New York

Dangling Modifiers   **255**

Dangling Modifiers   **255**

Knowing you deserve the best, Brilliant Shine shampoo is for you.

After evaluating the facts, our trucks will be chosen by people like you.

Allow students class time to share their slogans. Then, discuss with them the idea that although informal language is acceptable, even desirable, in marketing, clarity is always crucial.

POSSIBLE ANSWERS
continued

3. The size of the Great Plains, which extends farther north and south than I had thought, especially surprised me.

4. A picture of a Sioux encampment caught my attention while I was thumbing through the book.

5. Farming was the main activity of most of these peoples, who lived much of the year in villages.

6. I read, however, that they hunted buffalo during the summer.

7. Hunting for survival instead of sport, they killed fewer buffalo than European settlers did.

8. Characterized by a strong sense of independence, the Plains peoples practiced a form of democracy.

9. To make key decisions, they cast votes at council meetings.

10. Having read this fascinating book about the peoples of the Plains, I'm going to find out more about such peoples as the Crow and Cheyenne.

EXTENSION

Critical Thinking

Analysis. Ask students to explain the difference between how misplaced and dangling modifiers are corrected. [*A misplaced modifier needs only to be moved to the proper place, whereas a sentence containing a dangling modifier must be reworded.*]

at the map. [3] The size of the Great Plains especially surprised me, extending farther north and south than I had thought. [4] While thumbing through the book, a picture of a Sioux encampment caught my attention. [5] Living much of the year in villages, farming was the main activity of most of these peoples. [6] However, I read during the summer they hunted buffalo. [7] Hunting for survival instead of sport, fewer buffalo were killed by them than were killed by European settlers. [8] Characterized by a strong sense of independence, a form of democracy was practiced by the Plains peoples. [9] To make key decisions, votes were cast at council meetings. [10] I'm going to find out more about such peoples as the Crow and Cheyenne, having read this fascinating book about the peoples of the Plains.

Chapter Review

A. Revising Sentences by Correcting Misplaced and Dangling Modifiers

The following sentences contain misplaced and dangling modifiers. Revise each sentence so that its meaning will be clear on first reading.

1. The Kovaks gave a toy robot to one of their children with a square glass head and flashing red eyes.

2. Pounding the piano keys with all her might, the chords of the prelude resounded through the concert hall.

3. We saw a herd of sheep on the way to our hotel in Wales.

4. To succeed in college, a great deal of time must be spent studying.

5. Dipped in yogurt, many people love fresh strawberries.

6. When only five years old, Dad took me camping on the Fort Apache Reservation in Arizona.

7. While trying to get ready for school, the doorbell rang suddenly.

8. Elaine told Joanne after the first act the drama gets more exciting.

9. By putting money aside regularly, a small savings account will grow steadily larger.

10. A tarantula bit one of the dockworkers that had a hairy, huge body as big as a man's hand.

B. Revising Sentences by Correcting Misplaced and Dangling Modifiers

The following sentences contain misplaced and dangling modifiers. Revise each sentence so that its meaning will be clear on first reading.

11. Jody said on Saturday Fred should go to the classic car show.

12. Seeing a red 1928 Hispano-Suiza motorcar, his family's minivan seemed bulky and drab to Rick.

13. The Volkswagen Beetle remains one of the world's most popular cars first made in Germany in 1938.

14. Captivated by the Italian sports cars, the 1938 Alfa Romeo impressed Mark.

15. Mr. Reynolds showed a Model T Ford to his daughter that came off the assembly line in 1924.

ASSESSING

Monitoring Progress

Chapter Review. To assess student progress, you may want to compare the types of items missed on the **Diagnostic Preview** to those missed on the **Chapter Review.** If students have not made significant progress, you could refer them to **Chapter 16: Correcting Common Errors, Exercises 19–20** for additional practice.

Chapter Review A

POSSIBLE ANSWERS

1. . . . robot with a square glass head and flashing red eyes to one. . . .
2. The chords . . . concert hall as the pianist pounded . . . all her might.
3. On the way . . . Wales, we saw a herd of sheep.
4. . . . in college, a student must spend a great . . . time studying.
5. Many people love fresh strawberries dipped in yogurt.
6. When I was only five years old, Dad took me camping. . . .
7. While I was trying. . . .
8. Elaine told Joanne that the drama gets more exciting after the first act.
9. If you put money aside regularly, your small savings account will grow steadily larger.
10. A tarantula that had . . . hand bit . . . dockworkers.

Chapter Review B

POSSIBLE ANSWERS

11. On Saturday, Jody said Fred. . . .
12. After seeing a . . . motorcar, Rick thought his family's minivan seemed bulky and drab.
13. First made in Germany in 1938, the Volkswagen Beetle remains one . . . cars.
14. Captivated . . . cars, Mark was impressed by the 1938 Alfa Romeo.
15. Mr. Reynolds showed his daughter a Model T Ford that came off. . . .

USAGE

Chapter Review B

POSSIBLE ANSWERS
continued

16. Would you please tell Thelma that after lunch Mary plans to watch the . . . motorcars?

17. To . . . condition, the owner often needs much money and patience.

18. During the parade, I got a chance to ride . . . had restored.

19. After . . . motorcars, I became especially interested in the 1940 . . . Lagonda De Ville.

20. Looking . . . exhibits, I could easily see why . . . carriages.

Chapter Review C

POSSIBLE ANSWERS

21. During Christmas vacation, Jorie wrote a report. . . .

22. After dinner, Mom said my brother and I should wash the dishes.

23. Repeating . . . higher, the vocalist performed the song brilliantly.

24. Jim told Mimi that they would go to the ice-skating show during the holidays.

25. Every player who wants to make the team needs . . . coach.

26. Jo thinks her cat's coloring with clearly defined stripes is prettier. . . .

27. Having learned . . . sit, the dog had completed its training.

28. After Ernesto and Claudia saw the film, they nearly had an argument about. . . .

29. Before Thanksgiving dinner, Alejandro discussed with his mother the proper . . . turkey.

30. Because I was anxious about this morning's history test, . . .

31. Remember . . . manager the coach wants to see him before the game.

---

16. [10b]
17. [10c]
18. [10a]
19. [10c]
20. [10c]

16. Would you please tell Thelma after lunch Mary plans to watch the documentary about the history of U.S. motorcars?

17. To keep a classic car in excellent condition, much money and patience often are needed.

18. I got a chance to ride in a 1914 Rolls-Royce Continental that the Arnolds had restored during the parade.

19. After writing a report about classic luxury motorcars, the 1940 Packard and 1938 Lagonda De Ville were of special interest to me.

20. Looking at the various exhibits, it is easy to see why very early cars were called horseless carriages.

C. Revising Sentences by Correcting Misplaced and Dangling Modifiers

The following sentences contain misplaced and dangling modifiers. Revise each sentence so that its meaning will be clear on first reading.

21. [10a]
22. [10b]
23. [10c]
24. [10b]
25. [10a]
26. [10c]
27. [10c]
28. [10c]
29. [10a]
30. [10c]
31. [10b]

21. Jorie wrote a report about the Battle of Gettysburg during Christmas vacation.

22. Mom said after dinner my brother and I should wash the dishes.

23. Repeating the chorus an octave higher, the song was performed brilliantly.

24. Jim told Mimi during the holidays they would go to the ice-skating show.

25. Every player needs to prove her ability to the coach who wants to make the team.

26. With her clearly defined stripes, Jo thinks her cat's coloring is prettier than that of her friend's cat.

27. Having learned to heel, fetch, and sit, the dog's training was done.

28. After seeing the film, an argument nearly broke out between Ernesto and Claudia about what the message was.

29. Before Thanksgiving dinner, Alejandro discussed the proper method of stuffing a turkey with his mother.

30. Anxious about this morning's history test, thoughts raced through my head, and sleep did not come easily.

31. Remember to tell the equipment manager before the game the coach wants to see him.

32. Blowing steadily off the ocean, we had a difficult time walking into the wind.

33. Having learned the facts about Dutch elm disease, a program to save the trees was formulated by the members of the neighborhood association.

34. Professor Dellamorte said throughout class some students were not taking notes.

35. Whistling through the trees and between the buildings, the wind's force scattered loose trash in the street.

 ## Writing Application

Using Modifiers in a News Report

Correct Placement of Modifiers   Scientists have just discovered an entirely new life form in the Florida Everglades. You have been assigned the job of reporting the news to the public. You will need to describe not only the new creature but also the environment in which it was found and the methods used to find it.

Prewriting   First, you will need to decide what your creature is and what made it so difficult to discover for so long. Then, you will need to decide the conditions in which your creature lives. Finally, decide how the scientists made the discovery. You may wish to research recent discoveries to find out how actual scientists work.

Writing   Begin with a brief paragraph describing the new creature. Explain what makes this creature so different from previously known species. Then, give the details about how and where the creature lives and how it was discovered. You will need to use vivid modifiers to attract and keep your readers' attention.

Revising   Evaluate the written version of your article for believability and clarity. Remember that this information is entirely new and potentially confusing, so you will need to make sure your modifiers are placed carefully.

Publishing   Proofread your work for errors in grammar, spelling, and punctuation. You and your classmates may want to collect the fictional news reports in a booklet about recent discoveries. Add illustrations of the different creatures you have described. Work together to write an introduction explaining the nature of the scientific discovery.

32. [10c]
33. [10c]
34. [10b]
35. [10c]

Chapter Review C

POSSIBLE ANSWERS
continued

32. We had a difficult time . . . wind that was blowing . . . ocean.

33. Having . . . disease, the members . . . association formulated a program . . . trees.

34. Professor Dellamorte said that some students were not taking notes throughout class.

35. Whistling through the trees and between the buildings, the wind scattered . . .

APPLICATION

Writing Application

Prewriting Tip. You may want to have students do research on the environment and the animals of the Florida Everglades to get ideas for their news reports. They could look on the Internet or consult reference books and magazine articles in a library.

Scoring Rubric. While you will want to pay particular attention to students' placement of modifiers, you will also want to evaluate overall writing performance. You could give a split score to assess development and clarity of the composition separately from skill in usage.

Chapter Review   **259**

CHAPTER

11

A Glossary of Usage

Common Usage Problems

┌─HELP─
Some of the sentences in the Diagnostic Preview, Part A, may be revised in more than one way. You need to give only one revision for each sentence.

Terms in brackets refer to concepts tested by items in the Diagnostic Preview.
1. to [*try and, try to*]
2. ought not [*had ought, hadn't ought*]
3. effect [*affect, effect*]
4. doesn't [*don't, doesn't*]
5. I [*myself, ourselves*]
6. can hardly [double negative]
7. [*he, she, it, they* (double subject)]

Diagnostic Preview

A. Correcting Errors in Usage

Most of the following sentences contain ~~errors in the use of standard, formal English~~. If a sentence contains an error, revise the sentence. If a sentence is already correct, write *C*.   Answers may vary.

EXAMPLE   1. I was surprised to learn that Roberto's parents are wealthy; he doesn't act like he's rich.

    1. *I was surprised to learn that Roberto's parents are wealthy; he doesn't act as if he's rich.*

1. Please enclose a copy of your birth certificate, and we will try ~~and~~ return the document to you as soon as possible.
2. You ~~hadn't ought~~ to be so careless with your new watch.
3. The Student Council's arguments had little ~~affect~~ on the faculty's vote on the new dress code for school dances.
4. Theo ~~don't~~ care what others think; he has the courage to say what he believes.
5. Tricia, Angelo, Candace, and ~~myself~~ have tickets to the White Sox game next Saturday.
6. Whenever I feel sad, I ~~can't hardly~~ wait to talk with my friend Marcus, who always cheers me up.
7. Arthur Fiedler ~~he~~ made the Boston Pops' concerts popular with millions of people all over America.

8. The reason we're so late is ~~because~~ our car battery was dead.
9. We didn't know whether the light was a ~~phenomena~~ of nature or a UFO.
10. I had never seen this kind of insect before.
11. Because Eula made a mistake when she dropped the film cartridge ~~in~~ the camera, none of her pictures could be developed.
12. ~~Being as~~ we haven't seen Tim since he moved to New Mexico, we plan to visit him very soon.
13. She asked Tom whether he would be going to the dance, and he ~~says~~, "Maybe I'll go, and maybe I won't."
14. Where was Beth ~~at~~ last night when we went to the game?
15. Our teacher said we ~~done~~ a creditable job on our project.

B. Correcting Errors in Usage

Each of the sentences in the following paragraph contains an error in the use of standard, formal English. Identify and correct each error.
Answers may vary.

EXAMPLE   **[1] The number of versions of the Cinderella story are quite surprising.**

1.   *The number . . . are—The number . . . is*

[16] There are hardly ~~no~~ other tales in the world that are as popular as the story of Cinderella. [17] Almost ~~everywheres~~, people tell some version of this folk tale. [18] The ~~reason for the story's popularity is~~ probably because its themes of love and wealth appeal universally. [19] However, each culture ~~adopts~~ the tale by changing the heroine's name and other details. [20] Data collected by folklorists indicates that almost seven hundred versions of the Cinderella story exist. [21] In the English version, Cinderella is granted a wish by her fairy godmother; in Scotland, Rashin Coatie wishes on a dead calf's bones; and in Italy, it is a magic date tree ~~who~~ grants Zezolla's wish. [22] In the Chinese version, perhaps the oldest Cinderella story, the main character is Yeh-Shen, who is ~~prosecuted~~ by her stepmother. [23] In this ~~here~~ version, the stepmother, notorious for her cruelty, gives Yeh-Shen the dangerous task of drawing water from very deep wells. [24] As in other Cinderella stories, a slipper drops off ~~of~~ Yeh-Shen's foot on her way back from a festival. [25] The endings of all the stories are the same— the mistreated heroine, no matter what type name she has, finds love and happiness with the man who searches for the owner of the slipper.

8. that [*because*]
9. phenomenon [*phenomena*]
10. C [*kind(s), sort(s), type(s); kind of a(n), sort of a(n)*]
11. into [*in, into*]
12. Because [*being as, being that*]
13. said [*say*]
14. [*at*]
15. did [*done*]

16. any [*double negative*]
17. delete [*anyways, anywheres, etc.*]
18. story is popular [*because*]
19. adapts [*adapt, adopt*]
20. delete [*data*]
21. that [*who, which, that*]
22. persecuted [*persecute, prosecute*]
23. delete [*this here, that there*]
24. delete [*of*]
25. of [*type, type of*]

Differentiating Instruction

■ *Developmental Language & Sentence Skills,* pp. 105–112

■ *Developmental Language & Sentence Skills Guided Practice Teacher's Notes and Answer Key,* pp. 27–28

Assessment

■ *Holt Handbook Chapter Tests with Answer Key,* pp. 21–22, 54

Reference Note

For information about **words often confused,** such as *already* and *all ready*, see page 410.

PRETEACHING

Lesson Starter

Prior Knowledge. Ask students how they determine whether a speaking or writing opportunity calls for formal usage. Have them label the following situations as either formal or informal.

1. socializing with friends

2. giving a public speech

3. writing an essay to go into a time capsule

4. meeting a new teenage neighbor

5. meeting a new adult neighbor

Ask students to suggest additional situations in which formal or informal usage is appropriate.

A, An—A While, Awhile

(pp. 262–267)

O B J E C T I V E

- **To identify correct usage in sentences**

About the Glossary

This chapter provides a compact glossary of English usage. A *glossary* is an alphabetical list of special terms or expressions with definitions, explanations, and examples. You will notice that some examples in this glossary are labeled *nonstandard, standard, formal,* or *informal.* The label *nonstandard* identifies usage that does not follow the guidelines of standard English usage and is suitable only in the most casual speaking situations and in writing that attempts to re-create casual speech. The label *standard* identifies usage that is grammatically correct and appropriate in formal and informal situations. The label *formal* identifies language that is appropriate in serious speaking and writing situations (such as in speeches and in compositions for school). The label *informal* indicates standard usage common in conversation and in everyday writing such as personal letters. In doing the exercises in this chapter, be sure to use only standard English.

The following are examples of formal and informal English.

Formal	Informal
angry	steamed
unpleasant	yucky
agreeable	cool
very impressive	totally awesome
accelerate	step on it
request	put in for
in serious trouble	up a creek

Reference Note

For more information about **articles,** see page 12.

a, an   These *indefinite articles* refer to one of the members of a general group. Use *a* before words beginning with a consonant sound. Use *an* before words beginning with a vowel sound.

EXAMPLES   It was **an** honor and **a** surprise to receive **an** award last night for my work as **a** hospital volunteer. [The *h* in *honor* is silent; therefore, the word begins with a vowel sound. The *h* in *hospital* is not silent; therefore, the word begins with a consonant sound.]

The report of **a** unicorn came from **an** unnamed source. [The word *unicorn* begins with a consonant sound. The word *unnamed* begins with a vowel sound.]

RESOURCES

A, An—A While, Awhile

Practice

- *Language & Sentence Skills Practice,* p. 240

Differentiating Instruction

- *Developmental Language & Sentence Skills,* pp. 105–106

accept, except   *Accept* is a verb meaning "to receive." *Except* may be a verb or a preposition. As a verb, *except* means "to leave out." As a preposition, *except* means "excluding."

EXAMPLES   Did you **accept** the gift?

Does the new census **except** homeless people? [verb]

We were busy every night **except** Tuesday. [preposition]

adapt, adopt   *Adapt* means "to change or adjust something in order to make it fit or to make it suitable." *Adopt* means "to take something and make it one's own."

EXAMPLES   The play was **adapted** from a popular book.

My aunt and uncle in New York **adopted** a nine-year-old boy from Guatemala.

affect, effect   *Affect* is a verb meaning "to influence." *Effect* may be used as a verb or a noun. As a verb, *effect* means "to bring about [a desired result]" or "to accomplish." As a noun, *effect* means "the result [of an action]."

EXAMPLES   Try not to let unkind remarks **affect** you.

The board **effected** drastic changes in the budget. [verb]

The **effects** of the hurricane were evident. [noun]

ain't   *Ain't* is nonstandard. Avoid *ain't* in formal speaking and in all writing other than dialogue.

all ready, already   See page 410.

all right   *All right* means "satisfactory," "unhurt," "safe," "correct," or, as a reply to a question or to preface a remark, "yes." Although some dictionaries include *alright* as an optional spelling, it has not become standard usage.

EXAMPLES   The firefighters found that everyone in the building was **all right.**

All right, you may go to the movie, but be sure to be home by ten o'clock.

all together, altogether   See page 410.

DIRECT TEACHING

Modeling and Demonstration

A, An. Model how to identify and correct commonly misused words by using the example *Market Avenue is a one-way street.* First, ask students whether *one-way* begins with a vowel or a consonant sound. [*consonant sound*] Next, ask whether *a* is used correctly. [*yes*] Then, ask whether *a* could be replaced with *an* here. [*no*] *A* is used before words beginning with a consonant sound, and *an* is used before words beginning with a vowel sound. Point out that the sound that begins a word, and not the actual letter, is what determines whether *a* or *an* should be used. Now, have a volunteer use another example from this chapter to demonstrate how to identify and correct commonly misused words.

DIFFERENTIATING INSTRUCTION

English-Language Learners

Cantonese. Cantonese does not have the equivalent of the English articles *a, an,* or *the.* Students may omit articles *(I like book),* add articles unnecessarily *(She goes to the school every morning),* or confuse the two main types of articles *(Please lend me the pen and the piece of paper).* Articles are unstressed in English and difficult to hear for those whose language does not use articles. When introducing nouns, use the article with the noun. *(This is a noun, and this is an adjective.)* Also, have students practice the definite article *the* by using it to point to specific items.

Teacher: Which book do you want?

Student: The one with the red cover.

DIFFERENTIATING INSTRUCTION

Advanced Learners

Looking at Language. Explain to the class that *colloquialisms* are words and phrases of conversational language and that the word *colloquial* is derived from a Latin word meaning "conversation." Students might have seen or heard the colloquialism *y'all* for *all of you* or *you all*. Used appropriately, colloquialisms can give writing and speech a lively, personal tone, but colloquialisms are inappropriate in formal writing and speaking. You might want to ask students to listen for colloquialisms for a week or so and to add any they hear or read to a list on a bulletin board in the classroom.

MEETING THE CHALLENGE

What would you think if you picked up a newspaper and read the headline "Local Executive Busted for Embezzling Funds"? Most newspapers and magazines avoid nonstandard usage because they like to keep a professional image. Try this experiment: Working with a partner, edit a short, published article—only this time, replace correct usage with nonstandard usage. Keep the Glossary of Usage handy as you search for words and phrases to "edit." Present both articles to the class, and discuss the effects of usage on the impression the story makes.

ANSWER

Results will vary, but students should be able to find and explain several examples of Glossary of Usage terms. Original published articles will sound more professional and authoritative than the students' doctored, nonstandard versions.

all the farther, all the faster   These expressions are used informally in some parts of the United States. In formal situations, use *as far as* or *as fast as*.

INFORMAL   Thirty miles per hour was all the faster the first airplane could travel.

FORMAL   Thirty miles per hour was **as fast as** the first airplane could travel.

allusion, illusion   An *allusion* is an indirect reference to something. An *illusion* is a mistaken idea or a misleading appearance.

EXAMPLES   Amy Tan's writings include numerous **allusions** to Chinese folklore and mythology.

At one time, many people shared the **illusion** that the earth was flat.

The movie's special effects created the **illusion** of space travel.

a lot   Always write the expression *a lot* as two words. In informal situations, *a lot* may be used as a noun meaning "a large number or amount" or "a great deal" or as an adverb meaning "a great deal" or "very much." Avoid using *a lot* in formal situations.

INFORMAL   I have a lot of homework to do tonight. [noun]

FORMAL   I have **a great deal** of homework to do tonight.

INFORMAL   The final exam was a lot easier than I had expected. [adverb]

FORMAL   The final exam was **much** easier than I had expected.

alumni, alumnae   *Alumni* (ə • lumˊ • nī) is the plural of *alumnus* (a male graduate). *Alumnae* (ə • lumˊ • nē) is the plural of *alumna* (a female graduate). Considered as a group, the graduates of a coeducational school are referred to as *alumni*.

EXAMPLES   Both men are **alumni** of Harvard University.

All of my sisters are **alumnae** of Hollins University.

My parents went to their **alumni** reunion.

NOTE   In informal usage, the graduates of a women's college may be called *alumni*. In formal situations, however, the form *alumnae* should be used.

among   See **between, among.**

amount, number   Use *amount* to refer to a singular word. Use *number* to refer to a plural word.

EXAMPLES   The **amount** of research on stress has increased. [*Amount* refers to the singular word *research*.]

A large **number** of studies have been conducted. [*Number* refers to the plural word *studies*.]

and etc.   *Etc.* is an abbreviation of the Latin words *et cetera*, which mean "and others" or "and so forth." Since *and* is part of the definition of *etc.*, using *and* with *etc.* is redundant.

EXAMPLE   This unit discusses writers associated with the Harlem Renaissance: Countee Cullen, Langston Hughes, Zora Neale Hurston, **etc.** [not *and etc.*]

anyways, anywheres   Omit the final *s* from these words and others like them (*everywheres, nowheres, somewheres*).

EXAMPLE   I couldn't find my keys **anywhere** [not *anywheres*]; I looked **everywhere** [not *everywheres*], but they were **nowhere** [not *nowheres*] in the house.

as   See **like, as.**

as if   See **like, as if, as though.**

as though   See **like, as if, as though.**

assure, ensure, insure   *Assure* means "to state with confidence" or "to promise." *Ensure* means "to make certain." *Insure* means "to arrange for monetary payment in case of loss."

EXAMPLES   Marion **assured** me that she would bring the book with her.

I **ensured** that Bret had his lunch before I left.

Chris **insured** her car against damage and theft.

at   Avoid using *at* after a construction beginning with *where*.

NONSTANDARD   Where do most Navajo live at now?
STANDARD   **Where** do most Navajo live now?

a while, awhile   The noun *while*, often preceded by the article *a*, means "a period of time." *Awhile* is an adverb meaning "for a short time."

EXAMPLES   For **a while** Delia was the band's lead vocalist. [noun]

They lived **awhile** in Dallas before settling in Chicago. [adverb]

STYLE   **TIP**

Many style guides advise against using *etc.* in formal writing. Whenever possible, revise your sentences to avoid using *etc.*

ORIGINAL
Shelley uses rhyme, alliteration, onomatopoeia, etc., to create sound images that complement his visual images.

REVISED
Shelley uses sound devices **such as** rhyme, alliteration, and onomatopoeia to create sound images that complement his visual images.

USAGE

PRACTICE

Guided and Independent

Exercise 1 You may want to use the first ten sentences in **Exercise 1** as guided practice and then have students complete the last ten sentences of **Exercise 1** as independent practice.

HOMEWORK

Exercise 1 **Identifying Correct Usage**

For each of the following sentences, choose the correct word or words in parentheses.

EXAMPLE 1. After practicing law for (*a while, awhile*), Mr. Milano decided that he would rather be a teacher.

  1. *a while*

1. Some pets (*ain't, aren't*) suited for life in a small apartment.
2. I own a large (*number, amount*) of campaign buttons.
3. During my travels in Mexico, I met (*a lot, alot*) of Canadian students in Jalisco.
4. Everyone I know likes peanut butter (*accept, except*) you.
5. One line appears to be longer because the drawing is an optical (*allusion, illusion*).
6. Do you know whether or not Anderson Boulevard will be turned into (*a, an*) one-way street?
7. The research committee's job is to analyze the possible long-term (*affects, effects*) of acid rain on European forests.
8. Four hundred miles is (*all the farther, as far as*) this car will go on one tank of gas.
9. Were any crops (*affected, effected*) by this year's dry spell?
10. The expression "lock, stock, and barrel" is an (*allusion, illusion*) to the parts of a flintlock rifle.
11. What (*affect, effect*) will new telecommunications options have on your future?
12. We've ordered balloons, streamers, paper napkins, paper cups, (*and etc., etc.*)
13. On behalf of Miss West, I am honored to (*accept, except*) this award.
14. A vast (*amount, number*) of this mineral may well be buried under the ocean floor.
15. The animal shelter has plenty of cats that you could (*adopt, adapt*).
16. Where are the Canary Islands (*located, located at*)?
17. That's all right; I was going to the mall (*anyway, anyways*).
18. Is everything (*allright, all right*) here, Tony?
19. Several of the (*alumni, alumnus*) have donated money for the new scoreboard.
20. For centuries, scholars have been fascinated by the pyramids, mummies, and scrolls of ancient Egypt, but new discoveries and techniques (*assure, ensure*) that the search for their secrets will continue for a long time.

Exercise 2 Identifying Correct Usage

For each sentence in the following paragraphs, choose the correct word or words in parentheses.

EXAMPLE   [1] By developing, marketing, and selling shampoos, lotions, oils, (*and etc., etc.*), Madame C. J. Walker became a successful businesswoman.

1. *etc.*

[1] At one time, the name Madame C. J. Walker was known by black women just about (*everywhere, everywheres*) in America and Europe. [2] Walker's likeness, which you can see in this photo of her driving a car, was familiar, too, because it appeared on each of the huge (*amount, number*) of packages of beauty products that she manufactured. [3] For eighteen years, Walker washed clothes for a living, but she never believed people who said she had gone (*all the farther, as far as*) a black woman could go in business. [4] Eventually, she invested in a sizable (*number, amount*) of oils, shampoos, and lotions and began experimenting with them in her washtub. [5] When she was done, Walker had a formula that softened hair; later, she would patent (*an, a*) hair-straightening comb that gave users soft, manageable coiffures. [6] The public, however, was reluctant to (*accept, except*) Walker's new products, and she had to go door-to-door to sell her system of hair care. [7] The success of her dynamic personal demonstrations enabled Walker to purchase (*a, an*) office. [8] Before long, her offices, laboratory, manufacturing plant, (*and etc., etc.*) took up a city block, and thousands of Walker's sales representatives canvassed the United States and Europe, where the performer Josephine Baker used the Walker method. [9] A pioneer in the development, sales, and marketing of cosmetics, Madame Walker insisted that her salespeople (*adopt, adapt*) a strict program of hygiene, a requirement that later became part of state cosmetology laws. [10] As a wealthy older woman, she did not forget her years of poverty and toil, and many (*alumnae, alumnus*) of Tuskegee Institute and Palmer Memorial Institute have been grateful for the scholarships that Walker funded for young women.

DIFFERENTIATING INSTRUCTION

Advanced Learners

Exploring the Subject. Sarah McWilliams (1869–1919) was born near Delta, Louisiana. Not much is known of her early life except that she was orphaned at age seven, married at age fourteen, and was left a widow with a small child at age twenty.

After moving to St. Louis, McWilliams married Charles J. Walker. Under the name of Madame C. J. Walker, she began manufacturing her hair preparations. She later added a complete line of toiletries and cosmetics and established the Walker beauty schools. Walker was the first African American woman to become a millionaire.

Bad, Badly—Good, Well
(pp. 268–273)

OBJECTIVES

- To identify correct usage in sentences
- To correct errors in usage by revising sentences

DIFFERENTIATING INSTRUCTION

English-Language Learners

Spanish. Students whose first language is Spanish may need further explanation of the difference between *among* and *between* because in Spanish the single word *entre* fulfills the function of both *among* and *between*.

RETEACHING

Between and Among

Mnemonics. Some students may find it helpful to concentrate on spelling associations to determine the correct usage of *between* and *among*.

beTWeen TWo
aMOng MOre

STYLE TIP

Using *borrow* to mean *lend* is nonstandard. *Loan,* which is a noun in formal English, is sometimes used in place of the verb *lend* in informal situations.

NONSTANDARD
Will you borrow me a couple of dollars?

INFORMAL
Will you loan me a couple of dollars?

FORMAL
Will you **lend** me a couple of dollars?

---

bad, badly   See page 232.

because   In formal situations, do not use the construction *reason . . . because*. Instead, use *reason . . . that*.

INFORMAL   The reason I'm late is because my car had a flat tire.

FORMAL   The reason I'm late is **that** my car had a flat tire. [This sentence can also be revised to make the statement more direct: *I'm late because my car had a flat tire.*]

being as, being that   Avoid using either of these expressions for *since* or *because*.

EXAMPLE   **Because** [not *Being as*] Elena lived in Mexico until she was almost eight years old, she can speak fluent Spanish.

beside, besides   *Beside* is a preposition meaning "by the side of" or "next to." *Besides* may be used as a preposition or an adverb. As a preposition, *besides* means "in addition to" or "except." As an adverb, *besides* means "moreover."

EXAMPLES   Who sits **beside** you in English class?

Besides my homework, I still have chores to do. [preposition]

This soup is cold; **besides,** I didn't order it. [adverb]

between, among   Use *between* when referring to only two items or when referring to more than two items when each is being discussed in relation to each of the others individually.

EXAMPLES   The final chess match was **between** Anne and Lisa.

Do you know when the borders **between** the northwestern states were drawn? [*Between* is used because each border lies between two states.]

Use *among* when you are referring to more than two items and are not considering each item separately in relation to each of the others.

EXAMPLE   He decided **among** thousands of qualified applicants.

borrow, lend   *Borrow* means "to take [something] temporarily." *Lend* means "to give [something] temporarily." Its principal parts are *lend, (is) lending, lent, (have) lent*.

EXAMPLES   May I **borrow** your tennis racket?

Will you **lend** me your tennis racket?

268   **Chapter 11**   A Glossary of Usage

RESOURCES

Bad, Badly—Good, Well
Practice
- *Language & Sentence Skills Practice,* p. 241

Differentiating Instruction
- *Developmental Language & Sentence Skills,* pp. 107–108

bring, take *Bring* means "to come carrying something." *Take* means "to go carrying something."

EXAMPLES When you come to my house tonight, please **bring** your collection of Black Heritage postage stamps.

Please **take** the recycling bin out to the curb.

bust, busted Do not use these words as verbs in formal situations. Use a form of *break* or *burst* or *catch* or *arrest*, depending on the meaning.

EXAMPLES How were your glasses **broken** [not *busted*]?

My car's radiator hose **burst** [not *busted*].

Roxanne **caught** [not *busted*] her little sister reading her diary.

Have the police **arrested** [not *busted*] anyone for that car theft?

but, only See **The Double Negative,** page 286.

can, may See page 218.

can't hardly, can't scarcely See **The Double Negative,** page 286.

could of See **of.**

credible, creditable, credulous *Credible* means "believable." *Creditable* means "praiseworthy." *Credulous* means "inclined to believe too readily."

EXAMPLES The children gave a **credible** excuse for being late.

Her quick thinking and competent action were **creditable.**

The **credulous** listeners thought that the Martians really had invaded Earth.

data *Data* is the plural form of the Latin *datum*. In standard, informal English, *data* is frequently used as a collective noun, with singular pronouns and verbs. In formal usage, *data* takes plural pronouns and verbs.

INFORMAL As soon as the census data was published, it was challenged by several scientists.

FORMAL As soon as the census **data were** published, **they** were challenged by several scientists.

A Glossary of Usage **269**

discover, invent   *Discover* means "to learn of the existence of [something]." *Invent* means "to bring [something new] into existence."

EXAMPLES   Engineers **discovered** oil deposits in Michigan.

Sequoyah **invented** a written Cherokee language based on the spoken Cherokee language.

done   *Done* is the past participle of *do*. When used as a main verb, *done* requires a helping, or auxiliary, verb. Avoid using *done* for *did*, which does not require an auxiliary verb.

NONSTANDARD   We done all of our chores today.
STANDARD   We **have done** all of our chores today.
STANDARD   We **did** all of our chores today.

don't, doesn't   *Don't* is the contraction of *do not*. *Doesn't* is the contraction of *does not*. Use *doesn't*, not *don't*, with singular subjects except *I* and *you*.

EXAMPLES   Franklin **doesn't** [not *don't*] often complain.

Our local grocery store **doesn't** [not *don't*] carry mangoes.

effect   See **affect, effect.**

emigrate, immigrate   *Emigrate* means "to leave a country or a region to settle elsewhere." *Immigrate* means "to come into a country or a region to settle there."

EXAMPLES   The war forced people to **emigrate** from their homeland.

Marie's grandparents **immigrated** to the United States.

ensure   See **assure, ensure, insure.**

etc.   See **and etc.**

everywheres   See **anyways, anywheres.**

except   See **accept, except.**

famous, notorious   *Famous* means "widely known." *Notorious* means "widely but unfavorably known."

EXAMPLES   Gloria Steinem is a **famous** leader of the women's movement in the United States.

Al Capone was a **notorious** gangster in the 1920s.

farther   See **all the farther, all the faster.**

┌ H E L P ─

If you have trouble remembering the difference between *emigrate* and *immigrate*, think of the word *in*. *In* sounds similar to the prefix *im–*, and a person who *immigrates* comes *in*to a country.

USAGE

fewer, less Use *fewer*, which tells "how many," to modify a plural noun. Use *less*, which tells "how much," to modify a singular noun.

EXAMPLES   I worked **fewer** hours this week than last week.

              I worked **less** time this week than last week.

good, well See page 233.

Oral Practice **Identifying Correct Usage**

Read each of the following sentences aloud, giving the correct word or word group in parentheses.

EXAMPLE   **1.** I'm surprised that this cookbook (*doesn't, don't*) include a recipe for the Middle Eastern dish *baba ghanouj.*

            1. *I'm surprised that this cookbook doesn't include a recipe for the Middle Eastern dish* baba ghanouj.

1. (*Being that, Because*) Eric is shy, he doesn't say much.
2. When the car finally broke down, they had only thirteen dollars (*between, among*) the six of them.
3. (*Beside, Besides*) coordinating our volunteer work, our club sponsors an annual ski trip.
4. Please (*bring, take*) your guitar when you come to my party.
5. Jon is so (*credulous, credible, creditable*) that he believed Barbara's outrageous story.
6. They sold (*fewer, less*) new cars than used cars.
7. In what year was the automobile (*invented, discovered*)?
8. Their reason for being late to the rehearsal was (*because, that*) they missed their bus.
9. Did Carla (*bring, take*) her camera on her trip to Panama?
10. This is a picture of me (*beside, besides*) our pony.
11. All the film critics praised his (*creditable, credulous*) performance in his most recent movie.
12. They (*done, did*) well in the playoffs.
13. Angie forgot to (*bring, take*) her homework assignment when she went to school this morning.
14. We divided the tasks (*among, between*) the four of us.
15. Please (*lend, borrow*) me five dollars; I'll pay you back tomorrow.
16. Lupe's family (*emigrated, immigrated*) from the Philippines when she was nine years old.
17. I had (*fewer, less*) cavities than my sister.

DIRECT TEACHING

Correcting Misconceptions

Students may generally assume that most printed, published, or posted information is in standard English. Divide the class into groups of three, and ask the groups to find printed examples of the words presented in this segment. Students might look in newspapers, magazines, and advertisements. They may find examples of both standard and nonstandard use. For example, ask students if they have ever seen a sign at a grocery-store checkout register that reads "Fifteen items or less." Discuss with them the error in usage in this sign. [*The word* less *modifies a plural noun; therefore,* less *should be changed to* fewer.] After students have completed their research, have a spokesperson from each group report on the group's findings.

18. Alan Shepard, Jr., became (*famous, notorious*) as the first American in space.
19. Kristine decided to (*invent, discover*) a computer game of her own.
20. Cold weather (*don't, doesn't*) bother him very much.

Exercise 3 Correcting Errors in Usage

Most of the following sentences contain errors in the use of standard, formal English. If a sentence contains an ~~error~~, revise the sentence. If a sentence is already correct, write *C*.   Answers may vary.

EXAMPLE   **1.** We excepted the telegram nervously.
          1. *We accepted the telegram nervously.*

1. Frank has ~~less~~ hobbies than his friend.   **1.** fewer
2. ~~Being as~~ Bernard Malamud is my favorite writer, I was excited to find one of his novels on sale at my local bookstore.   **2.** Because
3. Would you please take this monstrosity out of here?   **3.** C
4. I think someone ~~busted~~ the culprits.   **4.** arrested
5. One of the main reasons for the widespread concern for eagles is ~~because~~ many are dying from lead poisoning.   **5.** that
6. The manager divided the work ~~between~~ the four of us.   **6.** among
7. The Chinese ballet dancer ~~immigrated~~ from his homeland to find creative freedom.   **7.** emigrated
8. Have any of you ~~did~~ your research for your report yet?   **8.** done
9. To prepare her report, Judy used current data that were published by the Department of the Treasury.   **9.** C
10. Roy told me that he ~~don't~~ care, but I know that he does. **10.** doesn't

Review A Correcting Errors in Usage

Most of the sentences in the following paragraphs contain ~~errors~~ in the use of standard, formal English. Revise each sentence that contains an error. If a sentence is already correct, write *C*.   Answers may vary.

EXAMPLE   **[1]** Do you know where the famous painting on the next page was discovered at?
          1. *Do you know where the famous painting on the next page was discovered?*

[1] One of the most powerful works of art anywheres, the bull shown here was painted some fifteen thousand years ago in Lascaux, France. [2] The painting remained hidden until 1940, when a dog named Robot darted down a hole and the four young men following him

---

DIFFERENTIATING INSTRUCTION

Special Education Students
Some students may have difficulty working with blocks of text such as the lengthy paragraphs in **Review A.** Suggest that students use sheets of paper to uncover one sentence at a time.

accidentally ~~invented~~ these marvelous cave paintings. **[3]** According to one of these boys, Marcel Ravidat, it was he who painstakingly enlarged the hole and wriggled down into the now ~~notorious~~ caverns. **[4]** With only a weak light to guide him, he soon tripped and fell; luckily, his flashlight was not ~~busted~~. **[5]** When Ravidat aimed the light at the walls, ~~an~~ herd of animal figures leapt into view. **[6]** As the other boys joined him, the sight of the giant bulls, cows, elk, stags, ~~and etc.~~, filled the young men with joy and wonder, prompting them to celebrate with a wild dance. **[7]** With difficulty, the boys got out of the cavern, promising to return and admonishing each other, "Don't tell anyone about this!"

[8] When they left home the next day, the boys ~~brought~~ a stronger light with them. **[9]** They investigated the cave excitedly until they found a passage that was so deep and dark that no one ~~accept~~ Ravidat would enter it. **[10]** Using a rope, the boys lowered him down the dangerous vertical passage ~~all the farther~~ he could go.
[11] At the bottom, Ravidat hardly knew where he was ~~at~~, but gradually he began to explore this new area. **[12]** Soon, a picture of a human body with a bird's head appeared, and though it spanned ~~less~~ feet than the great bulls, it was just as awesome. **[13]** One by one, the other boys came down to glimpse the image of the strange creature, which is shown being knocked over by a bison. **[14]** This eerie figure ~~effected~~ the boys; instead of feeling triumphant, they were left shaken and pale.

[15] For Ravidat and his friends, these days were sometimes frightening ~~beside~~ being joyous and exciting. **[16]** Quite possibly, the artists who ~~done~~ the paintings hoped to instill these very emotions in viewers long ago. **[17]** Despite all the data that ~~has~~ been collected about the age and meaning of the paintings, much about them remains uncertain. **[18]** Some scientists believe that the purpose of the paintings was to initiate young hunters; others think that the paintings were a form of magic meant to increase the ~~amount~~ of game animals; but most scientists do agree that the paintings were considered sacred and were kept secret. **[19]** The reason they have survived for so long is ~~because~~ they were hidden away in dark caves, protected from light and kept at a constant humidity. **[20]** ~~Being as~~ modern-day tourists have introduced destructive microorganisms into the Lascaux caverns, the caves are now, unfortunately, closed to the public.

2. discovered

3. famous

4. broken   5. a

6. etc.

7. C

8. took

9. except

10. as far as

12. fewer

13. C

14. affected

The Granger Collection, New York.

15. besides
16. did

17. have

18. number

19. that

20. Because

DIFFERENTIATING INSTRUCTION

Advanced Learners

About the Artwork. These cave paintings, rendered by prehistoric people, have been the subject of intense speculation. Although no clear explanation has been developed, some scientists believe that the caves were used mainly for ceremonial purposes. Animals are the most common subjects of cave paintings, and scientists postulate that prehistoric people invested animals with spiritual significance.

Had of—Myself, Ourselves

(pp. 274–279)

OBJECTIVES

- To identify correct usage in sentences

- To revise sentences in a paragraph to correct errors in usage

DIRECT TEACHING

Modeling and Demonstration

He, She, It, They. Model how to identify and correct common usage errors by using the incorrect example *Annika Sorenstam she is my favorite golfer.* First, ask students what the pronoun *she* refers to in this sentence. [*Annika Sorenstam*] Next, ask what the subject of the sentence is. [*Annika Sorenstam*] Then, ask what function *she* has in the sentence. [She *is also a subject.*] Point out that a pronoun (in this case *she*) should not be used along with its antecedent in a double subject. Ask students how the sentence can be written. [*Annika Sorenstam is my favorite golfer* or *She is my favorite golfer.*] Now, have a volunteer use another example from this chapter to demonstrate how to identify and correct common usage errors.

DIFFERENTIATING INSTRUCTION

English-Language Learners

Asian Languages. Several Asian languages, such as Chinese, Japanese, and Korean, have a sentence structure in which one first states the topic and then comments on it: "My aunt, she's coming to visit tomorrow." Speakers of such languages may transfer this structure to English sentences. Offer students extra written or oral practice, as necessary.

---

had of See **of.**

had ought, hadn't ought Do not use *had* or *hadn't* with *ought*.

NONSTANDARD	You had ought to be more patient.
STANDARD	You **ought** to be more patient.

NONSTANDARD	I hadn't ought to spend any more money on Jason's birthday party.
STANDARD	I **ought not** to spend any more money on Jason's birthday party.

hardly See **The Double Negative,** page 286.

he, she, it, they Avoid using a pronoun along with its antecedent as the subject of a verb. Such an error is sometimes called a *double subject.*

NONSTANDARD	Faith Ringgold, who was featured in a one-woman show, she designs remarkable story quilts.
STANDARD	Faith Ringgold, who was featured in a one-woman show, designs remarkable story quilts.

hisself, theirself, theirselves Avoid using these nonstandard words for *himself* and *themselves.*

EXAMPLE   Lou built the shed **himself** [not *hisself*].

hopefully *Hopefully* is an adverb meaning "in a hopeful manner."

EXAMPLE   We waited **hopefully** for the announcement of the election results last night.

illusion See **allusion, illusion.**

immigrate See **emigrate, immigrate.**

imply, infer *Imply* means "to suggest something indirectly." *Infer* means "to interpret" or "to draw as a conclusion."

EXAMPLES   Mayor Hanson **implied** during yesterday's press conference that she would run for reelection.

I **inferred** from the mayor's comments that she would run for reelection.

in, into *In* means "within." *Into* means "from the outside to the inside." In formal situations, avoid using *in* for *into.*

STYLE TIP

Some authorities do not approve of the use of "hopefully" to mean "it is to be hoped." Therefore, it is generally best to avoid using "hopefully" in this sense in formal speech and writing.

INFORMAL
Hopefully, the election results will be announced soon.

FORMAL
I hope the election results will be announced soon.

RESOURCES

Had of—Myself, Ourselves

Practice

- *Language & Sentence Skills Practice,* pp. 242–243

Differentiating Instruction

- *Developmental Language & Sentence Skills,* pp. 107–108

INFORMAL	Feeling nervous, Jim opened the door and walked in the personnel office.
FORMAL	Feeling nervous, Jim opened the door and walked **into** the personnel office.

insure   See **assure, ensure, insure.**

invent   See **discover, invent.**

it   See **he, she, it, they.**

its, it's   See page 413.

kind(s), sort(s), type(s)   With the singular form of each of these nouns, use *this* or *that*. With the plural form, use *these* or *those*.

EXAMPLES   **This kind** of package is recyclable, but **those kinds** are not.

These types of examples are helpful.

kind of, sort of   In formal situations, avoid using *kind of* or *sort of* for the adverb *somewhat* or *rather*.

INFORMAL	You look kind of nervous.
FORMAL	You look **rather** [or **somewhat**] nervous.

kind of a(n), sort of a(n)   In formal situations, omit the *a(n)*.

INFORMAL	What kind of a car is that?
FORMAL	What **kind of** car is that?

learn, teach   *Learn* means "to gain knowledge." *Teach* means "to provide with knowledge."

EXAMPLE   If you will **teach** me how to play the guitar, I will **learn** some traditional Mexican folk songs.

leave, let   *Leave* means "to go away." *Let* means "to permit" or "to allow." Do not use *leave* for *let*.

EXAMPLES   **Let** [not *Leave*] us finish our dinner.

I knew I shouldn't have **let** [not *left*] them borrow my car.

lend   See **borrow, lend.**

less   See **fewer, less.**

liable   See **likely, liable.**

lie, lay   See page 194.

DIFFERENTIATING INSTRUCTION

Learners Having Difficulty

Activity. Let students use a chart like the following one to interview one another about their use of non-standard constructions in everyday, informal communication. The interviewer should circle N for *never,* S for *sometimes,* or F for *frequently,* depending on the interviewee's response to the main question.

How frequently would you express yourself this way?

1. Leave me be.   N S F
2. I'm sort of glad.   N S F
3. She's liable to go.   N S F
4. Learn me how.   N S F
5. Larry he knows.   N S F

Be sure to include in your students' interview charts any nonstandard expressions that are used locally or regionally. Discuss with the class the extra challenge in changing usage patterns that are reinforced locally.

Reference Note

For more information about **subordinate clauses,** see page 83.

Reference Note

For more about **personal pronouns and reflexive and intensive pronouns,** see page 150.

like, as   In formal situations, do not use *like* for the conjunction *as* to introduce a subordinate clause.

INFORMAL   The plan to win the election worked like they had thought it would.

FORMAL   The plan to win the election worked **as** they had thought it would.

like, as if, as though   In formal situations, avoid using *like* for the conjunction *as if* or *as though* to introduce a subordinate clause.

INFORMAL   I feel like I have the flu.

FORMAL   I feel **as if** [or **as though**] I have the flu.

likely, liable   In informal situations, *likely* and *liable* are interchangeable. However, in formal situations, use *likely* to express simple probability and *liable* to express probability with potential harm or misfortune.

EXAMPLES   Ginny is **likely** to arrive any minute.

The children playing in the abandoned building are **liable** to get hurt.

Liable is also used to mean "responsible" or "answerable."

EXAMPLE   The Smiths are **liable** for the damages that their dog has caused.

literally, figuratively   *Literally* means "following the letter" or "in a strict sense." *Figuratively* means "metaphorically" or "not literally."

EXAMPLES   I was **literally** hopping mad—jumping up and down and hollering at the broken computer.

Figuratively speaking, I was paralyzed, each day a little less able to act decisively.

may   See page 218.

might of, must of   See **of.**

myself, ourselves   Avoid using pronouns ending in *–self* or *–selves* (reflexive and intensive pronouns) in place of personal pronouns.

EXAMPLES   Amy and **I** [not *myself*] appreciate your help.

Could you do a favor for Wanda and **us** [not *ourselves*]?

For each of the following sentences, choose the word or word group in parentheses that is correct according to the rules of standard, formal English.

EXAMPLE   **1.** What (*kind of a, kind of*) computer did you buy?

        1. kind of

1. In his address to Congress, the president (*implied, inferred*) that an economic reversal might occur soon.
2. When you have time, will you (*learn, teach*) me to sew?
3. He slipped on the wet deck and fell (*in, into*) the water.
4. We (*ought, had ought*) to have asked Allison for the recipe.
5. You look (*like, as if*) you've just seen a ghost!
6. Doyle and (*I, myself*) worked together on this project.
7. You (*ought, had ought*) to have asked me; I would have told you.
8. Have you been changing the oil (*as, like*) you're supposed to do?
9. (*Leave, Let*) them stay if they don't want to go with us.
10. Her recordings are (*liable, likely*) to become classics.
11. As for Ted and (*myself, me*), we're going to the dance.
12. This (*kind of a, kind of*) figure decorates many Navajo rugs.
13. (*Figuratively, Literally*) then, the singer was catapulted to fame.
14. From the evidence, we may (*imply, infer*) the presence of a much older civilization.
15. Mr. Hashem had an assignment for Emilio and (*ourselves, us*).
16. The new mare (*had, she had*) a foal this morning, a paint filly.
17. Glasses like these (*had ought, ought*) to be washed by hand.
18. Those (*kind, kinds*) of cats have bobtails.
19. I checked the meter daily, (*like, as*) I was instructed to do.
20. Did you hear that Tom got (*himself, hisself*) a new job?

Exercise 5 | Correcting Errors in Usage

Each sentence in the following paragraph contains an error in the use of standard, formal English. Revise each sentence to correct the error.

EXAMPLE   **[1]** Leave me explain the painting technique called pointillism.

        1. Let me explain the painting technique called pointillism.

[1] Georges Seurat ~~he~~ spent his short career studying the mysteries of light, color, and the human eye. [2] One of the results of his study is

EXTENSION

Relating to Literature
Ask students to brainstorm a list of characters in literature who rise in education, social expectation, or public trust. Their suggestions may include Pip in Charles Dickens's *Great Expectations,* Eliza Doolittle in Bernard Shaw's *Pygmalion,* or Michael Henchard in Thomas Hardy's *The Mayor of Casterbridge.* Ask students to find quotations that were appropriate for the character before his or her rise in station and then to find quotations that reflect the character's refined speech after his or her change in social status.

USAGE

2. rather

this painting, which is composed of thousands, perhaps millions, of <u>kind of</u> small dots. **[3]** This sort of ~~a~~ technique is called pointillism; the name is derived from the small points of color on the canvas.

4. themselves

5. as

[4] Rather than mix paint <u>theirselves</u>, artists using this technique let the viewer's eyes blend the colors. **[5]** Seen from a certain distance, the small points of color flow together and become solid, <u>like</u> the pixels on a computer screen or the dots of a printed photograph do. **[6]** In fact, some critics believe that observations of modern printed photographs

6. taught

8. types

<u>learned</u> Seurat all about pointillism. **[7]** However, these critics ~~had~~ ought to examine Seurat's painting more closely. **[8]** Unlike some of his contemporaries, Seurat was interested in photographic technology; however, the dots that make up his paintings are rather large, and obviously these <u>type</u> of points are not meant to appear completely solid.

9. kinds

[9] If you go to a museum to see one of these <u>kind</u> of paintings, estimate the diagonal length of the picture and then step back about three

10. likely

times that distance. **[10]** From this viewpoint, a pointillist painting is <u>liable</u> to flicker or shimmer with the very vibrancy of life itself.

DIFFERENTIATING INSTRUCTION

Advanced Learners

Viewing the Art. Georges Seurat (1859–1891) was an artist who integrated art with science. Seurat used the latest scientific discoveries about the perception of color and light to develop his artistic technique, called pointillism. Seurat produced a number of masterpieces during his short lifetime (he died at the age of thirty-one). The painting reproduced here is considered Seurat's greatest work and one of the landmarks of modern art.

Review B Correcting Errors in Usage

Most of the following sentences contain <u>errors</u> in the use of standard, formal English. If a sentence contains an error, revise the sentence. If a sentence is already correct, write *C*.   Answers may vary.

EXAMPLE   **1.** Hopefully, the working conditions in the factory will continue to improve.

         1. We hope the working conditions in the factory will continue to improve.

1. The magician dazzled us with flawless <u>allusions</u>.   **1.** illusions
2. The cat jumped from the chair and leaped <u>in</u> my arms.   **2.** into
3. The children helped <u>theirselves</u> to more vegetable curry.   **3.** themselves
4. Your room looks <u>like</u> it's been hit by a tornado.   **4.** as though
5. What can you infer from the refrain in the poem "Sympathy"?   **5.** C
6. You <u>hadn't ought</u> to complain so much.   **6.** ought not
7. Jane and <u>myself</u> are the editors of our yearbook.   **7.** I
8. What sort of a CD player does Margaret plan to buy with her Christmas bonus?
9. I asked my boss whether he would let me have the day off.   **9.** C
10. Some people <u>they're</u> always making a fuss about nothing.   **10.** are

nauseated, nauseous   Informally, *nauseated* and *nauseous* are often used interchangeably. In formal English, however, *nauseated* means "sick," while *nauseous* means "disgusting" or "sickening."

EXAMPLES   After riding the roller coaster, the child became **nauseated.**

        The chemical reaction gave off a **nauseous** odor.

no, nobody, none, no one, not, nothing, nowhere
See **The Double Negative,** page 286.

nor   See **or, nor.**

notorious   See **famous, notorious.**

nowheres   See **anyways, anywheres.**

number   See **amount, number.**

number of   Use a singular verb after the expression *the number of.* Use a plural verb after the expression *a number of.*

EXAMPLES   **The number of** candidates **was** surprising.

        A **number of** candidates **were nominated**.

Nauseated, Nauseous—Your, You're
(pp. 279–285)

OBJECTIVE

■ To revise sentences to correct errors in usage

DIFFERENTIATING INSTRUCTION

Learners Having Difficulty
Motivating. Students may not understand why it is important for them to be able to use standard English. Explain that the ability to use standard English will serve them well when they are applying for jobs or for further schooling. To emphasize this point, you could have students imagine they are applying for the jobs of their dreams. Have students write letters of application for their dream jobs.

RESOURCES

Nauseated, Nauseous—Your, You're
Practice
■ *Language & Sentence Skills Practice,* pp. 244–245
Differentiating Instruction
■ *Developmental Language & Sentence Skills,* pp. 109–110

USAGE

of   *Of* is a preposition. Do not use *of* in place of *have* after verbs such as *could, should, would, might, must,* and *ought* [*to*]. Also, do not use *had of* for *had.*

NONSTANDARD	You could of told me that you were hungry.
STANDARD	You **could have** told me that you were hungry.

NONSTANDARD	You ought to of seen the look on his face.
STANDARD	You **ought to have** seen the look on his face.

NONSTANDARD	If Amy had of heard that the party was casual, she wouldn't of worn that dressy outfit.
STANDARD	If Amy **had** heard that the party was casual, she **wouldn't have** worn that dressy outfit.

Avoid using *of* after other prepositions such as *inside, off,* or *outside.*

EXAMPLE   Leslie turned **off** [not *off of*] the parkway.

off, off of   Do not use *off* or *off of* for *from.*

NONSTANDARD	I got some good advice off that mechanic.
STANDARD	I got some good advice **from** that mechanic.

or, nor   Use *or* with *either;* use *nor* with *neither.*

EXAMPLES   **Either** Jennifer **or** Gloria will bring the book.

Neither Gwen **nor** Lily has been absent this term.

ought   See **had ought, hadn't ought.**

ought to of   See **of.**

persecute, prosecute   *Persecute* means "to attack or annoy someone constantly." *Prosecute* means "to bring legal action against someone for unlawful behavior."

EXAMPLES   The dictator **persecuted** those who opposed him.

The district attorney **prosecuted** the person caught looting.

phenomena   *Phenomena* is the plural form of *phenomenon.* Do not use *phenomena* as a singular noun.

PLURAL	We have been studying those **phenomena** of nature, which are quite rare.
SINGULAR	We have been studying that **phenomenon** of nature, which is quite rare.

MINI-LESSON **Usage**

Subject-Verb Agreement. Point out to students that in each example sentence under *or, nor,* there is a compound subject with a singular verb. Each subject appears plural, but in the first sentence, *Jennifer* and *Gloria* are singular, not plural. In the

reason . . . because   See **because.**

Reverend, Honorable   Do not use either of these titles before a person's last name alone. Also, be sure to use the word *the* before the title.

NONSTANDARD	My grandfather remembers meeting both Reverend King and the Honorable Inouye.
STANDARD	My grandfather remembers meeting both **the Reverend** Martin Luther King, Jr. [or **the Reverend Dr. King**] and **the Honorable** Daniel K. Inouye [or **the Honorable Mr. Inouye,** or **the Honorable Sen. Inouye**].

rise, raise   See page 196.

say   Do not use *say* or *says* after a past-tense verb. Use *said.*

NONSTANDARD	Then she glared at me and says, "Where have you been?"
STANDARD	Then she glared at me and **said,** "Where have you been?"

scarcely   See **The Double Negative,** page 286.

she   See **he, she, it, they.**

should of   See **of.**

sit, set   See page 194.

slow, slowly   See page 233.

some, somewhat   In formal situations, avoid using *some* to mean "to some extent." Use *somewhat.*

INFORMAL	Tensions between the nations began to ease some.
FORMAL	Tensions between the nations began to ease **somewhat.**

somewheres   See **anyways, anywheres.**

sort(s)   See **kind(s), sort(s), type(s)** and **kind of a, sort of a.**

sort of   See **kind of, sort of.**

supposed to, used to   When writing the past form of *suppose* or *use,* especially before the word *to,* be sure to add the *–d* ending.

EXAMPLES   Desmond is **supposed to** [not *suppose to*] be in charge of the props for the senior play.

I **used to** [not *use to*] work part time at that store.

take   See **bring, take.**

teach   See **learn, teach.**

Reference Note

For information about forming the **past tense of regular verbs,** see page 176.

A Glossary of Usage   **281**

---

second sentence, *Gwen* and *Lily* are singular as well. Review with the class the following rule: Singular subjects joined by *or* or *nor* take a singular verb. For more information on subject-verb agreement, refer students to **Chapter 5: Agreement**.

DIFFERENTIATING INSTRUCTION

English-Language Learners

Vietnamese. Vietnamese students may confuse similar sounding words in English, such as *sit* and *set,* because Vietnamese lacks the vowel sounds found in *sit, had, fire,* and *hour.* With certain words, Vietnamese-speaking students may substitute similar sounds for these vowel sounds and then confuse these words with similar sounding words.

Also, Vietnamese uses a limited number of consonant sounds at the ends of words, which may cause problems with students' grammar and ability to comprehend English. Vietnamese students need opportunities to practice spoken English in an encouraging environment where correct pronunciation is modeled. They should work in groups with native English speakers whenever possible.

DIRECT TEACHING

Modeling and Demonstration

Suppose to, Supposed to, Use to, Used to. Model how to identify and correct common usage errors by using the incorrect example *I was suppose to be home by dinner.* First, ask students what word or word group makes up the verb in this sentence. [*suppose to be*] Next, ask whether this verb phrase is in the correct form. [*no*] Ask what the correct form is. [*supposed to be*] Point out that the *d* should not be left off the verb *supposed* in *supposed to,* and the *d* should not be left off the verb *used* in *used to.* Now, have a volunteer use another example from the chapter to demonstrate how to identify and correct common usage errors.

RETEACHING

Than and Then

Mnemonic. The following tip may help students remember when to use *than* and when to use *then.*

1. *Th**e**n* tells wh**e**n.

2. *Th**a**n* comp**a**res or contr**a**sts.

There, Their, and They're

Mnemonic. To help students differentiate among the often misused words *there, their,* and *they're,* present the following helpful tips.

1. Remember the word *here* in *there* when writing about a place.

2. Remember the *heir* in *their* when writing about possession.

3. If *they are* can be substituted, use *they're.*

Reference Note

For information about **subordinating conjunctions,** see page 26. For information on **adverbs,** see page 20.

than, then   *Than* is a subordinating conjunction used in comparisons. *Then* is an adverb telling *when.*

EXAMPLES   Tyrone is more studious **than** I am.

Take your diploma in your left hand, and shake hands with the principal; **then** leave the stage, and return to your seat.

that   See **who, which, that.**

their, there, they're   See page 417.

theirself, theirselves   See **hisself, theirself, theirselves.**

them   Do not use *them* as an adjective. Use *those.*

EXAMPLE   Have you seen **those** [not *them*] murals by Judith Baca at the art museum?

they   See **he, she, it, they.**

this here, that there   Avoid using *here* or *there* after the demonstrative adjective *this* or *that.*

EXAMPLE   **This** [not *This here*] magazine has an article about the Japanese koto player Kazue Sawai.

this, that, these, those   See **kind(s), sort(s), type(s).**

try and, try to   Use *try to,* not *try and.*

EXAMPLE   Did anyone **try to** [not *try and*] help Ted?

type(s)   See **kind(s), sort(s), type(s).**

type, type of   Avoid using *type* as an adjective. Add *of* after *type.*

NONSTANDARD   That's the type job I'd like to have.
STANDARD   That's the **type of** job I'd like to have.

used to   See **supposed to, used to.**

ways   Use *way,* not *ways,* when referring to distance.

EXAMPLE   At dusk we were still a long **way** [not *ways*] from home.

well, good   See page 233.

what   Use *that,* not *what,* to introduce an adjective clause.

EXAMPLE   The song **that** [not *what*] Annie has chosen to sing in the talent show is "Anytime You Need a Friend."

282   Chapter 11   A Glossary of Usage

Learning for Life   Continued on pp. 283–284

Formal English. Work with students on a list of future circumstances or requirements for which formal writing skills may be necessary. Add to their ideas any of the following that they may have overlooked.

- description of experience on a job application
- personal essay for admittance to college
- account of achievement for job or school

when, where   Unless you are defining a time or place, do not use *when* or *where* to begin a definition.

STANDARD	Two o'clock is **when** we will have the next meeting.
STANDARD	This is **where** the new high school will be built.

NONSTANDARD	A hurricane is when a tropical cyclone has winds of 74 miles (118 kilometers) per hour or greater.
STANDARD	A hurricane is **a tropical cyclone that has winds of 74 miles (118 kilometers) per hour or greater.**

NONSTANDARD	An implosion is where something bursts inward.
STANDARD	An implosion is **an inward burst.**

where   Do not use *where* for *that*.

EXAMPLE   I read **that** [not *where*] the Smithsonian Institution has sixteen museums and galleries.

where . . . at   See **at.**

who's, whose   See page 418.

who, which, that   *Who* refers to persons only. *Which* refers to things only. *That* may refer to either persons or things.

EXAMPLES   Shah Jahan was the Indian ruler **who** [*or* **that**] built the Taj Mahal. [The antecedent is *ruler,* a person.]

The monument, **which** is a tomb, is near the city of Agra. [The antecedent is *monument,* a thing.]

It is a building **that** is much admired for its beautiful architecture. [The antecedent is *building,* a thing.]

who, whom   See page 152.

would of   See **of.**

your, you're   See page 418.

Exercise 6   Correcting Errors in Usage

Most of the sentences on the following page contain errors in the use of standard, formal English. If a sentence contains an error, revise the sentence. If a sentence is already correct, write *C*.   Answers may vary.

EXAMPLE   **1.** Can you name all of the American astronauts which have walked on the surface of the moon?

   1. *Can you name all of the American astronauts who have walked on the surface of the moon?*

┌HELP─

Some sentences in Exercise 6 may be correctly revised in more than one way. You need to give only one revision for each sentence.

- report or research paper
- self-evaluation for a job
- proposal for a project
- letter of recommendation
- acceptance letter or speech
- formal letter of thanks or appreciation
- request for a grant or scholarship

EXTENSION

Critical Thinking

Analysis. Tell students that English is a dynamic language in which standard usage changes over the course of time. Often, standard usage changes to correspond with popular usage. For example, *dove* as the past tense form of *dive* used to be nonstandard; now it is considered to be standard usage, and both *dove* and *dived* are correct.

Discuss with the class which of the nonstandard usages in this chapter will probably be considered standard one day. Ask students to give reasons for their opinions.

Ask students if their criteria for judgment included any of the following factors:

- tendency for language to become simpler
- personal preference for certain spoken patterns
- power of words to communicate

1. I was <u>suppose</u> to meet Jade here.   **1.** supposed
2. Backlighting is <u>when</u> the main source of light <u>is placed</u> in back of the subject being photographed.   **2.** the placement of
3. Why don't you borrow some change <u>off of</u> Rhoda?   **3.** from
4. A number of unusual themes <u>has</u> already been proposed for the senior prom.   **4.** have
5. Neither Chico <u>or</u> Robert has any albums by Tish Hinojosa.   **5.** nor
6. Sharon turned to me and <u>says</u>, "Did you see the beautiful sari that woman was wearing?"   **6.** said
7. You should <u>of</u> seen the premiere last night.   **7.** have
8. The aurora borealis is a spectacular <u>phenomena</u> of nature.   **8.** phenomenon
9. We stayed up to watch the late-night horror movie, which wasn't worth the loss of sleep.   **9.** C
10. It's a long <u>ways</u> to Memphis from Denver.   **10.** way
11. This type inscription is common in the Mayan records.   **11.** of
12. Deleting files will help <u>some</u> with the space problem on your hard drive.   **12.** somewhat
13. After some discussion, the district attorney decided not to <u>persecute</u>.   **13.** prosecute
14. The smell of sour milk makes some people <u>nauseous</u>.   **14.** nauseated
15. Take this <u>here</u> hose around to the back, and water the lawn.
16. Did you read <u>where</u> the new highway will bypass the town?   **16.** that
17. Many household cleansers are poisons <u>what</u> should be handled with caution.   **17.** that
18. Is Sudan bigger <u>then</u> Ethiopia, Nathan?   **18.** than
19. These phenomena have attracted astronomers' attention for decades.   **19.** C
20. She had long wanted to meet the woman <u>which</u> had done so much to register voters.   **20.** who

Exercise 7 Correcting Errors in Usage

Most of the sentences in the following paragraphs contain <u>errors</u> in the use of standard, formal English. If a sentence contains an error, revise the sentence. If a sentence is already correct, write *C*.

Answers may vary.

EXAMPLE   [1] I wish you could of gone with us on our trip to Alaska.

    1. I wish you could have gone with us on our trip to Alaska.

1. the

2. phenomenon

3. was

[1] Several years ago, I accompanied Reverend Alan Kemp and his wife, Angela, on a sightseeing trip to Alaska in July. [2] On our flight to Fairbanks, we saw a double rainbow—a marvelous <u>phenomena</u> that we felt was a lucky sign. [3] At the hotel, we began to plan what we would do the next day, but the number of possibilities <u>were</u> huge, and we

Learning for Life

Continued from p. 283

Ask each student to choose from the list a situation that seems relevant to his or her life. Then, ask each student to write a paragraph or two for the situations he or she has chosen.

Remind students that a written document is likely to make a lasting impression, and point out that every time they pass something they've written on to an audience, they are essentially publishing their work.

didn't know where to start. [4] Finally, we decided that we would neither stay in our rooms or eat dinner at the hotel; instead, we would go for a drive that evening. [5] As we headed for the car, I noticed on a poster where the World Eskimo-Indian Olympics were being held that very day. [6] "Doesn't this here event sound like fun?" I asked, showing Mrs. Kemp the advertisement for the games.

[7] The Kemps agreed, and as soon as we arrived at the fairgrounds, we introduced ourselves to a woman named Mrs. McBride. [8] She was a friendly woman which was happy to tell us about the games. [9] I was surprised some by the many different events that had been scheduled. [10] These games included tests of skill, such as the notorious Alaskan high kick, and tests of strength, such as drop-the-bomb.

[11] The Alaskan high kick is where a person sitting on the ground tries to kick a ball suspended in midair. [12] An event requiring exceptional balance, the Alaskan high kick is an example of the type skills that were traditionally developed by Alaska's native peoples. [13] The drop-the-bomb competition begins when three men lift another man off of the ground. [14] The man, who is held by his wrists and ankles, must remain perfectly horizontal while them three other men carry him. [15] The contestant who is carried the longest ways without sagging wins the event.

[16] As Mrs. McBride finished describing the games, she smiled and says, "This is the thirty-first year we've held these Eskimo Olympic games." [17] Than she proudly pointed out Cecelia Chanerak, who was sailing through the air during the blanket toss. [18] This event is when a group of people stretch out a hide blanket and throw a man or a woman as high as possible; the winner is whoever soars the highest and keeps the best balance. [19] I must confess that I got a bit nauseous watching people fly up so far in the air, but I managed to snap a picture anyway. [20] That there day was one of the best of our trip, and when I got back home, I eagerly described the Eskimo-Indian Olympics to my family and friends.

4. nor

5. that

7. C

8. who
9. somewhat
10. famous

11. a game in which

12. types of
14. the
15. way
16. said

17. Then
18. a game in which
19. nauseated

Exercise 7

DISTRIBUTED REVIEW
For a review of appositives, have students find an appositive and an appositive phrase in sentences 1 and 12. Ask them to determine which words are identified or explained by the appositive or appositive phrase.

1. Angela—wife
12. An event requiring exceptional balance—kick

The Double Negative

(pp. 286–287)

OBJECTIVE

■ To identify correct usage in sentences

DIFFERENTIATING INSTRUCTION

English-Language Learners

Spanish. The use of double and triple negatives is standard in Spanish. Therefore, you may need to work closely with some students to help them avoid using multiple negatives in their writing in English.

STYLE TIP

Double negatives were acceptable during Shakespeare's time, but they are now considered nonstandard.

EXAMPLE

If this be error, and upon me be proved,
I never writ, nor no man ever loved.

William Shakespeare,
Sonnet 116

The Double Negative

A **double negative** is a construction in which two or more negative words are used to express a single negative idea.

Common Negative Words		
barely	never	not (–n't)
but (meaning "only")	no	nothing
	nobody	nowhere
hardly	none	only
neither	no one	scarcely

NONSTANDARD	She has never missed none of the reunions.
STANDARD	She has **never** missed **any** of the reunions.
STANDARD	She has missed **none** of the reunions.

NONSTANDARD	I have not said nothing about your plans.
STANDARD	I have **not** said **anything** about your plans.
STANDARD	I have said **nothing** about your plans.

WINTHROP reprinted by permission of Newspaper Enterprise Association, Inc.

NOTE Avoid the common error of using *–n't,* the contraction of *not,* with another negative word, such as *barely, hardly,* or *scarcely.*

NONSTANDARD	I can't hardly see anything in this fog.
STANDARD	I can **hardly** see anything in this fog.

NONSTANDARD	Our lunch break was so short that we didn't scarcely have time to eat.
STANDARD	Our lunch break was so short that we **scarcely** had time to eat.

RESOURCES

The Double Negative

Practice

■ *Language & Sentence Skills Practice,* p. 246

Differentiating Instruction

■ *Developmental Language & Sentence Skills,* pp. 111–112

The words *but* and *only* are considered negative words when they are used as adverbs meaning "no more than." In such cases, the use of another negative word with *but* or *only* is considered informal.

INFORMAL   I don't have but one pair of dress shoes.
  FORMAL   I have **but** one pair of dress shoes.
  FORMAL   I have **only** one pair of dress shoes.

Exercise 8 Identifying Correct Usage

For each of the following sentences, choose the correct word from the pair given in parentheses.

EXAMPLE   1. The club doesn't have (*any, no*) funds left in its treasury.
          1. *any*

1. Benjamin will never get (*nowhere, anywhere*) until he starts believing in himself.
2. Luís (*can, can't*) hardly keep from being proud of you.
3. I was so sleepy that I (*could, couldn't*) hardly keep my eyes open.
4. The detectives (*haven't, have*) no clues in the case.
5. There (*is, isn't*) no good reason for your being late.
6. We hadn't (*ever, never*) tasted papaya before.
7. Neither of them wants (*nothing, anything*) to do with the prank you're planning.
8. We (*had, hadn't*) but one choice to make.
9. The candidates (*have, haven't*) only three minutes each to state their positions.
10. The manager insisted that there wasn't (*any, no*) reason for making the customers wait so long.
11. We didn't see (*anybody, nobody*) there, so we came home.
12. By the time those boys were through, there (*wasn't, was*) barely enough tuna salad left for a sandwich.
13. I wouldn't go (*nowhere, anywhere*) wearing that outfit.
14. Wouldn't (*any, none*) of those shoes suit you?
15. There shouldn't be (*no one, anyone*) here who doesn't have a solid background in experimental design.
16. Aren't you (*ever, never*) going to be ready to go?
17. Nothing we did made (*no, any*) difference.
18. They (*weren't, were*) finding scarcely any traces of copper in that mine.
19. There (*was, wasn't*) no way I was riding in that contraption.
20. Do not touch (*nothing, anything*) on my desk!

CONTENT-AREA CONNECTIONS

Mathematics
Double Negatives. Point out to students that the double negative in English has an effect similar to the doubling of negative signs in mathematics. Write the following

expression on the chalkboard, and ask students what it means.

– (–6) = 6 [*The negative of negative 6 is the same as positive 6.*]

Nonsexist Language
(pp. 288–290)

OBJECTIVE

- To revise sentences to eliminate gender-specific and awkward expressions

Nonsexist Language

Nonsexist language is language that applies to people in general, both male and female. For example, the nonsexist terms *humanity, human beings,* and *people* can substitute for the gender-specific term *mankind.*

In the past, many skills and occupations were generally closed to either men or women. Expressions like *seamstress, stewardess,* and *mailman* reflect those limitations. Since most jobs can now be held by both men and women, language is adjusting to reflect this change.

When you are referring generally to people, use nonsexist expressions rather than gender-specific ones. Following are some widely used non-sexist terms that you can use to replace the older, gender-specific ones.

Gender-Specific	Nonsexist
businessman	executive, businessperson
chairman	chairperson, chair
deliveryman	delivery person
fireman	firefighter
foreman	supervisor
housewife	homemaker
mailman	mail carrier
mankind	humankind, people
man-made	synthetic, manufactured
manpower	workers, human resources
May the best man win!	May the best person win!
policeman	police officer
salesman	salesperson, salesclerk
seamstress	needleworker
steward, stewardess	flight attendant
waiter, waitress	server
watchman	security guard

If the antecedent of a pronoun may be either masculine or feminine, use both masculine and feminine pronouns to refer to it.

EXAMPLES   **Anyone** who wants to purchase a class T-shirt must bring **his or her** money to Room 307 by Friday.

Any **student** may bring the money with **him or her** to Room 307.

RESOURCES

Nonsexist Language
Practice
- *Language & Sentence Skills Practice,* p. 246
Differentiating Instruction
- *Developmental Language & Sentence Skills,* pp. 111–112

Often, you can avoid the awkward *his or her* construction (or the alternative *his/her*) by substituting an article (*a, an,* or *the*) for the construction. You can also rephrase the sentence, using the plural forms of both the pronoun and its antecedent.

EXAMPLES   Any **student** who wants to purchase a class T-shirt must bring **the** money to Room 307 by Friday.

All **students** who want to purchase a class T-shirt must bring **their** money to Room 307 by Friday.

Exercise 9   Using Nonsexist Language

Rewrite each of the following sentences to avoid using <u>gender-specific terms and awkward expressions.</u>   Answers may vary.

EXAMPLE   **1.** Many parking garages hire watchmen to deter thieves.

     1. Many parking garages hire security guards to deter thieves.

1. More and more <u>man-made</u> objects are littering outer space.   1. synthetic
2. The Boston Marathon got underway to cries of "May the best <u>man</u> win!"   2. person
3. Being a <u>foreman</u> in a factory must be a tough job.   3. supervisor
4. The lobby of the office tower was full of <u>businessmen</u> arriving for appointments.   4. businesspeople
5. One problem the team faced was a shortage of <u>manpower.</u>   5. workers
6. Anyone who wants to audition for the play must be sure that <u>s/he</u> can memorize long passages of dialogue.   6. he or she
7. In the last century or so, fewer and fewer women have chosen to become <u>seamstresses.</u>   7. needleworkers
8. The airline we took to Mexico had very courteous <u>stewardesses.</u>   8. flight attendants
9. There was a fascinating TV program last night about a day in the life of a <u>fireman.</u>   9. firefighter
10. Dr. Zaharias has told her close associates that she is interested in becoming <u>chairman</u> of the department.   10. chairperson

Review C   Correcting Errors in Usage

Most of the following sentences contain <u>errors</u> in the use of standard, formal English. If a sentence contains an error, revise the sentence. If a sentence is already correct, write *C.*

EXAMPLE   **1.** An allegory is where a story's characters and events symbolize abstract ideas or moral principles.

     1. An allegory is a story in which the characters and events symbolize abstract ideas or moral principles.

| STYLE   TIP |

Avoid using the awkward expressions *s/he* and *wo/man.*

1. allusion

1. The professor made an <u>illusion</u> to Ralph Ellison's novel *Invisible Man.*
2. We had to adapt the stage lighting for the rock concert.   **2.** C
3. The organization helped a large <u>amount</u> of Asian refugees find work.

   3. number
4. Where did you stay <u>at</u> over Thanksgiving?
5. Everyone except Tim has <u>excepted</u> the invitation.   **5.** accepted
6. <u>Among</u> the two performers, I prefer Keb' Mo'.   **6.** Between
7. The data on acid rain <u>is</u> not complete.   **7.** are

   8. emigrated
8. My parents <u>immigrated</u> from Cuba before I was born.
9. Have you ever read about the nurse Florence Nightingale, who is <u>notorious</u> for having modernized the nursing profession?**9.** famous
10. Were you credulous enough to believe the fortuneteller?   **10.** C
11. My sister ~~she~~ attends Iowa State University.

    12. inferred
12. We <u>implied</u> from Rudy's comment that the movie was dull.
13. The Coopers grew all the vegetables <u>theirselves</u>.   **13.** themselves
14. I <u>had ought</u> to spend more time with my friends.   **14.** ought
15. He has been the catcher every inning so far, and he is beginning to look <u>kind of</u> tired.   **15.** rather
16. Ms. Robinson <u>learned</u> me all I know about botany.   **16.** taught
17. I think I just <u>busted</u> my watch, Marilyn.   **17.** broke
18. At the assembly yesterday, the Honorable John Murphy encouraged students to register to vote as soon as they turn eighteen.   **18.** C
19. A number of suggestions have been submitted to the prom decorations committee.   **19.** C
20. There were four freshmen <u>which</u> made the basketball team.

    20. who

11

Terms in brackets refer to concepts tested by items in the Chapter Review.

1. [double negative]
2. [in, into]
3. [all right]
4. [being as, being that]
5. [likely, liable]
6. [ways]
7. [like, as if, as though]
8. [fewer, less]
9. [kind(s), sort(s), type(s); kind of a(n), sort of a(n)]
10. [had ought, hadn't ought]
11. [some, somewhat]
12. [bring, take]
13. [affect, effect]
14. [of]
15. [imply, infer]
16. [amount, number]
17. [credible, cred- itable, credulous]
18. [supposed to, used to]
19. [off, off of]
20. [Reverend, Honorable]

Chapter Review

A. Identifying Correct Usage

For each of the following sentences, choose the <u>correct word or words</u> in parentheses. Base your answers on the rules of standard, formal usage.

1. We (*can't hardly, <u>can't</u>*) help feeling proud of our team.
2. The lifeguard dived (*<u>into</u>, in*) the water to rescue the child.
3. Did we do (*alright, <u>all right</u>*), Coach Garcia?
4. (*Being as, Being that, <u>Because</u>*) he was a good actor, he got the lead role in the play.
5. You are (*<u>likely</u>, liable*) to go far if you apply yourself.
6. We hiked a long (*<u>way</u>, ways*) before we found a suitable campsite.
7. The rescuers looked (*like, <u>as if</u>, as*) they had not slept.
8. There are (*less, <u>fewer</u>*) students in the senior class this year.
9. (*Those kinds of, That kind of a, <u>This kind of</u>*) movie is fun.
10. We (*hadn't ought, <u>ought not</u>*) to spill any of this paint on the floor.
11. The temperature has warmed (*some, <u>somewhat</u>*).
12. Please (*bring, <u>take</u>*) this report to Mr. Benson when you go.
13. The audience was deeply (*<u>affected</u>, effected*) by her speech.
14. We (*<u>could have</u>, could of, should of*) done a better job.
15. Kim's letter (*<u>implied</u>, inferred*) that she would be paying us a visit soon.
16. We received a large (*amount, <u>number</u>*) of offers.
17. Ana has done a very (*credible, <u>creditable</u>, credulous*) job.
18. Liev was (*suppose to, <u>supposed to</u>*) bring his pictures of Bali.
19. Do you remember borrowing a dollar (*off, off of, <u>from</u>*) me?
20. The first speaker will be (*Reverend Jackson, the Reverend Jackson, <u>the Reverend Edward Jackson</u>*).

B. Correcting Errors in Usage

Most of the sentences on the following page contain <u>errors</u> in the use of standard, formal English. If a sentence contains an error, revise the sentence. If a sentence is already correct, write *C*.   Answers may vary.

Chapter Review   **291**

ASSESSING

Monitoring Progress

Chapter Review. To assess student progress, you may want to compare the types of items missed on the **Diagnostic Preview** to those missed on the **Chapter Review.** If students have not made significant progress, you could refer them to **Chapter 16: Correcting Common Errors, Exercises 21–24** for additional practice.

USAGE

RESOURCES

A Glossary of Usage

Review
■ *Language & Sentence Skills Practice*, pp. 247–249

Assessment
■ *Holt Handbook Chapter Tests with Answer Key*, pp. 21–22, 54

21. as though [*like, as if, as though*]
22. [*at*]
23. among [*between, among*]
24. had [*double negative*]
25. Except [*accept, except*]
26. C [*because*]
27. affected [*affect, effect*]
28. Bring [*bring, take*]
29. to [*try and, try to*]
30. immigrated [*emigrate, immigrate*]
31. rather [*kind of, sort of*]
32. Besides [*beside, besides*]
33. C [*don't, doesn't*]
34. [*he, she, it, they (double subject)*]
35. a while [*a while, awhile*]
36. burst [*bust, busted*]
37. allusion [*allusion, illusion*]
38. C [*persecute, prosecute*]
39. said [*say*]
40. I [*myself, ourselves*]
41. [*who, which, that*]
42. [*discover, invent*]
43. [*than, then*]
44. [*he, she, it, they (double subject)*]
45. [*amount, number*]

21. After the play, Shirley acted <u>like</u> she were a movie star.
22. Do you know where the tape is <u>at</u>?
23. The other waiters and I divide the tips evenly <u>between</u> ourselves.
24. When the bill came, I realized that I <u>hadn't</u> scarcely any money.
25. <u>Accept</u> for Carlos and Glenn, everyone went to the fair.
26. The reason he left is that he felt tired.
27. Hasina and I are <u>effected</u> differently by the same song.
28. <u>Take</u> your dog with you when you come over to my house.
29. Could you try <u>and</u> help me move this table?
30. Both of Emily's grandmothers <u>emigrated</u> here in the 1940s.
31. We were <u>kind of</u> disappointed with the results.
32. <u>Beside</u> Ted and Ann, who else knows?
33. Doesn't a hot summer day make you long for an ice-cold drink?
34. My aunt Beverly, who was born in 1949, <u>she</u> served in the army.
35. The repair will take <u>awhile</u>.
36. Both tires <u>busted</u> when the bicycle rolled over the broken glass.
37. In his speech, Mr. Marlowe made an <u>illusion</u> to Shakespeare.
38. Finally, the gangster was successfully prosecuted for tax evasion.
39. After that the director <u>says</u> to me, "Just stay in the chariot, Chuck. I'll make sure you win the race."
40. Tony and <u>myself</u> are responsible for clearing the brush.

C. Identifying Correct Usage

For each sentence in the following paragraph, choose the <u>correct word or words</u> in parentheses.

[41] Even during ancient times, people (*which, who*) were sweltering in the heat found ways to cool off. [42] Around 3000 B.C., the Egyptians beat the heat when they (*discovered, invented*) the cooling effect of evaporation. [43] The Egyptians poured water into shallow trays made of clay; (*than, then*) they put the trays on a layer of straw. [44] As the temperature dropped during the night, the (*water it, water*) quickly evaporated and formed a thin layer of ice, which was eagerly gathered early the next morning. [45] Because more ice forms in very dry air, the (*amount, number*) of ice depended on the dryness of the air.

[46] A thousand years later, wealthy Babylonians would use the (*effects*, *affects*) of evaporation to cool their homes. [47] At twilight, they had the exterior walls and interior floors doused with water; as it evaporated from these surfaces, the houses cooled down (*some*, *somewhat*). [48] In ancient India, the same (*type*, *type of*) system was adapted for home cooling. [49] Wet grass mats hung in windward windows were (*liable*, *likely*) to create a considerable drop in temperature inside the house—as much as thirty degrees. [50] To maintain cooling, either someone kept the mats wet during the nights, or (*a*, *an*) reservoir over the windows slowly dripped water onto the mats.

46. [*affect, effect*]
47. [*some, somewhat*]
48. [*type, type of*]
49. [*likely, liable*]
50. [*a, an*]

Writing Application
Using Standard English in a Story

Standard and Nonstandard English   Recently you heard about a strange, inspiring, or funny experience. You have decided to write a fictional narrative based on the event. You may use non-standard English in dialogue, but be sure to write the rest of the story in standard English.

Prewriting   Think about something strange, inspiring, or funny that happened to you or to someone you know. Decide on the setting, the characters, and the point of view of the story. Finally, create a brief plot outline.

Writing   Using your prewriting notes, write a draft of your story. Expand on your original ideas by inventing vivid details.

Revising   Read your story aloud to friends and ask them to tell you which part held their interest and which parts did not. Revise accordingly.

Publishing   Be sure to use the **Glossary of Usage** to help you correct unintentional nonstandard usages. Then, proofread your story for errors in grammar, usage, spelling, and punctuation. Be sure that you have placed quotation marks around dialogue. You and your classmates may wish to collect all of the class's stories in a booklet and add illustrations or photographs.

Reference Note

For more about **using quotation marks,** see page 365.

APPLICATION

Writing Application

Prewriting Tip. To help students choose experiences on which to base their stories, you might ask them to think about personal experiences, such as their happiest moments or strange events that they have witnessed.

Writing Tip. To help students create three-dimensional characters, have them develop character sketches. You may want to provide the following questions for students to answer about each of their characters (explain that they need not include all such details in their narratives).

1. Is the character shy or outgoing?

2. Does the character cry during sad movies?

3. Is the character afraid of anything?

Scoring Rubric. While you will want to pay particular attention to standard and nonstandard usage in students' narratives, you will also want to evaluate overall writing performance. You could give a split score to assess development and clarity of the composition separately from skill in usage.

CHAPTER

12

Capitalization
Standard Uses of Capital Letters

Numerals in brackets refer to rules tested by the items in the Diagnostic Preview.

1. [12e, d]
2. [12d(2)]
3. [*or* President . . . Vice President] [12d, f(1)]
4. [12f(3), d(2)]
5. [12d(2)]
6. [12d(8,2)]
7. [12d (2)]
8. [*or* Democratic Party . . . Republican Party] [12d(3)]

Diagnostic Preview

A. Using Standard Capitalization

Many of the following sentences contain at least one error in capitalization. For each error, write the correct form of the word. If a sentence is already correct, write *C*.

EXAMPLE   **1.** Manolo Cruz will be attending Stanford university in the Fall.

     1. University, fall

1. I am studying russian, English, and Art this Semester.
2. Go north for two Streets and then turn east on Central Avenue.
3. In U.S. History, only one person, Gerald R. Ford, has held the nation's highest office without being elected president or Vice President.
4. Last summer I enjoyed reading *To Kill A Mockingbird*, a novel by the southern writer Harper Lee.
5. I have fished from the sea wall on the shore of lake Pontchartrain.
6. The first American woman in space, Sally Ride, was a member of the crew aboard the space shuttle *challenger*, launched from cape Canaveral, Florida, on June 18, 1983.
7. The Mountain Ranges in the West offer a variety of hiking experiences for those who love the outdoors.
8. Local representatives from the democratic party and the republican party worked together to increase voter registration.

9. Because Michael's letter was addressed to 730 Lexington Place instead of to 730 Lexington Court, it was delayed.

10. The United States' political and economic interests are closely tied to those of its northern neighbor, Canada, and to those of its southern neighbors, Mexico and the central American countries.

B. Proofreading Paragraphs for Correct Capitalization

Proofread the following paragraphs. Write the words that are incorrectly capitalized, changing capital letters to lowercase letters and lowercase letters to capital letters where necessary. If a sentence is already correct, write *C*.

EXAMPLE   **[1]** Chattanooga, Tennessee, is the seat of Hamilton county.

       1. County

[**11**] Chattanooga, on the Georgia border in Southeast Tennessee, is building its future by inviting visitors to explore its past. [**12**] The city has been welcoming tourists since at least 1866, when an ad in the *Chattanooga Times* invited people from the north to visit with the assurance that the Ku Klux Klan had no power in Chattanooga. [**13**] Today a multimillion-dollar plaza on the banks of the Tennessee river marks the city's original site, a landing established about 1815 by a trader named john Ross. [**14**] exhibits throughout the plaza depict the city's history, including the 1838 forced removal of the Cherokee to the area now known as Oklahoma. [**15**] Ross, who was himself part Cherokee and who vehemently protested the removal, led that tragic journey, which became known as the trail of Tears.

[**16**] Chattanooga's Terminal Station on Market Street, now a hotel, was a stop for the *Chattanooga Choo Choo*, the first train to provide passenger service between the north and the south. [**17**] Chattanooga's status as a rail center made the City strategically important to both sides during the Civil War. [**18**] As the junction point for railroads to Atlanta, Memphis, Nashville, and Knoxville, Chattanooga provided a vital link for the movement of confederate troops and equipment. [**19**] In fact, the struggle for control of the railroads in the fall of 1863 led to a series of battles that took place in and around the city and that may have determined the outcome of the war. [**20**] It was general William Tecumseh Sherman's victory in the last of those confrontations, the Battle of Missionary Ridge on November 24–25, that cleared the way for his devastating march through Georgia to the Sea.

9. C [12a, d(1,2)]
10. [12d(2)]

11. [12d(2)]
12. [12d(2)]
13. [12d(2,1)]
14. [12a]
15. [12d(4)]
16. [12d(2)]
17. [12d(2)]
18. [12d(3)]
19. C [12a, d(4,2)]
20. [12f(1), d(2)]

Entry-Level Assessment

Diagnostic Preview. If students are having problems with capitalization in their writing, the **Diagnostic Preview** can help you to identify particular areas in which students need instruction and practice. The preview assesses understanding of all the rules of capitalization presented in this chapter. You can assess students' responses to determine which rules students need to review.

PRETEACHING

Lesson Starter

Motivating. Students might enjoy participating in a capitalization bee. Following the rules of a spelling bee, divide the class into two teams and present words and phrases to each team alternately. Have a student from either team tell which of the given words should be capitalized and why. Give each team a point for a correct response and no points for an incorrect response. Continue the game until one team has scored thirty points.

MECHANICS

Differentiating Instruction

■ *Developmental Language & Sentence Skills,* pp. 113–126

■ *Developmental Language & Sentence Skills Guided Practice Teacher's Notes and Answer Key,* pp. 29–32

Assessment

■ *Holt Handbook Chapter Tests with Answer Key,* pp. 23–24, 54

Using Capital Letters Correctly

In your reading, you may notice variations in the use of capital letters. Most writers, however, follow the rules presented in this chapter. In your own writing, following these rules will help you communicate clearly with the widest possible audience.

12a. Capitalize the first word of every sentence.

EXAMPLES **R**eading the article, I learned about the Blessingway and other traditional Navajo ceremonies.

What is the formula for converting degrees Celsius to degrees Fahrenheit?

(1) Capitalize the first word of a sentence following a colon.

EXAMPLE We have one important recommendation: **I**n light of the statistics, four-way stop signs should be installed.

(2) Capitalize the first word of a resolution following the word *Resolved.*

EXAMPLE Resolved: **T**hat government support of the arts be increased.

(3) Capitalize the first word of a quoted sentence.

The first word of a quoted sentence should begin with a capital letter, whether or not the quotation comes at the beginning of your sentence.

EXAMPLE In one of his essays, Sir Francis Bacon wrote, "**S**ome books are to be tasted, others to be swallowed, and some few to be chewed and digested."

When quoting only part of a sentence, capitalize the first word of the quotation if the person you are quoting capitalized it or it is the first word of your sentence.

EXAMPLES To which books do you think Bacon was referring when he wrote "**s**ome few [are] to be chewed and digested"?

"**S**ome few to be chewed and digested" refers to books that should be read carefully and studied.

NOTE Capitalize the first word of a sentence fragment used in dialogue.

EXAMPLE When I asked Julia how many of Sir Francis Bacon's essays she had read, she replied, "**F**our of them."

┌HELP

Do not capitalize the first word of a list following a colon unless it would be capitalized otherwise.

EXAMPLES
Bring the following items to practice every day: **r**acquet, court shoes, towels.

In this unit, we will be reading the following poets: **M**arlowe, Raleigh, and the metaphysical poets.

Reference Note

For more about **capitalizing** and **punctuating direct quotations,** see page 365.

First Words, Pronoun *I,* Interjection *O,* Proper Nouns, and Proper Adjectives
Rules 12a–d *(pp. 296–307)*

O B J E C T I V E S

- To identify standard uses of capitalization
- To use standard capitalization rules to correctly capitalize words

DIFFERENTIATING INSTRUCTION

Learners Having Difficulty
To prevent students from being overwhelmed by capitalization rules, you may want to teach only the rules pertaining to situations that occur frequently in everyday writing.

MECHANICS

RESOURCES

First Words, Pronoun *I,* Interjection *O,* Proper Nouns, and Proper Adjectives

Practice
- *Language & Sentence Skills Practice,* pp. 255–263

Differentiating Instruction
- *Developmental Language & Sentence Skills,* pp. 113–124

Traditionally, the first word in each line of a poem is capitalized.

EXAMPLE   **H**e clasps the crag with crooked hands;
                Close to the sun in lonely lands,
                Ringed with the azure world, he stands.

                The wrinkled sea beneath him crawls;
                He watches from his mountain walls,
                And like a thunderbolt he falls.
                         Alfred, Lord Tennyson, "The Eagle"

For reasons of style, however, some writers do not follow this rule.

EXAMPLE   **T**he art of losing isn't hard to master;
                so many things seem filled with the intent
                to be lost that their loss is no disaster.
                       Elizabeth Bishop, "One Art"

When quoting from another writer's work, always use capital letters as the writer does.

(4) Capitalize the first word of a statement or question inserted without quotation marks into a sentence.

EXAMPLE   My question is, **W**ill this action solve the problem?

12b. Capitalize the pronoun *I* and the interjection *O*.

The interjection *O* is usually used only for invocations and is followed by the name of the person or thing being addressed. Do not confuse *O* with the common interjection *oh*, which is generally not capitalized and which is usually set off with punctuation.

EXAMPLES   Where could **I** have put my book report?

             Rejoice in the Lord, **O** ye righteous!

             He was driving, **oh,** about thirty-five miles an hour.

12c. Capitalize the first word in both the salutation and the closing of a letter.

EXAMPLES   **D**ear Ms. Wong: **S**incerely yours,

             My dear Caroline,   **B**est regards,

             Dear Principal Cuneo:

Reference Note

For more about **punctuating salutations and closings,** see pages 348 and 360.

EXTENSION

Relating to Literature

You may want to direct students to poems that use conventional capitalization and poems that do not. You can find many suitable examples in literature anthologies. For instance, poets sometimes capitalize words in the middle of sentences and lines to emphasize the words or to elevate their meanings by using them as proper nouns or proper adjectives. Students might want to read "When I Have Fears" by John Keats or "Ode to the West Wind" by Percy Bysshe Shelley for examples of internal capitalization. Discuss with students how this style of capitalization affects their appreciation of the poetry.

MECHANICS

Using Capital Letters Correctly   **297**

RETEACHING

Proper Nouns and Proper Adjectives

Activity. Have students practice capitalizing proper nouns and proper adjectives by playing a game. Assign each student a letter of the alphabet, and have students write on their papers both a proper noun and a proper adjective that begin with the letter. For example, for the letter *C* students can write *Carolina* and *Chinese*. Ask students to show their correctly capitalized answers and continue playing until every student has shared a proper noun and proper adjective.

Reference Note

For more about **common and proper nouns,** see page 4.

─HELP─

If you are not sure whether to capitalize a word, look it up in an up-to-date dictionary.

12d. Capitalize proper nouns and proper adjectives.

A *common noun* names any one of a group of persons, places, things, or ideas. A *proper noun* names a particular person, place, thing, or idea. A *proper adjective* is formed from a proper noun.

Common nouns are capitalized only if they begin a sentence (also, in most cases, a line of poetry), begin a direct quotation, or are part of a title.

Common Nouns	Proper Nouns	Proper Adjectives
a king	**K**ing **A**rthur	**A**rthurian legend
a country	**T**hailand	**T**hai restaurant
a city	**M**oscow	**M**uscovite voters
a people	**A**lgonquians	**A**lgonquian customs
a religion	**B**uddhism	**B**uddhist shrine

In proper nouns made up of two or more words, do not capitalize

- articles (*a, an, the*)
- short prepositions (those with fewer than five letters, such as *at, of, for, with*)
- coordinating conjunctions (*and, but, for, nor, or, so, yet*)

EXAMPLES International Union **f**or **t**he Conservation **o**f Nature **a**nd Natural Resources

Gulf **o**f Oman

Alfred **t**he Great

NOTE Some proper nouns and proper adjectives have lost their capital letters after long usage.

EXAMPLES a **c**ardigan (sweater)   **c**hina (dishes)

morocco leather   **w**atts

Others may be written with or without capital letters.

EXAMPLES **R**oman (**r**oman) numerals   **V**enetian (**v**enetian) blinds

plaster of **P**aris (**p**aris)   **G**othic (**g**othic) style

(1) Capitalize the names of persons and animals. Capitalize initials in names and abbreviations that either precede or follow names.

Persons	Marco Martínez	Dr. Lee Tseng
	St. Francis of Assisi	C. S. Lewis
	Christina Youngblood	Jamaal Johnson, Jr.
Animals	Babe	Polly
	Wishbone	Morris the Cat
	Trigger	Mr. Ed

NOTE Some names may contain more than one capital letter. If you are not sure about the spelling of a name, check with the person or consult a reference source.

EXAMPLES

De La Tour	Von Ryan	Morning Star
de la Tour	von Ryan	Morningstar
La Fontaine	Dupont	MacKenzie
Lafontaine	du Pont	Mackenzie

(2) Capitalize geographical names.

Type of Name	Examples	
Towns and Cities	Campbellsville	Pigeon Forge
	Stratford-on-Avon	San Juan
Counties, Townships, and Parishes	Maricopa County	Orleans Parish
	Concord Township	Lawrence Township
States and Provinces	Alaska	South Carolina
	Manitoba	District of Columbia
Regions	the South	Western Hemisphere
	Great Plains	the Pacific Rim

NOTE Words such as *north*, *eastern*, and *southwestern* are not capitalized when they indicate direction.

EXAMPLE flying **s**outh for the winter

Reference Note

For more information about **capitalizing abbreviations such as** *Dr.* and *Jr.,* see page 330.

COMPUTER TIP

The range of correct spellings of personal names can challenge even the best computer spellchecker. One way to avoid this problem is to customize your spell-checker. If your software allows, add to it any frequently used names that you have difficulty spelling or capitalizing correctly.

Reference Note

The abbreviations of the names of states are capitalized. For more about **using and punctuating state abbreviations,** see page 331.

DIFFERENTIATING INSTRUCTION

Advanced Learners

If you feel that students have a good understanding of the basic rules of capitalization, you may want to have them review the rules on their own so that you can devote class time to discussing the **Notes** under some of the textbook rules.

MECHANICS

EXTENSION

Relating to Writing

Ask students, working individually or in groups of three or four, to write a brief travel article for a specific local geographical region; each article should include information about a town or city or about a geographical feature such as a lake, river, mountain range, or cave. The article could mention specific historical sites or recreational and entertainment facilities. You could also have students provide directions to each attraction. Remind students to capitalize geographical names correctly. Ask each student or group to submit an illustration to accompany the article.

Reference Note

In addresses, abbreviations such as *St., Blvd., Ave., Dr., Ct.,* and *Ln.* are capitalized. For more information about **abbreviations,** see page 329.

┌─ TIPS & TRICKS ─┐

Avoid including the type of geographical name, such as *mountain, desert,* or *river,* as part of the proper noun if the proper noun already indicates the type of name.

EXAMPLES
Fujiyama or **Mount Fuji** [not *Mount Fujiyama,* because *yama* is Japanese for "mountain"]

Sahara [not *Sahara Desert,* because *sahara* is Arabic for "desert"]

Rio Grande [not *Rio Grande River,* because *rio* is Spanish for "river"]

┌─HELP─┐

If you are not sure about the spelling or capitalization of a geographical name, check in a dictionary or an encyclopedia.

Type of Name	Examples	
Countries	**Z**imbabwe	**S**audi **A**rabia
Continents	**A**ntarctica	**N**orth **A**merica
Islands	**I**sle of **W**ight	**S**olomon **I**slands
Mountains	**M**ount **S**t. **H**elens	**S**ierra **M**adre
	Pobeda **P**eak	**S**ugarloaf **M**ountain
Bodies of Water	**A**rctic **O**cean	**A**mazon **R**iver
	Lake **H**uron	**P**ersian **G**ulf
	Dead **S**ea	**G**uanabara **B**ay
Parks and Forests	**L**ake **C**lark **N**ational **P**ark	**O**uachita **N**ational **F**orest
Roads, Streets, and Highways	**R**oute 66	**R**aintree **R**oad
	Interstate 10	**B**luegrass **P**arkway
	Quail **B**riar **D**rive	**F**ifth **A**venue
	East **T**hird **S**treet	**G**ulf-to-**B**ay **B**oulevard
Other Geographical Names	**P**ainted **D**esert	**K**eweenaw **P**eninsula
	Palo **D**uro **C**anyon	**D**ismal **S**wamp
	Longhorn **C**averns	**S**hip **R**ock

NOTE The second word in a hyphenated street number begins with a lowercase letter.

EXAMPLE   Twenty-**s**econd Street

A word such as *city, lake, park,* or *street* is capitalized only when it is part of a proper noun.

Common Nouns	Proper Nouns
in the **c**ity	in **S**ioux **C**ity
near the **l**ake	near **L**ake **O**keechobee
through the **p**ark	through **M**esa **V**erde **N**ational **P**ark
on the next **s**treet	on **D**unbar **S**treet

Exercise 1   Identifying Correct Uses of Capitalization

For each of the following pairs of items, select the (letter) of the item that is correctly capitalized.

EXAMPLES

   1. a. the gulf of Mexico
     b. the Gulf of Mexico

   1. b

   2. a. Yours truly,
     b. yours truly,

   2. a

1. **a.** the Nile river
  b. the Nile River
2. **a.** She said, "Tell me, too."
  b. She said, "tell me, too."
3. **a.** Bering strait
  b. Bering Strait
4. **a.** Fifty-Second Street
  b. Fifty-second Street
5. **a.** a German movie
  b. a german movie
6. **a.** Charles Adams, Jr.
  b. Charles Adams, jr.
7. **a.** New Jersey Turnpike
  b. New Jersey turnpike
8. **a.** cedar rapids, Iowa
  b. Cedar Rapids, Iowa
9. **a.** a United States Citizen
  b. a United States citizen
10. **a.** Los Angeles
     County highways
  b. Los Angeles
     County Highways
11. **a.** east of the river
  b. East of the river
12. **a.** the Iberian peninsula
  b. the Iberian Peninsula
13. **a.** people of the Far East
  b. people of the far east
14. **a.** a cat named Banjo
  b. a cat named banjo

15. **a.** an Irish setter
  b. an Irish Setter
16. **a.** Billy The Kid
  b. Billy the Kid
17. **a.** We heard him say he was
     "pleased to be here."
  b. We heard him say he was
     "Pleased to be here."
18. **a.** dear Mr. Faust:
  b. Dear Mr. Faust:
19. **a.** Give me, oh, ten or so.
  b. Give me, Oh, ten or so.
20. **a.** the grand Canyon
  b. the Grand Canyon
21. **a.** Follow me!
  b. follow me!
22. **a.** The problem is, How do we
     fund the project?
  b. The problem is, how do we
     fund the project?
23. **a.** Jake and i planted several
     trees.
  b. Jake and I planted several
     trees.
24. **a.** a Shakespearean actor
  b. a shakespearean actor
25. **a.** Resolved: That educational
     funding should be increased.
  b. Resolved: that educational
     funding should be increased.

DIFFERENTIATING INSTRUCTION

Learners Having Difficulty

To help students learn capitalization rules, assign two rules to each student. Then, ask students to find examples of the rules in magazines and newspapers and to use the examples to assemble a bulletin board display of capitalization rules.

While searching for illustrations of the capitalization rules, students might find examples that contradict the rules they have learned. Explain that newspapers and magazines sometimes use styles of their own, which may differ from standard use.

MECHANICS

EXTENSION

Critical Thinking

Metacognition. After students have completed the **Oral Practice,** ask them to use the following questions to analyze the process they used to determine the correct capitalization for each item.

- Do you check a word at a time or do you look for connections between the words?

- Do you refer to the rules if you have any doubt about an answer?

- Do you recheck each item to make sure you have not overlooked a correction?

Students can discuss their answers to the questions to determine how they can improve the process they use.

Oral Practice | **Capitalizing Words and Names Correctly**

Read aloud each of the following items, saying where capital letters are needed.

EXAMPLE **1.** horseshoe mountain

1. Horseshoe Mountain

1. cook county
2. an african village on the atlantic
3. four miles south of route 10
4. ranching in the south
5. forty-ninth street
6. olympic national park
7. a city like new orleans, louisiana
8. along the mississippi river
9. coffee from colombia
10. st. paul, minnesota
11. new zealand
12. boats on the coral sea
13. lake Placid
14. Hear us, o mighty ruler!
15. Carson city
16. a pacific island
17. Here's a clue: the answer is round.
18. the great lakes
19. a cottage on the isle of man
20. Angel falls, Venezuela

(3) Capitalize the names of organizations, teams, institutions, and government bodies.

Type of Name	Examples	
Organizations	National Collegiate Athletic Association	
	League of Women Voters	
	Humane Society of Austin	
	National Forensic League	
Teams	Detroit Red Wings	San Antonio Spurs
	Seattle Seahawks	Oak Ridge Rangers
Institutions	Beverly Hills High School	
	Catawba Valley Technical College	
	Smithsonian Institution	
	Massachusetts General Hospital	
Government Bodies	House of Representatives	
	Federal Aviation Administration	
	Department of Commerce	
	Peace Corps	

NOTE The names of some organizations and government bodies are often abbreviated as a series of capital letters.

EXAMPLES   **N**ational **O**rganization for **W**omen   **NOW**

Federal **C**ommunications **C**ommission   **FCC**

Generally, the letters in such abbreviations are not followed by periods. If you are not sure whether an abbreviation requires periods, look it up in an up-to-date dictionary or other reliable source.

Do not capitalize a word such as *association, school, hospital,* or *department* unless it is part of a proper noun.

Common Nouns	Proper Nouns
a member of the **a**ssociation	**A**merican **M**edical **A**ssociation
a nearby **h**igh **s**chool	**W**ebster **H**igh **S**chool
at the **h**ospital	**G**ates **M**emorial **H**ospital
working in the **d**epartment	**D**epartment of **T**ransportation

"After working all day on my MBA, I hop into my BMW and race home to watch PBS on my VCR—OK?"

© 1990; reprinted courtesy of Bunny Hoest and Parade magazine.

Reference Note
For more about **punctuating abbreviations,** see page 329.

MEETING THE CHALLENGE

Acronyms are formed from the first letters of words in an organization's or place's name. Some acronyms are initalisms—letter combinations that cannot be pronounced as words, as in *BJH* (Bedford Junior High). Other acronyms, however, spell out catchy "words," like *SADD* (Students Against Drunk Driving). Experiment with making your own acronyms for groups at your school—perhaps your marching band is actually an EMU (Excellent Marching Unit). When your list includes ten to twenty acronyms, share them with your classmates.

ANSWER
Acronyms will vary.

MECHANICS

English-Language Learners

General Strategies. In some languages such as French, Spanish, and Vietnamese, days of the week, months, and nationalities used as proper adjectives begin with lowercase letters, as in "On the first monday in april, we're going to watch a french film." Acknowledge the fact that students are being asked to reverse rules they have already mastered in their native languages. You could involve students in the lesson by giving them the opportunity to be the experts. Ask them to teach you and the class the words in their first languages for the days of the week.

| STYLE | TIP |

The word *party* in the name of a political party may or may not be capitalized; either way is correct. However, you should be consistent within pieces of writing.

| STYLE | TIP |

The words *black* and *white* may or may not be capitalized when they refer to races; either way is correct. However, you should be consistent within pieces of writing.

NOTE Do not capitalize words such as *democratic, republican,* and *socialist* when they refer to principles or forms of government. Capitalize such words only when they refer to the political parties.

EXAMPLES   a **d**emocratic policy   the **D**emocratic **P**arty (*or* **p**arty)

(4) Capitalize the names of historical events and periods, special events, and holidays and other calendar items.

Type of Name	Examples	
Historical Events and Periods	**V**ietnam **W**ar **R**enaissance	**A**merican **R**evolution **B**ronze **A**ge
Special Events	**S**uper **B**owl **S**pecial **O**lympics	the **B**oston **M**arathon **C**onference on **W**orld **H**unger
Holidays and Other Calendar Items	**L**abor **D**ay **M**onday **D**ecember	**P**residents' **D**ay **F**ourth of **J**uly **H**ispanic **H**eritage **M**onth

NOTE Do not capitalize the name of a season unless the season is being personified or is being used as part of a proper noun.

EXAMPLES   an early **w**inter

"O wild West Wind, thou breath of **A**utumn's being, . . ."
Percy Bysshe Shelley, "Ode to the West Wind"

the **S**uncoast **S**ummer **F**estival

(5) Capitalize the names of nationalities, races, and peoples.

EXAMPLES
Asian	**H**ispanic	**O**jibwa
Zulu	**N**orse	**A**frican **A**merican
Caucasian	**A**ztec	**S**wedish

(6) Capitalize the names of religions and their followers, holy days and celebrations, holy writings, and specific deities.

Type of Name	Examples	
Religions and Followers	**C**hristianity	**C**onfucian
	Judaism	**M**ethodist
	Hinduism	**T**aoist
Holy Days and Celebrations	**C**hristmas	**R**amadan
	Purim	**R**osh **H**ashana
Holy Writings	**T**orah	**N**ew **T**estament
	Veda	**T**ao **T**e **C**hing
Specific Deities	**A**llah	**Y**ahweh
	God	**B**rahma

The words *god* and *goddess* are not capitalized when they refer to deities of ancient mythology. However, the names of specific mythological gods and goddesses are capitalized.

EXAMPLE　　Cassandra could foretell the future but was condemned by the **g**od **A**pollo never to be believed.

NOTE　Some writers always capitalize pronouns that refer to a deity. Other writers capitalize such pronouns only if necessary to prevent confusion.

EXAMPLE　　The priest asked God to bring peace to **H**is people. [The capitalization of *His* shows that the pronoun refers to God, not the priest.]

(7) Capitalize the names of businesses and the brand names of business products.

Type of Name	Examples
Businesses	**P**rocter & **G**amble **C**ompany®
	International **B**usiness **M**achines®
	Southwest **A**irlines®
	Uptown **D**iscount **S**hoe **S**tore
Business Products	**P**olaroid® camera
	Xerox® copier
	Nintendo® video game
	Jif® peanut butter

DIFFERENTIATING INSTRUCTION

Advanced Learners

Some brand names have been used so often that they have come to stand for the products themselves and have become common nouns. You may want to read the following clues to your class and ask students to identify the nouns.

1. a moving stairway [*escalator*]

2. a synthetic material [*nylon*]

3. a bran cereal with raisins [*raisin bran*]

4. a device used to fasten two edges of material together [*zipper*]

5. a commonly used pain-relieving medicine [*aspirin*]

Have students generate a list of brand names that are used to stand for the products or processes themselves, such as the names for tissues and copying machines. Ask the class to name other brand names that they think will eventually become or be used as if they were common nouns.

DIFFERENTIATING INSTRUCTION

Learners Having Difficulty
Have students use a graphic organizer to distinguish between common nouns and proper nouns. In a circle labeled "buildings," for example, students can list the proper names of specific buildings. Lead students to recognize that capitalization sets apart a specific proper noun within a general category of common nouns. Then, ask students to label other circles with categories and to fill in the circles with proper nouns.

TECHNOLOGY TIP
Spellchecking programs may catch some errors in capitalization. Though a program might draw a writer's attention to an uncapitalized *africa,* it might let *empire state building* pass. Students should not expect such programs to catch all their errors, and they should proofread their writing carefully.

Notice that a common noun that follows a brand name is not capitalized, but the name of a trademarked product is capitalized.

EXAMPLES   Nintendo **v**ideo **g**ame   Nintendo **G**ameboy

(8) Capitalize the names of ships, trains, aircraft, spacecraft, and other vehicles.

Type of Name	Examples	
Ships	*Merrimac*	*Cunard Princess*
Trains	*Orient Express*	*North Coast Limited*
Aircraft	*Spirit of St. Louis*	*Air Force One*
Spacecraft	*Atlantis*	*Saturn 5*

Reference Note
For more about the **use of italics,** see page 362.

NOTE   Notice above that the names of individual ships, trains, aircraft, and spacecraft are not only capitalized but also italicized. The names of the make and the model of a vehicle, though, are capitalized but not italicized.

EXAMPLES   **H**onda **A**ccord   **F**ord **E**xplorer

(9) Capitalize the names of buildings and other structures.

EXAMPLES   **S**hubert **T**heatre   **G**olden **G**ate **B**ridge

Plaza **H**otel   **L**eaning **T**ower of **P**isa

Hoover **D**am   **H**adrian's **W**all

(10) Capitalize the names of monuments, memorials, and awards.

Type of Name	Examples	
Monuments	**M**ontezuma **C**astle	**S**tatue of **L**iberty
Memorials	**L**incoln **M**emorial	**C**ivil **R**ights **M**emorial
Awards	**A**cademy **A**ward	**P**ulitzer **P**rize

Reference Note
For more about **common nouns and proper nouns,** see page 4.

NOTE   Do not capitalize a word such as *building, monument,* or *award* unless it is part of a proper noun.

(11) Capitalize the names of planets, stars, constellations, and other heavenly bodies.

Type of Name	Examples	
Planets	**N**eptune	**M**ercury
Stars	**S**irius	the **N**orth **S**tar
Constellations	**C**assiopeia	**C**anis **M**ajor

NOTE Generally, the words *sun* and *moon* are not capitalized. The word *earth* is not capitalized unless it is used along with the name of another heavenly body that is capitalized.

EXAMPLES   gazing at the **s**un, **m**oon, and stars

below the surface of the **e**arth

the distance between **V**enus and **E**arth

12e. Do not capitalize the names of school subjects, except course names that include a number and the names of language classes.

EXAMPLES   **a**rt   **a**lgebra   **c**hemistry

              Art 102   **A**lgebra I   **C**hemistry II

              English   **S**panish   **G**erman

NOTE Generally, a singular noun identified by a number or letter is capitalized.

EXAMPLES   **R**oom 31   **F**igure B   **S**chool **D**istrict 18   **C**hapter 4

However, the word *page* is usually not capitalized when followed by a number or letter, nor is a plural noun followed by two or more numbers or letters capitalized.

EXAMPLE   Look at **f**igures A and B on **p**age 327.

Do not capitalize the class name *senior, junior, sophomore,* or *freshman* unless it is part of a proper noun.

EXAMPLES   The **j**uniors and the **s**eniors will hold their talent show on May 4.

The **J**unior-**S**enior Revue will be held on May 4.

Languages, School Subjects, and Titles
Rules 12e, f *(pp. 307–315)*

OBJECTIVE

■ **To use standard capitalization rules to correctly capitalize words**

APPLICATION

Capitalization

Activity. You may want to obtain copies of different kinds of application forms such as those for jobs, schools, and driver's licenses. Ask students to fill out the forms and then to exchange forms to check for correct use of capital letters. Point out that correct capitalization will often be important to the people evaluating these types of applications.

MECHANICS

Special Education Students

When you give examples of titles to capitalize, use actual names and titles that are familiar to students. You may want to brainstorm with your class and to list suggestions on the chalkboard.

Learners Having Difficulty

Ask students if they would introduce one person to another with a common noun or a proper noun. Would they say "This is a doctor," or "This is Doctor Rodriguez"? Point out to students that they should use proper names and titles when introducing a person by name. Both the title and name of the person are capitalized.

Exercise 2 Capitalizing Words Correctly

Write the following items, using capital letters correctly. If an item is already correct, write *C*.

EXAMPLE　　**1.** earth science I

　　　　　　1. *Earth Science I*

1. itawamba junior college
2. a hotel across town **2.** C
3. central high school
4. the world series
5. medal of freedom
6. a ford ranger
7. winter blizzard **7.** C
8. the barclay hotel
9. trigonometry **9.** C
10. physics I
11. labor day
12. history class **12.** C
13. ibm computer
14. senior career day
15. bureau of the census
16. *zephyr* (train)
17. the crusades
18. She is a junior. **18.** C
19. newport athletic club
20. the rings of saturn
21. a methodist minister
22. one saturday in October
23. Chinese families **23.** C
24. the industrial revolution
25. a trophy for the Johnson High School wildcats

Review A Proofreading a Paragraph for Correct Capitalization

Proofread the following paragraph. Write each word that is incorrectly capitalized, changing capital letters to lowercase letters and lowercase letters to capital letters where necessary. If a sentence is already correct, write *C*.

EXAMPLE　　**[1]** Only well-educated, highly skilled candidates are chosen as mission specialists with Today's National Aeronautics and Space administration (NASA).

　　　　　　1. *today's, Administration*

[1] A physician who speaks four languages and is trained in modern dance, dr. Mae Jemison (right) is one of NASA's most sought-after speakers. [2] Jemison, the first African american female astronaut, grew up in Chicago and won a scholarship to Stanford university in California. [3] At Stanford she turned her attention to chemical engineering and African and african American studies. [4] Later, while earning her Medical degree at Cornell University in Ithaca, new York, she worked at a refugee camp in Thailand. [5] After obtaining her degree, she served in the Peace corps in the African nations of Sierra

leone and Liberia. **[6]** Jemison joined NASA in 1987 while working as a general practitioner and attending graduate Engineering classes in Los angeles. **[7]** With her first spaceflight on *Endeavor* in the Fall of 1992, she sought to bring people "A view of the space program they may not [otherwise] get." **[8]** As the United States gets closer to completing a space station and sending crews to the Moon and to Mars, the number of mission specialists is expected to increase dramatically. **[9]** As a result, more opportunities will be available to all candidates who excel in research, science, and engineering. **[10]** "everyone has skills and talents," 9. C Jemison emphasizes, "and no one has a lock on scientific ability or physical ability."

12f. Capitalize titles.

(1) Capitalize a person's title when the title comes before the person's name.

EXAMPLES   **C**aptain Valdés   **J**ustice O'Connor

               Senator Inouye   **P**resident White Feather

Generally, do not capitalize a title used alone or following a person's name.

EXAMPLES   the **c**aptain of the ship

               every **j**ustice of the U.S. Supreme Court

               Daniel Inouye, a **s**enator from Hawaii

               Uta White Feather, the class **p**resident

For clarity or special emphasis, however, you may capitalize a title used alone or following a person's name. In addition, a few titles are always capitalized. If you are unsure of whether to capitalize a title, look it up in a current dictionary.

EXAMPLES   Both the **P**resident and the **V**ice **P**resident met with the **P**rime **M**inister of Israel.

               The **S**urgeon **G**eneral addressed the assembly.

Relating to Writing

To practice Rules **12d(2)** and **12f**, students might try writing folk tales that include the following words: south, North, sister, king, King, Grandmother.

DIRECT TEACHING

Modeling and Demonstration

Titles. Model how to correct capitalization errors by using the example *Have you read the poem "ode on a grecian urn" by John Keats?* First, ask if the poem's title should be capitalized. [*yes;* "Ode on a Grecian Urn"] Point out that an article (*a, an,* or *the*) is only capitalized in a title when it is the first word. Now, have a volunteer use another example from this chapter to demonstrate how to correct capitalization errors.

MECHANICS

Reference Note

For more about **articles,** see page 12. For more about **prepositions,** see page 23. For more about **coordinating conjunctions,** see page 25.

DIFFERENTIATING INSTRUCTION

English-Language Learners

Spanish. In Spanish, only the first letter of the first word of the title of a book, article, or movie is capitalized, as in the title of the Mexican novel *Los de abajo* (*The Underdogs,* literally "the ones from below") by Mariano Azuela. When Spanish-speaking students are writing in English, they might have difficulty determining which words in titles to capitalize. Help students by showing them a variety of titles so that the students get a sense of which words in titles are capitalized in English.

Generally, capitalize a title when using it alone in direct address.

EXAMPLES   Goodbye, **P**rofessor.

                Thank you, **S**ir [or **s**ir].

NOTE Do not capitalize prefixes such as *ex–,* suffixes such as *–elect,* or the words *former* or *late* when using them with titles.

EXAMPLES   the governor-**e**lect

                ex-President Carter

                former Prime Minister Thatcher

                the **l**ate Senator Humphrey

(2) Capitalize a word showing a family relationship when the word is used before or in place of a person's name, unless the word is preceded by a possessive.

EXAMPLES   **U**ncle Juan   **C**ousin Denisa   **G**randpa

                my **a**unt Eunice   Jay's **c**ousin Ramón   your **m**other

(3) Capitalize the first and last words and all important words in titles and subtitles.

Unimportant words in a title include

- articles (*a, an, the*)
- short prepositions (those with fewer than five letters, such as *in, of, to, for, from, with*)
- coordinating conjunctions (*and, but, for, nor, or, so, yet*)

Type of Title	Examples
Books	*A **P**ortrait of the **A**rtist as a **Y**oung **M**an* *M**odern **P**oetry: **A**merican and **B**ritish*
Chapters and Other Parts of Books	"**T**he 1920s: **A** **T**urbulent **D**ecade" "**G**lossary of **U**sage"
Periodicals	*The **S**an **D**iego **T**ribune* *P**eople **W**eekly*

MINI-LESSON Mechanics

Punctuating Titles. Students may be confused about when to use italics (underlining) with titles and when to use quotation marks. Be sure that students understand that they should use italics (underlining) for titles of books, periodicals, films, television programs, and works of art and that they should use quotation marks to enclose the

Type of Title	Examples
Poems	"**O**de on a **G**recian **U**rn" *I **A**m **J**oaquín*
Short Stories	"**T**he **O**ld **M**an at the **B**ridge" "**T**he **T**rain from **R**hodesia"
Plays	*The **M**erchant of **V**enice* *A **L**and **B**eyond the **R**iver*
Historical Documents	**D**eclaration of **I**ndependence **M**agna **C**arta
Movies	*It's a **W**onderful **L**ife* *Air **B**ud: **G**olden **R**eceiver*
Radio and TV Series	*Billboard's **T**op 40 **C**ountdown* *The **T**onight **S**how*
Videos and Video Games	*Leonard **B**ernstein: **R**eaching for the **N**ote* *Asteroids*
Computer Programs and Games	*Infopedia 2.0* *Tom **C**lancy's **R**ainbow **S**ix*
Comic Strips	*Hi and **L**ois* *Dennis the **M**enace*
Works of Art	*Nike of **S**amothrace* [sculpture] *I and the **V**illage* [painting]
Musical Compositions	*Ragtime **D**ance* "**T**he **S**ky **I**s **C**rying"
Audiotapes and CDs	*Gershwin's **S**ongbook* *These **A**re **S**pecial **T**imes*

> **NOTE** Capitalize an article (*a, an,* or *the*) in a title or subtitle only if the article is the first word of the official title or subtitle. The official title can usually be found in the table of contents or in the masthead, the section of a periodical that lists the publisher, the editor, the owner, and other information.
>
> EXAMPLES **t**he *Science Digest*   *The Spectator*   *A Farewell to Arms*

titles of short works such as articles, short stories, poems, and songs. For more information on punctuating titles, refer students to **Chapter 14: Punctuation.**

RETEACHING

Proper Nouns

Mnemonics. Point out to students that the words not capitalized in proper nouns can be remembered by using the acronym *CAP4* for *coordinating conjunctions, articles,* and *prepositions with four or fewer letters.*

DIRECT TEACHING

Correcting Misconceptions

Capitalizing Titles. Students may believe that all very short words in titles, except for the first word and any nouns, should not be capitalized. One reason for confusion may be that an article capitalized at the beginning of a title is not capitalized in the middle of the title: *The Old Man and the Sea,* for example. Another problem is that a short word such as *is* is capitalized in the middle of a title but the longer *with* is not capitalized.

Have students generate a list of titles of popular books, movies, and television shows. Write each title on the chalkboard, and ask students if each word should be capitalized. If the answer for any word is *no,* students should be able to identify the word as a coordinating conjunction, an article, or a preposition with fewer than five letters. Challenge the class to think of at least two titles containing each type of word and to identify each word that is not capitalized. Students can record their examples in a chart such as the one shown below.

CONJUNCTIONS	ARTICLES	PREPOSITIONS

MECHANICS

APPLICATION

Capitalizing Titles

Activity. Have students practice conducting interviews with at least five people to get answers to the following questions.

1. What is your favorite book?

2. What is your favorite magazine?

3. What is your favorite song?

4. What is your least favorite song?

5. What is your favorite television show?

Remind students to capitalize titles correctly as they record responses.

PRACTICE

Guided and Independent

Review B Since **Review B** provides a review of all the rules presented in the chapter so far, you may want to use the first ten sentences as guided practice and then have students complete the last ten sentences as independent practice.

HOMEWORK

Exercise 3 Capitalizing Titles Correctly

Write each of the following items, using capital and lowercase letters where they are needed. If an item is already correct, write *C*.

EXAMPLE   1. governor Nellie Tayloe Ross
          1. *Governor Nellie Tayloe Ross*

1. captain Ahab
2. *guernica* (painting)
3. a Sergeant in an army
4. the club president **4.** C
5. aunt Betty
6. senator Campbell
7. mayor Fulton of Nashville
8. *down and out in paris and london* (book title)
9. *All In the Family* (television series)
10. Rabbi Klein, a military chaplain **10.** C
11. former president Jimmy Carter
12. the leader of a brass band **12.** C
13. Ms. Solomon, the center director **13.** C
14. mayor-elect Marc Morial
15. the bill of rights
16. your Aunt Shirley
17. the *Los Angeles times*
18. duties of a legislator
19. former Golf Champion Annika Sörenstam
20. "the world is too much with us" (poem)
21. a recipe in *Family Circle* (magazine) **21.** C
22. "All summer in a day" (short story)
23. "The Monsters are Due On Maple Street" (television episode)
24. *The Life and times of Rosie The Riveter* (film)
25. Please come in, doctor.

Review B Capitalizing Words Correctly

For each of the following sentences, correctly write the words that should be capitalized.

EXAMPLE   1. My best friend, alonzo, played the part of petruchio in the senior class's production of shakespeare's comedy *the taming of the shrew.*
          1. *Alonzo, Petruchio, Shakespeare's,* The Taming, Shrew

---

Learning for Life

Continued on pp. 313–315

Writing a Personal Statement. To help students understand the importance of correct capitalization outside the classroom, have them write personal statements as part of applications for jobs or college. Assemble a number of college and job applications that require written statements, and display the forms in the classroom.

Then, brainstorm with students a list of the kinds of information to be included in a personal statement—for example, goals,

1. In their english classes this term, the juniors have read *o pioneers!*, a novel written by willa cather about swedish immigrants in the state of nebraska.
2. A recent report from the secretary of labor includes the following statement: "most of the new jobs in the next decade will be in service fields."
3. According to professor De La Rey, the first poems of Alfred, lord Tennyson's *idylls of the king* were published in 1859, the same year as the publication of Charles Darwin's *the origin of species*, George Eliot's *adam bede*, and Charles Dickens's *a tale of two cities*.
4. In "canto I" the poet Ezra Pound describes an ominous sea voyage to one of the same mythical lands visited by the hero Odysseus in the *Odyssey*, an epic by the greek poet Homer.
5. Speaking to a reporter from the *County Clarion*, coach Sheila Smith explained the debate team's latest resolution, which read, in part, "Resolved: that we will win all of our debates next year."
6. In ancient egypt the people worshiped many gods equally until the sun god Ra became the principal deity.
7. Dr. Bruce Jackson, jr., the principal of the high school, formerly taught mathematics I classes and an introductory class in computer science offered to sophomores and juniors.
8. From the St. Croix island national monument in Maine to the Huleia wildlife refuge in Hawaii, public lands managed by the federal government, including the military, equal a large percentage of the nation's total acreage.
9. Suzanne o'Rourke, the president of the jogging club, has an exercise route that takes her three times a week through Myers park, down Carriage street, and then back west to Dean avenue.
10. The will of the swedish industrialist and inventor of dynamite, Alfred Nobel, established the Nobel prize to honor those who have done great service for the world in the areas of literature, medicine, physics, chemistry, and peace; a prize in economics was added in 1969.
11. Calvin Peete, the first african american to succeed on the professional golf tour, earned hundreds of thousands of dollars at events like the greater milwaukee open and walked away with awards like the vardon trophy.
12. did corporal Myers receive a radio transmission from squad 5?
13. While cousin Marty and I were at the Capital theater seeing *Mr. Smith goes to Washington* at the Frank Capra festival, we saw Mayor Balard and his wife.

2. [*or* secretary of labor]

Review B

DISTRIBUTED REVIEW
To provide students with a review of verb tense and voice, ask them to identify the main verb in sentences 1 and 3 and to tell the verb's tense and voice.

1. have read—past perfect—active

3. were published—past—passive

MECHANICS

inspiration, role models, and interests. Record ideas on the chalkboard in a graphic organizer such as the following web diagram.

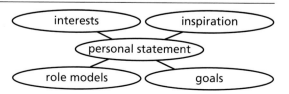

Relating to Writing

Give the class practice in using the rules of capitalization presented in this chapter by having the students write letters to imaginary pen pals in foreign countries. Students should give personal information that they are comfortable sharing. They may want to include what subjects they are studying in school and what their ambitions are for the future. Before students begin the activity, you may wish to review the standard form for writing a personal letter.

14. Although Paula Gunn Allen is sioux, scottish, and lebanese, she grew up around the pueblo indian culture; later, she made a career of her fascination with her native american heritage by writing, among other things, *Studies in american indian Literature.*

15. That their living room was decorated in the victorian style was a little strange considering that a Packard Bell computer was under a lace cover and the ruffled curtains over the front window concealed a view of a military base full of jets and helicopters.

16. Around the world, jewish people observe yom kippur, during which they remember and fast in reparation for their failings.

17. The treaty of Versailles simultaneously put an end to world war I and inaugurated the league of nations.

18. The voting rights act of 1965 ensured the registration of many voters by outlawing literacy tests and other unfair practices.

19. It's a good thing that doctor Daniel Hale Williams III decided not to become a shoemaker as his father had planned; otherwise, open-heart surgery might not have gotten its start in 1893, and the Provident hospital and medical center, where so many African American interns and nurses trained, might not have been built.

20. Commanded by general Dwight D. Eisenhower, the Allies mounted the multifaceted attack known as the normandy invasion.

Review C Proofreading Paragraphs for Correct Capitalization

Proofread the following paragraphs, and change capital letters to lowercase letters and lowercase letters to capital letters as necessary. If a sentence is already correct, write *C*.

EXAMPLE **[1]** An intriguing museum in Western Oklahoma celebrates the diversity and vitality of American Indian Culture.

1. *western, culture*

[1] The Southern Plains Indian Museum on Highway 62, East of Anadarko, Oklahoma, was founded in 1947. [2] Administered by the Indian arts and crafts board, an agency of the U.S. department of the Interior, the museum showcases the creative achievements of the Kiowa, Comanche, Kiowa-Apache, Southern Cheyenne, Southern Arapaho, Wichita, Caddo, Delaware, and Ft. Sill Apache. [3] A display of authentically detailed traditional costumes highlights the Museum's permanent

Learning for Life *Continued from p. 313*

Have students complete their own web diagrams, and then ask them to write personal statements of two pages or less and to include in the statements three titles, one company or university name, two geographical names, and the names of at least three people.

Remind students that the personal statement is an opportunity to present themselves to people who will otherwise know very little about them, an opportunity they should use wisely. Incorrect capitalizacollection. [4] Also on permanent display are four dioramas and a mural by the nationally renowned Artist and sculptor Allen Houser, a Ft. Sill Apache; these exhibits illustrate the traditional social and ceremonial customs of the region's peoples. [5] The museum also offers changing exhibits of contemporary arts and crafts, including painting, beadwork, metalwork, and featherwork.

[6] These displays, as well as frequent one-person shows and demonstrations, are held in cooperation with the Oklahoma Indian Arts and Crafts cooperative, an independent business owned and operated by American indian artists and craftworkers. [7] The Cooperative operates the museum's gift shop and certifies the authenticity of all products sold there. [8] One special attraction during the Summer is a display on the museum grounds of full-scale tepees, like these, painted by contemporary artists. [9] Another attraction is the week-long American Indian Expo held each August at the Caddo county Fairgrounds adjacent to the museum. [10] The largest gathering of native American peoples in the State of Oklahoma, the exposition features dance contests, a pageant, horse races, and parades.

5. C

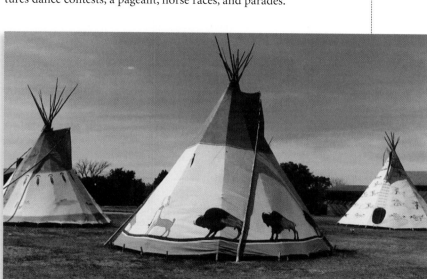

DIFFERENTIATING INSTRUCTION

Learners Having Difficulty

Activity. Some students might benefit from an oral exercise in which they generate proper nouns from common nouns. Begin with a general category, and ask a volunteer to name a proper noun in that category. If you were to say "river," for example, a student might say "Allegheny River." Repeat this exercise until you think students understand the difference between common and proper nouns.

tion will not make a good impression.

Have students exchange statements to check each other's capitalization; then, have students keep their personal statements on file for possible future use.

Abbreviations

An *abbreviation* is a shortened form of a word or phrase.

12g. Generally, abbreviations are capitalized if the words that they stand for are capitalized.

Personal Names

Abbreviate given names only if the person is most commonly known by the abbreviated form of the name. Capitalize initials.

EXAMPLES **W.E.B.** DuBois   **T. S.** Eliot   **D. H.** Lawrence

> **NOTE** Leave a space between two initials, but not between three or more.

Titles

Abbreviate and capitalize social titles whether used before the full name or before the last name alone.

EXAMPLES	**Mr.** Jon Ferguson	**Sra.** (Señora) Santiago
	Sr. (Señor) Aguilar	**Ms.** Cohen
	Mrs. Douglass	**Dr.** Jefferson

You may abbreviate civil and military titles used before full names or before initials and last names. Spell them out before last names alone. Capitalize the title whether or not it is abbreviated.

EXAMPLES	**Sen.** Joseph Biden	**Senator** Biden
	Prof. I. B. Haro	**Professor** Haro
	Gen. George Patton	**General** Patton

Abbreviate and capitalize titles and academic degrees that follow proper names.

EXAMPLES	Cuba Gooding, **Jr.**	Sara Kincaid, **M.D.**
	Lon Chaney, **Sr.**	Rafael Castillo, **D.V.M.**
	Giselle Richard, **D.D.S.**	Kuri Asato, **Ph.D.**

─HELP─
If you are not sure about the capitalization or punctuation of an abbreviation, look it up in a current dictionary.

Reference Note
For information on **forming the plurals of abbreviations,** see page 379.

─STYLE─────TIP─
Only a few abbreviations are appropriate in the text of a formal paper written for a general audience. In tables, notes, and bibliographies, abbreviations are used more freely to save space.

Abbreviations

Rule 12g *(pp. 316–320)*

OBJECTIVE

- To correct errors in sentences in the use of abbreviations and capitalization

MECHANICS

RESOURCES

Abbreviations

Practice

- *Language & Sentence Skills Practice,* pp. 266–268

NOTE Do not include the titles *Mr., Mrs., Ms., Sr., Sra.,* or *Dr.* when you use a title or degree after a name.

EXAMPLE **Dr.** Joanna Wilde *or* Joanna Wilde, **M.D.** [not *Dr. Joanna Wilde, M.D.*]

Agencies and Organizations

An **acronym** is a word formed from the first (or first few) letters of a series of words. Acronyms are usually capitalized and written without periods. After spelling out the first use of the names of agencies, organizations, and other things commonly known by their acronyms, abbreviate these names.

EXAMPLE My cousin applied for a job with the **Internal Revenue Service (IRS).** She said that working for the **IRS** would allow her to use the math skills she has worked so hard to develop.

HUD	Department of Housing and Urban Development
OPEC	Organization of Petroleum Exporting Countries
ACLU	American Civil Liberties Union
PBS	Public Broadcasting Service
MDOT	Michigan Department of Transportation
JAG	judge advocate general
MVP	most valuable player
VCR	videocassette recorder
HMO	health maintenance organization

Geographical Terms

In regular text, spell out names of states and other political units whether they stand alone or follow other geographical terms. Abbreviate them in tables, notes, and bibliographies. Generally, you should use the same capitalization rules for the abbreviations as you use for the full words.

STYLE TIP

Many common abbreviations are capitalized though the spelled-out words are not. If you are not sure whether to capitalize an abbreviation, look it up in a current dictionary.

STYLE TIP

A few acronyms, such as *radar, laser,* and *sonar,* are now considered common nouns. They do not need to be spelled out on first use and are no longer capitalized. When you are not sure whether an acronym should be capitalized, look it up in a current dictionary.

MINI-LESSON Mechanics

Punctuation. Remind students of the following rule: When an abbreviation that ends with a period is the last word in a statement, do not add another period as an end mark. However, do add a question mark or an exclamation point if one is needed. For more on punctuating abbreviations, refer students to **Chapter 13: Punctuation.**

Abbreviations for States

Activity. Remind students that each state in the United States has two abbreviations. One is a traditional abbreviation of the state's name and is always followed by a period. The second is a two-letter postal code and does not require a period. Many students' parents or grandparents will remember a time before ZIP Codes and two-letter abbreviations for states were in use. Have students research when ZIP Codes and two-letter abbreviations for state names were instituted.

Have the class name the two abbreviations for as many states as they can. Have a volunteer record responses. Then, divide the class into five groups, and have each group look up the two abbreviations for ten states. After all groups have finished, they can check to see how accurate their original list was. Finally, have students create a chart of all the abbreviations for the states.

In regular text, you should include the traditional abbreviation for the District of Columbia, *D.C.,* with the city name *Washington* to distinguish it from the state of Washington.

COMPUTER TIP

Publishers usually set time abbreviations as small capital letters—uppercase letters of a smaller font size. If you use a computer, your word-processing software may offer small capitals as a style option. If it does not, or if you are writing by hand, you may use either uppercase or lowercase letters for time abbreviations as long as you are consistent within each piece of writing.

TEXT	Edgar Allan Poe spent his early years in Richmond, Virginia, and Boston, Massachusetts.
	On their tour of the United Kingdom, they visited Belfast, the capital of Northern Ireland.

TABLE	Liverpool, **U.K.**	Santa Fe, **N. Mex.**
	Vancouver, **B.C.**	Columbia, **N.C.**

FOOTNOTE	[3]Clemens's letters, literary manuscripts, and scrapbooks are kept at the Univ. of **Calif.,** Berkeley.

BIBLIOGRAPHY ENTRY	"The Last Honest Man." Editorial. *Ledger-Tribune* [Tucson, **Ariz.**] 29 Mar. 1997:30.

In regular text, spell out every word in an address. Such words are generally abbreviated in letter and envelope addresses and may be abbreviated in tables and notes.

TEXT	They live at 4726 South Oak Street.
	Send the package to Wharton Court, Suite 101, San Diego, California.

ENVELOPE	4726 **S.** Oak **St.**

TABLE	Wharton **Ct.**	San Diego, **Calif.**

NOTE Two-letter state abbreviations without periods are used only when the ZIP Code is included.

EXAMPLE   Wilmington, **DE** 19899-8962

Time

Abbreviate the two most frequently used era designations, *A.D.* and *B.C.* The abbreviation *A.D.* stands for the Latin phrase *anno Domini,* meaning "in the year of the Lord." It is used with dates in the Christian era. When used with a specific year, *A.D.* precedes the number. When used with the name of a century, it follows the name.

EXAMPLES   The Middle Ages is usually considered to have begun in Britain in **A.D.** 1066, with the Norman Conquest.

        The fifteenth century **A.D.** saw the beginnings of the Renaissance in England.

CONTENT-AREA CONNECTIONS

Home Economics, Math, Science
Abbreviations of Measures. To help students review proper use of abbreviations, have the class supply recipes to identify and compare abbreviations. Encourage students to bring a variety of recipes, including handwritten family recipes, recipes from books or magazines, and foreign recipes that use metric measurements. First, have students compare the different ways abbreviations have been written in the recipes. Then, if metric and nonmetric recipes are for

The abbreviation *B.C.*, which stands for *before Christ*, is used for dates before the Christian era. It follows either a specific year number or the name of a century.

EXAMPLES   The Roman poet Virgil was born in 70 **B.C.**

Tutankhamen ruled Egypt for a short time during the fourteenth century **B.C.**

In regular text, spell out the names of months and days whether they appear alone or in dates. Both types of names may be abbreviated in tables, notes, and bibliographies.

TEXT   The project is due on Thursday, March 14.

NOTE   **Thurs., Mar.** 14

BIBLIOGRAPHY   "The Last Honest Man." Editorial. *Ledger-Tribune*
ENTRY   [Tucson, Ariz.] 29 **Mar.** 1997:30.

Abbreviate the designations for the two halves of the day measured by clock time. The abbreviation *A.M.* stands for the Latin phrase *ante meridiem*, meaning "before noon." The abbreviation *P.M.* stands for *post meridiem*, meaning "after noon." Both abbreviations follow the numerals designating the specific time.

EXAMPLES   The alarm goes off at 8:00 **A.M.**

By 5:30 **P.M.**, Sandy has completed most of her work for the day.

Units of Measurement

In regular text, spell out the names of units of measurement whether they stand alone or follow a spelled-out number or a numeral. Such names may be abbreviated in tables and notes when they follow a numeral. Most abbreviations for units of measurement are not capitalized.

TEXT   In town, the speed limit is generally twenty-five **miles per hour** [not *mph*].

The tent measured ten **feet** [not *ft*] by twelve.

TABLE

| 1 **tsp** salt | 2 **tbsp** oil | 26° **F** |
| 6 **ft** 1 **in.** | 6 **oz** lemon juice | 5 **mph** |

STYLE   TIP

In your reading, you may come across the abbreviations *C.E.* and *B.C.E.* These abbreviations stand for *Common Era* and *Before Common Era*. These abbreviations are sometimes used in place of *A.D.* and *B.C.*, respectively, and are used after the date.

EXAMPLES
The Saxon king Egbert ruled England from 829 to 839 **C.E.**

Hannibal and his elephants entered Italy in 218 **B.C.E.**

STYLE   TIP

Do not use *A.M.* and *P.M.* with numbers spelled out as words or as substitutes for the words *morning, afternoon,* and *evening.*

EXAMPLES
The rally will begin at **8:00 A.M. (or eight o'clock in the morning)** Sunday [not *eight A.M.*].

Her letter vividly describes the fog on an **evening** [not *on a P.M.*] in London.

similar products, have students try to figure out if the amount of ingredients in each is similar. A math teacher could assist students with charts of equivalents for converting measurements from one system to another.

Perhaps a science or a home economics teacher could supply measuring vessels and scales so students can compare metric amounts with standard measures.

NOTE As the examples on the preceding page show, the abbreviations of most units of measurement do not include periods. To prevent confusion with the word *in,* however, writers should include a period in the abbreviation of *inch* or *inches* (*in.*).

Exercise 4 Using Abbreviations and Correct Capitalization

For the following sentences, correct any errors in the use of abbreviations and capitalization. If a sentence is already correct, write *C.*

EXAMPLE
1. Dad was born in new london, WI.

1. *New London, Wisconsin*

1. C

2. 49 B.C.

3. A.D.

4. Michigan, Indiana, Illinois, and Wisconsin

5. Elm Street

8. VCR

9. C

10. General

1. Tomorrow, the lecture begins at 10:30 A.M.
2. Julius Caesar started the Roman Civil War by crossing a small river, the Rubicon, in B.C. 49.
3. The Hundred Years' War between England and France began in A.D. the fourteenth century.
4. Lake Michigan, the largest body of fresh water in the United States, touches four states: MI, IN, IL, and WI.
5. Sandy has moved from elm st. to Sycamore avenue.
6. Have you asked ms. Pellitier about the results?
7. The blueprint says "32 FT by 60 FT."
8. My father still has not figured out how to set the clock on the new v.c.r.
9. The guest speaker will be Juanita Acosta, Ph.D.
10. Please call gen. Rogers tomorrow.

12

1. [12d(4)]
2. [12f(2)]
3. [12d(7)]
4. [12b]
5. [12d(10)]
6. [12c, g, d(1)]
7. [12e]
8. [12d(2)]
9. [12d(2)]
10. [12d(3)]
11. [12d(4)]
12. [12d(8)]
13. [12e]
14. [12d(6)]
15. [12d(2)]
16. [12d(2)]

Chapter Review

A. Identifying Correct Uses of Capitalization

For each of the following pairs of items, select the letter of the item that is correctly capitalized.

1. **a.** Battle of the Coral sea
   b. Battle of the Coral Sea
2. **a.** my uncle Francis
   b. my Uncle Francis
3. **a.** Maytag washer and dryer
   b. Maytag Washer and Dryer
4. **a.** Hearken to me, o Israel!
   b. Hearken to me, O Israel!
5. **a.** the Nobel prize
   b. the Nobel Prize
6. **a.** Dear Ms. Evans,
   b. dear ms. evans,
7. **a.** English, Math I, Science
   b. English, Math I, science
8. **a.** a chinese elm tree
   b. a Chinese elm tree
9. **a.** live in Buffalo County
   b. live in Buffalo county
10. **a.** Davis High School in Alton
    b. Davis high school in Alton
11. **a.** in honor of Arbor Day
    b. in honor of Arbor day
12. **a.** the train known as the *city of New Orleans*
    b. the train known as the *City of New Orleans*
13. **a.** took courses in English, Spanish, and chemistry
    b. took courses in English, Spanish, and Chemistry
14. **a.** the islamic sacred month called Ramadan
    b. the Islamic sacred month called Ramadan
15. **a.** at the intersection of Sixth avenue and Market street
    b. at the intersection of Sixth Avenue and Market Street
16. **a.** a trip to Yosemite National Park
    b. a trip to Yosemite national park

MECHANICS

17. [12d(3, 2)]
18. [12f(3)]
19. [12d(9)]
20. [12d(11)]

17. **a.** the Roosevelt hotel in New York city
    (b.) the Roosevelt Hotel in New York City
18. **a.** enjoyed Toni Morrison's novel *the Bluest Eye*
    (b.) enjoyed Toni Morrison's novel *The Bluest Eye*
19. **a.** a visit to the Empire State building
    (b.) a visit to the Empire State Building
20. **(a.)** the moons of Jupiter
    b. the Moons of Jupiter

B. Identifying and Correcting Errors in Capitalization

Most of the following items contain one or two errors in capitalization. Correct each error, using capital letters and lowercase letters where they are necessary.

21. [12d(4)]
22. [12f(2), d(3)]
23. [12d]
24. [12d(2)]
25. [12a(2)]
26. [12f(3)]
27. [12d(3, 9)]
28. [12d]
29. [12d(4)]
30. [12f(1)]
31. [12c, g]
32. [12d(9, 2)]
33. [12d(3)]
34. [12a(3)]
35. [12f(1), g]

21. Father's day is observed on the third Sunday in June.
22. For years uncle Wyatt was in the Mesa Garden club.
23. I work in a Drugstore on Breakstone Parkway.
24. When we traveled on the Continent of europe, we especially enjoyed seeing the Swiss Alps.
25. Resolved: that freedom of speech is the foundation of our liberty.
26. Booker T. Washington, an African American educational leader in the late 1800s, wrote *Up from slavery*.
27. The Western High school volleyball team is playing the championship game tonight in Davis gymnasium.
28. The local Post Office is being remodeled by Teller Construction.
29. The revolutionary war was fought in North America more than two centuries ago.
30. Ms. Li is now a Professor of music at Lawson College.
31. sincerely yours,
    Fouad Hussein, m.d.
32. Is the British museum on Great Russell street in London?
33. The Saint Angelica choir performed there on Friday.
34. She said, "that is easy."
35. In 1998, senator John Glenn participated in a Nasa mission.

C. Using Abbreviations and Correct Capitalization

For the following sentences, correct any errors in the use of abbreviations and capitalization.

36. I read that the second millennium began in ~~1001 A.D.~~

37. My father was born in Woodland, ~~MI,~~ on ~~Sept.~~ 13, 1958.

38. Try to remember the following: the rental truck cannot be driven any faster than 55 ~~mph.~~

39. After the Civil war, General Ulysses s. Grant became the eighteenth president of the United States.

40. I believe the vcr was shipped on August 23 from San diego, CA.

36. A.D. 1001 [12g]

37. Michigan/ September [12g]

38. miles per hour [12a(1), g]

39. [or President] [12d(4), g]

40. California [12g, d(2)]

Writing Application

Using Capital Letters in a Letter

Standard Capitalization   Write a letter to the school librarian, recommending five books, periodicals, or videocassettes. Briefly describe each one, telling why you think it would be a worthwhile addition to the library. Be sure to use correct capitalization.

Prewriting   Write down a list of novels, biographies, newspapers, literary journals, educational videocassettes, and other materials that you think would be helpful additions to the library. Choose five titles from your list. Note whether each is a book, a periodical, or a videocassette. Briefly describe the subject matter of each.

Writing   Use your notes to help you write your first draft. Give clear, specific information about each suggested item to convince the librarian to acquire it.

Revising   Read your draft critically. Is your letter persuasive? Does it follow the proper form for a business letter? Be sure that all of your information is accurate and complete.

Publishing   Make sure you have spelled each title correctly, followed the rules of standard capitalization, and italicized each title or enclosed it in quotation marks correctly. Be sure you have corrected any errors in grammar, usage, spelling, and punctuation. Show your letter to the school librarian. Ask him or her what is most effective in the letter and what could be improved to make it more persuasive.

Reference Note

For more about **using italics and quotation marks,** see pages 362 and 365.

MECHANICS

CHAPTER

Punctuation
End Marks and Commas

Diagnostic Preview

A. Correcting Punctuation Errors in Sentences

Rewrite the following sentences, adding, deleting, or changing periods, question marks, exclamation points, and commas as necessary.

Numerals in brackets refer to rules tested by items in the Diagnostic Preview.

1. [13i, m]
2. [13f, a]
3. [13j(4), a]
4. [13j(1), j(4), k(2), a]
5. [13e, l(3, 1), i, k(1), a]
6. [13i, e, l(1)]
7. [13c, c(2), d]
8. [13j(3)]

EXAMPLE
  1. My best friend has moved to 9782, Revere Avenue, New York NY 10465-2879

   1. *My best friend has moved to 9782 Revere Avenue, New York, NY 10465-2879.*

Optional commas are underscored.

1. Marilyn and Antonio who both work at a nearby child-care center greatly enjoy inventing and playing games with the children.
2. Unfolding the solar panels placing satellites into orbit and conducting medical experiments had kept the space shuttle crew busy.
3. Because we had to rekindle the fire twice our cookout was delayed.
4. Well if you apply to all eight colleges Paul you will pay a sizable sum in application fees.
5. "It is my pleasure to introduce Vernon K. Foster, Jr. who has recently returned from a visit to Nairobi Kenya," said Adele Peters the president of our school's Student Foreign Exchange League.
6. The diplomats both educated at American University in Washington D.C. were assigned posts in Athens Greece and Nicosia Cyprus.
7. "The house is on fire" shouted my father. "Everyone get out of here right now."
8. On the far wall to the right of the entrance you will see a striking oil painting done in matte black, ash white, and neutral gray.

---

9. Studying *Beowulf* for the first time,the class particularly enjoyed Grendel,the grim,gruesome monster⊙

10. The treasurer's report did,I believe,make it clear that the senior class has been very successful in its fund-raising activities this year.

11. Interrupting his friends,Philip asked, "Are you ready to leave?,"

12. We spent the morning cleaning the basement and sorting boxes,and in the afternoon we rode our bikes along lovely country roads.

13. My sister's class decided to hold its first class reunion on July 4,2010,at the Bollingbroke Hotel in San Francisco,California⊙

14. Using hyperbole,the store claimed in a colorful full-page newspaper ad that it would be having the "World's Most Spectacular Labor Day Sale."

15. When they went to the prom,did Martha wear a lavender gown with blue satin ribbons,and did George wear a light gray tuxedo?

B. Correcting Errors in the Use of End Marks and Commas in a Paragraph

Rewrite the following paragraph, adding, deleting, or changing any end marks and commas to correct the numbered word groups that are incorrectly punctuated.   Optional commas are underscored.

EXAMPLE   **[1]** In looking through a United States atlas have you ever been tempted to use it, as a menu to create a meal of places named for foods.

    1. *In looking through a United States atlas, have you ever been tempted to use it as a menu to create a meal of places named for foods?*

[16] For an appetizer,that will take the edge off your family's hunger,without filling them up,why not serve a relish tray assembled from Pickleville in Utah, Olive in Montana, and Pepperton in Georgia, along with Rolls from Arizona and Indiana and Butters from North Carolina?**[17]** You might follow that opener with a salad made with Tomato from Mississippi and dressed with Mayo from Maryland, Thousand Island from New York, or French from New Mexico,or Wyoming. **[18]** Seafood-loving families won't be disappointed,for you can find Whitefish in Montana, Salmon in Idaho, Haddock in Georgia, and Trout in Louisiana. **[19]** Families that enjoy red meat can savor selections from Rib Lake in Wisconsin, Lambs Junction in South Carolina, Rabbithash in Kentucky, or,indeed,Beef Island in the Virgin Islands. **[20]** If your family prefers poultry,on the other hand, consider

9. [13j(2), k(1), g, a]
10. [13k(3)]
11. [13j(2), b, b(3)]
12. [13h]
13. [13l(1)]
14. [13j(2)]
15. [13j(4), h, b]

16. [13i, m, j(3), b]
17. [13m]
18. [13h, f]
19. [13k(3)]
20. [13k(3), d]

Diagnostic Preview   **325**

| STYLE   TIP |

In speaking, the tone and pitch of your voice, the pauses in your speech, and your gestures and expressions all help to make your meaning clear. In writing, marks of punctuation signal these verbal and nonverbal cues.

However, if the meaning of the sentence is unclear in the first place, punctuation will usually not clarify it. Whenever you find yourself struggling to punctuate a sentence correctly, take a closer look at your arrangement and choice of words. Often you can eliminate the punctuation problem by rewriting the sentence.

ASSESSING

Entry-Level Assessment
Diagnostic Preview. You may want to use the results of the **Diagnostic Preview** in conjunction with an assessment of students' papers to determine whether students need to review the rules for using end marks and commas in punctuating sentences. Even students who do well on the preview may have trouble using punctuation marks correctly in their own writing. You may wish to have students record errors made on recent writing assignments and use the results as a basis for assessing their progress.

PRETEACHING

Lesson Starter
Motivating. To emphasize the importance of punctuation, especially commas, in making meaning clear, write the following sentences on the chalkboard and ask students to explain how the meanings of the sentences would be different if the commas were deleted.

1. No, children are allowed to see movies that carry a PG rating. [*The comma indicates that* No *is an introductory element. If the comma*

(continued)

Differentiating Instruction
■ *Developmental Language & Sentence Skills,* pp. 127–144
■ *Developmental Language & Sentence Skills Guided Practice Teacher's Notes and Answer Key,* pp. 33–36

Assessment
■ *Holt Handbook Chapter Tests with Answer Key,* pp. 25–26, 54

21. [13k(3), h]
22. [13g, j(3)]
23. [13a]
24. [13d]
25. [13m]

were deleted, the sentence would state that children are not permitted to see movies rated PG under any circumstances.]

2. The officer, who works with street gangs, coaches a soccer team in his spare time. [*The commas set off a nonessential clause. If the commas were deleted, it would be understood that the clause was needed to distinguish the particular officer being discussed from other officers.*]

End Marks

Rules 13a–e *(pp. 326–333)*

O B J E C T I V E S

■ **To correct a passage by adding appropriate end marks**

■ **To rewrite sentences, correcting errors in the use of abbreviations**

DIFFERENTIATING INSTRUCTION

English-Language Learners

General Strategies. Punctuation marks differ from language to language. For example, a period is equivalent to a vertical line in Hindi and to a circle in Japanese. In languages such as Greek, Korean, Persian, and Arabic, the period is slightly raised. The Greek question mark looks like an English semicolon, and Spanish interrogative and exclamatory sentences have end marks at both ends of the interrogative and exclamatory parts, with the first mark inverted. Encourage students to discuss differences in punctuation between their native languages and English. Such discussion will aid some students in remembering English punctuation rules and may increase other students' awareness of such variations among languages.

Reference Note

For information on how sentences are **classified according to purpose,** see page 97.

MECHANICS

Chicken from Alaska, or Duck or Turkey from North Carolina. **[21]** You'll want to serve some vegetables, too, so choose your family's favorites from Corn in Oklahoma, Bean City in Florida, Greens in Kansas and Michigan, and Pea Patch Island in Delaware. **[22]** For a delicious, nourishing side dish, look no further than Noodle in Texas, Rice in Minnesota or Virginia, or Wild Rice in North Dakota. **[23]** Milk River in Montana, Goodwater in Alabama, and Tea in South Dakota will remind you to include a beverage or two. **[24]** Round out your satisfying meal with Oranges, which you'll find in both California and Vermont, and Almonds from Alabama and Wisconsin. **[25]** When your little brother raves about the meal, but complains about having to do the dishes, simply suggest that he get out the atlas and see how far it is to Soap Lake, Washington.

End Marks

An **end mark**—a period, a question mark, or an exclamation point — is used to indicate the purpose of a sentence. A period is also used at the end of many abbreviations.

Sentences

13a. A statement (or declarative sentence) is followed by a period.

EXAMPLES   Mexico City is the home of the Ballet Folklórico.

My words are like the stars that never change.
Chief Seattle, "Speech of Chief Seattle"

13b. A question (or interrogative sentence) is followed by a question mark.

EXAMPLES   When will Terrell prepare the wild rice?

Have you read Lorraine Hansberry's *To Be Young, Gifted, and Black*?

(1) Do not use a question mark after a declarative sentence containing an indirect question.

INDIRECT QUESTION   Mariana wants to know when Junko Tabei climbed Mount Everest.

QUESTION   In what year did Junko Tabei climb Mount Everest?

RESOURCES

End Marks

Practice

■ *Language & Sentence Skills Practice,* pp. 277–282

Differentiating Instruction

■ *Developmental Language & Sentence Skills,* pp. 127–132

(2) In informal writing, a polite request in question form may be followed by either a question mark or a period.

EXAMPLE   Would you please return these books and videotapes to the media center?

or

Would you please return these books and videotapes to the media center.

In formal writing, an interrogative sentence should always be followed by a question mark.

(3) A question mark should be placed inside the closing quotation marks when the quotation itself is a question. Otherwise, it should be placed outside the closing quotation marks.

EXAMPLES   Cara asked, "Did Scott Joplin compose the opera *Treemonisha*?" [The quotation is a question.]

Do you agree with the Spanish proverb "Whoever gossips to you will gossip about you"? [The entire sentence, not the quotation, is a question.]

13c. An exclamation (or exclamatory sentence) is followed by an exclamation point.

EXAMPLES   What a talented artist Frida Kahlo was!

I can't stand that noise!

(1) An interjection at the beginning of a sentence is generally followed by a comma or an exclamation point.

EXAMPLES   Ah, there you are!

Ah! There you are! [Notice that an exclamation point may be used after a single word as well as after a sentence.]

(2) An exclamation point should be placed inside the closing quotation marks when the quotation itself is an exclamation. Otherwise, it should be placed outside the closing quotation marks.

EXAMPLES   "What a good movie that was!" exclaimed Natalie as she left the theater. [The quotation is an exclamation.]

How quickly she said, "I'll take it"! [The entire sentence, not the quotation, is an exclamation.]

Reference Note

For more about the **placement of end marks with closing quotation marks,** see page 367.

S T Y L E   T I P

In informal writing and dialogue, almost any mark of punctuation can be used after an interjection, depending on the meaning of the sentence.

EXAMPLES

"Hmm. You might be right after all, Geraldo," Angelo mused.

"Well? What's your answer?" inquired Sarah.

"Hey—I mean, Sir—can you help me?" asked Kris.

"Wow . . . that's incredible!" Judi exclaimed.

Reference Note

For information on **dashes** and **ellipsis points,** see pages 384 and 371.

End Marks   **327**

DIFFERENTIATING INSTRUCTION

Advanced Learners
Relating to Literature. If "The Tyger" by William Blake is available to students, have them read the poem and discuss Blake's use of exclamation points and question marks. Ask students to consider, for example, how the poem would be different without the exclamation points in the first line. [*Students might point out that the exclamation points show the emphatic nature of the speaker's address and heighten the sense of energy and tension in the poem. Students might find that the numerous question marks in the poem emphasize the wonder and fear the tiger inspires in the speaker.*]

MECHANICS

CONTENT-AREA CONNECTIONS

Math
Periods. Point out to students that the period is used differently in math than it is in reading and writing. In reading and writing, the period is used to indicate the end of a sentence or that a word has been abbreviated. In math, the period is used to indicate decimals and is called the *decimal point.* It can be read as *and* or *point.* For example, *4.3* is read as "four and three tenths" or as "four point three." Ask volunteers to write on the chalkboard examples of decimals in tenths and hundredths.

DIFFERENTIATING INSTRUCTION

Learners Having Difficulty

Activity. Have students work in groups of three or four to write short skits or songs that each include at least two questions, two exclamations, and two commands. Ask students to perform their skits or songs for the class. Tell students to use intonation, body language, and facial expressions to convey the sense of each sentence. Each student in the group should take part in the writing and performance of the skit or song.

EXTENSION

Critical Thinking

Metacognition. After students have completed their skits or songs, have them analyze the process they used to write their pieces. Students can use the following prompts to write their analyses:

- Did some sentences take more time than others to write? Why?

- How did you fit the different types of sentences together to make them form a skit or song?

- Did you refer to the textbook for help in writing the sentences?

- What could you have done to make the activity go more quickly or smoothly?

PRACTICE

Guided and Independent

Exercise 1 You may want to use the first ten sentences of **Exercise 1** as guided practice and then assign the last fifteen sentences as independent practice. **HOMEWORK**

S T Y L E   T I P

Do not overuse exclamation points. Use an exclamation point only when the expression is obviously emphatic.

When they are used too frequently, exclamation points lose their effect.

OVERUSED

Last Sunday, we went tubing! In some places, the rapids got very rough! By the time we landed, we were all thoroughly soaked!

IMPROVED

Last Sunday, we went tubing. In some places, the rapids got very rough. By the time we landed, we were all thoroughly soaked!

13d. A request or a command (or imperative sentence) is followed by either a period or an exclamation point.

A request or a mild command is generally followed by a period. A strong command is generally followed by an exclamation point.

EXAMPLES   Please write me a letter. [request]

Turn to page 126. [mild command]

Hold that line! [strong command]

HI & LOIS reprinted with special permission of King Features Syndicate, Inc.

Exercise 1   **Correcting a Passage by Adding End Marks**   Some answers may vary.

Many periods and all exclamation points and question marks have been omitted from the following passage. Write each word that should be followed by an end mark, add the appropriate end mark, and as needed, capitalize the first word of the sentence following the end mark. For any quotation requiring an end mark, include the closing quotation marks to show the proper placement of the end mark.

EXAMPLES   **[1]** Dr. Lynn Block, director of research for the Larson Soap Company, looked at her appointment book

    1. book.

    [2] "oh, no" she groaned

    2. "Oh, no!"; groaned.

[1] Today she must conduct interviews to hire a new secretary. [2] she thought, "How nerve-racking it is when an applicant is unprepared" [3] nonetheless, she was ready for the 9:00 A.M. interview.
[4] At 9:35 A.M., the receptionist ushered in the late arrival. [5] "Oh, dear," thought Dr. Block as she surveyed the young man's torn jeans, unironed T-shirt, and shaggy hair. [6] to questions about his qualifications, the young man answered only yes or no instead of mentioning

specific details, and he did not apologize for his lateness[7] "Well," Dr. Block puzzled, "this person has much experience and good typing skills, but he certainly doesn't seem to want the job"

[8] The next applicant, Ms. Smith, entered wearing a professional tool belt with carpentry tools around her waist[9] she said, "I'm so sorry to disturb you[10] I'm interested in the maintenance position being advertised[11] I must have taken a wrong turn when I got off the elevator"

[12] "I'll say" exclaimed Dr. Block[13] she directed the woman to the maintenance office on the other side of the building and wished her luck[14] To herself, she mused, "Whew at this rate, I may never get a secretary" [15] By then, the next interviewee had arrived—on time [16] Dr. Block wondered, "Now what? [17] Looking up to see a neatly dressed young man, she asked, "Are you sure you're in the right place? [18] it's been a highly unusual morning so far"

[19] he replied, "Oh, yes, I'm applying for the secretarial position [20] he gave brief, helpful explanations and asked appropriate questions about the job. [21] About his career plans, he said, "I would someday like to be an office manager[22] I like office work and believe good management is vital to a smooth operation"

[23] "You're right about that" exclaimed Dr. Block. [24] After the interview ended, Dr. Block pondered her choices[25] she thought, "Well, he doesn't have as much experience or quite as high a typing rate as the first interviewee, but I know whom I'm going to hire"

Abbreviations

13e. **Many abbreviations are followed by a period.**

An ***abbreviation*** is a shortened form of a word or phrase. Notice how periods are used with abbreviations in the following examples.

Personal Names

Abbreviate given names only if the person is most commonly known by the abbreviated form of the name.

EXAMPLES   Ida **B.** Wells   **E. M.** Forster   **W.E.B.** DuBois

             F. Scott Fitzgerald   Harry **S.** Truman   **M.F.K.** Fisher

NOTE Leave a space between two such initials, but not between three or more.

STYLE TIP

Sometimes (most often in dialogue), a writer will use more than one end mark to express intense emotion or a combination of emotions.

EXAMPLES

More and more loudly, the team's fans cheered, "We're number one!!" [intense emotion]

"You had to pay how much?!" Steven exclaimed. [combination of curiosity and surprise]

Using such double end punctuation is acceptable in most informal writing. However, in formal writing, you should use only one end mark.

HELP

If a statement ends with an abbreviation, do not use an additional period as an end mark. However, do use a question mark or an exclamation point if one is needed.

EXAMPLES

The new president is Daniel Franklin, **Jr.**

Is the new president Daniel Franklin, **Jr.?**

DIFFERENTIATING INSTRUCTION

Advanced Learners

Relating to Literature. Few poems include abbreviations; however, "The Unknown Citizen" by W. H. Auden does include one. Have students read the poem, and ask them to consider Auden's use of the abbreviation *Inc.* Ask students what they think the theme of the poem is and how the use of an abbreviation supports that theme. [*One possible response is that the theme is the anonymity of the individual in a bureaucratic, impersonal world, in which people are valued on the basis of productivity and conformity. The use of the abbreviation supports this theme because abbreviations—used for the sake of efficiency—are seen as impersonal and result from the desire to enhance speed and, therefore, productivity.*]

Critical Thinking

Synthesis. Challenge students to combine the rules from **Chapter 12: Capitalization** with the rules for end marks. Point out to students that one of the many places where the rules overlap is in abbreviated names and titles, which are capitalized and followed by a period. Have students share their findings in small groups.

DIFFERENTIATING INSTRUCTION

Advanced Learners

Library Activity. Discuss with students the trend among organizations to create acronyms in which the letters form or sound like an existing word. Share the following examples:

Navy SEAL (Sea, Air, Land)

MADD (Mothers Against Drunk Driving)

SADD (Students Against Drunk Driving)

Have the class discuss why these organizations chose those particular words. Then, have students research directories of organizations to find other examples of this kind of acronym.

STYLE   TIP

Only a few abbreviations are appropriate in the text of a formal paper written for a general audience. In tables, notes, and bibliographies, abbreviations are used more freely in order to save space.

HELP

Roman numerals that follow a proper name do not end with periods. Also, they are not separated from the name by a comma.

EXAMPLES
Davis Love **III**

Pope John Paul **II**

HELP

A few acronyms, such as *radar, laser,* and *sonar,* are now considered common nouns. They do not need to be spelled out on first use and are no longer capitalized. When you are not sure whether an acronym should be capitalized, check a recent dictionary.

Titles

Abbreviate social titles whether used before the full name or before the last name alone.

EXAMPLES   **Mr.** John Kelley   **Mrs.** Rachel Draper   **Ms.** Young

Sr. (Señor) Reyes   **Sra.** (Señora) Jiménez   **Dr.** Jefferson

You may abbreviate civil and military titles used before full names or before initials and last names. Spell them out before last names used alone.

EXAMPLES   **Gen.** H. Norman Schwarzkopf   **General** Schwarzkopf

Sen. Daniel K. Akaka   **Senator** Akaka

Prof. Samuel Isaacharoff   **Professor** Isaacharoff

Abbreviate titles and academic degrees that follow proper names.

EXAMPLES   Marco Lopez, **Jr.**   Jeremy Stone, **M.D.**

NOTE   Do not include the titles *Mr., Mrs., Ms.,* or *Dr.* when you use a title or degree after a name.

EXAMPLE   Dr. Jeremy Stone *or* Jeremy Stone, **M.D.** [not *Dr. Jeremy Stone, M.D.*]

Agencies, Organizations, and Acronyms

After spelling out the first use of the names of agencies and organizations, abbreviate these names.

EXAMPLE   Janelle was researching the International Monetary Fund and learned that the United Nations created the **IMF** to promote international economic cooperation.

An *acronym* is a word formed from the first (or first few) letters of a series of words. Notice that acronyms are written without periods.

ADA American Dental Association	**OAS** Organization of American States
PRI Public Radio International	**HUD** Department of Housing and Urban Development
ERIC Educational Resources Information Center	**CPB** Corporation for Public Broadcasting

Geographical Terms

In regular text, spell out names of states and other political units whether they stand alone or follow other geographical terms. Abbreviate them in tables, notes, and bibliographies.

TEXT Rudyard Kipling was born in Bombay, India, and was educated in England.

Our tour included stops in Olympia, Washington; Salem, Oregon; and Sacramento, California.

CHART

Mumbai, Ind.	Sacramento, Calif.
London, U.K.	Piedras Negras, Mex.

FOOTNOTE ³The Stanford University Libraries in Stanford, Calif., hold a special collection of Irish literature.

BIBLIOGRAPHY ENTRY Johansen, Bruce. Forgotten Founders. Boston, Mass.: The Harvard Common Press, 1982.

NOTE Include the traditional abbreviation for the District of Columbia, *D.C.*, with the city name *Washington* to distinguish it from the state of Washington.

In regular text, spell out every word in an address. Such words may be abbreviated in letter and envelope addresses as well as in tables and notes.

TEXT Our new house is located at 1492 Columbia Avenue, Fort Myers, Florida.

For more information, write us at Park Drive in Laredo, Texas.

ENVELOPE 1492 Columbia Ave.
Fort Myers, **FL** 33906

TABLE

Park Dr.	Laredo, Tex.
Columbia Ave.	Durham, N.C.

NOTE Two-letter state abbreviations without periods are used only when the ZIP Code is included.

EXAMPLE Yorba Linda, **CA 92886**

Reference Note
For information on **capitalizing geographical terms,** see page 299.

End Marks **331**

In your reading, you may see the abbreviations *B.C.E.* (Before the Common Era) and *C.E.* (Common Era). These abbreviations should be placed after the year.

EXAMPLES

The city of Rome was founded in 753 **B.C.E.**

Genghis Khan began his conquest of Asia in the late twelfth century **C.E.**

COMPUTER TIP

Publishers usually print time abbreviations as small capitals—uppercase letters that are slightly smaller than standard uppercase letters. Your word processor may offer small capitals as a style option. If it does not, or if you are writing by hand, you may use either uppercase or lowercase letters for time abbreviations, as long as you are consistent.

Time

Abbreviate the two most frequently used era designations, A.D. and B.C. The abbreviation A.D. stands for the Latin phrase *anno Domini,* meaning "in the year of the Lord." It is used with dates in the Christian era. When used with a specific year number, A.D. precedes the number. When used with the name of a century, it follows the name.

EXAMPLES   Attila the Hun began his reign in **A.D.** 433.

The first books printed from wood blocks were produced in China in the tenth century **A.D.**

The abbreviation B.C., which stands for "before Christ," is used for dates before the Christian era. It follows either a specific year number or the name of a century.

EXAMPLES   In 55 **B.C.**, Julius Caesar invaded Britain.

The first Olympic games were held in Greece during the eighth century **B.C.**

In regular text, spell out the names of months and days whether they appear alone or in dates. Both types of names may be abbreviated in tables, notes, and bibliographies.

TEXT   The convention will begin Thursday, February 4, in the Civic Center.

NOTE   Thurs., Feb. 4

Abbreviate the designations for the two halves of the day measured by clock time. The abbreviation A.M. stands for the Latin phrase *ante meridiem,* meaning "before noon." The abbreviation P.M. stands for *post meridiem,* meaning "after noon." Both abbreviations follow the numerals designating the specific time.

EXAMPLES   The meeting will pause for lunch at 11:30 **A.M.**

The video must be returned by 10:00 **P.M.** tomorrow.

Units of Measurement

Abbreviations for units of measurement are usually written without periods. However, do use a period with the abbreviation for inch (*in.*) to prevent confusing it with the word *in.*

EXAMPLES   mm, kg, ml, tsp, doz, yd, ft, lb

In regular text, spell out the names of units of measurement whether they stand alone or follow a spelled-out number or a numeral. Such names may be abbreviated in tables and notes when they follow a numeral.

TEXT The speed limit in the mall's parking lot is five **miles per hour** [not *mph*].

She wanted a rug that was at least five **feet** [not *ft*] by seven.

TABLE

2 **tsp** pepper	47° **C**
8 **ft** 2 **in.**	6 **oz** shredded cheese

Exercise 2 Using Abbreviations

Rewrite the following sentences, correcting errors in the standard, formal use of abbreviations.

EXAMPLE
   1. The next stop for the train is Cincinnati, OH.
   1. *Cincinnati, Ohio.*

1. The bus is leaving at 7:30 A.M. in the morning.
2. Scientists found enough clues to date the artifact B.C. 1124.
3. Shakespeare's first play was produced sometime before 1592 A.D.
4. In 1975, Jim Sparks of Visalia, CA, set a record by sitting in a tree for almost sixty-two days.
5. The race would begin on Franklin St. and finish on Euclid Ave.
6. I'll be there at 7:00 A.M..
7. Dr. Sylvia Irving, DVM, was a guest for career day.
8. Marshall refused to trade his Ken Griffey, Junior, rookie card.
9. Very few of the residents have forgotten the time when Moses Hazard Robinson, III, passed through their town.
10. A. Lincoln was the sixteenth president of the United States.

Commas

Items in a Series

13f. Use commas to separate items in a series.

EXAMPLES She had been a correspondent for the wire service in London, Paris, Rome, and Madrid. [words in a series]

STYLE   TIP

Do not use *A.M.* or *P.M.* with numbers spelled out as words or as a substitute for the word *morning*, *afternoon*, or *evening*.

EXAMPLE
The parade began at **9:00 A.M.** (or **nine o'clock in the morning**) Friday [not *nine A.M. Friday*].

Also, do not use the word *morning*, *afternoon*, or *evening* with numerals followed by *A.M.* or *P.M.*

INCORRECT
The results should be in by 2:30 P.M. in the afternoon.

CORRECT
The results should be in by **2:30 P.M.** (or **two-thirty in the afternoon.**)

Exercise 2 Using Abbreviations

ANSWERS

1. The bus is leaving at 7:30 A.M. *or* The bus is leaving at 7:30 in the morning.
2. Scientists found enough clues to date the artifact 1124 B.C.
3. Shakespeare's first play was produced sometime before A.D. 1592.
4. In 1975, Jim Sparks of Visalia, California, set a record by sitting in a tree for almost sixty-two days.
5. The race would begin on Franklin Street and finish on Euclid Avenue.
6. I'll be there at 7:00 A.M.
7. Sylvia Irving, D.V.M., was a guest for career day. *or* Dr. Sylvia Irving was a guest for career day.
8. Marshall refused to trade his Ken Griffey, Jr., rookie card.
9. Very few of the residents have forgotten the time when Moses Hazard Robinson III passed through their town.
10. Abraham Lincoln was the sixteenth president of the United States.

Commas
Rules 13f–m *(pp. 333–350)*

OBJECTIVES

■ To correct sentences by adding and deleting commas

■ To identify essential and nonessential clauses and phrases and to add commas in sentences where needed

---

DIRECT TEACHING

Modeling and Demonstration

Commas. Model how to proofread sentences for correct use of commas by using the example *The reporter wanted to know who I was, where I went to school, and how I felt about getting my driver's license.* Ask if there is a series of three or more items in the sentence. [*yes; who I was, where I went to school, how I felt about getting my driver's license*] Then, ask whether this series is made up of individual words, phrases, or clauses. [*clauses*] Next, ask if all the items in the series are joined by *and, or,* or *nor.* [*no*] Therefore, the items in the series need to be separated by commas. Now, have a volunteer use another example from this chapter to demonstrate how to proofread sentences for correct use of commas.

EXTENSION

Relating to Dictionary Skills

The word *comma* has an interesting etymology. Have students look up *comma* in a dictionary to discover the word's origin. [*Comma comes from the Greek word* komma, *meaning "that which is cut off," from the Greek word* koptein, *meaning "to cut or split."*] Discuss with students how the origin of the word *comma* relates to the function of the comma in writing.

STYLE TIP

Words customarily used in pairs, such as *bag and baggage, law and order,* and *macaroni and cheese,* are set off as one item in a series.

EXAMPLE
    For supper they served a tossed salad, **spaghetti and meatballs,** garlic bread, milk, and fruit.

STYLE TIP

A comma before the conjunction in a series of three or more items is not incorrect. If you have any doubt about the clarity of the sentence without the comma, add the comma.

Reference Note

For more information about punctuating **nouns of direct address,** see page 344.

Reference Note

For more about **using semicolons to separate independent clauses,** see page 356.

I studied for the test on the way to school, during homeroom, and in study hall. [phrases in a series]

The reporter wanted to know who I was, where I went to school, and how I felt about getting my driver's license. [clauses in a series]

NOTE   Do not use a comma before the first item or after the final item in a series.

INCORRECT   The students in auto mechanics class learned, to replace the spark plugs, to check the fluid levels, and to change the oil, in several makes of cars.

CORRECT   The students in auto mechanics class learned to replace the spark plugs, to check the fluid levels, and to change the oil in several makes of cars.

When *and, or,* or *nor* joins the last two items in a series, writers sometimes omit the comma before the conjunction if the comma is not needed to make the meaning of the sentence clear.

CLEAR   Soccer, basketball and lacrosse are my favorite sports. [The meaning of the sentence is clear without a comma before the conjunction *and.*]

UNCLEAR   Joetta, Lucia and Ben are rehearsing a scene from the musical *Grease.* [The meaning of the sentence is unclear: Are three people rehearsing a scene, or is Joetta being addressed?]

CLEAR   Joetta, Lucia, and Ben are rehearsing a scene from the musical *Grease.* [The sentence clearly states that all three people are rehearsing a scene.]

CLEAR   Lucia and Ben are rehearsing a scene from the musical *Grease,* Joetta. [The sentence clearly indicates that Joetta is being addressed. *Joetta* is a noun of direct address.]

If all the items in a series are joined by *and, or,* or *nor,* do not use commas to separate them.

EXAMPLE   Derrick **and** Han **and** Jina will represent the senior class.

Short independent clauses in a series may be separated by commas.

EXAMPLE   I came, I saw, I conquered.

Long independent clauses separated by commas can be difficult to read. To make the break between clauses more distinct, use semicolons instead of commas.

334   Chapter 13   Punctuation

13g. Use a comma to separate two or more adjectives preceding a noun.

EXAMPLES   Katherine Dunham is a creative, talented dancer and choreographer.

        Did you see that boring, silly, worthless movie?

Do not use a comma before the final adjective in a series if the adjective is thought of as part of the noun.

EXAMPLES   Lawanda hung colorful, delicate Chinese lanterns around the patio. [*Chinese lanterns* is regarded as a compound noun.]

        It was a crisp, clear fall day. [*Fall day* is considered one item.]

NOTE A word that modifies one of the adjectives in a series is an adverb, not another adjective. Do not separate the adverb from the adjective with a comma.

EXAMPLE   Why did he wear a **bright red** cap?

Exercise 3 **Correcting Sentences by Adding Commas**

For each of the following sentences, write each <u>word that should be</u> <u>followed by a comma</u>, and place a comma after it. If a sentence is already correct, write *C*.   Optional commas are underscored.

EXAMPLE   1. The firefighters arrived promptly extinguished the blaze and returned to the station.

           1. *promptly, blaze,*

1. She is a bright, charming woman.
2. Albert Cunningham prepared a tossed green salad, ham and cheese sandwiches, and iced tea.
3. Armando sang, danced, and juggled in the talent show.
4. My parents always ask me where I'm going, who will be there, and when I'll be home.
5. Should we go to the mall or to the park or to Yoko's house?   **5.** C
6. Study this ancient, complex pattern for any thematic repetitions from right to left.
7. That station airs jazz, rock-and-roll, rhythm and blues, and just about everything else.
8. Wouldn't a light blue-green color look nice on the wall in the new family room?   **8.** C

MECHANICS

9. My little sister said, "I want a book and a puzzle and a doll and a big sand castle and a rocket ship and a puppy and a cell phone for my birthday."   **9.** C

10. There was confetti on the floor‸in our hair‸on every stick of furni-ture‸and even under the sofa.

Independent Clauses

13h. Use a comma before a coordinating conjunction (*and, but, for, nor, or, so,* or *yet*) when it joins independent clauses.

EXAMPLES   The sky looks clear‚ yet rain has been forecast.

I saw a performance of August Wilson's *Fences*‚ and now I am eager to read his other plays.

NOTE   Always use a comma before *for, so,* or *yet* joining independent clauses. The comma is sometimes omitted before *and, but, or,* or *nor* when the independent clauses are very short and the meaning of the sentence is clear without the comma.

CLEAR   We didn't enjoy the film but you might.

UNCLEAR   I will work with Emma and Josh will help Madison.
CLEAR   I will work with Emma‚ and Josh will help Madison.

Do not confuse a compound sentence with a simple sentence that contains a compound verb.

COMPOUND SENTENCE   Ashley and I looked everywhere for the sheet music‚ but we couldn't find it. [two independent clauses]

SIMPLE SENTENCE   Ashley and I looked everywhere for the sheet music but couldn't find it. [one independent clause with a compound verb]

Also, keep in mind that compound subjects and compound objects are not separated by commas unless they are made up of three or more items.

EXAMPLES   When you begin a project and when you finish it are closely related. [two subordinate clauses serving as a compound subject]

Dave planned to watch both the Super Bowl and the Pro Bowl. [two compound nouns serving as a compound object]

Reference Note

For more information about **compound subjects** and **compound verbs,** see page 40. For information about **compound sentences,** see page 94.

S T Y L E   T I P

It is not incorrect to use a comma before a coordinating conjunction separating independent clauses. If you are not sure that the meaning of the sentence would be clear without a comma, use a comma.

DIFFERENTIATING INSTRUCTION

English-Language Learners

Spanish. In Spanish, commas are often used between independent clauses, as in "The rain was falling steadily, it looked as if the game would be canceled." Using the comma in this way in English is a mechanical error called a comma splice. Suggest that students proof-read for such errors and replace the commas with periods (capitalizing the word after the period) or add coordinating conjunctions after the commas.

MINI-LESSON   Grammar

Grammar. Students may need a quick review of some grammatical terms used in this lesson, such as *independent clause, subordinate clause, participial phrase,* *prepositional phrase,* and *adverb clause.*

Divide the class into groups, and assign each group one of the terms that you feel students may need to review. Each group

My Three Sons, *I Love Lucy,* and *The Dick Van Dyke Show*
are all considered television classics. [compound subject
made up of three items]

Exercise 4 **Correcting Sentences by Adding Commas**

For each of the following sentences, write the <u>word that should be
followed by a comma</u>, and place a comma after it. If a sentence is
already correct, write *C.*

EXAMPLE   **1.** My aunt Rosa used to be a flight attendant but now she
        owns and manages a travel agency.

    1. *attendant,*

1. Are you busy Friday <u>night</u>or would you like to go to the movies?
2. I'm eating dinner now but will call you back as soon as I finish.   **2.** C
3. Don't forget to take your history book home this <u>weekend</u>for the
    test is Monday.
4. The recipes in *Spirit of the Harvest: North American Indian
    Cooking* are adapted for modern <u>cooks</u>yet the ingredients listed
    are all traditional.
5. Quilting is a practical folk <u>art</u>and it is also a relaxing and enjoy-
    able pastime.
6. We shivered and clutched our jackets <u>close</u>for the wind had picked
    up, and the sea had grown troubled and crashed against the rocks
    by the cliff.
7. The Yaqui of Mexico have always maintained their social <u>organiza-
    tion</u>so their traditions have remained largely intact to this day.
8. They did not go to <u>sleep</u>nor did they stop talking till dawn that
    first night in the college dorm.
9. Back in 1865, Maria Mitchell had the distinction of being a profes-
    sor of astronomy and of becoming the first U.S. woman in the
    American Academy of Arts and Sciences.   **9.** C
10. A tiger slept in the shade under dense green <u>leaves</u>yet her cubs
    were busy investigating several large beetles.

Review A **Correcting Errors in the Use of
        Commas in a Paragraph**

Rewrite the paragraph on the following page, adding or deleting commas in order to correct sentences that are incorrectly punctuated. If a
sentence is already correct, write *C.*

MECHANICS

EXAMPLE   **[1]** Do you know what the second-largest, Russian city is?

1. Do you know what the second-largest Russian city is?
Optional commas are underscored.

[1] In 1697, Czar Peter I of Russia toured western Europe, liked what he saw and determined to remodel his nation along Western lines. **[2]** Six years later, he decreed that an entirely new city be built at the eastern end of the Gulf of Finland on land that had recently been controlled by Sweden. **[3]** Peter hired leading Russian, French, and Italian architects to create a city with planned squares, wide avenues, and extensive parks and gardens. **[4]** He named the city St. Petersburg and in 1712 moved the capital there from Moscow. **[5]** The German name of the capital was kept for two centuries but in 1914 was Russianized to *Petrograd* by Czar Nicholas II.

[6] Three years later, the city witnessed both the abdication of Nicholas and the return from exile of the Russian Marxist revolutionary V. I. Lenin. **[7]** Petrograd served as the first capital of Soviet Russia after the Communist Revolution of 1917 but lost that status to Moscow early the following year. **[8]** Then, in 1924, the Second Congress of the Soviets of the U.S.S.R. changed the city's name to Leningrad to honor the recently deceased Lenin. **[9]** Further name changes seemed unlikely once the Communist system became firmly entrenched. **[10]** In 1991, however, the Russian people went to the polls, repudiated the name Leningrad and reclaimed their beautiful historic city's original name—St. Petersburg.

7. C

9. C

Nonessential Elements

13i. Use commas to set off nonessential subordinate clauses and nonessential participial phrases.

A *nonessential* (or *nonrestrictive*) clause or participial phrase contains information that is not necessary to the meaning of the sentence.

Reference Note

For more information about **subordinate clauses,** see page 83. For more about **participial phrases,** see page 65.

NONESSENTIAL CLAUSES	Carla Harris**,** **who was offered scholarships to three different colleges,** will go to Vassar in the fall.
	The word *telethon***, which is a combination of the words *television* and *marathon*,** is an example of a portmanteau word.
NONESSENTIAL PHRASES	Antonio**, following his grandmother's recipe,** prepared *arroz con pollo* for his cooking class.
	Frightened by the thunder, both of the kittens jumped into my lap.

Each nonessential clause or phrase in the examples above can be omitted without changing the main idea expressed in the rest of the sentence.

EXAMPLES	Carla Harris will go to Vassar in the fall.
	The word *telethon* is an example of a portmanteau word.
	Antonio prepared *arroz con pollo* for his cooking class.
	Both of the kittens jumped into my lap.

An *essential* (or *restrictive*) subordinate clause or participial phrase is not set off by commas because it contains information that is necessary to the meaning of the sentence.

ESSENTIAL CLAUSES	Carla Harris is the only senior **who was offered scholarships to three different colleges.**
	Mercury is the planet **that is closest to the sun.**
ESSENTIAL PHRASES	Any student **wanting to learn about the new reference database** should sign up in the library by Friday.
	The lines **cited at the beginning and the end of the speech** are from Omar Khayyám's *Rubáiyát.*

Notice below how the omission of the essential clause or phrase affects the main idea of each example above.

EXAMPLES	Carla Harris is the only senior.
	Mercury is the planet.
	Any student should sign up in the library by Friday.
	The lines are from Omar Khayyám's *Rubáiyát.*

⌐ TIPS & TRICKS ⌐

A subordinate clause or a participial phrase that tells *which one(s) of two or more* is generally essential. Furthermore, a subordinate clause beginning with *that* and modifying a noun or pronoun is generally essential. A subordinate clause or a participial phrase that modifies a proper noun is generally nonessential.

Commas   **339**

DIRECT TEACHING

Modeling and Demonstration

Nonessential Elements. Model how to proofread sentences for correct use of commas by using the example *My sister, who lives in Delaware, is a nurse.* First, ask whether the clause *who lives in Delaware* is essential or nonessential. [*nonessential*] Point out that the meaning of the sentence is not changed if the nonessential clause is omitted. [*My sister is a nurse.*] Next, ask if the clause *who lives in Delaware* should be set off by commas. [*yes*] Explain that commas should be used to set off nonessential subordinate clauses and nonessential participial phrases. Now, have a volunteer use another example from this chapter to demonstrate how to proofread sentences for correct use of commas.

RETEACHING

Essential Elements

Activity. If students have trouble distinguishing between essential and nonessential elements, try the following approach. Have students look up the word *essential* in a dictionary. Then, ask students to give examples of things that are essential, such as eggs in an omelet. As students call out examples, have two or three volunteers write lists on the chalkboard. Remind students that, similarly, if a clause or phrase is essential, it is a necessary part of the sentence and is not separated from the rest of the sentence by commas. Nonessential clauses or phrases, on the other hand, are not necessary to the sentence and are separated from the rest of the sentence by commas.

Commas appear throughout our daily lives—on billboards, on restaurant menus, and on movie posters, for example. You can even find commas in mathematic formulas. Record several examples of the commas you encounter on a given day, and then compile the results for your class. When you show the class each comma you've found, explain its function and tell whether or not it is used correctly.

ANSWER
Sets of sentences will differ, but students should show an understanding of the comma rules in this chapter.

Some subordinate clauses and participial phrases may be either essential or nonessential. The presence or absence of commas tells the reader how the clause or phrase relates to the main idea of the sentence.

ESSENTIAL	Dave took his problem to the librarian **who is an authority on children's literature.** [The library has more than one librarian, but only one is an authority on children's literature.]
NONESSENTIAL	Dave took his problem to the librarian**,** **who is an authority on children's literature.** [The library has only one librarian.]
ESSENTIAL	The squirrel **with its bushy tail twitching** was nibbling on an acorn. [More than one squirrel was visible, but only one had its tail twitching.]
NONESSENTIAL	The squirrel**,** **with its bushy tail twitching,** was nibbling on an acorn. [Only one squirrel was in view.]

Exercise 5 **Identifying Essential and Nonessential Subordinate Clauses and Participial Phrases**

In each of the following sentences, identify the italicized clause or phrase as *essential* or *nonessential*. Add commas where they are needed, or write *no comma needed*.

EXAMPLES
1. Do you know the name of the actor *who provides the voice for the title character in the new animated film*?

1. essential—no comma needed

2. Sisyphus *who had been a greedy king of Corinth* was doomed to push a heavy stone uphill, only to have it always roll down again.

2. nonessential—Sisyphus, Corinth,

1. n.c.n.
2. n.c.n. *(marginal note — unclear)*
3. n.c.n.
4. n.c.n.
6. n.c.n.

1. Employees *who always have a ready smile* make the job seem easier.
2. Toni Morrison has been widely praised for her novel Beloved, *which is one of my favorite books.*
3. Tortellini *that is filled with garden vegetables* is one of Eduardo's favorite meals.
4. People *who are overly nervous* may not make good drivers.
5. The Federal Reserve System, *serving as the central bank of the United States,* monitors money and credit growth.
6. Cities *that seem alike* may require a closer look.
7. Lake Chad, *covering an area of about six thousand square miles,* is West Africa's largest body of water.

Placement of Modifiers. Remind students to avoid misplaced modifiers by placing modifying phrases and clauses as close as possible to the words being modified.

For more information on misplaced modifiers, refer students to **Chapter 10: Placement of Modifiers.**

8. Human adults, *whose development has been studied and recorded over time,* continue to mature, usually in predictable stages, after the age of eighteen.

9. That law, *which may have met a real need one hundred years ago,* should be repealed or rewritten to deal with today's situation.

10. The Suez Canal, *extending more than a hundred miles,* links the Mediterranean Sea and the Red Sea.

Review B **Correcting Errors in the Use of Commas in a Paragraph**

Rewrite the following paragraph, adding or deleting commas to correct sentences that are incorrectly punctuated. If a sentence is already correct, write *C*.   Optional commas are underscored.

EXAMPLE   **[1]** Rona asked me when the Old, Spanish Days fiesta is.

1. *Rona asked me when the Old Spanish Days fiesta is.*

[1] Each August, visitors are welcomed to the Old Spanish Days fiesta, which is sponsored by the city of Santa Barbara in California. **[2]** The festival, lasting five days, attracts nearly half a million people. 2. C **[3]** It honors the Spaniards, who colonized the area, beginning in the early 1700s. **[4]** The festivities start on Wednesday with blessings and singing and dancing at *La Fiesta Pequeña,* which is Spanish for "Little Festival," outside Mission Santa Barbara on East Los Olivos and Laguna streets. **[5]** This mission, founded in 1786, is one of the best preserved of the twenty-one missions, that the Spanish established in California between 1769 and 1823. **[6]** Costumed dancers and colorful floats enliven Thursday's *Desfile Histórico* ("Historic Parade"), which recounts how the Spanish conquistador Sebastian Vizcaino sailed into the nearby bay in 1602, why he named the bay Santa Barbara, and what drew settlers to the area. **[7]** A free, variety show that begins later in the day and continues nightly features Spanish flamenco dancers and Mexican folkloric dancers like those, pictured here. **[8]** On the weekend, artists and craftworkers set up booths along Cabrillo Boulevard and State

TEACHING TIP

Review B   In sentence 3, students must delete the second comma. Some students might leave the first comma in the sentence because they define the *who* clause as nonessential. If students can explain the rationale (the festival honors all Spaniards, not just the particular ones who colonized the area), their answers should be accepted.

DIFFERENTIATING INSTRUCTION

Advanced Learners
Viewing the Illustration. Ask students to consider the various metaphors that have been used to describe society in the United States. An early metaphor compares society in the United States to a melting pot, emphasizing the blending of ethnic and national groups into a homogeneous country. Other more recent metaphors compare society in the United States to a salad bowl or stew, in which separate ingredients retain their qualities yet combine to form a whole. Another metaphor compares culture in the United States to a mosaic, in which pieces that are different from one another are put together to form a picture.

After discussing the ideas about unity and diversity suggested by these metaphors, ask students to write persuasive paragraphs that state and support their opinions as to which of these metaphors is most accurate.

Street, and sell handmade items. [9] Fiesta-goers needn't go hungry, for authentic Latin foods, such as tortas, tacos, enchiladas, flautas, and tamales, are sold in the two open-air markets. [10] What an eventful, fun-filled five days Old Spanish Days provides!

Introductory Elements

13j. Use a comma after certain introductory elements.

(1) Use a comma after *yes, no,* or any mild exclamation such as *well* or *why* at the beginning of a sentence.

EXAMPLES **Yes,** you are welcome to join us.

Well, what do you think?

Why, the whole story sounds suspicious!

(2) Use a comma after an introductory participle or participial phrase.

EXAMPLES **Beaten,** I shook hands with my opponent and walked off the court.

Proofreading my report, I saw that I had written *gorilla,* instead of *guerrilla,* before the word *warfare.*

Almost hidden by the dense brush, the tiny rabbit sat absolutely still.

NOTE Do not confuse a gerund phrase used as the subject of a sentence with an introductory participial phrase.

GERUND PHRASE **Planting the Japanese quinces along the fence** took several hours.
PARTICIPIAL PHRASE **Planting the Japanese quinces along the fence,** I stepped on a mound of fire ants.

(3) Use a comma after two or more introductory prepositional phrases or after one long introductory prepositional phrase.

EXAMPLES **In the park near my house,** a music festival will take place this weekend.

Near the beginning of the trail, the scout leader found an overturned canoe.

On the day when the last autumn leaf finally fell, I packed my bags.

NOTE A single short introductory prepositional phrase does not require a comma unless the phrase is parenthetical or unless the sentence is confusing or awkward without the comma.

EXAMPLES **During spring break** we're going camping in the mountains. [clear without comma]

By the way, you're late. [The comma is needed because the phrase is parenthetical.]

From Laura, Lee had borrowed a sleeping bag and a flashlight. [The comma is needed to avoid reading "Laura Lee."]

Reference Note

For more information about **parenthetical expressions,** see page 345.

(4) Use a comma after an introductory adverb clause.

An introductory adverb clause may appear at the beginning of a sentence or before any independent clause in the sentence.

EXAMPLES **While the orchestra tuned their instruments,** the stagehands checked the curtain.

My friends came over, and **as soon as we finished eating,** we cleared the table for a game of mah-jongg.

Reference Note

For more about **adverb clauses,** see page 90.

Exercise 6 **Correcting Sentences by Adding Commas**

For each of the following sentences, write the word that should be followed by a comma, and place a comma after it.

EXAMPLE 1. On your trip to Washington, D.C., last summer did you visit either the Library of Congress or the Folger Shakespeare Library?

1. *summer,*

1. When they had finished playing the musicians moved their instruments offstage to make room for the dancers.
2. By the end of the second day of school nearly all of the students seemed to have found their assigned classrooms, teachers, and lockers.
3. Oh I meant to ask Gloria whether she had watched the Chinese New Year parade.
4. In the second half of the third quarter Johnson caught a twenty-yard pass and raced into the end zone.
5. After a lengthy discussion of the options the committee voted to reject both of the themes proposed for the prom and to seek fresh ideas.

┌ **TIPS** & **TRICKS** ┐

Generally, an appositive or appositive phrase that identifies or describes a proper noun is nonessential; an appositive or appositive phrase that tells *which one(s) of two or more* is essential.

NONESSENTIAL
An interview with Florence Cohen**,** **the well-known landscape architect,** will appear in the *Herald.*

ESSENTIAL
An interview with the well-known landscape architect **Florence Cohen** will appear in the *Herald.*

Reference Note

For more information about **appositives** and **appositive phrases,** see page 73.

6. Following the example of ancestors who had served in the Revolutionary War⌄Susie King served in the Civil War as a nurse.
7. Just as I came into the house⌄the phone rang.
8. Yes⌄we will be happy to refund your money.
9. To Linda⌄Ramón sent a video of his family in Puerto Rico.
10. Having taken the prerequisite course⌄Jason registered for the advanced section.

Interrupters

13k. **Use commas to set off an expression that interrupts a sentence.**

(1) **Use commas to set off nonessential appositives and appositive phrases.**

An ***appositive*** is a noun or a pronoun placed beside another noun or pronoun to identify or describe it. An ***appositive phrase*** consists of an appositive and its modifiers.

A ***nonessential*** (or ***nonrestrictive***) appositive or appositive phrase provides information that is unnecessary to the meaning of the sentence. In other words, the basic meaning of the sentence is the same, with or without the appositive or appositive phrase.

EXAMPLES   An interview with Florence Cohen**,** **the well-known landscape architect,** will appear in the *Herald.*

Sipa**,** **a game similar to volleyball,** is a popular sport in the Philippines.

An ***essential*** (or ***restrictive***) appositive adds information that makes the noun or pronoun it identifies or describes more specific. In other words, without the appositive, the sentence loses necessary information or changes meaning. Therefore, an essential appositive should not be set off by commas.

EXAMPLES   We are studying the works by the landscape artist **Fernando Amorsolo.**

James Baldwin wrote the novel ***Go Tell It on the Mountain.***

(2) **Words used in direct address are set off by commas.**

A ***noun of direct address*** is a word that names the person or persons being spoken to.

EXAMPLES   Will you explain to the class, **Lena,** how you solved the
            last problem?

            Dexter, please help your brother set the table.

            You seem upset, **my friend.**

(3) Parenthetical expressions are set off by commas.

A *parenthetical expression* is a side remark that adds information or
shows a relationship between ideas.

Commonly Used Parenthetical Expressions		
after all	I believe	naturally
at any rate	incidentally	nevertheless
by the way	in fact	of course
consequently	in general	on the contrary
for example	in the first place	on the other hand
for instance	meanwhile	that is
however	moreover	therefore

EXAMPLES   The train heading toward Edinburgh will, **I am sure,**
            be on time today.

            On the contrary, exercise is relaxing.

            Jameson was the first of the senior students to solve the
            puzzle, **naturally.**

Some of these expressions are not always parenthetical. When an
expression is not used parenthetically, it is not set off by commas.

EXAMPLES   My grandfather, **by the way,** created these colorful sand
            paintings. [parenthetical, meaning "incidentally"]

            We could see **by the way** Melinda worked that she wanted
            to do her best. [not parenthetical, meaning "by the manner
            in which"]

NOTE A contrasting expression introduced by *not* is parenthetical and
should be set off by commas.

EXAMPLE   Frank Robinson, **not Jackie Robinson,** was the first African
           American to manage a major-league baseball team.

Reference Note

Some parenthetical
expressions, such as
*consequently, however,
moreover,* and *therefore,*
are **conjunctive
adverbs.** See page 356.

Reference Note

Parentheses and **dashes**
are sometimes used to set
off parenthetical expres-
sions. See page 384.

RETEACHING

Parenthetical Expressions
Activity. Students may have difficulty grasping the concept of parenthetical expressions if they do not
use them in their own writing. Assign
each student an expression from the
list on this page. Each student should
write a sentence using his or her
assigned expression. Students can
then read their sentences aloud in
turn as the class identifies the parenthetical expression in each sentence.

MECHANICS

RETEACHING

Uses of Commas

To help students visualize some of the uses of commas, show examples of comma usage in four columns on the chalkboard. Label the columns *independent clauses, nonessential clauses, introductory elements,* and *interrupters.* Then, work with students to generate examples of each usage, and write the examples under the appropriate headings on the chalkboard.

Exercise 7 **Correcting Sentences by Adding Commas**

For the following sentences, write each word that should be followed by a comma, and place a comma after it. If a sentence is already correct, write *C*.

EXAMPLE **1.** My take-home pay at any rate is less than yours.

　　　1. pay, rate,

1. The Red Sea, not the Black Sea, separates Northeast Africa and the Arabian Peninsula.
2. My father's youngest sister, Pilar, is an architect in New Orleans.
3. The future, of course, is largely in your hands.
4. Certainly, well-nourished babies have a better chance of surviving infancy, Thomas.
5. Call Felipe as soon as you can, Hope.
6. A rose window, by the way, resembles an open rose.
7. The Chiricahua Apache leader Geronimo took part in President Theodore Roosevelt's inaugural procession in 1901.　**7.** C
8. In college, however, students usually arrange their own schedules.
9. Alex Haley, the author of *Roots*, attributed his interest in writing to stories his grandmother and great-aunts told.
10. I believe the fairy tale "Cinderella" originated in ninth-century China.　**10.** C

Oral Practice **Correcting Sentences by Adding Commas**

Read each of the following sentences aloud. Then, for each sentence, say each word that should be followed by a comma. If a sentence is already correct, say "correct."　Optional commas are underscored.

EXAMPLE **1.** The students read William Shakespeare's *Hamlet* watched the most recent film adaptation of the play and discussed the similarities and differences between the two.

　　　1. Hamlet, play,

1. If you give us your application now, our office will process it before the deadline, which is this afternoon.
2. The plot of that book, a murder mystery, is far too complicated, in my opinion.
3. Ancient Mayan ruins, tropical rain forests, and beautiful mountains are just a few of the beautiful sights I saw in Guatemala, where my cousins live.

Learning for Life **Continued on pp. 347–349**

Writing an Article. Explain to students that in their adult lives, they may occasionally be called on to write articles. Even if students have no interest in a career in journalism, they may belong to organizations—unions or other professional organizations, neighborhood associations, book clubs, charitable organizations, and so on—that might ask their members to contribute articles. Ask students to write according to

4. Please understand, friends, that as much as I would like to, I cannot be at the picnic, the game, and the track meet all at the same time.

5. The people riding in the front seat of the roller coaster were the ones who screamed the loudest.   **5. C**

6. Hiroshi, whom you met last night, is an exchange student from Kyoto, a large city in Japan.

7. Looking for economical transportation, Harry, who had never bought a car before, nervously investigated all of the possibilities at Country Motors.

8. Before you start putting that jigsaw puzzle together, Rosa, make sure that all of it will fit on the table.

9. When Jamie had finished, the chicken and salad were all gone; the beans, carrots, and potatoes, however, had been left untouched.

10. In my opinion, *My Fair Lady*, not *Breakfast at Tiffany's*, is Audrey Hepburn's best movie.

Conventional Uses

13l. Use commas in certain conventional situations.

(1) Use commas to separate items in dates and addresses.

EXAMPLES Hawaii achieved statehood on August 21, 1959, and became the fiftieth state. [Notice that a comma separates the final item in a date (*1959*) from the words that follow it.]

Write to me at 423 Twentieth Street, Salt Lake City, UT 84101-0423, after the first of May. [Notice that a comma separates the final item in an address (*84101-0423*) from the words that follow it.]

Do not use a comma to separate

• the month from the date

EXAMPLE We began rehearsals on **June 20.**

• the date from the month when the date is given before the month

EXAMPLE After many years of foreign rule, the Philippines became an independent nation on **4 July 1946.**

• the month from the year when no date is given

EXAMPLE Did a severe storm hit Luzon in **October 1999?**

| COMPUTER TIP

If you use a computer, you may want to create a file of the parenthetical expressions listed on page 345. Refer to this file as you proofread your writing, and be sure that you have punctuated these expressions correctly. Use the search function to speed up your proofreading. The computer will search for and highlight each occurrence of whatever expression you select.

PRACTICE

Punctuation
Activity. You may want to have students practice using correct punctuation to complete various standard forms, such as applications for employment.

MECHANICS

the following prompt: "You belong to an organization that has asked you to write an article for that organization's newsletter. You are writing the article because you are the one who knows most about the topic—

either because you were an eyewitness to an event, because you have researched the topic, or because you are heavily involved in planning an activity." After students have selected suitable topics, have them

Relating to Writing

Have students write brief personal letters in which they demonstrate correct conventional comma uses. Ask for volunteers to share their letters with the class.

DIRECT TEACHING

Modeling and Demonstration

Unnecessary Commas. Model how to proofread sentences for unnecessary commas with the example *My brother, and I, both enjoy hiking, and last summer we spent a week, in Arizona, exploring the Grand Canyon.* First, ask if the comma between *hiking* and *and* is necessary. [*yes*] Then, ask why this comma is needed. [*A comma should be used before* and, but, for, nor, or, so, *or* yet *when it joins independent clauses.*] Next, ask if there are any rules requiring the other commas in this sentence. [*no*] Point out that no punctuation should be inserted when there is no rule requiring punctuation and when the sentence is clear without it. Now, have a volunteer use another example from this chapter to demonstrate how to proofread sentences for unnecessary commas.

- a house number from a street name

EXAMPLE   Their address is **531 Belmont Avenue,** St. Louis, MO 53308-3150.

- a state abbreviation from a ZIP Code

EXAMPLE   Is 1208 Elmhurst Drive, Seattle, **WA 43211-8614,** the correct address?

- items joined by prepositions

EXAMPLE   Joanna lives **at 301 Green Street in San Diego.**

Reference Note

Use a **colon** after the salutation of a business letter. For more about **colons,** see page 359.

(2) Use a comma after the salutation of a personal letter and after the closing of any letter.

EXAMPLES   Dear Angela,   Sincerely yours,

(3) Use a comma to set off a title, such as *Jr., Sr.,* or *Ph.D.,* that follows a person's name.

EXAMPLES   Peter Grundel, Jr.   Lorraine Henson, Ph.D.

NOTE Within a sentence, a comma appears both before and after a title following a person's name.

EXAMPLE   Hazel Sellers, M.D., will be the guest speaker.

Unnecessary Commas

13m. Do not use unnecessary commas.

Too many commas can be as confusing as too few. Use a comma only when a rule requires one or when the meaning of the sentence would be unclear without one.

CONFUSING   Amy, and I put a videocassette, and a fashion catalog in the time capsule.

CLEAR   Amy and I put a videocassette and a fashion catalog in the time capsule.

Exercise 8 Using Commas Correctly

Write the following sentences and word groups, adding and deleting commas where needed.

Learning for Life   **Continued from p. 347**

work in groups to make sure they can answer the *5W-How?* questions on their topics.

Remind students that the clarity of their articles depends not only on the information they use but also on the way in which they express themselves. Proper use of end marks and commas is important in making sure their readers understand what they write. Incorrect use of punctuation marks

     1. On our road trip from Durham North Carolina to Salt Lake City Utah we traveled through twelve states.

     1. On our road trip from Durham, North Carolina, to Salt Lake City, Utah, we traveled through twelve states.

1. Mr. Boyd still talks about the "blue moon" of March, 1998.

2. Sammy Davis, Jr., was one of the stars in that musical.

3. Our new apartment at 310 Columbia Avenue, Fort Wayne, Indiana, is comfortable; however, I wish we were still living at 2125 West Third Street in Omaha, Nebraska.

4. Did you and Maureen know that Jay Carson, Sr., arranged the benefit concert and helped with the financing?

5. In the summer of 1936, the library staff at the *Tribune* began recording copies of every issue from October 14, 1858, up to the most recent one.

6. Dear Aunt Judy,

7. That restaurant can be found at 2904 Barton Avenue, in Austin.

8. Yours truly,

9. My mother's diploma is dated 29 May, 1980.

10. Are you certain you addressed it to 4900 Elm Street, Kansas City, MO 64112-1278?

Review C   **Correcting Errors in the Use of Commas in a Paragraph**

Rewrite the following paragraph, adding, deleting, or changing any commas to correct each sentence that is incorrectly punctuated. If a sentence is already correct, write *C*.

EXAMPLE   **[1]** The Japan America Theatre is the performing arts stage of the Japanese American Cultural and Community Center in Los Angeles California.

     1. The Japan America Theatre is the performing arts stage of the Japanese American Cultural and Community Center in Los Angeles, California.

   [1] Since it opened in 1984, the theater has won worldwide acclaim for the quality and scope of its productions. **[2]** Those productions range from all-male casts (such as the one shown on the next page) performing works in the sixteenth-century Grand Kabuki tradition to U.S. premieres of contemporary works by leading Japanese choreographers. **[3]** The theater doesn't just book productions; it works closely with the artists, whom it presents. **[4]** In fact, according to the managing director for programs, between 60 and 70 percent of the theater's presentations

2. *C*

DIRECT TEACHING

Correcting Misconceptions

Unnecessary Commas. Some students may operate under the theory "when in doubt, add a comma." Explain to students that too many commas may be as troublesome as too few. Point out that oral language came before written language and that written language attempts to record the spoken sentence. Stress that commas are not placed arbitrarily; in general, commas are used to indicate a pause for breath. Encourage students to read their problem sentences aloud and to place commas where they would naturally pause for breath.

DIFFERENTIATING INSTRUCTION

Learners Having Difficulty

Activity. Have students look in newspapers and magazines for some examples of each type of comma usage discussed in this chapter. Students could then cut out the sentences that contain the examples and create charts containing those sentences. On their charts, students should label each comma according to which comma rule it exemplifies.

MECHANICS

---

can detract from the clarity of their articles. After they have finished writing, students could work with partners or in small groups to proofread each other's articles for standard use of end marks and commas. Finally, students could compile a booklet containing the revised articles or could display the articles in the classroom.

are developed in partnership with the artists. [5] In 1988, for example, the theater staged the first, Broadway-style Japanese musical, *Utamoro: The Musical,* which is Tako Izumi's story of the eighteenth-century woodcut artist Utamoro. [6] In order to make the work more accessible to American audiences, the Los Angeles production pared down the slang from the Tokyo version, emphasized movement and gesture more, and provided narration, and supertitles in English. [7] It also used more elaborate costumes, wigs, and masks, to convey the splendor of the Edo period. [8] Recognizing that outstanding art transcends national boundaries, the theater features performing artists of all nationalities. [9] In recent years, for example, both New York City's Theater of the Open Eye and the Los Angeles Chamber Ballet have performed there. [10] In addition, a few years ago the Indian sitar player Ravi Shankar, working with American musicians, created a composition incorporating classical Japanese instruments into an Indian musical form.

9. C

13

Numerals in brackets refer to rules tested by items in the Chapter Review.

1. [13a]
2. [13a, b(1)]
3. [13c(1), c]
4. [13e]
5. [13b, b(3), a, c(2)]
6. [13e, b]
7. [13a]
8. [13d]
9. [13b(3)]
10. [13e, a]

Chapter Review

A. Using Periods, Question Marks, and Exclamation Points

Rewrite the following sentences, adding, deleting, or changing punctuation as necessary.

1. The Andromeda Galaxy is the galaxy closest to the Milky Way.
2. Paolo wants to know what you are bringing to the party.
3. Yes! That was a spectacular touchdown!
4. Mr. Simon Clark, Jr. would like to speak to you.
5. "Have you ever seen *The Wizard of Oz*?" asked Tasha. "What a wonderful movie it is!"
6. Didn't Dr. Sanchez used to work for NATO?
7. The women's rights activist Anna Howard Shaw grew up near Big Rapids, Michigan.
8. Look out for that car!
9. Who first said, "A penny saved is a penny earned"?
10. We will meet you in front of the school at 8:00 A.M. tomorrow.

B. Correcting Sentences by Adding or Deleting Commas   Optional commas are underscored.

Most of the following sentences contain errors in the use of commas. Write the word preceding each error, and add or delete punctuation to correct the error. If a sentence is already correct, write *C*.

11. [13i]
12. [13k(2), f]
13. [13g, m]
14. [13j(4)]
15. [13j(1)]
16. C [13k(3)]
17. [13i, l(1)]
18. [13m]

11. We asked our class advisor, who had several suggestions.
12. Randy, please lend me some paper, tape, and paint.
13. It was a raw, blustery, night when Kahlil met me in Edgewater.
14. After she listened to the players' strategy, the coach nodded.
15. Yes, our second composition assignment is due tomorrow.
16. My theory, unfortunately, was disproved by new research.
17. Salim, who was born on Friday, September, 13, 1985, has never been superstitious about the number thirteen.
18. That our candidate was fighting a losing battle for political office, was evident to most of the campaign staff.

Chapter Review   **351**

ASSESSING

Monitoring Progress

Chapter Review. To assess student progress, you may want to compare the types of items missed on the **Diagnostic Preview** to those missed on the **Chapter Review.** If students have not made significant progress, you could refer them to **Chapter 16: Correcting Common Errors, Exercises 26** and **27,** for additional practice.

MECHANICS

RESOURCES

Punctuation

Review
■ *Language & Sentence Skills Practice,* pp. 291–293

Assessment
■ *Holt Handbook Chapter Tests with Answer Key,* pp. 25–26, 54

19. I had worked with her at the resort for three summers, and I admired her determination to put herself through college.

20. John Buse, the president of our class, asked me to sell tickets for the benefit concert.

C. Correcting Errors in the Use of Periods, Question Marks, Exclamation Points, and Commas in Sentences

Add, delete, or change punctuation to correct any of the following sentences that contain punctuation errors. If a sentence is already correct, write *C*.

21. [13e, k(2), b]
22. [13c(1), d]
23. [13j(2)]
24. *or* niece, P.J.,
    [13k(1), e, a]
25. C [13f, a]

21. Mr. Stanton, will you please give me a reference. ?

22. Ouch! Watch where you're going!

23. Hoping to meet Oprah Winfrey, we got tickets to a taping of her show.

24. My niece P.J. will celebrate her twenty-first birthday tomorrow.

25. Mom or Dad or Uncle Paul will cook dinner tonight.

D. Correcting Errors in the Use of Commas in Paragraphs

Optional commas are underscored.

Add or delete commas in the following paragraphs to correct sentences that are incorrectly punctuated. If a sentence is already correct, write *C*.

26. [13i, m]
27. C [13j(2)]
28. [13i, m, k(1)]
29. [13g]
30. [13i, m]
31. [13h]
32. [13k(1), i, m]
33. [13k(3), f]
34. [13j(4), k(1)]

[26] Sports medicine is a branch of medicine concerned with preventing and treating injuries, suffered during participation in sports. [27] Initially practiced by doctors working with professional sports teams, the practice of sports medicine has grown rapidly as interest in amateur sports and physical-fitness programs has increased.

[28] One ailment that doctors, who specialize in sports medicine, frequently encounter is tendinitis, the inflammation of a tendon. [29] Tendons are the tough, fibrous, inelastic tissues that connect muscles to bones or other body parts. [30] Tennis elbow is a form of tendinitis caused by straining the tendons, that attach the muscles of the lower arm at the elbow.

[31] You don't have to be active in sports to benefit from advances in sports medicine, for those advances are now being applied in the workplace. [32] Repetitive strain injury (RSI), a disorder caused by tendinitis, can afflict anyone, whose job requires performing the same motion hundreds or even thousands of times a day. [33] In fact, RSI strikes workers as varied as meat packers, word processors, fruit pickers, supermarket checkout clerks, and musicians. [34] Because permanent

disability can set in if RSI is left untreated͵physicians are teaming up with ergonomists͵scientists who adapt working conditions or the work itself to prevent injuries. **[35]** Employers͵ are finding that preventive measures are a sound investment͵not a waste of money, paying for them-selves many times over in increased productivity͵reduced turnover͵and lower medical costs.

35. [13m, k(3), f]

Writing Application
Using Commas in Instructions

Commas for Clarity   You and some friends are planning to study together for an important final exam. To make the study sessions more interesting, you have decided to create a game using the information to be covered on the exam. As you write the instructions for playing the game, include at least five adverb clauses. Be sure to use commas correctly.

Prewriting   First, write down several ideas for a game based on one of your school subjects. Then, decide which idea you want to develop. What are the rules of the game? Take notes for your instruc-tions. Arrange the information in an easy-to-follow order.

Writing   Begin by giving a brief, general description of the game. Then, give complete step-by-step instructions for playing the game. Be sure to explain the game clearly so that a reader can easily learn to play it from your instructions.

Revising   To help you evaluate your instructions, ask a friend to read them. Can your friend follow the instructions easily? As you revise, try to combine sentences to make the instructions more concise. Be sure you have used at least five adverb clauses.

Publishing   Read your instructions for errors in grammar, usage, punctuation, and spelling. Pay special attention to your use of commas with introductory elements, interrupters, and items in a series. You may want to publish your game by distributing the instructions to your classmates so they can use the game as a study tool.

Reference Note

For more information about **adverb clauses,** see page 90.

MECHANICS

INTRODUCING THE CHAPTER

- Although students may understand the uses of semicolons, colons, and quotation marks, they may need to refer to the material in this chapter for information on the uses of other punctuation marks presented.

- This chapter begins by explaining the use of the semicolon, the colon, italics (underlining), and quotation marks, Then, the chapter covers ellipsis points, apostrophes, hyphens, dashes, parentheses, and brackets.

- The chapter concludes with a **Chapter Review** including a **Writing Application** feature that asks students to write a short research report, using apostrophes correctly to form the possessive case.

- For help in integrating this chapter with writing assignments, see the **Teaching Strands** chart on pp. T24–T25.

Punctuation
Other Marks of Punctuation

Diagnostic Preview

A. Proofreading Sentences for Correct Punctuation

Each of the following sentences contains at least one error in the use of semicolons, colons, dashes, parentheses, ellipsis points, brackets, italics (underlining), quotation marks, apostrophes, or hyphens. Rewrite each sentence, punctuating it correctly. Hyphens are indicated by the $\wedge$ symbol.

EXAMPLE   1. Why did you wait until the last minute? asked my friend Tanya when I told her my problem.

1. *"Why did you wait until the last minute?" asked my friend Tanya when I told her my problem.*

Numerals in brackets refer to rules tested by items in the Diagnostic Preview.

1. [14g]
2. [14e(1), d]
3. [14t]
4. [14x]
5. [14j]
6. [14b]
7. [14m(6)]

1. When I read The Hobbit, my favorite chapter was the one in which Bilbo meets Gollum.
2. Among the members of the Fine Arts Commission who met in New York City were some very talented people:Diane Keaton, actress:Paul McCartney, musician:Paul Taylor, choreographer:and Lee Krasner, artist.
3. My brothers and sisters and I have been encouraged to be self$\wedge$reliant since we were children.
4. The rapid spread of the bacterial infection(see the time line and the map below)posed a grave puzzle to the medical experts.
5. "We're going to win this championship!" said the soccer coach to the newspaper sportswriter.
6. Paulette sent in her application before the deadline;however, she neglected to put a stamp on the envelope.
7. Finally, his mother said, "Well . . . . . . I guess it will be okay."

CHAPTER RESOURCES

Internet
- Web resources: go.hrw.com

go.hrw.com

Practice & Review
- *Language & Sentence Skills Practice,* pp. 299–331
- *Language & Sentence Skills Practice Answer Key,* pp. 117–126

Application & Enrichment
- *Language & Sentence Skills Practice,* pp. 298, 332, 333–334, 335
- *Language & Sentence Skills Practice Answer Key,* pp. 117, 126–127

8. "The packages sitting over there are your's," said Tamala.

9. Although the contract had not been renewed, the oil company made a delivery the customers complained when they received the bill.

10. The mayor-elect met for two hours yesterday afternoon with members of the Allentown Youth Council see the picture on page 17)

11. At Book Lore the bookstore where I work we sold twenty-seven copies of that book in one day.

12. I'll never forget the first time I read Walt Whitmans poem Song of Myself said Megan It made me think about self-acceptance in a new way.

13. Within the next three week's, new television stations will begin broadcasting from the following cities Kalamazoo, Michigan Salinas, California and Fairbanks, Alaska.

14. Helena knew the day would be less than perfect when she heard herself saying Don't forget to dot your ts and cross your is.

15. In 1813, Governor Claiborne offered a reward for the capture of Jean Laffitte (Laffitte 1780?–1826 was a pirate who in 1814 fought for the U.S. at the battle of New Orleans).

B. Proofreading a Paragraph for Correct Punctuation

Rewrite the following paragraph, punctuating each sentence correctly.
Hyphens are indicated by the - symbol.

EXAMPLE **[1]** A list of composers of extraordinary talent and I am sure most of you will agree would include Mozart, Bach, Beethoven, and Chopin.

1. A list of composers of extraordinary talent—and I am sure most of you will agree—would include Mozart, Bach, Beethoven, and Chopin.

[16] When you hear the word *composer*, you probably think of the world-renowned musical masters of long ago Mozart, Bach, Beethoven, and Chopin, among others. **[17]** However, you dont really have to think that far back the twentieth century also has produced some outstanding talents. **[18]** Youll probably recognize at least one of these modern composers George Gershwin, Benjamin Britten, Leonard Bernstein, Richard Rodgers, or Paul McCartney. **[19]** Yes, McCartney and other rock musicians have produced many memorable compositions for example, McCartney and his longtime composing partner John Lennon gave us such popular ballads as Yesterday and Michelle. **[20]** Richard Rodgers worked with the lyricist Oscar Hammerstein II on many projects including the following musical plays Oklahoma, South Pacific, The King and I, and The Sound of Music. **[21]** Leonard

8. [14n(3)]
9. [14a]
10. [14t, x]
11. *or* (the bookstore where I work)[14w, x, r]
12. [14j, o, n(1), k, j(7), j(4)]
13. [14n(2), e(1), d]
14. [14j, i, p]
15. [14y]

16. [14s, e(1)]
17. [14o, a]
18. [14o, e(1)]
19. [14b, k]
20. [14e(1), g]
21. [14g]

Entry-Level Assessment

Diagnostic Preview. The **Diagnostic Preview** has two parts which involve editing sentences for the correct use of semicolons, colons, dashes, parentheses, ellipsis points, brackets, italics (underlining), quotation marks, apostrophes, and hyphens.

The results of this preview will indicate students' skill levels by identifying which students have mastered the use of the less common punctuation marks and which students need a rule-by-rule explanation.

PRETEACHING

Lesson Starter

Motivating. Instead of having students read all the rules and examples and then take a test on them, you may wish to assign students the rules you want them to master. Review the rules with the class, and use the textbook for reference, or model the rules with examples related to a form of writing students are currently studying. Then, have each student write a composition in which he or she uses an example of each rule assigned. For easier grading, have students label each rule in their compositions.

Differentiating Instruction

■ *Developmental Language & Sentence Skills,* pp. 145–166

■ *Developmental Language & Sentence Skills Guided Practice Teacher's Notes and Answer Key,* pp. 37–41

Assessment

■ *Holt Handbook Chapter Tests with Answer Key,* pp. 27–28, 54

Diagnostic Preview   **355**

22. [14b]
23. [14n(1), a, g]
24. [14x, n(1), s]
25. [14g, t, k]

Bernstein, too, was involved in many musical productions, but perhaps his most famous is West Side Story. [22] Both Bernstein and Rodgers are known primarily for their Broadway musicals; however, much of their music is popular outside the theater. [23] Benjamin Britten, on the other hand, is often ranked as England's greatest technical composer; his difficult operas, such as Death in Venice, are performed only by highly skilled musicians and vocalists. [24] George Gershwin (1898–1937) was one of America's finest and best-loved composers. [25] He wrote the opera Porgy and Bess, which contains the all-time classic song "Summertime."

Semicolons

Rules 14a–d *(pp. 356–359)*

O B J E C T I V E

■ To correct sentences by adding semicolons

DIRECT TEACHING

Modeling and Demonstration

Semicolons. Model how to use semicolons correctly with the example *Josie is an excellent dancer; last year she won a national dance competition.* First, ask if there are two independent clauses in the example. [*yes*] Next, ask if the two clauses are joined by a coordinating conjunction. [*no*] Then, ask if the two independent clauses are closely related in thought. [*yes*] Ask if the semicolon after *dancer* is used correctly here. [*yes*] Explain that semicolons can be used between independent clauses that are closely related in thought and are not joined by a coordinating conjunction. Now, have a volunteer use another example from the chapter to demonstrate how to use semicolons correctly.

APPLICATION

Semicolons

Activity. Point out to students that semicolons connect closely related independent clauses. Give students practice with semicolons by having them write sentences that express cause-and-effect relationships. Write this example on the chalkboard:

> After the first race I trained harder and more frequently; at the starting line of the second race, I knew I could win.

Have students write their own cause-and-effect sentences with semicolons. Ask for volunteers to share their sentences with the class.

Reference Note
For information on **clauses,** see page 80.

Reference Note
For more information on **conjunctive adverbs** and **transitional expressions,** see page 95.

Semicolons

14a. Use a semicolon between independent clauses that are closely related in thought and are not joined by a coordinating conjunction *(and, but, for, nor, or, so, or yet).*

EXAMPLES   "No man is an island entire of itself; every man is a piece of the continent, a part of the main."

John Donne, "Meditation 17"

Three candidates have filed for the new commission seat; all of them have experience in public office.

Do not use a semicolon to join independent clauses unless there is a close relationship between the main ideas of the clauses.

INCORRECT   Madagascar is a small nation made up of several islands; for many years, scientists have studied this country because of its unusual wildlife.

CORRECT   Madagascar is a small nation made up of several islands. For many years, scientists have studied this country because of its unusual wildlife.

14b. Use a semicolon between independent clauses joined by a conjunctive adverb or a transitional expression.

A *conjunctive adverb* or a *transitional expression* indicates the relationship between the independent clauses that it joins.

EXAMPLES   The speech was long and repetitious; **consequently,** people in the audience began fidgeting in their seats and whispering among themselves.

RESOURCES

Semicolons
Practice
■ *Language & Sentence Skills Practice,* pp. 299–301
Differentiating Instruction
■ *Developmental Language & Sentence Skills,* pp. 145–148

"To excel the past we must not allow ourselves to lose contact with it; **on the contrary,** we must feel it under our feet because we raised ourselves upon it."

José Ortega y Gasset, "In Search of Goethe from Within, Letter to a German"

Commonly Used Conjunctive Adverbs

accordingly	however	moreover
besides	indeed	nevertheless
consequently	instead	otherwise
furthermore	meanwhile	therefore

Commonly Used Transitional Expressions

as a result	for instance	on the contrary
for example	in fact	that is

When a conjunctive adverb or a transitional expression is used between independent clauses, it is preceded by a semicolon and followed by a comma.

EXAMPLES The leaders of the two nations saw no hope for a settlement; **however,** they were willing to meet again.

The leaders of the two nations saw no hope for a settlement; **on the other hand,** they were willing to meet again.

When used within a clause, a conjunctive adverb or a transitional expression is set off by commas.

EXAMPLES The leaders of the two nations saw no hope for a settlement; they were willing, **however,** to meet again.

The leaders of the two nations saw no hope for a settlement; they were, **on the other hand,** willing to meet again.

14c. You may need to use a semicolon (rather than a comma) before a coordinating conjunction to join independent clauses that contain commas.

EXAMPLE Stephen Foster wrote many songs, including "Oh! Susanna," "Camptown Races," and "Beautiful Dreamer"; **but,** as I recall, he is best remembered for "My Old Kentucky Home."

When the independent clauses contain only one or two commas, the semicolon may not be needed. However, a semicolon is required when a sentence would be confusing without a semicolon.

Semicolons   **357**

MINI-LESSON Grammar

Classifying Sentences According to Structure. Remind students that a sentence containing two independent clauses is a compound sentence. If such a sentence also contains a subordinate clause, the sentence is compound-complex. For more information on sentences classified according to structure, refer students to **Chapter 4: The Clause.**

Use a semicolon between items in a series if the items contain commas.

EXAMPLES   Winners in the competition were Alina Murphy, first place;
             Jeff Bates, second place; and Eduardo Davis, third place.

             On our trip to South America, we visited Santiago, Chile;
             Bogotá, Colombia; and Lima, Peru.

Exercise 1

DISTRIBUTED REVIEW
For a review of complements, ask students to examine sentences 1 and 4 and to find a compound predicate nominative, an indirect object, and two direct objects.

1. Tony Fleming, Donna Lee Bryant, and Phyllis Ward—compound predicate nominative

4. father—indirect object; gifts—direct object; present—direct object

---

Exercise 1 **Correcting Sentences by Adding Semicolons**

Rewrite the following sentences, using semicolons where they are needed.

EXAMPLE   **1.** An allegory is a story in which the characters, settings, and events stand for abstract or moral concepts one of the best-known allegories is *The Pilgrim's Progress* by John Bunyan.

             1. *An allegory is a story in which the characters, settings, and events stand for abstract or moral concepts; one of the best-known allegories is* The Pilgrim's Progress *by John Bunyan.*

1. Performers in the show were Tony Fleming, trumpet and trombone; Donna Lee Bryant, clarinet and saxophone; and Phyllis Ward, drums and steel guitar.
2. The first Alaskans most likely traveled to North America from Asia around twenty thousand years ago; they may have been following caribou herds.
3. The new republic at once began increasing production and distribution of goods; furthermore, it also appealed to other nations for financial assistance.
4. I bought my father several gifts, including a book, a shirt, and a battery charger; but, to my dismay, I couldn't find a present for my sister.
5. Our dates of birth are as follows: September 27, 1969; September 2, 1957; October 27, 1967; and March 27, 1960.
6. Some scientists believe that once, long ago, all the earth's land was joined into one continent; that continent is known as Pangaea.
7. Savannas, which are valuable grasslands, may be found in tropical or subtropical climates; and, I believe, they are known variously as prairies, veldts, pampas, and chaparrals.
8. The expression "gung-ho," which is used to describe an exceptionally hard worker, was originally Chinese; U.S. troops made it their motto during World War II.

9. She bought a shirt, $19.98**;** jeans, $34.79**;** and socks, $3.98.

10. Louise has already been working on that spreadsheet for hours**:** however, we need to change the format.

Colons

14e. Use a colon to mean "note what follows."

(1) Use a colon before a list of items, especially after expressions like *as follows* and *the following.*

EXAMPLES The volumes in Edward Brathwaite's autobiographical trilogy are as follows**:** *Rights of Passage, Masks,* and *Islands.*

Central America comprises seven countries**:** Belize, Costa Rica, El Salvador, Guatemala, Honduras, Nicaragua, and Panama.

NOTE Do not use a colon before a list that serves as a complement or an object of a preposition.

INCORRECT We collected: blankets, canned goods, and clothing.
CORRECT We collected blankets, canned goods, and clothing. [The list is the direct object of the verb *collected.*]

INCORRECT The concert included performances by: Placido Domingo, Luciano Pavarotti, and José Carreras.
CORRECT The concert included performances by Placido Domingo, Luciano Pavarotti, and José Carreras. [The list is the object of the preposition *by.*]

(2) Use a colon before a long, formal statement or quotation.

EXAMPLE The Gettysburg Address, delivered by President Lincoln during the American Civil War, begins with these words**:** "Four score and seven years ago our fathers brought forth on this continent a new nation, conceived in liberty, and dedicated to the proposition that all men are created equal."

(3) Use a colon between independent clauses when the second clause explains or restates the idea of the first.

EXAMPLES Those hanging lamps are the most popular kind**:** They are inexpensive, available in many colors, and easy to install.

"A cutting word is worse than a bowstring**:** A cut may heal, but the cut of the tongue does not."

African proverb

Reference Note
For more information on **using long quotations,** see page 368.

Colons   359

Colons
Rules 14e, f *(pp. 359–362)*
OBJECTIVE
■ **To use colons correctly**

DIRECT TEACHING

Modeling and Demonstration
Colons. Model how to add colons to sentences by using the example *Central America comprises seven countries: Belize, Costa Rica, El Salvador, Guatemala, Honduras, Nicaragua, and Panama.* First, ask if the sentence contains a list of items. [yes] Next, ask if the list is the object of a preposition, since a colon should not come between a preposition and its object. [no] Then, ask if the list is the object of a verb, since a colon should not come between a verb and its object. [no] Therefore, the colon belongs after *countries* to signal that more information follows. Now, have a volunteer use an example from this chapter to demonstrate correct colon usage.

RETEACHING

Colons Between Clauses
Activity. Students may find that deciding when a colon is needed between independent clauses is difficult. Students often have difficulty telling when the second clause explains or restates the idea of the first. Simplify the matter for students by pointing out that a colon is appropriate when the second clause answers a question such as *why* or *how.*

Analyze with students the example sentences for **Rule 14e(3)** to show how the second independent clause in each sentence answers the question *why* or *how.* Then, have students work in pairs or small groups to compose two sentences, each containing two independent clauses joined by a colon.

MECHANICS

Colons   359

English-Language Learners

General Strategies. Students may not have a problem understanding the colon itself, but they might get confused when they try to use a colon with the expressions *as follows* and *the following*. It might help students to show them how the expressions are used in sentences.

1. NOUN + LINKING VERB + *as follows:*
   Supplies are as follows: . . .
                    or
   The qualities she admires are as follows: . . .

2. VERB + *the following* + NOUN:
   Bring the following supplies: . . .
                    or
   Learn to spell the following new words: . . .

NOTE The first word of a sentence following a colon is capitalized.

EXAMPLES Luisa felt a great sense of accomplishment**:** **S**he had successfully developed and printed her first roll of film.

It was a poor lunch**:** **T**he paper sack held a soggy sandwich, a bruised banana, and a few pieces of limp celery.

14f. Use a colon in certain conventional situations.

(1) Use a colon between the hour and the minute.

EXAMPLES 8**:**00 A.M.   9**:**30 in the evening

(2) Use a colon between a chapter and verse in referring to passages from the Bible.

EXAMPLES Proverbs 3**:**3   Ecclesiastes 3**:**1–8

(3) Use a colon between a title and subtitle.

EXAMPLES "Ghosts and Voices**:** Writing from Obsession" [article]

*Middlemarch***:** *A Study of Provincial Life* [novel]

*Billie Holiday***:** *The Golden Years* [recording]

(4) Use a colon after the salutation of a business letter.

EXAMPLES Dear Ms. Ayala**:**   To Whom It May Concern**:**

Dear Sir or Madam**:**   Dear Editor**:**

NOTE Use a comma after the salutation of a personal letter.

EXAMPLE Dear Grandma and Grandpa**,**

Exercise 2 **Using Colons Correctly**

Rewrite the following items, adding colons where they are needed.

EXAMPLE 1. Your assignment is to read the following poems "Ode on a Grecian Urn," "Ode to a Nightingale," and "Ode to the West Wind."

1. *Your assignment is to read the following poems: "Ode on a Grecian Urn," "Ode to a Nightingale," and "Ode to the West Wind."*

1. For a more thorough discussion of the woman who was pharaoh of Egypt, read *Hatchepsut***:***The Female Pharaoh.*

2. Two of my favorite stories from the Bible are the story of the battle between David and Goliath in I Samuel 17:4–58 and the story of the good Samaritan in Luke 10:25–37.

3. Groups of art students, all going to see Egyptian, Assyrian, and Greek exhibits, boarded the buses at 8:30 A.M. and arrived at the museum at 10:00 A.M.

4. She revised her report three times: She looked first at the content, then considered organization, and then read the report for style.

5. Our local paper is divided into the following five sections: news, features, business, sports, and classified advertising.

6. Not surprisingly, my mom, who was a big fan of *Star Trek* during the '60s, regularly watched *Star Trek: The Next Generation* in the '90s.

7. The chairperson rose and read the mission statement: "We dedicate ourselves to the education of young people and commit ourselves to providing them with every opportunity to prepare for tomorrow's world."

8. So far, I've lived in three places: Phoenix, Arizona; Williamsburg, Pennsylvania; and Sarasota, Florida.

9. Your reading assignment is as follows: pages 217–232, pages 275–302, and pages 335–410.

10. Dear Sir or Madam:

Review A — Correcting Paragraphs by Adding Semicolons and Colons

Rewrite the following paragraphs, adding semicolons and colons where they are needed.

EXAMPLE   [1] Arthur Mitchell was more than a talented ballet dancer He was a pioneer in the world of ballet.

      1. *Arthur Mitchell was more than a talented ballet dancer: He was a pioneer in the world of ballet.*

[1] Arthur Mitchell blazed new trails in the world of ballet: He became the first African American male dancer to become a permanent member of a major ballet company, the New York City Ballet, and he founded the Dance Theatre of Harlem. [2] As a young man, Mitchell studied tap dance, modern dance, and ballet at a special high school for the performing arts: the challenges of ballet especially appealed to him. [3] After graduation from high school in 1952, Mitchell enrolled in the School of American Ballet, part of the New York City Ballet; however, he continued performing modern dance with other companies.

MECHANICS

[4] Mitchell's fine technique and commanding style, evident in the photograph at left, were impressive consequently, he was invited to join the New York City Ballet in 1955. **[5]** Director George Balanchine admired Mitchell's talent as a result, Balanchine choreographed dances for Mitchell and cast him in many leading roles. **[6]** Among the New York City Ballet productions featuring Mitchell were these *Agon, Arcade, The Nutcracker,* and *Creation of the World.* **[7]** The company was often criticized for showcasing an African American dancer nevertheless, Balanchine remained adamant in his support for Mitchell.

[8] During his years with the New York City Ballet, Mitchell broke racial barriers, received much praise on foreign tours, and helped organize ballet companies in many countries and in 1968 Mitchell decided to form his own ballet company and school, which became the Dance Theatre of Harlem. **[9]** The ballet company quickly established a name for itself in fact, it is acclaimed throughout the world. **[10]** Critics and audiences have responded enthusiastically to such productions as the following *Creole Giselle, Fancy Free,* and *Firebird.*

Italics (Underlining)

Italics are printed characters that slant to the right. To indicate italics in handwritten or typewritten work, use underlining.

PRINTED   *The Once and Future King* was written by T. H. White.

TYPED   <u>The Once and Future King</u> was written by T. H. White.

14g. Use italics (underlining) for titles and subtitles of books, plays, long poems, periodicals, works of art, films, radio and television series, long musical works and recordings, videos, video and computer games, and comic strips.

Type of Title	Examples
Books	*Blue Highways: A Journey into America* *Wuthering Heights*
Plays	*The King and I* *Barefoot in the Park*
Long Poems	*I Am Joaquín* *The Song of Roland*

Italics (Underlining)
Rules 14g–i *(pp. 362–365)*

OBJECTIVE

- To correct sentences by underlining words that should be italicized

MECHANICS

DIFFERENTIATING INSTRUCTION

English-Language Learners
General Strategies. Because the textbook's use of the terms *underlining* and *italics* for the same treatment may be confusing to students, you may want to clarify the difference between these two terms. Explain that italics are used in publishing and word processing, and that underlining is used to indicate italics when writing by hand or when typing on a typewriter that does not have the capability of creating italic type.

COMPUTER TIP

If you use a personal computer, you may be able to set words in italics. Most word-processing software and many printers can produce italic type.

RESOURCES

Italics (Underlining)

Practice
- *Language & Sentence Skills Practice,* pp. 305–307

Differentiating Instruction
- *Developmental Language & Sentence Skills,* pp. 151–152

Type of Title	Examples
Periodicals	*San Diego Tribune*
	The New Yorker
Works of Art	*Nocturne in Black and Gold: The Falling Rocket*
	The Thinker
Films	*Hank Aaron: Chasing the Dream*
	The Maltese Falcon
Radio and TV Series	*The Lone Ranger*
	Seinfeld
Long Musical Works and Recordings	*Appalachian Spring*
	La Bohème
	Miracles: The Holiday Album
Videos	*How to Get Fit Fast*
	Animal Bloopers
Video and Computer Games	*Madden Football 99*
	Escape Velocity
Comic Strips	*Jump Start*
	Doonesbury

The titles of poems that are long enough to be published as separate volumes should be italicized. Such poems are usually divided into titled or numbered sections, such as cantos, parts, or books. The titles of these sections should be enclosed in quotation marks.

EXAMPLES   *The Faerie Queene*   "Canto IV"

            the *Iliad*   "Book I"

NOTE   The articles *a, an,* and *the* before a title are italicized and capitalized only if the article is part of the official title.

EXAMPLES   I found some good ideas in several back issues of **the** *Chicago Tribune* and ***The*** *Wall Street Journal.*

          Jason did not immediately understand that Swift's ***A*** *Modest Proposal* was a satire.

STYLE   **TIP**

On the cover page or title page of a paper of your own, do not use italics for your paper's title. However, if your title contains a title that belongs in italics, you will need to use italics for that part of the title.

EXAMPLES
   Shakespeare's Tragic Heroines [contains no title that belongs in italics]

   Cordelia in *King Lear:* A Daughter's Love [contains a title that belongs in italics]

   Be creative when giving your paper a title. Avoid using the title of another work as the complete title of your paper.

Reference Note

For information about **titles** that are not italicized but are **enclosed in quotation marks,** see page 369.

HELP

The official title of a periodical can usually be found in the masthead, the section of the newspaper or magazine that lists the publisher, the editor, the owner, and other information about the periodical.

Italics (Underlining)   **363**

DIFFERENTIATING INSTRUCTION

Learners Having Difficulty

Some students might have difficulty with the examples in **Rule 14g** because the items listed might not seem to have any connection to each other. Students may find it helpful to have an overall characterization of the rule governing the list—that italics are usually used for long works, while quotation marks are used for parts of works and short works.

You may wish to put the list on a large poster as a handy reference in the classroom and as an aid to visual learners, or let the students make posters for themselves.

MECHANICS

When words that should be italicized appear in a sentence that is already italicized, use roman letters for those words to contrast them with the rest of the italicized sentence.

EXAMPLE
(*Note: The class will have finished reading* Othello *before beginning the research project.*)

HELP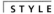

If you are not sure whether to italicize a foreign word, look it up in an up-to-date dictionary.

Do not use italics for titles of religious texts or of legal or historical documents.

RELIGIOUS TEXTS	New Testament
	Veda
LEGAL OR HISTORICAL DOCUMENTS	Treaty of Medicine Lodge
	Declaration of Independence

14h. Use italics (underlining) for the names of trains, ships, aircraft, and spacecraft.

Type of Title	Examples	
Trains, Ships	*Orient Express*	*Queen Mary*
Aircraft	*Enola Gay*	*Hindenburg*
Spacecraft	*Atlantis*	*Skylab 1*

14i. Use italics (underlining) for words, letters, symbols, and numerals referred to as such and for foreign words that have not been adopted into English.

EXAMPLES   The most common word in English is ***the;*** the letters used most frequently are ***e*** and ***t;*** and the numerals most often confused are ***7*** and ***9.***

The symbol ***&*** means "and."

According to the recipe, the pasta should be ***al dente,*** so be careful not to overcook it.

Exercise 3   **Correcting Sentences by Adding Underlining**

Rewrite the following sentences, underlining each word or word group that should be italicized.

EXAMPLE   1. Didn't Joseph Conrad write the novel Heart of Darkness?

1. Didn't Joseph Conrad write the novel *Heart of Darkness*?

1. Is the <u>Pietà</u> the only work Michelangelo ever signed?
2. For my birthday I received a print of Rousseau's <u>The Jungle</u> and a tape of the soundtrack for the musical <u>Cats</u>.
3. <u>Die dulci fruere</u> means "Have a nice day" in Latin, according to the book <u>Latin for All Occasions</u> by Henry Beard.

4. Chris Burke, who was born with Down's syndrome, became a successful actor in the TV series <u>Life Goes On</u>.

5. Frank Capra, a Sicilian immigrant, made such film classics as <u>It's a Wonderful Life</u> and <u>Mr. Smith Goes to Washington</u>.

6. Try to vary your transitional expressions; I counted five <u>so</u>'s on this page alone.

7. Mr. Lawrence, do you have the latest copy of <u>Popular Mechanics</u>?

8. Out of necessity, the USSR developed the world's foremost ice-breaker technology; the Soviet ship <u>Arktika</u> was the first surface vessel to reach the North Pole.

9. Last summer, Dad and Uncle Jim built an ultralight airplane that they call <u>Firefly</u>.

10. Whenever I try to write <u>&</u>'s, I end up writing cursive <u>S</u>'s.

Quotation Marks

14j. Use quotation marks to enclose a ***direct quotation***—a person's exact words.

Be sure to place quotation marks both before and after a person's exact words.

EXAMPLES   Eleanor Roosevelt said, **"**No one can make you feel inferior without your consent.**"**

          "People are trapped in history and history is trapped in them,**"** wrote the author James Baldwin in *Notes of a Native Son*.

Do not use quotation marks to enclose an ***indirect quotation***—a rewording of a direct quotation.

DIRECT QUOTATION   Natalie said, "My favorite singer is Whitney Houston."

INDIRECT QUOTATION   Natalie said that her favorite singer is Whitney Houston.

(1) A direct quotation generally begins with a capital letter.

EXAMPLE   In *Up from Slavery,* Booker T. Washington writes, "**S**uccess is to be measured not so much by the position that one has reached in life as by the obstacles which he has overcome while trying to succeed."

| STYLE   TIP |

Writers sometimes use italics (underlining) for emphasis, especially in written dialogue. The italic type shows how the sentence is supposed to be spoken. Read the following sentences aloud. Notice that by italicizing different words, the writer can change the meaning of the sentence.

EXAMPLES
"*Is* he going to buy the car?" Sharon asked. [Will he buy the car, or will he not?]

"Is *he* going to buy the car?" Sharon asked. [Will he buy the car, or will someone else?]

"Is he going to *buy* the car?" Sharon asked. [Will he buy the car, or will he just borrow it?]

Italicizing (underlining) words for emphasis is a handy technique that should not be overused. It can quickly lose its impact.

MECHANICS

Quotation Marks
Rules 14j–l *(pp. 365–371)*

O B J E C T I V E

■ **To correct sentences by adding quotation marks, other punctuation marks, and capitalization**

DIRECT TEACHING

Quoted Material
Activity. Ask students if they have ever heard a TV news anchor use the words *quote . . . unquote*. Discuss with students the importance of determining the exact wording of a person's statement and of attributing quoted material to the right person.

RESOURCES
Quotation Marks
Practice
■ *Language & Sentence Skills Practice,* pp. 308–312
Differentiating Instruction
■ *Developmental Language & Sentence Skills,* pp. 153–156

English-Language Learners

General Strategies. Students sometimes make mistakes when using the verbs *said* and *told*, resulting in sentences such as "He said me, 'Look out!'" Give the following examples of how these verbs differ, and lead students to see that *told* usually takes an indirect object.

1. He said, "Look out!" [*He told me that I should look out.*]

2. Maria said, "This is a good book." [*Maria told us that this is a good book.*]

Vietnamese. Though Vietnamese has no official conventions of punctuation, the language uses a punctuation system inherited from the French. Instead of using quotation marks, as English does, Vietnamese uses a dash in direct speech: —*I saw the game.* Quotation marks resemble marks used in French: << >>.

Students need to be able to identify quotation marks, to explain their uses, and to use those marks correctly in their own writing. Those students who do not write Vietnamese will learn punctuation much like English-speaking students do. Point out the use of quotation marks in books the students read in class, and provide students with exercises to reinforce the use of quotation marks.

When writing only a part of a quoted sentence, do not begin the quotation with a capital letter unless the person you are quoting capitalized it or it is the first word in your sentence.

EXAMPLES A film critic has called the movie "**a** futile attempt by the director to trade on his reputation as a creator of blockbusters."

I'm sure the expression she used in her essay was "**L**affite's exile."

"**M**y all-time favorite dish" was how Martha described the entree.

(2) When a quoted sentence is interrupted by an expression that identifies the speaker, the second part of the quotation begins with a lowercase letter.

EXAMPLE "When we do the best that we can," explained Helen Keller, "**w**e never know what miracle is wrought in our life, or in the life of another." [Notice that each part of the divided quotation is enclosed in quotation marks.]

When the second part of a divided quotation is a new sentence, it begins with a capital letter.

EXAMPLE "Please don't open the door!" Albert shouted. "**W**e're developing film."

NOTE When a direct quotation of two or more sentences is not divided, only one set of quotation marks is used.

EXAMPLE "Please don't open the door! We're developing film!" Albert shouted.

(3) A direct quotation is set off from the rest of the sentence by a comma, a question mark, or an exclamation point, but not by a period.

EXAMPLES "For tomorrow, please read the article about the Sherpas of Nepal**,**" requested Ms. Estevan.

"Who do you think is the current president of the Philippines**?**" asked Nathan.

"The Wildcats have upset the Rockets**!**" exclaimed the sportscaster.

NOTE Do not set off a quotation that is clearly an integral part of the sentence you are writing. Generally, such a quotation is a word or phrase that would require no pause before or after it.

EXAMPLE   In his speech, Enrique said that "one for all and all for one" is the key to a successful club.

(4) When used with quotation marks, other marks of punctuation are placed according to the following rules:

- Commas and periods are placed inside closing quotation marks.

EXAMPLE   "Generosity," said Nathaniel Hawthorne, "is the flower of justice."

- Semicolons and colons are placed outside closing quotation marks.

EXAMPLES   "Eva," my grandmother said, "you should keep up with your chores"; then she reminded me to vacuum.

Gail Sloan described the following as "deserted-island reading": *An Encyclopedia of World History,* the complete works of Shakespeare, and *Robinson Crusoe.*

- Question marks and exclamation points are placed inside closing quotation marks if the quotation is a question or an exclamation. Otherwise, they are placed outside.

EXAMPLES   The teacher asked me, "Where did you find this information about José Rizal?"

Someone behind me shouted, "Watch out!"

Did Franklin Roosevelt say, "The only thing we have to fear is fear itself"?

How proud and happy Colleen was when her supervisor told her, "You deserve a raise"!

NOTE In a sentence that ends with a quotation, only one end mark is necessary.

INCORRECT   Have you ever asked yourself, "Where will I be ten years from now?"?

CORRECT   Have you ever asked yourself, "Where will I be ten years from now?"

DIFFERENTIATING INSTRUCTION

Advanced Learners

Relating to Literature. Ask students how direct speech is written in the script of a play. You may want to review the text of a play to show students that quotation marks are not used to set off one character's words from another's. Then, contrast the dialogue in a play with direct quotations in prose. Point out to students that because everything in a play except the stage directions is a quotation, quotation marks are not needed. Only in prose, when quotations are mixed with descriptions, are quotation marks necessary to set off characters' speech.

EXTENSION

Relating to Writing

Activity. Divide the class into groups of three students each. Have students create imaginary situations in which they are defrauded, deceived, or shortchanged in a consumer transaction. Have each group role-play the encounter. Then, have group members collaborate on writing a complaint letter to a consumer protection agency, a newspaper consumer column, or the consumer advocate of a local TV station. Have students write the letter using both direct and indirect quotations to describe the transaction. One student in each group can be responsible for the role-play, another for writing the quotations, and the third student for writing the final draft of the letter.

(5) When writing dialogue, begin a new paragraph every time the speaker changes, and enclose each speaker's words in quotation marks.

EXAMPLE   "Don't stand chattering to yourself like that," Humpty Dumpty said, looking at her for the first time, "but tell me your name and business."

"My *name* is Alice, but—"

"It's a stupid name enough!" Humpty Dumpty interrupted impatiently. "What does it mean?"

"*Must* a name mean something?" Alice asked doubtfully.

"Of course it must," Humpty Dumpty said with a short laugh: " *My* name means the shape I am—and a good handsome shape it is, too. With a name like yours, you might be any shape, almost."

Lewis Carroll, *Through the Looking-Glass*

(6) When quoting a passage that consists of more than one paragraph, place quotation marks at the beginning of each paragraph and at the end of only the last paragraph in the passage.

EXAMPLE   "The engine cuts again, and then catches, and each time it spurts to life I climb as high as I can get, and then it splutters and stops and I glide once more toward the water, to rise again and descend again, like a hunting sea bird.

"I find the land. Visibility is perfect now and I see land forty or fifty miles ahead. If I am on my course, that will be Cape Breton. Minute after minute goes by. The minutes almost materialize; they pass before my eyes like links in a long slow-moving chain, and each time the engine cuts, I see a broken link in the chain and catch my breath until it passes."

Beryl Markham, *West with the Night*

A long passage quoted from a published source is often set off from the rest of the text. According to some style guides, the entire passage should be indented. When a passage is set off in this way, no quotation marks are necessary to indicate that it is a quotation. However, if there are quotation marks in the passage, be sure to include them.

EXAMPLE

```
    In the following passage, Markham uses
vivid imagery and intense verbs to draw the
reader into the action:
        The engine cuts again, and then
        catches, and each time it spurts to
        life I climb as high as I can get, and
```

```
        then it splutters and stops and I glide
        once more toward the water, to rise
        again and descend again, like a hunting
        sea bird.
            I find the land. Visibility is per-
        fect now and I see land forty or fifty
        miles ahead. If I am on my course, that
        will be Cape Breton. Minute after
        minute goes by. The minutes almost
        materialize; they pass before my eyes
        like links in a long slow-moving chain,
        and each time the engine cuts, I see a
        broken link in the chain and catch my
        breath until it passes.
```

(7) Use single quotation marks to enclose a quotation within a quotation.

EXAMPLES   Mrs. Winters said, "Cristina, please tell us what you think Alexander Pope meant when he said, 'To err is human, to forgive divine.'" [Notice that the period is placed inside the single quotation mark.]

Mrs. Winters asked, "Do you think the moral of the story could be 'To err is human, to forgive divine'?" [Notice that the question mark is placed between the single quotation mark and the double quotation marks because only Mrs. Winters' words, not Pope's, are a question.]

How did Cristina respond when Mrs. Winters said, "Please explain what Alexander Pope meant when he said, 'To err is human, to forgive divine'"? [Notice that the question mark is placed outside both the single and double quotation marks because the whole sentence, not the words of Mrs. Winters or of Pope, is a question.]

NOTE Be sure to reproduce quoted material as it appears in the original. If the original contains an error, write *sic* in brackets directly after the error to indicate that you have not made the error.

EXAMPLE   The drama critic continued, "In Act III, the young soldier must chose [*sic*] between equally disagreeable alternatives."

14k. Use quotation marks to enclose titles (including subtitles) of short works, such as short stories, short poems, essays, articles and other parts of periodicals, songs, episodes of radio and television series, and chapters and other parts of books.

Reference Note

For information on using **brackets,** see page 385.

Reference Note

For examples of **titles that are italicized,** see page 362.

Quotation Marks   **369**

RETEACHING

Titles

Activity. To help students distinguish between titles that are italicized (underlined) and those that are enclosed in quotation marks, have them create guides they can keep in their notebooks to refer to when punctuating titles in their writing. List on the chalkboard all the categories of names and titles in the examples for **Rules 14g, 14h,** and **14k.** Have students copy the lists and illustrate their guides with pictures or icons.

EXTENSION

Relating to Listening

Divide the class into groups of three students each. In each group, have two of the students ask each other three or four questions and give answers while the third group member takes notes on the conversation. Then, have the three students work together to turn the notes into a dialogue, using quotation marks and identifying the speakers. Next, have the third student read the dialogue aloud while the other two group members listen carefully to check the passage for accuracy. Finally, groups could share their dialogues with the rest of the class.

STYLE TIP

Generally, do not use quotation marks for the title of a paper you are writing. However, if your title contains a title that belongs in quotation marks, you should use quotation marks for that part of your title.

EXAMPLES

King Arthur: Real or Mythical? [contains no title that belongs in quotation marks]

"Do Not Go Gentle into That Good Night": An Analysis of a Villanelle [contains a title that belongs in quotation marks]

Be creative when giving your paper a title. Avoid using the title of another work as the complete title of your own work.

STYLE TIP

Avoid using slang words in formal speaking and writing whenever possible. When using technical terms, be sure to explain their meanings. If you are not sure whether a word is appropriate or its meaning is clear, consult an up-to-date dictionary. If the dictionary labels a word *slang* or *colloquial,* it probably is inappropriate in formal speaking and writing.

Type of Title	Examples
Short Stories	"Raymond's Run" "Chee's Daughter" "The Necklace" "A Worn Path"
Short Poems	"My Mother Pieced Quilts" "The Eagle: A Fragment"
Essays	"A Child's Christmas in Wales" "Old English: Where English Came From"
Articles and Other Parts of Periodicals	"How to Choose a Career" "Water: Not as Cheap as You Think"
Songs	"We Are the World" "The Star-Spangled Banner"
Episodes of Radio and Television Series	"The All-Night Listener: A Mystery" "Secret of the Dead Sea Scrolls"
Chapters and Other Parts of Books	"The War in the Persian Gulf" "Biology: The Study of Life"

14l. Use quotation marks to enclose slang words, invented words, technical terms, dictionary definitions of words, and any expressions that are unusual in standard English.

EXAMPLES   In the drama club's latest production, Dylan plays the role of Lyndon, a "nerd."

The running of the bulls through the streets (one might say "bullevards") of Pamplona, Spain, is an annual event.

What do you mean by "looping" the computer instructions?

The name *Arkansas* is derived from the Sioux word for "downstream people."

What do Southerners mean when they say they are "fixing to" do something?

Exercise 4   Correcting Sentences by Adding Quotation Marks, Other Punctuation Marks, and Capitalization

Revise the following sentences, correctly using quotation marks, other marks of punctuation, and capitalization.

EXAMPLE 1. Jim asked have you read James Alan McPherson's story Why I Like Country Music.

1. *Jim asked, "Have you read James Alan McPherson's story 'Why I Like Country Music'?"*

1. How many of you, Mrs. Martínez asked, have studied a foreign language for more than two years?
2. Nice try, Donna, was what the coach said.
3. We should have started our homework earlier, said Beth; we have answered only three questions so far.
4. Where have you been? she asked.
5. It is said that someone once asked Bernard Shaw how old he was, and he answered, I'm as old as my tongue and a few years older than my teeth.
6. Can you please tell me, asked Mrs. Ross, how many syllables are in a haiku?
7. Was it Elizabeth Barrett Browning, asked Lani, who wrote the poem Cry of the Children?
8. My baby brother calls elephants elephanuts.
9. Would you let us hand in our research papers next week, Ms. Lewis? we asked; none of the books we need are in the library.
10. Alice whispered, thank you for lending me the article Is There Life on Other Planets?

Ellipsis Points

14m. Use ellipsis points to mark omissions from quoted material and pauses in a written passage.

ORIGINAL   At Lincoln, making us into Americans did not mean scrubbing away what made us originally foreign. The teachers called us as our parents did, or as close as they could pronounce our names in Spanish or Japanese. No one was ever scolded or punished for speaking in his native tongue on the playground. Matti told the class about his mother's down quilt, which she had made in Italy with the fine feathers of a thousand geese. Encarnación acted out how boys learned to fish in the Philippines. I astounded the third grade with the story of my travels on a stagecoach, which nobody else in the class had seen except in the museum at Sutter's Fort. After a visit to the Crocker Art Gallery and its collection of heroic paintings of the golden age of California, someone showed a silk scroll with a Chinese painting. Miss Hopley herself had a way of expressing wonder over these matters before a class, her eyes wide open until they popped slightly. It was easy for

Ellipsis Points

Rule 14m *(pp. 371–374)*

O B J E C T I V E

■ To use ellipsis points correctly in sentences

DIFFERENTIATING INSTRUCTION

English-Language Learners
General Strategies. Some students may have trouble deciding which words in a sentence or passage can be replaced with ellipsis points. It may be helpful to discuss summarization and the difference between general and specific details to help students understand when to use ellipsis points to replace unnecessary details.

MECHANICS

STYLE ✏️ **TIP**

When using ellipsis points, be sure to leave a space before, between, and after the points.

Reference Note

For information on using **brackets,** see page 385.

HELP 🛟

If you omit words from a quoted passage, be absolutely certain that you are not changing the meaning of the passage.

MISLEADING

"I astounded the third grade with the story of my travels on a stage-coach . . . in the museum at Sutter's Fort." [Galarza did not say or mean that he had traveled on a stagecoach in a museum.]

If you have any doubt about whether your omission changes the meaning, do not omit anything.

---

me to feel that becoming a proud American, as she said we should, did not mean feeling ashamed of being a Mexican.

Ernesto Galarza, *Barrio Boy*

(1) When you omit words from the middle of a sentence, use three spaced ellipsis points.

EXAMPLE   In his autobiography, Galarza recalls, "It was easy for me to feel that becoming a proud American . . . did not mean feeling ashamed of being a Mexican."

(2) When you omit words at the beginning of a sentence within a quoted passage, keep the previous sentence's end punctuation and follow it with the points of ellipsis.

EXAMPLE   Galarza remembers that his teachers encouraged him and his classmates to share stories about their families and backgrounds: "Matti told the class about his mother's down quilt, which she had made in Italy with the fine feathers of a thousand geese. Encarnación acted out how boys learned to fish in the Philippines. I astounded the third grade with the story of my travels on a stagecoach, which nobody else in the class had seen except in the museum at Sutter's Fort. . . . [S]omeone showed a silk scroll with a Chinese painting."

Notice in the above example that the *s* beginning *someone* has been capitalized because it begins the sentence following the ellipsis points. Brackets are used around the *S* to show that *someone* was not capitalized in the original passage.

(3) When you omit words at the end of a sentence within a quoted passage, keep the sentence's end punctuation and follow it with the points of ellipsis.

EXAMPLE   Miss Hopley herself had a way of expressing wonder over these matters before a class. . . . It was easy for me to feel that becoming a proud American, as she said we should, did not mean feeling ashamed of being a Mexican.

(4) When you omit one or more complete sentences from a quoted passage, keep the previous sentence's end punctuation and follow it with the points of ellipsis.

EXAMPLE   About Lincoln School, Galarza writes, "At Lincoln, making us into Americans did not mean scrubbing away what made us originally foreign. . . . It was easy for me to feel that becoming a proud American, as she [the principal] said we should, did not mean feeling ashamed of being a Mexican."

Notice in the previous example that the words *the principal* are included to identify *she*. The words are enclosed in brackets to show that they have been inserted into the quotation and are not the words of the writer.

(5) To show that a full line or more of poetry has been omitted, use an entire line of spaced periods.

ORIGINAL   I dream of Hanoi:
           Co-ngu Road
           ten years of separation
           the way back sliced by a frontier of hatred.
           I want to bury the past
           to burn the future
           still I yearn
           still I fear
           those endless nights
           waiting for dawn.

                      Nguyen Thi Vinh, "Thoughts of Hanoi"

WITH OMISSION   I dream of Hanoi:
                . . . .
                ten years of separation
                . . . .
                still I yearn
                still I fear
                those endless nights
                waiting for dawn.

(6) Use three spaced ellipsis points (. . .) to indicate a pause in written dialogue.

EXAMPLE   "Well, . . . I don't know what to say," Sarah answered.

Exercise 5 Using Ellipsis Points Correctly

Rewrite the following passages, omitting the italicized parts and using ellipsis points to punctuate each omission correctly.

EXAMPLE   **1.** This thief during the last months had broken into the sheepfolds of the neighborhood like a wolf, *had killed and dragged away his prey like a wolf,* and like a wolf had left no trace after him.

                      Isak Dinesen, "The Ring"

           1. *This thief during the last months had broken into the sheepfolds of the neighborhood like a wolf . . . and like a wolf had left no trace after him.*

⌐HELP──

Notice in the example to the left that each line of spaced periods is as long as the line of poetry above it.

⌐HELP──

You may keep or omit internal sentence punctuation, such as commas, depending on whether that punctuation is necessary to the meaning of the sentence with the omission.

EXTENSION

Critical Thinking

Analysis. When a student is writing a research paper, he or she will have to analyze sources of information for relevance to his or her thesis statement. Often, only a portion of the information is needed; sometimes, only part of a sentence will apply. Tell students to use as much information as is relevant to the topic and to replace unnecessary phrases and sentences with ellipsis points.

DIFFERENTIATING INSTRUCTION

Advanced Learners

Looking at Language. Have students consult dictionaries to find the etymology of *ellipsis*. Then, have them find the etymology of *elision*. Discuss with the class the odd coincidence of two words in English having related meanings and similar spellings but completely different origins.

TEACHING TIP

Exercise 5 You may want to point out to students that usage varies on whether to retain the comma before ellipsis points. Other punctuation may be used on either side of the ellipsis points if it is necessary to the sense of the passage.

1. It was nearly the time of full moon, and *on this account, though the sky was lined with a uniform sheet of dripping cloud,* ordinary objects out of doors were readily visible.

   1. and . . . ordinary   Thomas Hardy, "The Three Strangers"

2. The old native stood, *breath blowing out the skin between his ribs, feet tense,* balanced in the sand, smiling and shaking his head.

   2. stood . . . balanced   Nadine Gordimer, "The Train from Rhodesia"

3. In the world's broad field of battle,
   In the bivouac of Life,
   Be not like dumb, driven cattle!
   Be a hero in the strife!

   3. In the world's broad field of battle,
   . . . .
   Be a hero in the strife!

   Henry Wadsworth Longfellow,
   "A Psalm of Life"

4. Remember, I am not recording the vision of a madman. *The sun does not more certainly shine in the heavens, than that which I now affirm is true. Some miracle might have produced it, yet the stages of the discovery were distinct and probable.* After days and nights of incredible labor and fatigue, I succeeded in discovering the cause of generation and life; nay, more, I became myself capable of bestowing animation upon lifeless matter.

   4. madman. . . . After   Mary Shelley, *Frankenstein*

5. When the lights went on, little boys like a bevy of flies assembled around the lamppost for gossip and stories. *Elsewhere in a similar manner men gathered to throw dice or cut cards or simply to talk.* The spectacle repeated itself at each crossing where there was a street lamp ringed to a post.

   5. stories. . . . The   George Lamming, *In the Castle of My Skin*

Apostrophes

Possessive Case

The **possessive case** of a noun or a pronoun shows ownership or possession.

EXAMPLES   Alice Walker**'s** poetry   Crowfoot**'s** family

the students**'** suggestions   five dollars**'** worth

your opinion   my grandparents

MECHANICS

Apostrophes
Rules 14n–p *(pp. 374–380)*

OBJECTIVES

- To use apostrophes in forming possessive nouns and indefinite pronouns

- To proofread sentences and phrases for correct use of apostrophes

RESOURCES
Apostrophes
Practice
- *Language & Sentence Skills Practice,* pp. 314–321
Differentiating Instruction
- *Developmental Language & Sentence Skills,* pp. 159–162

14n. Use an apostrophe to form the possessive of nouns and indefinite pronouns.

(1) To form the possessive of most singular nouns, add an apostrophe and an *s*.

EXAMPLES   the senator**'s** comments   Charles**'s** grades

               tennis racquet**'s** size   player**'s** turn

> **NOTE** When forming the possessive of a singular noun ending in an *s* sound, add only an apostrophe if the noun has two or more syllables and if the addition of an apostrophe and an *s* would make the noun awkward to pronounce. Otherwise, add an apostrophe and an *s*.
>
> EXAMPLES   for goodness**'** sake
>
>   Achilles**'** battles
>
>   the Netherlands**'** exports

(2) To form the possessive of a plural noun ending in *s*, add only an apostrophe.

EXAMPLES   the girls**'** team   the Millses**'** backyard

              the winners**'** trophy   the governors**'** conference

The few plural nouns that do not end in *s* form the possessive by adding an apostrophe and an *s*.

EXAMPLES   those sheep**'s** wool   children**'s** playground

> **NOTE** Generally, you should not use an apostrophe and an *s* to form the plural of a noun.
>
> INCORRECT   Two of the novel's that Jean Rhys wrote are *Wide Sargasso Sea* and *Voyage in the Dark.*
>
> CORRECT   Two of the **novels** that Jean Rhys wrote are *Wide Sargasso Sea* and *Voyage in the Dark.*

(3) Do not use an apostrophe with possessive personal pronouns or with the possessive pronoun *whose*.

INCORRECT   We thought the top score was her's.
CORRECT   We thought the top score was **hers.**

INCORRECT   I have witnessed democracy at it's best.
CORRECT   I have witnessed democracy at **its** best.

Reference Note

For information about using **apostrophes to form plurals of letters, numerals, symbols, and words used as such,** see page 379.

MECHANICS

Apostrophes   **375**

Reference Note

For information about how to distinguish the **possessive pronouns** *your, their, its,* and *whose* from the **contractions** *you're, they're, it's,* and *who's,* see pages 413, 417, and 418.

	INCORRECT	Who's notebook is this?
	CORRECT	**Whose** notebook is this?

Possessive Personal Pronouns					
First Person	my	mine	our	ours	
Second Person	your	yours			
Third Person	his	her	hers	its	their	theirs

(4) To form the possessive of an indefinite pronoun, add an apostrophe and an *s.*

EXAMPLES **No one's** contribution was overlooked.

She consented to **everybody's** request for a class meeting.

Reference Note

For a list of **indefinite pronouns,** see page 10.

NOTE For the expressions *anyone else* and *somebody else,* the correct possessives are *anyone else's* and *somebody else's.*

(5) Generally, in compound words, in names of organizations and businesses, and in word groups showing joint possession, only the last word is possessive in form.

EXAMPLES father-in-law's hobby

the Economic and Social Council's members

Lewis and Clark's expedition

Reference Note

For information on **compound nouns,** see page 5.

When a possessive pronoun is part of a word group showing joint possession, each noun in the word group is also possessive.

EXAMPLE **Lusita's, Joshua's,** and **my** report

Reference Note

For information on **acronyms,** see page 330.

NOTE The possessive of an acronym is formed by adding an apostrophe and an *s.*

EXAMPLES NATO's membership   NBC's prime-time programs

(6) Form the possessive of each noun in a word group showing individual possession of similar items.

EXAMPLE **Maria Bethania's** and **Aster Aweke's** albums

MECHANICS

(7) Use an apostrophe to form the possessives of words that indicate time, such as *minute, hour, day, week, month,* and *year,* and of those that indicate an amount in cents or dollars.

EXAMPLES
a **minute's** work	five **minutes'** work
a **day's** rest	three **days'** rest
one **cent's** worth	five **cents'** worth

ME AND WALLY'S PRODUCE

maslin

"Sorry, but I'm going to have to issue you a summons for reckless grammar and driving without an apostrophe."

STYLE TIP

If a possessive form sounds awkward to you, use a phrase beginning with *of* or *for* instead.

AWKWARD
my sister's best friend's photograph

IMPROVED
a photograph of my sister's best friend

Exercise 6 Forming Possessive Nouns and Pronouns

Each of the following groups of words expresses a possessive relationship by means of a prepositional phrase. Revise each word group so that a possessive noun or pronoun expresses the same relationship.

EXAMPLE
1. a vacation of two weeks
   1. a two weeks' vacation

1. hats of the firefighters
2. dressing room of the star
3. job of my sister-in-law
4. character of a person
5. business of Jorge and her
6. speech of the mayor-elect
7. a pause of a moment
8. owner of the Doberman pinscher
9. highlights of the film
10. kimonos of the women
11. costumes of the matadors
12. worth of four dollars
13. admission prices for adults and children
14. prize of Ralph Bunche
15. sides of it
16. trip of Maria and Cam
17. a wait of an hour
18. responsibility of everyone
19. CD of the group Depression Glass
20. the charter of the Organization of American States

Apostrophes   **377**

MECHANICS

Exercise 6 Forming Possessive Nouns and Pronouns

ANSWERS

1. the firefighters' hats
2. the star's dressing room
3. my sister-in-law's job
4. a person's character
5. Jorge's and her business
6. the mayor-elect's speech
7. a moment's pause
8. the Doberman pinscher's owner
9. the film's highlights
10. the women's kimonos
11. the matadors' costumes
12. four dollars' worth
13. adults' and children's admission prices
14. Ralph Bunche's prize
15. its sides
16. Maria and Cam's trip
17. an hour's wait
18. everyone's responsibility
19. the group Depression Glass's CD
20. the Organization of American States' charter

EXTENSION

Relating to Writing

Activity. You could have students write short poems using possessive pronoun/contraction homonyms such as *their/they're, whose/who's,* and *your/you're.* Tell students to begin a new line each time they use one of these homonyms. You may want to write the following example on the chalkboard.

> You're too quick to give up
> Your dreams.
> They're here to offer you
> Their guidance.
> Who's going to reach
> Your dreams if not you?
> Whose dreams will you reach if not
> Your own?

DIRECT TEACHING

Correcting Misconceptions

Contractions. Some students may confuse the contractions and possessive pronouns that sound alike, such as *who's* and *whose* and *you're* and *your.* Suggest that students read aloud all contractions and possessive pronouns that they write as if they are two words. If the two words make sense in context, then the word is a contraction and should have an apostrophe.

┌─ STYLE ──────── TIP ─┐
Contractions are acceptable in most informal writing and speaking. However, many people consider them inappropriate in formal writing, such as school essays and business letters. Therefore, it is generally best to avoid using contractions in formal situations.

Contractions

14o. Use an apostrophe to show where letters, numerals, or words have been omitted in a contraction.

A **contraction** is a shortened form of a word, word group, or numeral in which an apostrophe takes the place of all the letters, words, or numerals that are omitted.

EXAMPLES

I am. . . . . I'm	they had . . . . .they'd
he has. . . . . he's	where is. . . . . where's
let us. . . . . let's	we are . . . . we're
of the clock. . . . . . o'clock	we have. . . . . we've
1950s. . . . . '50s	you will. . . . . .you'll

The word *not* can be shortened to *n't* and added to a verb, usually without any change in the spelling of the verb.

EXAMPLES

is not. . . . . isn't	has not . . . . hasn't
does not. . . . . . . doesn't	should not. . . . . . .shouldn't
do not. . . . . don't	were not. . . . . weren't
was not. . . . . wasn't	had not . . . . hadn't
have not. . . . . . . haven't	would not. . . . . . . wouldn't

EXCEPTIONS will not. . . . . won't   cannot. . . . . can't

Do not confuse contractions with possessive pronouns.

Contractions	Possessive Pronouns
It's [*It is*] time to go.	**Its** diameter is almost 2,290 kilometers.
It's [*It has*] been snowing since noon.	
Who's [*Who is*] the captain?	**Whose** umbrella is this?
Who's [*Who has*] been using the computer?	
You're [*You are*] late.	**Your** skates are in the attic.
They're [*They are*] in the gym.	We are learning about **their** customs.
There's [*There is*] only one left.	This equipment is **theirs**.

Plurals

14p. Use an apostrophe and an *s* to form the plurals of all lower-case letters, of some capital letters, of numerals, of symbols, and of words referred to as words.

EXAMPLES   *Hawaii* ends with two *i*'**s.** [Without the apostrophe, the plural of *i* would spell *is*.]

        Not many names begin with *U*'**s,** but the names of my oldest sister's favorite bands do—U2 and UB40. [Without the apostrophe, the plural of *U* would spell *Us*.]

        Jeremy's *No want to*'**s** are just a sign that he's a normal two-year-old.

        Make sure your *1*'**s** do not look like your *7*'**s**.

Writers sometimes add only an s to form the plurals of such items—except lowercase letters—if the plural forms cannot be misread.

EXAMPLE   Most of his grades this term are **Cs.**

Be sure to use apostrophes consistently.

EXAMPLE   The printed *T*'**s** look like *I*'**s.** [Without the apostrophe, the plural of *I* would spell *Is*. The apostrophe in the plural of *T* is included for consistency.]

> **NOTE** To form the plurals of abbreviations that end with a period, add an apostrophe and an *s*.
>
> EXAMPLES   Ph.D.'**s**   M.A.'**s**
>
>   To form the plurals of abbreviations not followed by periods, add either an apostrophe and an *s* or just *s*.
>
> EXAMPLES   VCR'**s** *or* VCR**s**   CD'**s** *or* CD**s**

Reference Note

For more information about forming the **plurals of abbreviations,** see page 406.

Exercise 7   **Proofreading for the Correct Uses of the Apostrophe**

Write the following phrases and sentences, adding apostrophes where they are needed. If an item is already correct, write *C*.

EXAMPLE   **1.** Hes sure those are *us*.
          1. He's sure those are u*'s.*

1. Its a pagoda, isn't it?
2. shouldnt be disrespectful
3. How many CPAs are here? **3.** [*or* C]
4. sand in its gears **4.** C

APPLICATION

Critical Thinking

Challenge each student to write a sentence that contains an apostrophe used to form the possessive case, an apostrophe in a contraction, and an apostrophe in a plural. [*For example, Mrs. Brown's students won't receive any A's unless they work hard.*] Students can exchange sentences and identify how each apostrophe is used.

PRACTICE

Guided and Independent

Exercise 7   You may want to use the first ten items in **Exercise 7** as guided practice and then have students complete the last fifteen items as independent practice.

HOMEWORK

5. She's wearing a sari, I'm sure.
6. If he lets you, you'll go, too.
7. His choices were the same
   as hers. 7. C
8. Let's see what's going on.
9. I've found it's no help.
10. could've fainted 10. C
11. What's its title?
12. Your handwritten *win*'s look
    like *urn*'s.
13. the tornadoes of '99
14. Who's on the bicycle?

15. How many *um*'s did you hear?
16. How many *i*'s are there in
    Mississippi? 17. [*or* C]
17. Did the *Titanic* send out *SOS*'s?
18. His grades in French are all A's.
19. Are these *l*'s or *I*'s?
20. It's lost its shine.
21. Back in '77, disco was popular.
22. Yes, we've called everyone.
23. Of course, you're invited!
24. Doesn't he have two Ph.D.'s?
25. Cross these *t*'s.

Hyphens

14q. Use a hyphen to divide a word at the end of a line.

When dividing a word at the end of a line, remember the following rules:

- Do not divide a one-syllable word.

INCORRECT   Alicia chose to write her report about the pli-
            ght of the homeless.

CORRECT   Alicia chose to write her report about the
            plight of the homeless.

- Divide a word only between syllables.

INCORRECT   Isn't Ethan running for student council presid-
            ent this year?

CORRECT   Isn't Ethan running for student council presi-
            dent this year?

NOTE Generally, if a word of more than one syllable contains double consonants, you may divide the word between those consonants.

EXAMPLES swi**m-m**ing   syl-lable

Similarly, as a rule, you may divide a word with an affix (prefix or suffix) between the affix and the base word or root.

EXAMPLES pre-heat [prefix]

          allow-ance [suffix]

Hyphens
Rules 14q–u (pp. 380–383)

OBJECTIVE

■ To hyphenate words correctly

DIFFERENTIATING INSTRUCTION

English-Language Learners
General Strategies. Students some-times do not know how to divide an English word into syllables, and this problem leads students to hyphenate improperly at the end of a line. Let students know that there are some basic rules for the division of words (one vowel sound per syllable; divide between a double consonant) and that they can always check in a dic-tionary for correct word divisions.

HELP

When you are not sure about how to divide a word, look it up in a current dictionary that shows word division.

RESOURCES

Hyphens

Practice

■ *Language & Sentence Skills Practice*, pp. 322–324

Differentiating Instruction

■ *Developmental Language & Sentence Skills*, pp. 163–164

- Divide an already hyphenated word at the hyphen.

INCORRECT   Hirohito was the emperor of Japan for six-
            ty-three years.

CORRECT   Hirohito was the emperor of Japan for sixty-
            three years.

- Do not divide a word so that one letter stands alone.

INCORRECT   Proofreading my report, I saw that I had o-
            mitted an important quotation.

CORRECT   Proofreading my report, I saw that I had
            omitted an important quotation.

CORRECT   Proofreading my report, I saw that I had omit-
            ted an important quotation.

14r. Use a hyphen with compound numbers from *twenty-one* to *ninety-nine* and with fractions used as modifiers.

EXAMPLES   **forty-two** applicants

about **three-fourths** empty [*Three-fourths* is an adverb modifying *empty*.]

a **two-thirds** majority [Here, *two-thirds* is an adjective modifying *majority*.]

two thirds of the voters [Here, *two thirds* is not a modifier. *Thirds* is a noun modified by the adjective *two* and the prepositional phrase *of the voters*.]

14s. Hyphenate a compound adjective when it precedes the word it modifies.

EXAMPLES   a **well-liked** author   an author who is **well liked**

a **world-renowned** composer   a composer who is **world renowned**

the **less-appreciated** services   the services that are **less appreciated**

NOTE   Some compound adjectives are always hyphenated whether they precede or follow the words they modify.

EXAMPLE   a **well-balanced** meal   a meal that is **well-balanced**

If you are unsure about whether a compound adjective is usually hyphenated, look up the word in a current dictionary.

STYLE TIP

The prefix *half–* often requires a hyphen, as in *half-life, half-moon,* and *half-truth.* However, sometimes *half* is used without a hyphen, either as a part of a single word (*halftone, halfway, halfback*) or as a separate word (*half shell, half pint, half note*). If you are not sure how to spell a word containing *half*, look up the word in a current dictionary.

Do not use a hyphen if one of the modifiers preceding a noun is an adverb ending in –ly.

EXAMPLE   a **highly polished** surface

14t. Use a hyphen with the prefixes *ex–, self–, all–,* and *great–;* with the suffixes *–elect* and *–free;* and with all prefixes before a proper noun or proper adjective.

EXAMPLES

ex-mayor	president-**elect**	**non-**European
self-control	mayor-**elect**	**anti-**Soviet
all-star	fat-**free**	**pro-**Canadian
great-grandson	sugar-**free**	**Pan-**American

14u. Use a hyphen to prevent confusion or awkwardness.

EXAMPLES   re-collect [prevents confusion with *recollect*]

de-icer [avoids the awkwardness of *deicer*]

Reference Note

For more about adding **prefixes** and **suffixes** to words, see page 398.

STYLE TIP

Although you may see a variety of spellings for some words (*reelect, re-elect*), the preferred style is to make most prefixes not listed in Rule 14t part of single, unhyphenated words.

EXAMPLES
biannual   reevaluate

semiarid   miniseries

COMPUTER TIP

Some software programs can evaluate your writing for common errors in the use of punctuation marks. Such programs can help you proofread your writing, but remember that they cannot find every error. You should still proofread your work carefully.

Exercise 8 Using Hyphens

Rewrite the following groups of words, adding hyphens where they are needed and correcting any incorrect uses of hyphens. If a word group is already correct, write *C*.   Placement of hyphens is indicated by carets. Word breaks may vary.

EXAMPLE   1. a self cleaning oven

1. *a self-cleaning oven*

1. almost two⌄thirds full
2. pre⌄Columbian artifact
3. well⌄spoken individual
4. a highly motivated employee
5. anti⌄imperialism   4. C
6. burrowing under the gro–
   und   6. ground
7. a new form of tran–
   sportation   7. trans-portation
8. stepped into the aren–
   a   8. are-na
9. one hundred fifty⌄five years
10. three fourths of the crowd
    at the fair   10. C

11. recreation of a historical event
12. building an adob–
    e house   12. ado-be
13. part⌄time job
14. one⌄fourth completed
15. great⌄grandfather
16. since she's a doctor of o–
    ptometry   16. op-tometry
17. treasurer⌄elect
18. a singer who is world famous   18. C
19. an anti⌄inflammatory ointment
20. a dictionary that is up⌄to⌄date

CONTENT-AREA CONNECTIONS

Science

Hyphens. Point out to students that scientists often use the same prefixes, roots, and suffixes repeatedly when naming similar compounds. Sometimes these common word parts are separated by hyphens and sometimes the parts are run together. Scientists may even use hyphens with numbers to differentiate among similar chemicals. Ask students to find examples of such scientific compounds. A good place to look is on the lists of ingredients on shampoo bottles or on the packages of over-the-counter medicines.

Correcting Paragraphs by Adding Italics (Underlining), Quotation Marks, Ellipsis Points, Apostrophes, and Hyphens

Rewrite the following paragraphs, adding italics (underlining), quotation marks, ellipsis points, apostrophes, and hyphens where they are needed. Hyphens are indicated by the ‸ symbol.

EXAMPLES [1] This is one of Georgia O'Keeffes paintings, isnt it, Anthony? asked Darla.

1. *"This is one of Georgia O'Keeffe's paintings, isn't it, Anthony?" asked Darla.*

[2] Anthony said Youve been studying, havent you?

2. *Anthony said, "You've been studying, haven't you?"*

[1] "This painting, <u>Cow's Skull: Red, White, and Blue</u>, really intrigues me; Im sure its extremely symbolic, Darla said. [2] What do you think of it?"

[3] Youve asked the right person, replied Anthony, because Georgia O'Keeffe is one of my favorite painters. [4] One biography of her, which is simply titled <u>Georgia O'Keeffe</u>, tells how shed collect horses and cows skulls in New Mexico and then paint pictures of them. [5] This well-known work, which she painted in 1931, is symbolic; the paintings colors represent O'Keeffe's pro-American feelings.

[6] "I like this photograph of O'Keeffe, too, Darla added. [7] Dont you think she looks extremely self-reliant and self-assured?"

[8] "Well, . . . thats probably an understatement, chuckled Anthony. [9] O'Keeffe, who was born in Wisconsin in 1887, developed her own independent style in art and life. [10] Shes best known for her abstract paintings, especially the ones of flowers and of New Mexico desert scenes, such as her painting <u>Ranchos Church—Taos</u>."

Georgia O'Keeffe, *Cow's Skull: Red, White, and Blue* (1952). Oil on canvas, 39½" x 35⅞". The Metropolitan Museum of Art, The Alfred Stieglitz Collection (52.203). Photograph © 1994 The Metropolitan Museum of Art.

Laura Gilpin, *Georgia O'Keeffe* (1953). Sat. neg. (P 1979.230.4297). © 1981, Laura Gilpin Collection, Amon Carter Museum, Fort Worth, Texas.

Hyphens   **383**

MECHANICS

Dashes, Parentheses, and Brackets
Rules 14v–y *(pp. 384–388)*

O B J E C T I V E

- To correct sentences by adding dashes, parentheses, and brackets

DIRECT TEACHING

Dashes and Parentheses
Motivation. Ask students to think of times they have given directions or told a story and have had to interrupt themselves briefly to explain something. Point out that they probably used hand gestures or words such as *anyway,* or they may have changed the tone of their voices to signal that they were adding something parenthetical to the main idea. Then, ask students what marks of punctuation serve the same function in writing as the gestures, words, or change in voice tone does in speaking. [*Students should name dashes and parentheses.*]

TECHNOLOGY TIP

Typewriters and some word-processing programs are not capable of making dashes. Instead, dashes are indicated by using two hyphens without any spacing before, between, or after them. If students are unaware of this convention, point it out to them and remind them of it when they proofread.

Some programs use a combination of keys to create dashes. You may want to make sure students know the key combinations for dashes if their software has that capability.

COMPUTER TIP

Many computer programs are capable of setting dashes. If your computer program does not set dashes, type two hyphens to represent a dash. Do not leave a space before, between, or after the hyphens. When you write a dash by hand, use an unbroken line about as long as two hyphens.

Dashes

Sometimes a word, phrase, or sentence is used parenthetically; that is, it breaks into the main thought of a sentence. Most parenthetical elements are set off by commas or by parentheses.

EXAMPLES   Jorge**, however,** had already finished his work.

Karina's idea **(that we each work on a separate part of the project)** made sense to all of us.

Sometimes, though, such elements call for a sharper separation from the rest of the sentence. In such cases, dashes are used.

14v. Use a dash to indicate an abrupt break in thought or speech.

EXAMPLES   The director of the film—I can't recall his name—said that there would be a sequel.

The truth is—and you probably already know this—we can't finish the project on time.

14w. Use a dash to mean *namely, in other words,* or *that is* before an explanation.

EXAMPLES   It was a close call—the sudden gust of wind pushed the helicopter to within inches of the power line.

Early Native American civilizations—the Mayan, the Incan, and the Aztec—relied on farming for their livelihood.

Parentheses

14x. Use parentheses to enclose informative or explanatory material of minor importance.

EXAMPLES   The late Representative Barbara Jordan **(Texas)** was on that committee.

The length of the Mekong River is 4,186 kilometers **(about 2,600 miles).**

Be sure that the material within parentheses can be omitted without losing important information or changing the basic meaning or structure of the sentence.

INCORRECT   Tina had been shopping (in that store) most of her life.
[The idea in parentheses is important to the meaning of the sentence.]

CORRECT   Tina had been shopping in that store **(Mr. Dan's)** most of her life.

A sentence enclosed in parentheses may fall within another sentence or may stand by itself.

(1) A parenthetical sentence that falls within another sentence

- should not begin with a capital letter unless it begins with a word that should be capitalized
- should not end with a period but may end with a question mark or an exclamation point

EXAMPLES   The largest island of the Solomon Islands **(see the map on page 453)** is Guadalcanal.

I hope I persuaded Alex **(is he a senior?)** to help us.

(2) A parenthetical sentence that stands by itself

- should begin with a capital letter
- should end with a period, a question mark, or an exclamation point before the closing parenthesis

EXAMPLES   The largest island of the Solomon Islands is Guadalcanal. **(See the map on page 453.)**

Alex asked me if he could help us. **(What do you think I said?)**

NOTE When parenthetical material falls within a sentence, punctuation should not come before the opening parenthesis but may follow the closing parenthesis.

INCORRECT   According to this article about Grandma Moses, (1860–1961) she began to paint in her seventies.

CORRECT   According to this article about Grandma Moses (1860–1961), she began to paint in her seventies.

Brackets

14y. Use brackets to enclose an explanation within quoted or parenthetical material.

EXAMPLES   Ms. Grayson was quoted as saying in her acceptance speech: "I am honored by this **[the award]**, and I would like to share the recognition with those who made my work possible."

MEETING THE CHALLENGE

Parentheses, dashes, and ellipses have conventional uses in various types of writing. Scriptwriting, for example, has specific uses for each of these types of punctuation. Explore some of these uses by examining a movie script, which you can check out of a large library or view online. What kinds of information do these punctuation marks indicate? Generalize about their uses; then, write a short skit and practice using these marks of punctuation as scriptwriters do.

ANSWER
Skits will vary. Students should notice that dashes and parentheses are used to indicate prop specifics and directions, while ellipses denote passage of time and scene-to-scene transitions, as well as pauses within dialogue.

DIFFERENTIATING INSTRUCTION

English-Language Learners
General Strategies. Some students may occasionally use a double subject. For example, the construction "My mother, she . . ." contains a double subject. Students who use this feature may have trouble telling the difference between a double subject and a parenthetical element. Point out that a sentence with a double subject is correct with either subject, but not with both.

Learners Having Difficulty
Activity. Encourage students to read sentences aloud to each other. Have the listener pay close attention to hear the drop in the reader's voice when he or she reads parenthetical expressions.

EXTENSION

Relating to Writing
Activity. Tell students that good writing is smooth writing; too many parenthetical expressions interrupt the flow of ideas. Divide the class into groups of three or four, and have each student write five sentences that contain too many parenthetical expressions. Then, have the group members exchange papers and rewrite the sentences to make them smoother, without losing any of the information in the parentheses. Each student can present to the group his or her original and revised sentences.

MECHANICS

Learning for Life   *Continued on pp. 386–388*

Creating a Newsletter. Explain to students that many organizations have newsletters that are produced by the members of the organization. Have students look at a number of examples of newsletters from companies, neighbor- hoods, interest groups such as the Sierra Club, and so on. If possible, invite a parent or community member who is involved in publishing a newsletter to speak to the class about the publishing process and about the importance of correct punctuation.

By a vote of 5 to 4, the Supreme Court overturned the lower court's ruling. (See page 149 **[Diagram A]** for a chronology of the case.)

Use brackets and the Latin word *sic* to indicate that an error existed in the original version of a quoted passage.

EXAMPLE   As one critic has said, "The publication of 'The Raven' in 1846 **[sic]** ensured Poe's lasting literary fame but did little for his immediate financial needs." [The publication date should be 1845, but the critic being quoted used the wrong year.]

Reference Note

For information on **italicizing foreign words and phrases,** see page 364.

Exercise 9 **Correcting Sentences by Adding Dashes, Parentheses, and Brackets**

Rewrite each of the following sentences, adding or replacing dashes, parentheses, and brackets as needed.

EXAMPLE   1. One of the most prolific writers of England's Victorian Period most of the nineteenth century was Charles Dickens.

1. *One of the most prolific writers of England's Victorian Period (most of the nineteenth century) was Charles Dickens.*

Answers may vary.

1. Dr. Percy Lavon Julian, who was born in Montgomery, Alabama, is noted for developing helpful drugs from this surprised me, too soybeans.

2. My cousin Matthew my father's brother's son plans to open an aerobics and yoga center on the north side of town.

3. Some offspring of famous performers Michael Douglas, Liza Minnelli, Jeff and Beau Bridges, and Jane Fonda, for example have established distinguished careers for themselves.

4. Christine was quoted as saying in her valedictory speech: "We seniors are not at an ending but a beginning, and it graduation marks an exciting time of change in our lives."

5. For the new course on government and society, students are required to analyze the nonfiction writings of Ayn Rand 1905–1982 and to read her novel *Anthem.*

6. The parenthetical annotation said, "(please direct your attention to Figure C page 764)."

7. Babysitters in my neighborhood all quake at the very mention of one name Tanyisha.

Learning for Life **Continued from p. 385**

Then, discuss with students some possible ideas for newsletters. Narrow the suggestions to a few of the most popular topics, and have students work in groups of four or five to produce newsletters. Using the community newsletters they studied as models, each group should make a list of tasks and divide the tasks among the group members. Encourage students to be creative and to invent the schedule and minutes of past meetings or to make up interviews with experts or authors.

8. "Wait until you meet Annie—oh, Annie, there you are," said Tom.

9. At this time, the power of Carthage (see Appendix III on page 579) rivaled that of Rome.

10. The word *pants* derives from the name of a character called Pantaloon—an old man in the commedia dell'arte whose preference for the garment became well known.

Oral Practice **Proofreading a Paragraph for Correct Punctuation**

Read aloud each sentence of the following paragraph. Then, tell where end marks, semicolons, dashes, parentheses, apostrophes, and hyphens are needed in each sentence. If a sentence is already correct, say *correct.*

Hyphens are indicated by the ∧ symbol

EXAMPLE   [1] Jim Thorpe 1888–1953 was named our nations most outstanding athlete for the first half of the twentieth century.

    1. Parentheses are needed around 1888–1953; an apostrophe is needed before the s in nations.

[1] As you can see in the picture at right, Jim Thorpe (his American Indian name was Wa-tho-huck) looked exactly like what he was—a strong athlete. [2] No discussion of Americas outstanding sports figures would be complete without reference to Thorpe, who in 1950 was voted the greatest athlete of the centurys first half. [3] He achieved unique feats in football, track, and baseball and, as I read recently, his strength and speed are legendary. [4] Born of Irish, French, and Native American heritage and reared in Prague, Oklahoma, Thorpe began **4. C** earning honors early in his life. [5] He was an all-American halfback for two years while playing for a local school and broke all previous records in winning the gold medals for the pentathlon and the decathlon at the 1912 Olympic Games, where he was hailed as the greatest athlete in the world. [6] Because hed already begun playing professional baseball, however, he was forced to return his medals a year later. [7] (They were restored in 1982 posthumously) [8] Thorpe spent six outstanding years in professional baseball, but he became best known as a football player who could do everything well—run, pass, catch, punt, and more. [9] He played professional football for more **9. C** than ten years. [10] In 1969, sixteen years after his death and on the National Football Leagues fiftieth birthday, Thorpe was named to footballs all-time all-professional team.

Students should use punctuation correctly in their newsletters. Descriptions from events or meetings might use quotation marks, brackets, and ellipsis points to report comments; lists might make use of colons and commas; and a summary of resources and other materials might contain italics (underlining) and apostrophes in possessive-case nouns and indefinite pronouns.

After students have worked individually to produce their parts of the project, have

EXTENSION

Critical Thinking

Metacognition. After students have completed **Review C,** have them analyze the processes they used to proofread a dialogue for correct punctuation and capitalization. Have partners work together to discuss and answer the following questions:

- Did you check one word at a time, or did you read an entire sentence or paragraph before starting to make corrections? Did this procedure work for you, and why?

- Did you note corrections of items that gave you trouble, in order to return to them?

- Did you refer to the rules in the textbook?

- Did you recheck your work to see if you may have overlooked a correction?

- What part of your procedure might you change to make your strategies more effective?

Review C Proofreading a Dialogue for Correct Punctuation and Capitalization

Rewrite the following dialogue, adding commas, semicolons, quotation marks, apostrophes, and capital letters where they are needed. If a sentence is already correct, write C.

EXAMPLE   **[1]** Roger thought to himself I think that Ms. Zimsky will be pleased with these business letters.

     1. *Roger thought to himself, "I think that Ms. Zimsky will be pleased with these business letters."*

1. C   **[1]** Feeling proud of himself, Roger Morton sat back for a moment. **[2]** Have you finished those sample business letters yet asked Ms. Zimsky, the typing teacher. **[3]** Yes Roger replied. **[4]** I think Ive improved the format, too. **[5]** See how much space Ive saved on each page!

6. C   **[6]** Ms. Zimsky glanced down. **[7]** These arent done the way they
8. C   are in the book. **[8]** Just do them that way for now. **[9]** You need to finish this chapter today, or youll be far behind. **[10]** Theres no time to talk about format.

11. C   **[11]** Embarrassed and tired, Roger later told his friend Annette about the incident.

     [12] Your problem she explained isnt that you improved the letters
13. C   its that you didn't get Ms. Zimskys permission first. **[13]** I learned that any time you want to change a procedure, no matter how great an improvement the change will make, you should first talk your idea over with the person who will need to approve it. **[14]** Try discussing your suggestions again when Ms. Zimsky has more time.

15. C   **[15]** Roger went back to the typing classroom after school, and Ms. Zimsky listened to his ideas.

     [16] Oh, I see what youre doing she said. **[17]** Its really a very good idea in fact, I'd like you to share it with the whole class tomorrow. **[18]** See you then, Roger.

     [19] See you tomorrow said Roger and thanks for listening, Ms. Zimsky. **[20]** If I think of any other improvements, Ill be sure to discuss them with you first.

Learning for Life

Continued from p. 387

them exchange work and proofread the work of their peers.

Groups can assemble their newsletters as separate printed pages stapled together or lay them out using a desktop-publishing computer program, complete with graphics and illustrations. Allow groups to present their newsletters to the class. Students may decide that they want to continue publishing a newsletter for a group or club.

Chapter Review

A. Using Semicolons and Colons Correctly

Most of the following sentences have either a comma or no mark of punctuation at all where a semicolon or a colon should be used. Write the <u>word preceding each error</u>, and add the semicolon or colon. If a sentence is already correct, write *C*.

1. William Faulkner is remembered today for such novels as *Light in August, The Sound and the Fury,* and *As I Lay Dying*<u>;</u>but, as I remember, during his lifetime he cowrote screenplays, including the scripts for *The Big Sleep, To Have and Have Not,* and *Land of the Pharaohs.*

2. My grandparents were born and raised in a little town in the south of <u>France</u><u>;</u>however, they speak English with only a slight accent.

3. Several people contributed to the <u>book</u><u>:</u>Dr. Newman, who did the <u>research</u><u>;</u>Ms. Lewis, who provided the <u>photographs</u><u>;</u>and Mr. Jung, who wrote the introduction.

4. The town has four landmarks: the town hall, the Baptist church, Butler Memorial Library, and the Sheraton House.

5. Some people can play musical instruments by ear without formal <u>training</u><u>;</u>others need years of lessons and practice to play an instrument well.

6. He was tired and greatly in need of a warm place to <u>rest</u><u>;</u>nevertheless, he refused to ask anyone for help.

7. The finalists for the Northwestern States Debating Team were from American Falls, <u>Idaho</u><u>;</u> Medicine Bow, <u>Wyoming</u><u>;</u>and Sunburst, Montana.

8. Stella has the following considerate <u>habits</u><u>;</u>knocking before entering my room and asking before borrowing my things.

9. Juanita went home right after softball <u>practice</u><u>;</u>she was expecting an important phone call.

10. I have applied for the following <u>jobs</u><u>:</u>delivery person for a greenhouse, dishwasher at a restaurant, clerk at a drugstore, and packer at a supermarket.

Chapter Review **389**

MECHANICS

B. Using Italics, Quotation Marks, and Ellipsis Points Correctly

Rewrite each of the following sentences, correctly using underlining (italics), quotation marks, and ellipses. Be careful to show the correct position of quotation marks in relation to other punctuation.

11. [14j]
12. [14k]
13. [14j, i]
14. [14j, g, h]
15. [14i]
16. [14j, g]
17. [14j]
18. • • • [14j, m(6)]
19. [14j, g]
20. [14j, j(7), j(4)]

11. "Do not rush into anything," Leroy warned, "that you are not willing to finish."

12. Marguerita said that "An Apology for Idlers," by Robert Louis Stevenson, is one of her favorite essays.

13. Emily asked, "Have you ever used the word ineluctable or ineffable in a sentence?"

14. "In his novel Moby-Dick," said Professor Donadio, "Herman Melville writes about life on the whaling ship Pequod."

15. Did you know that the word Texas comes from the Caddo language?

16. "I would like to read the magazine Computer Digest," Phoebe said, "because I want to understand more of the technical terms that are related to computers."

17. "I do not like that dress," Wanda sighed. "However, I will wear it to please my mother."

18. "Well," Kelly hesitated, and then said, "I suppose I could have done a better job."

19. "We will be rehearsing The Long Christmas Dinner for two more weeks," replied the drama coach.

20. "Then, a boy standing across the street yelled, 'Are you hurt?' David told the reporter.

C. Using Apostrophes, Hyphens, Dashes, Parentheses, and Brackets Correctly

Rewrite the following sentences, adding apostrophes, hyphens, dashes, parentheses, and brackets where needed. Answers may vary. Hyphens are indicated by the ‿ symbol.

21. [14v, r]
22. [14n(7), p]
23. [14n(1), r]

21. Everyone—this means you, too, Carla—needs to rest for twenty‿five minutes before we continue the hike.

22. After a minute's consideration, Mark realized that there were as many *s*'s as *i*'s in Mississippi.

23. The shop's plainly marked sale tags showed a one‿third discount on seasonal gift items.

24. We enjoyed Glenda's and Maraya's speeches more than anyone else's at the assembly.

25. My sister-in-law's reaction to her new computer's user-friendly features was relief.

26. The grain companies' vice presidents met recently to discuss marketing strategies for Europe. (See the article on page 3 of the Business Section.)

27. Can't you tell me which bicycle is Victor's and which one is hers?

28. One of the measures of distance in astronomy is the light-year, which is the distance light travels in a vacuum in a year (about 5,880,000,000,000 miles).

29. I think Poe (Edgar Allan Poe [1809–1849]) wrote the first modern detective story.

30. The results of our survey are—and let me be absolutely clear about this—rather distressing for the company's long-term prospects.

D. Proofreading Sentences for Correct Punctuation

The following sentences contain errors in the use of semicolons, colons, dashes, parentheses, brackets, italics (underlining), quotation marks, apostrophes, and hyphens. Rewrite the sentences, correcting each error. Hyphens are indicated by the ‿ symbol. Some answers may vary.

31. Traffic was stopped for the city's Dr. Martin Luther King, Jr., Day parade; consequently, a massive traffic jam developed.

32. One of my favorite Biblical passages is the story of Jesus and the Samaritan woman in John 4:5–42.

33. Since Bethany visited Europe last summer, she has been using foreign expressions such as bonjour and arrivederci.

34. "How long will it take for these three rolls of film to be developed?" I asked.

35. Our English class agrees that the short story "The Rockpile" by James Baldwin (1924–1987) is one of the best we have ever read.

36. Please turn up the radio; I'd like to hear the governor-elect's speech.

37. The confusion occurred because I thought that the briefcase was yours, not Dorothy's.

38. Very successful people, whether they excel in politics, the arts, or sports, are expert at self-motivation.

24. [14n(6), n(4)]
25. [14n(5), s]
26. [14n(2), x]
27. [14o, n(1)]
28. [14x]
29. [14y]
30. [14v, s]

31. [14n(1), b]
32. [14f(2)]
33. [14i]
34. [14j(4)]
35. [14k, x]
36. [14a, o, t, n(5)]
37. [14n(3)]
38. [14t]

39. [14v]
40. [14y, j(4)]

39. We might and, according to the tour schedule, should have a free afternoon in Rome, the first city on the tour.

40. The newspaper quoted Mr. Bowen as saying, "People who take it [Introduction to Auto Mechanics] usually are glad they did."

E. Proofreading Paragraphs for Correct Punctuation

Hyphens are indicated by the ‿ symbol. Some answers may vary.

Rewrite the following paragraphs, adding, changing, or deleting semicolons, colons, italics (underlining), quotation marks, apostrophes, hyphens, dashes, and parentheses as needed.

41. [14x, a, o]
42. [14v]
43. [14s, n(1)]
44. [14s, k, g]
45. [14n(1, 2)]
46. [14o, a, s]
47. [14n(1), g, b]
48. [14w]
49. [14e(1), n(1)]
50. [14d]

[41] The National Museum of American History (formerly the National Museum of History and Technology) is a fascinating place; its part of the Smithsonian Institution in Washington, D.C. **[42]** You may ask I know I did what makes the museum so fascinating. **[43]** The museum offers changing displays on various themes represented by extremely‿diverse artifacts of the United State's culture. **[44]** When we visited the three‿story building, we saw the actual flag that inspired Francis Scott Key to write "The Star-Spangled Banner" and a pair of ruby slippers that Judy Garland wore in the film The Wizard of Oz. **[45]** Another crowd pleaser was the museums collection of First Ladies' gowns. **[46]** Children shouldnt miss the Hands-On History Room; they can explore our history and culture there in well‿planned, creative ways.

[47] We spent all day looking for such cultural keepsakes as the Fonz's jacket from the television show Happy Days; however, there were also many scientific and technological displays to see. **[48]** One of these displays the Foucault Pendulum was almost impossible to overlook upon entering the building. **[49]** Some of the other scientific treasures were: Henry Fords Model T, our country's oldest working steam engine, cotton gins, and Samuel Morse's telegraph. **[50]** We also allowed time for such interesting displays as the National Philatelic Collection, which was especially popular with stamp collectors like my dad; a country store post office, which came from a West Virginia town; and a variety of other wonderful exhibits.

Writing Application
Using Apostrophes in a Report

Using Correct Punctuation   In biology class you have learned that a *community* is a group of living things that forms a system of production, consumption, and decomposition. Now your biology teacher wants you to observe a community and write a report on your findings. Here is your assignment:

- Identify a community of organisms, and form a hypothesis about how the organisms interact.
- Observe their interactions for at least ten minutes a day for several days in a row.
- Take notes on your observations.
- Decide whether the data you collect support your hypothesis.
- Write your hypothesis, observations, and conclusions in a brief report. (Be sure to use apostrophes correctly to form the possessive case of nouns and pronouns.)

Prewriting   Choose a community that you can observe easily. Record the date and time of each observation. After you have completed your observations, review your notes carefully. What tentative conclusions can you draw about how the community functions?

Writing   Write a draft of your report. State your hypothesis, present your observations, state your conclusions, and then explain how your conclusions differ from or support your hypothesis. Finally, write your report in formal English appropriate for scientific writing.

Revising   Check your draft against your notes. Do your conclusions follow clearly from your observations? Revise your report as necessary.

Publishing   Proofread your report for errors in grammar, usage, spelling, and punctuation. You may want to attach your report to poster board and illustrate it with photographs or drawings. With your teacher's permission, display your poster in the classroom.

Reference Note

For information on **formal English,** see page 262.

MECHANICS

Spelling
Improving Your Spelling

INTRODUCING THE CHAPTER

- This chapter focuses on spelling rules and strategies students can use if they are uncertain about the correct spelling of a word. The chapter also clarifies distinctions between words whose spellings and meanings are often confused. In addition, the chapter provides a list of **300 Spelling Words** that students can study and master over the course of a semester or year.

- The chapter concludes with a **Chapter Review** including a **Writing Application** feature that asks students to write a letter of application for a job.

- For help in integrating this chapter with writing assignments, see the **Teaching Strands** chart on pp. T24–T25.

Numerals and terms in brackets refer to rules and concepts tested by items in the Diagnostic Preview.

1. seventeenth/passed [15n; *passed, past*]
2. hopped [15j]
3. loaves/surely [15k(5), e, g]
4. fifth [15n]
5. personal [*personal, personnel*]
6. brief [15a]
7. conscience [15b]
8. toys/truly [15k(3), g]
9. clothes [*clothes, cloths*]
10. Who's [*who's, whose*]
11. compliment [*complement, compliment*]

Diagnostic Preview

Proofreading Sentences for Correct Spelling

Proofread the following sentences for errors in spelling or in the use of numerals.

EXAMPLE   1. The 3 mooses were startled by the plain roaring overhead.

     1. *three, moose, plane*

1. After the 17th boxcar past us, we knew we were in for a wait.
2. Oh, no, one of the mice must have hoped out of the cage somehow.
3. A half dozen loafs of raisin bread sat cooling on the kitchen counter; surly no one could be expected to resist just a little piece.
4. For the 5th time, the band's conductor raised his arms and said, "All together now."
5. Keep your personnel property safely locked in a drawer.
6. In my opinion, this issue could be resolved in a series of breif meetings.
7. Surely, your consceince will guide you through this situation.
8. Chris makes toyes that are truely clever.
9. These cloths that you made for us to wear in the play look quite authentic.
10. Whose next in line for tickets?
11. Be sure to complement Justin on his new glasses.

12. ~~I~~ of the miners refused to ~~waist~~ a moment and quickly filled cart after cart with coal.
13. Of course, Isaac and his friends will be ~~their~~.
14. ~~Its~~ almost time for the first hard frost of the season.
15. The plows were working hard to keep the roads clear, but the snow was falling ~~to~~ fast.
16. The ~~principal~~ of osmosis can be difficult to comprehend.
17. The corn is ready, but the ~~tomatos~~ are not sliced yet.
18. Why do some lowercase ~~as~~ look almost like upside-down ~~es~~?
19. I've never known friendlier people ~~then~~ your cousins.
20. As you probably ~~all ready~~ have discovered, sometimes an ~~ilogical~~ solution works best.
21. The parade will ~~procede~~ as planned.
22. Who said that the only sure things in life are death and ~~taxs~~?
23. Are they going to the movie ~~altogether~~?
24. The ~~morale~~ of the story is that you shouldn't judge a book by its cover.
25. Didn't the ~~Davis'~~ order ~~72~~ 8-foot sections of fence?

Good Spelling Habits

Using the following techniques will improve your spelling.

1. Pronounce words carefully.

EXAMPLES   ath•let•ic [*not* a•the•let•ic]

soph•o•more [*not* soph•more]

jew•el•ry [*not* jew•le•ry]

2. Spell by syllables. A *syllable* is a word part that can be pronounced as one uninterrupted sound.

EXAMPLES   prob•a•bly [three syllables]

dip•lo•ma•tic [four syllables]

co•in•ci•den•tal [five syllables]

3. Use a dictionary. Do not guess about correct spelling. Look up any words you are unsure of how to spell. Using a dictionary to check the spelling of one word may help you spell other words. For example, by checking the spelling of *criticism*, you will see that the word ends in *–ism*, not *–isim*. Learning this spelling may help you spell other words ending in *–ism*, such as *patriotism*, *skepticism*, and *socialism*.

12. One/waste [15l, m; *waist, waste*]
13. there [*their, there, they're*]
14. It's [*its, it's*]
15. too [*to, too, two*]
16. principle [*principal, principle*]
17. tomatoes [15k(7)]
18. *a's/e's* [15k(13)]
19. than [*than, then*]
20. already/illogical [*all ready, already;* 15d]
21. proceed [15c]
22. taxes [15k(2)]
23. all together [*all together, altogether*]
24. moral [*moral, morale*]
25. Davises/seventy-two [*or* 72 eight-foot] [15k(2), l]

─HELP─

If you are not sure how to pronounce a word, look in a dictionary. In the dictionary, you will usually find the pronunciation given in parentheses after the word. The information in parentheses often shows the sounds used, the syllable breaks, and any accented syllables. A guide to the pronunciation symbols is usually found at the front of the dictionary.

ASSESSING

Entry-Level Assessment
Diagnostic Preview. In the **Diagnostic Preview,** students are asked to proofread sentences for errors in spelling or in the use of numerals. The preview assesses understanding of all the rules of spelling presented in this chapter. You can assess students' responses to determine which rules students need to review.

PRETEACHING

Lesson Starter
Background. A review of dictionary and glossary skills may be helpful to students. To ensure that they understand dictionary abbreviations and other indications of pronunciation and meaning, you can create a simple key as a handout.

Good Spelling Habits
(pp. 395–397)

OBJECTIVE

■ **To divide words into syllables**

Differentiating Instruction
■ *Developmental Language & Sentence Skills,* pp. 167–182
■ *Developmental Language & Sentence Skills Guided Practice Teacher's Notes and Answer Key,* pp. 42–44

Assessment
■ *Holt Handbook Chapter Tests with Answer Key,* pp. 29–30, 54

DIRECT TEACHING

Spelling Strategies

Activity. You may wish to offer the following additional spelling strategies to students.

1. Periodically review spelling notebooks for duplicate entries. Duplicate entries might suggest that particular spelling rules should be reviewed.

2. Write particularly troublesome spelling words on index cards to post in prominent places.

3. Generate mnemonic aids. For example, you might use the sentence *We are weird* to help students remember that the word *weird* begins with *we*.

Modeling and Demonstration

Spelling Rules. Model how to spell correctly words that contain *ie* or *ei* by using the examples *brief, deceit, veil, foreign, protein,* and *friend*. First, ask what sound *ie* makes in *brief*. [*long* e] Point out that a word is spelled with *ie* when the sound is *long e*. Next, ask what sound *ei* makes in *deceit*. [*long* e] Explain that after *c* the *long e* sound is spelled *ei*. Point out that *ei* is also the correct spelling when the sound is not *long e*, or when the sound is *long a*. [*foreign, veil*] Show that *protein* and *friend* represent exceptions to these rules. Now, have a volunteer use another example from this chapter to demonstrate how to spell words with *ie* or *ei*.

STYLE TIP

Becoming a careful speller takes a little practice, but the results are certainly worth the effort. Because readers constantly base assumptions about writers on their writing, looking good on paper is important.

If, for example, a written passage contains misspellings, a reader may suspect that the writer was careless about other information in the passage. By correcting misspelled words, the writer helps to focus the reader's attention on what is being said.

---

4. Proofread for careless spelling errors. Always re-read what you have written so that you can eliminate careless spelling errors, such as typos (*trail* for *trial*), missing letters (*goverment* for *government*), and the misuse of words that sound the same (*except* for *accept*).

5. Keep a spelling notebook. Divide each page into four columns.

COLUMN 1   Write correctly any word you find troublesome.

COLUMN 2   Write the word again, dividing it into syllables and marking the stressed syllable(s). (You may need to use a dictionary.)

COLUMN 3   Write the word again, circling the part(s) causing you trouble.

COLUMN 4   Jot down any comments that will help you remember the correct spelling.

Correct Spelling	Syllables and Accents	Trouble Spot	Comments
emperor	em´•per•or	emper(or)	Pronounce clearly.
awfully	aw´•ful•ly	awfu(ll)y	Study rule 15e.

NOTE In some names, diacritical marks (marks that show pronunciation) are as essential to correct spelling as the letters themselves. If you are not sure about the spelling of a name, check with the person who has that name or consult a reference source.

EXAMPLES   François   d'Alembert   Muñoz   Lemaître

           Janáček   Dalén   Fu'ād   Rölvaag

Exercise 1   Spelling Words by Syllables

Without using a dictionary, divide each of the following words into syllables, inserting a hyphen between syllables. Be sure that the division of each word includes all the letters of the word. When you have finished, use a dictionary to check your work.

EXAMPLE   **1.** evacuate   Vertical lines indicate syllable divisions.

            1. e-vac-u-ate

RESOURCES

Good Spelling Habits

Practice

■ *Language & Sentence Skills Practice,* p. 337

1. annotate
2. similar
3. library
4. surprise
5. privilege
6. disastrous
7. quiet
8. embarrassing
9. perspiration
10. boundary
11. candidate
12. equipment
13. recognize
14. business
15. representative
16. entrance
17. accidentally
18. mischievous
19. government
20. unnecessary
21. establishment
22. unnerving
23. attempt
24. happiness
25. modern

Spelling Rules

ie and *ei*

15a. Write *ie* when the sound is long *e*, except after *c*.

EXAMPLES th**ie**f   bel**ie**ve   c**ei**ling   rec**ei**ve   dec**ei**ve

EXCEPTIONS s**ei**ze   **ei**ther   l**ei**sure   n**ei**ther   prot**ei**n

15b. Write *ei* when the sound is not long *e*, especially when the sound is long *a*.

EXAMPLES forf**ei**t   n**ei**ghbor   fr**ei**ght   h**ei**ght   w**ei**gh

EXCEPTIONS anc**ie**nt   consc**ie**nce   misch**ie**f   fr**ie**nd   rev**ie**w

B.C. by Johnny Hart. By permission of Johnny Hart and Creators Syndicate.

MECHANICS

Spelling Rules
Rules 15a–o *(pp. 397–409)*

OBJECTIVES

- To spell correctly *ie* and *ei* words
- To spell correctly words with prefixes and suffixes
- To spell correctly the plural forms of nouns
- To use correctly numbers in sentences

DIFFERENTIATING INSTRUCTION

Learners Having Difficulty
Many students will benefit from hearing words pronounced and spelled aloud. To help students spell syllable by syllable, they can emphasize syllable breaks as they read aloud.

Learners Having Difficulty
Activity. Encourage students to create rhymes about particular spelling rules, using the old standard "*i* before *e*" rhyme as a model:

I before *e* except after *c*
or when sounded like *a*
as in *neighbor* and *weigh*.

Students can share their rhymes with the class or display them on a bulletin board.

MECHANICS

DIRECT TEACHING

Prefixes

To help students expand their vocabularies and improve their spelling, have them learn the meanings of prefixes. The following prefixes are grouped according to meaning.

Prefixes That Show Quantity

Prefix	Meaning
semicircle	half
unicycle	one

Prefixes That Show Negation

Prefix	Meaning
unhappy	not, lack of
disrespect	
misunderstanding	
antiwar	opposite or against

Prefixes That Show Time

Prefix	Meaning
forecast	before
predate	
postwar	after
review	again, repeated

Prefixes That Show Direction or Position

Prefix	Meaning
supervise	above, over
transport	across, over
coexist	together

You could have students suggest words containing these prefixes and then have them supply the words' meanings.

─HELP─

Different dictionaries show variations in spelling in different ways. To understand your dictionary's presentation of such variations, check the guide that explains how to use the book (usually found in the front).

When you look up the spelling of a word, make sure that its use is not limited by a label such as *British* or *chiefly British* (*flavour* for *flavor*), *obsolete* (*vail* for *veil*), or *archaic* (*spake* for *spoke*). In general, optional spellings that are not labeled, such as *cargos/cargoes*, are equally correct.

NOTE Rules 15a and 15b apply only when the *i* and the *e* are in the same syllable.

Exercise 2 Spelling *ie* and *ei* Words

Spell each of the following words correctly by supplying *ie* or *ei*.

EXAMPLE 1. f . . . ld
1. *field*

1. for . ei . gn
2. br . ie . f
3. rel . ie . ve
4. s . ie . ge
5. v . ei . l
6. n . ie . ce
7. sl . ei . gh
8. gr . ie . f
9. p . ie . ce
10. retr . ie . ve

11. counterf . ei . t
12. ach . ie . ve
13. handkerch . ie . f
14. perc . ei . ve
15. conc . ei . ve
16. . ei . ther
17. rec . ei . pt
18. bel . ie . f
19. f . ie . nd
20. ch . ie . f

21. sold . ie . r
22. h . ei . r
23. sh . ie . ld
24. s . ei . ze
25. c . ei . ling

–cede, –ceed, and –sede

15c. The only English word that ends in *–sede* is *supersede.* The only words ending in *–ceed* are *exceed, proceed,* and *succeed.* Most other words with this sound end in *–cede.*

EXAMPLES ac**cede** con**cede** inter**cede**
pre**cede** re**cede** se**cede**

Adding Prefixes

A ***prefix*** is a letter or group of letters added to the beginning of a word to create a new word that has a different meaning.

15d. When adding a prefix, do not change the spelling of the original word.

EXAMPLES a + moral = a**moral** il + legal = il**legal**
mis + spell = mis**spell** in + elegant = in**elegant**
re + print = re**print** im + movable = im**movable**
over + rule = over**rule** un + necessary = un**necessary**

398 Chapter 15 Spelling

398 Spelling

Adding Suffixes

A *suffix* is a letter or group of letters added to the end of a word to create a new word with a different meaning.

15e. When adding the suffix *–ness* or *–ly,* do not change the spelling of the original word.

EXAMPLES
mean + ness = **mean**ness	royal + ly = **royal**ly
open + ness = **open**ness	social + ly = **social**ly
dry + ness = **dry**ness	sly + ly = **sly**ly

EXCEPTIONS For most words that have two or more syllables and end in *y,* change the *y* to *i* before adding *–ness* or *–ly:*

heavy + ness = heav**iness**	steady + ly = stead**ily**
happy + ness = happ**iness**	busy + ly = bus**ily**
empty + ness = empt**iness**	easy + ly = eas**ily**

Exercise 3 Spelling Words with Prefixes and Suffixes

Spell correctly each of the following words, adding the prefix or suffix given.

EXAMPLES
1. un + known
  1. unknown
2. happy + ness
  2. happiness

Except for numbers 10, 20, and 23, the correct spelling of each word is formed by adding the prefix/suffix to the root word without changing the spelling of the root word.

1. over + rate
2. habitual + ly
3. green + ness
4. im + material
5. dis + appoint
6. mis + apprehend
7. practical + ly
8. un + abated
9. un + natural
10. silly + ness
11. il + legible
12. in + appropriate
13. dis + appear

14. mis + step
15. re + construct
16. in + animate
17. dis + similar
18. keen + ness
19. un + avoidable
20. merry + ly
21. dry + ness
22. actual + ly
23. happy + ly
24. safe + ly
25. thin + ness

10. silliness
20. merrily
23. happily

15f. Drop the final silent *e* before adding a suffix that begins with a vowel.

EXAMPLES   care + ing = **car**ing   use + able = **us**able

active + ity = **activ**ity   large + er = **larg**er

EXCEPTIONS   1. Keep the final silent *e* in most words ending in *ce* or *ge* before a suffix that begins with *a* or *o*: notic**eable**; courag**eous.** Sometimes the *e* becomes *i*, as in *spacious* and *gracious.*

2. To avoid confusion with other words, keep the final silent *e* in some words: *dyeing* and *dying, singeing* and *singing.*

3. mile + age = mileage

NOTE   When adding *–ing* to words that end in *ie,* drop the *e* and change the *i* to *y.*

EXAMPLE   lie + ing = l**ying**   tie + ing = t**ying**

15g. Keep the final silent *e* before adding a suffix that begins with a consonant.

EXAMPLES   use + less = us**eless**   care + ful = car**eful**

nine + ty = nin**ety**   amuse + ment = amus**ement**

EXCEPTIONS   nine + th = nin**th**   argue + ment = argu**ment**

true + ly = tru**ly**   awe + ful = aw**ful**

NOTE   Certain words that end with a silent *e* can drop or keep the final *e* when a suffix is added. Either spelling is acceptable.

EXAMPLES   acknowledge + ment = acknowledg**ment** *or* acknowledg**ement**

judge + ment = judg**ment** *or* judg**ement**

15h. For words ending in *y* preceded by a consonant, change the *y* to *i* before adding any suffix that does not begin with *i.*

EXAMPLES   funny + er = funn**ier**   twenty + eth = twent**ieth**

reply + ed = repl**ied**   reply + ing = repl**ying**

NOTE   Some one-syllable words do not follow Rule 15h.

EXAMPLES   dry + ness = dry**ness**   shy + ly = sh**yly**

15i. For words ending in *y* preceded by a vowel, keep the *y* when adding a suffix.

EXAMPLES   gray + est = gra**yest**   convey + ing = conve**ying**

                   pay + ment = pa**yment**   employ + ed = emplo**yed**

EXCEPTIONS   lay—la**id**   pay—pa**id**   say—sa**id**   day—da**ily**

15j. Double the final consonant before adding a suffix that begins with a vowel if the word both (1) has only one syllable or has the accent on the final syllable and (2) ends in a single consonant preceded by a single vowel.

EXAMPLES   slim + er = sli**mmer**   prefer + ing = prefe**rring**

                 excel + ed = exce**lled**   forget + able = forge**ttable**

Do not double the final consonant unless the word satisfies both of the conditions.

EXAMPLES   benefit + ed = benefi**ted** [*Benefit* ends in a single consonant preceded by a single vowel but does not have the accent on the final syllable.]

                 select + ing = selec**ting** [*Select* has the accent on the final syllable but does not end in a single consonant.]

When a word satisfies both conditions but the addition of the suffix causes the accent to shift, do not double the final consonant.

EXAMPLES   refer + ence = refe**rence** [*Refer* has the accent on the final syllable, but *reference* has the accent on the first syllable.]

                 prefer + able = prefe**rable** [*Prefer* has the accent on the final syllable, but *preferable* has the accent on the first syllable.]

EXCEPTIONS   excel—exce**llent**, exce**llence**, exce**llency**

NOTE The final consonant of some words may or may not be doubled. Either spelling is acceptable.

EXAMPLES   cancel + ed = cance**led** *or* cance**lled**

                 travel + ing = trave**ling** *or* trave**lling**

                 program + er = progra**mer** *or* progra**mmer**

If you are not sure whether you should double the final consonant, consult a dictionary.

MEETING THE CHALLENGE

Some words are intentionally misspelled in ads and product names. You've probably seen supermarket products listed as "lite," and you may occasionally take advantage of a "drive-thru window." Spend some time looking for deliberate misspellings, listing those you see. Compile your list with other students' findings; then, discuss these questions: What do advertisers gain by intentionally misspelling words? What do advertisers risk?

ANSWER
Lists will vary, but students should note that advertisers use misspellings to catch readers' attention, to simplify language for less proficient readers, and to avoid duplicating other product names. These advertisers risk losing sales to readers who are annoyed by the misspellings.

MECHANICS

Exercise 4 Spelling Words with Suffixes

ANSWERS

1. deferred
2. deference
3. hoping
4. approval
5. discoverer
6. safety
7. preparing
8. obeying
9. spicier
10. propelling
11. desired
12. controlled
13. hopeless
14. greener
15. duly
16. running
17. singeing
18. remotest
19. tying *or* tieing
20. reddest
21. daily
22. chosen
23. defiance
24. courageous
25. employable

Review A Proofreading a Paragraph to Correct Misspelled Words

ANSWERS

1. mixed; rebelled
2. conquered
3. seized; died
4. C
5. re-establishing
6. brief; plotted; chief
7. C

—HELP—

No proper nouns in Review A are misspelled.

Exercise 4 Spelling Words with Suffixes

Spell each of the following words, adding the suffix given.

EXAMPLE   1. swim + ing

1. *swimming*

1. defer + ed
2. defer + ence
3. hope + ing
4. approve + al
5. discover + er
6. safe + ty
7. prepare + ing
8. obey + ing
9. spicy + er
10. propel + ing
11. desire + ed
12. control + ed
13. hope + less
14. green + er
15. due + ly
16. run + ing
17. singe + ing
18. remote + est
19. tie + ing
20. red + est
21. day + ly
22. chose + en
23. defy + ance
24. courage + ous
25. employ + able

Review A Proofreading a Paragraph to Correct Misspelled Words

Proofread the following paragraph, correcting any misspelled words. If all the words in a sentence are already spelled correctly, write *C*.

EXAMPLE   [1] Accordding to legend, Jean-Jacques Dessalines created the Haitian flag by removeing the white panel from the French flag.

1. *According, removing*

[1] When news of the French Revolution reached the colony of Saint Domingue on the Caribbean island of Hispaniola, the African slaves and the freed islanders of mixxed ancestry rebeled against the French colonists. [2] Uniting the two rebel groups, the man shown here, General François Dominique Toussaint-L'Ouverture, conquerred the entire island and abolished slavery in 1802. [3] The next year, however, Toussaint was siezed by the French and deported to France, where he dyed a prisoner. [4] General Jean-Jacques Dessalines then declared the island independent and renamed it Haiti. [5] Declaring himself emperor, Dessalines ordered that a fortress, the Citadelle, and a series of smaller fortresses be built to prevent the Europeans from restabishing power on the island. [6] Dessalines' breif reign lasted until 1806, when he was assassinated in an uprising believed to have been ploted by his cheif rival, General Henri Christophe. [7] Christophe, unable to control the legislature, in 1807 set up a separate state in northern Haiti and had himself

crowned Henri I, King of Haiti. [8] Convinced that imposing structures such as the Citadelle shown here would boost his nation's stature, Christophe launched an extensive building program <u>carryed</u> out by forced labor. [9] Hospitals and schools sprang up, and work on the Citadelle progressed <u>steadyly</u>, but <u>eventualy</u> the people <u>rebeled</u>. [10] In 1820, having <u>sufferred</u> a series of strokes, Christophe, the last of the revolution's three great generals, took his own life.

Forming the Plurals of Nouns

15k. Remembering the following rules will help you spell the plural forms of nouns.

(1) For most nouns, add *s*.

SINGULAR	artist	song	lake	flower	muscle	Wilson
PLURAL	artist**s**	song**s**	lake**s**	flower**s**	muscle**s**	Wilson**s**

(2) For nouns ending in *s, x, z, ch,* or *sh,* add *es*.

SINGULAR	dress	box	waltz	birch	bush	Ruíz
PLURAL	dress**es**	box**es**	waltz**es**	birch**es**	bush**es**	Ruíz**es**

> **NOTE** Some one-syllable words ending in *z* double the final consonant when forming plurals.
>
> EXAMPLES   quiz—qui**zz**es   fez—fe**zz**es

(3) For nouns ending in *y* preceded by a vowel, add *s*.

SINGULAR	monkey	journey	essay	decoy	alley	Friday
PLURAL	monkey**s**	journey**s**	essay**s**	decoy**s**	alley**s**	Friday**s**

(4) For nouns ending in *y* preceded by a consonant, change the *y* to *i* and add *es*.

SINGULAR	fly	enemy	lady	trophy	ally	theory
PLURAL	fl**ies**	enem**ies**	lad**ies**	troph**ies**	all**ies**	theor**ies**

For most proper nouns, add *s*.

EXAMPLES   Brady—Brady**s**   Mallory—Mallory**s**

MECHANICS

DIFFERENTIATING INSTRUCTION

Advanced Learners

Looking at Language. Students might wonder why there has been no attempt to make English spelling more consistent. Tell students that several campaigns have been mounted to simplify English spellings. One of the most famous proponents of a simplified spelling system was Bernard Shaw (1856–1950). He felt that time and effort were wasted in spelling and campaigned for a new alphabet. Challenge interested students to discover more about Shaw's ideas for reform. Students could then present their findings to the class.

─HELP─

If you are not sure about how to spell the plural of a noun ending in *f* or *fe*, look up the word in a dictionary.

(5) For some nouns ending in *f* or *fe*, add *s*. For others, change the *f* or *fe* to *v* and add *es*.

SINGULAR	roof	chief	carafe	knife	loaf
PLURAL	roof**s**	chief**s**	carafe**s**	kni**ves**	loa**ves**

For proper nouns, add *s*.

EXAMPLES   Cardiff—Cardiff**s**   Wolfe—Wolfe**s**

(6) For nouns ending in *o* preceded by a vowel, add *s*.

SINGULAR	radio	studio	cameo	stereo	igloo	Matsuo
PLURAL	radio**s**	studio**s**	cameo**s**	stereo**s**	igloo**s**	Matsuo**s**

(7) For many nouns ending in *o* preceded by a consonant, add *es*.

SINGULAR	tomato	potato	hero	veto	torpedo	echo
PLURAL	tomato**es**	potato**es**	hero**es**	veto**es**	torpedo**es**	echo**es**

For some common nouns, especially those referring to music, and for most proper nouns, add *s*.

SINGULAR	burrito	silo	photo	piano	soprano	Yamamoto
PLURAL	burrito**s**	silo**s**	photo**s**	piano**s**	soprano**s**	Yamamoto**s**

NOTE   For some nouns ending in *o* preceded by a consonant, you may add either *s* or *es*.

SINGULAR	motto	tornado	mosquito	zero	banjo
PLURAL	motto**s**	tornado**s**	mosquito**s**	zero**s**	banjo**s**
	or	*or*	*or*	*or*	*or*
	motto**es**	tornado**es**	mosquito**es**	zero**es**	banjo**es**

If you are in doubt about the plural form of a noun ending in *o*, check the spelling in a dictionary.

│ STYLE   TIP │

When it refers to a computer device, the word *mouse* can be made plural in either of two ways— *mouses* or *mice.* Someday, one of these forms may be the preferred style. For now, either is correct.

(8) The plurals of a few nouns are formed irregularly.

SINGULAR	mouse	woman	tooth	foot	child
PLURAL	m**ice**	wom**en**	t**ee**th	f**ee**t	child**ren**

(9) For a few nouns, the singular and the plural forms are the same.

SINGULAR AND PLURAL	sheep	deer	species	trout
	moose	aircraft	Chinese	Sioux

(10) For most compound nouns, form the plural of only the last word of the compound.

SINGULAR	bookshelf	two-year-old	seat belt	baby sitter
PLURAL	bookshel**ves**	two-year-old**s**	seat belt**s**	baby sitter**s**

(11) For many compound nouns in which one of the words is modified by the other word or words, form the plural of the noun modified.

SINGULAR	sister-in-law	runner-up	passer-by	senior citizen
PLURAL	sister**s**-in-law	runner**s**-up	passer**s**-by	senior citizen**s**

NOTE Some compound nouns have two acceptable plural forms.

SINGULAR	attorney general	court-martial	notary public
PLURAL	attorney general**s**	court-martial**s**	notary public**s**
	or	or	or
	attorney**s** general	court**s**-martial	notarie**s** public

(12) For some nouns borrowed from other languages, the plural is formed as in the original language.

SINGULAR	alumnus [male]	alumna [female]	phenomenon
PLURAL	alumn**i** [male]	alumn**ae** [female]	phenomen**a**

NOTE When referring to graduates of both genders, use *alumni*.

A few nouns borrowed from other languages have two acceptable plural forms. For each of the following nouns, the plural form preferred in English is given first.

SINGULAR	index	stigma	formula	cactus	seraph
PLURAL	index**es**	stigma**s**	formula**s**	cactus**es**	seraph**s**
	or	or	or	or	or
	indi**ces**	stigma**ta**	formula**e**	cact**i**	seraph**im**

(13) To form the plurals of numerals, most uppercase letters, symbols, and most words referred to as words, add an *s* or both an apostrophe and an *s*.

SINGULAR	5	1990	B	+	and
PLURAL	5**s**	1990**s**	B**s**	+**s**	and**s**
	or	or	or	or	or
	5**'s**	1990**'s**	B**'s**	+**'s**	and**'s**

HELP

Check an up-to-date dictionary whenever you are in doubt about the plural form of a compound noun.

STYLE TIP

Some people use *phenomenons* as an alternative plural form, but this spelling has not become accepted in standard, formal English.

Reference Note

For information on **using italics with words, letters, and numerals referred to as such,** see page 364.

DIFFERENTIATING INSTRUCTION

Advanced Learners

Activity. Students may want to make a list of commonly used English words borrowed from other languages. Students can construct charts showing the singular and plural forms of the words, the words' languages of origin, and the meanings of the words. Display students' charts in the classroom.

EXTENSION

Relating to Dictionary Skills

Have students look up the etymologies of the words *alumnus, alumna,* and *phenomenon.* [*Two of these words have Latin origins, and one is of Greek origin.*] Students might be interested in finding the etymologies of some other groups of words in order to detect any patterns. For example, students might research the etymologies of several nouns that form their plurals in irregular ways—such as *child, ox, woman, tooth, mouse,* and *foot*—to discover whether any of these words have similar origins.

MECHANICS

MINI-LESSON   Mechanics

Italics (Underlining). As students study **Rule 15k (13),** you may want to review the following rule on italics: Use italics (underlining) for words, letters, symbols, foreign words, and numerals referred to as such.

EXAMPLES
The word *robot* is derived from the Czech *robota,* meaning "forced labor."
There are two *i*'s in *idyllic.*
How many *5*'s and *3*'s can you see?
See **Chapter 14: Punctuation.**

Review B — Explaining the Spellings of Words

ANSWERS

1. *misstate:* **Rule 15d.** When adding a prefix, do not change the spelling of the original word.

2. *stubbornness:* **Rule 15e.** When adding the suffix *–ness* or *–ly,* do not change the spelling of the original word.

3. *peaceable:* **Rule 15f.** Keep the final silent e in most words ending in *ce* or *ge* before a suffix that begins with *a* or *o.*

4. *ladies:* **Rule 15k(4).** For nouns ending in *y* preceded by a consonant, change the *y* to *i* and add *es.*

5. *alumnae:* **Rule 15k (12).** For some nouns borrowed from other languages, the plural is formed as in the original language.

6. *niece:* **Rule 15a.** Write *ie* when the sound is long e, except after c.

7. *occurred:* **Rule 15j.** Double the final consonant before adding a suffix that begins with a vowel if the word both (1) has only one syllable or has the accent on the final syllable and (2) ends in a single consonant preceded by a single vowel.

8. *writing:* **Rule 15f.** Drop the final silent e before adding a suffix that begins with a vowel.

9. *roofs:* **Rule 15k (5).** For some nouns ending in f or fe, add s.

10. *weigh:* **Rule 15b.** Write *ei* when the sound is not long e, especially when the sound is long a.

MECHANICS

TIPS & TRICKS

It is not incorrect to add both an apostrophe and an s to form the plurals of numerals, letters, symbols, and words referred to as words. Therefore, if you have any doubt about whether or not to use the apostrophe, use it.

Reference Note

For more information about **forming the plurals of numerals, letters, symbols, and words referred to as words,** see page 379.

2. sheep
4. aircraft
5. *buts* [or but's]
11. flies
14. shelves
15. #s [or #'s]
20. geese
22. passers-by
23. alumni
25. mediums [or media]

HELP

To form the plural of an abbreviation that includes periods, add both an apostrophe and an s. To form the plural of an abbreviation that does not include periods, add both an apostrophe and an s, or add only an s.

EXAMPLES
Ph.D.—Ph.D.'s
CD—CD's *or* CDs

To prevent confusion, add both an apostrophe and an s to form the plural of all lowercase letters, certain uppercase letters, and some words referred to as words.

EXAMPLES The word *Philippines* contains three **p's** and three **i's.** [Both letters are lowercase.]

Most of her grades are **A's.** [Without an apostrophe the plural of *A* could be confused with the word *As.*]

In the last paragraph of your story, I can't tell which woman the **her's** refer to. [Without an apostrophe the plural of *her* could be confused with the possessive pronoun *hers.*]

Exercise 5 — Spelling the Plural Forms of Nouns

Spell the plural form of each of the following nouns.

EXAMPLE   1. alto
            1. *altos*

1. turkeys
2. sheep
3. hairdos
4. aircraft
5. *but*
6. videos
7. *6s* [or 6's]
8. beliefs
9. embargoes
10. foxes
11. fly
12. sopranos
13. ponchos
14. shelf
15. #
16. editorsin chief
17. spoonfuls
18. twelfth-graders
19. Gomezes
20. goose
21. *I's*
22. passer-by
23. alumnus
24. heroes
25. medium

Review B — Explaining the Spellings of Words

By referring to the rules on the preceding pages, explain the spelling of each of the following words.

EXAMPLE   1. living
            1. *Drop the final silent e before adding a suffix that begins with a vowel.*

1. misstate
2. stubbornness
3. peaceable
4. ladies
5. alumnae
6. niece
7. occurred
8. writing
9. roofs
10. weigh

MINI-LESSON Mechanics

Hyphenating Numbers. You may want to remind students of the rule for hyphenating numbers: Use a hyphen with compound numbers from *twenty-one* to *ninety-nine* and with fractions used as modifiers. The compound numbers from *twenty-one* to *ninety-nine* are also hyphenated when they are part of another number that needs to be written out, as on a check—for example, *four hundred twenty-three.* In a *two-thirds*

Writing Numbers

15l. Spell out a *cardinal number*—a number that states how many—if it can be expressed in one or two words. Otherwise, use numerals.

EXAMPLES   **thirteen** seniors   **forty-four** days   **one hundred** books

                  313 seniors   **344** days   **1,100** books

> **NOTE**   Generally, you should not spell out some numbers and use numerals for others in the same context. If numerals are required for any of the numbers, use numerals for all of the numbers.

INCONSISTENT   The Congress of the United States is composed of one hundred senators and 435 representatives.

CONSISTENT   The Congress of the United States is composed of **100** senators and **435** representatives.

However, to distinguish between numbers that appear beside each other but that count different things, spell out one number and use numerals for the other.

EXAMPLES   We bought **seven 15**-pound sacks of birdseed.

                              or

           We bought **7 fifteen**-pound sacks of birdseed.

15m. Spell out a number that begins a sentence.

EXAMPLE   **Four hundred twenty-one** students participated in the contest.

If a number appears awkward when spelled out, revise the sentence so that it does not begin with the number.

AWKWARD   Two hundred twenty-three thousand six hundred thirty-one votes were cast in the election.

IMPROVED   In the election, **223,631** votes were cast.

15n. Spell out an *ordinal number*—a number that expresses order.

EXAMPLES   Junko Tabei, the **first** [not *1st*] woman who climbed Mount Everest, was born in Japan in 1939.

            Of the fifty states, Tennessee ranks **thirty-fourth** [not *34th*] in total land area.

Reference Note

For information about **hyphenating compound numbers,** see page 381.

STYLE TIP

For large round numbers, you may use words, numerals, or a combination of words and numerals.

EXAMPLES

thirty trillion dollars *or* **30 trillion** dollars

10,800,000 people *or* **10.8 million** people

EXTENSION

Critical Thinking

Synthesis and Evaluation. Ask each student to choose five of the rules in the chapter and to write an expressive or narrative paragraph using five words that exemplify those rules but that are intentionally misspelled. (You may wish to have students write series of sentences instead of paragraphs if time is limited.)

Ask students to trade papers and underline each word that is misspelled in their partners' paragraphs, give the number of the rule that applies to each misspelled word, and correct the spelling.

MECHANICS

majority, two-thirds is hyphenated because it is an adjective modifying *majority.* In *two thirds of the group, two thirds* is not hyphenated because it is not a modifier; *two* is an adjective modifying the noun *thirds.* For more information on hyphenating numbers, refer students to **Chapter 14: Punctuation.**

Spelling Rules   **407**

Spelling Rules   **407**

DIFFERENTIATING INSTRUCTION

Special Education Students

Some students might benefit from multisensory strategies when they try to identify errors in exercises and in their own writing. One strategy is to have students use rulers or pieces of paper to cover all sentences but the one on which they are working. Another strategy is to have students point to words as they proofread. This might help them isolate words that do not sound or look correct.

Exercise 6

DISTRIBUTED REVIEW

For a review of the use of modifiers, ask students to identify two subordinate clauses in sentence 1 and a participial phrase in sentence 3, to give the part of speech each modifier functions as, and to tell what word or words it modifies.

[**1.** *When you go to Washington, D.C.*—adverb—*modifies* visit; *which is located at 1411 W Street SE*—adjective—*modifies* Frederick Douglass National Historical Site

3. *setting an attendance record for the community theater*—adjective—*modifies* people]

15o. Use numerals to express numbers in conventional situations.

Type of Number	Examples		
Identification Numbers	Room 12 Channel 4	pages 246–315 State Road 541	Model 19-A lines 3–19
Measurements, Statistics	72 degrees 14 percent	6½ yards 84 years old	32.7 ounces ratio of 6 to 1
Dates	July 4, 1776	1200 B.C.	A.D. 2000
Addresses	345 Lexington Drive Tampa, FL 33628-4533		Route 6 P.O. Box 105
Times of Day	8:20 P.M. 7:35 A.M.		4:00 EST

NOTE Spell out a number used with *o'clock.*

EXAMPLE **ten** [not *10*] o'clock

Exercise 6 Using Numbers in Sentences

Each of the following sentences contains at least one error in the use of numbers. Revise each sentence to correct the error(s).

EXAMPLE **1.** In the bottom of the 9th inning, the Wildcats scored 7 runs and won the playoff.

1. In the bottom of the ninth inning, the Wildcats scored seven runs and won the playoff.

1. 1411

1. When you go to Washington, D.C., visit the Frederick Douglass National Historic Site, which is located at One Thousand Four Hundred Eleven W Street SE.

2. fifteen/first

2. Since he was 15, my brother's 1st choice as a college major has been computer science, and his second choice has been mathematics.

3. Five hundred ninety/4

3. 590 people attended the play on opening night, September fourth, setting an attendance record for the community theater.

4. 97

4. Did you realize that ninety-seven percent of the earth's water supply is salt water?

5. 3/51

5. According to the chart on page three, only fifty-one of the company's 360 products are sold in this region.

6. seventy

6. That summer they sailed approximately 70 miles along the Carolina coastline.

7. 50 [*or* fifty 2-inch]

7. Please get fifty two-inch nails and a new claw hammer, Rita.

8. There's plenty of time; the show doesn't start until 9 o'clock.

9. It was only a 3rd-place ribbon, but I had never even placed before.

10. Fully seventy-five percent of the sample were tested without problems.

8. nine
9. third
10. 75

┌HELP┐
All of the proper nouns in Review C are spelled correctly.

Review C   Proofreading Paragraphs to Correct Misspelled Words and Errors in the Use of Numbers

Proofread the following paragraphs, correcting any misspelled words or errors in the use of numbers.

EXAMPLE   **[1]** 5 days ago, members of my family joined in a lovly birthday celebration for my great-auntes.

1.   *Five; lovely; great-aunts*

[1] Last Sunday my grandmother's sisters, Aunt Maeve and her twin Aunt Margaret, celebrated their <u>seventyeth</u> birthdays in an enormous family gathering at La Vista Park. [2] Since I am almost <u>16</u> years old and have my <u>learnner's</u> permit, Mom let me drive to the park. [3] My aunts and uncles on Mom's side of the family were there with their husbands and <u>wifes</u>. [4] <u>6</u> of my cousins, all but Erin, whom I had been especially <u>hopeing</u> to see, attended the celebration. [5] Unfortunately, the flights from Chicago, where Erin goes to nursing school, had been canceled because it had snowed <u>heavyly</u> that night. [6] Although I missed Erin, I enjoyed visiting with many of the <u>85</u> friends and family members who had come to the celebration. [7] Aunt Maeve and Aunt Margaret had insisted that birthday gifts were <u>unecessary</u>, but this time they were overruled. [8] You could tell that they were <u>truely</u> stunned when they opened the gift and found plane tickets to Dublin, Ireland, which is where they were born. [9] Mom and her sisters had <u>chiped</u> in to buy them a <u>2-week</u> vacation. [10] Everyone had such a good time that we have already started <u>planing</u> for Aunt Maeve and Aunt Margaret's <u>71st</u> birthday party on May <u>fourth</u>, 2002.

Spelling Rules   **409**

Review C   Proofreading Paragraphs to Correct Misspelled Words and Errors in the Use of Numbers

1. seventieth
2. sixteen; learner's
3. wives
4. Six; hoping
5. heavily
6. eighty-five
7. unnecessary
8. truly
9. chipped; two-week
10. planning; seventy-first; 4

TEACHING (TIP)

Review C   Students may think that the word *canceled* in item 5 is spelled incorrectly. Point out that both *canceled* and *cancelled* are correct.

EXTENSION

Critical Thinking
Metacognition. After students have completed **Review C,** have them ask themselves the following questions to analyze the strategies they used to proofread for misspelled words.

• Were some words unfamiliar or more difficult to correct than others?

• Do you think you have improved upon your original weaknesses in spelling? What strategies do you think have been most helpful?

• Did you refer to any of the rules in the textbook while correcting the paragraph?

• Did you recheck your work?

• How can you further improve your spelling?

Words Often Confused

(pp. 410–420)

OBJECTIVE

- To distinguish between words whose spellings or meanings are often confused

DIRECT TEACHING

Modeling and Demonstration

Words Often Confused. Model the correct use of commonly confused words with the example *The builders did not alter the historic altar in that church.* First, point out that correct use can often be determined by asking what the confusing words mean in a sentence. Ask what *alter* means. [*change*] Ask what *alter* is or does in the sentence. [*is part of the verb* did alter] Next, ask what *altar* means. [*a table used in a religious ceremony*] Ask what *altar* does in the sentence. [*It is the direct object of the verb.*] *Altar* is a noun and should be used only as a noun. Now, have a volunteer demonstrate the correct use of confusing words, using another example from this chapter.

Reference Note

If there is a word that you cannot find in the list of words often confused, refer to Chapter 11 or look up the word in a dictionary.

Reference Note

For more information about using **all right,** see page 263.

─HELP─

Notice that both *born* and *borne* are past participles of *to bear.* The definition you mean determines the spelling you should use.

Words Often Confused

all ready	[adjective] *all prepared*
	Give the signal when you are *all ready.*
already	[adverb] *previously*
	I had *already* read several articles about the customs of the Micmac people of Canada.
all right	[adjective] *satisfactory;* [adverb] *satisfactorily*
	I did *all right* on the quiz.
	[Although the spelling *alright* is in some dictionaries, it has not become standard usage.]
all together	[adverb] *in unison;* [adjective] *in the same place*
	Please sing *all together,* now.
	We were *all together* for the holidays.
altogether	[adverb] *entirely*
	Her reaction was *altogether* unexpected.
altar	[noun] *a table or stand at which religious rites are performed*
	The priest was standing beside the *altar.*
alter	[verb] *to change*
	If we are late, we will *alter* our plans.
assure	[verb] *to make certain by removing doubt or suspense; to promise*
	Did she *assure* you that the problem would be resolved by tomorrow?
ensure	[verb] *to make certain by protecting; to guarantee*
	Doesn't the First Amendment *ensure* U.S. citizens the freedom of speech?
insure	[verb] *to arrange for monetary payment in case of loss, accident, or death*
	Did you speak to an insurance agent to see what the cost to *insure* both vehicles would be?
born	[verb, past participle of *bear*] *given birth*
	Where was Zora Neale Hurston *born*?
borne	[verb, past participle of *bear*] *carried; endured*
	The people there have *borne* many hardships.

RESOURCES

Words Often Confused

Practice

- *Language & Sentence Skills Practice,* pp. 355–359

Differentiating Instruction

- *Developmental Language & Sentence Skills,* pp. 177–182

brake	[verb] *to slow down or stop;* [noun] *a device for slowing down or stopping*
	Remember to *brake* cautiously on wet roads.
	The report concluded that a defective *brake* caused the accident.
break	[verb] *to cause to come apart; to shatter;* [noun] *a fracture*
	Try not to *break* any dishes as you clear the table tonight.
	The doctor says that the X-ray shows a *break* in your left fibula.
capital	[adjective or noun; spelling used in all cases except when referring to a building in which a legislature meets]
	Washington, D.C., has been the *capital* of the United States since 1791. [*city*]
	Do you think they have enough *capital* to start their business? [*wealth*]
	In most states, first degree murder is a *capital* offense. [*punishable by death*]
	That idea is *capital*. [*of major importance*]
	Proofread your work to be sure that every sentence begins with a *capital* letter. [*uppercase*]
capitol	[noun] *a building in which a legislature meets* [capitalized when it refers to a building for a national legislature]
	The *capitol* faces a park.
	On our visit to Washington, D.C., we toured the *Capitol*.
choose	[verb, rhymes with *shoes*]
	Did you *choose* the movie for today?
chose	[verb, past tense of *choose*, rhymes with *shows*]
	Who *chose* the movie yesterday?
clothes	[noun] *wearing apparel*
	Should these *clothes* be dry-cleaned, or can I put them in the washing machine?
cloths	[noun] *pieces of fabric*
	Use these *cloths* to dust the furniture.

TIPS & TRICKS

To remember the spelling of *capitol*, use this sentence: The capit**o**l has a d**o**me.

TIPS & **TRICKS**

You can remember the difference in spelling between *complement* (something that completes) and *compliment* (an expression of affection or respect) by remembering that a compl**e**ment compl**e**tes a sentence.

Exercise 7 **Distinguishing Between Words Often Confused**

From the choices in parentheses, select the correct word or words for each of the following sentences.

EXAMPLE   **1.** He writes poetry with no (*capital, capitol*) letters.

   1. *capital*

1. Mother was (*all together, altogether*) too surprised to protest.
2. (*All right, Alright*), I'll wrap the package now.
3. What was the Supreme Court decision on (*capital, capitol*) punishment?
4. Did you (*chose, choose*) the green one?
5. We polished the car with (*cloths, clothes*).
6. They will (*altar, alter*) the building to suit tenants.
7. How have we (*born, borne*) such disrespect?
8. For how much did you (*assure, ensure, insure*) the jewels, sir?
9. If you (*brake, break*) a window, you will pay for it.
10. Are the sandwiches (*already, all ready*) prepared?

coarse	[adjective] *rough; crude* This fabric is as *coarse* as burlap.
course	[noun] *path of action; part of a meal; series of studies* [also used after *of* to mean *naturally* or *certainly*] What *course* should I follow to find a job? Soup was the first *course.* I am taking a *course* in creative writing. Of *course,* I'll help you set the table.
complement	[noun] *something that makes whole or complete;* [verb] *to make whole or complete* The *complement* of a 50° angle is a 40° angle. [The two angles complete a 90° angle.] Her part of this job *complements* mine. [Together the parts complete the job.]
compliment	[noun] *praise; a courteous act or expression;* [verb] *to express praise or respect* Thank you for the *compliment.* The tennis coach *complimented* me on my backhand.

consul	[noun] *a person appointed by a government to serve its citizens in a foreign country*
	The American *consul* helped us during our visit.
council	[noun] *a group gathered to accomplish a job*
	The *council* met to vote on the proposal.
councilor	[noun] *a member of a council*
	Did each *councilor* vote in favor of the proposal?
counsel	[noun] *advice;* [verb] *to advise*
	I accepted the wise *counsel* of Ms. Ariyoshi.
	Ms. Ariyoshi had *counseled* me to take Algebra II.
counselor	[noun] *one who gives advice*
	Ms. Ariyoshi is my guidance *counselor*.
desert	[noun, pronounced des'•ert] *a dry region*
	The Sahara is the world's largest *desert*.
desert	[verb, pronounced de•sert'] *to leave or abandon*
	She would never *desert* her friends.
dessert	[noun, pronounced des•sert'] *the sweet, final course of a meal*
	For *dessert* we had strawberry yogurt.
formally	[adverb] *in a proper or dignified manner, according to strict rules*
	The Nobel Prizes are *formally* presented on December 10.
formerly	[adverb] *previously; in the past*
	Katherine Ortega was *formerly* the U.S. treasurer.
its	[possessive form of *it*] *belonging to it*
	The community is proud of *its* school system.
it's	[contraction of *it is* or *it has*]
	It's a symbol of peace.
	It's been a long time since your last visit.
later	[adjective or adverb] *more late*
	We will send the package at a *later* time.
	I will help you *later*.
latter	[adjective] *the second of two*
	When given the choice of a volleyball or a tennis racket, I chose the *latter*.

(continued)

—HELP—

The adjective *latter* is often used as the opposite of *former* to indicate which of two items is being discussed. In the example to the left, *latter* means *tennis racket*, as opposed to *volleyball*, which would be the *former*.

MECHANICS

DIRECT TEACHING

Commonly Confused Words

Activity. Divide the class into small groups. Have each group divide the list of commonly confused words from this chapter equally among its members. Students should write their words on a separate sheet of paper. Then, each student should write on another sheet of paper a sentence using one of his or her words. Students should pass their sentences to the left, as in a round robin, and each student should add another sentence, using a different word from his or her list. Students should try to make the sentences tell a story. Group members should keep passing their sentence pages until they have used all of their words once. Then, ask students to underline the commonly confused words in the story to which they have last added a sentence and to read the story to the rest of the group.

(continued)

lead	[verb, pronounced "leed"] *to go first; to guide*
	Who will *lead* the parade?
led	[verb, past form of *lead*]
	She *led* the team to victory.
lead	[noun, pronounced "led"] *a heavy metal; graphite in a pencil*
	The alchemist truly believed that he would one day transform *lead* into gold.
	I bought new *leads* for my mechanical pencil.

Exercise 8   Distinguishing Between Words Often Confused

From the choices in parentheses, select the correct word for each of the following sentences.

EXAMPLE   1. We decided to make baklava for (*desert, dessert*).

1. *dessert*

1. These supplies will (*complement, compliment*) those that you already have.
2. How long will it take Art to cross the (*dessert, desert*)?
3. Why does he use such (*course, coarse*) language?
4. I do not enjoy parties conducted as (*formally, formerly*) as this one.
5. We are not sure which (*course, coarse*) to follow.
6. Are you sure (*its, it's*) not too late?
7. I worked last summer as a camp (*councilor, counselor*).
8. He spoke to both the mayor and the school superintendent, and the (*later, latter*) was more helpful.
9. Last season, Albert (*lead, led*) the team to a championship.
10. Our (*consul, counsel*) in China has returned to Washington.

loose	[adjective, rhymes with *noose*] *free; not close together; not firmly fastened*
	The *loose* chickens roamed the barnyard.
	They stumbled in the *loose* sand.
	Some of the shingles on the roof are *loose*.
lose	[verb, rhymes with *shoes*] *to suffer loss of*
	When did you *lose* your books?

miner	[noun] *a worker in a mine*
	Her father is a coal *miner*.
minor	[noun] *a person under legal age;* [adjective] *less important*
	A *minor* cannot vote in local, state, or federal elections.
	They raised only *minor* objections.
moral	[adjective] *good; virtuous;* [noun] *a lesson of conduct*
	His conduct throughout the situation showed him to be a *moral* person.
	The class understood the *moral* of the story.
morale	[noun] *spirit; mental condition*
	The victory boosted the team's *morale*.
passed	[verb, past form of *pass*] *went beyond*
	The red car *passed* me at the finish line.
past	[noun] *time gone by;* [adjective] *of a former time;* [preposition] *beyond*
	To understand the present, you need to study the *past*.
	For some people, *past* events are much more interesting than present ones.
	After you drive *past* the shopping mall, turn right at the first traffic light.
peace	[noun] *calmness* (as opposed to *war* or *strife*)
	Doesn't everyone prefer *peace* to war?
piece	[noun] *a part of something*
	I fed the dog a boneless *piece* of turkey as a special treat.
personal	[adjective] *individual; private*
	The celebrity declined to answer any *personal* questions.
personnel	[noun] *a group of people employed in the same work or service*
	The *personnel* of the company ranged in age from sixteen to sixty-four.

(continued)

TIPS & TRICKS

Here is a way to remember the difference between *peace* and *piece*. You eat a p**ie**ce of p**ie**.

Words Often Confused **415**

plain	[adjective] *not fancy; clear;* [noun] *an area of flat land*
	The tourist cabin was small and *plain* but quite comfortable.
	Our problem is *plain* to see.
	The *plain* stretched before them for miles.
plane	[noun] *a flat surface; a woodworking tool; an airplane*
	Geometry is the study of imaginary flat surfaces, or *planes.*
	The carpenter used a *plane* to smooth the edge of the board.
	Waiting for the fog to lift, the *plane* circled the airport for an hour.
principal	[noun] *the head of a school;* [adjective] *main or most important*
	Jorge's mom, Mrs. Pacheco, is the assistant *principal* at our school.
	The *principal* cause of accidents is carelessness.
principle	[noun] *a rule of conduct; a fact or a general truth*
	The plaintiff accused the defendant of having no *principles.*
	We have been studying many of the *principles* of aerodynamics.
quiet	[adjective] *still; silent*
	The library is usually *quiet,* but it wasn't today.
quite	[adverb] *completely; rather; very*
	I had *quite* forgotten her advice.
	Angela's report on the lifestyle of the Amish was *quite* interesting.

DIFFERENTIATING INSTRUCTION

Learners Having Difficulty

Activity. Have each student choose a group of often-confused words to illustrate on poster board. For example, a student might illustrate *peace* and *piece* by drawing a large peace symbol and a piece of pie.

Advanced Learners

Activity. Students could create cartoons that feature puns based on the words in this lesson. For example, a student might draw and label a cartoon showing someone lost in a *dessert* or depicting a car *breaking* at a stoplight.

MECHANICS

TIPS & TRICKS

Here is an easy way to remember the difference between *principal* and *principle.* The princi**pal** is your **pal.**

Exercise 9 Distinguishing Between Words Often Confused

From the choices in parentheses, select the correct word for each of the following sentences.

EXAMPLE **1.** The jigsaw puzzle consisted of more than one thousand (*peaces, pieces*).

1. *pieces*

Learning for Life

Continued on pp. 417–419

Writing a Letter to the Editor. Explain to students that a letter to the editor is an effective way to have one's opinion read by many people. Some people frequently write letters to the editor, and some write only when they feel very strongly about an issue and they want to influence its outcome or resolution. Bring to class the editorial pages from a number of issues of the local newspaper and of other newspapers from your area. Divide the class into small groups to read and discuss the letters to the

1. All three nations signed a (*peace*, *piece*) treaty to end the long-standing conflict.
2. Do these printed instructions seem (*plain*, *plane*) to you?
3. This store's sales (*personal*, *personnel*) have been very helpful every time I've shopped here.
4. The (*principal*, *principle*) underlying solar energy is not difficult to understand.
5. If you (*loose*, *lose*) your concentration, you might (*loose*, *lose*) the tennis match.
6. What are the (*principal*, *principle*) parts of the verb *shrink*?
7. Mrs. Wilson insists that students remain absolutely (*quiet*, *quite*) during study period.
8. Does every fable have a (*moral*, *morale*)?
9. On my way to school every day, I always walk (*passed*, *past*) the bakery.
10. Now that he is officially no longer a (*miner*, *minor*), he can vote in the upcoming election.

stationary	[adjective] *in a fixed position*
	Is that a new *stationary* bicycle in the gym?
stationery	[noun] *writing paper*
	I received a box of *stationery* at Christmas.
than	[conjunction used for comparisons]
	Jupiter is larger *than* any other planet in our solar system.
then	[adverb] *at that time; next*
	First, make an outline; *then*, write the composition according to the outline.
their	[possessive form of *they*] *belonging to them*
	The performers made *their* own costumes.
there	[adverb] *at that place;* [expletive used to begin a sentence]
	We were *there* at two o'clock.
	There were four of us in the final round of competition.
they're	[contraction of *they are*]
	They're going with us to the jazz festival.

(continued)

TIPS & TRICKS

Here is an easy way to remember the difference between *stationary* and *stationery*. You write a lett**er** on station**er**y.

Reference Note

For more about **expletives,** see page 42.

RETEACHING

Homonyms

Activity. Many of the often-confused words in this chapter are homonyms—they sound alike but have different spellings and meanings. Have students work in groups of three or four to think of and list as many homonyms as possible in a given period of time. Then, have groups compare lists and delete any homonyms that two or more groups have in common. Groups with homonyms nobody else has listed should share their words with the rest of the class by writing the words on the chalkboard.

editor. Each group should then choose a well-written, thoughtful letter on an important topic and appoint a spokesperson to read the letter to the class.

Then, tell students they will each be writing a one-page letter to the editor. Ask them each to think of topics they feel strongly about to use as the subjects of letters to the editor. They should be able to supply logical reasoning to support their stances on their topics. Encourage them to write letters they will actually want to send.

to	[preposition; part of the infinitive form of a verb]
	Are you going *to* Puerto Rico this summer?
	My father showed me how *to* prepare sushi.
too	[adverb] *also; more than enough*
	Lamont is a senior, *too.*
	It is *too* late to go now.
two	[adjective] *totaling one plus one;* [noun] *the number between one and three*
	We had only *two* dollars.
	Two of my favorite singers are Whitney Houston and Sheryl Crow.
waist	[noun] *the midsection of the body*
	She wore a colorful obi around her *waist.*
waste	[noun] *unused material;* [verb] *to squander*
	Pollution can be caused by industrial *wastes.*
	Don't *waste* your time.
who's	[contraction of *who is* or *who has*]
	Who's in charge of the recycling program?
	Who's been using my computer?
whose	[possessive form of *who*] *belonging to whom*
	Whose castanets are these?
your	[possessive form of *you*] *belonging to you*
	Wasn't that *your* cue?
you're	[contraction of *you are*]
	You're a true friend.

Exercise 10 Distinguishing Between Words Often Confused

From the choices in parentheses, select the correct word for each of the following sentences.

EXAMPLE   1. (*Who's, Whose*) the captain of the team?

   1. *Who's*

1. They had neglected to close (*there, their*) lockers.
2. I wanted to go to camp, (*to, two, too*).
3. Tie the rope around your (*waist, waste*).

Advanced Learners

Looking at Language. If possible, have volunteers read aloud different stanzas of Lewis Carroll's poem "Jabberwocky." Note that in creating original words, Carroll followed the logic of the English language. For example, although *slithy* and *mimsy* are "portmanteau" words—blending *lithe* and *slimy* on the one hand and *flimsy* and *miserable* on the other— they have recognizable English endings. Carroll also followed English suffix rules in other word formations. Note that *toves* is a plural noun. Ask volunteers to apply spelling rules to other original words in the poem. For example, ask "How would you spell the present participle of the verb *gimble* [*gimbling*]? the comparative form of the adjective *mimsy* [*mimsier* or *more mimsy*]? the plural of *bandersnatch* [*bandersnatches*]?"

MECHANICS

Learning for Life   *Continued from p. 417*

Remind students that a successful letter contains precise, thoughtful language. Students should strive to use appropriate language and should not try to use words they do not fully understand. Students should also be very careful to use correct spelling.

Have students write their letters, and after they have finished writing, have them exchange letters with partners. Partners should read the letters for clarity and reasoning and should also check for spelling errors. Students can refer to a dictionary or

4. The platform, we discovered, was (*stationary*, *stationery*).
5. No one could remember (*whose*, *who's*) name had been drawn first.
6. As soon as (*their*, *they're*) printed, we will ship the books.
7. Write your letters on business (*stationery*, *stationary*).
8. (*Your*, *You're*) lucky to have such a good job.
9. I cannot do any more (*than*, *then*) I have done.
10. I was surprised at (*you're*, *your*) attitude.

Oral Practice **Distinguishing Between Words Often Confused**

Read each of the following sentences aloud. Then, say which term in the parentheses correctly completes each sentence.

EXAMPLE   1. Which math (*coarse*, *course*) are you taking?

    1. *course*

1. Columbia is the (*capital*, *capitol*) of South Carolina.
2. Aaron, have you discussed this problem with your guidance (*councilor*, *counselor*)?
3. The amount of vegetation in the (*dessert*, *desert*) surprised us.
4. My companion (*lead*, *led*) me down a dark passage.
5. We were (*all ready*, *already*) to start before dawn.
6. Try not to (*lose*, *loose*) your keys.
7. Each success helps to build (*moral*, *morale*).
8. Members of the (*counsel*, *council*) are elected annually.
9. My red scarf (*complements*, *compliments*) my outfit.
10. The peace-keeping mission was accomplished without loss of (*personal*, *personnel*).
11. Do not (*altar*, *alter*) any part of the contract.
12. The wheels screamed as the train's engineer hit the (*brakes*, *breaks*).
13. She doesn't just design her own (*stationary*, *stationery*); she makes the paper.
14. (*Who's*, *Whose*) books are these on the kitchen counter?
15. I thought the word problems on this test would be hard, but (*they're*, *their*, *there*) easy.
16. Will *x* be greater (*than*, *then*) *y* in this equation?
17. Discuss the (*principal*, *principle*) historical events in Africa during the twelfth century.
18. Suddenly, four boys on skateboards zoomed (*passed*, *past*) us.
19. The compressor has been delivered, but (*it's*, *its*) installation has been delayed.
20. You may use the potter's wheel now, if (*you're*, *your*) interested.

EXTENSION

Relating to Literature
If possible, play for the class selected scenes from a professional recording of Bernard Shaw's satire *Pygmalion*. You could also use the film version starring Wendy Hiller and Leslie Howard. Include Act I, the first part of Act II (in which Eliza visits Higgins at home), and Act III (the garden party). Discuss with the class Shaw's notion of the link between proper diction and success. Have the class discuss the relationships between speaking (pronunciation) and writing skills (spelling).

You could also bring a copy of the play *Pygmalion* to class. Note that Shaw insisted his plays be printed according to his own views on simplifying spelling. Help the students find examples of his refusal to use apostrophes in contractions and his dropping the silent *e* from *Shakespeare* (near the end of Act III). You might also note his use of phonetic spelling to convey accents (Act I). Have students discuss whether Eliza's pronunciation might have had any effect on the spelling skills she exhibits.

to the spelling rules in this chapter to answer any questions about correct spelling.

Students who do not mail their letters can display them on a bulletin board. Those students who do send their letters to newspapers can scan the editorial pages each day for their letters or for letters on the same topic.

1. their
2. course/
   all together
3. its

4. formally/
   it's
5. believed

6. altar

7. to/
   later
8. two/
   quiet
9. there/
   forty-five

10. It's/quite/
    too/their

Review D   Proofreading Paragraphs to Correct Misspelled Words

Proofread the following paragraphs, correcting all of the misspelled or incorrectly used words or numerals.

EXAMPLE   **[1]** We spent this passed weekend in San Francisco.

    1. past

[1] Many of the more than 100,000 Hispanics who live in San Francisco make they're homes in the Mission District. [2] They come from many different countries, of coarse, but altogether they've created one of San Francisco's most inviting areas. [3] Comprising twenty square blocks on the city's south side, the district takes it's name from the mission founded in 1771 by the Franciscan missionary Junípero Serra.

[4] The whitewashed adobe mission is formerly named Mission San Francisco de Asís, but its popularly known as Mission Dolores after the name of a nearby stream. [5] One of the few structures that survived the devastating earthquake of 1906, it's beleived to be the oldest intact building in the city. [6] Its gilded alter was among the most ornate in the twenty-one Spanish missions Fray Junípero founded in what is now California. [7] The basilica, the grander church next door, too the original mission, was demolished in the 1906 earthquake but was latter rebuilt. [8] Nestled between the to buildings, a small park invites visitors to spend a quite moment resting before exploring further.

[9] Even the most un-observant visitor can't fail to notice the striking outdoor murals, like the one here, which brighten walls throughout the neighborhood; all together, their are 45 of these murals. [10] Its not surprising that quiet a few well-known Hispanic artists, including Amalia Mesa-Bains, Enrique Chagoya, and to many others to list here, launched they're careers there.

Numerals and terms in brackets refer to rules and concepts tested by items in the Chapter Review.

1. immovable [15d]
2. 9:27 [15o]
3. argument [15g]
4. funniest [15h]
5. Four hundred [15l, m]

6. queries [15k(4)]
7. [15k(3)]
8. leaves [15k(5)]
9. spacecraft [15k(9)]
10. [15k(2)]
11. quanta [15k(12)]
12. fathers-in-law [15k(11)]
13. [15k(1)]
14. *but*s [or *but*'s] [15k(13)]
15. [15k(7)]

16. [*stationary, stationery*]
17. [*all ready, already*]
18. [*plain, plane*]

Chapter Review

A. Proofreading Sentences for Correct Spelling

Proofread the following sentences for errors in spelling or the use of numbers.

1. "Have you ever wondered what would happen," asked the philosopher, "if an irresistible force met an ~~imovable~~ object?"

2. The space shuttle took off at exactly ~~nine twenty-seven~~ A.M. on Thursday.

3. Ken and Teresa finally resolved their ~~arguement~~ about sports by agreeing to disagree.

4. Who was the ~~funnyest~~ comedian we saw on television last night—Whoopi Goldberg, Billy Crystal, or Robin Williams?

5. ~~400~~ readers wrote to the newspaper to praise its coverage of the recent flood.

B. Spelling the Plural Form of Nouns

Spell the plural form of each of the following nouns.

6. query
7. valleys
8. leaf
9. spacecraft
10. toothbrushes
11. quantum
12. father-in-law
13. Smiths
14. *but*
15. burritos

C. Distinguishing Between Words Often Confused

In each of the following sentences, write the correct word or words in parentheses.

16. Having been (*stationary, stationery*) for quite a while, the mannequin in the shop window suddenly blinked and looked right at me.

17. Have you (*all ready, already*) picked up your graduation invitations?

18. Because of the storms, the (*plain, plane*) waited on the runway for an hour before being cleared for take-off.

Chapter Review   **421**

19. [*personal, personnel*]
20. [*brake, break*]
21. [*capital, capitol*]
22. [*its, it's*]
23. [*who's, whose*]
24. [*consul, council, councilor, counsel, counselor*]
25. [*principal, principle*]
26. [*than, then*]
27. [*complement, compliment*]
28. [*all together, altogether*]
29. [*assure, ensure, insure*]
30. [*quiet, quite*]

─HELP─

All of the proper nouns in Part D are spelled correctly.

31. 160 [15l]
32. excelled [15j]
33. radios [15k(6)]
34. freight [15b]
35. usually [15e]

19. If our company is to meet these deadlines, management will need to add (*personal, personnel*).
20. Yesterday there was an unexpected (*break, brake*) in the transmission of satellite signals.
21. Alec hopes to have enough (*capital, capitol*) to invest in his friends' auto parts business this spring.
22. (*Its, It's*) true that the Rosetta Stone was the key to understanding Egyptian hieroglyphics.
23. Coach Russell wants to know (*whose, who's*) truck is blocking the entrance to the playing field.
24. Only one (*counselor, councilor*) voted against the mass transit plan during the meeting of the city's leaders Tuesday night.
25. Mr. Davidson is the (*principal, principle*) of our school and our school's only algebra teacher.
26. I think this video is a little longer (*then, than*) the one we watched last night.
27. I think *The Hobbit* is an entertaining novel in itself, not just a (*complement, compliment*) to *The Lord of the Rings*.
28. Will the family be (*all together, altogether*) for Aunt Minnie's birthday?
29. This policy (*ensures, insures*) that your family will be taken care of in case you become seriously ill.
30. The concert last night was (*quite, quiet*) loud, don't you think?

D. Proofreading a Paragraph to Correct Misspelled Words and Errors in the Use of Numbers

Identify the spelling errors and errors in the use of numbers in the following paragraph. Then, write the correct spellings and numbers.

[31] For more than one hundred sixty years, women have been working on the railroad. [32] Women have exceled in all kinds of railroad work, from domestic service jobs to engineering and executive jobs. [33] Before radioes were used by railroads, telegraph operators were essential to railway safety. [34] Ella Campbell, a young telegraph operator at a Pennsylvania depot, prevented a collision between a westbound frieght train and an eastbound passenger train. [35] In the nineteenth century, female railroad workers usualy were telegraph operators, or

"ops." **[36]** Historians ~~beleive~~ believe that Ida Hewitt of West Virginia was the first female locomotive engineer in the United States. **[37]** Before 1900, she was ~~emploied~~ employed, like her father, by the Calico Railroad. **[38]** One of the ~~1st~~ first women to be president of a railroad company was Sarah Clark. **[39]** Clark was ~~nameed~~ named president of the Nevada County Narrow Gauge in 1901. **[40]** An estimated 27,000 women work for the railroads today, and many are ~~succeeding~~ succeeding in a variety of important jobs.

36. believe [15a]
37. employed [15i]
38. first [15n]
39. named [15f]
40. succeeding [15c]

Writing Application

Using Correct Spelling in an Application Letter

Spelling Words   Imagine the best job you could have. Then, write the letter of application that will get you that job. The letter should be short—no longer than two paragraphs—and should be as clear as possible. In your letter use ten words from the spelling list on page 424.

Prewriting   Start by making a list of five jobs that might interest you. Do some research in specialist publications or on the Internet on the major requirements of your dream job so that you can use professional terms authoritatively in your letter. Once you have drawn up a list of dream jobs, choose one job and freewrite about it. Write down as many details as you can to describe the job, its responsibilities, and where you see the job taking you in the future.

Writing   Use your freewriting notes to help you write the first draft of your letter. You may want to begin your letter by stating how you learned of the job opening. Then, go on to explain how your training and experience make you suited for this particular job.

Revising   Ask a classmate to play the part of a personnel officer, and read your letter to him or her. Rearrange or cut details to make the letter more effective.

Publishing   Be sure that all words are spelled correctly. Proofread your letter for any errors in grammar, usage, and mechanics. With your teacher's approval, you might suggest a contest among your classmates to determine which students get their dream jobs. Post the completed letters on the class bulletin board or Web page, and follow up with the announcement of the successful applicants.

Writing Application

Writing Tip. Divide the class into groups of three or four, and have students brainstorm about writing job application letters. You could have groups exchange letters and take turns acting as applicants and employers, commenting on the strengths and weaknesses of the job applications.

Scoring Rubric. While you will want to pay particular attention to students' spelling, you will also want to evaluate overall writing performance. You could give a split score to assess development and clarity of the composition separately from skill in spelling.

MECHANICS

The following list contains three hundred words that are commonly misspelled.

abundant	beggar	cruelty	familiarize
academically	beneficial	curriculum	fascination
accelerator	bibliography		fascism
accessible	biscuit	deceitful	feminine
accidentally	blasphemy	decision	financier
acclimated	boulevard	definitely	fission
accommodation	buffet	descendant	forfeit
accompaniment	bureaucrat	desirable	fulfill
accomplishment	burial	despair	fundamentally
accuracy	business	desperately	
acknowledge		detrimental	galaxy
acquaintance	calculation	devastation	gauge
adequately	camouflage	devise	government
admission	capable	dilemma	grammatically
admittance	capitalism	diligence	guaranteed
adolescence	carburetor	disagreement	guidance
advantageous	caricature	disastrous	
advertisement	catastrophe	disciple	harassment
aerial	cellar	discrimination	hereditary
allege	cemetery	dissatisfied	hindrance
allegiance	changeable		horizontal
alliance	chassis	ecstasy	hygiene
allotting	Christianity	efficiency	hypocrisy
annihilate	circumstantial	embarrassment	
anonymous	colossal	emperor	ideally
apologetically	commercial	emphasize	immediate
apparatus	communist	endeavor	incidentally
apparent	competition	enormous	independent
arrangement	complexion	entertainment	indispensable
atheistic	conceivable	enthusiastically	inevitable
atmosphere	connoisseur	entrance	inexperienced
attendance	conscientious	environment	influential
awfully	consciousness	especially	ingenious
	consistency	espionage	initiative
background	controlling	exercise	innocent
ballet	controversy	exhaustion	institution
bankruptcy	courtesy	exhibition	intellectual
barbarian		expensive	interference
			irrelevant

irresistible
irritating

kerosene

laborious
larynx
license
liquor
livelihood
luxurious

magistrate
magnificence
maintenance
malicious
manageable
maneuver
marriageable
martyrdom
materialism
meadow
mediocre
melancholy
melodious
metaphor
miniature
mischievous
misspelled
mortgage
mosquito
municipal
mysterious

naive
necessary
neurotic
noticeable
nucleus
nuisance
nutritious

obedience

occasionally
occurrence
omitting
opportunity
orchestra
outrageous

pageant
pamphlet
paralysis
parliament
pastime
peasant
pedestal
penicillin
perceive
permanent
permissible
persistent
perspiration
petition
phenomenon
physician
picnicking
playwright
pneumonia
politician
precede
presence
prestige
presumption
prevalent
privilege
probably
procedure
propaganda
prophesy
psychoanalysis
pursue

quietly

rebellion
receive
recommendation
recruit
reference
referred
refrigerator
rehearsal
relieve
reminiscent
representative
responsibility
restaurant

safety
seize
separation
sergeant
siege
significance
souvenir
specimen
sponsor
statistics
straight
strategic
stubbornness
succeed
succession
summed
superintendent
supersede
suppress
surprise
surroundings
susceptible
symbolic
symmetrical
synonymous

tariff
temperament

temperature
tendency
theoretical
tolerance
tomorrow
tortoise
traffic
tragedy
transcend
transparent
tried
twelfth
tyranny

undoubtedly
universal
unmistakable
unnatural
unnecessary
unscrupulous

vaccine
vacuum
variation
vaudeville
vegetable
vehicle
vengeance
versatile
vigilance
villain
vinegar
visage

welcome
whisper
whistle
withhold

yacht
yawn
yield

16 Correcting Common Errors

┌ H E L P ─

Remember that the exercises in Chapter 16 test your knowledge of the rules of **standard, formal English.** These are the rules you should follow in your schoolwork.

Reference Note

For more about **standard** and **nonstandard English** and **formal** and **informal English,** see page 262.

Key Language Skills Review

This chapter reviews key skills and concepts that pose special problems for writers.

- Sentence Fragments and Run-on Sentences
- Subject-Verb and Pronoun-Antecedent Agreement
- Pronoun Forms and Clear Pronoun Reference
- Verb Forms
- Comparison of Modifiers
- Misplaced and Dangling Modifiers
- Standard Usage
- Capitalization
- Punctuation—End Marks, Commas, Semicolons, Colons, Quotation Marks, and Apostrophes
- Spelling

Most of the exercises in this chapter follow the same format as the exercises found throughout the grammar, usage, and mechanics sections of this book. You will notice, however, that two sets of review exercises are presented in standardized test formats. These exercises are designed to provide you with practice not only in solving usage and mechanics problems but also in dealing with such problems on standardized tests.

Exercise 1 Identifying and Correcting Sentence Fragments

For each of the following word groups, identify and revise each sentence fragment to make it a complete sentence. If a word group is already a complete sentence, write *C*.

EXAMPLE   **1.** Since the invention of plastic.

        1. Since the invention of plastic, technology has come a long way.

1. Frances Perkins, who, in 1933, was the first woman to serve as a Cabinet member.
2. Pausing before he answered their question about his experimental method.
3. The perfect symmetry of the room imparted a certain serenity to those who entered it.
4. Within a small box that had been hidden in the chimney of the old cottage that had stood unchanged since the Civil War.
5. The boy in the striped shirt playing guitar under the oak trees on the quadrangle between the buildings.
6. Spanning a chasm this wide required a new engineering solution and new technology.
7. That first expedition to venture so far into the Arctic.
8. Her all-consuming goal to become an astronaut.
9. Surprising to no one who knew him.
10. Quechua, the ancient Incan language that is still used widely in the Andes of South America.

Exercise 2 Identifying and Revising Run-on Sentences

Most of the word groups on the following page are run-on sentences. Revise each run-on sentence to make it at least one complete sentence. If a word group is already correct, write *C*.   Revisions will vary.

EXAMPLE   **1.** Many varieties of fish inhabit this coral reef a number of them are vividly colored.

        1. Many varieties of fish inhabit this coral reef, and a number of them are vividly colored.

                          or

        Many varieties of fish inhabit this coral reef. A number of them are vividly colored.

Reference Note

For information on correcting **sentence fragments,** see page 480.

Reference Note

For information about correcting **run-on sentences,** see page 483.

HELP

Although the example in Exercise 2 gives two possible answers, you need to give only one for each item.

Exercise 1

OBJECTIVE

■ **To identify and revise sentence fragments**

Exercise 1 Identifying and Correcting Sentence Fragments

POSSIBLE ANSWERS

1. Frances Perkins, who was named to her post in 1933, was the first woman to serve as a Cabinet member.
2. Pausing before he answered their question about his experimental method, the scientist smiled at the reporters.
3. C
4. We found the emerald ring within a small box that had been hidden in the chimney of the old cottage that had stood unchanged since the Civil War.
5. I know the boy in the striped shirt playing guitar under the oak trees on the quadrangle between the buildings.
6. C
7. Who led that first expedition to venture so far into the Arctic?
8. Her all-consuming goal is to become an astronaut.
9. Joseph's achievements were surprising to no one who knew him.
10. My aunt Martha is studying Quechua, the ancient Incan language that is still used widely in the Andes of South America.

Exercise 2

OBJECTIVE

■ **To identify and revise run-on sentences**

1. I don't know how he does that trick I'd like to find out.
2. Cedar panels lined all four walls of the room, they had been fashioned from trees that grew right there on the property.
3. Luckily, Mr. Hawkins is a skilled metalworker, so he made another part; the line was up and running in less than two hours.
4. A cold, wicked wind blew through the dark trees, and the horses stamped nervously in the stables.
5. An accomplished actress, Ida Lupino was Hollywood's only female director for some time, she also worked as a writer and producer.
6. Take these to the supervisor; she's expecting them.
7. Act Three begins with a complete reversal of fortunes notice the parallels between the two families.
8. A ridge of mountains rose before them, yet they pressed on, for winter was near.
9. The stones of the ancient fortress had been placed with extraordinary precision; the archaeologist realized that the masonry was more sophisticated than she had thought.
10. Kofi Atta Annan assumed the office of secretary general of the United Nations in 1997, prior to that time he had held many positions at the United Nations.

Exercise 3

OBJECTIVE

- To identify and revise sentence fragments and run-on sentences

Exercise 3 — Identifying and Correcting Sentence Fragments and Run-on Sentences

POSSIBLE ANSWERS

1. We are enjoying a bounty harvested from the orchards on the coast.
2. Domestic canaries are usually yellow, but they may be bright orange if red peppers are part of their diet.
3. Noelle is one of the fastest runners and usually the winner in races.
4. The fertile land in the river valley had never been farmed before.
6. The huge gears had long ago become rusty, and they groaned as the blades of the windmill turned.
8. An old oak grew there; it had survived being struck by lightning.
9. The Black Hills are in southwestern South Dakota. Southeast of the Black Hills are the Badlands.
10. Calamity Jane, born in 1852 near Princeton, Missouri, is someone about whom many wild stories are told.

Reference Note

For information on correcting **sentence fragments** and **run-on sentences,** see pages 480 and 483.

Exercise 3 — Identifying and Correcting Sentence Fragments and Run-on Sentences

Each numbered item below is a sentence fragment, a run-on sentence, or a complete sentence. First, identify the item by writing *F* for a sentence fragment, *R* for a run-on sentence, or *S* for a complete sentence. Then, rewrite each sentence fragment or run-on sentence to make at least one complete sentence.

EXAMPLE
1. Rice and potatoes, two food staples of the world.
   1. *F—Rice and potatoes are two food staples of the world.*

1. Enjoying a bounty harvested from the orchards on the coast. **1.** F
2. Domestic canaries are usually yellow, they may be bright orange if red peppers are part of their diet. **2.** R
3. One of the fastest runners and usually the winner in races. **3.** F
4. Because the fertile land in the river valley had never been farmed before. **4.** F
5. To go home was all Dorothy wanted. **5.** S
6. The huge gears had long ago become rusty, they groaned as the blades of the windmill turned. **6.** R

7. After twenty years had passed, he no longer recognized the prince.

8. An old oak grew there, it had survived being struck by lightning.

9. The Black Hills are in southwestern South Dakota, southeast of the Black Hills are the Badlands.

10. Calamity Jane, born in 1852 near Princeton, Missouri, about whom many wild stories are told.

7. S
8. R
9. R
10. F

Exercise 4 Revising Sentence Fragments and Run-on Sentences in a Paragraph

The paragraph below contains complete sentences, sentence fragments, and run-on sentences. Rewrite the paragraph to correct each sentence fragment and run-on sentence.

EXAMPLE
[1] Sculptors in Benin create extremely detailed statues, they use the lost-wax process of bronze casting to do so.

1. *Using the lost-wax process of bronze casting, sculptors in Benin create extremely detailed statues.*

[1] To begin the process, a sculptor forms a core figure from loamy soil and water, after the figure has dried, the sculptor coats it with beeswax. [2] Which is quite easy to shape. [3] The sculptor can then add details to the wax figure. [4] With knives and modeling tools. [5] When the design is complete, it must be sealed, the sculptor presses a smooth coating of soil all over the beeswax and then leaves the figure to dry. [6] After applying three such layers. [7] The sculptor heats the sealed figure in a hot fire, and all of the wax melts and runs out of a channel formed in the base. [8] Creating a hollow mold, which is buried upside down. [9] Next, the sculptor heats bronze until it lique-fies, pouring molten bronze into the upside-down mold, the sculptor fills the hollow area left by the "lost" wax. [10] Once the mold is cool, the sculptor breaks it with a hammer, to complete the process, the sculptor cleans and polishes the finished bronze figure.

Exercise 5 Choosing Verbs That Agree in Number with Their Subjects

Choose the verb in parentheses that correctly completes each of the sentences on the following page.

EXAMPLE
1. (*Has, Have*) you or your sister ever been in a play?

1. *Have*

Reference Note

For information on correcting **sentence fragments** and **run-on sentences,** see pages 480 and 483.

Reference Note

For information on **subject-verb agreement,** see page 106.

Grammar and Usage **429**

Exercise 4

OBJECTIVE

■ To revise a paragraph to correct sentence fragments and run-on sentences

Exercise 4 Revising Sentence Fragments and Run-on Sentences in a Paragraph

POSSIBLE ANSWERS

[1] To begin the process, a sculptor forms a core figure from loamy soil and water. After the figure has dried, the sculptor coats it with beeswax, [2] which is quite easy to shape. [3] The sculptor can then add details to the wax figure [4] with knives and modeling tools. [5] When the design is complete, it must be sealed, so the sculptor presses a smooth coating of soil all over the beeswax and then leaves the figure to dry. [6] After applying three such layers, [7] the sculptor heats the sealed figure in a hot fire. All of the wax melts and runs out of a channel formed in the base, [8] creating a hollow mold, which is buried upside down. [9] Next, the sculptor heats bronze until it liquefies. Pouring molten bronze into the upside-down mold, the sculptor fills the hollow area left by the "lost" wax. [10] Once the mold is cool, the sculptor breaks it with a hammer. To complete the process, the sculptor cleans and polishes the finished bronze figure.

Exercise 5

OBJECTIVE

■ To select verbs that agree in number with their subjects

1. My friend and I (*takes*, *take*) English literature every semester.
2. Charles Dickens's *Great Expectations* (*is*, *are*) the novel that we are studying now.
3. Our class, fortunate enough to have several talented drama students, (*plans*, *plan*) to dramatize Dickens's novel.
4. We hope that raising funds (*don't*, *doesn't*) prove very difficult.
5. Do you think four dollars (*is*, *are*) too much for an advance ticket?
6. We're going to see whether the PTA (*has*, *have*) any resources available for a project like this.
7. Hawkins Lumber and Tools (*has*, *have*) promised to donate some building supplies.
8. One thing we've learned in producing this play is that economics (*needs*, *need*) to be considered carefully.
9. Even scissors (*costs*, *cost*) three dollars apiece, and we need six pairs.
10. All the students and adults helping to put on the show (*has*, *have*) been working to make the production well worth the time and resources our class and community have been investing in it.
11. The director and production consultant for the set designers (*is*, *are*) Teresa Gonzales, who is a senior.
12. (*Don't*, *Doesn't*) she have a brother with the Little Theater who might loan us some sound equipment?
13. (*There's*, *There are*) still openings for the stage crew.
14. All of the roles (*has*, *have*) been assigned, but we might be able to put you in the chorus.
15. Many of the costumes (*is*, *are*) just our everyday street clothes.
16. (*Here's*, *Here are*) the bluejeans and work shirt Pip will wear.
17. Several of the costumes (*was*, *were*) borrowed from our teacher.
18. Jimmy and James, who are writing the lyrics for all the songs, (*don't*, *doesn't*) have them finished yet.
19. Neither the actors nor the director (*knows*, *know*) what the audience's reaction to a twenty-first century *Great Expectations* will be.
20. The goal of every member of the team (*has*, *have*) two parts—happy memories and pride in a job well done.

Exercise 6 Correcting Errors in Subject-Verb Agreement

Reference Note

For information on **subject-verb agreement,** see page 106.

Most of the following sentences contain verbs that do not agree with their subjects. Identify each verb that does not agree with its subject, and give the correct form of the verb. If a sentence is already correct, write C.

430   Correcting Common Errors

COMMON ERRORS

Exercise 6

OBJECTIVE

■ To correct errors in subject-verb agreement

DIFFERENTIATING INSTRUCTION

Learners Having Difficulty

If you would like to give students extra practice with subject-verb agreement before they complete **Exercise 6,** you could write a list of subjects and a list of verbs on the chalkboard. Ask students to work in pairs to compose sentences showing combinations of various subjects and verbs. Tell the paired students to write sentences showing two verb choices (one correct, one incorrect) in parentheses. Students should write one of each of the following types of sentences: sentences with compound subjects, sentences with phrases between the subjects and verbs, and sentences with the subjects following the verbs. Then, have the student pairs present their sentences as a challenge to other class members.

EXAMPLE   1. Don't he want to go to the Renaissance Fair?

          1. *Don't—Doesn't*

1. Admission to most movie theaters now cost more than one hundred times the price of attending a nickelodeon movie theater in 1905.
2. The Schomburg collection of books and other materials about Africa and Africans are owned by the New York Public Library.
3. Pilot-training programs incorporating virtual-reality technology have recently been improved.
4. The writers and painters of the Pre-Raphaelite Brotherhood was determined to reform English art.
5. The red doors along the hallway open into classrooms.
6. A number of brightly colored fish swims among the coral and kelp.
7. Mr. Blake said that *Elemental Odes* contain many of Pablo Neruda's most eloquent poems.
8. The class president or the members of the French Club usually announces the results of the election at the assembly.
9. Each of the men know my uncle Louis.
10. There are among many cultures all over the world a great respect for the elderly.

1. costs

2. is

3. C

4. were

5. C
6. swim
7. contains

8. announce

9. knows

10. is

Exercise 7 Correcting Errors in Pronoun-Antecedent Agreement

The following sentences contain errors in pronoun-antecedent agreement. If a pronoun does not agree with its antecedent, rewrite the sentence to correct the error.

EXAMPLE   1. Jim Gatacre founded the Handicapped Scuba Association (HSA), which opened their doors in 1981.

          1. *Jim Gatacre founded the Handicapped Scuba Association (HSA), which opened its doors in 1981.*

1. Currently, more than a dozen diver-certification agencies exist, and each one makes sure that their divers meet rigorous standards.
2. In addition to getting regular certification, all HSA students and instructors agree to make sure his or her dives meet HSA standards.
3. HSA has set these standards to help ensure that their members have safe and rewarding dives.
4. Everyone who becomes certified through HSA learns to plan dives according to the level of assistance that they will need from team members.
5. No one, not even a Level A diver, goes on their dives alone.

─HELP─

In Exercise 7, you may need to revise the wording, especially in sentences that are awkward or misleading.

Reference Note

For information on **pronoun-antecedent agreement,** see page 124.

Grammar and Usage   **431**

Exercise 7

OBJECTIVE

■ To correct errors in pronoun-antecedent agreement

Exercise 7 Correcting Errors in Pronoun-Antecedent Agreement

POSSIBLE ANSWERS

1. Currently, more than a dozen diver-certification agencies exist, and each one makes sure that its divers meet rigorous standards.

2. In addition to getting regular certification, all HSA students and instructors agree to make sure their dives meet HSA standards.

3. HSA has set standards to help ensure that its members have safe and rewarding dives.

4. Everyone who becomes certified through HSA learns to plan dives according to the level of assistance that he or she will need from team members.

5. No one, not even a Level A diver, goes on his or her dives alone.

COMMON ERRORS

Grammar and Usage   **431**

Exercise 7 Correcting Errors in Pronoun-Antecedent Agreement

POSSIBLE ANSWERS continued

6. Additionally, Level B and Level C divers are required to take extra precautions; for example, they must always be part of a three-person team.

7. A Level C diver always has a trained Rescue Diver as one of his or her team members.

8. However, neither instructors nor students are required by law to make their dives in accordance with those standards.

9. Every diver must have great control over his or her movements.

10. Most people who have had physical therapy know how to focus their effort and attention; this ability can be of great importance in disorienting underwater environments.

Exercise 8

OBJECTIVE

■ To identify and correct errors in pronoun-antecedent agreement in sentences

HELP

In Exercise 8, you may need to revise the wording, especially in sentences that are awkward or misleading. Although two revisions are shown in the example, you need to give only one for each sentence.

Reference Note

For information on **pronoun-antecedent agreement,** see page 124.

1. everyone
2. his or her
3. his
4. her
5. they
6. Both/they
7. its
8. who/is

6. Additionally, Level B and Level C divers are required to take extra precautions; for example, he or she must always be part of a three-person team.

7. A Level C diver always has a trained Rescue Diver as one of their team members.

8. However, neither instructors nor students are required by law to make his or her dives in accordance with those standards.

9. Every diver must have great control over their movements.

10. Most people who have had physical therapy know how to focus his or her effort and attention; this ability can be of great importance in disorienting underwater environments.

Exercise 8 Correcting Errors in Pronoun-Antecedent Agreement

Most of the following sentences contain errors in pronoun-antecedent agreement. If a pronoun does not agree with its antecedent, rewrite the sentence to correct the error. If a sentence is already correct, write *C*.

EXAMPLE Revisions may vary.
1. Ellen is organizing our senior class picnic, and she needs somebody to bring their grill.

1. *Ellen is organizing our senior class picnic, and she needs somebody to bring his or her grill.*

or

Ellen is organizing our senior class picnic, and she needs somebody to bring a grill.

1. Nobody wanted to be left out, so they all called Ellen and volunteered to help with the preparations.

2. Everyone wants to do their part to make the class picnic a success.

3. Michael or Don has offered to spend their afternoon today planning the schedule and assigning the teams for the volleyball tournament.

4. Ellen is bringing a stereo, and each of the Mullaney girls will bring their favorite CDs.

5. All of the members of the Art Club said that he or she will help make a banner for the occasion.

6. Mr. Johnston and Miss Sidney say that he or she both can chaperon our picnic.

7. By the way, the parks commission has already given their permission.

8. If anybody wants to play music, they are welcome to bring an instrument.

9. All seven drivers will be at the school by 10:30 A.M. this Saturday to pick up their passengers.

10. I heard that anyone in the senior class can attend and bring ~~their~~ friends, too.

Reference Note
For information on **pronoun-antecedent agreement,** see page 124.

Exercise 9 Correcting Errors in Pronoun-Antecedent Agreement

Most of the following sentences contain pronouns that do not agree with their antecedents. Identify and correct each pronoun that does not agree with its antecedent. If a sentence is already correct, write *C*.

EXAMPLE **1.** A number of students here plan to make computer animation his or her career.

　　　　　1. *his or her—their*

1. Be sure to review the statistics; it revealed some interesting trends.
2. After the short meeting, the staff returned to its offices.
3. Not only has the price of binoculars dropped, but technology has improved it as well.
4. You'll need to take ethics; the summer session at the community college offers them this year.
5. A jury summons is a serious obligation, and it should not be ignored.
6. Yes, I read *The Three Musketeers* years ago and remember them quite well.
7. Many a young person learns their full potential in the armed services.
8. She left the pliers downstairs; it should still be there.
9. If anyone has lost a backpack, they must go to Ms. Kasmarski's room to claim it.
10. The number of applications has risen for two years, and they may do so again this year.

1. they
2. their
3. them
4. it
5. C
6. it
7. his or her
8. they
9. he or she
10. it

Exercise 10 Correcting Errors in the Use of Pronouns

Most of the sentences on the following page contain errors in the use of pronoun forms. Identify and correct each error. If a sentence is already correct, write *C*.

EXAMPLE **1.** John is going to let me know when Greg and him are planning to go hiking in Big Bend National Park.

　　　　　1. *him—he*

Reference Note
For information on **using pronouns correctly,** see Chapter 6.

Exercise 9

OBJECTIVE

■ To identify and correct errors in pronoun-antecedent agreement

Exercise 10

OBJECTIVE

■ To identify and correct errors in the use of pronoun forms

COMMON ERRORS

1. me
2. them
3. he
4. me
5. C
6. me
7. us
8. they
9. her/them
10. We
11. C
12. us
13. she
14. her
15. I
16. you
17. she
18. her
19. who
20. myself

1. Did he say that the guest of honor at the banquet will be seated near Ann and I?
2. Which members of the chorus, besides they, do you want to invite to the auditions?
3. In the story, the butler arrives at the worst possible moment and asks, "Pardon, Madame, are you expecting Mr. Forster? It is him at the door."
4. When large drops began to pelt Christy and I, we ran for cover.
5. Mrs. Blair gave Richard and him several fifty-cent pieces to take with them.
6. Did Scott remember to write down directions for her and I, or should we remind him?
7. Donna sent her and we postcards from Moscow.
8. Was it them who arranged the interview with her?
9. Here's a picture of she and they standing in front of the entrance to the New Orleans World's Fair.
10. Us soloists need another practice session before we have the dress rehearsal.
11. To whom should we assign the research?
12. Mr. Laughlin gave Mother and we a tour of the museum grounds and the special exhibit.
13. Didn't Fran and her do their report on the rise and fall of the Ottoman Empire?
14. Wow! Who taught Linda and she how to mix tracks?
15. Yes, my brother and me are great admirers of Isaac Stern's violin technique.
16. Will the cancellation affect yourself at all?
17. Nobody, not even those politicians on television, can give a speech better than her.
18. I suspect that, in any debate between Danielle and she, Shannon would always win.
19. Let the victory go to those whom have met the challenge.
20. No, it's not for you, old pal; I'm fixing this tuna fish and tomato sandwich for me.

Reference Note

For information on **clear reference,** see Chapter 7.

Exercise 11 Revising Sentences to Correct Faulty Pronoun References

Rewrite the following sentences to correct each ambiguous, general, weak, or indefinite pronoun reference.

Exercise 11

OBJECTIVE

■ To identify and correct faulty pronoun references

Exercise 11 Revising Sentences to Correct Faulty Pronoun References

POSSIBLE ANSWERS

1. Although the delegates discussed the issues, nothing was settled, and no agreement was reached.
2. Jonathan likes watching archaeological films and hopes to become an archaeologist someday.

EXAMPLE

1. Kaitlin gave Lynda the photographs just before she went to lunch.

1. *Just before Kaitlin went to lunch, she gave Lynda the photographs.*

or

Just before Lynda went to lunch, Kaitlin gave her the photographs.

1. Although the delegates discussed the issues, it didn't settle anything, and no agreement was reached.
2. Jonathan likes watching archaeological films and hopes to become one someday.
3. The singing was so loud that they were heard three blocks away.
4. In this article, it describes the Genroku Era in Japan.
5. When my mom and Aunt Lil spend the afternoon baking, they usually let us have some.
6. Reporters mobbed the jurors until the police led them away.
7. In A.D. 900 in Europe, you usually never travelled more than ten miles from your birthplace.
8. Amber spoke with Mrs. Davison about her plans for the summer.
9. Last Saturday, we pulled weeds in the garden, but it took longer than we had planned.
10. Clowns were performing acrobatics on the median, and that slowed traffic all morning.

Exercise 12 Rewriting Sentences to Correct Faulty Pronoun References

Rewrite the following sentences to correct each ambiguous, general, weak, or indefinite pronoun reference.

EXAMPLE

1. Good roads promote communication and trade. This was well understood by many ancient peoples.

1. *Many ancient peoples understood well that good roads promote communication and trade.*

or

That good roads promote communication and trade was well understood by many ancient peoples.

1. In the Roman Empire, they had some 50,000 miles of road connecting the distant points of their domain.
2. Some of these roads, which once stretched from Scotland to North Africa, can still be seen, and this is a testament to the skill of the builders.

─HELP─

Although the example in Exercise 11 shows two revisions, you need to give only one for each sentence.

─HELP─

Although the example in Exercise 12 shows two revisions, you need to give only one for each item.

Reference Note

For information about **clear reference,** see Chapter 7.

Grammar and Usage **435**

Exercise 11 Revising Sentences to Correct Faulty Pronoun References

POSSIBLE ANSWERS continued

3. Those singing were so loud that they were heard three blocks away.
4. This article describes the Genroku Era in Japan.
5. When my mom and Aunt Lil spend the afternoon baking, they usually let us have some of what they make.
6. Reporters mobbed the jurors until the police led the jurors away.
7. In A.D. 900 in Europe, a person usually never travelled more than ten miles from his or her birthplace.
8. Amber spoke with Mrs. Davison about Amber's plans for the summer.
9. Last Saturday, pulling weeds in the garden took us longer than we had planned.
10. Traffic was slow all morning because clowns were performing acrobatics on the median.

Exercise 12

OBJECTIVE

■ To revise sentences by correcting faulty pronoun references

Exercise 12 Rewriting Sentences to Correct Faulty Pronoun References

POSSIBLE ANSWERS

1. The Roman Empire had some 50,000 miles of road connecting the distant points of its domain.
2. Some of these roads, which once stretched from Scotland to North Africa, can still be seen, and their durability is a testament to the skill of the builders.

Exercise 12 Rewriting Sentences to Correct Faulty Pronoun References

ANSWERS continued

3. As the Romans discovered, sound foundations and good drainage are critical features of a good roadway. These features ensure longevity.

4. Without drainage, water collects on a road, causing the surface to deteriorate and creating hazards for travelers.

5. The Roman roads were constructed to bear heavy chariot and cart traffic, but the Incas did not use such vehicles.

6. Two roads tied together the Incas' far-flung empire: One of the most famous ran more than 2,200 miles along the coast, while another snaked along the Andes.

7. In relays, Incan runners would cover distances of up to 1,200 miles, sometimes in as few as five days.

8. In various civilizations, roads paved with stone slabs withstood much wear from wheeled carts and wagons, and those roads are still sometimes used.

9. Improperly designed roads are soon marred by puddles and ruts that cause travelers much inconvenience.

10. Layers of sand, gravel, and concrete used in modern road construction help make road foundations strong and stable.

Exercise 13

OBJECTIVE

■ To use the correct past or past participle forms of irregular verbs

---

3. As the Romans discovered, sound foundations and good drainage are critical features of a good roadway. It ensures longevity.

4. Without drainage, water collects on a road, which causes the surface to deteriorate and creates hazards for travelers.

5. The Roman roads were constructed to bear heavy chariot and cart traffic, but in the Incan civilization, they did not use such vehicles.

6. One of the most famous Incan roads ran more than 2,200 miles along the coast, while another snaked along the Andes, which tied together their far-flung empire.

7. In relays, Incan runners would cover distances of up to 1,200 miles, which sometimes took as few as five days.

8. In various civilizations, roads paved with stone slabs withstood much wear from wheeled carts and wagons, and they are still sometimes used.

9. Improperly designed roads are soon marred by puddles and ruts, and this causes travelers much inconvenience.

10. Layers of sand, gravel, and concrete used in modern road construction help make its foundation strong and stable.

Exercise 13 Using Past and Past Participle Forms of Irregular Verbs Correctly

Reference Note

For information on **using verbs correctly,** see Chapter 8.

For each of the following sentences, fill in the correct past or past participle form of the italicized verb.

EXAMPLE 1. *bind* Libraries existed long before books were printed and _____.

1. *bound*

1. held

2. saw

3. forbade [or forbad]

4. made

5. lost

6. kept

1. *hold* Ancient libraries in Mesopotamia and Egypt _____ collections of inscribed clay tablets and papyrus scrolls.

2. *see* The Alexandrians, whose library was famous, _____ the rival library at Pergamum as a threat to their prestige.

3. *forbid* Therefore, the Alexandrians _____ the export of any papyrus to Pergamum.

4. *make* The citizens of Pergamum substituted parchment, which they _____ from dried animal skins, for the papyrus.

5. *lose* The world _____ a great storehouse of knowledge when the library at Alexandria was destroyed in 47 B.C.

6. *keep* One of the greatest manuscript collections in the Americas was _____ at Maní, in what is now Mexico.

7. *leave*   Unfortunately, most of the manuscripts at Maní were burned; today, only three are ____.   **7. left**

8. *write*   Prior to the invention of the printing press, monks copied by hand what scholars had ____.   **8. written**

9. *strike*   Before they ____ Monte Cassino monastery by air in 1944, the Allied forces warned the monks, thereby giving them the chance to protect manuscripts at the monastery.

10. *tell*   My grandmother, who has seen the manuscripts at Monte Cassino, has ____ me that they are very ornate.

   9. struck   10. told

Exercise 14   Correcting Errors in the Use of Past and Past Participle Verb Forms

Identify the incorrect verb form in each of the following sentences, and then provide the correct verb form.

EXAMPLE   1.   The brothers had ran all the way to the ballpark before they found out that the game had been canceled.

   1.   *ran—run*

1. The snow that fell in early spring had froze the blossoms.
2. He beared his burdens with such great dignity that the emperor finally forgave him.
3. His terrier has stole a dog biscuit and has run out the door.
4. The tomb had laid undisturbed for centuries before the archaeologist found it.
5. After she won the first race, she done her best to win the next two.
6. Have they sprang the trap and caught the thief yet?
7. The goldfish they bought at the fair swum round and round in its new home.
8. I met Mr. Russell last fall when he teached math at my brother's middle school.
9. Before the sun had rose, we had already driven many miles toward Ontario.
10. Someone set on my sunglasses, which were lying on the couch.
11. The expedition had came in search of gold but found something far more valuable.
12. I don't know why, but that cat has never hurted my little brother's hamster; in fact, the two seem to be friends.
13. Alberto must have rode by that store a hundred times without noticing it.

Reference Note

For information on **using verbs correctly,** see Chapter 8.

1. frozen
2. bore
3. stolen
4. lain
5. did
6. sprung
7. swam
8. taught
9. risen
10. sat
11. come
12. hurt
13. ridden

DIFFERENTIATING INSTRUCTION

Learners Having Difficulty

As students work through **Exercises 13** and **14,** have them list irregular verbs that are problematic for them. Students could make charts with the base, past, and past participle forms of the verbs and keep the charts in their notebooks for reference when they are completing writing assignments.

Exercise 14

OBJECTIVE

■ **To correct errors in the use of past and past participle verb forms**

COMMON ERRORS

14. saw
15. cut
16. done

17. given

18. taken
19. won
20. found

14. Is that the same movie you seen in Mexico last summer?
15. Who cutted this wonderful design in the stencil?
16. His friends and he were sure they had did everything they could to help the Pakistani exchange student feel at home.
17. Have you and your opponent already finished your match and gave the results to the officials?
18. Yes, I have already took Spanish II.
19. "Aw," she answered, "it was a draw, so nobody winned."
20. Just then, a first-grader holding up a purple Easter egg yelled that she had finded one.

Exercise 15

OBJECTIVE

- **To correct errors in the use of past and past participle verb forms**

APPLICATION

Relating to Dictionary Skills

Point out to students that when they have questions about the principal parts of irregular verbs, they can look up the verbs in a dictionary. Explain that the entry word in a dictionary is the base form and that the past, past participle, and present participle forms of irregular verbs are listed following the entry word. For example, if students look up *sing,* they will find *sang, sung,* and *singing.* Have each student choose two or three irregular verbs to look up in a dictionary. Students should write each verb's principal parts.

Reference Note

For information on **using verbs correctly,** see Chapter 8.

1. chosen

2. kept

3. brought

4. worn

Exercise 15 Correcting Errors in the Use of Past and Past Participle Verb Forms

Identify the incorrect verb form in each of the following sentences, and then provide the correct form.

EXAMPLE
    1. By the time the Spanish come to the desert country of the Southwest, the Navajo had already been living there for at least a hundred years.

    1. come—came

1. The Navajo learned to weave from the Pueblo people, many of whom had chose to live with the Navajo in northern New Mexico.
2. The Spanish, Navajo, and Pueblo cultures influenced one another, but each one also keeped its own traditions.
3. The Spanish had brung with them a breed of sheep, the churro, which thrived in the high deserts of New Mexico.
4. Woven from the wool of these sheep, the Navajo blanket was often wore as a robe.

5. The Navajo could also lie wide blankets, known as chief's blankets, on the ground and use them as rugs.

6. While we often think of blankets as ordinary household items, these blankets were greatly valued and sometimes costed as much as twenty horses.

7. Since the mid-1800s, the Navajo have maked weaving a major commercial enterprise.

8. The Navajo drawed on new markets for designs and soon found ways to incorporate trains, flags, and other elements into their traditional designs.

9. In the last century and a half, the market for these useful and durable blankets has growed rapidly.

10. Many Navajo blankets and rugs are buyed by art lovers, crafts-people, and others who particularly admire things that have both beauty and utility.

5. lay

6. cost

7. made

8. drew

9. grown

10. bought

Reference Note

For information on **using tenses consistently,** see page 206.

Exercise 16 Revising a Paragraph for Consistent and Logical Use of Tenses

The verb tenses in the following paragraph are not used consistently and logically. Rewrite the paragraph to correct errors in the use of tense.

EXAMPLE [1] The name *Haiti* came from the Arawak word *Ayiti,* which means "land of high mountains."

1. The name Haiti *comes from the Arawak word* Ayiti, *which means "land of high mountains."*
Some answers may vary.

[1] Haiti's natural resources—ranging from mahogany forests and Caribbean coral reefs to mountain slopes where farmers grow coffee and cacao—have been remarkably diverse. [2] Today, Haiti's environment has been under serious threat. [3] Only 10 percent of Haiti's once lush forests were remaining. [4] Similarly, waters that will have been teeming with fish no longer yielded rich catches. [5] However, efforts were now underway to protect and restore Haiti's lands and waters. [6] For instance, several groups had supported the creation of a marine conservation park at Les Arcadins Bank. [7] Also, fine-mesh nets that will harvest young fish before they have reproduced had already been outlawed. [8] Fishing boats were working in deeper waters now so that fish can grow and spawn in shallow waters. [9] Schoolchildren were being taught about the value of the forests and waters. [10] These efforts and others, it is hoped, will have helped to conserve and restore Haiti's natural resources.

1. are

2. is

3. remain

4. teemed/yield

5. are

6. have

7. reproduce/ have

8. are

9. are

10. help

COMMON ERRORS

Exercise 17

OBJECTIVE

- To use verb tenses correctly in sentences

Exercise 18

OBJECTIVE

- To correct errors in the use of modifiers and comparisons

COMMON ERRORS

Reference Note

For information on **using verbs correctly,** see Chapter 8.

Exercise 17 Using Tenses Correctly

Each of the following sentences contains an error in the use of tenses. Rewrite the sentences to correct the errors. Answers may vary.

EXAMPLE 1. Once the rain stopped, we had a picnic.

     1. Once the rain had stopped, we had a picnic.

1. had
2. sanded
3. walking
4. had
5. had

6. had

7. are

8. Having read
9. hadn't

10. have been

1. The project would have been more profitable if they ~~would have~~ consulted the experts.
2. While I ~~sand~~ one board, Kathy stained the other.
3. While ~~having walked~~ through the park, Debra saw a nest of red squirrels near the ranger station.
4. If you ~~would have~~ asked me, I would have helped you.
5. Even though we already ~~have~~ tickets, we waited in line for almost an hour just to enter the arena.
6. My mom and I just finished painting the boat when the rain started to fall.
7. Because fire ants' stings ~~were~~ painful, we were especially careful to avoid ant mounds when we worked in the yard yesterday.
8. ~~Reading~~ the novel last year, I am eagerly awaiting the film version.
9. Detectives examined the evidence left at the crime scene and decided that the butler ~~hasn't~~ committed the crime.
10. On the first of next month, Nelson's Deli on First Street will ~~be~~ open for forty years.

Reference Note

For information on **using modifiers correctly,** see Chapter 9.

Exercise 18 Using Modifiers and Comparisons Correctly

Some of the following sentences contain errors in the standard, formal use of modifiers. Revise each incorrect sentence to correct the error. If a sentence is already correct, write *C*. Answers may vary.

EXAMPLE 1. Of the McDonald twins, Jessica is the best basketball player.

     1. Of the McDonald twins, Jessica is the better basketball player.

1. more careful

3. less
4. most

1. Try to be ~~carefuller~~ the next time you stack dishes in the sink.
2. For almost two days, the sea had been ~~more~~ calmer than the captain had thought it would be.
3. Which is ~~least~~ expensive—the tall vase or the music box?
4. After watching the litter awhile, we chose the ~~more~~ playful one of the three kittens.

5. The speech you gave today was better than any I've heard this week.
6. My stepsister thinks it's ~~real~~ easy to put together a jigsaw puzzle.
7. Is this the ~~most~~ narrowest stretch of the trail?
8. Joshua usually finishes his worksheets faster than anyone in his math class.
9. We tried green lampshades, but I like the warm look of the red ones better.
10. During the dinner hour, a number of our customers prefer lighting that is less ~~brighter.~~
11. Everybody knows that Scott is better than anyone at identifying bacteria.
12. Of Jorge Luis Borges, Gabriel García Márquez, and Pablo Neruda, I like Borges ~~better.~~
13. Let's move ~~more~~ closer to the stage; I can't understand what they're saying.
14. Keep going; the cabin's just a little ~~more~~ farther down this road.
15. The weather forecasters said driving conditions would be ~~more~~ worse today, but, thank goodness, they were wrong.
16. At last, it was official—Maria was a faster runner than any other girl in town.
17. The plan sounds ~~badly~~ to me; do you think it will work as they hope it will?
18. Seemingly from out of nowhere floated the ~~beautifulest~~ flute music.
19. Which of the two do you like ~~best~~—the Persian rug or the Chinese one?
20. I didn't know you could speak Italian so ~~good.~~

5. other
6. really
8. else
9. C
10. bright
11. else
12. best
16. C
17. bad
18. most beautiful
19. better
20. well

Exercise 19 **Revising Sentences to Correct Misplaced Modifiers and Dangling Modifiers**

Each of the sentences on the following page contains a misplaced or dangling modifier. Revise each sentence so that its meaning is clear and correct.

EXAMPLE
   1. When training animals, firm and consistent commands should be used.
   1. *When training animals, a person should use firm and consistent commands.*

            or

   A person who is training animals should use firm and consistent commands.

Grammar and Usage   **441**

For information on the **correct placement of modifiers,** see Chapter 10.

HELP
Although the example in Exercise 19 shows two revisions, you need to give only one for each sentence.

OBJECTIVE

■ To revise sentences to correct misplaced and dangling modifiers

Exercise 19 **Revising Sentences to Correct Misplaced Modifiers and Dangling Modifiers**

POSSIBLE ANSWERS

1. Since I had seen the video before, it didn't seem very exciting.
2. On the way to the mall in San Jose, we saw a flock of geese.
3. Even buses seemed small as I looked down from the thirtieth story.
4. Several meetings have been scheduled for us to discuss this issue adequately.
5. Pulling twelve boxcars, the train sped past the van.
6. Absolute silence is required of bystanders while recording is taking place in the studio.
7. To assign priorities, you must have clear goals.
8. Your idea is even more practical than mine.

Grammar and Usage   **441**

Exercise 19 Revising
Sentences to Correct Misplaced
Modifiers and Dangling Modifiers

POSSIBLE ANSWERS
continued

9. While performing a routine safety
check, the inspector found a leak
in the duct.

10. Growing at a remarkable rate, the
ivy soon covered the fence around
the backyard.

Exercise 20

OBJECTIVE

■ To revise sentences by correcting
misplaced and dangling modifiers

Exercise 20 Revising
Sentences to Correct Misplaced
Modifiers and Dangling Modifiers

POSSIBLE ANSWERS

1. Last week Mr. Smith's class
watched a movie about how electricity was first used.

2. According to our debate schedule,
your rebuttal will be limited to
only three minutes.

3. Practicing for the piano recital, Sara
found the out-of-tune key very
bothersome.

4. When conducting an experiment,
you should keep precise notes.

5. Hanging from the crane at the top
of the building, the boom swung
wildly over the crowd.

6. Mrs. Chamberlin said my assignment is due on Thursday.

7. My neighbor's advice came to
mind while I was pondering how
to proceed.

8. You should dial 911 only in an
emergency.

9. After I studied all week, the test
was easy for me.

10. Before we drove into the park,
the ranger told us not to feed
the bears.

1. Having seen the video before, it didn't seem very exciting.
2. We saw a flock of geese on the way to the mall in San Jose.
3. Looking down from the thirtieth story, even buses seemed small.
4. To discuss this issue adequately, several meetings have been scheduled.
5. The train sped past the van pulling twelve boxcars.
6. While recording in the studio, absolute silence is required of bystanders.
7. To assign priorities, your goals must be clear.
8. Your idea is more practical even than mine.
9. While performing a routine safety check, a leak was found in the duct.
10. Growing at a remarkable rate, the fence around the backyard was soon covered with ivy.

Reference Note
For information about correct **placement of modifiers,** see Chapter 10.

Exercise 20 Revising Sentences to Correct Misplaced Modifiers and Dangling Modifiers

Each of the following sentences contains a misplaced or dangling modifier. Revise each sentence so that its meaning is clear and correct.

EXAMPLE
1. There was only one glitch in this computer program that we could find.

1. *There was only one glitch that we could find in this computer program.*

1. Mr. Smith's class watched a movie about how electricity was first used last week.
2. According to our debate schedule, your rebuttal will only be limited to three minutes.
3. Practicing for the piano recital, the out-of-tune key was very bothersome.
4. When conducting an experiment, precise notes should be kept.
5. The boom swung wildly over the crowd hanging from the crane at the top of the building.
6. Mrs. Chamberlin said on Thursday my assignment is due.
7. While pondering how to proceed, my neighbor's advice came to mind.
8. You should only dial 911 in an emergency.
9. Having studied all week, the test was easy for me.
10. The ranger told us not to feed the bears before we drove into the park.

Exercise 21 Correcting Errors in Usage

Most of the following sentences contain an error in usage. If a sentence contains an error, revise the sentence. If a sentence is already correct, write *C.* Some answers may vary.

EXAMPLE   **1.** Where were you at when I called?

           1. *Where were you when I called?*

1. There are less ingredients in this recipe than you think there are.
2. Being as you have studied programming, could you help us install the new software?
3. I did good on the quiz because I've been paying attention in class.
4. We had ought to take a map with us.
5. Several dinosaur skeletons have been discovered besides the river near here.
6. A team of three screenwriters will adapt the novel for a three-part television miniseries.
7. Douglas is more skillful at flying model airplanes then John is.
8. No one yet knows how the World Wide Web will ultimately effect our culture.
9. Many a traveler has been fooled by the type of allusion commonly known as a mirage.
10. Few stores specialize in these kind of programs.

Exercise 22 Correcting Errors in Usage

Each of the following sentences contains an error in usage. Rewrite each sentence to correct the error. Some answers may vary.

EXAMPLE   **1.** Both French and Spanish are understood in Andorra, an European country between France and Spain.

           1. *Both French and Spanish are understood in Andorra, a European country between France and Spain.*

1. I read where the settlement that became St. Paul, Minnesota, used to be known as "Pig's Eye," which was the nickname of Pierre Parrant, the settlement's founder.
2. The reason ice floats on water is because water expands and becomes less dense as it freezes.
3. Rita implied from Avi's letter that he had decided to stay somewhere in Montana for the summer.
4. Between the thirty theories, there were only three that gave credible explanations for those phenomena.

Reference Note

For information about **common usage errors,** see Chapter 11.

1. fewer
2. Since
3. well

5. beside

6. C

7. than
8. affect

9. illusion

10. kinds

Reference Note

For information about **common usage errors,** see Chapter 11.

1. that

3. inferred

4. Among

Exercise 21

O B J E C T I V E

■ To revise sentences by correcting errors in usage

Exercise 22

O B J E C T I V E

■ To revise sentences by correcting errors in usage

5. I

7. As

8. fewer

9. nor

10. have

5. Lisa and myself were just wondering when the scholarship committee would begin accepting applications.
6. A number of penguins dove off of the huge chunk of floating ice.
7. Like Mr. Faust indicated, the eruption of Mount Vesuvius covered the city of Pompeii not with lava but with ashes.
8. Amy said that less people visit the gallery on Thursdays than on Fridays.
9. Neither the first or the last person in line knew when the tickets were supposed to go on sale.
10. Joey ought to of written the address on the notepad beside the phone.

Exercise 23

OBJECTIVE

■ **To identify and correct errors in usage**

Reference Note

For information about **common usage errors,** see Chapter 11.

1. said

2. everywhere

3. were

4. I

5. break

7. have
8. take

9. [or reason . . . that]

Exercise 23 Correcting Errors in Usage

Each of the following sentences contains an error in usage. Identify and correct each error.

EXAMPLE   1. Has that phenomena ever been explained?
     1. *phenomena—phenomenon*

1. Then, right after both of us had lost our passports, Erin says, "I just knew this would happen."
2. Richard looked everywheres for Maria and Laura and then asked the information clerk to page them.
3. A number of trout was feeding on the minnows under the lights at the end of the pier.
4. Simone and myself will narrate the tale while Nicole and Peter present it in pantomime.
5. Be careful that you don't bust that mirror.
6. The mechanic told my brother Tim that we had ought to change the oil every three thousand miles.
7. The papers must of blown off the table.
8. If you go to the library tomorrow afternoon, will you bring these videotapes back for me?
9. The reason Jackson Street is closed to vehicles is because a parade will be passing there soon.
10. Where was the Hope diamond found at?

Exercise 24

OBJECTIVE

■ **To correct sentences with double negatives and other errors in usage**

Reference Note

For information about **common usage errors,** see Chapter 11.

Exercise 24 Correcting Double Negatives and Other Errors in Usage

Rewrite the sentences on the following page, eliminating the double negatives and other errors in usage. Some answers may vary.

EXAMPLE   **1.** Megan doesn't want no more mashed potatoes.

            1. Megan doesn't want any more mashed potatoes.

1. You can't never tell what will happen.   **1.** can
2. I still haven't had a chance to see none of this summer's block-buster movies yet. **2.** any
3. The travelers walked a long ways to reach their destination. **3.** way
4. We looked all over, but neither my books nor my papers were nowhere in the library. **4.** anywhere
5. After working outside all morning in the wind and rain, he isn't feeling good.   **5.** well
6. Mr. Lee hadn't hardly started class before the bell rang for a fire drill.   **6.** had
                                               7. have
7. The power outage couldn't of lasted longer than a minute or so.
8. I did well on every test accept this last one. **8.** except
9. Were you in the kitchen when the china teapot fell off of the counter?
10. None of the clerks remembered nothing about our order.
                          10. anything

BORN LOSER reprinted by permission of Newspaper Enterprise Association, Inc.

Although some sentences in Exercise 24 can be corrected in more than one way, you need to give only one revision for each sentence.

DIFFERENTIATING INSTRUCTION

English-Language Learners

Spanish. The double negative is perfectly acceptable in Spanish (as it is in Russian, French, and a number of other languages). You may want to observe students to identify those who are transferring this usage to English, especially with words such as *nothing, none,* or *nobody.* Begin by asking questions that call for negative answers, such as "Did you meet anyone famous today?" or "Did you go abroad last weekend?" Require students to answer in complete sentences. Give additional written practice to students who are having trouble.

Grammar and Usage   **445**

Grammar and Usage   **445**

COMMON ERRORS

Grammar and Usage Test: Section 1

DIRECTIONS Read the paragraph below. For each numbered blank, select the word or group of words that best completes the sentence. Indicate your response by shading in the appropriate oval on your answer sheet.

EXAMPLE Have you ever wondered __(1)__ systems for classifying fingerprints?

1. (A) who discovered the first
   (B) whom discovered the first
   (C) who invented the first
   (D) whom invented the first
   (E) who first invented the

ANSWER 1. (A) (B) (C) (D) (E)

Fingerprinting __(1)__ a significant role in investigative work ever since the late nineteenth century, when Sir Francis Galton, a British anthropologist, determined that __(2)__ identical fingerprints. Building upon the research of Galton, Juan Vucetich of Argentina and Sir Edward R. Henry of Great Britain __(3)__ fingerprint classification systems during the 1890s. Fingerprints are one of the __(4)__ of identification because a person's fingerprints are unlikely to change during __(5)__ lifetime. Thus, when working to solve crimes, __(6)__ find fingerprints that identify people and place them at crime scenes. Sometimes such fingerprints are clearly visible, but other times __(7)__ cannot be seen. Most latent, or hidden, fingerprints __(8)__ detected until they have been covered with colored powder or special chemicals. Moreover, there are some types of latent fingerprints __(9)__ with a laser beam. Fingerprints, which are also used to identify victims of tragedies such as fires and plane crashes, __(10)__ to be an invaluable tool for more than a century.

1. (A) has played
   (B) played
   (C) plays
   (D) had played
   (E) will have played

2. (A) no two people never have
   (B) people they never have
   (C) two people don't have no
   (D) no two people don't have
   (E) no two people have

3. (A) introduced his
   (B) introduced their
   (C) were introducing his
   (D) had introduced their
   (E) have introduced their

4. (A) more useful type
   (B) usefuller types
   (C) most usefullest types
   (D) most useful types
   (E) usefullest types

5. **(A)** his or her
    (B) her
    (C) there
    (D) their
    (E) they're

6. **(A)** investigators they try and
    (B) investigators try and
    (C) investigators try to
    (D) investigators they try to
    (E) those investigators try to

7. **(A)** they
    (B) no fingerprints
    (C) these here fingerprints
    (D) these kind of fingerprints
    (E) those type of fingerprints

8. **(A)** can't hardly be
    (B) can't in no way be
    (C) can hardly be
    (D) they can't hardly be
    (E) can't scarcely be

9. **(A)** that only can be seen
    (B) that can be seen only
    (C) what can be seen only
    (D) only that can be seen
    (E) what can only be seen

10. **(A)** has proven
    (B) proves
    (C) will have proven
    (D) proved
    (E) have proven

Grammar and Usage Test: Section 2

DIRECTIONS   In the following sentences, either part or all of each sentence is underlined. Using the rules of standard, formal English, choose the answer that most clearly expresses the meaning of the sentence. If there is no error, choose *A*. Indicate your response by shading in the appropriate oval on your answer sheet.

EXAMPLE   **1.** Gail told Wendy that the tryout had gone so <u>well that she was sure she got</u> the part of Emily in *Our Town*.

    (A) well that she was sure she got
    (B) good that she was sure Wendy had got
    (C) well that she was sure Wendy had got
    (D) well that Wendy was sure she had got
    (E) good that Gail was sure she had got

ANSWER   **1.** A B C D E

1. On the other side of <u>these here mountains lie</u> some of the richest farmland in the world.

    (A) these here mountains lie
    (B) these mountains lie
    (C) these mountains lies
    (D) these mountains lay
    (E) these mountains lays

2. The myelin sheath which surrounds nerve cells and helps to speed up nerve impulses.
   (A) The myelin sheath which surrounds nerve cells and helps to speed up nerve impulses.
   (B) The myelin sheath surrounding nerve cells, which helps to speed up nerve impulses.
   (C) The myelin sheath which surrounding nerve cells and helping to speed up nerve impulses.
   (D) The myelin sheath, which surrounds nerve cells, helps to speed up nerve impulses.
   (E) Helping speed up nerve impulses, the myelin sheath surrounding nerve cells.

3. Arnie carves soapstone beautifully; he plans to give them to his friends.
   (A) them
   (B) these
   (C) carvings
   (D) it
   (E) ones

4. Beaming proudly, a medal hung around her neck at the ceremony.
   (A) Beaming proudly, a medal hung around her neck at the ceremony.
   (B) At the ceremony, a medal hung around her neck, beaming proudly.
   (C) At the ceremony, she wore a medal around her neck beaming proudly.
   (D) Beaming proudly, she wore a medal around her neck at the ceremony.
   (E) Beaming proudly at the ceremony, a medal hung around her neck.

5. The contract between him and them is quite complex.
   (A) between him and them
   (B) between him and they
   (C) between he and them
   (D) among him and them
   (E) among he and they

6. I can't hardly believe that less people than we had predicted turned out for today's carnival.
   (A) I can't hardly believe that less people than
   (B) I can hardly believe that fewer people then
   (C) I can hardly believe that less people then
   (D) I can't hardly believe that fewer people than
   (E) I can hardly believe that fewer people than

7. <u>In 1824, I read that a fifteen-year-old student who was blind, Louis Braille, developed a system of reading that used raised dots.</u>

   (A) In 1824, I read that a fifteen-year-old student who was blind, Louis Braille, developed a system of reading that used raised dots.

   (B) I read in 1824 that a fifteen-year-old student who was blind, Louis Braille, developed a system of reading that used raised dots.

   (C) I read that in 1824 a fifteen-year-old student who was blind, Louis Braille, developed a system of reading that used raised dots.

   (D) I read that Louis Braille, a fifteen-year-old student who was blind in 1824, developed a system of reading that used raised dots.

   (E) I read that a fifteen-year-old student who was blind, Louis Braille, developed a system of reading that used raised dots in 1824.

8. In golf, a "mulligan" is <u>when a player is given a free shot after having made a</u> poor shot.

   (A) when a player is given a free shot after having made

   (B) where a player is given a free shot after having made

   (C) when a player is given a free shot after he or she has made

   (D) a free shot given to a player after he or she has made

   (E) that a player is given a free shot after having made

9. <u>Skimming through the magazine, there were two articles I found for my report on Marcus Garvey.</u>

   (A) Skimming through the magazine, there were two articles I found for my report on Marcus Garvey.

   (B) While skimming through the magazine, there were two articles I found for my report on Marcus Garvey.

   (C) Skimming through the magazine, I found two articles for my report on Marcus Garvey.

   (D) I found two articles for my report on Marcus Garvey skimming through the magazine.

   (E) Two articles for my report on Marcus Garvey were found skimming through the magazine.

10. <u>Each of the athletes in the Olympics wore their</u> nation's jersey.

   (A) Each of the athletes in the Olympics wore their

   (B) Each of the athletes in the Olympics wore his or her

   (C) Every athlete in the Olympics wore their

   (D) All of the athletes in the Olympics wore their

   (E) All of the athletes in the Olympics wore his or her

COMMON ERRORS

Exercise 25

OBJECTIVE

■ To correct errors in capitalization

DIFFERENTIATING INSTRUCTION

English-Language Learners

Spanish and French. In some languages, days of the week, months, and proper adjectives are lowercased. The following sentence is an example of how words would be capitalized if the sentence were written in French or Spanish.

"On the first monday in april, we're going to watch a french film." In French, the sentence would read, "Le premier lundi d'avril, nous allons regarder un film français"; in Spanish, "En el primer lunes de abril, vamos a mirar una película francesa." Your acknowledgment to students that they are being asked to reverse rules they may already have mastered in their native languages may help them deal independently with the difference in English capitalization rules.

Exercise 26

OBJECTIVE

■ To correct sentences by adding or deleting commas

Reference Note

For information on **capitalization,** see Chapter 12.

Reference Note

For information on **using commas,** see page 333.

Exercise 25 Using Standard Capitalization

For each of the following items, correct any errors in capitalization by changing lowercase letters to capital letters or capital letters to lowercase letters as necessary. If an item is already correct, write *C*.

EXAMPLE
1. tests in Physics, history IV, and spanish

1. *tests in physics, History IV, and Spanish*

1. business in latin America
2. the middle ages
3. a book called *Everyday life of The Aztecs*
4. on Lake Texcoco **4.** C
5. the north American Free Trade Agreement
6. American broadcasting company, inc.
7. my uncle Matthew **7.** C
8. Carol Williams, m.d.
9. ancient toltec peoples
10. the sinai peninsula
11. the university of Michigan
12. the organization habitat for humanity
13. dr. j. s. ramírez, jr.
14. a roman catholic church
15. East of the Jordan River
16. the Nobel Prize **16.** C
17. at aunt Susan's house
18. queen Elizabeth I
19. 87 Thirty-Third street
20. a Bakery in New York city
21. the Capital theater
22. Harley-davidson motorcycles
23. Benjamin Franklin high school
24. travis county
25. my irish setter

Exercise 26 Correcting Errors in the Use of Commas

For each of the following sentences, add or delete commas to correct each error in the use of commas. If a sentence is already correct, write *C*.

Optional commas are underlined.

EXAMPLE
1. Wearing a gorilla suit Joe put aside his stage fright, and stepped into the spotlight.

1. *Wearing a gorilla suit, Joe put aside his stage fright and stepped into the spotlight.*

1. Thunder clapped, lightning flashed, and rain pounded the roof.
2. Lewis, having read the book, was especially eager to see the film adaptation.
3. The conference, Mr. Cherensky, will focus on technological advances in medicine.
4. Scheduled to employ some 1,200 people, the factories will open in Dayton, Ohio, and Phoenix, Arizona.
5. Copies of the videotape have been sent to Michael Tan, M.D., and Cindy Lowe, Ph.D.
6. Yes, we still need people to play the roles of Diana, and Pan, and Apollo in next month's production.
7. Actually John Adams, not Thomas Jefferson, was the second president of the United States.
8. Hey, have you read about the African American leader Malcolm X?
9. Robert Penn Warren, who was a poet, novelist, and essayist, was the first official U.S. poet laureate.
10. That is one of the oldest, most valuable paintings in the collection, I believe.

8. C

Exercise 27 · Correcting Errors in the Use of Commas

Rewrite the following sentences, adding or deleting commas as necessary.
Optional commas are underlined.

EXAMPLE 1. "Wow" said Ms. Gage "just listen to those, African drummers!"

1. "Wow," said Ms. Gage, "just listen to those African drummers!"

1. The oldest musical instrument, the drum, is a percussion instrument.
2. Of the musical instruments that have come from Africa, percussion instruments are probably the most common.
3. Percussion instruments, those that are tapped, shaken, or struck, include drums, bells, and xylophones.
4. The banjo, which was brought to this country from Africa, is a modified percussion instrument.
5. Although, the banjo is generally considered a string instrument, its body is actually a small drum with a tightly stretched skin on one side.
6. Maurice, have you noticed that African drums have many different shapes, and sizes?
7. Drums are often shaped like cones or cylinders, and some, such as ceremonial drums, are decorated with complex, fanciful carvings.

Reference Note

For information on **using commas,** see page 333.

Mechanics   **451**

Exercise 27

OBJECTIVE

- To correct errors in the use of commas

DIFFERENTIATING INSTRUCTION

Learners Having Difficulty

You may want to help students visualize some of the uses of commas by showing examples of comma usage in six columns on the chalkboard. Label the columns *items in a series, independent clauses, nonessential clauses, introductory elements, interrupters,* and *conventional uses.* Work with students to generate examples to go in each column. Write the examples under the appropriate headings on the chalkboard.

You may then want to assign **Exercise 27** for homework and go over the answers with students in class. Survey the class for error patterns and review those rules of comma usage that seem to be giving students problems.

COMMON ERRORS

8. Reserved for special occasions, ceremonial drums, can be quite elaborate.
9. Drums can be made from hollow logs, cooking pots, tin cans, or even oil drums.
10. The steel drum, which is a 55-gallon oil drum that has been carefully tuned to produce a full range of notes, was invented on the islands of Trinidad and Tobago in the 1930s.

Reference Note

For information about **semicolons** and **colons**, see page 356 and page 359.

Exercise 28 **Correcting Sentences by Adding Semicolons and Colons**

Rewrite the following sentences, replacing commas with semicolons and colons and adding semicolons and colons as necessary.

EXAMPLE
1. The house is in need of very few cosmetic repairs, furthermore, the foundation is sound.

1. *The house is in need of very few cosmetic repairs; furthermore, the foundation is sound.*

1. Three books sat on Ethan's desk his journal, a dictionary, and a copy of *Middlemarch A Study of Provincial Life.*
2. Leather car seats require upkeep for instance, they should be cleaned regularly and kept out of direct sunlight.
3. The prizes are as follows first prize, $500; second prize, $200; and third prize, $100.
4. This setback doesn't mean that the project is over on the contrary, we'll be reorganizing it and redoubling our efforts.
5. Here are our next reading assignments pages 51–67, pages 110–130, and pages 185–200.
6. Baby-sitting can be profitable and enjoyable however, it entails a great deal of responsibility.
7. The following students should report to the front office Kyle Werner, Brian Weber, and Amanda Lawrence.
8. The unconscious mind is said to contain all the forgotten experiences of a person's lifetime psychologists are seeking ways to tap that knowledge.
9. Performances will be given in several major cities Atlanta, Georgia Orlando, Florida San Francisco, California and Seattle, Washington.
10. One of Shakespeare's best-known soliloquies includes these three lines "Tomorrow, and tomorrow, and tomorrow / Creeps in this petty pace from day to day, / To the last syllable of recorded time."

Exercise 28

OBJECTIVE

■ To correct sentences by adding semicolons and colons

DIFFERENTIATING INSTRUCTION

Learners Having Difficulty

Some students might confuse the colon with the semicolon or think that the two are interchangeable. Tell your class that a colon ordinarily points to the part of a sentence the writer wants to emphasize, whereas a semicolon helps the reader avoid confusion by separating ideas or items.

Learners Having Difficulty

If students need additional practice with semicolon use, collect from several essays a few sentences that contain comma splices or lack needed semicolons and have students correct errors by inserting semicolons. You may also want to enter students' sentences into a word-processing program and have students make corrections on the screen by adding semicolons.

Exercise 29 Proofreading a Dialogue for Correct Punctuation and Capitalization

Rewrite the following dialogue, adding or deleting paragraph indents, commas, end marks, and quotation marks where necessary. You may also need to replace some lowercase letters with capital letters.

EXAMPLE   **[1]** Hey, Annie, look at this sari my aunt brought me from India" Irene said.

1.   *"Hey, Annie, look at this sari my aunt brought me from India," Irene said.*

[1] "Wow, how do you put it on? Annie asked." **[2]** "You just wrap it around yourself and put the end over your shoulder," Irene answered.

[3] "It's beautiful! Annie declared. What was your aunt doing in India"?

[4] "She's a professor, and she's studying ancient Hindu texts and manuscripts." "She translated some of her favorite passages and wrote them in a little book for me".

[5] Annie said, "Oh, how nice of her! **[6]** "Yes, it was Irene replied "she also brought back a number of other interesting things—earrings, wooden carvings, clothes, and recipes." **[7]** "I'd love to see them." Annie remarked.

[8] Sure, Irene said, tonight she's going to teach me to cook a whole Indian dinner.

Have you ever had Indian food? **[9]** "No" Annie answered.

[10] "Well, stay for dinner tonight! You can help us cook and eat!

Exercise 30 Proofreading for the Correct Use of Quotation Marks, Other Marks of Punctuation, and Capitalization

Rewrite each of the following sentences, correcting any error in the use of quotation marks, capitalization, commas, or end marks.

EXAMPLE   1. "Since it's sunny, she said Let's take a walk."

1. *"Since it's sunny," she said, "let's take a walk."*

1. Did the flight attendant just say, "This is the last call for passengers boarding Flight 304?"
2. "Next week's story," Ms. Sorvino said "Will be "The Ring."
3. Mr. Keith posted Christine's latest essay, Reading for Life, outside the classroom.

Reference Note

For information on **quotation marks,** see page 365.

Reference Note

For information on **using quotation marks,** see page 365. For information on **capitalization,** see Chapter 12.

COMMON ERRORS

Exercise 29

OBJECTIVE

■ To punctuate and capitalize written dialogue correctly

Exercise 29 Proofreading a Dialogue for Correct Punctuation and Capitalization

ANSWERS

1. ¶"Wow, how do you put it on?" Annie asked.

2. ¶"You just wrap it around yourself and put the end over your shoulder," Irene answered.

3. ¶"It's beautiful!" Annie declared. "What was your aunt doing in India?"

4. ¶"She's a professor, and she's studying ancient Hindu texts and manuscripts. She translated some of her favorite passages and wrote them in a little book for me."

5. ¶Annie said, "Oh, how nice of her!"

6. ¶"Yes, it was," Irene replied. "She also brought back a number of other interesting things—earrings, wooden carvings, clothes, and recipes."

7. ¶"I'd love to see them," Annie remarked.

8. ¶"Sure," Irene said. "Tonight she's going to teach me to cook a whole Indian dinner. Have you ever had Indian food?"

9. ¶"No," Annie answered.

10. ¶"Well, stay for dinner tonight! You can help us cook and eat!"

Exercise 30

OBJECTIVE

■ To correct errors in the use of quotation marks, other marks of punctuation, and capitalization

Exercise 30 Proofreading for the Correct Use of Quotation Marks, Other Marks of Punctuation, and Capitalization

ANSWERS

1. Did the flight attendant just say, "This is the last call for passengers boarding Flight 304"?

2. "Next week's story," Ms. Sorvino said, "will be 'The Ring.'"

3. Mr. Keith posted Christine's latest essay, "Reading for Life," outside the classroom.

4. What are "green bytes" in a computer file?

5. "Are you really going to write music for Robert Frost's poem 'Fire and Ice'?" Paul asked.

6. Didn't he say that there will be a test this Friday?

7. Jethro always called the swimming pool behind his house the "cement pond."

8. Yesterday's review called the novel "immature"; however, I think the novel is fresh and spontaneous.

9. Jonathan asked me whether I knew the lyrics to the second verse of "America the Beautiful."

10. The next chapter, "Healthy Teeth and Gums," details basic dental hygiene.

Exercise 31

OBJECTIVE

■ To correct errors in the use of apostrophes

4. What are 'green bytes' in a computer file?

5. "Are you really going to write music for Robert Frost's poem "Fire and Ice"? Paul asked.

6. Didn't he say that "There will be a test this Friday"?

7. Jethro always called the swimming pool behind his house the 'cement pond.'

8. Yesterday's review called the novel "immature;" however, I think the novel is fresh and spontaneous.

9. Jonathan asked me whether I knew the lyrics to the second verse of America the Beautiful.

10. The next chapter, Healthy Teeth and Gums, details basic dental hygiene.

Exercise 31 Using Apostrophes Correctly

Rewrite the following word groups and sentences, adding or deleting an apostrophe to correct each error. If an item is already correct, write C.

EXAMPLE   1. a boys' trousers

      1. *a boy's trousers*

1. Angelas room
2. mices exercise wheel
3. Ours are here, but yours are missing.
4. anybody's suggestion **4.** C
5. somebody elses turn
6. her two brothers-in-laws dogs
7. Theres the bell!
8. Susie's and Bill's haircuts **8.** C
9. both gymnasts routines
10. Dont say *can't* to me!
11. Dot your is so that they don't look like ls.
12. Its six oclock.
13. Youre right again.
14. Were ready to go!
15. Whos next on the tryout list?
16. Youd need two Ph.D.s to program these VCRs! **16.** [*or* VCR's]
17. twenty-five cents worth
18. a friend of theirs
19. Lisa and Tom's uniforms **19.** 's
20. The blouse is hers.

HELP

You may need to change the spelling of some words in Exercise 31.

Reference Note

For information on **apostrophes**, see page 374.

21. the runner's-up prize   21. 's
22. Mom's and Dad's car
23. Aren't those women's shoes on sale?
24. Greg and Paul's lab table   24. C
25. two weeks' time

Exercise 32 Proofreading Sentences to Correct Misspelled Words

Rewrite the following sentences, correcting any misspelled words or incorrectly used numerals. If a sentence contains no errors, write *C*.

EXAMPLE   **1.** Do you have a reciept for the loafs of bread?

    1. receipt, loaves

1. If you are still mispelling many words, study your spelling rules more carefuly.
2. With 3 of the bookshelfs almost complete, our job was nearly finished.
3. "Julia has always exceled at math," her mother replyed.
4. How many solos will there be in tonight's recital?
5. Dishs filled with appetizeing foods of all kinds covered the banquet table.
6. The Welchs looked at several stereoes and chose the one with the bigest speakers.
7. Approximatly half of the precincts have already reported election results.
8. My uncle Bill is the editor in cheif of the local newspaper.
9. "Ladys and gentlemen," the speaker said, "we have a tie for 3rd place!"
10. Let's cook five or six potatos to serve with the sea trouts Timothy caught.
11. Companies must give satisfaction to those few disatisfied customers that they have.
12. They had made a couragous decision, but it created numerous political difficulties.
13. His opponent failed to appear and forfieted the race.
14. The soft yellow glow from the oil lamp made us look forward to expereincing another power failure.
15. Two soldeirs stood at attention beside the guard house.

Reference Note

For information on **spelling,** see Chapter 15.

Exercise 32

OBJECTIVE

- To correct errors in spelling in sentences

1. misspelling/ carefully
2. three/book-shelves
3. excelled/ replied
4. C
5. Dishes/appetiz-ing
6. Welches/stereos/ biggest
7. Approximately
8. editor in chief
9. Ladies/third
10. potatoes/trout
11. dissatisfied
12. courageous
13. forfeited
14. experiencing
15. soldiers

COMMON ERRORS

16. swimming

17. careful

18. seize

19. C

20. paid

16. As we watched, a family of dolphins began ~~swiming~~ swimming around a school of mullet.

17. Be ~~carful~~; you can easily miss the turn to State Road 13.

18. Does that expression actually mean "~~sieze~~ the day"?

19. These oxen have been trained to pull a plow.

20. "I have already ~~payed~~, though," insisted the moviegoer who had stepped outside to turn his car's headlights off and was now trying to return to his seat in the theater.

Reference Note

For information on **words often confused,** see page 410.

Exercise 33 Distinguishing Between Words Often Confused

Choose the correct word from the choices in parentheses in the following sentences.

EXAMPLE   1. Yesterday we borrowed (*their, they're*) bicycles to go to the movies.

1. *their*

1. The (*principals, principles*) of calculus are generally more difficult to master than those of algebra.
2. I have (*already, all ready*) told them that we are ready to go.
3. (*Your, You're*) performance in the play was terrific!
4. In order to obtain water, a mesquite tree in a (*desert, dessert*) may extend its roots more than 250 feet into the ground.
5. Rather (*then, than*) read a report, they're going to give a live demonstration.
6. Can you tell me (*who's, whose*) in charge of personnel?
7. Do you expect that the team will break the record for this (*coarse, course*)?
8. The scout leader carefully (*lead, led*) our troop to the top of the mountain.
9. Have you decided (*weather, whether*) you're going to the gym?
10. We must have (*past, passed*) twenty motels before we found one with a "Vacancy" sign.
11. Leave your completed application with the receptionist at the front desk in the (*personal, personnel*) office.
12. A sign above the delicate glass figurines read, "If you (*brake, break*) it, you buy it."
13. Before them stretched a great (*plane, plain*) dotted with gazelles.
14. Don't (*waist, waste*) time; our flight leaves in fifteen minutes.

15. Somehow the sash became (*loose, lose*), and, right in the middle of my big scene, the curtain dropped and almost knocked me over.

16. Would you care for a (*peace, piece*) of this mandarin orange?

17. Oh, Uncle Jim and the others are still getting (*their, there, they're*) luggage.

18. Except for the rippling of the water over the rocks, all nature was (*quiet, quite*) that summer afternoon.

19. I can't decide between the convertible and the compact, although the (*later, latter*) would cost less to maintain.

20. The hawk turned (*its, it's*) keen eyes toward the perch swimming just below the surface.

458 Correcting Common Errors

TEACHING TIP

Using the Mechanics Tests.
A **Correcting Common Errors
Standardized Test Answer Sheet**
that students may use for this
Mechanics Test is provided in the **Holt
Handbook** *Chapter Tests* booklet.

Mechanics Test: Section 1

DIRECTIONS   Each of the following sentences contains an underlined group of
words. Choose the answer that shows the correct capitalization, punctuation, and
spelling of the underlined part. If there is no error, choose answer E (*Correct as is*).
Indicate your response by shading in the appropriate oval on your answer sheet.

EXAMPLE   **1.** The nearest mailbox is on <u>Twenty-First Street</u>.

    (A) Twenty-first street

    (B) Twenty first Street

    (C) Twenty First Street

    (D) Twenty-first Street

    (E) Correct as is

ANSWER   **1.**   (A)   (B)   (C)   **(D)**   (E)

1. Have you ever been to my <u>brother-in-laws repair shop, Gus's Garage</u>?

  (A) brothers-in-law's repair shop,
     Gus's garage

  (B) brother-in-laws repair shop,
     Gus' Garage

  (C) brother in law's repair shop,
     Gus' garage

  (D) brother-in-law's repair shop,
     Gus's Garage

  (E) Correct as is

2. Please read the next <u>chapter *Filing Your Income Tax.*</u>

  (A) chapter, *Filing your Income Tax.*

  (B) chapter "Filing Your
     Income Tax."

  (C) chapter, "Filing your Income Tax."

  (D) chapter, "Filing Your Income Tax."

  (E) Correct as is

3. Volunteers should <u>bring: hammers,</u> wrenches, and screwdrivers.

  (A) bring hammers,

  (B) bring—hammers,

  (C) bring; hammers,

  (D) bring, hammers,

  (E) Correct as is

4. Mrs. Hendrix <u>said that "The Chemistry II exam will be next Wednesday."</u>

  (A) said, "The Chemistry II exam
     will be next wednesday."

  (B) said that the Chemistry II exam
     will be next Wednesday.

  (C) said that the chemistry II exam
     will be next Wednesday.

  (D) said that "The chemistry II exam
     will be next Wednesday."

  (E) Correct as is

5. "Next, we will visit the Moody <u>Museum of Art.</u>" said Mr. Singh.

(**A**) Museum Of Art,"

(**B**) Museum of Art"

(**C**) Museum of Art,"

(**D**) Museum of Art",

(**E**) Correct as is

6. "I don't want to hear any <u>*if*'s, *and*'s, or *but*'s," my Aunt Marjorie</u> said to my cousin and me.

(**A**) *if*'s, *and*'s, or *but*'s," my aunt Marjorie

(**B**) *if*'s *and*'s or *but*'s," my Aunt Marjorie

(**C**) *if*s', *and*s', or *but*s'," my aunt Marjorie

(**D**) *if*s, *and*s, or *but*s" my Aunt Marjorie

(**E**) Correct as is

7. Honeybees live and work <u>together, however, the</u> majority of the world's bees are solitary.

(**A**) together, however the

(**B**) together; however, the

(**C**) together however, the

(**D**) together; however the

(**E**) Correct as is

8. "Did you see," asked Tom, "the television <u>movie Gulliver's Travels?"</u>

(**A**) movie "Gulliver's Travels"?

(**B**) movie *Gulliver's Travels*?"

(**C**) movie, "Gulliver's Travels,"?

(**D**) movie, *Gulliver's Travels*?

(**E**) Correct as is

9. The state of Michigan borders all of the <u>Great Lakes except lake Ontario.</u>

(**A**) Great lakes except lake Ontario

(**B**) great lakes except Lake Ontario

(**C**) great Lakes except lake Ontario

(**D**) Great Lakes except Lake Ontario

(**E**) Correct as is

10. <u>More than nine million people live in Mexico City one</u> of the largest cities in the world.

(**A**) More then 9 million people live in Mexico City, one

(**B**) More than 9 million people live in Mexico city one

(**C**) More than nine million people live in Mexico City, one

(**D**) More then nine million people live in Mexico City, one

(**E**) Correct as is

Mechanics Test: Section 2

DIRECTIONS Each numbered item below contains an underlined group of words. Choose the answer that shows the correct capitalization, punctuation, and spelling of the underlined part. If there is no error, choose answer E (*Correct as is*). Indicate your response by shading in the appropriate oval on your answer sheet.

EXAMPLE [1] St. Paul MN, 55101

1. (A) St. Paul MN 55101
   (B) St. Paul, MN 55101
   (C) St. Paul Minn. 55101
   (D) St. Paul, Minnesota, 55101
   (E) Correct as is

ANSWER 1. Ⓐ Ⓑ Ⓒ Ⓓ Ⓔ

---

[1] April 7. 2001

Ms. Luisa Gibson
Amalgamated Automation, Inc.
[2] 8723 Forty-Third Street

St. Paul, MN 55101

[3] Dear Ms. Gibson

We would like to thank you for coming to speak to our chapter of the Future Businesspeople [4] club and for sharing your guidelines on [5] principals of good business management. At our meeting the [6] week after your talk, we had a very, lively discussion about the information you had given us. It is always helpful for our group to hear from [7] someone who has already succeded in doing what we hope to accomplish. We especially appreciated your insights concerning [8] government agencies and their regulations regarding business practices. We are looking forward to seeing you again at the upcoming Small Business Association Summer Conference at [9] the Leicester hotel and, of course, would be happy to have you speak to our chapter in the future.

[10] Yours sincerely,

Alfonso Santiago

Alfonso Santiago
President, Future Businesspeople Club

1. **(A)** April Seventh 2001
   (B) April 7th, 2001
   (C) April, 7 2001
   (D) April 7, 2001
   (E) Correct as is

2. **(A)** 8723 Forty-third Street
   (B) 8723 Forty third Street
   (C) 8723 Forty Third Street
   (D) 8723 Fortythird Street
   (E) Correct as is

3. **(A)** Dear Ms. Gibson:
   (B) Dear Ms. Gibson,
   (C) Dear Ms Gibson:
   (D) Dear Ms Gibson,
   (E) Correct as is

4. **(A)** club and for sharing you're
   (B) Club and for sharing you're
   (C) club and for shareing your
   (D) Club and for sharing your
   (E) Correct as is

5. **(A)** principals of good business
       managment
   (B) principles of good business
       management
   (C) principals of good busyness
       management
   (D) principles of good business
       managment
   (E) Correct as is

6. **(A)** week after your talk we had a
       very lively
   (B) week after your talk we had a
       very, lively
   (C) week after your talk, we had a
       very lively
   (D) week after your talk, we had a
       very livly
   (E) Correct as is

7. **(A)** someone who has all ready
       suceded
   (B) someone who has all ready
       succeeded
   (C) someone, who has already
       succeded
   (D) someone who has already
       succeeded
   (E) Correct as is

8. **(A)** goverment agencies and they're
   (B) goverment agencys and their
   (C) government agencies and
       they're
   (D) government agencys and their
   (E) Correct as is

9. **(A)** The Leicester hotel and, of
       course
   (B) the Leicester Hotel and, of
       coarse,
   (C) the Leicester Hotel and, of
       course,
   (D) the Leicester hotel and, of
       coarse,
   (E) Correct as is

10. **(A)** Your's sincerely:
    (B) Yours' sincerely,
    (C) Yours sincerely:
    (D) Yours sincerly,
    (E) Correct as is

RESOURCES

Correcting Common Errors
Review
- *Language & Sentence Skills Practice,* pp. 403–405

Assessment
- *Holt Handbook Chapter Tests with Answer Key,* pp. 31–32, 55

PART 2

Sentences

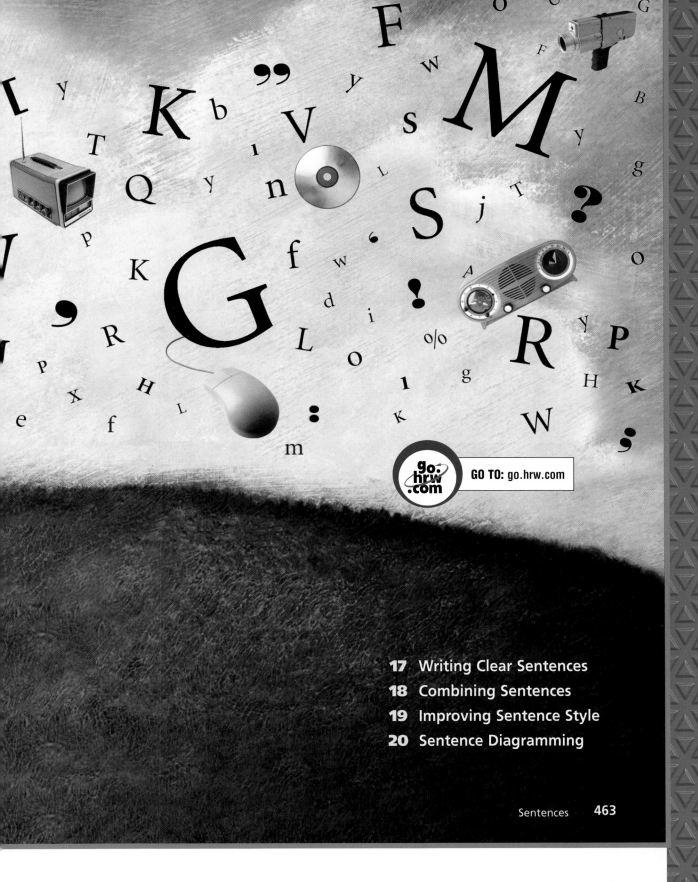

GO TO: go.hrw.com

Sentences **463**

CHAPTER

17

Writing Clear Sentences

INTRODUCING THE CHAPTER

■ The focus in this chapter is on writing clear sentences. Students will learn how to link ideas by coordinating and subordinating clauses and phrases. They will also learn to convey thoughts clearly by recognizing and correcting sentence fragments, run-ons, and faulty parallelism. Because sentence clarity is the backbone of good writing, it will be useful to review these exercises later when students are working on paragraph structure.

Diagnostic Preview

A. Choosing Appropriate Conjunctions and Connectives

Complete each of the following sentences by supplying an appropriate conjunction or other connecting word or word groups. Be sure you include any needed punctuation with the conjunction or connective you choose. Here are possible answers.

Terms in brackets refer to concepts tested by the items in the Diagnostic Preview.

1.–5. [coordinating and subordinating ideas]
1. After
2. , but
3. because
4. ; however,
5. If

EXAMPLE   **1.** We missed our connecting flight in Chicago _____ our flight left Philadelphia an hour later than scheduled.

1. *We missed our connecting flight in Chicago because our flight left Philadelphia an hour later than scheduled.*

1. _____ we waited in line for an hour, the airline agent booked a new flight for us.

2. Unfortunately, we were assigned separate seats _____ at least we were able to get home that night.

3. We arrived without our luggage _____ it could not be transferred to our new flight in time.

4. The agent told us that we could come back for our suitcases the next afternoon _____ our house is more than two hours' drive from the airport.

5. _____ we could wait another day, the agent told us, the airline would have the luggage delivered to our house.

CHAPTER RESOURCES

Internet
■ Web resources: go.hrw.com

Practice & Review
■ *Language & Sentence Skills Practice,* pp. 411–432

■ *Language & Sentence Skills Practice Answer Key,* pp. 158–165

B. Using Parallel Structure

Revise the following sentences by correcting faulty parallelism. You may need to delete, add, or move some words to bring the ideas into balance.

Possible answers follow.

EXAMPLE 1. I called to tell Jo about our new car, about my report card, and to wish her a happy birthday.

    1. I called to tell Jo about our new car and my report card and to wish her a happy birthday.

6. Craig planned to spend the weekend finishing his science project and ~~to~~ work on his college applications.

7. His father reminded him to select some additional items for his portfolio and ~~that he still needed to~~ write one essay.

8. He had applied to one college that is well known for its graphic-design program and ~~because it~~ is near Boston.

9. Craig was ~~both~~ satisfied that his portfolio was varied and representative of his best work.

10. He realized, however, that ~~expressing himself well in~~ his essay was as important to the admissions panel as his portfolio.

6. ing [parallel structure]

7. that he still needed [parallel structure]

8. that [parallel structure]

9. both [parallel structure]

10. [parallel structure]

C. Identifying Sentences, Sentence Fragments, and Run-on Sentences

Identify each of the following word groups as a *sentence*, a *sentence fragment*, or a *run-on sentence*. Then, if a word group is a fragment, revise the word group to make it a complete sentence. If a word group is a run-on, revise it to make one or more complete sentences.

Possible revisions follow.

EXAMPLE 1. Megan, almost ready to leave the flea market, when she spotted the old dresser.

    1. fragment—Megan was almost ready to leave the flea market when she spotted the old dresser.

11. The piece of furniture was in good condition, someone had painted it a horrible, muddy green.

12. The dresser barely in the back of the car, so Megan had to tie the lid of the trunk closed.

13. Decided to paint the dresser pale yellow, and figured several coats of paint would be necessary to cover the awful green.

14. Sanding is tedious work, Megan listened to the radio while she worked, and the hours flew by.

15. Picturing the freshly painted dresser in her bedroom, Megan was inspired to keep working all weekend.

11. run-on—Although [run-on]

12. fragment—fit [fragment]

13. fragment—She, she [fragment]

14. run-on—but [run-on]

15. sentence [sentence]

Differentiating Instruction

- *Developmental Language & Sentence Skills,* pp. 185–190

- *Developmental Language & Sentence Skills Guided Practice Teacher's Notes and Answer Key,* p. 46

Assessment

- *Holt Handbook Chapter Tests with Answer Key,* pp. 33–36, 54

ASSESSING

Entry-Level Assessment

Diagnostic Preview. You may want to use the **Diagnostic Preview** to identify areas in which students need instruction and practice in writing effective sentences. You could use the results of the preview to decide which lessons to teach to the entire class and which ones to assign to small groups.

PRETEACHING

Lesson Starter

Motivating. Write the following quotation on a chalkboard.

> ❝ Ah, the simple rapture of fulfillment at my work being understood that cold morning. What unutterable reward for my labor.❞
>
> (Sylvia Ashton-Warner, 1908–1984, New Zealand educator and writer)

Ask students to remember and write about a positive experience when someone understood their motives, ideas, or goals. Explain that good writers strive to create clear, effective sentences to gain such understanding from their readers.

D. Revising Sentences to Eliminate Unnecessary Shifts in Sentences

Revise each of the following sentences to eliminate unnecessary shifts in subject or in verb tense or voice. You may need to add, delete, or rearrange words in the sentence. Possible revisions follow.

EXAMPLE
1. He bought that CD with some money he got for his birthday, and now the CD is played all the time.

   1. *He bought that CD with some money he got for his birthday, and now he plays the CD all the time.*

16. ed [verb tense shift]
17. fastening [subject shift]
18. took [verb tense shift]
19. he gave us [subject shift/verb voice shift]
20. [verb tense shift]

16. The child climbed into the big red wagon and patiently waits for someone to give him a ride.
17. The cast on her wrist made tying her shoelaces difficult, and the buttons on her jacket were impossible.
18. The engine was making a high-pitched, whining noise, so John takes it to the shop.
19. The ranger stopped us at the park entrance, and our camping permit was obtained from him.
20. In the next scene the two sisters come into the room, sit down at the dining-room table, and picked up their forks at exactly the same time.

Ways to Achieve Clarity

OBJECTIVES

- **To use appropriate connectives to show addition, contrast, choice, or result**
- **To choose appropriate subordinating conjunctions to show time, cause, purpose, or condition**
- **To revise sentences by inserting adverb clauses**
- **To subordinate ideas by using adjective clauses**
- **To revise sentences by correcting faulty coordination**
- **To revise sentences by correcting faulty parallelism**

Ways to Achieve Clarity

Have you ever stepped from a warm room into the surprisingly cold, crisp air outside? Did everything seem sharper, your mind suddenly alert and focused? Like the first cold snap of fall, clear writing also commands our attention. Clarity is essential in conveying information, whether your purpose is to explain the steam engine or to describe your new neighborhood. One of the best ways to bring clarity to your writing is to show the appropriate relationships between ideas. To do this, you must adjust and revise the structure of each sentence until it accurately communicates your message. *Coordinating* and *subordinating* ideas are two ways to sharpen and clarify your writing.

Coordinating Ideas

Ideas that are equally important—or that carry the same weight—in a sentence are called ***coordinate*** ideas. To show that ideas are coordinate, you link them with a coordinating conjunction, such as *and* or *but* or another connective. Sometimes the connective may simply be a punctuation mark, such as the semicolon in the second example that follows.

EXAMPLES   The Pathfinder lander was sending back its first images of the surface of Mars**, and** everyone was focused on the television screens.

Matthew P. Golombek, "The Mars Pathfinder Mission," *Scientific American*

Crisp foods have to be loud in the upper register**;** foods which generate low-frequency rumblings are crunchy, or slurpy, but not crisp.

David Bodanis, *The Secret House*

The connective you use shows the relationship between the ideas. For example, *and* links similar ideas, while *but* links contrasting ideas. The following chart lists connecting words you can use to show *addition, contrast, choice,* and *result.*

Addition	Contrast	Choice	Result
also	but	either . . . or	accordingly
and	however	neither . . . nor	consequently
as well as	nevertheless		for
besides	still	nor	hence
both . . . and	yet	or	so
		otherwise	therefore
			thus

Reference Note

For more information about **conjunctions,** see page 25.

When you use connectives to join words, phrases, or subordinate clauses (clauses that do not express complete thoughts), the result is a compound element in your sentence; these compound elements may be subjects, verbs, modifiers, or complements. When you use coordination to join complete thoughts, or independent clauses, the result is a compound sentence.

CONTRAST   Elijah **slurped** his soup **but wiped** his mouth neatly afterward. [compound verb]

CHOICE   **Either Regina or Bookie** will go to the movie with me. [compound subject]

ADDITION   Basketball players are generally **tall, fit, and quick.** [compound predicate adjective]

RESULT   **Mack's hair was uncombed;** consequently, **he looked too messy for the photo.** [compound sentence]

EXTENSION

Relating to Literature

Have students analyze the way author Naguib Mahfouz uses coordinate ideas in "The Cairo Rooftop" from *Palace Walk.* Start by showing students some examples from the story, and then discuss the types of coordinate ideas the connectives convey: addition, contrast, choice, or result. [*For example:* "They were content to be ruled by her, and Aisha would not question her assignment." And *joins, or adds, the ideas contained in the two independent clauses.*]

Have students work on their own to locate two more sentences from the story that use connectives. Ask students to take turns sharing their sentences and discussing how the connective changes or enhances a reader's understanding of the ideas in the sentence.

Be sure to choose a connective that shows the correct relationship between the linked ideas. Otherwise, your meaning will not be clear to your readers.

UNCLEAR   Nell looked for her wallet, and she couldn't find it anywhere.
CLEAR   Nell looked for her wallet**, but** she couldn't find it anywhere.
          [contrast]

UNCLEAR   Floss your teeth, yet you might get gum disease.
CLEAR   Floss your teeth**; otherwise,** you might get gum disease.
          [choice]

NOTE When you use a coordinating conjunction to link independent clauses, put a comma before the conjunction unless the clauses are very short.

EXAMPLES   Vikram made peach cobbler**,** and he brought it to the picnic.

           Carly drove and Sandra slept.

When you use a conjunctive adverb to join independent clauses, put a semicolon before the adverb and a comma after it.

EXAMPLE   Francine studied hard for the driving exam**;** however**,** she overslept on the day of the test.

Reference Note

For more about **punctuating compound sentences,** see page 336.

Exercise 1

DISTRIBUTED REVIEW
Have each student develop a thesis statement based on Kaiulani's experiences as related in **Exercise 1.** Emphasize the importance of writing a clear and concise thesis statement that will provide an overview of the content in all ten sentences. [*Though young and far from her homeland, Princess Kaiulani was concerned about the fate of Hawaii.*]

Princess Kaiulani

Exercise 1 **Using Appropriate Connectives**

Complete each of the following sentences by deciding which connecting word(s) will best fit in the blank(s). Remember to use the correct punctuation with the connective you choose. Possible answers follow.

EXAMPLE   **1.** Princess Kaiulani was King Kalakaua's niece _____ Hawaii's last princess.

          1. *and*

1. Fourteen-year-old Kaiulani was quite young to travel long distances _____ she was sent to Great Britain from Hawaii anyway.
2. Kaiulani's family wanted to prepare her to assume the role of queen of Hawaii _____ Kaiulani was sent to Great Britain for a traditional education.   **1.** , but   **2.** ; accordingly,
3. Kaiulani was halfway across the world from Hawaii _____ she managed to keep in touch with Hawaiian events through letters.
4. _____ friends _____ family members kept her informed of events in her homeland.   **3.** ; nevertheless,   **4.** Both/and

5. Kaiulani was glad to hear from her friends and family ____ she was unhappy to hear of increasing trouble with American business leaders known as *haoles* (pronounced HOU-LEES), or "foreigners." **5.** , but **6.** ; consequently, **7.** ; however,/and

6. These haoles wanted to annex Hawaii to the United States ____ Kaiulani's uncle considered them his enemies.

7. Many Hawaiians resisted annexation to the United States ____ in 1893, a group of powerful haoles overthrew the royal family ____ took control of the government.

8. In 1893, Kaiulani was still only a teenager ____ she acted decisively when she heard the news. **8.** ; still,

9. She went to New York in March 1893 ____ read a statement addressed "to the American People." **9.** and

10. Kaiulani's persuasive statement gained the support of many Americans ____ the forces of annexation triumphed ____ in 1898, Hawaii was transferred to the United States.

10. , but/, and

King Kalakaua

Subordinating Ideas

Not all ideas are created equal. Sometimes, one idea in a sentence is more important than another, and you will want to downplay, or *subordinate,* the less important idea.

One way to subordinate an idea is to place it in a *subordinate clause.* Used as part of a sentence, the subordinate clause elaborates on the thought expressed in an independent clause.

EXAMPLES   Petra, **who is learning how to scuba dive,** took a trip to the coast.

Michael likes going to the coast **because the beaches are clean and uncrowded.**

The kinds of subordinate clauses you will use most often are *adverb clauses* and *adjective clauses.*

Adverb Clauses

An *adverb clause* modifies a verb, an adjective, or another adverb in a sentence. You introduce an adverb clause with a subordinating conjunction such as *although, after, because, if, when,* or *while.* The conjunction shows how the adverb clause relates to the main clause.

Reference Note

For more about the **types of subordinate clauses,** see page 83.

DIRECT TEACHING

Modeling and Demonstration

Subordinating Ideas. Model how to subordinate ideas by using the example

I enjoyed my senior year

my friends and I planned the senior prom

Ask whether the two word groups are about the same subject and what they are about generally. [*yes; senior year*] Next, ask whether the word groups are equal and could reasonably be joined by a coordinating conjunction. [*As stated, the ideas may appear to be equal because each expresses a complete thought, but adding coordinating conjunctions does not create a coherent sentence.*] Last, ask what subordinating conjunction could be used to join the two ideas into one sentence. [*because*] Point out that the resulting sentence *I enjoyed my senior year because my friends and I planned the senior prom* is a complex sentence with one independent clause and one subordinate adverb clause. Now, have a volunteer use another example from this chapter to demonstrate how to subordinate ideas.

RETEACHING

Subordination

Giving students an alternate means of understanding emphasis and subordination may be helpful. Bring in examples of paintings in which the artist, such as Rembrandt, uses light for emphasis, thereby subordinating the other subject matter in the painting. Compare the light and dark areas in the painting to sentence clauses; though the darker material is subordinate to the lighter, it nonetheless adds meaning to the painting and describes the scene.

DIFFERENTIATING INSTRUCTION

English-Language Learners

Cantonese. Cantonese sentences are sometimes patterned in ways that allow an adverbial clause to act as a coordinating rather than a subordinating element. *Although I worked on my science project,* **but *I did not finish.***

Show students that complex sentences that begin with a subordinating conjunction, or connecting word, cannot also have *and* or *but* between clauses.

STYLE TIP

An adverb clause can appear at the beginning, the middle, or the end of a sentence. Read the sentence aloud with the clause in each position to see which sounds best. Remember to use commas to set off the clause, where needed.

Usually, the conjunction shows a relationship of *time, cause or reason, purpose or result,* or *condition.*

TIME   At Bonanza Creek, **while our socks dried by the fire,** we fished for arctic grayling.

Barry Lopez, *Crossing Open Ground*

CAUSE OR REASON   **Because it is a direct reflection of the pressure and movement of the artist's hand across the surface of the painting,** brushwork is one of the most intimate links that we, as viewers, have with the artist's mind at work.

Dawson W. Carr and Mark Leonard, *Looking at Paintings*

PURPOSE OR RESULT   A synergy kicks in, **so that when you're finished, you drag yourself to the locker room in a state of euphoria, amazed at what you've done, completely drained.**

John Davidson, "Reach Your Peak," *Self*

CONDITION   He ran so hard that he could feel the sweat fly from his head and arms, **though it was winter and the air was filled with snow.**

N. Scott Momaday, *House Made of Dawn*

The following chart lists subordinating conjunctions you can use to show each kind of relationship.

Time	Cause	Purpose	Condition
after	as	in order that	although
as	because	so that	despite
before	even though	such that	if
since	since	that	provided that
until	unless		though
when	whereas		
whenever	while		
while			

Oral Practice   **Choosing Appropriate Subordinating Conjunctions**

Each of the following sentences is missing a subordinating conjunction. Decide what relationship exists between the independent clause and the subordinate clause. Then, choose a subordinating conjunction that clearly shows that relationship, and read the completed sentence aloud.

Possible answers follow.

EXAMPLE   1. _____ we were studying ecology, we learned about
              the ozone layer.

           1. *When we were studying ecology, we learned about the*
              ozone layer.

1. _____ atmospheric scientists discovered a large hole in the
   ozone layer in the 1980s, people have been concerned about
   ozone depletion. **1.** Since   **2.** Although   **3.** because

2. _____ scientists disagree about the exact cause of ozone depletion,
   many attribute the phenomenon to the effects of pollution.

3. Ozone depletion is a concern _____ ozone in the stratosphere
   protects the earth from the sun's harmful ultraviolet radiation.

4. _____ ultraviolet radiation is necessary to life on earth, overexposure to it is known to cause skin cancer among people and the
   destruction of many plant and animal species. **4.** Though

5. _____ the ozone layer is depleted, the risk of overexposure for
   humans and other species increases dramatically. **5.** After

6. _____ scientists discovered the hole in the ozone layer, people
   feared that the hole would spread to other parts of the world.

7. Chlorofluorocarbons (CFCs) are believed by some to be   **6.** When
   responsible _____ these CFCs may break down ozone. **7.** as

8. CFCs are released into the atmosphere _____ things such as
   aerosol spray cans, refrigerants, and other manufacturing
   products are used. **8.** whenever

9. _____ there has been disagreement over the exact cause of ozone
   destruction, industrial countries took steps to reduce the use of
   CFCs during the 1980s and 1990s. **9.** Although

10. In 1994, Germany banned CFC production _____ depletion of
    the ozone layer might be prevented. **10.** so that

Exercise 2   **Revising Sentences by Inserting**
                 Adverb Clauses

Revise each of the following sentences by adding an adverb clause. Use a
different subordinating conjunction for each sentence. (Note: Remember
to add a comma if you place the clause at the sentence's beginning.)

EXAMPLE   **1.** Photography is a fun activity.

           1. *Photography is a fun activity because it allows you to be*
              creative.

1. We tried to take some photographs outside.
2. We learned how to control the film's exposure to light.

STYLE   **TIP**

It is possible to use too
many subordinate clauses
in a sentence. Excessive
subordination occurs when
too many subordinate
clauses are strung together.
This type of sentence
makes it difficult for the
reader to keep track of
the main idea of the
independent clause.

HELP

You don't
need to know anything
about photography to
revise the sentences for
Exercise 2. Just use your
imagination.

PRACTICE

Relating to Writing
To give students practice using
subordinate clauses, invite them to
stage a letter-writing campaign. As
a class, discuss how easy or difficult
students perceive voter registration
to be. Do students believe that voters
should be able to register to vote up
until election day? Divide students
into groups of four, and have each
group compose a letter that advo-
cates a position on the issue. Make
sure the letters include at least four
sentences with subordinate clauses
that represent contributions from
each student. Allow time for groups
to share their letters with the class
before sending them to appropriate
state or national elected officials
either through the postal service
or via e-mail.

Exercise 2   **Revising**
Sentences by Inserting Adverb
Clauses

ANSWERS
Here are some possible answers.

   1. We tried to take some pho-
      tographs outside even though it
      was about to rain.

   2. While we were taking a photogra-
      phy class last semester, we learned
      how to control the film's exposure
      to light.

Exercise 2 Revising Sentences by Inserting Adverb Clauses

ANSWERS continued

3. Because you enjoy photographing things in motion, you should try taking photographs of animals sometime.

4. Even though I command Molly to sit still, my dog sometimes tries to sniff or even lick the camera.

5. I have taken several blurry photos of my sister's pet rabbit, Scooter, because I did not use the correct lens.

6. Many schools offer courses in photography in order that students can gain some experience in a practical field.

7. As soon as the Canada geese began migrating last fall, Roseanne's father used a tele-photo lens to take some beautiful photographs of the birds.

8. If there are no reasons not to do so, Dan likes to use black-and-white film.

9. I have used a digital camera since I bought my first computer.

10. Although I bought expensive new equipment, some of the best photos I have taken were shot with an inexpensive camera.

Reference Note
For more about **combining sentences by subordinating ideas,** see page 504.

3. You should try taking photographs of animals sometime.
4. My dog Sunshine sometimes tries to sniff or even lick the camera.
5. I have taken several blurry photos of my sister's pet rabbit, Scooter.
6. Many schools offer courses in photography.
7. Roseanne's father used a telephoto lens to take some beautiful photographs of birds.
8. Dan likes to use black-and-white film.
9. I have used a digital camera.
10. Some of the best photos I have taken were shot with an inexpensive camera.

Adjective Clauses

You can also subordinate an idea by placing it in an *adjective clause,* a subordinate clause that modifies a noun or a pronoun in a sentence. An adjective clause usually begins with *who, whom, whose, which, that,* or *where.*

EXAMPLE   I propped myself against the brick wall of the schoolhouse, **where the school delinquent found me.**

Henry Louis Gates, Jr., "A Giant Step," *The New York Times*

Before you use an adjective clause in a sentence, you need to decide which idea in the sentence you want to subordinate. Suppose you wanted to combine these two ideas in one sentence:

Albert Einstein was born in 1879. He is considered one of the greatest scientists of the twentieth century.

If you wanted to emphasize that Einstein was born in 1879, you would put that information in an independent clause and the other information in an adjective clause.

Albert Einstein, **who is considered one of the greatest scientists of the twentieth century,** was born in 1879.

To emphasize that Einstein is considered one of the greatest scientists of the twentieth century, put his birth information in an adjective clause.

Albert Einstein, **who was born in 1879,** is considered one of the greatest scientists of the twentieth century.

MINI-LESSON   Grammar

Punctuating Adjective Clauses. Review with students the difference between an essential clause and a nonessential clause. [*Essential clauses contain information that is necessary to convey the sentence's meaning. Nonessential clauses offer additional* *information and are not necessary to complete the sentence.*] Point out to students that the nonessential clause is set off by commas.

Write the following sentences on the chalkboard, and ask students to determine

Exercise 3 Subordinating Ideas by Using Adjective Clauses

Use adjective clauses to combine the following pairs of sentences.

EXAMPLE
1. My grandmother was born in 1947. She is a baby boomer.
1. *My grandmother, who is a baby boomer, was born in 1947.*

1. The term *baby boom* refers to the generation born in the United States between the late 1940s and the early 1960s. Most people recognize the term *baby boom.*
2. The previous generation had lived through the economic hardships of the 1930s and early 1940s. Many members of that generation put off having children until the end of World War II.
3. These children are called baby boomers because of their generation. They were born in the stable years following World War II.
4. Many of the baby boomers grew up during relatively peaceful and prosperous times. They saw themselves as very different from people in their parents' generation.
5. The baby boom generation is best known for rebelling against the previous generation's traditions. It created a widespread youth culture during the 1960s and 1970s.
6. Advertisers are eager to reach the millions of baby boomers. These advertisers have developed special marketing campaigns targeting that age group.
7. The baby boom generation was much larger than the preceding generation. The baby boom generation had its own specific problems.
8. For instance, existing school systems were built to accommodate the previous generation. These school systems were not large enough or plentiful enough to hold all the baby boom students.
9. Many baby boomers have chosen to have families late in life. Some of them come from large families.
10. Baby boomlets are increases in the birthrate that are not as large as the increase during the baby boom. Boomlets have occurred in recent decades.

Correcting Faulty Coordination

In everyday speech, we tend to be casual about stringing together ideas with *and.* In writing, though, it is essential to show clearly the relationships among ideas. If you use a coordinating conjunction to join ideas that are not coordinate, or equal, you end up with **faulty coordination.**

—HELP—

When completing Exercise 3, you may have to delete or add some words or change the word order.

if each adjective clause is essential or nonessential. If it is nonessential, instruct students to insert punctuation where it is needed.

1. Large, old trees and fragrant flowers[,] which were in bloom[,] grew in the park. [*nonessential*]

2. My favorite movie star always plays the character who saves the day. [*essential*]

3. A good friend of mine works in Zelli's deli[,] where we always go after our softball games. [*nonessential*]

Exercise 3 Subordinating Ideas by Using Adjective Clauses

ANSWERS

1. Most people recognize the term *baby boom,* which refers to the generation born in the United States between the late 1940s and the early 1960s.

2. The previous generation, which had put off having children until the end of World War II, had lived through the economic hardships of the 1930s and early 1940s.

3. These children, who were born in the stable years following World War II, are called baby boomers because of their generation.

4. Many of the baby boomers, who saw themselves as very different from people in their parents' generation, grew up during relatively peaceful and prosperous times.

5. The baby boom generation, which created a widespread youth culture during the 1960s and 1970s, is best known for rebelling against the previous generation's traditions.

6. Advertisers who are eager to reach the millions of baby boomers have developed special marketing campaigns targeting that age group.

7. The baby boom generation, which was much larger than the preceding generation, had its own specific problems.

8. For instance, existing school systems, which were built to accommodate the previous generation, were not large enough or plentiful enough to hold all the baby boom students.

9. Many baby boomers, some of whom come from large families, have chosen to have families late in life.

10. Baby boomlets, which have occurred in recent decades, are increases in the birthrate that are not as large as the increase during the baby boom.

To avoid faulty coordination, check each compound sentence to see if the ideas are really equal in importance. If they are not, subordinate the less-important idea by placing it in a subordinate clause or a phrase. You may need to add, delete, or rearrange words in the sentence.

FAULTY   This male butterfly is distinguishable from females of its species, and its wings reflect ultraviolet light.

REVISED   **Because its wings reflect ultraviolet light,** this male butterfly is distinguishable from females of its species. [adverb clause]

FAULTY   Malaria is a serious infectious disease, and it can be transmitted to humans through mosquito bites.

REVISED   Malaria, **which can be transmitted to humans through mosquito bites,** is a serious infectious disease. [adjective clause]

FAULTY   The light was at the end of the pier, and it showed us how far we had walked.

REVISED   The light **at the end of the pier** showed us how far we had walked. [prepositional phrase]

FAULTY   Tama was the lifeguard on duty that day, and she saved the drowning child.

REVISED   Tama, **the lifeguard on duty that day,** saved the drowning child. [appositive phrase]

NOTE   After revising a sentence, re-read it within the context of the longer passage to make sure the relationship between ideas is accurately conveyed.

Butterfly under normal light

Butterfly under ultraviolet light

---HELP---

In Exercise 4, you may need to add or delete some words or change the punctuation.

Exercise 4   Revising Sentences by Correcting Faulty Coordination

ANSWERS

Possible answers are shown below.

1. Both Charlotte and Emily Brontë, who were sisters, produced novels of enduring popularity and significance.

2. They lived in Yorkshire, a former county in England.

3. Yorkshire, which is now divided into three counties, is in an area on the North Sea.

Exercise 4   Revising Sentences by Correcting Faulty Coordination

Revise each of the following sentences by placing one of the ideas in a subordinate clause or in a phrase. Make sure each revised sentence shows the relationship between ideas that you think is most accurate.

EXAMPLE   **1.** I went to the library, and I checked out books.

       1. I went to the library to check out books.

1. Charlotte and Emily Brontë were sisters, and they both produced novels of enduring popularity and significance.

2. They lived in Yorkshire, and Yorkshire is a former county in England.

3. Yorkshire is now divided into three counties, and the area is on the North Sea.

4. Emily and Charlotte Brontë wrote novels, and the novels depict the complicated emotional lives of their characters.

5. Both authors drew upon the Yorkshire moors as a setting, and they wrote passionately about the landscape.

6. They had a brother, and his name was Branwell.

7. Their sister Anne also published novels, *Agnes Grey* and *The Tenant of Wildfell Hall,* and they are not as widely read as the novels Emily and Charlotte wrote.

8. Charlotte sometimes worked as a governess, and her novel *Jane Eyre* is about a young woman who works as a governess.

9. Emily wrote the novel *Wuthering Heights,* and it has been made into a movie many times.

10. The Brontë family lived in a town called Haworth at a parsonage, and you can still visit that parsonage.

Using Parallel Structure

To create clarity and rhythm in a sentence, it is important to express similar ideas in similar grammatical forms. For example, pair an adjective with an adjective, a prepositional phrase with a prepositional phrase, and a noun clause with a noun clause. When you use the same grammatical form for similar ideas, you create *parallel structure.*

EXAMPLES   He had come to tell his brother **that power corrupts, that a man who fights for justice must himself be cleansed and purified, that love is greater than force.**

Alan Paton, *Cry, the Beloved Country*

Scribes were needed **to send messages, to convey news, to take down the king's orders, to register the laws.** . . .

Alberto Manguel, *A History of Reading*

He was the **weather-beaten, brown-faced, black-eyed** Cupid of the community.

Jovita González, "The Mail Carrier"

Remember to use parallel structure when you link coordinate ideas, as the following examples show.

FAULTY   Amanda's favorite forms of exercise are swimming and to run.
         [gerund paired with infinitive]

PARALLEL   Amanda's favorite forms of exercise are **swimming** and **running.** [gerund paired with gerund]

Exercise 4 Revising Sentences by Correcting Faulty Coordination

ANSWERS continued

4. Emily and Charlotte Brontë wrote novels that depicted the complicated emotional lives of their characters.

5. Both authors, who drew upon the Yorkshire moors as a setting, wrote passionately about the landscape.

6. They had a brother named Branwell.

7. Although their sister Anne also published novels, including *Agnes Grey* and *The Tenant of Wildfell Hall,* her books are not as widely read as the novels Emily and Charlotte wrote.

8. Charlotte, who sometimes worked as a governess, wrote *Jane Eyre* about a young woman who also worked as a governess.

9. Emily wrote the novel *Wuthering Heights,* which has been made into a movie many times.

10. The Brontë family lived in a town called Haworth at a parsonage, which you can still visit.

CONTENT-AREA CONNECTIONS

Math

Parallel Structures. Remind students of parallel structures in geometry. Quadrilaterals such as the rhombus, rectangle, and parallelogram are symmetrically formed by combining pairs of parallel lines. Students may also know about rotational symmetry, in which an object looks the same after a rotation of less than 360 degrees. An example of rotational symmetry includes the starfish, which has a parallel structure as a result of its repeated patterns.

DIFFERENTIATING INSTRUCTION

English-Language Learners

General Strategies. Some students may not readily recognize the grammatical forms commonly used to create parallel structures in English. Help students complete the sentences below by using noun clauses, infinitives, and gerunds. As they complete the sentences, point out the grammatical forms used in these parallel structures.

1. Anna told me three things: that she was tired, that . . . [*noun clauses*]

2. Saturday morning I plan to sleep late, to . . . [*infinitives*]

3. Boris spends his free time reading, . . . [*gerunds*]

Then, ask students to create original sentences containing these parallel structures.

| TIPS & TRICKS |

To check for faulty parallelism in your writing, look for the words *and* and *or*. Then check on each side of these words to see that the items joined are parallel. If the two items on either side of *and* are not parallel, revise one of them.

FAULTY
She walked *proudly* and *in a big hurry*.

PARALLEL
She walked *proudly* and *swiftly*.

FAULTY	Derrick's editorial shows his knowledge and that he is passionate about the subject. [noun paired with noun clause]
PARALLEL	Derrick's editorial shows **that he is knowledgeable about the subject** and **that he is passionate about it.** [noun clause paired with noun clause]

Use parallel structure when you compare or contrast ideas.

FAULTY	Reading novels no longer interests me as much as to read poems. [gerund contrasted with infinitive]
PARALLEL	**Reading novels** no longer interests me as much as **reading poems.** [gerund contrasted with gerund]
FAULTY	In sports, enthusiasm is as important as that you have skill. [noun paired with noun clause]
PARALLEL	In sports, **enthusiasm** is as important as **skill**. [noun paired with noun]

Use parallel structure when you link ideas with correlative conjunctions (*both . . . and, either . . . or, neither . . . nor,* and *not only . . . but also*).

FAULTY	The medicine woman was revered not only for her healing abilities but also because she possessed wisdom. [prepositional phrase correlated with adverb clause]
PARALLEL	The medicine woman was revered not only **for her healing abilities** but also **for her wisdom.** [prepositional phrase correlated with prepositional phrase]

To avoid awkwardness and confusion, place correlative conjunctions directly before the parallel terms.

UNCLEAR	Shawna considered both pursuing careers in law and in journalism.
BETTER	Shawna considered pursuing careers **both** in law **and** in journalism.
UNCLEAR	Our choice of eight o'clock movies either was *Slime* or *Return of the Insect People.*
BETTER	Our choice of eight o'clock movies was **either** *Slime* **or** *Return of the Insect People.*
UNCLEAR	I asked Chi to not only join our band but also to be the lead vocalist.
BETTER	I asked Chi **not only** to join our band **but also** to be the lead vocalist.

When you create parallel structure, you often need to repeat an article, a preposition, or a pronoun before each of the parallel terms to make your meaning clear. Notice how the first version of each of the following sentences might be misread.

UNCLEAR   Before leaving the store, I talked with the clerk and manager.

BETTER   Before leaving the store, I talked with **the** clerk and **the** manager.

UNCLEAR   This Elvis biography reveals more about the era of the 1950s than the singer himself.

BETTER   This Elvis biography reveals more **about** the era of the 1950s than **about** the singer himself.

To clarify your meaning, you will often need to add a few words to the second part of a sentence that uses parallel structure.

UNCLEAR   I enjoyed the singing of the opera's soprano more than the tenor.

BETTER   I enjoyed the singing of the opera's soprano more than **that of** the tenor.

NOTE   For many writers, parallel structure is an important stylistic tool. Parallelism creates natural rhythm and flow in both prose and poetry. In the following stanza, notice that a string of parallel phrases follows the preposition *between.*

> On visiting days with aunts and uncles,
> I was shuttled back and forth—
> between Chavez bourgeois in the city
> and rural Lucero sheepherders,
> new cars and gleaming furniture
> and leather saddles and burlap sacks,
> noon football games and six packs of cokes
> and hoes, welfare cards and bottles of goat milk.
>
> Jimmy Santiago Baca, "Martín &
Meditations on the South Valley"

When you use parallelism as a stylistic device in your own writing, revise by reading your work aloud, listening for a strong and consistent rhythm. If you cannot hear the rhythm of parallel statements, rework your sentences.

┌ H E L P ─

Creating sentences in which elements are parallel in form but not parallel in meaning is a common mistake. Remember that it is necessary to compare like, or similar, things. Comparing unlike things will not make sense to your readers.

Look at how the first example below compares two unlike things:

FAULTY
Arthur's pitching skills are better than the batting skills of Steve.

PARALLEL
Arthur's pitching skills are better than those of Steve.

Ways to Achieve Clarity   **477**

Exercise 5 Revising Sentences by Correcting Faulty Parallelism

ANSWERS

Possible answers are shown below. The parallel elements are underlined.

1. Kwame Nkrumah is known <u>not only as the first prime minister of the African country Ghana but also as the person who led the country to independence from British rule</u>.

2. Ghana interests many <u>because it was called the Gold Coast by the British</u> and <u>because it was the first of Britain's colonies to achieve independence after World War II</u>.

3. Nkrumah's educational influences included <u>his study in the United States</u> and <u>his interest in Pan-Africanism</u>.

4. After <u>studying in the United States</u> and <u>attending a Pan-African conference in Great Britain in 1945</u>, Nkrumah returned to the Gold Coast in 1947.

5. During the late 1940s, Nkrumah became the leader of the Gold Coast nationalist movement, <u>not only because of his organizing ability but also because of his great determination</u>.

6. Nkrumah's goals included <u>gathering wide popular support for the nationalist movement</u> and <u>gaining self-government apart from the British</u>.

7. C

8. Although the British jailed him, Nkrumah and the CPP were successful both <u>popularly</u> and <u>politically</u>.

9. Because of this pressure, the British agreed <u>both to allow national elections and to grant a self-governing constitution in 1951</u>.

10. Nkrumah's leadership led <u>not only to CPP victory in the elections but also to the Gold Coast's full self-government</u>, which Britain granted in 1957.

┌HELP──

In Exercise 5, remember to check the placement of correlative conjunctions.

MEETING THE CHALLENGE

Parallelism can be one of the more difficult style elements to master, but excellent parallelism makes writing memorable. Go on a scavenger hunt for ten sentences that employ effective parallelism. Look for well-written examples of parallelism in everything you read, prose and poetry, and copy these sentences into a journal. (Hint: Speeches are an especially good source.) Include the author, source, and date of publication for each sentence. Compile your findings with other students'. When you need inspiration for your own writing, return to some of the excellent model sentences you have collected.

ANSWER
Compilations will vary.

Exercise 5 Revising Sentences by Correcting Faulty Parallelism

Some of the following sentences are unclear because they lack parallel structure. Revise each faulty sentence by putting parallel ideas into the same grammatical form. Add, delete, move, and replace words and punctuation as necessary. If a sentence is already in parallel form, write *C* for *correct*.

EXAMPLE 1. We are studying geography, history, and learning about famous people.

1. *We are studying geography, history, and famous people.*

1. Kwame Nkrumah is known not only as the first prime minister of the African country Ghana but also because he led the country to independence from British rule.

2. Ghana interests many because it was called the Gold Coast by the British and then was the first of Britain's colonies to achieve independence after World War II.

3. Nkrumah's educational influences included studying in the United States and that he was interested in Pan-Africanism.

4. After his study in the United States and attending a Pan-African conference in Great Britain in 1945, Nkrumah returned to the Gold Coast in 1947.

5. During the late 1940s, Nkrumah became the leader of the Gold Coast nationalist movement, not only through his organizing ability but also because he had great determination.

6. Nkrumah's goals were to gather wide popular support for the nationalist movement and gaining self-government apart from the British.

7. Nkrumah established the Convention People's Party, or CPP, in 1949 and led demonstrations and strikes in support of the cause.

8. Although the British jailed him, Nkrumah and the CPP were successful both popularly and as far as becoming major political forces.

9. Because of this pressure, the British both agreed to allow national elections and to grant a self-governing constitution in 1951.

10. Nkrumah's leadership led to CPP victory in the elections and that Britain granted the Gold Coast full self-government in 1957.

Review A Revising Paragraphs for Clarity

The following paragraphs are confusing because they contain faulty coordination and faulty parallelism. Using what you have learned, make each faulty sentence smoother and clearer. Remember to add, delete, or rearrange words and punctuation marks as necessary.

EXAMPLE

Sherman Alexie has earned awards not only for his writing but also because of his filmwork.

Sherman Alexie has earned awards not only for his writing but also for his filmwork.

Sherman Alexie is an American Indian of Spokane and Coeur d'Alene ancestry, and he writes powerfully about the experiences of American Indians. He is a prolific writer, and Alexie's writings include poetry, novels, short stories, essays, and screenplays. Alexie is known for his writing as well as producing and directing films based on his work. Alexie's depictions of American Indian life are sometimes grim, but the grittiness is often tempered by Alexie's wit and being humorous.

Alexie wrote and produced the movie Smoke Signals, and the film was released in 1998. Smoke Signals is the first Native American–produced, Native American–directed feature film written by an American Indian. The two lead characters in the film are American Indian men in their twenties who travel by bus across the country. One is sullen and angry, and he finds an outlet in playing basketball. The other one likes to tell long, involved stories and talking about his grandmother's frybread. These characters reflect Alexie's fresh and confident point of view and that he consciously works against the stereotypes of American Indians that have prevailed in our culture.

Alexie's portrayals of American Indians have won him acclaim from many critics, and they have also drawn reproach. Some people find Alexie's works dark, and they believe

Sherman Alexie

Review A Revising Paragraphs for Clarity

ANSWERS
Possible revisions follow.

Sherman Alexie is an American Indian of Spokane and Coeur d'Alene ancestry who writes powerfully about the experiences of American Indians. He is a prolific writer of poetry, novels, short stories, essays, and screenplays. Alexie is also known for producing and directing films based on his work. Although Alexie's depictions of American Indian life are sometimes grim, the grittiness is often tempered by his wit and humor.

Alexie wrote and produced the movie Smoke Signals, released in 1998, which is the first feature film written, produced, and directed by an American Indian. The two lead characters in the film are American Indian men in their twenties who travel by bus across the country. One is sullen and angry, but he finds an outlet in playing basketball. The other one likes to tell long, involved stories and talk about his grandmother's frybread. These characters reflect Alexie's fresh and confident point of view and his conscious work against the stereotypes of American Indians prevalent in our culture.

Alexie's portrayals of American Indians have won him both critical acclaim and reproach. Some people who find Alexie's works dark believe he should write more optimistically about life for American Indians. Alexie has said that he wants people to be provoked by what he writes, and he seems comfortable with making people uncomfortable at times. As a talented and productive writer who enjoys both critical success and a good fight, Alexie is likely to continue to shape the way we see contemporary American Indians.

Obstacles to Clarity

OBJECTIVE

- To identify and revise sentence fragments, run-on sentences, and unnecessary shifts in subject, tense, and voice

Lesson Starter

Motivating. Write the following quotation on the chalkboard.

❝The greatest of faults, I should say, is to be conscious of none.❞

(Thomas Carlyle, 1795–1881, Scottish essayist and historian)

Ask students to discuss what they think Carlyle is saying. How might this idea be applied to revising sentence fragments and run-on sentences? [*Before students can correct sentences that are fragments or run-ons, they must first be able to recognize these errors.*]

Correcting Misconceptions

Subordinating Ideas. Some students may insist that they speak in fragments all the time and that they are understood. Explain that speaking in fragments may create clear communication with people who are familiar with the speaker, the topic, or the manner of delivery, but that in written communication we cannot take for granted that the reader will automatically be able to fill in the missing words. Encourage students to listen to conversations randomly and to notice whether they are always able to fill in the unstated sentence parts.

Alexie should write more optimistically about the life for American Indians. Alexie has said that he wants people to be provoked by what he writes and he seems comfortable with making people uncomfortable at times. As a talented and productive writer, who both enjoys critical success and a good fight, Alexie is likely to continue to shape the way we see contemporary American Indians.

Obstacles to Clarity

In this part of the chapter, you will learn how to check your writing for some common obstacles to clarity: *sentence fragments*, *run-on sentences*, and *unnecessary shifts*.

Sentence Fragments

A sentence expresses a complete thought. If you punctuate a part of a sentence as if it were a whole sentence, you create a **sentence fragment**. Fragments are usually confusing because the reader has to puzzle out the missing information.

FRAGMENT	In 1929, the global economy into a worldwide depression. [missing verb]
SENTENCE	In 1929, the global economy **collapsed** into a worldwide depression.
FRAGMENT	We observing the bacteria through a powerful microscope. [missing helping verb]
SENTENCE	We **were** observing the bacteria through a powerful microscope.
FRAGMENT	Photographed families who were victims of the Great Depression. [missing subject]
SENTENCE	**Dorothea Lange** photographed families who were victims of the Great Depression.
FRAGMENT	By closing the park to bicycle riders and skateboarders. [not a complete thought—missing subject and verb]
SENTENCE	**The city tried to cut down on accidents** by closing the park to bicycle riders and skateboarders.

Obstacles to Clarity

Practice

- *Language & Sentence Skills Practice,* pp. 425–432

Differentiating Instruction

- *Developmental Language & Sentence Skills,* pp. 187–190

Phrase Fragments

A *phrase* is a group of words that does not have a subject and a verb. When a phrase is separated from the sentence it belongs with, it becomes a *phrase fragment.*

FRAGMENT   I found my sister in the den. **Making origami swans out of blue and green paper.** [participial phrase fragment]

SENTENCE   I found my sister in the den making origami swans out of blue and green paper.

FRAGMENT   My sister is good at figuring out how to do things. **With very little instruction.** [prepositional phrase fragment]

SENTENCE   My sister is good at figuring out how to do things with very little instruction.

FRAGMENT   She just sits down and gives herself enough time. **To ensure her success.** [infinitive phrase fragment]

SENTENCE   She just sits down and gives herself enough time to ensure her success.

FRAGMENT   Later, my sister made me two beautiful objects. **An origami snail and a fish.** [appositive phrase fragment]

SENTENCE   Later, my sister made me two beautiful objects, an origami snail and a fish.

Subordinate Clause Fragments

A **subordinate clause** has a subject and a verb but does not express a complete thought. Unlike an independent clause, a subordinate clause cannot stand on its own as a sentence.

FRAGMENT   Sea urchins have long, moveable spines. **Which they use to push themselves across the ocean floor.** [adjective clause fragment]

SENTENCE   Sea urchins have long, moveable spines, which they use to push themselves across the ocean floor.

FRAGMENT   Sea urchins can also be eaten in sushi. **After they have been harvested from the sea and properly prepared.** [adverb clause fragment]

SENTENCE   Sea urchins can also be eaten in sushi, after they have been harvested from the sea and properly prepared.

Sea Urchin

Obstacles to Clarity   **481**

EXTENSION

Critical Thinking

Analysis. Help students see that punctuation is not arbitrary but rather a tool for creating meaning in written language. Write the following sentence on the chalkboard:

Tom felt he could win if he could just pass Geraldo it would be easy.

Point out that merging two thoughts together like this can be confusing for the reader. In fact, the example has two different possible meanings, depending on where the period is inserted. [*The period could follow* win *or* Geraldo.] Discuss how making *it would be easy* a separate sentence would suggest much more confidence on Tom's part than placing the period after *win.* Students might enjoy creating similar sets of clauses.

NOTE A complete sentence is usually the clearest way to express a thought. However, experienced writers sometimes use fragments for stylistic effect. For example, in the following passage, notice how each fragment creates a precise image and how, grouped together, the fragments recreate the rhythm of a child's day.

> There had been a fight about who was to be "It" next. It had been so fierce that their mother had emerged from her bath and made them change to another game. Then they had played another and another. Broken mulberries from the tree and eaten them. Helped the driver wash the car when their father returned from work. Helped the gardener water the beds till he roared at them and swore he would complain to their parents. The parents had come out, taken up their positions on the cane chairs. They had begun to play again, sing and chant. All this time no one had remembered Ravi. Having disappeared from the scene, he had disappeared from their minds. Clean.
>
> Anita Desai, "Games at Twilight"

You can use fragments occasionally in expressive and creative writing such as journal entries and short stories. For example, you might use fragments in dialogue to capture the natural sounds of your characters' speech. You can also use fragments in classified ads and other types of writing where an informal, shorthand style is appropriate. However, avoid fragments in informative writing such as research papers and reports. Because your readers expect formal, straightforward language in this type of writing, fragments may confuse your message.

Exercise 6 Revising to Eliminate Fragments

Some of the following items contain sentence fragments. Revise each item by combining any fragments with the adjoining sentences. Move or add words and punctuation marks as necessary. If the item is already correct, write *C*. Here are possible revisions.

EXAMPLE **1.** We are studying Elizabeth Blackwell. This week in class.

1. *This week in class, we are studying Elizabeth Blackwell.*

1. Elizabeth Blackwell was born in 1821, And died in 1910.
2. In 1832, her parents immigrated with their eight children to New York, To escape an unpleasant social and political situation in Bristol, England.
3. Because of the financial plight of her family, Blackwell and her mother established a boarding school.
4. A friend of Blackwell's encouraged her to become a doctor. At first, Blackwell totally rejected this suggestion. **4.** C
5. Eventually, ~~Blackwell became interested~~ in the idea of becoming a doctor, ~~Leading~~ her to investigate the possibility of a woman studying medicine. **5.** Blackwell's interest/led
6. She became even more determined to follow her friend's advice, After she was told that a woman could not become a doctor.
7. In 1847, Elizabeth Blackwell was admitted to the Medical Institution of Geneva College, Which is now known as Hobart College.
8. She became the first woman in the United States to earn an M.D. degree, When she graduated in 1849 at the head of her class.
9. Elizabeth was not content with these honors. She spent the next two years doing graduate work in Europe. **9.** C
10. In 1857, Elizabeth Blackwell established the New York Infirmary for Women and Children, a hospital staffed by women. She opened the hospital on May 12, the birthday of her friend Florence Nightingale. **10.** C

Run-on Sentences

A **run-on sentence** is just the opposite of a fragment. It is made up of two complete sentences run together as if they were one sentence. Most run-ons are **comma splices**—two complete thoughts that have only a comma between them. Other run-ons, called **fused sentences,** have no punctuation between the two thoughts. The following examples show four ways to correct run-ons.

| RUN-ON | Naomi longed to make the basketball team, to achieve her goal, she practiced every afternoon. |
| CORRECT | Naomi longed make the basketball team**.** **To** achieve her goal, she practiced every afternoon. [two sentences] |

| RUN-ON | She tried several exercises, her skills showed no improvement. |
| CORRECT | She tried several exercises**,** **but** her skills showed no improvement. [compound sentence with comma and coordinating conjunction] |

DIFFERENTIATING INSTRUCTION

Learners Having Difficulty
Point out that revising for clarity generally eliminates passive and ambiguous sentences. However, some forms of writing—such as government documents, "academese," or "legalese"—are full of passive constructions. Obtain for the class a few sample paragraphs of inflated writing. Have students work together in groups to rewrite the paragraphs clearly and concisely. Allow time for groups to present their rewrites to the class.

⌈ TIPS ⅋ T R I C K S ⌉

Like fragments, run-ons usually occur when you are writing in a hurry. To avoid fragments and run-ons, give yourself enough time to draft complete, effective sentences and to revise them for clarity. It may help to put your draft away for a day, and then return to it with fresh eyes.

Obstacles to Clarity **483**

RUN-ON	Naomi worked hard, she was persistent.
CORRECT	Naomi worked hard**;** she was persistent. [compound sentence with semicolon]

RUN-ON	Her hard work paid off later she made the team.
CORRECT	Her hard work paid off**;** **later,** she made the team. [compound sentence with semicolon plus conjunctive adverb]

Exercise 7 Revising Run-on Sentences

Revise each of the following run-ons by using one of the methods you have learned. Use each of the four methods at least once.

Possible revisions appear below.

EXAMPLE 1. I run cross-country on my school's team, I get regular exercise.

1. *I run cross-country on my school's team, so I get regular exercise.*

1. Exercise can increase the efficiency of your muscles, it can increase your muscles' strength and size. **1. and**

2. Aerobic exercise helps your body supply oxygen to muscles, it increases the efficiency of the production of ATP, adenosine triphosphate. **2. and**

3. ATP is a biological molecule scientists consider it the cell's fuel.

4. Some of the energy from food molecules is stored in ATP a steady supply of ATP is essential to cell functioning.

5. With aerobic exercise the heart pumps more efficiently then the number of blood vessels in your muscles increases.

6. Aerobic activities include walking, biking, jogging, and swimming people who regularly exercise aerobically can expect such activities to become easier over time.

7. Exercise has beneficial psychological effects, too it improves mood and reduces depression and anxiety.

8. Regular exercise boosts your resistance to fatigue it also decreases tension and sleeplessness.

9. People just starting an exercise program should build gradually from an easier workout to a harder one trying to do too much too soon can leave a beginner quite sore.

10. and

10. Stretching before and after exercise improves flexibility and lessens the chance of injury, cooling down prevents dizziness, muscle cramps, and nausea.

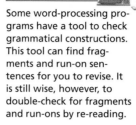

COMPUTER TIP

Some word-processing programs have a tool to check grammatical constructions. This tool can find fragments and run-on sentences for you to revise. It is still wise, however, to double-check for fragments and run-ons by re-reading.

Unnecessary Shifts in Sentences

For clarity, it is usually best to keep the same subject and the same verb form throughout a sentence. Unnecessary shifts in subject, tense, or voice can make a sentence awkward to read.

Shifts in Subject

Note that sometimes, especially in short compound sentences, a shift in subject is necessary to express your intended meaning. In the following sentences, the shift in subject is natural.

NATURAL SHIFT   Jessica jumped off the high diving board, but no one saw her.

I'll paint the background, and you can paint the birds and trees.

Most often, though, a shift in subject is awkward and unnecessary. In the following examples, notice that each sentence is much clearer when it has the same subject throughout.

AWKWARD   The Mullaneys have a new puppy, and the shelter is where they found it.

BETTER   **The Mullaneys** have a new puppy, and **they** found it at the shelter.

AWKWARD   All runners should be at the track by 7:00 so that you can pick up your registration forms.

BETTER   **All runners** should be at the track by 7:00 so that **they** can pick up their registration forms.

Shifts in Verb Tense and Voice

Unnecessarily changing verb tense or voice in midsentence can also create awkwardness and confusion. Stick to the tense and voice you start with unless you have a good reason for changing.

AWKWARD   Aldo talked about going to the North Pole, but then he goes to the Antarctic. [shift from past tense to present tense]

BETTER   Aldo **talked** about going to the North Pole, but then he **went** to the Antarctic. [past tense used in both clauses]

AWKWARD   The cat asks to go out, and then it always wanted to come back in.

BETTER   The cat asks to go out, and then it always wants to come back in.

TIPS & TRICKS

Often, the best way to correct a shift in subject and voice in a compound sentence is to create a compound verb. Just omit the second subject and place the second verb in the same voice as the first.

AWKWARD

Julio Cortázar attended the University of Buenos Aires, and then literary translation work was done.

BETTER

Julio Cortázar attended the University of Buenos Aires and then **did** literary translation work.

Reference Note

For more about **tense**, see page 198. For more about **active and passive voice**, see page 211.

Exercise 8 **Eliminating Unnecessary Shifts in Subject, Tense, and Voice**

ANSWERS

Possible revisions are given below.

1. The only creatures that have conquered the air are insects, pterosaurs, birds, and bats.

2. These flying animals share striking similarities, but they also have major differences.

3. Birds possess feathers, a unique, beneficial feature.

4. Feathers are well-suited to flight and are easily replaced.

5. Scientists think a creature called Archaeopteryx is the earliest known bird, and they estimate that it lived about 150 million years ago.

6. Archaeopteryx was roughly the size of a crow and shared features with some of the smaller dinosaurs.

7. Archaeopteryx had teeth, a tail, and, unlike present-day birds, solid bones.

8. However, this creature possessed feathers, which dinosaurs did not have, and wishbones, which were also part of their skeletal structure.

9. Some biologists have called birds "feathered dinosaurs"; however, most biologists classify birds in a separate class, *Aves*.

10. C

EXTENSION

Critical Thinking

Analysis. Students should be able to identify what should be corrected in each sentence in **Exercise 8** and explain why. Review the exercise as a class, and ask volunteers to describe what revision technique makes each unclear sentence smoother.

| AWKWARD | Volunteers made the dangerous journey after dark, but no wolves were encountered. [shift from active voice to passive voice] |
| BETTER | Volunteers **made** the dangerous journey after dark, but they **encountered** no wolves. |

A shift in voice usually causes a shift in subject, too. Notice that in the awkward sentence in the last pair, the shift from active to passive voice results in a shift from the subject *volunteers* to the subject *wolves.*

Exercise 8 **Eliminating Unnecessary Shifts in Subject, Tense, and Voice**

Most of the following sentences contain unnecessary shifts in subject or in verb tense or voice. Revise each awkward sentence, adding, deleting, or rearranging words as necessary. If a sentence does not need to be revised, write *C* for *correct.*

EXAMPLE
1. My teacher Mr. Rogers has a fossil collection; most of the fossils in it were collected by him when he was studying to be a geologist.

1. *My teacher Mr. Rogers has a fossil collection; he collected most of the fossils when he was studying to be a geologist.*

1. Only four types of creatures have conquered the air, and this group is comprised of insects, pterosaurs, birds, and bats.

2. These flying animals share striking similarities, but major differences have also been found among them.

3. Birds possess feathers, and this unique feature is beneficial to birds.

4. Feathers are well-suited to flight and are easily replaceable.

5. Scientists think a creature called Archaeopteryx is the earliest known bird, and they estimated that it lived about 150 million years ago.

6. Archaeopteryx was roughly the size of a crow, and it has shared features with some of the smaller dinosaurs.

7. Archaeopteryx had teeth and a tail, and, unlike present-day birds, solid bones were also characteristic of the creature.

8. However, this creature possessed feathers, which dinosaurs do not have, and wishbones were also part of their skeletal structure.

9. Some biologists have called birds "feathered dinosaurs"; however, birds are classified in a separate class, *Aves,* by most biologists.

10. Within this class, there are 28 orders of birds and about 8,800 species.

Fossil of Archaeopteryx

Review B **Revising Paragraphs for Clarity**

Fragments, run-ons, and unnecessary shifts in subject, tense, and voice make the following paragraphs awkward and unclear. Using the methods you have learned, revise the sentences to eliminate these obstacles to clarity. Notice how much smoother the paragraphs sound when you are finished.

EXAMPLE   Désirée is working on a short story, she plans to submit it to our school's literary magazine.

Désirée is working on a short story, and she plans to submit it to our school's literary magazine.

```
        Dorothy West began writing stories when
she was seven, and several Boston Post prizes
were won by her while she was a teenager.
Opportunity published West's story "The
Typewriter." Which later appeared in The Best
Short Stories of 1926.
        West born in Boston but eventually settled
in New York City, there West met many writers
of the Harlem Renaissance. Including Zora
Neale Hurston and Langston Hughes. In the early
1930s, she founded Challenge, a magazine that
published the works of young African American
writers. Because many Harlem Renaissance writ-
ers were published in West's magazine, West
```

Dorothy West

Obstacles to Clarity   **487**

Review B Revising **Paragraphs for Clarity**

ANSWERS
Possible revisions follow.

Dorothy West began writing stories when she was seven, and she won several <u>Boston Post</u> prizes while she was a teenager. <u>Opportunity</u> published West's story "The Typewriter," which later appeared in <u>The Best Short Stories of 1926</u>.

West was born in Boston, but she eventually settled in New York City. There she met many writers of the Harlem Renaissance, including Zora Neale Hurston and Langston Hughes. In the early 1930s, she founded <u>Challenge</u>, a magazine that published the works of young African American writers. Because West's magazine published the works of many Harlem Renaissance writers, West is often considered a member of that group. However, her own writing was published long after the height of the Harlem Renaissance movement. West stopped publishing <u>Challenge</u> in 1937 and started a new, more political magazine named <u>New Challenge</u> later that same year. Her new magazine published the work of Richard Wright and Ralph Ellison.

After West's magazine ventures failed, she took a job as a welfare investigator in Harlem. She later joined the Federal Writers' Project and became a contributor to the <u>New York Daily News</u>, which published many of her stories. In 1945, West moved to Martha's Vineyard, where she wrote her novel <u>The Living Is Easy</u>.

Her most successful novel, <u>The Wedding</u>, which was published in 1995, tells the story of a young woman of the Vineyard's black elite who marries a poor white jazz musician. West died in 1998 at the age of ninety-one.

is often considered a member of that group. However, her own writing published long after the height of the Harlem Renaissance movement. West stopped Challenge in 1937 and started a new, more political magazine named New Challenge later that same year it published the work of Richard Wright and Ralph Ellison.

After West's magazine ventures failed. She took a job as a welfare investigator in Harlem, she later joined the Federal Writers' Project. She became a contributor to the New York Daily News. Which published many of her stories. In 1945 West moved to Martha's Vineyard, where her novel The Living Is Easy was written.

Her most successful novel, The Wedding, was published in 1995, and West tells the story of a young woman of the Vineyard's black elite who marries a poor white jazz musician in The Wedding. West died in 1998. At the age of ninety-one.

Chapter Review

A. Using Coordination and Subordination

Use coordination and subordination to combine the following sentences. For each sentence, be sure to choose a coordinating conjunction, correlative conjunction, or subordinating conjunction that expresses the logical relationship between the ideas. You may rearrange or delete words if necessary.

1. Dana is my cousin. She lives in California now.
2. Marcy will rent a movie. She might bring a game instead.
3. The dragon was huge. It was also scaly and green.
4. Kris asked for a new book to read. We brought her one from the library.
5. That pumpkin weighs nearly fifteen pounds. It grew from a seed Jimmy planted.
6. The sky grew dark. The wind picked up.
7. Eleanor Roosevelt worked to further human rights. She is one of my heroes.
8. We planted tomatoes in the back garden. We planted basil and oregano in the front beds.
9. The movie won several prestigious awards. It was also a box-office hit.
10. I thought that the camera was broken. It just needed a new battery.

B. Revising Paragraphs for Clarity

Revise the following paragraphs to eliminate any problems with faulty coordination, faulty parallelism, or unnecessary shifts in subjects or in verb tense or voice. You may need to add, delete, or rearrange words in the sentences.   Possible revisions follow.

      The Komodo dragon is the largest living
lizard species, ~~but~~ _∧and it exists only on a few
islands of Indonesia. The lizard, now pro-
tected, is threatened by ~~losing~~ its habitat
_∧the loss of
and the depletion of its prey. The Komodo
dragon may reach over 9 feet in length,_∧
330 to 350 pounds ~~may be its weight~~, and ~~it~~
weigh
lives for up to 100 years, although the

(margin notes: and | the loss of | weigh)

ASSESSING

Monitoring Progress

Chapter Review. To assess student progress, you may want to compare the types of items missed on the **Diagnostic Preview** to those missed on the **Chapter Review.** If students have not made significant progress, you may want to provide them with additional practice.

Chapter Review

A. Using Coordination and Subordination

ANSWERS
Possible revisions follow.

1. Dana, who is my cousin, lives in California now.
2. Marcy will rent a movie, or she might bring a game instead.
3. The dragon, which was huge, was also scaly and green.
4. Kris asked for a new book to read, so we brought her one from the library.
5. That pumpkin, which grew from a seed Jimmy planted, weighs nearly fifteen pounds.
6. The sky grew dark, and the wind picked up.
7. Eleanor Roosevelt, who is one of my heroes, worked to further human rights.
8. After we planted tomatoes in the back garden, we planted basil and oregano in the front beds.
9. Not only did the movie win several prestigious awards, it was also a box-office hit.
10. I thought the camera was broken, but it just needed a new battery.

average life span is much shorter. The lizard can run swiftly, reaching speeds of 12 miles per hour, but ^its stealth, strength, and acute senses ~~are relied on~~ for hunting.

it relies on

^Komodos eat mostly carrion, ~~but~~ their living prey includes deer, boar, goats, and even ~~cannibalizing~~ other members of their own species. Attacks on humans are known ~~and~~ not common. The Komodo dragon's basic hunting strategy is ^attack~~ing~~ the prey's feet first and to knock it off balance. ^The lizard's claws are powerful, ~~and~~ its teeth are a more dangerous weapon. The Komodo's teeth are not only sharp and curved, ~~and their~~ serrated ^edges ~~also~~ provide a breeding ground for numerous bacteria. Even if the prey escapes the Komodo, researchers believe, infections from the deadly bacteria kill~~ed~~ it sooner or later. ^Other Komodos~~, however,~~ are immune to infection from the Komodo bite, ~~so~~ researchers ^search^ for special antibodies in Komodo blood.

Although

but
to
Although

but also are
,/ing

Because

are/ing

As early as 1915, local rulers and the Dutch colonial government acted to protect the Komodo dragon. Today, the Komodo is internationally protected) and ^the World Conservation Union ~~officially considers it vulnerable~~. Much of the known population lives on islands that make up the Komodo Island National Park. On other islands, however, the Komodo dragon continues to face challenges, ~~yet~~ poachers have depleted the Komodo's natural prey, especially deer, and ~~forests~~ have ~~been~~ cleared ~~by settlers~~. In the past twenty years, habitat loss on one island has caused the species to disappear from about 93 miles of the coast.

officially considered vulnerable by

since

settlers/forests

C. Revising Paragraphs to Eliminate Fragments and Run-on Sentences

Revise the following paragraphs to eliminate any sentence fragments and run-on sentences. You may need to add, delete, or rearrange words in the sentences.   Possible revisions follow.

The Louvre, the national museum and art gallery of France, may be the largest museum in the world,∧ its collections of paintings, sculptures, tapestries, furniture, jewelry, and antiquities are famous all over the world. Many people are familiar with at least some of the Louvre's treasures∧ for example, Leonardo da Vinci's *Mona Lisa* is housed there∧ Along with the *Venus de Milo.*

The Louvre, or *Grand Louvre,* as it is known in French∧ ~~It~~ was not originally intended to be a museum. In 1546, King Francis I began to build his royal residence, the Louvre, on the bank of the Seine◦ almost every later French monarch added to the structure, and in the seventeenth century, Kings Louis XIII and Louis XIV made major additions to the complex. The Louvre was no longer a royal residence⌐ After Louis XIV moved his court to Versailles in 1682. The idea of using the Louvre to house and display the royal collections was born in the mid-1700s,∧ the collections were not accessible to the public⌐ Until the French revolutionary government opened the Grande Galerie in 1793. Further major additions were made under Napoleon I⌐ And under Napoleon III.

Beginning in the 1980s, the French government undertook a billion-dollar remodeling and restoration of the Louvre complex◦ a huge, new underground complex of exhibition space and support facilities was constructed. The entire palace, part of which had been occupied by government offices, is now devoted to the museum. The rebuilt Richelieu wing, which had housed the Ministry of Finance, was opened in 1993 on the museum's two-hundredth anniversary, providing 230,000 square feet of new exhibition space◦ major restoration and reorganization continued into 2000.

and

but

CHAPTER

Combining Sentences

Diagnostic Preview

A. Combining Sentences by Inserting Words and Phrases

Combine the sentences in the following items by inserting words or phrases from one sentence into the other sentence. You may need to change the form of some words.　Here are possible revisions.

EXAMPLE　　1. Mike looked up from the book he was reading. He shrugged but didn't say a word.

　　　　　　1. *Looking up from the book he was reading, Mike shrugged but didn't say a word.*

1. Cheryl closed the curtains and brought up the house lights. ~~She was the stage manager.~~
2. The horse stood quietly a little outside the gate. Its broken tether dangled in the dusty road.
3. The kitten was stuck in a high branch of the tree. ~~It was mewing piteously.~~
4. Several city council members opposed the zoning ordinance. ~~They opposed it strenuously.~~
5. Ray finally made his way to the barn. Snow and ice ~~were~~ lashing at his bare face and hands.
6. Mrs. Jackson is my Latin teacher and a good friend of my family. She occasionally writes a column for the newspaper.
7. Christina found this old diary at a junk shop. ~~The diary was in a stack of books and papers.~~

8. The shovel‸had obviously been left outside for a long time. ~~It was corroded and covered with mud.~~

9. Refreshments will be available‸during intermission. ~~You can get refreshments in the lobby of the theater.~~

10. Upon hearing the punch line, the‸audience exploded with laughter. ~~The entire audience was laughing.~~

8. , corroded and covered with mud,

9. in the lobby of the theater

10. entire

B. Combining Sentences by Coordinating Ideas

Combine the sentences in each of the following items by forming a compound subject, a compound verb, a compound object, or a compound sentence. Possible revisions follow.

EXAMPLE   1. Have you seen that new movie? Has Karen seen it yet?

    1. *Have either you or Karen seen that new movie yet?*

11. Each member of my family has specific chores to do‸Everyone pitches in to help with some big jobs.

12. Rachel tried to see the back of her dress in the full-length mirror‸She couldn't get a good view.

13. ‸I have applied for early admission to the university. ~~My cousin Neil has applied there for early admission, too.~~

14. Liam has an internship at the museum this summer‸His friend Kyle will be working as a lifeguard.

15. The travel agent sent my uncle‸some tour brochures. ~~She sent the same brochures to my grandmother.~~

11.–15. [coordinating ideas]

11. , but

12. but

13. My cousin Neil and

14. , and

15. and my grandmother the same

C. Combining Sentences by Subordinating Ideas

Combine the sentences in each of the following items by subordinating one of the sentences to the other. Possible revisions follow.

EXAMPLE   1. I twisted my ankle playing volleyball. It still aches sometimes.

    1. *My ankle, which I twisted playing volleyball, still aches sometimes.*

16. The class had to postpone the field trip‸The bus driver became ill at the last minute.

17. Martin will be our class valedictorian‸He ~~would have to~~ flunk‸all his classes this semester ~~not to be.~~

18. ‸I finished mowing the lawn and clipping the hedge‸I needed a big drink of water.

16.–25. [subordinating ideas]

16. because

17. unless/s

18. After

Diagnostic Preview   **493**

Differentiating Instruction

- *Developmental Language & Sentence Skills,* pp. 191–196

- *Developmental Language & Sentence Skills Guided Practice Teacher's Notes and Answer Key,* p. 47

Assessment

- *Holt Handbook Chapter Tests with Answer Key,* pp. 37–41, 54

ASSESSING

Entry-Level Assignment
Diagnostic Preview. Use the Diagnostic Preview to identify areas in which students need instruction and practice in combining sentences. You could use the results of the preview to decide which lessons to teach to the entire class and which ones to assign to small groups.

PRETEACHING

Lesson Starter
Motivating. Write the following quotation on the chalkboard.

❝The only thing that makes life possible is permanent, intolerable uncertainty; not knowing what comes next.❞

(Ursula K. Le Guin, 1929–   , American writer)

Ask students whether they would enjoy listening to music and watching movies if every song had the same melody and every movie had the same plot. Explain that just as one tires of the same melodies or movie plots, readers grow bored with sentences that all have the same structure.

19. , whose mother was trying her best to ignore him,
20. The fire chief explained to the reporter that
21. I can't understand why
22. that/is loose again
23. , who/, should do well in calculus
24. when
25. , which

19. The child was fidgeting. ~~Her mother was trying her best to ignore him.~~
20. The fire was caused by faulty wiring. ~~The fire chief explained that to the reporter.~~
21. That movie still isn't available on video. ~~I can't understand the reason.~~
22. That dog ~~is loose again.~~ It always manages to dig its way out of the yard.
23. Rita ~~should do well in calculus.~~ She has always gotten the highest grades in her math classes.
24. My father guessed that we were planning a surprise party for him. He saw all the bags of supplies and the cake.
25. Cory finished saving for his airline tickets. ~~The tickets~~ will cost him over five hundred dollars.

Modeling and Demonstration

Combining Sentences. Model how to combine sentences by using the following sentences.

Fungi secrete enzymes to get their food.

The enzymes are digestive.

First, ask whether the two sentences are about the same subject. [*yes; enzymes*] Next, ask what information could be moved from the second sentence to the first sentence. [*the word* digestive, *which describes the enzymes*] Point out that the revision *Fungi secrete digestive enzymes to get their food* provides the same information as the two original sentences, but it conveys the information more concisely and effectively. Finally, ask a volunteer to combine the following sentence with the revision created in this activity.

Their food is organic.

[*Fungi secrete digestive enzymes to get their organic food.*]

Combining for Variety

Have you ever found your mind drifting while reading, despite real efforts to concentrate? (Be honest.) Choppy sentences can make it hard to concentrate. Of course, a short, simple sentence is sometimes just the thing you want; short sentences can be used to create emphasis. If you use only short sentences, however, you probably will not hold your reader's attention for very long. Take a look at the following passage. Does its style help hold your attention, or do you find it hard to focus on the paragraph's meaning?

> The sinking of the <u>Titanic</u> was one of the worst maritime disasters in history. The <u>Titanic</u> was the largest ship of its time. It was the most luxurious ship of its time. The <u>Titanic</u> was on its maiden voyage. The ship struck an iceberg. The iceberg was located off the Grand Banks of Newfoundland. The accident happened on the night of April 14, 1912. The night was clear and cold. The <u>Titanic</u>'s hull had sixteen watertight compartments. The iceberg punctured five compartments. The ship sank in less than three hours.

When some of the sentences are combined to create longer, more varied ones, the passage sounds smoother and more interesting.

The sinking of the <u>Titanic</u>, the largest and most luxurious ship of its time, was one of the worst maritime disasters in history. On the clear, cold night of April 14, 1912, the ship, which was on its maiden voyage, struck an iceberg off the Grand Banks of Newfoundland. The iceberg punctured five of the sixteen watertight compartments in the ship's hull, and the ship sank in less than three hours.

Sentence-combining techniques can help you create balance, rhythm, and precision in your writing. In this chapter, you will learn several techniques for combining sentences to improve variety and style.

Inserting Words and Phrases

Sometimes, a sentence adds only a little information to a more important idea that appears before or after it. Instead of giving a small detail a sentence of its own, you can insert that detail into another sentence as a word or phrase. By combining the sentences, you eliminate extra words and repeated ideas. (Notice, for example, how many words are repeated in the four sentences printed below.)

FOUR SENTENCES	The surgeon considered doing the operation. The operation would be simple. The surgeon was experienced. She thought the operation would go smoothly.
ONE SENTENCE	**Thinking it would go smoothly,** the **experienced** surgeon considered doing the **simple** operation.

or

The **experienced** surgeon considered doing the **simple** operation, **as she thought it would go smoothly.**

Often, the words or phrases you are inserting can be placed in several different ways. Just make sure your combined sentence sounds clear and expresses the meaning you intend. Watch out for awkward, confusing combinations like this one: *Thinking it would go smoothly, the surgeon, who was experienced, considered doing the operation, which would be simple.*

MEETING THE CHALLENGE

A paragraph of short, choppy sentences can be improved by adding information to some of the sentences. How much information, however, is too much? Find a partner. Write a simple sentence, and give it to your partner to expand by adding a phrase, a clause, or modifiers. Then, add more information to the sentence yourself. Take turns until the sentence is packed with information. Using this method, write a total of three sentences. Now look over the sentences. At what point does a well-written, informative sentence turn into a long, overwhelming one? How long can a reader keep from losing track of the meaning? In a small group, generalize some ground rules for knowing when it's time for an end mark and a new beginning.

ANSWER
Sentences will vary, but students should note that bulky sentences are likely to require readers to hold too much information in mind at once, thus hindering comprehension.

Inserting Words and Phrases

OBJECTIVES

- To combine sentences by inserting adjectives, adverbs, and prepositional phrases

- To combine sentences by using participial and absolute phrases

- To combine sentences by using appositive phrases

STYLE | TIP

Single-word modifiers enable you to pack sentences with meaning. Most readers find brevity a relief, and using adverbs and adjectives to combine sentences can add conciseness and zip to your writing.

Single-Word Modifiers

Before you take a word from one sentence and insert it into another sentence, check to make sure the word can act as a modifier in the second sentence. You may need to change the word into an adverb or adjective before you insert it.

USING THE SAME FORM

ORIGINAL   Angela de Hoyos is a Mexican American poet. She is an award-winning poet.

COMBINED   Angela de Hoyos is an **award-winning** Mexican American poet.

ORIGINAL   De Hoyos has spoken out against racism and social oppression. She has spoken out publicly.

COMBINED   De Hoyos has spoken out **publicly** against racism and social oppression.

CHANGING THE FORM

ORIGINAL   She was involved in the revolution of the 1960s. It was a revolution of the culture.

COMBINED   She was involved in the **cultural** revolution of the 1960s.

ORIGINAL   In her poetry de Hoyos often explores themes through humor. The humor is based on irony.

COMBINED   In her poetry de Hoyos often explores themes through **ironic** humor.

Reference Note

For more about **prepositional phrases,** see page 23.

Prepositional Phrases

Usually, you can insert a prepositional phrase without any change in form.

ORIGINAL   Ole likes contemporary American films. He likes the ones with ensemble casts.

COMBINED   Ole likes contemporary American films **with ensemble casts.**

Sometimes you can change a part of one sentence into a prepositional phrase and then insert it into another sentence.

ORIGINAL   These movies make Ole weep. He cries tears of joy.

COMBINED   These movies make Ole weep **with tears of joy.**

COMPUTER TIP

Use a word-processing program's cut and paste features to move words or phrases as you combine sentences. If you change your mind, you can always move the text again.

496   **Chapter 18**   Combining Sentences

MINI-LESSON   Grammar

Using Gerund and Infinitive Phrases.
You may want to introduce students to two other phrases that can be used to combine sentences or to reduce wordiness. Explain to students that a gerund phrase includes a verb form ending in *–ing* that is used as a noun and an infinitive phrase contains a verb form, usually beginning with *to,* that is used as a noun, an adjective, or an adverb. Write the following sentences on the chalkboard, and work with students to reduce and/or combine sentences by using gerund and infinitive phrases.

Exercise 1 **Combining Sentences by Inserting Adjectives, Adverbs, and Prepositional Phrases**

Combine each of the following groups of short sentences by inserting adjectives, adverbs, or prepositional phrases from one sentence into the other. Read your combined sentences aloud to make sure the meaning is clear. *Here are possible combinations.*

EXAMPLE   **1.** Fungi make up one of the kingdoms of life. There are several kingdoms of life. Most fungi are multicellular organisms.

　　　　　 1. *The mostly multicellular fungi make up one of the several kingdoms of life.*

1. Biologists used to recognize only two kingdoms of life, the animal kingdom and the plant kingdom. ~~That was before the 1960s.~~

2. Many biologists use a system consisting of five kingdoms of organisms. ~~It is a system of classification.~~

3. The animal kingdom, Animalia, is the largest kingdom. ~~It is a kingdom with more than one million named species.~~

4. Trees, shrubs, grasses, mosses, and many other chlorophyll-containing organisms are part of another kingdom. ~~They are part of the second-largest kingdom.~~

5. We are studying the Fungi kingdom, which contains more than 100,000 known species. ~~We are currently studying this kingdom in my AP biology class.~~

6. Fungi secrete enzymes that break down organic matter. ~~The organic matter is broken down~~ into simple compounds.

7. Fungi, which include mushrooms, molds, and mildews, live all over the world. ~~They live on land and in water.~~

8. The Protista kingdom includes thousands of species of algae as well as sporozoans and flagellates. ~~The algae in this kingdom include species of green, golden, red, and brown algae.~~

9. Another kingdom, Prokaryotae, contains bacteria, including cyanobacteria (also known as blue-green algae). ~~The bacteria are various.~~

10. Scientific classification of organisms changes as biologists learn more about the creatures that make up these kingdoms. ~~The changes are continual.~~

1. Before the 1960s,
2. classification
3. With more than one million named species,
4. , second-largest,
5. In my AP biology class, / currently
7. on land and in water
8. green, golden, red, and brown
9. various
10. continually

---

1. That she finished her book was important. [*Finishing her book was important;* gerund phrase]

2. Yosef gave a birthday party. He wanted to surprise his brother. [*To surprise his brother, Yosef threw a birthday party;* infinitive phrase]

Then, have students working in groups compose three or four sentences of their own that contain gerund and infinitive phrases. Groups can share their sentences with the class.

Reference Note

For more about **participles** and **participial phrases,** see page 64.

Participial Phrases

A *participial phrase* contains a participle and its modifiers and complements. Participial phrases act as adjectives in a sentence. They help develop concrete details that elaborate on a sentence's main idea and so can add interest to your writing.

EXAMPLE   Sometimes their mother sat in the room behind them, sewing, or **dressing their younger sister,** or **nursing the baby, Paul.**

James Baldwin, "The Rockpile"

Often, you can lift a participial phrase from one sentence and insert it directly into another sentence without a change in form.

ORIGINAL   Constance set out to conquer the wilds of Alaska. She set out armed with only a backpack and a strong will.

COMBINED   Constance, **armed with only a backpack and a strong will,** set out to conquer the wilds of Alaska.

Sometimes you will need to change a verb into a participle before inserting the idea into another sentence.

ORIGINAL   Constance arrived in Alaska early in the morning. She gripped her guidebook and a photo of home.

COMBINED   Constance, **gripping her guidebook and a photo of home,** arrived in Alaska early in the morning.

NOTE   Place a participial phrase beside the noun or pronoun you want it to modify. Otherwise, you may give your sentence a meaning you did not intend. Notice how the placement of the modifier makes a difference in the meaning of the following sentence.

MISPLACED   Buried inside her backpack, Constance tried to find the trail map.

CORRECT   Constance tried to find the trail map **buried inside her backpack.**

Absolute Phrases

An *absolute phrase* consists of (1) a participle or a participial phrase, (2) a noun or a pronoun that the participle or participial phrase modifies, and (3) any other modifiers of that noun or pronoun. The entire word group is used as an adverb to modify the independent clause of a sentence.

Participial Phrases. Review with students the definition and function of participles. Point out that participles are verb forms that can be used as adjectives in sentences. Write the following sentences on the chalkboard:

The water was **running** over the cliff.

The water **running** over the cliff was cool and clear.

In the first sentence, *running* is part of the verb. In the second sentence, *running* is a participle modifying *water.*

DIRECT TEACHING

Correcting Misconceptions

The words "absolute phrase" may suggest to students that the phrase is total or final. To increase understanding, explain that the term *absolute* can mean "separate." An absolute phrase is separate in the sense that it has no grammatical connection with any word in the clause it modifies. Remind students that the noun or pronoun of an absolute phrase is different from the subject in the independent clause of the sentence. Then, have students identify the noun or pronoun of the phrase and the subject of the independent clause in the following sentence.

The wind gusting, Constance returned home.

CONTENT-AREA CONNECTIONS

Social Studies

Phrases. Point out that in addition to creating interest, participial, absolute, and appositive phrases pack a lot of information into individual sentences. Have students monitor newspaper coverage of a current event over several days. Then, ask students to work in small groups to compose five-hundred-word summaries of the event. The summaries should use participial, absolute, and appositive phrases where appropriate. Have groups exchange summaries to identify and tally the phrases used.

Absolute phrases express something about the time, cause, or circumstances of the action in the independent clause. Absolute phrases are easy to spot because they always contain a noun that is different from the subject of the independent clause. Using absolute phrases is another way to combine sentences.

ORIGINAL   The wind started gusting. Constance returned home.
COMBINED   **The wind gusting,** Constance returned home.

Exercise 2 Combining Sentences by Using Participial and Absolute Phrases

Combine each of the following pairs of sentences by reducing one sentence to a participial or an absolute phrase and inserting the phrase into the other sentence.

EXAMPLE   1. Marian Anderson demonstrated her love for music at an early age. She sang in the church choir.
           1. *Singing in the church choir, Marian Anderson demonstrated her love for music at an early age.*

1. Anderson traveled to Europe to study for a year when she was twenty-two. She was awarded a fellowship to do so.
2. European audiences received her warmly. Anderson became famous.
3. She returned to the United States for a recital in 1935. American opera lovers were eager to hear her.
4. Anderson sang on the steps of the Lincoln Memorial in protest on Easter morning of 1939. She had been banned from singing at Constitution Hall because she was black.
5. Seventy-five thousand people came to hear the Easter morning concert. They expressed their disapproval of the discriminatory treatment.
6. Anderson received the Spingarn Medal in 1939. She was chosen, like other recipients of that award, for outstanding achievement in a particular field.
7. The conductor Arturo Toscanini praised her voice as the kind "that comes along once in a hundred years." Anderson received praise from many of the best musicians and conductors of the time.
8. She earned fame mainly as a concert performer. Anderson went on to become a delegate to the United Nations.

─HELP─
When you change a verb form into a participle, you may also have to delete some words from a participial or absolute phrase to avoid an awkward combination. Remember to use correct punctuation in the combined sentence.

Exercise 2 Combining Sentences by Using Participial and Absolute Phrases

ANSWERS
Possible sentence combinations follow.

1. Awarded a fellowship, Anderson traveled to Europe to study for a year when she was twenty-two.
2. Received warmly by her European audiences, Anderson became famous.
3. American opera lovers being eager to hear her, she returned to the United States for a recital in 1935.
4. Banned from singing at Constitution Hall because she was black, Anderson sang on the steps of the Lincoln Memorial in protest on Easter morning of 1939.
5. Seventy-five thousand people, expressing their disapproval of the discriminatory treatment, came to hear the Easter morning concert.
6. Receiving the Spingarn Medal in 1939, Anderson was chosen, like other recipients of that award, for outstanding achievement in a particular field.
7. Adding to the praise of many of the best musicians and conductors of the time, conductor Arturo Toscanini praised Anderson's voice as the kind "that comes along once in a hundred years."
8. Earning fame mainly as a concert performer, Anderson went on to become a delegate to the United Nations.
9. Remembered today for her vocal virtuosity and her contributions to civil and human rights, this talented woman won the UN Peace Prize in 1977.
10. Born in 1897, she lived through World War I, the Great Depression, World War II, the civil rights movement, and more.

DIFFERENTIATING INSTRUCTION

Advanced Learners

Some appositives are so closely related to the word or words they modify that they should not be set off by commas. Such appositives are called *restrictive appositives.* Show students the following examples:

1. Yoshi's friend Claire went with us. (Yoshi has more than one friend.)

2. I loved Dylan Thomas's poem "Fern Hill." (Dylan Thomas wrote more than one poem.)

3. She always forgets how to spell the word *weird.* (She remembers how to spell other words.)

For more information on appositives, see pp. 73–76.

9. This talented woman won the UN Peace Prize in 1977. She is remembered today for her vocal virtuosity and her contributions to civil and human rights.

10. She was born in 1897. She lived through World War I, the Great Depression, World War II, the civil rights movement, and more.

Appositive Phrases

An ***appositive phrase*** is made up of an appositive and its modifiers. Appositive phrases add detail by identifying or describing a noun or pronoun in a sentence. For clear meaning, insert an appositive phrase directly before or after the noun or pronoun it identifies or describes.

EXAMPLE   You can also imagine the enormous statue-filled gate that once dominated the place and marked the beginning of Watling Street, **the road that still takes you through London to the northwest of England.**

Benedict Nightingale, "The Garden of England," *Gourmet*

You can combine sentences in a variety of ways by using appositive phrases.

TWO SENTENCES   Isabella d'Este was a ruler of the Italian city-state Mantua during the Renaissance. She actively supported many great artists and writers of the time.

ONE SENTENCE   **A ruler of the Italian city-state Mantua during the Renaissance,** Isabella d'Este actively supported many great artists and writers of the time.

or

Isabella d'Este, **an active supporter of many great artists and writers of the time,** was a ruler of the Italian city-state Mantua during the Renaissance.

In the second combination, the verb *supported* was changed into the noun *supporter* to create the appositive phrase. Notice that each combination emphasizes a different idea.

Reference Note

For more about **punctuating appositive phrases** in sentences, see page 344.

NOTE   Set an appositive phrase off from the rest of the sentence with a comma—or two commas if you place the phrase in the middle of the sentence.

EXAMPLE   The town of Canterbury, **the ancient religious center of England,** attracted many pilgrims during the Middle Ages.

500   **Chapter 18** Combining Sentences

Exercise 3 Combining Sentences by Using Appositive Phrases

To combine the following pairs of sentences, turn one of the sentences into an appositive phrase and insert it into the other sentence. Be sure to check your punctuation.   Sample combinations appear below.

EXAMPLE   **1.** Pierre Roux helped develop an antitoxin to combat diphtheria in 1894. He was a French bacteriologist.

   1. *Pierre Roux, a French bacteriologist, helped develop an antitoxin to combat diphtheria in 1894.*

1. ~~Diphtheria is a serious and highly infectious disease.~~ Diphtheria particularly affects children.
2. ~~Toxoids are harmless forms of diphtheria toxin.~~ Toxoids have become more effective in treating the disease than the original antitoxin.
3. German measles is most common among teenagers and rarely affects babies. ~~German measles is a contagious disease caused by a viral infection.~~
4. The virus that causes German measles was discovered and isolated in 1961. ~~German measles is a disease that is also called rubella.~~
5. A vaccine for mumps was approved in 1967. ~~Mumps is an infectious disease that attacks gland and nerve tissue.~~
6. A red rash that appears several days after the other symptoms is the distinguishing feature of fifth disease. ~~Fifth disease is~~ an illness that gets its name from being counted among five very common childhood infections.
7. Fifth disease is caused by a parvovirus. ~~A parvovirus is~~ a very small virus that causes disease in mammals.
8. Chickenpox does not come from chickens; it gets its name from the word *cicer.* ~~Cicer is~~ the Latin word for chickpeas.
9. People with chickenpox generally develop red spots. ~~These are~~ blisters that were once thought to resemble chickpeas.
10. My doctor says that she sees fewer cases of chickenpox now than she used to. ~~My doctor is a pediatrician.~~

1. , a serious and highly infectious disease,
2. , harmless forms of diphtheria toxin,
3. , a contagious disease caused by a viral infection,
4. , a disease also called rubella,
5. , an infectious disease that attacks gland and nerve tissue,
10. , a pediatrician,

Review A Combining Sentences

Combine some of the sentences in the following passage by using the methods you have learned. Use your judgment about which sentences to combine and how to combine them. When you are finished, the paragraphs should have a smoother, livelier style.

> ⌐TIPS & TRICKS⌐
>
> When revising for style, first combine ideas that strike you as flowing together naturally. Then, read over the revised passage to see where else you can make changes to add variety to your work.

Review A   Combining
Sentences

Review A   **Combining Sentences**

ANSWER
A possible revision appears below.

The surface of the planet Mars can be seen through a telescope from Earth. Reddish in color, the planet was named after the ancient Romans' red god of war. Mars, maintaining a distance of at least 128 million miles from the sun, travels in an elliptical orbit around it.

Part of the planet's surface is covered with craters caused by meteors. Mars also has canyons and deep gorges. Such features seem to support the view of some scientists that large quantities of water once flowed on the planet's surface. Mars also has windblown plains. The plains are covered by sand dunes and jagged rocks.

Coordinating and Subordinating Ideas

OBJECTIVES

- To combine sentences by coordinating ideas

- To combine sentences by subordinating ideas

Reference Note

For more about **coordination,** see page 466.

EXAMPLE   I am interested in astronomy. Astronomy is the science dealing with matter in outer space.

I am interested in astronomy, the science dealing with matter in outer space.

The surface of the planet Mars can be seen through a telescope. The surface can be seen from Earth. The planet is reddish in color. It was named after the ancient Romans' red god of war. Mars travels in an elliptical orbit. It travels around the sun. It maintains a distance of at least 128 million miles from the sun.

Part of the planet's surface is covered with craters. These craters were caused by meteors. Mars also has canyons and gorges. The gorges are deep. Such features seem to support the view that large quantities of water once flowed on the planet's surface. This is the view of some scientists. Mars also has plains. The plains are windblown. They are covered by sand dunes and rocks. The rocks are jagged.

Coordinating Ideas

You can join equally important words, phrases, or clauses by using coordinating conjunctions (such as *and, but, or, for, yet*) or correlative conjunctions (such as *both . . . and, either . . . or, neither. . . nor*). When you combine sentences in this way, you will usually create a compound subject, a compound verb, a compound object, or a compound sentence.

ORIGINAL   Ella is an aikido expert. Sebastian is also an aikido expert.

COMBINED   **Both Ella and Sebastian** are aikido experts. [compound subject]

ORIGINAL   Many people who have fibromyalgia experience great pain. However, they lead active, productive lives.

COMBINED   Many people who have fibromyalgia **experience great pain yet lead active, productive lives.** [compound verb]

ORIGINAL   We saw the man on the moon. We also saw the meteor shower.

COMBINED   We saw **the man on the moon and the meteor shower.** [compound direct object]

RESOURCES

Coordinating and Subordinating Ideas
Practice
- *Language & Sentence Skills Practice,* pp. 441–448
Differentiating Instruction
- *Developmental Language & Sentence Skills,* pp. 193–196

ORIGINAL	Mrs. Granger gave Vinnie tickets to see the new exhibit at the museum. She gave me tickets, too.
COMBINED	Mrs. Granger gave **Vinnie and me** tickets to see the new exhibit at the museum. [compound indirect object]

ORIGINAL	Jaya ran to catch the train. She got there too late.
COMBINED	Jaya ran to catch the train, **but** she got there too late. [compound sentence]

To form a compound sentence, you can also link independent clauses with a semicolon and a conjunctive adverb or with just a semicolon.

Reference Note
For a list of **conjunctive adverbs,** see page 357.

EXAMPLES   Winston had never made the smallest effort to verify his guess**;** **indeed,** there was no way of doing so.

George Orwell, *1984*

The mall is a common experience for the majority of American youth**;** they have probably been going there all their lives.

William Severini Kowinski, *The Malling of America*

Oral Practice   Combining Sentences by Coordinating Ideas

Read aloud each of the following pairs of sentences. Then, aloud, combine each pair by creating a compound subject, a compound verb, a compound object, or a compound sentence. Make sure any connectives you use show the proper relationship between the ideas.

Possible combinations appear below.

EXAMPLE   1. Connie Chung is a famous Chinese American. Amy Tan is another famous Chinese American.

1. *Connie Chung and Amy Tan are famous Chinese Americans.*

1. Between 1840 and 1850, Canton Province in China experienced severe economic problems. Large numbers of Chinese peasants emigrated to the United States.   **1.** , and
2. During the 1850s, more than 41,000 Chinese made their way to this country. ~~They~~ joined the great gold rush of that time.   **2.** and
3. Most of these early Chinese immigrants found ~~no~~ gold. ~~They found no~~ reliable employment.   **3.** neither/nor
4. They came seeking prosperity. They found only hard work and discrimination.   **4.** , but
5. The transcontinental railroad system was being built in the 1850s. Cheap labor was in great demand.   **5.** , and

Oral Practice

DISTRIBUTED REVIEW
Have students combine each pair of sentences in the **Oral Practice** by turning one sentence into a participial or absolute phrase. Students can then create a paragraph from the resulting sentence combinations.

6. Ten thousand laborers built the Union Pacific railroad. Nine thousand of them were of Chinese descent.

7. The railroad builders of America initially favored Chinese immigration. The sentiment changed when the railroad system was finished.   **7.** ; however,

8. In 1869, the tracks of the Central Pacific joined those of the Union Pacific in Ogden, Utah. Thousands of Chinese laborers were immediately out of work.   **8.** , and

9. Most new immigrants in the nineteenth century lacked education. ~~They possessed few skills.~~   **9.** skills and

10. Despite their hardships, many Chinese immigrants stayed in the United States. ~~They~~ began to make it their home.   **10.** and

Subordinating Ideas

When two related sentences contain ideas of unequal importance, you can combine the sentences by making the less important idea into a subordinate clause (an *adjective clause*, an *adverb clause*, or a *noun clause*). The use of subordination will help show the relationships between the ideas.

In the following sentences, notice how each subordinate clause begins with a connecting word that shows how the clause relates to the main idea.

EXAMPLES   Mustangs comprise a fascinating chapter in the story of the modern horse, **whose ancestors evolved here and then migrated over the Bering land bridge to Asia, Africa, and Europe.** [adjective clause]

> Yva Mamatiuk, "Mustangs on the Move,"
> *Smithsonian*

If birders can learn to distinguish dozens of characteristic songs and telegraphers could handle Morse code, we should be able to cope with a few simple electronic warbles and trills. [adverb clause]

> James Gleick, "What the Beep Is Going On?"
> *The New York Times Magazine*

Other studies along these lines have shown **that extroverts have greater pain tolerance than introverts.** [noun clause]

> Atul Gawande, "The Pain Perplex,"
> *The New Yorker*

Reference Note

For more about **subordination,** see page 469.

TIPS & TRICKS

Besides connecting the subordinate clause to the independent clause, subordinators explain relationships:
- To describe a person use *who, whose*
- To describe a thing, use *which, that*
- To show why, use *as, since, because*
- To show how or where, use *if, how, as though*
- To show when, use *after, as, whenever, while*
- To show under what condition, use *although, if, though, unless*

Learning for Life

Writing a Cover Letter for a Résumé. Prospective employers frequently ask job applicants to submit a résumé, or summary of personal information (education, skills, work experience, other activities, and interests). A cover letter should always accompany a résumé. The cover letter is an opportunity for the applicant to catch the employer's attention by highlighting skills and qualifications that make the applicant the best choice for the job.

Adjective Clauses

An *adjective clause* modifies a noun or pronoun and usually begins with *who, whose, which, where,* or *that.* To combine sentences by using an adjective clause, first decide which sentence you want to subordinate. Then, change that sentence into an adjective clause and insert it into the other sentence.

ORIGINAL   Mammals alone possess hair. Hair is really filaments made mainly of dead cells filled with protein.

COMBINED   Hair, **which mammals alone possess,** is really filaments made mainly of dead cells filled with protein.

ORIGINAL   Because hair is made of dead cells, I do not believe my friend Dante. He says it hurts when he gets his hair cut.

COMBINED   Because hair is made of dead cells, I do not believe my friend Dante, **who says it hurts when he gets his hair cut.**

NOTE   Use a comma or commas to set off an adjective clause that is not essential to the meaning of the sentence.

ESSENTIAL   The computer **that is most reliable** is most likely to rank first in the survey.

NONESSENTIAL   That computer, **which Edgar just bought,** is fairly reliable.

Reference Note

For more about **adjective clauses,** see page 84.

Reference Note

For more about **punctuating adjective clauses,** see page 338.

Adverb Clauses

An *adverb clause* modifies a verb, an adjective, or an adverb in a sentence. To form an adverb clause, add a subordinating conjunction (such as *although, after, because, if, when, where,* or *while*) to the beginning of the sentence you want to subordinate. Then, attach the adverb clause to a related sentence. You may need to delete or replace some words to form a clause.

ORIGINAL   Carlos left the store. He could not find the CD he wanted.
COMBINED   Carlos left the store **because he could not find the CD he wanted.**

ORIGINAL   There may not be any racquetball courts open. In that case, we will go to the park and play tennis.
COMBINED   **If there are no racquetball courts open,** we will go to the park and play tennis.

HELP

When you combine sentences by using an adverb clause, make sure that the subordinating conjunction reflects the proper relationship between the ideas in the two clauses.

Reference Note

For more about **adverb clauses** and **subordinating conjunctions,** see pages 90 and 469.

DIFFERENTIATING INSTRUCTION

Learners Having Difficulty
Before studying adjective clauses, students may benefit from a review of the difference between phrases and clauses and a review of the relative pronouns *who, whose, which, where,* and *that.* Discuss as a class which pronouns describe people [*who, whose*] and which describe things or places [*which, where, that*]. Then, ask students to construct simple sentences using each of these pronouns.

RETEACHING

Coordinating and Subordinating Ideas
To help students understand the desirability of varied sentence structures, you could discuss the sentence structures used in Doris Lessing's "No Witchcraft for Sale," if it is included in your literature textbook. Have students read the selection, and then have them analyze a portion of it for compound subjects and verbs, compound sentences, and subordinate clauses. Examples include "Mr. and Mrs. Farquar went to Gideon in the kitchen and thanked him over and over again" [*compound verb*] and "Their feelings over the miracle (that was how they thought of it) were so strong and deep and religious, that it was distasteful to them to think of money" [*subordinate clauses*]. Ask students how the selection would be different if it consisted only of simple sentences.

Have each student compose a résumé and a cover letter for a summer job he or she would like to have. The cover letter should demonstrate a variety of sentence-combining techniques to engage the interest of the employer and lead him or her to look closely at the résumé. Post students' résumés and cover letters for the class to examine. Students might vote on the three cover letters with the most appealing and varied sentence style.

Critical Thinking

Synthesis. Remind students that adjective and noun clauses may be introduced by *that,* which can sometimes be omitted from the sentence without any confusion. Have students formulate two sentences with noun clauses and two sentences with adjective clauses from which *that* has been omitted. Ask the class to identify which of the students' sample sentences contain noun clauses and which contain adjective clauses.

─HELP─

You may need to add, delete, or rearrange some words in Exercise 4.

Noun Clauses

A **noun clause** is a subordinate clause used as a noun. It usually begins with *that, what, whatever, why, whether, how, who, whom, whoever,* or *whomever.*

EXAMPLES   **Whatever Mimi does** will have an impact on this situation. [noun clause as subject]

Many people do not realize **that Jim is a champion chess player.** [noun clause as direct object]

People were talking about **how Hugo ate twelve sandwiches.** [noun clause as object of a preposition]

Sometimes you can drop the introductory word, such as *that, whom,* or *which,* from a noun clause without any confusion.

EXAMPLE   Irma told me [that] **I should get a haircut.**

You can combine sentences by turning one sentence into a noun clause and attaching it to the other sentence.

ORIGINAL   Cruciferous vegetables are good for your health. The magazine article explained the reason this is true.

COMBINED   The magazine article explained **why cruciferous vegetables are good for your health.**

ORIGINAL   Broccoli is a cruciferous vegetable. Vernon said he had heard this fact.

COMBINED   Vernon said he had heard **that broccoli is a cruciferous vegetable.**

Exercise 4   **Combining Sentences by Subordinating Ideas**

Combine each of the following pairs of sentences. Change one sentence into a subordinate clause, and attach the clause to the other sentence. Remember to choose connectives carefully, and check your combined sentences for correct punctuation.

EXAMPLE   1. I am a member of a film buffs' society. It meets regularly to watch and discuss interesting films.

1. *I am a member of a film buffs' society that meets regularly to watch and discuss interesting films.*

1. Akira Kurasawa was Japan's most influential movie director. He died in 1998 at 88 years of age.
2. His first internationally known film was *Rashomon. Rashomon* portrays the same event from four different points of view.
3. Kurasawa's interests linked East and West. He was interested in Japanese folk tales, American westerns, and such authors as Shakespeare and Dostoyevsky.
4. Kurasawa's movie *Throne of Blood* is based on Shakespeare's *Macbeth*. One should not be surprised.
5. Early in his career, Kurasawa was interested in making beautiful films. Then he became more interested in realism.
6. Kurasawa wanted *Throne of Blood* to be realistic. Kurasawa required his lead actor to wear a protective vest so he could be shot with real arrows.
7. As a teenager, Kurasawa learned about film from his brother. His brother was a *benshi*, or silent film narrator.
8. In 1936, Kurasawa answered a movie studio advertisement for apprentice movie directors. He was desperate for money.
9. *Star Wars* was inspired by Kurasawa's movie *The Hidden Fortress. Star Wars* replaces the bickering peasants with bickering robots.
10. In *The Hidden Fortress*, the peasants help free a princess. *The Hidden Fortress* is an adventure film made in 1958.

Akira Kurasawa and an actor on set (above); film still from Throne of Blood *(below).*

 Review B **Combining Sentences by Coordinating and Subordinating Ideas**

Combine each of the following pairs of sentences by either coordinating or subordinating ideas. You may see more than one way to combine a sentence pair. If so, combine the sentences in the way that reads best to you.

EXAMPLE
    1. Japanese comic books are a multibillion dollar industry. Japanese comic books are called *manga*.

    1. Japanese comic books, which are called manga, *are a multibillion dollar industry.*

ANSWERS
Possible revisions appear below.

1. Akira Kurasawa, who died in 1998 at 88 years of age, was Japan's most influential movie director.

2. *Rashomon*, which was his first internationally known film, portrays the same event from four different points of view.

3. Kurasawa's interests, which included Japanese folk tales, American westerns, and such authors as Shakespeare and Dostoyevsky, linked East and West.

4. One should not be surprised that Kurasawa's movie *Throne of Blood* is based on Shakespeare's *Macbeth*.

5. Although early in his career Kurasawa was interested in making beautiful films, he became more interested in realism.

6. Because Kurasawa wanted *Throne of Blood* to be realistic, he required his lead actor to wear a protective vest so he could be shot with real arrows.

7. As a teenager, Kurasawa learned about film from his brother, who was a *benshi*, or silent film narrator.

8. In 1936, Kurasawa answered a movie studio advertisement for apprentice movie directors because he was desperate for money.

9. *Star Wars*, which was inspired by Kurasawa's movie *The Hidden Fortress*, replaces Kurasawa's bickering peasants with bickering robots.

10. In *The Hidden Fortress*, which is an adventure film made in 1958, the peasants help free a princess.

Review B **Combining Sentences by Coordinating and Subordinating Ideas**

ANSWERS

Possible answers are shown below.

1. *Manga* look like American comics because both have sequential panels and word balloons.

2. Modern *manga* are related to ancient illustrated scrolls and ancient humorous woodblock prints.

3. The *manga* process has roots in American comics, which were first translated into Japanese in the 1920s.

4. Early Japanese comic books really were books, for they had as many pages as a novel and had hard covers.

5. After World War II, Osamu Tezuka, who was influenced by U.S. movie animation, became the major creator of *manga.*

6. Tezuka, whose works are sometimes hundreds or thousands of pages long, expanded the story lines of *manga.*

7. Tezuka made a comic book of *Crime and Punishment,* which is a novel by the Russian writer Feodor Dostoyevsky.

8. Today, *manga* first come out in magazines and are later collected and presented in book form.

9. Americans can find *manga* in translation and see cartoons based on them.

10. Many people think reading *manga* is like reading novels or watching movies.

1. *Manga* look like American comics. *Manga* have sequential panels and word balloons.

2. Modern *manga* are related to ancient illustrated scrolls. They are also related to ancient humorous woodblock prints.

3. The *manga* process has roots in American comics. In the 1920s, American comics were first translated into Japanese.

4. Early Japanese comic books really were books. They had as many pages as a novel and had hard covers.

5. After World War II, Osamu Tezuka became the major creator of *manga.* He was influenced by U.S. movie animation.

6. Tezuka expanded the story lines of *manga.* Tezuka's works are sometimes hundreds or thousands of pages long.

7. Tezuka made a comic book of the novel *Crime and Punishment.* The novel is by the Russian writer Feodor Dostoyevsky.

8. Today, *manga* first come out in magazines. The material in magazines is later collected and presented in book form.

9. Americans can find *manga* in translation. They can see cartoons based on *manga.*

10. Many readers think *manga* are like novels. Many people also think reading *manga* is like watching movies.

18

Terms in brackets refer to concepts tested by the items in the Chapter Review.

Chapter Review

A. Revising Sentences by Subordinating Ideas

The clauses in each of the following sentences have been combined by coordinating ideas. Revise each of the sentences by subordinating one of the clauses to the other.   Possible revisions follow.

1. Matt wants to join the navy, ~~for~~ his father and his grandfather served in the navy.

2. Simone will have to buy her own car, ~~but~~ her parents have agreed to pay for the insurance for a year.

3. That parakeet is Mrs. Popakowski's pet, ~~and it~~ seems never to tire of chattering.

4. I knew ~~something about the situation, and that thing was~~ that we would soon have a chance to explain ourselves.

5. Sarah had spent hours on her French homework, ~~yet~~ she still couldn't remember parts of some of the irregular verbs.

6. My sister had a dentist's appointment this morning, ~~so~~ she didn't get to school until after ten o'clock.

7. A new teacher has just been hired, ~~and that teacher speaks Cantonese and Vietnamese~~.

8. Two of the newspaper's editors will be graduating, ~~but~~ the younger staff members who will take their places are talented.

9. Ben re-read the directions carefully, ~~for~~ he didn't want to get lost.

10. Mr. Catalano would especially like to thank ~~one person, and that person~~ anonymously donated a set of encyclopedias to the school library.

11. The ground was too soft and wet from the rain, ~~so~~ the farmer couldn't take the tractor into the field.

12. The mayor ~~made an announcement, and she said~~ that the city would begin using solar energy to power streetlights.

13. The singer was recovering from laryngitis, ~~but he~~ nevertheless performed beautifully.

14. Maria will live in Wyoming this summer and work on a ranch, ~~and you met Maria last night~~.

ASSESSING

Monitoring Progress

Chapter Review. To assess student progress, you may want to compare the types of items missed on the **Diagnostic Preview** to those missed on the **Chapter Review.** If students have not made significant progress, you may want to provide them with additional practice.

SENTENCES

RESOURCES

Combining Sentences

Assessment

■ *Holt Handbook Chapter Tests with Answer Key,* pp. 37–41, 54

Chapter Review

B. Revising Paragraphs by Combining Sentences

ANSWER

Here is a sample revision of the passage.

Although the western Roman Empire fell in A.D. 476, much of this civilization persisted. The European languages known as Romance languages are one legacy of the Roman Empire. The Romance languages, which include Italian, French, Spanish, Romanian, and Portuguese, developed from Latin, the language of Rome.

English developed from the Germanic languages, but some English also derives from Latin, in part because of England's close association with France during Norman times. Latin's influence can be seen in English in prefixes such as *pro–*; in church words such as *disciple, shrine,* and *bishop;* and in words such as *veto* and *curriculum,* which come directly from Latin.

Another legacy of the Roman Empire is architecture. Examples of Roman architecture can be seen throughout southern Europe as well as in North Africa and Southwest Asia. Roman bridges spanning rivers in France, Germany, and Spain are still used. The Romans rebuilt the cities they conquered and added their own city grid system, which consisted of roads, baths, theaters, and a central forum.

Even today, the round arch and the vault, the primary innovations of Roman architecture, are used in buildings and bridges. Roman buildings were often based on Greek models; the ruins of these buildings inspired later architects such as Thomas Jefferson. Jefferson studied Roman architecture before building his home, Monticello, in 1770.

15. After
16. Whoever has
17. when
18. , who
19. that
20. so that

15. Oscar fixed himself a snack, ~~and then~~ he started to write his research paper.

16. ~~The winner will be the person with~~ the best essay, ~~and that person~~ will win a gift certificate from a nearby bookstore.

17. Celia had to be at school at five o'clock, ~~for~~ the rehearsal was scheduled to begin.

18. Texas farmers have suffered through a terrible drought this year, ~~and they~~ are hoping for increased rainfall.

19. Kudzu is a fast-growing vine, ~~and it~~ was brought to the United States from Japan.

20. When you finish the weaving, clip the threads and weave them back in, ~~and that way~~ no one can see the loose ends.

B. Revising Paragraphs by Combining Sentences

Using the methods you have learned, combine the short sentences in the following passage to make more interesting sentences. In some cases you can combine more than just two sentences. Your combined sentences should add variety and improve the style of the passage. Remember to check for correct punctuation when you have finished.

> The western Roman Empire fell in A.D. 476. Much of this civilization persisted. One legacy of the Roman Empire lies in European languages. The Romance languages show this legacy. The Romance languages developed from Latin. Latin was the language of Rome. Romance languages include Italian, French, Spanish, Romanian, and Portuguese.
>
> English developed from the Germanic languages. Some English also derives from Latin. This fact is in part a result of England's close association with France during Norman times. Some English words reveal Latin's influence. You can see Latin's influence in prefixes such as *pro-*. Many church words also come from Latin. The words *disciple, shrine,* and *bishop* are examples. Other English words including *veto* and *curriculum* come from Latin. These words come directly from Latin.
>
> Another legacy of the Roman Empire is Roman architecture. Examples can be seen throughout southern Europe. Examples can also be seen in North Africa and Southwest Asia.

Roman bridges are still used. Many of these bridges span rivers in France, Germany, and Spain. The Romans rebuilt the cities they conquered. They added their own city grid system. This grid system consisted of roads, baths, theaters, and a central forum.

The round arch and the vault are innovations of Roman architecture. They are the primary innovations. They are used in buildings and bridges even today. Roman buildings were often based on Greek models. The ruins of these buildings inspired later architects. Thomas Jefferson built his home in 1770. He named the home Monticello. Before Jefferson built Monticello he studied Roman architecture.

Improving Sentence Style

Diagnostic Preview

A. Revising Sentences by Varying Sentence Beginnings

Each of the following sentences begins with the subject. Revise each sentence so that it begins with a single-word modifier, a phrase, or a clause. Possible revisions follow.

EXAMPLE
1. Nick, Daniel, and Ann are members of the planning committee for the class picnic. They were assigned the task of arranging the food for the picnic.

1. *Members of the planning committee for the class picnic, Nick, Daniel, and Ann were assigned the task of arranging the food for the picnic.*

1. ∧Daniel, Nick, and Ann were concerned ~~because they had not cooked for such a big group before.~~

2. ∧~~Mr. Crawford, the class sponsor, explained~~ that they didn't have to do the cooking themselves ∧~~and~~ put their minds at ease.

3. ∧They kept the menu for the picnic simple, ~~but~~ the quantities of food were still enormous.

4. ~~Daniel~~ spent hours on the telephone ∧~~and~~ called around for the best prices.

5. ∧Nick borrowed a pickup truck from his uncle ~~later,~~ and he and Ann bought the food and other supplies.

B. Revising Sentences to Reduce Wordiness

The following sentences are wordy. Revise each sentence, eliminating unnecessary words and reducing clauses and phrases to make the sentence more concise. Possible revisions follow.

EXAMPLE   **1.** At that point in time, it was necessary for students who had proceeded to sit in the first rows to find alternative seating in other parts of the auditorium.

       1. Then, students who were sitting in the first rows had to move to different seats.

6. Over the course of the next two or three minutes, our speaker, who is also our distinguished guest, will be commencing his arrival in the auditorium.

7. As the chief administrative and instructional official of your institution of learning, I am delighted, thrilled, excited, pleased, and privileged to offer a welcoming hand to the elected official who heads our city.

8. Students, please rise from a seating position and join together with me in singing our national anthem, in which we will be led by Natalie Cranwick, a member of our senior class who will be graduating this year.

9. At the close of the ceremonies that open this assembly, I myself will be personally presenting the awards to senior class members who have been selected for awards by their classmates.

10. I respectfully request that you do not display your appreciation of each of your classmates one at a time, but rather restrain yourselves until the last of the awards has been awarded to its recipients.

6.–10. [reducing wordiness]

6. In a few/distinguished guest arrive

7. your principal welcome our mayor

8. stand senior

9. After/opening senior class

10. Please hold your applause until all the awards have been given out.

C. Revising Paragraphs by Varying Sentence Structure.

The following paragraph is made up of simple sentences. Rewrite the paragraph, combining sentences and using a variety of sentence structures.   Possible revisions follow.

```
    Cappadocia was an ancient district in
Anatolia in Turkey. The name now refers to
a much smaller area. The name particularly
refers to a triangular area full of strange
rock formations, underground dwellings, and
hundreds of churches carved out of the rock.
The region has been inhabited since the Stone
Age. The area changed hands many times.
Cappadocia was dominated by the Hittites, the
Persians, the Greeks, and the Romans.
    The region of Cappadocia once contained
active volcanoes. Eruptions from the volcanoes
covered the area with tuff. Tuff is composed of
mud, ashes, and lava. Tuff is a soft rock. It
```

Although it has/it has been

which/a soft rock and which

Diagnostic Preview   **513**

Differentiating Instruction
- *Developmental Language & Sentence Skills,* pp. 197–202
- *Developmental Language & Sentence Skills Guided Practice Teacher's Notes and Answer Key,* p. 48

Assessment
- *Holt Handbook Chapter Tests with Answer Key,* pp. 42–46, 54

Revising for Variety

OBJECTIVES

- To revise sentences by varying their beginnings
- To revise a paragraph by varying sentence structure

PRETEACHING

Lesson Starter

Motivation. Write the following quotation on the chalkboard.

❝ Once you've finished writing for yourself and begin to write for your *reader,* your mumbo jumbo will start slowly turning into bona fide prose—i.e., sentences that make sense. ❞

(John R. Trimble, 1940–   , American writer and educator)

Ask students to reflect on the meaning of Trimble's words and their connection to revising sentences for style. Tell students that in the revision stage, writers often rearrange sentences and words to create effective writing.

DIRECT TEACHING

Modeling and Demonstration

Varying Sentence Beginnings. Model how to vary sentence beginnings by using the example *They choose to visit places new to them.* First, ask students how the sentence begins. [*with a subject followed by a verb*] Next, explain to students that if they have too many sentences that begin with a subject followed by a verb, their writing may be dull. Then, ask students to add a modifier to the beginning of the sentence. [*Answers will vary.*] Now, have a volunteer use another example from this chapter to demonstrate how to vary sentence beginnings.

---

and

and

and

is easy to carve. Wind and water carved spectac-ular gorges, valleys, and cliffs, ~~Wind and water~~ created the strange, pointed rock formations now called "fairy chimneys." The lack of trees in the area may have forced people there to seek shelter in the formations. The area may have been invaded often enough for people to seek secure hiding places. People still live in some of the old cave dwellings even today. Visitors to the region can tour the underground "cities" and the countless churches carved into the rock. The area also boasts Islamic architecture, Roman ruins, and spectacular natural scenery.

Revising for Variety

No one likes to read dull writing—not your cousin in Chicago, not your chemistry teacher, and not your colleagues at work. Whether you are writing a personal letter, a report on ions, or a memo about time-saving techniques, a versatile writing style will help you convey your message with punch and pizazz.

As you learn to evaluate and revise your writing, you can develop an eye for sentence style. The next time you draft an essay, examine how your sentences fit together. Do they add up to lively, natural-sounding paragraphs? If your writing sounds dull, you probably need to vary the beginnings and the structures of some of your sentences.

Notice how the varied sentences below work together to form a smooth, effective passage.

> Beyond the stream, the river calmed into a long, wide pool. We stopped paddling for a time and turned to see the setting sun dye river and sky in crimson. Air and water seemed all one, of one color and translucence. The wind had died; a great stillness enveloped us. We rested together, drifting slowly backward through fiery waters, content simply to gaze as the red waters of the river slipped away into reddening skies, briefly obstructed by a dark silhouetted line of leafless trees on the far bank.
>
> Steve Faulkner, "Common Water," *DoubleTake*

RESOURCES

Revising for Variety

Practice

- *Language & Sentence Skills Practice,* pp. 449–454

Differentiating Instruction

- *Developmental Language & Sentence Skills,* pp. 197–200

Varying Sentence Beginnings

Most sentences begin with a subject followed by a verb.

EXAMPLES   **Canoeing is** a popular activity.

            Some people prefer kayaking to canoeing.

While there is nothing wrong with this basic subject-verb pattern, it can begin to sound monotonous after a while. You can improve the style of your writing by beginning some sentences with introductory words, phrases, and clauses instead of with subjects. At the same time, you can make more effective connections between related sentences.

In each example below, the first version is clear. However, the second version brings the ideas into sharper focus by shifting the emphasis.

BLAND	Bernice won the sculpting contest. She told her best friend Emi as soon as she found out.
BETTER	Bernice won the sculpting contest. **As soon as she found out,** she told her best friend Emi.
BLAND	Emi was happy for Bernice. She told Ari the good news over the phone.
BETTER	Emi was happy for Bernice. **Over the phone,** she told Ari the good news.

Sometimes the best way to vary sentence beginnings is to reduce a short sentence to an introductory word, phrase, or clause and attach it to another sentence. This is where your sentence-combining skills come in handy.

BLAND	Emi kept Ari on the phone for an hour. She is talkative and sociable.
BETTER	**Talkative and sociable,** Emi kept Ari on the phone for an hour.
BLAND	Ari was excited to hear that Bernice had won. He wanted to congratulate her.
BETTER	**Excited to hear that Bernice had won,** Ari wanted to congratulate her.

NOTE Remember that there are many ways to combine sentences. In the second bland example above, another acceptable way to combine the two sentences would be *Ari was excited to hear that Bernice had won and wanted to congratulate her.*

Reference Note

For more information about **combining sentences,** see page 494.

DIFFERENTIATING INSTRUCTION

Advanced Learners

If the selection is available in your literature textbook, choose an excerpt from Virginia Woolf's "The Death of a Moth," and ask students to analyze it for variety in sentence beginnings and structure. Have students create charts or graphs showing how often Woolf uses each of the types of sentence beginnings shown on the chart on this page. Then, ask students to determine the number and order of short, medium, and long sentences Woolf incorporates in this excerpt.

In their analyses, students will discover that Woolf uses short, long, and medium sentences in random order. Explain that authors tend to use short sentences for emphasis, longer sentences for details and intensity, and medium-length sentences to balance the rhythm.

English-Language Learners

General Strategies. For **Exercise 1** on page 517, you may want to pair English-language learners needing assistance and peer tutors, preferably those who are proficient in organizing ideas and have an especially good command of English grammar. In this way, the tutors can review and deepen their knowledge, and the English-language learners can receive guidance.

TEACHING TIP

Review with students the use of the comma to punctuate sentence beginnings. The material on pp. 515–518 is a helpful reference.

Critical Thinking

Evaluation. Ask students to bring to class a piece of their writing, such as a lab report or a civics paper. Have students mark sentence beginnings and write self-evaluative paragraphs on the variety shown. Encourage students to revise their work based on their findings.

Varying Sentence Structure

Loose and Periodic Sentences. Work with students to practice varying sentences in their own writing through the use of loose and periodic sentences.

- A loose sentence is a basic statement with a string of details added at the end of the statement.

EXAMPLE: The waves crashed, filling the air with sea water and chasing the children back to their parents.

- A periodic sentence places additional details before the basic statement.

EXAMPLE: Unexpectedly, without even thinking about it, my mother chose the red roses.

Have students work in pairs to add details and revise wording to create a loose and a periodic sentence for each of these basic statements.

1. The young boy retold his story.

2. Mother repaired my broken bracelet.

3. Several soldiers received orders.

4. The dog helped the girl.

5. The choir waited.

A plant demonstrating phototropism.

The following chart gives some examples of how to vary sentence beginnings.

Varying Sentence Beginnings	
Sentence Connectives	A tropism is a growth response in which the direction a plant grows is determined by a particular stimulus. **Consequently,** phototropisms are growth responses to light.
	The growth of a plant toward light is called positive phototropism. **However,** the growth of a plant's roots away from light is called negative phototropism.
Appositives and Appositive Phrases	Another example of this phenomenon, **gravitropism,** is the growth of a plant in response to gravity.
	An example of positive gravitropism, the downward growth of roots occurs frequently.
Single-Word Modifiers	**Strangely,** some plants respond to touch.
	Curly and green, grapevines grow in response to touch and are therefore thigmotropic.
Phrase Modifiers	**From the window of my kitchen,** I can see many types of plants.
	Looking closely, I noticed that most of the plants were in need of water.
	To address this problem, I went outside and watered the plants.
Clause Modifiers	**Because I noticed the situation in time,** I was able to keep the plants from dying.
	Although I am not the best gardener, I am eager to learn more about plants.

NOTE Sentence connectives such as *and, but,* and *however* can help you make transitions between ideas. Usually, these connecting words link ideas within a sentence. Sometimes, though—especially in informal writing—they are used at the beginning of a sentence for variety and emphasis. For example, notice how the writer uses a sentence connective for emphasis in the following passage.

> It's crunch time for Julie Shama. Like thousands of high school seniors, she faces college-application deadlines in the next month. Julie's counselor at Brookline High, outside Boston, and her $300-a-session private college-application advisor are helpful. **But** they can't match the resources of the Internet.
>
> T. Trent Gegax, "www.Apply-Here.com,"
> *Newsweek*

Use sentence connectives sparingly and carefully to begin sentences. When you use them, be sure that the connective shows the appropriate relationship between your ideas. Also, note that in formal writing it is best not to begin sentences with coordinating conjunctions such as *and* and *but*.

Exercise 1 Varying Sentence Beginnings

Revise each of the following sentences so that it begins with an appositive, an appositive phrase, a single-word modifier, a phrase modifier, or a clause modifier.

EXAMPLE   1. We are studying the Revolutionary War in my history class this week.

1. *In my history class this week we are studying the Revolutionary War.*

1. African Americans, many experiencing great hardships, played an important role during the Revolutionary War.
2. George Washington ordered at the beginning of the war that no African American soldiers could serve in the Continental Army.
3. The Continental Army's troops, poorly trained and prone to disease, were also few in number.
4. The British army also suffered a shortage of troops, and the British made plans to recruit African Americans into their army in 1775.
5. Washington ordered the Continental Army to enlist free blacks to counter this move.
6. Many African Americans served in units with European Americans, and others served in separate African American companies.

The Granger Collection, New York

Exercise 1 Varying Sentence Beginnings

ANSWERS
Possible revisions follow.

1. Many experiencing great hardships, African Americans played an important role during the Revolutionary War.
2. At the beginning of the war, George Washington ordered that no African American soldiers could serve in the Continental Army.
3. Poorly trained and prone to disease, the Continental Army's troops were also few in number.
4. Also suffering a shortage of troops, the British made plans to recruit African Americans into their army in 1775.
5. To counter this move, Washington ordered the Continental Army to enlist free blacks.
6. Although some African Americans served in separate African American companies, many served in units with European Americans.

Exercise 1   **Varying Sentence Beginnings**

ANSWERS continued

7. At first, many of the white commanders of the all-black companies were reluctant to lead the groups.

8. Because of the notable courage of many African American troops, these commanders later changed their minds.

9. Numbering about 5,000, African American soldiers helped win the Revolutionary War.

10. Although many soldiers' heroic efforts went unacknowledged, a few black soldiers received official recognition for their outstanding bravery.

7. Most commanders of the all-black companies were white, and many of these commanders were reluctant to lead the groups at first.

8. These commanders later changed their minds because of the notable courage of many African American troops.

9. African American soldiers, numbering about 5,000, helped win the Revolutionary War.

10. A few black soldiers received official recognition for their outstanding bravery, although many soldiers' heroic efforts went unacknowledged.

Varying Sentence Structure

When you revise your writing for style, it is not always enough to vary your sentence beginnings. It is also important to vary sentence structures by using a mix of simple, compound, complex, and sometimes compound-complex sentences.

Read the following short paragraph, which contains only simple sentences.

Reference Note

For more information about the **four types of sentence structures,** see page 94.

> Quasars are the brightest, most distant objects in the sky. For decades they have puzzled and intrigued astronomers. Quasars may hold important clues to the birth and formation of galaxies. Astronomers believe this. Astronomers first observed quasars in 1963. Since then, they have discovered over one thousand of these objects. With the help of two segmented-mirror telescopes in Hawaii, astronomers hope to discover the power source of quasars. According to some astronomers, giant black holes produce the energy.

Now, read the revised version of the paragraph. Notice how the writer has made the paragraph smoother by including a variety of sentence structures.

> Quasars are the brightest, most distant objects in the sky. For decades they have puzzled and intrigued astronomers, who believe quasars may hold important clues to the birth and formation of galaxies. Astronomers first

---

MINI-LESSON   **Usage**

Active vs. Passive Voice. When revising for variety and style, students should avoid overuse of the passive voice. Passive constructions often sound awkward and lack impact. Active verbs, on the other hand, usually require fewer words to convey the point, and they make the writing style more lively.

Have students convert passive-voice verbs in the following sentences to active voice. Sample revisions are shown in brackets.

1. In 1929, the first Women's Air Derby, whose course runs from Santa Monica,

observed quasars in 1963, and since then, they
have discovered over one thousand of these
objects. With the help of two segmented-mirror
telescopes in Hawaii, astronomers hope to discover the power source of quasars, which some
believe to be giant black holes.

Complex sentences do more than add variety to your writing.
They also help bring your thoughts into focus by emphasizing main
ideas and subordinating less important ones. For example, in the
revised paragraph on quasars, notice how the complex sentence at the
end establishes a clear connection between the last two ideas. The relative pronoun in the subordinate clause relates the information in that
clause to *quasars*, the object of the preceding clause.

Reference Note

For more information
about **subordinating
ideas in sentences**, see
page 469.

Exercise 2 — Varying Sentence Structure

The following paragraph contains too many simple sentences. Improve
the paragraph by varying the structure of the sentences. You can add,
delete, or rearrange words as needed.

COMPUTER TIP

When you print out a draft
to revise, use double- or
triple-line spacing and wide
margins to allow room for
handwritten corrections.
Then, when you are ready
to print a final copy,
remember to reset the
spacing and margins.

EXAMPLE   Cynthia and Eddie are leaving soon for
           England. They will visit friends and hike
           in the rolling countryside.

           *Cynthia and Eddie are leaving soon for
           England, where they will visit friends and
           hike in the rolling countryside.*

Kent is a county in southern England. It is
known as "the garden of England" because of its
lush and serene countryside. Sir Thomas Wyatt
wrote fondly about Kent. Wyatt introduced the
sonnet to England. Wyatt lists the unbearable
faults of other European countries in one poem.
He also praises the virtues of Kent in this
poem. Kent has lovely hills and fields, old villages, and abundant flowers in the spring. Kent
has these today just as it did in Wyatt's time.
The historic town of Canterbury lies in Kent.
Canterbury was made famous by Geoffrey Chaucer's
tales. A journey through Kent rewards the visitor. The visitor enjoys history, as well as
robust food and beautiful country.

Exercise 2 — Varying Sentence Structure

ANSWER

Here is a sample revision.

Kent, a county in southern England,
is known as "the garden of England"
because of its lush and serene countryside. Sir Thomas Wyatt, who introduced the sonnet to England, wrote
fondly about Kent. In one poem,
Wyatt lists the unbearable faults of
other European countries and praises
the virtues of Kent. As it did in Wyatt's
time, Kent today has lovely hills and
fields, old villages, and abundant
flowers in the spring. Canterbury,
the historic town made famous by
Geoffrey Chaucer's tales, lies in Kent.
A journey through Kent rewards the
visitor with history as well as robust
food and beautiful country.

California, to Cleveland, Ohio, was
won by Louise Thaden. [*In 1929, Louise
Thaden won the first Women's Air
Derby, whose course runs from Santa
Monica, California, to Cleveland, Ohio.*]

2. A national organization for women
pilots was founded three months later
by twenty-six women fliers. [*Twenty-
six women fliers founded a national
organization for women pilots two
months later.*]

Review A Varying Sentence
Beginnings and Sentence
Structure

ANSWER
A sample paragraph follows.

Increasingly popular with television viewers, extreme sports, such as surfing, skateboarding, snowboarding, and mountain biking, require great physical agility and, often, risk. Although traditional sports, including basketball, football, and baseball, used to dominate television ratings, the big salaries and bad attitudes of many athletes in those sports have alienated viewers. Because extreme-sport athletes do not participate in their sports just for money, some viewers think these athletes take their sports more seriously. Extreme sports are especially popular among young viewers, and for this reason television analysts say that the traditional three-sport era may be over for good.

Revising to Reduce Wordiness

OBJECTIVES

- **To revise wordy sentences**
- **To revise a paragraph by eliminating unnecessary words**
- **To revise sentences through reduction**

┌─**HELP**─
When revising for style, be careful to retain the meaning you wish to convey. After you have made revisions, remember to re-read what you have written aloud purely for sense.

┌**TIPS** & **TRICKS**┐

When revising for wordiness, look for the following two types of problems:

- Redundant Pairs—words that imply each other

EXAMPLES
true facts

future plans

- Redundant Categories—words that designate their general categories

EXAMPLES
engineering field

large in size

Review A Varying Sentence Beginnings and
Sentence Structure

Using what you have learned about varying sentence beginnings and sentence structure, revise the following paragraph for style. Add, delete, and rearrange words wherever necessary to make the sentences more varied.

EXAMPLE   My sister prefers extreme sports. I prefer
sports like football and baseball.

*While my sister prefers extreme sports, I
prefer sports like football and baseball.*

Extreme sports are growing increasingly popular with television viewers. Extreme sports are called extreme because they require great physical agility and, often, risk. Extreme sports include surfing, skateboarding, snowboarding, and mountain biking, among other sports. Traditional sports such as basketball, football, and baseball used to dominate the television ratings. Many athletes in traditional sports, with their big salaries and bad attitudes, have alienated viewers. Some viewers think that extreme sports athletes take their sports more seriously because they do not participate in them just for money. Extreme sports are especially popular with young viewers. Television analysts say that the traditional three-sport era may be over for good.

Revising to Reduce Wordiness

Which would you rather read: a ten-page essay on the health benefits of broccoli or a one-or-two-paragraph statement on the subject? Skilled writers make every word count, suiting length to purpose. Your writing is most effective when it is clear, concise, and free of the clutter of unnecessary words. To avoid wordiness, keep these three points in mind.

- Use only the words you need to make your point.
- Avoid complicated words where simple ones will do.
- Do not repeat words unless it is absolutely necessary.

RESOURCES

Revising to Reduce Wordiness
Practice
■ *Language & Sentence Skills Practice*, pp. 455–462
Differentiating Instruction
■ *Developmental Language & Sentence Skills*, pp. 201–202

Sometimes you can fix a wordy sentence by taking out whole groups of unnecessary words. At other times you can revise by reducing clauses to phrases and both clauses and phrases to single words.

Eliminating Unnecessary Words

The following paragraph is an example of wordy writing. Lines have been drawn through the unnecessary words. First, read the paragraph aloud, including the words that have been crossed out. Then, read the shorter, more concise version. Notice the difference the revisions make in the sound of the paragraph.

> Anyone who has ever ~~in the course of his or her life~~ searched the World Wide Web knows how time-consuming the process ~~of searching~~ can be. Although ~~helpful~~ search engines can aid you in finding what you are looking for, often the specific information you seek remains elusive ~~and out of reach~~. At other times, a search can ~~yield far too much information and~~ overload you with tens of thousands of irrelevant Web sites ~~that are not important to your search~~. To address this problem, in 1998, researchers ~~working before the end of the millennium~~ developed a system called ARC, which stands for automatic resource compiler, in order to amend the situation. ARC ~~is a technique that~~ analyzes how Internet documents are linked to each other. Web pages are ~~categorized and~~ put into two separate types of sites: "authorities" and "hubs." Authorities ~~are called such because they~~ are sites that are cited by many other documents on the subject. Hubs are pages that link to a lot of authorities. By categorizing sites, ARC helps sort useful information from useless material ~~that will not help the searcher~~.

Following are more examples of how less can be more when it comes to sentences. Can you see other ways in which these sentences might be revised to reduce wordiness?

WORDY   Hiking in the wild, untamed, natural wilderness is, I believe, a great thing to do in my opinion.

BETTER   Hiking in the wilderness is, I believe, a great thing to do.

Revising to Reduce Wordiness   **521**

PRETEACHING

Lesson Starter
Motivation. Write the following quotation on a chalkboard.

❝ **Look for the clutter in your writing and prune it ruthlessly. Be grateful for everything you can throw away.** ❞

(William Zinsser, 1922– , American writer and teacher)

Compare clutter in writing to clutter in a garden or in personal space such as a locker, a car, a room, or a garage. Invite students to share stories of how weeding a garden or clearing out physical clutter enables them to reclaim space for more effective use. Explain that such clearing away in writing makes for more effective communication.

 MINI-LESSON **Grammar**   *Continued on p. 522*

Using Gerund and Infinitive Phrases. Introduce students to two additional types of phrases that can be used to reduce wordiness. Explain to students that a gerund phrase includes a verb form ending in *–ing* that is used as a noun. An infinitive phrase contains a verb form, usually beginning with *to,* that is used as a noun, an adjective, or an adverb. Write the following sentences on the chalkboard, and work with students to reduce sentences by using gerund and infinitive phrases.

Oral Practice **Revising Wordy Sentences**

ANSWERS

Here are possible revisions.

1. The poet William Shakespeare is known for his sonnets.

2. In 1609, Shakespeare published his sonnets in a collection.

3. Many questions about Shakespeare's sonnets remain unresolved.

4. There are conflicting theories about the identity of the speaker in the sonnets.

5. Despite the controversy, most scholars agree that the sonnets are extraordinary.

6. Another mystery is Shakespeare's physical appearance.

7. Even though Shakespeare is famous, no one is sure how he really looked.

8. From surviving portraits, he appears to have been a slim man of average height.

9. C

10. Although we may never learn more about Shakespeare the man, we can continue to learn about Shakespeare the writer by studying his magnificent works.

WORDY	From a great distance away, you can see for miles, looking at huge, enormous mesas that fill the expanse of the sky.
BETTER	From far away, you can see mesas that fill the expanse of sky.

Oral Practice **Revising Wordy Sentences**

Read aloud each of the following sentences, and revise it to reduce wordiness. Say your revision aloud. If a sentence is already concise, say *concise*.

EXAMPLE 1. Have you ever read any of the plays that are by William Shakespeare?

1. *Have you read any plays by William Shakespeare?*

1. One of the many things that the poet William Shakespeare is known for is his sonnets.
2. In 1609, Shakespeare published his sonnets all together in one collection during the early seventeenth century.
3. Much mystery surrounds Shakespeare's sonnets, as many questions about the sonnets remain debated, discussed, and unresolved.
4. Among the conflicting theories lies the question of who the speaker in the sonnets who voices concerns really is.
5. Despite the controversy, however, most scholars agree that the sonnets are examples of extraordinary writing in the English language.
6. Another Shakespeare mystery involves uncertainty regarding his physical appearance.
7. Even though Shakespeare is famous throughout the world everywhere, no one can be sure about how he really looked in actual life.
8. From portraits of Shakespeare that have survived and withstood the passage of time, he appears to have been a slim man of slight build and average height.
9. Artists rendered Shakespeare with well-proportioned features and expressive eyes.
10. Although we may never learn more about Shakespeare the man himself, we can continue to learn and gain information about Shakespeare the writer by studying his magnificent works.

Exercise 3 **Revising a Paragraph by Eliminating Unnecessary Words**

Revise the following paragraph to make it more concise. Eliminate unnecessary words, keeping the original meaning of each sentence. You may need to change some verb forms, too.

MINI-LESSON **Grammar** *Continued from p. 521*

1. That he completed his research report was important. [*Completing his research report was important; gerund phrase*]
2. Iqui wanted her mother to be surprised so she cleaned the house. [*To surprise her mother, Iqui cleaned the house; infinitive phrase*]

Then, have students work in groups to compose three or four sentences of their own that contain gerund and infinitive phrases. Groups can share their sentences with the class.

EXAMPLE   Over the years, athletes have set many
           impressive and noteworthy records for ath-
           letic achievements in their day.

           Athletes have set many noteworthy records.

Few athletes earn lasting reputations that endure in the record books and in the hearts of admirers. However, the accomplishments of athlete and Chicago Cubs baseball player Sammy Sosa will likely be remembered for a long and extensive time to come. It is true that in 1998 he broke the previous record for number of home runs in a season; until 2001, he was second only to Mark McGwire, who also broke the old record during the same season that Sosa broke the record. Sosa is also known as a compassionate, caring human being in his native Dominican Republic. Sosa grew up poor in his Dominican homeland and had to shine shoes to help his family. Now he invests in various businesses there, in order to create opportunities and positions for other poor and impoverished children.

Reducing Groups of Words

Writing concisely means using only as many words as you need. The following charts give examples of how you can trim away excess words from your writing.

Clauses Reduced to Phrases	
Clause	**When Jessica was doing algebra equations in the library,** she forgot the time.
Participial Phrase	**Doing algebra equations in the library,** Jessica forgot the time.

(continued)

Exercise 3 Revising a Paragraph by Eliminating Unnecessary Words

ANSWER
Here is a sample revision.

Few athletes earn lasting reputations in the record books and in their admirers' hearts. However, the accomplishments of Chicago Cubs' Sammy Sosa will probably be remembered for a long time. In 1998, he broke the record for home runs per season, until 2001, second only to Mark McGwire, who also broke the record that season. In his native Dominican Republic, Sosa is also known as a compassionate person. Sosa, who grew up poor and had to shine shoes to help his family, now invests in various businesses in his homeland to create opportunities for other impoverished children.

┌ **TIPS** & **TRICKS** ┐

You do not want to delete words that clarify your meaning or add interest to your sentences. When considering whether or not to take out a word or phrase, ask yourself if the sentence would mean the same thing without it.

Revising to Reduce Wordiness   **523**

Learning for Life

Continued on p. 524

Writing Memos. Concise writing is useful in the workplace, where people share a great deal of information. Intra-office memos, distributed through both print and electronic media, are one means of conveying information in the workplace.

Explain to students that the most effective memos communicate a message in as few words as possible. Have students form groups, and ask each group to compose a brief memo (forty or fewer words) relating to one of the following situations.

(continued)

Clauses Reduced to Phrases	
Clause	Earlier in the day, she had decided **that she wanted to visit Davida after school.**
Infinitive Phrase	Earlier in the day, she had decided **to visit Davida after school.**
Clause	The problems **that were about applied algebra** took forever to complete.
Prepositional Phrase	The problems **about applied algebra** took forever to complete.
Clause	Davida's sisters, **one of whom is Sarah and the other Suzanne,** walked into the library.
Appositive Phrase	Davida's sisters, **Sarah and Suzanne,** walked into the library.

Clauses and Phrases Reduced to Single Words	
Clause	**The hat that belongs to Mark** is the nicest.
Word	**Mark's** hat is the nicest.
Clause	Mark is a person **who keeps up with fashion.**
Word	Mark is a **fashionable** person.
Phrase	**Cherishing his sneakers,** he cleans them nightly.
Word	He cleans his **cherished** sneakers nightly.
Phrase	He appraises other people's wardrobes **in an expert manner.**
Word	He appraises other people's wardrobes **expertly.**

Following is a list of concise, one-word replacements for some common wordy phrases.

Wordy	Simpler
at which time	when
by means of	by
due to the fact that	because, since
in spite of the fact that	although
in the event that	if

MEETING THE CHALLENGE

One cause of wordiness is redundant phrasing. Have you ever taken on a "completely impossible" task or discovered that you have the "exact same" birthday as a friend? Particularly in formal writing, such as in a school essay or newspaper article, redundant word groups can clutter writing unnecessarily. Brainstorm in a small group and create a list of redundancies that creep into language. List these wordy phrases, along with suggested revisions. With your teacher's permission, post your list in the classroom as a reminder to avoid redundancy in writing.

ANSWER
Lists will vary, but students should work together in a group to create a list of acceptable length and content.

Learning for Life   **Continued from p. 523**

- Fire-alarm testing on Wednesday
- Meeting on changes in vacation policy
- Company picnic set for August
- Requests for office supplies due next week
- Seminar at noon on the new database
- Construction site is a hard-hat area only

Students may create scenarios and invent names and places as needed. Allow time for groups to share their memos.

Exercise 4 Revising Sentences Through Reduction

Reduce the following sentences by deleting, replacing, and rearranging words. Be sure to keep the original meaning of each sentence.

EXAMPLE
1. My friend Sean prefers to watch DVDs due to the fact that they provide a better picture and soundtrack than VHS videos do.

1. *My friend Sean prefers DVDs because they provide a better picture and soundtrack than VHS videos do.*

1. Movies were born in 1895, at which time two brothers who were named Louis and Auguste Lumière offered the first public screening in Paris.
2. That screening consisted of several one-minute film clips that showed workers who were leaving a factory and a baby who was having lunch.
3. Thomas Edison has also been cited as the inventor of movies due to the fact that he invented the Kinetoscope in 1889, but the fact is that his device could only be used by one viewer at a time.
4. In America, animation got its beginnings in 1906, and the beginning of animated features, which are full-length movies, was in 1918.
5. Animation has subjects that can be seen as both serious and comic; however, comedy seems ideally and naturally suited to animation.
6. The movies that were produced first had no sound, so actors who acted in an expressive and physically agile manner, one of whom was Charlie Chaplin and another Buster Keaton, became stars.
7. When sound was introduced with success in 1927, many movie directors thought it was horrible and awful.
8. Filmmakers from the early era preferred to make black-and-white movies; color seemed like an extra, added annoyance and nuisance that audiences would find annoying.
9. Three-dimensional movies that used three dimensions instead of two were new, trendy, and popular in the 1950s when they had their heyday.
10. Now, showing daily on huge screens as large as eight stories high are IMAX movies that have as their basis wide-screen technology.

Exercise 4 Revising Sentences Through Reduction

ANSWERS

Here are sample sentences.

1. Movies were born in 1895 when brothers Louis and Auguste Lumière offered the first public screening in Paris.
2. That screening consisted of several one-minute film clips showing workers leaving a factory and a baby having lunch.
3. Thomas Edison has also been cited as the inventor of movies because he invented the Kinetoscope in 1889, but his device could only be used by one viewer at a time.
4. American animation got its start in 1906, and full-length movies, or animated features, began in 1918.
5. Animation has both serious and comic subjects; however, comedy seems naturally suited to animation.
6. The first movies had no sound, so expressive and physically agile actors such as Charlie Chaplin and Buster Keaton became stars.
7. When sound was successfully introduced in 1927, many movie directors thought it was horrible.
8. Early filmmakers preferred to make black-and-white movies; color seemed like an annoyance for audiences.
9. Three-dimensional movies were trendy in the 1950s.
10. Now, IMAX movies, based on wide-screen technology, are shown daily on screens as large as eight stories high.

Review B Revising a Paragraph by Reducing Wordiness

ANSWER

Here is a sample revision.

As in ancient Mesopotamia and Egypt, early life in India developed in the basins of great rivers. The first civilization on the Indian subcontinent was located in the Indus River Valley, in present-day Pakistan. The Indus Valley is a broad plain bordered by desert in the east and mountains in the west. Geographically, it resembles the Nile, Tigris, and Euphrates valleys. Because the land was arid, settlers could clear it without difficulty. The Indus River flooded when the Himalayan snows melted and when the yearly rainy winds known as monsoons occurred. Flooding created the right conditions for agriculture, which led to settlement in the area.

Review B Revising a Paragraph by Reducing Wordiness

Revise the following wordy paragraph. Eliminate unnecessary words and reduce clauses and phrases to make the paragraph concise. You should be able to make at least five reductions.

EXAMPLE   Several rivers feed the Indus River, which is a river that flows to the Arabian Sea.

Several rivers feed the Indus River, which flows to the Arabian Sea.

As in the ancient cultures of Mesopotamia and Egypt that existed, early life in India developed in the basins of great rivers a long time ago. The first civilization to arise early on on the Indian subcontinent was located in the valley of the Indus River, which is in present-day Pakistan. The Indus Valley is a broad, vast plain bordered by desert, if you look eastward, and by mountains that rise up in the west. It resembles the valleys of other places such as those of the Nile, the Tigris, and the Euphrates, in terms of its geography. The land was arid, and people could clear it in order to settle it without too much difficulty. The Indus River flooded when mountain snows from the Himalayas melted and whenever monsoons, otherwise known as seasonal rainy winds, occurred as they did every year. Flooding of the river created the right conditions for agriculture to occur, which in turn fostered the situation which led to the growth of settlement in the area.

AFGHANISTAN

IRAN

PAKISTAN

CHINA

NEPAL

INDIA

Thar Desert

INDUS RIVER VALLEY

HIMALAYA

Indus R.

Jhelum R.

Chenab R.

Ravi R.

Sutlej R.

Jumna R.

Ganges R.

Chambal R.

Narbada R.

Ancient course of the Hakra River

Arabian Sea

Miles
0   200
0   200
Kilometers

Chapter Review

A. Revising Paragraphs to Vary Sentence Beginnings and Sentence Structure

Revise the following paragraphs, varying sentence beginnings and structures.

before it was
In fact,

Apparently,
and

and

Therefore,
However,

Interestingly,

and

Since

and

In fact,

> Who invented zero? The question is not easy to answer. The historical record indicates that zero appeared and disappeared many times. ~~Then, zero became~~ fully accepted. The histories of the two main uses of zero are quite different from each other. The use of zero as a place-holder ~~apparently~~ came first. The use of zero as a number came much later.
>
> Our number system is characterized as a "place-value" system. The usefulness of zero is apparent in our system in numbers like *1906*. We know that number is 1 thousand plus 9 hundreds plus 6 ones. We know the zero means "no tens." We couldn't tell the difference between 1906 and 196 if we didn't have zero. Zero seems necessary in our place-value number system. The Babylonians had a place-value number system without zero for over one thousand years. They understood the difference between numbers by the context in which the numbers were used. Around 700 B.C., some Babylonians put little hooks where we would put zero. Sometimes they used three hooks, sometimes one. Around 400 B.C., others used two wedge symbols to show an empty place. This place-holder never appeared as the last digit of a number. ~~It~~ was used only between two numbers. ~~That is interesting.~~
>
> The Greeks did not use a positional number system. Most of their mathematical achievements were in geometry. Greek mathematicians generally didn't need to name numbers. ~~They~~ worked with numbers as line lengths. Greek astronomers ~~were~~ an exception. ~~They~~ used a symbol O. They were the first to use anything that looks like our zero. Ptolemy, by A.D. 130,

ASSESSING

Monitoring Progress

Chapter Review. To assess student progress, you may want to compare the types of items missed on the **Diagnostic Preview** to those missed on the **Chapter Review**. If students have not made significant progress, you may want to provide them with additional practice.

SENTENCES

RESOURCES

Improving Sentence Style

Assessment

■ *Holt Handbook Chapter Tests with Answer Key,* pp. 42–46, 54

Although

was using the symbol as an empty place-holder between digits and at the end of numbers. ∧Some other astronomers did the same, ~~but~~ zero was still not widely accepted.

Zero made its most important appearance in India∧ ~~That is~~ where both our numerals and our number system were born. Historians who specialize in mathematics believe the Indians may have gotten zero from the Greek astronomers. ∧The Indians (certainly∧) took the idea of zero much further than the Greeks.

and

Islamic and Arabic mathematicians got zero from the Indians∧ ∧The ideas from India also spread east into China. One of the main people to bring zero and other new numerical concepts to Europe was Fibonacci∧ ~~Fibonacci was~~ an Italian who had grown up in North Africa. ~~He wrote~~ in 1200, ~~and~~ he introduced the nine Indian (Hindu-Arabic) numerals and the zero to Europe. ∧Fibonacci called zero a "sign∧" ~~He did~~ not ~~call it~~ a number. Zero did not become widely accepted until the 1600s.

However,

B. Revising Paragraphs to Reduce Wordiness

The following paragraphs are longer and wordier than necessary. Revise the paragraphs, eliminating unnecessary words and reducing clauses and phrases.

Botulism is a rare but ~~definitely very~~ serious illness caused by a toxin ~~that is~~ produced by the bacterium *Clostridium botulinum.* Of the three main types of botulism, most people are familiar with the food-borne type ~~of botulism~~. Another type occurs when a wound becomes infected with botulinum spores. In the third type, ~~which is known as~~ infant botulism, the botulinum spores are ingested and grow in the intestines, releasing the toxin.

Botulism~~, which can be fatal,~~ causes respiratory failure∧ ~~and~~ paralysis∧ and sometimes death. Recovery can take months ~~and months~~ and may require using a breathing machine, ∧~~which is often called a~~ ventilator. Botulinum antitoxins may be used to treat the botulism, but this treatment can be tricky∧ ~~due to the fact~~

or

because

~~that~~ the antitoxin has to be specific, as each
of the seven botulinum toxins responds only to
antitoxins made from specific⋀~~and~~ different
antibodies.

SENTENCES

Sentence Diagramming

The Sentence Diagram

A *sentence diagram* is a picture of how the parts of a sentence fit together and how the words in a sentence are related.

Subjects and Verbs

Reference Note

For more information about **subjects** and **verbs,** see page 37.

Every sentence diagram begins with a horizontal line intersected by a short vertical line, which divides the subject from the verb.

EXAMPLE   **William Faulkner wrote** *Light in August.*

William Faulkner	wrote

Understood Subjects

Reference Note

For more information about **understood subjects,** see page 41.

EXAMPLE   Open the window, please.

(you)	Open

Nouns of Direct Address

Reference Note

For more information about **nouns of direct address,** see page 42.

EXAMPLE   Give me the scissors, **Taylor.**

Taylor

(you)	Give

Compound Subjects

EXAMPLE   **Steven** and **Rachel** are flying kites.

Reference Note

For more information about **compound subjects,** see page 40.

Compound Verbs

EXAMPLE   Daphne **paints** and **sculpts.**

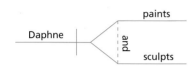

Reference Note

For more information about **compound verbs,** see page 40.

Compound Subjects and Compound Verbs

EXAMPLE   **Hornets** and **wasps can fly** and **sting.**

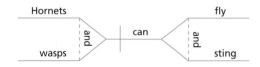

When the parts of a compound subject or a compound predicate are joined by a correlative conjunction, diagram the sentence this way:

EXAMPLE   **Both** James **and** Gina will **not only** cook **but also** serve.

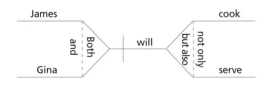

Reference Note

For more information about **correlative conjunctions,** see page 26.

Modifiers

Adjectives and Adverbs

Adjectives and adverbs are written on slanting lines beneath the words they modify.

EXAMPLE   **The small** bird **quickly** flew **away.**

An adverb that modifies an adjective or an adverb is placed on a line connected to the word it modifies.

EXAMPLE   The team played **very** energetically.

Here, There, and *Where* as Modifiers

EXAMPLES   **Here** comes the parade!

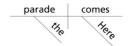

There goes the last blueberry bagel.

Where did the accident happen?

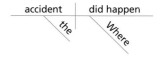

Reference Note

For more information about **adjectives,** see page 11. For more about **adverbs,** see page 20.

Reference Note

For more about questions and sentences beginning with **here** and **there,** see page 42.

NOTE Sometimes *there* begins a sentence but does not modify the verb. When used in this way, *there* is called an *expletive*. It is diagrammed on a line by itself.

EXAMPLE   **There** is one bathroom in my house.

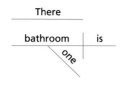

Subject Complements

A subject complement is placed after the verb on the same horizontal line as the simple subject and the verb. A line *slanting toward the subject* separates the subject complement from the verb.

Reference Note

For more information about **subject complements,** see page 49.

Predicate Nominatives

EXAMPLE   Some cats are good **climbers.**

Predicate Adjectives

EXAMPLE   These shoes are **uncomfortable.**

Compound Subject Complements

EXAMPLE   Miroslav Holub was both a **doctor** and a **poet.**

The Sentence Diagram   **533**

Objects

Direct Objects

Reference Note

For more information about **direct objects,** see page 45.

A direct object is placed after the verb on the same horizontal line as the simple subject and the verb. A *vertical* line separates the direct object from the verb.

EXAMPLE   Eric dropped the **book.**

Compound Direct Objects

EXAMPLE   They bought **fruit** and **vegetables.**

Indirect Objects

Reference Note

For more information about **indirect objects,** see page 45.

The indirect object is diagrammed on a horizontal line beneath the verb.

EXAMPLE   Natalie showed **me** her guitar.

Compound Indirect Objects

EXAMPLE   Tom gave **Keisha** and **me** tickets.

Phrases

Prepositional Phrases

The preposition is placed on a slanting line leading down from the word that the phrase modifies. The object of the preposition is placed on a horizontal line connected to the slanting line.

Reference Note

For more information about **prepositional phrases,** see page 60.

EXAMPLES   The fragile ecosystem **of the Everglades** is protected **by laws.** [adjective phrase modifying the subject; adverb phrase modifying the verb]

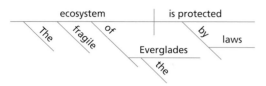

We worked long **into the night.** [adverb phrase modifying an adverb]

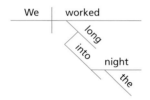

Mr. Benson explained the complicated equation to **Emily** and **Ross.** [compound object of preposition]

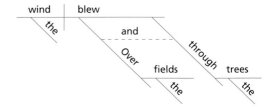

Over the fields and **through the trees** blew the wind. [two phrases modifying the same word]

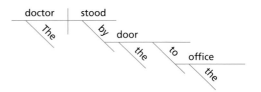

The doctor stood **by the door to the office.** [phrase modifying the object of another preposition]

Participles and Participial Phrases

Participles and participial phrases are diagrammed as follows.

EXAMPLES   We watched them **playing.**

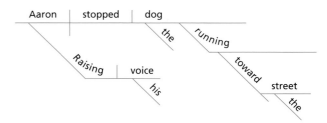

Raising his voice, Aaron stopped the dog **running toward the street.**

Notice above that the participle *Raising* has a direct object (*voice*), which is diagrammed in the same way that a direct object of a main verb is.

Reference Note

For more information about **participles** and **participial phrases,** see page 65.

SENTENCES

Gerunds and Gerund Phrases

Gerunds and gerund phrases are diagrammed as follows.

EXAMPLES **Yelling** is not polite. [gerund used as subject]

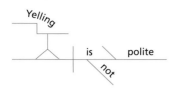

Reference Note

For more information about **gerunds** and **gerund phrases,** see pages 68 and 69.

Pedaling steadily for days is usually the only way of **winning the Tour de France.** [gerund phrases used as subject and as object of a preposition]

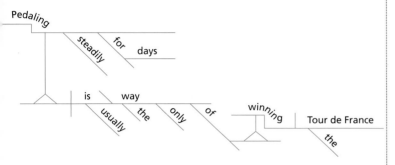

Notice above that the gerund *winning* has a direct object (*Tour de France*).

Infinitives and Infinitive Phrases

Infinitives and infinitive phrases used as modifiers are diagrammed in the same way as prepositional phrases.

EXAMPLE   He lives **to work.** [infinitive used as adverb]

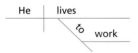

Reference Note

For more information about **infinitives** and **infinitive phrases,** see pages 70 and 71.

The Sentence Diagram   **537**

Infinitives and infinitive phrases used as nouns are diagrammed as follows.

EXAMPLES **To find a new planet** demands infinite patience. [infinitive phrase used as subject]

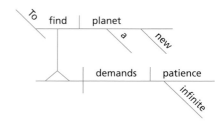

We expect **to see him eventually.** [infinitive phrase used as direct object]

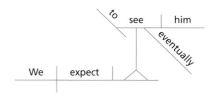

My father saw **me catch the football.** [infinitive clause with subject, *me,* and with *to* omitted]

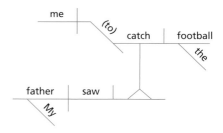

Reference Note

For more information about **appositives** and **appositive phrases,** see page 73.

Appositives and Appositive Phrases

Place the appositive in parentheses after the word it identifies or describes.

EXAMPLES   My sister **Jen** is a geologist.

Jan Kowalski comes from Warsaw, **a city in Poland.**

Subordinate Clauses

Adjective Clauses

An adjective clause is joined to the word it modifies by a broken line leading from the modified word to the relative pronoun.

EXAMPLES   The prize **that he won** was very valuable.

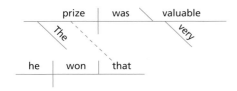

The cabinet, **which held the supplies,** was locked.

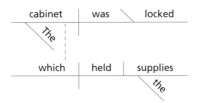

Reference Note

For more information about **adjective clauses,** see page 84.

The Sentence Diagram   **539**

He is the officer **from whom we received the helpful directions.**

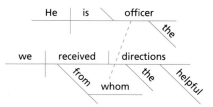

Adverb Clauses

Reference Note

For more information about **adverb clauses,** see page 90.

Place the subordinating conjunction that introduces the adverb clause on a broken line leading from the verb in the adverb clause to the word the clause modifies.

EXAMPLE   **When a tornado hits,** severe damage can result.

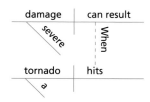

Noun Clauses

Reference Note

For more information about **noun clauses,** see page 87.

Noun clauses often begin with the word *that, what, who,* or *which.* These words may have a function within the subordinate clause or may simply connect the clause to the rest of the sentence. How a noun clause is diagrammed depends on how it is used in the sentence and whether or not the introductory word has a grammatical function in the noun clause.

EXAMPLES   **What they did** amazed us. [The noun clause is used as the subject of the independent clause. *What* functions as the direct object in the noun clause.]

Roger thought **that he saw a deer.** [The noun clause is the direct object of the independent clause. *That* has no grammatical function in the noun clause.]

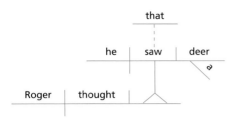

If the introductory word were omitted from the preceding sentence, the diagram would look like this.

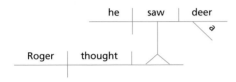

Sentences Classified According to Structure

Simple Sentences

Reference Note
For more information about **simple sentences,** see page 94.

EXAMPLES   The Mississippi is a mighty river. [one independent clause]

Craig sang a song. [one independent clause]

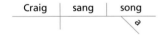

Reference Note

For more information about **compound sentences,** see page 94.

Compound Sentences

EXAMPLE The loud thunder scared us, and the lightning lit the sky. [two independent clauses]

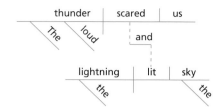

If the compound sentence has a semicolon and no conjunction, a straight broken line joins the two verbs.

EXAMPLE Frederick Douglass gave speeches in the 1800s; he was a famous, eloquent African American abolitionist.

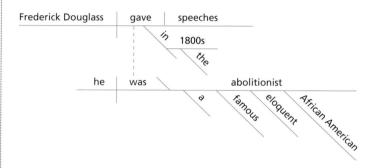

Notice above that the compound adjective *African American* is written on one slanted line.

If the clauses of a compound sentence are joined by a semicolon and a conjunctive adverb (such as *consequently, therefore, nevertheless, however, moreover,* or *otherwise*), place the conjunctive adverb on a slanting line below the verb it modifies.

Reference Note

For more information about **conjunctive adverbs,** see page 94.

EXAMPLE   Maria sometimes rushes through homework**; however,** she
           is trying to do a better job.

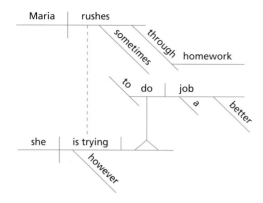

Complex Sentences

EXAMPLE   Once winter arrived, the weather turned nasty. [one
           independent clause and one subordinate clause]

Compound-Complex Sentences

EXAMPLE   The movie that we saw was creative, and we liked the
           actors. [two independent clauses and one subordinate
           clause]

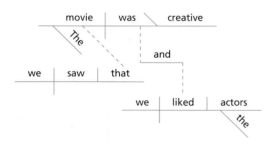

Reference Note

For more information about **complex sentences,** see page 95.

Reference Note

For more information about **compound-complex sentences,** see page 96.

The Sentence Diagram   **543**

GO TO: go.hrw.com

- **Manuscript Form**
- **The History of English**
- **Test Smarts**
- **Grammar at a Glance**

Manuscript Form

Why Is Manuscript Form Important?

What is manuscript form, and why should you care about it? **Manuscript form** refers to the overall appearance of a document. A legible, professional-looking manuscript gives the impression that the writer cares not only about what he or she has to say but also about what the reader thinks. A manuscript that is an illegible jumble, on the other hand, gives the impression that the writer is careless, is not thinking clearly, or does not respect the reader.

Such impressions affect our lives every day. For example, a busy employer faced with the task of evaluating multiple job résumés may simply discard the sloppy ones without ever reading them. If we value what we write and want others to understand and value it too, then we should present our ideas in the best form possible. To help you present your ideas as effectively as possible, this section of the book covers basic guidelines for preparing and presenting manuscripts and provides a sample research paper as a model.

General Guidelines for Preparing Manuscripts

The following guidelines are general style rules to use in formal, nonfiction writing. Such writing includes papers and reports for school, letters of application for jobs or colleges, letters to the editor, and press releases for clubs and other organizations.

Content and Organization

1. Begin the paper with an introductory paragraph that contains a thesis sentence.

2. Develop and support your thesis in body paragraphs.

3. Follow the principles of unity and coherence. That is, develop one and only one big idea (your thesis), and make sure that your paragraphs and sentences flow smoothly without any gaps in the sequence of ideas.

4. Place charts, graphs, tables, and illustrations close to the text they illustrate. Label and number each one.

RESOURCES

Manuscript Form

Practice

■ *Language & Sentence Skills Practice,* pp. 463–464

Differentiating Instruction

■ *Developmental Language & Sentence Skills,* pp. 203–204

5. Follow the conventions of standard grammar, usage, capitalization, punctuation, and spelling.

6. Include a conclusion.

Appearance

1. Submit manuscript that is legible. Type or print out your paper using black ink; or when your teacher permits handwriting, write neatly using blue or black ink. (Other colors are harder to read.) If the printer or typewriter you are using is printing words that are faint and hard to read, change the ink cartridge or the ribbon.

2. Keep all pages neat and clean. If you discover errors and if you are working on a word processor, you can easily correct the errors and print out a fresh copy. If you write your paper by hand or on a typewriter, you generally may make a few corrections with correction tape and insert the revisions neatly. To replace a letter, word, or phrase, neatly cross out what you want to replace. Then, insert a caret mark (∧) below the line, and write the inserted item above the line.

EXAMPLE

The ~~daily~~ ^weekly^ broadcasts continued all that summer.

Paper and Font

1. Use quality 8½ × 11 inch paper.
2. Use only one side of the paper.
3. When using a word processor, use an easy-to-read font size. Size twelve is standard.
4. Use a standard font, such as Times New Roman, that does not call attention to itself. Flowery, highly stylized fonts are hard to read. They look unprofessional, and they distract the reader from the ideas you are trying to convey.

Plagiarism

Do not plagiarize. Plagiarism is the unacknowledged borrowing of someone else's words or ideas and the submission of those words or ideas as one's own. Honest writers document all borrowings, whether those borrowings are quoted or merely paraphrased.

Back-up files

When you are ready to submit your work, be sure to save a copy—a printout, a photocopy, or an electronic file—for yourself.

Academic Manuscript Style

In school you will write some very formal papers—research reports or term papers, for example. For such assignments, you will need to follow not only general manuscript guidelines but also some very specific guidelines especially for academic manuscripts.

The academic manuscript style summarized on the following pages follows the style recommended by the Modern Language Association in the *MLA Handbook for Writers of Research Papers.* Two other popular manuscript styles are the format recommended by the American Psychological Association, known as APA style, and the one published in *The Chicago Manual of Style.* Style manuals are updated from time to time, so be sure you are using the most current version. When formatting papers for school, be sure to follow your teachers' instructions on which manuscript style to use.

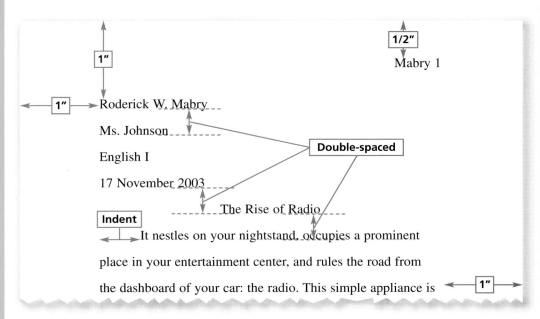

1/2″

Mabry 1

1″

1″ Roderick W. Mabry

Ms. Johnson

Double-spaced

English I

17 November 2003

Indent

The Rise of Radio

It nestles on your nightstand, occupies a prominent

place in your entertainment center, and rules the road from

the dashboard of your car: the radio. This simple appliance is   1″

Title Page, Margins, and Spacing

1. Leave one-inch margins on the top, sides, and bottom of each page.
2. Starting with the first page, number all your pages in the upper right-hand corner. Precede each page number with your last name. Computer software can help you create this "header."
3. Place your heading—your name, your teacher's name, your class, and the date—in the upper left-hand corner of the first page. (If your teacher requires a separate cover sheet, follow his or her instructions.)
4. Double-space between the header and the heading. Double-space the lines in the heading. Double-space between the heading and your title. (This rule does not apply if your teacher requires a cover sheet.)
5. Center the title, and capitalize the appropriate letters in it.

6. Double-space between the title and the body of the paper.
7. Do not underline or use quotation marks to enclose your own title at the head of your own paper. If you use someone else's title within your title, use quotation marks or underlining, as appropriate, with the other person's title only.

EXAMPLE

An Analysis of Symbolism in Yeats' "The Second Coming"

8. When typing or word-processing, always double-space the lines. (In a handwritten paper, skip every other ruled line unless your teacher instructs you otherwise.)
9. Do not use more than a double-space, even between paragraphs.
10. Indent the beginning of each paragraph one-half inch (five spaces).

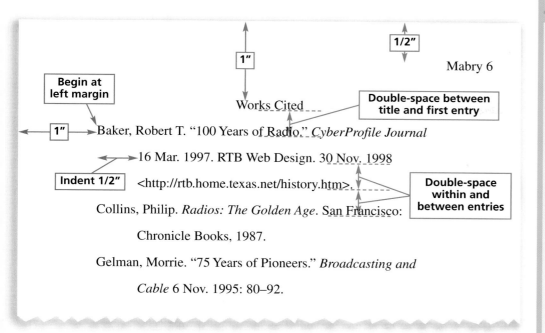

- 1/2" (top margin indicator)
- 1" (top margin indicator)
- Mabry 6
- Begin at left margin
- Double-space between title and first entry
- Works Cited
- 1" (left margin indicator)

Baker, Robert T. "100 Years of Radio." *CyberProfile Journal*

    16 Mar. 1997. RTB Web Design. 30 Nov. 1998

- Indent 1/2"
- Double-space within and between entries

    <http://rtb.home.texas.net/history.htm>.

Collins, Philip. *Radios: The Golden Age.* San Francisco:

    Chronicle Books, 1987.

Gelman, Morrie. "75 Years of Pioneers." *Broadcasting and*

    Cable 6 Nov. 1995: 80–92.

Documenting Sources

Works Cited Page

1. In a research paper or any other paper that incorporates information from other sources, add a works cited page at the end.
2. Continue numbering the pages of your paper through the works cited page.
3. The entries on the works cited page should be in alphabetical order, according to the last name of the author. For works with no author, the entry should be alphabetized according to the first main word in the title.
4. Do not number the sources on your works cited page.

Documentation in the Body of the Essay

1. Use parenthetical citations within the body of your paper to acknowledge any paraphrased idea or quotation that you have borrowed from someone else. The parenthetical citation refers to specific source documentation on the works cited page. Place the parenthetical citations at the **end** of the material that you borrowed from some other source.

EXAMPLE

Newspapers worried that radio would drive them out of business (Henderson 90).

2. If the citation appears at the end of a sentence, the citation comes before the closing period, as shown above. If the citation appears at the end of a dependent clause or after the first half of a compound sentence, the citation comes before the sentence comma.

EXAMPLE

Newspapers worried that radio would drive them out of business (Henderson 90), but it did not.

RESOURCES

3. For quotations of five or more lines, indent all of the lines one inch (about ten spaces) from the left margin. Do not use quotation marks to enclose indented quotations. Also, place end punctuation at the end of the quoted material, not after the closing parenthesis.

In the following passage, we see how effectively the author sets the mood. With a little imagination, we can almost feel the moist air and hear the murmured conversations.

|←——— 1" ———→| The streetlights along Toole Street, which meandered downhill from the Language Academy to the town, were already lit and twinkled mistily through the trees. Standing at the gates were small groups of students, clustered together according to nationality. As Myles passed by, he could not help overhearing intense conversations in Spanish, German, and Japanese; all of his students had momentarily abandoned English in the urgency of deciding where to go for the weekend and how to get there. (Boylan 58)

Model Research Paper

The following final draft of a research paper closely follows the guidelines for MLA style given on the preceding pages. (Note: The pages of the model paper are smaller than 8½ × 11, and the margins of the paper are less than one inch wide to allow room for annotations.)

Mabry 1

Roderick W. Mabry

Ms. Johnson

English I

17 November 2003

The Rise of Radio

It nestles on your nightstand, occupies a prominent place in your entertainment center, and rules the road from the dashboard of your car: the radio. This simple appliance is so common that most people take it for granted, yet radio is a relatively new invention. In fact, the first commercial radio station, KDKA in Pittsburgh, did not go on the air until 1920 (Stark 120). Before long, however, the new medium dramatically affected the nation's entertainment, information delivery, and economy.

The invention of radio was made possible by a number of earlier developments. German physicist Heinrich Hertz, drawing on established mathematical principles, discovered the existence of radio waves in 1887. Eight years later, in Italy,

HEADING

your name

your teacher's name

your class

date

THESIS SENTENCE:
tells focus of the paper

TOPIC SENTENCE:
tells focus of the paragraph and is a subtopic of the thesis

(continued)

(continued)

Mabry 2

Guglielmo Marconi successfully completed the first wireless transmission of Morse code signals. An American invention helped move radio closer to reality: Lee De Forest's 1907 Audion, which made it possible to transmit sounds, not just signals. A full decade before KDKA debuted, De Forest broadcast a live performance by famed Italian tenor Enrico Caruso from New York City's Metropolitan Opera House (Yenne 77).

Few people were equipped to hear that landmark broadcast, however, because radio was still very much a do-it-yourself project; most people built their own receivers. In 1921, one such "tinkerer," twenty-eight-year-old Franklin Malcolm Doolittle of New Haven, Connecticut, even used his homemade transmitter to broadcast the Yale-Princeton football game from his home (Gelman 80). The first commercially produced receivers became available in 1920, when a Pittsburgh department store began offering sets for ten dollars. The response was so enthusiastic that Westinghouse began mass producing the appliances (Baker).

When radio found its way into the majority of American households, it brought the nation together in an unprecedented

way. Radio reached into "once dreary homes, reducing the
isolation of the hinterlands and leveling class distinctions"
(Henderson 44). At first radio programming simply duplicated
existing forms of entertainment: singers, musicians, comedians,
lecturers. Coping with technical difficulties left little time for
creating new types of shows. Later, as the technical problems
were resolved, programmers began adapting existing formats
and experimenting with new types of shows, including variety
shows, serials, game shows, and amateur hours ("Radio as a
Medium of Communication"). As programming expanded,
radio truly became, in researcher Amy Henderson's words, "a
theater of the mind" (144).

   The introduction of radio also radically altered the way
people learned about events in the outside world. For the first
time in history, everyone could receive the same information
simultaneously. As sociologists Robert and Helen Lynd, writing
in the 1920s, noted, "With but little equipment one can call the
life of the rest of the world from the air . . ." (qtd. in Monk 173).
Live coverage gave news events an immediacy far greater than
newspapers or newsreels could provide. In fact, most people

> When parenthetical documentation follows closing quotation marks at the end of a sentence, the period should be placed after the parentheses.

> These parentheses contain only the page number because the author is named in the text.

> This citation tells us that the quotation from Robert and Helen Lynd was found in a book edited by Linda R. Monk.

(continued)

(continued)

Mabry 4

first learned of such historic events as the 1941 Japanese attack on Pearl Harbor from the radio (Stark 120).

> Note again how strong topic sentences control the content of the paragraph and develop a subtopic of the thesis sentence.

Equally important was radio's impact on the economy. The first, and most noticeable, effect was to add a new consumer product to people's wish lists. Most early sets were strictly functional—"a box, some wire, and headphones" (Baker). Once the initial demand was satisfied, however, manufacturers began stimulating repeat sales by offering new models each year, with the goal of placing a "radio in every room" (Collins 10).

The demand for sets was a boon to manufacturers, but it struck fear into some other segments of the economy. Newspapers worried that radio would drive them out of business (Henderson 90). Similarly, members of the traditional entertainment industry feared that the new technology would cut into the sales of tickets and recordings (Stark 120).

> The parenthetical citation for Henderson is placed directly at the end of the paraphrase.

Surprisingly, advertisers were slow to realize the opportunities radio offered. At first, most business people assumed that profits would come solely from the sale of sets and replacement parts. In addition, paid advertising was considered improper for what was initially viewed as a "new, pure instrument of democracy" (Weiner). Instead, early programs were underwritten by "sponsors," with companies receiving only a brief, discreet acknowledgment in return for their support. Eventually, however, this approach gave way to the direct advertising that is familiar today (Weiner).

Reviewing the rise of radio makes clear how instrumental the medium was in shaping the nation's entertainment, information delivery, and economy. Today, with the advent of television and the Internet, radio is no longer the primary source of news and entertainment for most people, nor is its impact on the economy as far-reaching. Still, each day millions of listeners wake, work, and play to the rhythms of radio, and many would be lost without it. The radio may have been muted, but it has not been unplugged.

Mabry ends his paper with a concluding paragraph that is entirely his own statement. First, he restates the thesis in the form of a conclusion. Then, he places the history of the radio in its modern context.

(continued)

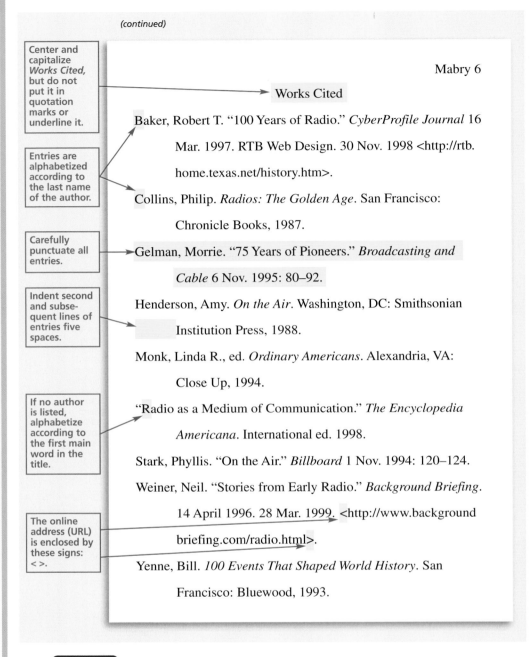

(continued)

Mabry 6

Center and capitalize *Works Cited,* but do not put it in quotation marks or underline it.

Entries are alphabetized according to the last name of the author.

Carefully punctuate all entries.

Indent second and subse-quent lines of entries five spaces.

If no author is listed, alphabetize according to the first main word in the title.

The online address (URL) is enclosed by these signs: < >.

Works Cited

Baker, Robert T. "100 Years of Radio." *CyberProfile Journal* 16

Mar. 1997. RTB Web Design. 30 Nov. 1998 <http://rtb.

home.texas.net/history.htm>.

Collins, Philip. *Radios: The Golden Age.* San Francisco:

Chronicle Books, 1987.

Gelman, Morrie. "75 Years of Pioneers." *Broadcasting and

Cable* 6 Nov. 1995: 80–92.

Henderson, Amy. *On the Air.* Washington, DC: Smithsonian

Institution Press, 1988.

Monk, Linda R., ed. *Ordinary Americans.* Alexandria, VA:

Close Up, 1994.

"Radio as a Medium of Communication." *The Encyclopedia

Americana.* International ed. 1998.

Stark, Phyllis. "On the Air." *Billboard* 1 Nov. 1994: 120–124.

Weiner, Neil. "Stories from Early Radio." *Background Briefing.*

14 April 1996. 28 Mar. 1999. <http://www.background

briefing.com/radio.html>.

Yenne, Bill. *100 Events That Shaped World History.* San

Francisco: Bluewood, 1993.

The History of English

Origins and Uses

The first appearance of the English language in writing occurred about thirteen hundred years ago, but the language was spoken long before that. The English language of a thousand years ago is so different from the language we speak today that it is almost like a foreign tongue. There is, however, some continuity across the ages. The history of the English language may be divided into four major periods: *Pre-English, Old English, Middle English,* and *Modern English*. The following time line shows approximately when English moved from one period to the next and when other languages influenced the development of English. It also indicates how the number of English speakers has grown over the centuries.

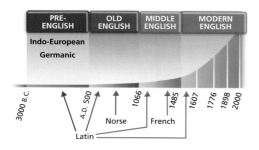

Pre-English

About five thousand years ago, migrating peoples in Asia Minor and southeast Europe spoke a language that became the ancestor of English and many other languages but of which no record exists. We call that parent language *Proto-Indo-European* because most of the languages of Europe, as well as many of those spoken in India and Iran, descended from it. (*Proto–* means "first," or "earliest.") As people migrated from their original homelands and settled in various parts of the Indo-European area, they developed their own *dialects,* or ways of speaking. One group of these migrating people, composed of three tribes—the Jutes, the Angles, and the Saxons—settled in northern Europe, along the coast of the North Sea. They spoke a version of Proto-Indo-European we call *Germanic,* from which Modern English is descended.

The *Anglo-Saxons,* as these tribes were collectively known, eventually came into contact with Latin-speaking Romans in southern Europe. From the Romans, the Anglo-Saxons adopted many words into their language. For example, the Latin words for *wine (vinum), cheese (caseus), pepper (piper), kettle (catillus),*

Origins and Uses   **557**

and *sack (saccus),* among many others, made their way into the language of the Anglo-Saxons. Words, such as these, that one language borrows from another are called **loanwords**. The following chart shows the origins of some present-day English words.

Proto-Indo-European
kwon
"dog"

OLD ENGLISH	GERMAN	WELSH	LATIN	GREEK
hund	*dachshund*	*corgi*	*canis,*	*kyon,*
		(corr + ci)	*caninus*	*kynikos*
"dog"	"badger-dog"	"dwarf dog"	"of dogs"	"doglike"
↓	↓	↓	↓	↓
hound	**dachshund**	**corgi**	**canine**	**cynic**

Old English

History Beginning around A.D. 450, the Angles, Saxons, and Jutes began invading Britain, taking over land that had been settled much earlier by the Celts, then colonized for centuries by the Romans. The separate dialects these tribes spoke eventually blended into one language—*Old English,* sometimes called *Anglo-Saxon.* (The words *English* and *England* come from *Englaland,* or "land of the Angles.") Later, Latin-speaking missionaries came to the island to convert the Anglo-Saxons to Christianity. Many Latin words associated with religion and other things came into English during this time. The following chart shows some of these Latin words and the changes they underwent on their way to Modern English.

Latin	Old English	Modern English
presbyter	preost	priest
apostolus	apostol	apostle
schola	scol	school

In the ninth to the eleventh centuries, Viking invaders from Scandinavia invaded Britain. Many of these Norse invaders then settled in Britain, introducing words from their language into Old English. For example, Norse provided English with such words as *give, skin, take, want,* and *window* and the pronouns *they, their,* and *them.*

Relationship to Modern English The English spoken by the Anglo-Saxons was very different from Modern English, so different that you would not recognize it. The Anglo-Saxons used sounds that have been lost over time, as in their word *cniht,* which meant "boy" but has evolved into the Modern English word *knight.* In Old English, *cniht* had an initial hard *c* or *k* sound, which we continue to spell although we do not pronounce it.

Written English was different, too. When Anglo-Saxons wrote at all, the alphabet they used was an angular-looking system of characters called *runes.* Later, the Irish monks who first converted the Anglo–Saxons to Christianity taught them to write a rounded form of letters called *insular hand.*

Old English also differed from Modern English in that it had word endings, or **inflections,** to show the grammatical function of certain words—nouns, pronouns, adjectives, and verbs—in a sentence. The grammatical function of Old English nouns was also indicated by one of the many different forms of the definite article (*the* in Modern English) that preceded it. In Old English, the order of the words in a sentence did not mean as much as these inflections and definite articles. The following two Old English sentences illustrate the way inflections and definite articles worked. (The letter þ in the examples is an Old English letter that does not exist in Modern English. It has been replaced by *th* and is called *thorn.*) The Modern

English meanings of the sentences are given in parentheses.

> Sē cyning þone guman andwyrde.
> (The king answered the man.)
> þone cyning sē guma andwyrde.
> (The man answered the king.)

In the first sentence, the Old English word for *the* is written as *sē* to tell us that *king (cyning)* is the subject and as *þone* to tell us that *man (guman)* is the direct object. The opposite is true of the second sentence. In the first sentence, *guman* is spelled with the *an* inflection to tell us it is the direct object. In the second, it is spelled with the *a* inflection to tell us it is the subject.

As the English language changed over the centuries, most of the inflections and the forms of the definite article were dropped. However, we still have a few inflections that we use every day in writing and speaking. For example, *s, es,* and *'s* indicate plurals and possessives, and *ed* indicates the past tense of regular verbs. Moreover, many of our most familiar, everyday words have been used by English speakers since the origin of the English language. The following chart shows the Old English and Modern English forms of several everyday words.

Old English	Modern English
finger	finger
fōt	foot
broþor	brother
hnutu	nut
hlaf (meaning "bread")	loaf
tūn (meaning "enclosed place")	town

Middle English

In 1066, the Normans, a French-speaking group of Norse who had settled earlier in France and adopted the French language, invaded and conquered England. For the next two centuries, the important languages of the country were French and Latin. The affairs of government, business, education, literature, and law were conducted in these languages rather than in English. At this time, many English words were replaced with French and Latin vocabulary. *Army, court, government, literature, mirror,* and *service* are a few French loanwords, for example. Here are some other French and Latin loanwords that entered English in the Middle English period.

French	Modern English	Latin	Modern English
cité	city	mercurius	mercury
contrée	country	scriba	scribe
juge	judge	sub poena	subpoena
libraire	library	("under penalty")	

Despite the importance of French and Latin, English, by now evolved into **Middle English,** was still the language of the common people. It did not die out under French rule, primarily because the English-speaking commoners outnumbered the French-speaking rulers. Another reason that English did not vanish was that the French-speaking rulers in England gradually lost contact with French culture and language. As a result, in the fourteenth century, English was once again recognized as the national language of England. By this time, however, it looked a great deal more like the English spoken today.

Modern English (1500–Present)

Despite the Scandinavian and Norman invasions of England, the Anglo-Saxons in England were relatively isolated and protected for nearly 1,200 years. Most of the Anglo-Saxons were illiterate. They had no need to read or write because books were not available to them.

Around 1475, however, the availability of books began to change when William Caxton published the first English book on a printing press in Belgium. Two years later, he began publishing books in England. Books, which previously had been hand copied and affordable only to the rich, became more available to the masses. This mass production of books resulted in an increase in literacy, which helped to standardize the English language and make universal education possible.

Shortly after the introduction of the printing press into England, the adventurous English began to explore the world. From the sixteenth century to the nineteenth century, English merchants, explorers, and settlers spread English to other parts of the globe. Englishmen settled in North America, first in 1607 at Jamestown, Virginia, and then thirteen years later at Plymouth, Massachusetts. Later, English settlers and traders traveled to virtually every part of the globe, including Canada, the Caribbean, India, Australia, New Zealand, and South Africa. English language and culture would permanently influence the native languages and cultures of all these places. In turn, the English travelers' interaction with other cultures brought many new loanwords into English. For example, the word *alligator* came from Spanish via Latin, *pariah* from Tamil, *caravan* from Persian, and *knapsack* from Dutch.

American English

English settlers in the North American colonies in the seventeenth and eighteenth centuries changed their language by necessity, eventually creating a new version of the language—*American English*. Separated from their homeland by an ocean and confronted by a land entirely new and different to them, the new Americans developed a variety of English clearly distinguishable from its British parent.

One of the many problems faced by English settlers in North America was to describe things and experiences never before seen or described by an English speaker. Often, they had to borrow words from the American Indians or to invent new words for new objects or situations. For example, to describe a nocturnal animal with a ringed, bushy tail and black marks around its eyes that made it look like a bandit wearing a mask, they adopted the Algonquian name for the creature, *ärähkun,* which the settlers imitated as *raccoon.*

With the signing of the Declaration of Independence in 1776 and the successful revolution that followed, the differentiation of American English from British English was greatly accelerated. The citizens of the new United States of America set about building a new nation, a new literature, and a new variety of the English language.

By the late nineteenth century, Americans began to turn their attention to other parts of the world. As the United States became an increasingly powerful influence in world affairs, the influence of American English on other varieties of English and on other languages around the world also increased. Other languages have had a corresponding effect on American English.

English: An International Language

In the contemporary world, English has three types of speakers. Many of the people living in the United States, Canada, the United Kingdom, Ireland, Australia, New Zealand, South Africa, Jamaica, and a number of other countries speak English as their native language.

Others use English as a second language. India, for example, has two official languages—Hindi and English—and many regional dialects, some totally unrelated to Hindi. Non-Hindi speakers often prefer English to Hindi for official business. No other language is used more as a first or second language than English.

Some people use English occasionally or for special purposes. It is the principal language of international commerce, communication, transportation, entertainment, science, technology, and scholarship all over the globe. A tour conductor in Spain speaks to a translator for a Japanese tour group in English, their only common language. The Japanese translator then speaks to the Japanese group in their own language. A Thai pilot speaks to an air traffic controller in the Netherlands in English. In total, about 500 million people use English fluently. About another 250 million use it with less fluency.

With so many people using English in so many places around the world, it is inevitable that new varieties and uses of the language will develop. Some people think that because of such new varieties, English will break up into a number of different and mutually incomprehensible languages. That is exactly what happened to Latin some 1,500 years ago when Italian, Spanish, French, Portuguese, Romanian, and other Romance languages began to develop out of local dialects of Latin.

Today, however, circumstances are different. All languages change constantly. They must in order to adapt to changes in human knowledge and society. Still, an international variety of the language is also developing. Because those who use that international variety communicate frequently with each other, it will stay relatively uniform, influencing the local varieties so that they do not turn into separate languages. What we are likely to see in the future is an international English that is pretty much the same all over the earth. Many local subvarieties of English will flourish, but they will be related to the central international variety as planets are to the sun.

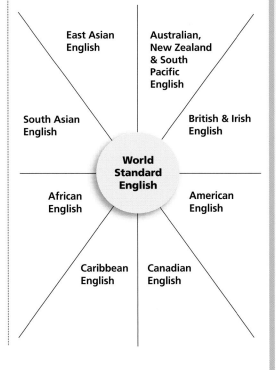

East Asian English

Australian, New Zealand & South Pacific English

South Asian English

British & Irish English

World Standard English

African English

American English

Caribbean English

Canadian English

Varieties of International English

American and British English are the two major varieties of English. Together they account for the vast majority of native English speakers. American and British English differ to some degree in pronunciation and accent. There are also differences in informal and specialized vocabulary. Because there are no significant differences in grammar, however, Americans and Britons have very little difficulty understanding each other in writing and not much difficulty in understanding each other's speech.

Here are some differences in word choices between British and American English.

British	American
beetroot	beet
biscuit	cracker or cookie
block of flats	apartment building
drawing pin	thumbtack
fiddle	swindle, cheat
hire (a car)	rent (a car)
mash	mashed potatoes
polling day	election day
rota	duty roster, work schedule
sister	nurse
toffee-nosed	snobbish, stuck-up
zip	zipper

Other varieties of international English have their own distinctive characteristics. Americans have "barbecues," but Australians have "barbies." When a New Zealander buys "kitset furniture," he or she knows that the furniture is "ready to assemble."

Varieties of American English

Dialects of American English

Like all languages, American English has many distinct versions of speech, called *dialects*. Each dialect has unique features of grammar, vocabulary, and pronunciation. Everyone uses a dialect, and these language variations can communicate much about us—our home locality, education, gender, and age, for example.

Ethnic Dialects *Ethnic dialects* are the speech patterns of particular communities that have preserved some of their ethnic heritage. Most people who have come to the United States have brought language characteristics of their original homeland. For example, English, Dutch, Welsh, French, Spanish, Scandinavian, German, Yiddish, Polish, Czech, Italian, Greek, Armenian, Chinese, Japanese, Korean, and Vietnamese have all influenced American English.

The two most prominent ethnic dialects in the United States are the African American and Hispanic dialects. African American English unites some features of West African languages, some features of early Southern United States speech, and other usages developed by speakers of the dialect themselves. Hispanic English includes Mexican-influenced English in the Southwest, Cuban-influenced English in Florida, and Puerto Rican-influenced English in New York City and Puerto Rico. Of course, not all African Americans or Hispanic Americans use the dialect associated with their ethnic groups, and some features of these dialects turn up in other speech communities, too. The boundaries of ethnic dialects, like those of regional dialects, are fluid and ever-changing.

Regional Dialects *Regional dialects* are based on four major geographic regions shown in the map below. The dialects of these four areas translate into the following categories: *the Northern, the Midland, the Southern,* and *the Western.* (Eastern New England is labeled to indicate where colonists first introduced the language.) Remember, however, that not everyone in a region speaks the dialect of that region, just as all members of a particular ethnic group do not speak the same way.

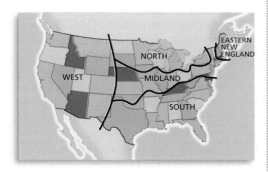

Within each of the major regions, there are also local dialects. Bostonians talk differently from New Yorkers; Charlestonians talk differently from New Orleanians. Furthermore, Northern Midland dialects often differ slightly from Southern Midland dialects, as shown in the chart at the bottom of the page. The chart shows some of the distinctive features of pronunciation, vocabulary, and grammar that distinguish a few regional dialects. (According to linguists, the Western dialect is still developing and is not yet as well-defined as other regional dialects; one clear difference is the tendency to pronounce words like *cot* and *caught* the same way.)

Standard English *Standard English* is the most useful and the most widely used variety of English. Unlike other dialects, it is not limited to a particular place or ethnic group. Because it is commonly understood, people from many different regions and cultures can communicate with one another clearly. In the United States, standard English is usually more a matter of writing than of speech. Standard English is especially appropriate for communicating with a general audience and with anyone outside a familiar circle of family and friends. People are expected to use standard English in most school and business situations. Standard English is also the written and spoken language of public affairs and education, of publications and television, of science and technology, and of

	Northern	Northern Midland	Southern Midland	Southern
Features of Regional Dialects				
Pronunciation	"greassy" "hahg" "pahked cah"	"greassy" "hahg" or hog parked car	"greazy" hog parked car	"greazy" "hawg" "pawked caw"
Word Choice	burlap bag or gunnysack pail	burlap bag bucket	burlap bag bucket	burlap bag or croker sack bucket
Grammar	quarter of/to you, youse	quarter to you	quarter til you, you'uns	quarter til/to you, y'all

business and government. This textbook presents and illustrates many of the rules and guidelines for using standard English. To identify the differences between standard English and other varieties of English, this book uses the labels *standard* and *nonstandard*. *Nonstandard* does not mean "wrong" language. It means "language that is inappropriate in situations where standard English is expected."

- **Formal English**   Like formal dress and formal manners, ***formal English*** is for special occasions, such as writing serious papers and reports or speaking at formal occasions. The sentence structure of formal English is often longer and more complex; word choice is precise, sometimes specialized; spelling is conventional and does not include contractions; and the tone is serious and dignified.

- **Informal English**   Everyday English is called ***informal English.*** Used for writing personal letters, journal entries, and many newspaper and magazine articles, informal English has a short and easy sentence structure and simple and ordinary word choices. Informal English often includes contractions, colloquialisms, slang, and a conversational tone.

  - ***Colloquialisms*** are the informal words and phrases of conversational language. If you say that the home team "bit the dust" in last night's basketball game, you are using a colloquialism. If you tell a friend that you "couldn't care less" about new fashions, you are using a colloquialism. Colloquialisms bring flavor and color to everyday speech and a friendly, conversational tone to writing. They also have a place in expressive and creative writing. Many colloquialisms are figures of speech, or idioms, that are not meant to be taken literally.

    EXAMPLES   When I told my friends where I was working, they thought I was **a couple of bricks shy of a load**.
    When the car stalled for the sixth time, I knew something was **out of whack**.

  - ***Slang*** is newly coined language or old words used in unconventional ways. Often a special language used by a specific group of people, such as students, musicians, or military personnel, slang is sometimes an indication of identification with a particular group. Closely related to this type of slang is ***argot,*** the made-up language of a secretive social group. Cockney slang, which probably originated from an argot, features words that rhyme with the words they represent. For example, *apples and pears* means "stairs" and *I suppose* means "nose."

    Some slang words have been around for centuries—for example, the slang word *lousy* dates back to the 1600s. However, most slang is short-lived. It rides a crest of popularity and then is quickly replaced.

    EXAMPLES
    chill out—relax
    bummer—disappointment
    awesome—very good
    lame—weak, pathetic
    zone out—relax

    Slang is considered highly informal and is inappropriate in most kinds of writing. However, like colloquial language, slang sometimes has a place in expressive and creative writing. In fictional dialogue, slang can make characters sound like real people.

Test Smarts
Taking Standardized Tests in Grammar, Usage, and Mechanics

TEACHING TIP

You can reinforce the material in this part of the book with practice tests found on pages 446–449 and 458–461 of the pupil's textbook and with chapter tests found in the ancillary booklet *Holt Handbook Chapter Tests.*

Becoming "Test-Smart"

Standardized achievement tests, like other tests, measure your skills in specific areas. Standardized achievement tests also compare your performance to the performance of other students at your age or grade level. Some language arts standardized tests measure your skill in using correct capitalization, punctuation, sentence structure, and spelling. Such tests sometimes also measure your ability to evaluate sentence style.

The most important part of preparing for any test, including standardized tests, is learning the content on which you will be tested. To do this, you must

- listen in class
- complete homework assignments
- study to master the concepts and skills presented by your teacher

In addition, you need to use effective strategies for taking a standardized test. The following pages will teach you how to become test-smart.

General Strategies for Taking Tests

1. **Understand how the test is scored.** If no points will be taken off for wrong answers, plan to answer every question. If wrong answers count against you, plan to answer only questions you know the answer to or questions you can answer with an educated guess.

2. **Stay focused.** Expect to be a little nervous, but focus your attention on doing the best job possible. Try not to be distracted with thoughts that aren't about the test questions.

Becoming "Test-Smart" **565**

3. **Get an overview.** Quickly skim the entire test to get an idea of how long the test is and what is on it.

4. **Pace yourself.** Based on your overview, figure out how much time to allow for each section of the test. If time limits are stated for each section, decide how much time to allow for each item. Pace yourself, and check every five to ten minutes to see if you need to work faster. Try to leave a few minutes at the end of the testing period to check your work.

5. **Read all instructions.** Read the instructions for each part of the test carefully. Also, answer the sample questions to be sure you understand how to answer the test questions.

6. **Read all answer choices.** Carefully read *all* of the possible answers before you choose an answer. Note how each possible answer differs from the others. You may want to make an *x* next to each answer choice that you rule out.

7. **Make educated guesses.** If you do not know the answer to a question, see if you can rule out one or more answers and make an educated guess. Don't spend too much time on any one item, though. If you want to think longer about a difficult item, make a light pencil mark next to the item number. You can go back to that question later.

8. **Mark your answers.** Mark the answer sheet carefully and completely. If you plan to go back to an item later, be sure to skip that number on the answer sheet.

9. **Check your work.** If you have time at the end of the test, go back to check your answers. This is also the time to try to answer any questions you skipped. Make sure your marks are complete, and erase any stray marks on the answer sheet.

Strategies for Answering Grammar, Usage, and Mechanics Questions

The questions in standardized tests can take different forms, but the most common form is the multiple-choice question. Here are some strategies for answering that kind of test question.

Correcting parts of sentences

One kind of question contains a sentence with an underlined part. The answer choices show several revised versions of that part. Your job is to decide which revised version makes the sentence correct or whether the underlined part is already correct. First, look at each answer carefully. Immediately rule out any answer in which you notice a grammatical error. If you are still unsure of the correct answer, try approaching the question in one of these two ways.

- **Think how you would rewrite the underlined part.** Look at the answer choices for one that matches your revision. Carefully read each possible answer before you make your final choice. Often, only tiny differences exist between the answers, and you want to choose the *best* answer.

- **Look carefully at the underlined part and at each answer choice, looking for one particular type of error, such as an error in capitalization or spelling.** The best way to look for a particular error is to compare the answer choices to see how they differ both from each other and from the underlined part of the question. For example, if there are differences in capitalization, look at each choice for capitalization errors.

After ruling out incorrect answers, choose the answer with no errors. If there are errors in each of the choices but no errors in the underlined part, your answer will be the "no error" or "correct as is" choice.

EXAMPLE

Directions: Choose the answer that is the **best** revision of the underlined words.

1. My neighbor is painting his <u>house and my brother helped him.</u>

   A. house; and my brother is helping him.

   B. house, and my brother had helped him.

   C. house, and my brother is helping him.

   D. Correct as is

Explanation: In the example above, the possible answers contain differences in punctuation and in verb tense. Therefore, you should check each possible answer for errors in punctuation and verb tense.

   A. You can rule out this choice because it has incorrect punctuation.

   B. This choice creates inconsistent verb tenses, so you can rule out this answer.

   C. This choice has correct punctuation and creates consistent verb tenses.

   D. You can rule out this choice because the original sentence lacks correct punctuation between the clauses and has inconsistent verb tenses.

Answer: Choice C is the only one that contains no errors, so the oval for that answer choice is darkened.

Correcting whole sentences

This type of question is similar to the kind of question previously described. However, here you are looking for mistakes in the entire sentence instead of just an underlined part. The strategies for approaching this type of question are the same as for the other kind of sentence-correction questions. If you don't see the correct answer right away, compare the answer choices to see how they differ. When you find differences, check each choice for errors relating to that difference. Rule out choices with errors. Repeat the process until you find the correct answer.

EXAMPLE

Directions: Choose the answer that is the **best** revision of the following sentences.

1. After Brad mowed the lawn, he swept the sidewalk and driveway, then he took a shower. And washed his hair.

   A. After Brad mowed the lawn, he swept the sidewalk and driveway. Then he took a shower and washed his hair.

   B. After Brad mowed the lawn, he swept the sidewalk and driveway. Then he took a shower, and washed his hair.

   C. After Brad mowed the lawn. He swept the sidewalk and driveway; then he took a shower and washed his hair.

   D. Correct as is

Explanation: The original word groups and answer choices have differences in sentence structure and punctuation, so you should check each answer choice for errors in sentence structure and punctuation.

   A. This choice contains two complete sentences and correct punctuation.

   B. This choice contains two complete sentences and incorrect punctuation.

   C. This choice begins with a sentence fragment, so you can rule it out.

   D. You can rule out this choice because the original version contains a sentence fragment.

Answer: Choice A is the only one that contains no errors, so the oval for that answer choice is darkened.

Identifying kinds of errors

This type of question has at least one underlined part. Your job is to determine which part, if any, contains an error. Sometimes, you also may have to decide what type of error (capitalization, punctuation, or spelling) exists. The strategy is the same whether the question has one or several underlined parts. Try to identify an error, and check the answer choices for that type of error. If the original version is correct as written, choose "no error" or "correct as is."

EXAMPLE

Directions: Read the following sentences and decide which type of error, if any, is in the underlined part.

1. Marcia, Jim, and Leroy are participating in <u>Saturday's charity marathon. they</u> are hoping to raise one hundred dollars for the new children's museum.
   - **A.** Spelling error
   - **B.** Capitalization error
   - **C.** Punctuation error
   - **D.** Correct as is

Explanation: If you cannot tell right away what kind of error (if any) is in the original version, go through each answer choice in turn.
   - **A.** All the words are spelled correctly.
   - **B.** The sentences contain a capitalization error. The second sentence incorrectly begins with a lowercase letter.
   - **C.** The sentences are punctuated correctly.
   - **D.** The sentences contain a capitalization error, so you can rule out this choice.

Answer: Because the passage contains a capitalization error, the oval for answer choice B is darkened.

Revising sentence structure
Errors covered by this kind of question include sentence fragments, run-on sentences, repetitive wording, misplaced modifiers, and awkward construction. If you don't immediately spot the error, examine the question and each answer choice for specific types of errors, one type at a time. If you cannot find an error in the original version and if all of the other answer choices have errors, then choose "no error" or "correct as is."

EXAMPLE

Directions: Read the following word groups. If there is an error in sentence structure, choose the answer that best revises the word groups.

1. Mary Lou arranged the mozzarella cheese and fresh tomatoes. On a platter covered with lettuce leaves.
   - **A.** Mary Lou arranged the mozzarella cheese and fresh tomatoes on a platter covered with lettuce leaves.
   - **B.** Mary Lou arranged the mozzarella cheese and fresh tomatoes, on a platter covered with lettuce leaves.
   - **C.** Mary Lou arranged the mozzarella cheese and fresh tomatoes; on a platter covered with lettuce leaves.
   - **D.** Correct as is

Explanation: The original word groups and answer choices have differences in sentence structure and punctuation.
   - **A.** This choice is correctly punctuated and contains a correct, complete sentence.
   - **B.** This choice contains an incorrect comma, so you can rule it out.
   - **C.** This choice contains an incorrect semicolon, so you can rule it out.
   - **D.** The original word groups contain a sentence fragment, so D cannot be correct.

Answer: Choice A is the only one that contains no errors, so the oval for that answer choice is darkened.

Questions about sentence style

These questions are often not about grammar, usage, or mechanics but about content and organization. They may ask about tone, purpose, topic sentences, supporting sentences, audience, sentence combining, appropriateness of content, or transitions. The questions may ask you which is the *best* way to revise the passage, or they may ask you to identify the *main* purpose of the passage. When you see words such as *best*, *main*, and *most likely* or *least likely*, you are not being asked to correct errors; you are being asked to make a judgment about style or meaning.

If the question asks for a particular kind of revision (for example, "What *transition* is needed between sentence 4 and sentence 5?"), analyze each answer choice to see how well it makes that particular revision. Many questions ask for a general revision (for example, "Which is the *best* way to revise the last sentence?"). In such situations, check each answer choice and rule out any choices that have mistakes in grammar, usage, or mechanics. Then, read each choice and use what you have learned in class to judge whether the revision improves the original sentence. If you are combining sentences, be sure to choose the answer that includes all important information, that demonstrates good style, *and* that is grammatically correct.

EXAMPLE

Directions: Choose the answer that shows the **best** way to combine the following sentences.

1. Jacques Cousteau was a filmmaker and author. Jacques Cousteau explored the ocean as a diver and marine scientist.

   A. Jacques Cousteau was a filmmaker and author; Jacques Cousteau explored the ocean as a marine scientist.

   B. Jacques Cousteau was a filmmaker and author, he explored the ocean as a diver and marine scientist.

   C. Jacques Cousteau was a filmmaker and author who explored the ocean as a diver and marine scientist.

   D. Jacques Cousteau was a filmmaker, author, diver, and scientist.

(A) (B) (C) (D)

Explanation:

A. Answer choice A is grammatically correct but unnecessarily repeats the subject *Jacques Cousteau* and leaves out some information.

B. Choice B is a run-on sentence, so it cannot be the correct answer.

C. Choice C is grammatically correct, and it demonstrates effective sentence combining.

D. Choice D is grammatically correct but leaves out some information.

Answer: Because answer choice C shows the best way to combine the sentences, the oval for choice C is darkened.

Fill-in-the-blanks

This type of question tests your ability to fill in blanks in sentences, giving answers that are logical and grammatically correct. A question of this kind might ask you to choose a verb in the appropriate tense. A different question might require a combination of adverbs (*first, next*) to show how parts of the sentence relate. Another question might require a vocabulary word to complete the sentence.

To approach a sentence-completion question, first look for clue words in the sentence. *But, however,* and *though* indicate a contrast; *therefore* and *as a result* indicate cause and effect. Using sentence clues, rule out obviously incorrect answer choices. Then, try filling in the blanks with the remaining choices to determine which answer choice makes the most sense. Finally, check to be sure your choice is grammatically correct.

EXAMPLE

Directions: Choose the words that **best** complete the sentence.

1. When Jack _____ the dog, the dog _____ water everywhere.
   A. washes, splashed
   B. washed, will be splashing
   C. will have washed, has splashed
   D. washed, splashed

Explanation:
   A. The verb tenses (present and past) are inconsistent.
   B. The verb tenses (past and future) are inconsistent.
   C. The verb tenses (future perfect and present perfect) are inconsistent.
   D. The verb tenses (past and past) are consistent.

Answer: The oval for choice D is darkened.

Using Your Test Smarts

Remember: Success on standardized tests comes partly from knowing strategies for taking such tests—from being test-smart. Knowing these strategies can help you approach standardized achievement tests more confidently. Do your best to learn your classroom subjects, take practice tests if they are available, and use the strategies outlined in this section. Good luck!

Grammar at a Glance

abbreviation An abbreviation is a shortened form of a word or a phrase.

- **capitalization of** (See page 316.)

TITLES USED WITH NAMES	**M**s.	**G**ov.	**S**r.	**M.B.A.**
KINDS OF ORGANIZATIONS	**C**o.	**I**nc.	**A**ssn.	**C**orp.
PARTS OF ADDRESSES	**B**lvd.	**A**ve.	**H**wy.	**P.O. B**ox
NAMES OF STATES	[without ZIP Codes]	**T**ex.	**A**la.	
		Ind.	**N. D**ak.	
	[with ZIP Codes]	**TX**	**AL**	
		IN	**ND**	
TIMES	**A.M.**	**P.M.**	**B.C.**	**A.D.**

- **punctuation of** (See page 329.)

WITH PERIODS	(See preceding examples.)			
WITHOUT PERIODS	PC	FM	GPA	VISTA
	DC (D**.**C**.** without ZIP Code)			
	ml	kb	lb	mph	mm
	[Exception: inch = in**.**]			

action verb An action verb expresses physical or mental activity. (See page 16.)

EXAMPLES   Every day, Eleanor **works** in the garden.

             I **remember** most of my lines.

active voice Active voice is the voice a verb is in when it expresses an action done by its subject. (See page 211. See also **voice.**)

EXAMPLE   We **planted** the oak next to the fence.

A

HELP

Grammar at a Glance is an alphabetical list of special terms and expressions with examples and references to further information. When you encounter a grammar or usage problem in the revising or proofreading stage of your writing, look for help in this section first. You may find all you need to know right here. If you need more information, **Grammar at a Glance** will show you where in the book to turn for a more complete explanation. If you do not find what you are looking for in **Grammar at a Glance,** turn to the index on page 599.

RESOURCES

adjective An adjective modifies a noun or a pronoun. (See page 11.)

EXAMPLE　　The **sturdy** horse showed **no** signs of tiring.

adjective clause An adjective clause is a subordinate clause that modifies a noun or a pronoun. (See page 84.)

EXAMPLE　　The school **that outperformed us** was our old rival.

adjective phrase A prepositional phrase that modifies a noun or a pronoun is called an adjective phrase. (See page 60.)

EXAMPLE　　Airbags **in cars** can be lifesavers.

adverb An adverb modifies a verb, an adjective, or another adverb. (See page 20.)

EXAMPLE　　I thought **quickly** before I gave my name.

adverb clause An adverb clause is a subordinate clause that modifies a verb, an adjective, or an adverb. (See page 90.)

EXAMPLE　　**After she comes home,** Katya is frequently too tired to go out.

adverb phrase A prepositional phrase that modifies a verb, an adjective, or an adverb is called an adverb phrase. (See page 62.)

EXAMPLE　　**Until the last possible moment,** the judges kept us guessing.

agreement Agreement is the correspondence, or match, between grammatical forms. Grammatical forms agree when they have the same number, gender, and person.

  ■ **of pronouns and antecedents** (See page 124.)

SINGULAR　　At the winter carnival, **Trenton** won first prize for **his** ice sculpture.

PLURAL　　At the winter carnival, the Duarte **twins** won first prize for **their** ice sculpture.

SINGULAR　　To go on the field trip, **each** of the students must return **his or her** permission slip to Mr. Wilkins by Friday.

PLURAL　　To go on the field trip, **all** of the students must return **their** permission slips to Mr. Wilkins by Friday.

| SINGULAR | **Neither Ling nor Soledad** has indicated what **her** major field of study in college will be. |
| PLURAL | **Both Ling and Soledad** have indicated what **their** major fields of study in college will be. |

■ **of subjects and verbs** (See page 106.)

SINGULAR	The yearbook **editor is working** hard to meet the publisher's deadline.
SINGULAR	The yearbook **editor,** as well as the other staff members, **is working** hard to meet the publisher's deadline.
PLURAL	The yearbook staff **members are working** hard to meet the publisher's deadline.
PLURAL	The yearbook staff **members,** especially the editor, **are working** hard to meet the publisher's deadline.
SINGULAR	**Each** of these garden tools **belongs** to my neighbor.
PLURAL	**All** of these garden tools **belong** to my neighbor.
SINGULAR	**Lauren or Amanda** usually **goes** snorkeling with me.
PLURAL	**Lauren and Amanda** usually **go** snorkeling with me.
SINGULAR	Here **is** a **snapshot** of the winners of the salsa dance contest.
PLURAL	Here **are** some **snapshots** of the winners of the salsa dance contest.
SINGULAR	**Two days is** not enough time to complete the project.
PLURAL	**Two days** in January **are** national holidays.
SINGULAR	*Gulliver's Travels* **includes** a satirical look at Great Britain's political system.
PLURAL	Gulliver's **travels include** voyages to Lilliput and Brobdingnag.
SINGULAR	One possible side **effect** of the medication **is** headaches.
PLURAL	**Headaches are** one possible side effect of the medication.
SINGULAR	Kelly is one freshman **who plays** on the varsity team.
PLURAL	Kelly is one of the freshmen **who play** on the varsity team.
SINGULAR	Kelly is the only one of the freshmen **who plays** on the varsity team.

ambiguous reference Ambiguous reference occurs when a pronoun incorrectly refers to either of two antecedents. (See page 163.)

AMBIGUOUS	A tortoise is different from a turtle only in that it lives on land, not in water.
CLEAR	A tortoise is different from a turtle only in that a tortoise lives on land, not in water.

antecedent An antecedent is the word or words that a pronoun stands for. (See page 7.)

EXAMPLE   **Mr. Haynes** sent the **winners** the photos **he** had taken of **them.** [*Mr. Haynes* is the antecedent of *he*. *Winners* is the antecedent of *them*.]

apostrophe

■ **to form contractions** (See page 378. See also **contractions.**)

EXAMPLES   isn•t   they•ll   let•s   •01

■ **to form plurals of numerals, symbols, and words referred to as words** (See page 379.)

EXAMPLES	*a*•s, *e*•s, *i*•s, *o*•s, and *u*•s	*A*•s, *I*•s, and *U*•s [*but Zs or Z*•s and Qs or Q*•s]
	1600•s [*or* 1600s]	SUV•s [*or* SUVs]
	%•s, +•s, and =•s	using &•s for *and*•s [*or* using &s for *and*s]

■ **to show possession** (See page 374.)

EXAMPLES   the doctor•s office
the doctors• offices
children•s rights
someone•s eyeglasses
my mother•s and father•s birthdays
my mother and father•s wedding anniversary
one month•s [*or* four weeks•] allowance

appositive An appositive is a noun or a pronoun placed beside another noun or pronoun to identify or explain it. (See page 73.)

EXAMPLE   Bernard, an aspiring **artist,** wants to study in New York.

appositive phrase An appositive phrase consists of an appositive and its modifiers. (See page 74.)

EXAMPLE   Anthony, **our track-and-field star,** has been awarded a scholarship.

article The articles, *a, an,* and *the,* are the most frequently used adjectives. (See page 12.)

EXAMPLE   **A** sudden gust of wind and **an** ominous rumbling in **the** distance were **the** first signs of **an** impending storm.

bad, badly (See page 232.)

NONSTANDARD   This chicken soup tastes badly.
STANDARD   This chicken soup tastes **bad.**

base form The base form, or infinitive, is one of the four principal parts of a verb. (See page 176.)

EXAMPLE   We heard Suzi **sing** the national anthem before last night's game.

brackets (See page 385.)

EXAMPLES   Ms. Kwan explained the Yoruban proverb "A river does not flow so far that it forgets its source" by rewriting it as follows: "A river **[**person**]** does not flow **[**travel**]** so far that it **[**he or she**]** forgets its source **[**his or her roots**]**."

              The first director of the Environmental Protection Agency (EPA **[**1970**]**) was William Ruckelshaus.

capitalization

- **of abbreviations and acronyms** (See page 316. See also **abbreviations.**)

- **of first words** (See page 296.)

 EXAMPLES   **I**n Greek mythology, Nike is the goddess of victory.

              Mr. Tyler asked, "**D**id you know that the human body has 206 bones and 650 muscles?"

              Dear Dr. Nunez:

              Best regards,

- **of proper nouns and proper adjectives** (See page 298.)

Proper Noun	Common Noun
Gen. **H. N**orman **S**chwarzkopf	leader
Edward the **C**onfessor	king

Proper Noun	Common Noun
North America	continent
New Zealand	country
Grenada County	county
Tsinghai Province	province
Kauai	island
Chang River	body of water
Lamotte Peak	mountain
Klondike Gold Rush National Historical Park	park
Argonne Forest	forest
Altamira	caves
Black Rock Desert	desert
Southwest	region
Twenty-ninth Street	street
Republican Party (or party)	political party
Operation Desert Storm	historical event
Stone Age	historical period
the Special Olympics	special event
Bastille Day	holiday
February	calendar item
Quiché Mayas	people
Hinduism	religion
Mormon	religious follower
God [*but* the Egyptian god Ra]	deity
Epiphany	holy day
Talmud	sacred writing
Casa Grande Ruins National Monument	monument
Water Tower Place	building
Bollingen Prize in Poetry	award
Pluto	planet
Vega	star
Crux, or Southern Cross	constellation
Lady of the Lake	ship
Galileo	spacecraft
Computer Science II (*but* computer science)	school subject

■ **of titles** (See page 309.)

EXAMPLES **G**overnor Benjamin Cayetano [preceding a name]

Benjamin Cayetano, the **g**overnor of Hawaii [following a name]

Welcome, **G**overnor. [direct address]

Uncle Cesare [*but* my **u**ncle Cesare]

***B*aseball: *A*n *I*llustrated *H*istory** [book]

***I*'ll *M*ake *M*e a *W*orld: *A* *C*entury of *A*frican-*A*merican *A*rts** [TV program]

***T*he *T*hinker** [sculpture]

***R*iders to the *S*ea** [musical composition]

"**B**ye **B**ye **L**ove" [song]

"**T**he **T**rain from **R**hodesia" [short story]

"**S**pring and **F**all: **T**o a **Y**oung **C**hild" [poem]

***C*onsumers *D*igest** [magazine]

the ***S*tar-*L*edger** [newspaper]

***D*oonesbury** [comic strip]

case of pronouns Case is the form a pronoun takes to show how the pronoun is used in a sentence. (See page 138.)

NOMINATIVE Terrell and **she** were named the athletes of the year.
The first and second runners-up were Dylan and **he,** respectively.
Both guest speakers, Mr. Jimenez and **she,** inspired their listeners with confidence.
We seniors met with the class sponsors to discuss the plans for Grad Night.
The last person **who** speaks to Prince Hamlet is Horatio.
Do you know **who** the chaperons will be?
I don't see Elise as often as **he.** [meaning *as often as he sees Elise*]

OBJECTIVE The helpful theater usher led **us** back to our seats.
Aunt Helen gave **me** a video camera for graduation.
Who won the jujitsu match between Aaron and **him**?
The band dedicated its last song to the prom's king and queen, Miguel and **her.**

As the principal handed **us** graduates our diplomas, she shook our hands and congratulated us.

A conversation with my great-uncle inspired **me** to chart my ancestry.

The last person to **whom** Prince Hamlet speaks is Horatio.

Among the members of the Ballets Russes dance company was Vaslav Nijinsky, **whom** many regard as the most talented dancer of the twentieth century.

I don't see Elise as often as **him.** [meaning *as often as I see him*]

POSSESSIVE **Your** poems are more imaginative than **mine** are.

Their winning the Pulitzer Prize in investigative reporting came as no surprise to their colleagues.

clause A clause is a group of words that contains a verb and its subject and that is used as a sentence or as part of a sentence. (See page 82.)

                                  S V

INDEPENDENT CLAUSE   Irv went to a Chinese restaurant for the first time last night

                                  S   V

SUBORDINATE CLAUSE   because Kris really enjoys Renaissance music and theater

colon (See page 359.)

   ■ **before lists**

EXAMPLES   On our cross-country road trip to see my parents in Seattle, we traveled through seven states**:** Oklahoma, Kansas, Colorado, Wyoming, Idaho, Oregon, and Washington.

    Some of the sites we visited along the way are as follows**:** Cherokee Cultural Center, Oklahoma; John Brown's cabin at Osawatomie, Kansas; and Mount Saint Helens, Washington.

   ■ **in conventional situations**

EXAMPLES   12**:**15 P.M.

    Luke 10**:**25–27

    *Bulfinch's Mythology***:** *The Age of Fable, The Age of Chivalry, Legends of Charlemagne*

    "First Aid**:** Principles and Practices"

    Dear Mrs. Komachi**:**

comma (See page 333.)

- **in a series**

  EXAMPLES   Among the species of flightless birds are the emu, ostrich, rhea, and penguin.

  Gina's hobbies include designing greeting cards on her computer, collecting coins, and piecing quilts.

- **in compound sentences**

  EXAMPLES   Dr. Mariano Azuela wrote several novels, but his most famous is *The Underdogs,* a novel about the revolution in Mexico during the early part of the twentieth century.

  Marta and I have not completed our woodworking project, and the deadline is Friday.

- **with nonessential phrases and clauses**

  EXAMPLES   Seeking fame, Gilgamesh travels with Enkidu to the cedar forest.

  West Side Story, which was written almost four hundred years later, is based on Shakespeare's *Romeo and Juliet.*

- **with introductory elements**

  EXAMPLES   In the summer of 1994, Dr. Chiaki Naito-Mukai became the first Japanese woman to travel in space.

  As my lab partner performed the chemistry experiment, I recorded the steps of the procedure.

- **with interrupters**

  EXAMPLES   The best program on television, in my opinion, is *Nova.*

  Did you know that some foods we call vegetables, such as tomatoes and lima beans, are actually fruits?

- **in conventional situations**

  EXAMPLES   On Saturday, October 7, 2000, they drove to West Lafayette, Indiana, to visit the campus of Purdue University.

  They mailed the letter to Dean of Admissions, Purdue University, West Lafayette, Indiana 47907-1080, on 5 February 2000.

comma splice A comma splice is a run-on sentence in which only a comma separates two independent clauses. (See page 483. See also **fused sentence, run-on sentence.**)

COMMA SPLICE	A haiku is a three-line poem that consists of seventeen syllables, the first and third lines contain five syllables each, the second line has seven.
REVISED	A haiku is a three-line poem that consists of seventeen syllables**;** the first and third lines contain five syllables each**, and** the second line has seven.
REVISED	A haiku is a three-line poem that consists of seventeen syllables**. T**he first and third lines contain five syllables each**;** the second line has seven.

comparison of modifiers (See page 236.)

■ comparison of adjectives and adverbs

Positive	Comparative	Superlative
dark	dark**er**	dark**est**
busy	bus**ier**	bus**iest**
imaginative	**more** imaginative	**most** imaginative
cautiously	**less** cautiously	**least** cautiously
far	**farther/further**	**farthest/furthest**
good/well	**better**	**best**

■ comparing two

EXAMPLES   This brand of orange juice tastes **tangier** than the brand we normally drink.

The team played **more aggressively** in the second half than in the first half.

■ comparing more than two

EXAMPLES   Weighing about three hundred pounds, the ostrich is the **largest** bird.

Of all of the species of birds that can swim, the penguin can propel itself underwater **most easily.**

complement A complement is a word or word group that completes the meaning of a verb. (See page 44. See also **direct object, indirect object, predicate nominative,** and **predicate adjective.**)

EXAMPLES   Tony gave **Suzanne** a **ring.**

It's not a dull **movie,** but it is **long.**

complex sentence A complex sentence has one independent clause and at least one subordinate clause. (See page 95.)

EXAMPLES My friend Kishi, who draws cartoons for the school newspaper, wants to become a professional animator.

When the school holds its annual Shakespeare Festival on April 23, the drama classes will perform excerpts from some of the plays by the honored dramatist.

compound-complex sentence A compound-complex sentence has two or more independent clauses and at least one subordinate clause. (See page 96.)

EXAMPLES Marcie had no difficulty downloading the article, but when she tried to e-mail it to her friend Will, who had requested it, her computer shut down.

When you are in Pittsburgh next summer, you should visit The Carnegie Museum of Art; it has impressive exhibits of American Indian and pre-Columbian artwork.

compound sentence A compound sentence has two or more independent clauses but no subordinate clauses. (See page 94.)

EXAMPLES The horse was the first animal to be featured on a United States postage stamp; the two-cent stamp was issued in 1869.

Last summer, John worked two jobs to earn money for his college expenses; during the day, he caddied at a local golf course, and at night he bagged groceries at a nearby supermarket.

conjunction A conjunction joins words or groups of words. (See page 25.)

EXAMPLES I am taking civics **and** art.

Shelley wants to **either** grow vegetables **or** raise pigs.

Sign the guest book **before** you go inside.

contraction A contraction is a shortened form of a word, a numeral, or a group of words. Apostrophes in contractions indicate where letters or numerals have been omitted. (See page 378. See also **apostrophe.**)

EXAMPLES	She'd [she had *or* she would]	there's [there is *or* there has]
	who's [who is *or* who has]	it's [it is *or* it has]
	haven't [have not]	they're [they are]
	can't [cannot]	won't [will not]
	'14–'18 war [1914–1918 war]	o'clock [of the clock]

dangling modifier A dangling modifier is a modifying word, phrase, or clause that does not clearly and sensibly modify a word or a word group in a sentence. (See page 252.)

DANGLING	Using deductive reasoning, the mystery was solved. [Who was using deductive reasoning?]
REVISED	Using deductive reasoning, **the detective** solved the mystery.

dash (See page 384.)

EXAMPLE	Among the pen names used by the Brontë sisters—Anne, Charlotte, and Emily—were Acton Bell, Currer Bell, and Ellis Bell, respectively.

declarative sentence A declarative sentence makes a statement and is followed by a period. (See page 97.)

EXAMPLE	The two countries with the highest life expectancy are Japan and Iceland**.**

direct object A direct object is a word or word group that receives the action of the verb or shows the result of the action. A direct object answers the question *Whom?* or *What?* after a transitive verb. (See page 45.)

EXAMPLE	Sandra bought **sunglasses.**

double comparison A double comparison is the nonstandard use of two comparative forms (usually *more* and *–er*) or two superlative forms (usually *most* and *–est*) to express comparison. In standard usage, the single comparative form is correct. (See page 239.)

NONSTANDARD	In classical mythology, was Hercules more stronger than Atlas?
STANDARD	In classical mythology, was Hercules **stronger** than Atlas?

double negative A double negative is the nonstandard use of two or more negative words to express a single negative idea. (See page 286.)

NONSTANDARD	Sitting at the back of the theater, I couldn't barely hear the actors' dialogue.
STANDARD	Sitting at the back of the theater, I **could barely** hear the actors' dialogue.

NONSTANDARD	Our library doesn't have no copies of August Wilson's most recent play.
STANDARD	Our library **doesn't have any** copies of August Wilson's most recent play.
STANDARD	Our library **has no** copies of August Wilson's most recent play.

double subject A double subject occurs when an unnecessary pronoun is used after the subject of a sentence.

NONSTANDARD	The oystercatcher it's a large shorebird that feeds mainly on bivalve mollusks, such as oysters.
STANDARD	**The oystercatcher** is a large shorebird that feeds mainly on bivalve mollusks, such as oysters.

elliptical construction An elliptical construction is a clause from which words have been omitted. (See page 149.)   **E**

EXAMPLE	Joel is much taller **than his brothers** [are tall].

end marks (See page 326.)

- **with sentences**

EXAMPLES	Weather permitting, the powwow will be held on the first Saturday in June**.**
	What is the difference between an endangered species and a threatened species**?**
	Bravo**!** What a heartfelt performance that was**!**
	Please tell us another story, Aunt Frida**.**

- **with abbreviations** (See **abbreviations.**)

EXAMPLES	In that movie, Tom Hanks portrays Commander James A. Lovell, Jr**.**
	In that movie, doesn't Tom Hanks portray Commander James A. Lovell, Jr**.?**

essential clause/essential phrase An essential, or restrictive, clause or phrase is necessary to the meaning of a sentence; it is not set off by commas. (See page 339.)

EXAMPLES   The person **who left a bag in the library** can claim it at the office. [essential clause]

The man **wearing a bowler hat** is my grandfather. [essential phrase]

exclamation point (See **end marks.**)

exclamatory sentence An exclamatory sentence expresses strong feeling and is followed by an exclamation point. (See page 98.)

EXAMPLE   What a beautiful sunset that is**!**

faulty coordination Faulty coordination occurs when unequal ideas are presented as though they were coordinate. Usually, the clauses are strung together with coordinating conjunctions like *and* or *but*. (See page 473.)

FAULTY   Daedalus warned Icarus to avoid flying too high, for the sun would melt the wax, causing the wings to fall off, but before they had flown very far, Icarus soared too close to the sun, and as his father had warned, the wax melted, and the wings dropped off, and Icarus fell into the sea and drowned.

REVISED   Dadealus warned Icarus to avoid flying too high because the sun would melt the wax, causing the wings to fall off. Before they had flown very far, however, Icarus soared too close to the sun. As his father had warned, the wax melted, the wings dropped off, and Icarus fell into the sea and drowned.

fragment (See **sentence fragment.**)

fused sentence A fused sentence is a run-on sentence in which no punctuation separates independent clauses. (See page 483. See also **comma splice, run-on sentence.**)

FUSED   The Vietnam Veterans Memorial in Washington, D.C., was built in the early 1980s the Civil Rights Memorial in Montgomery, Alabama, was constructed only a few years later both monuments had been designed by Maya Ying Lin.

REVISED   The Vietnam Veterans Memorial in Washington, D.C., was built in the early 1980s**, and** the Civil Rights Memorial in Montgomery, Alabama, was constructed only a few years later**;** both monuments had been designed by Maya Ying Lin.

REVISED   The Vietnam Veterans Memorial in Washington, D.C., was built in the early 1980s; the Civil Rights Memorial in Montgomery, Alabama, was constructed only a few years later. **B**oth monuments had been designed by Maya Ying Lin.

general reference A general reference is the incorrect use of a pronoun to refer to a general idea rather than to a specific noun. (See page 164.)

GENERAL   Yolanda, the team's star player, has been sidelined by a wrist injury. That may be the reason for her teammates' low morale.
[To what does *That* refer?]

REVISED   That Yolanda, the team's star player, has been sidelined by a wrist injury may be the reason for her teammates' low morale.

gerund A gerund is a verb form ending in *–ing* that is used as a noun. (See page 68.)

EXAMPLE   **Smoking** is prohibited on all commercial domestic flights.

gerund phrase A gerund phrase consists of a gerund and any modifiers and complements it has. (See page 69.)

EXAMPLE   On weekends, Alberto enjoys **sending his friends e-mail.**

good, well (See page 233.)

EXAMPLES   To say that Pete Sampras is a **good** tennis player is an understatement.

To say that Pete Sampras plays tennis **well** [not *good*] is an understatement.

hyphen (See page 380.)

- **to divide words**

EXAMPLE   Seeing the patches of daffodils dotting the hill-side reminded me of a Wordsworth poem.

- **in compound numbers**

EXAMPLE   By the time you graduate, will you have earned twenty-four credits?

- **with prefixes and suffixes**

EXAMPLES   The grand opening of the new shopping mall is scheduled for mid-October.

Janet handed the gavel to the president-elect.

imperative mood The imperative mood is used to express a direct command or request. (See page 215.)

EXAMPLES **Put** that magazine down!

Read what the sign says.

imperative sentence An imperative sentence gives a command or makes a request and is followed by either a period or an exclamation point. (See page 97.)

EXAMPLES List the first six presidents**.**

Be quiet**!**

indefinite reference An indefinite reference is the incorrect use of the pronoun *you*, *it*, or *they* to refer to no particular person or thing. (See page 168.)

INDEFINITE In this book they state that *The Mahabharata* is the longest poem ever written.

REVISED This book states that *The Mahabharata* is the longest poem ever written.

independent clause An independent, or main, clause expresses a complete thought and can stand by itself as a sentence. (See page 82.)

EXAMPLE **Egypt is an African nation,** but **it is an Arabic nation as well**.

indicative mood The indicative mood is used to express a fact, an opinion, or a question. (See page 215.)

EXAMPLES Flann O'Brien **was** the pen name of an Irish writer and journalist.

Jacques Villeneuve **is** a Canadian race-car driver.

Don't you **live** next door to the Sandovals?

indirect object An indirect object is a noun, pronoun, or word group that sometimes appears in sentences containing direct objects. An indirect object tells *to whom* or *to what* (or *for whom* or *for what*) the action of a transitive verb is done. Indirect objects generally precede direct objects. (See page 46.)

EXAMPLE Lucy cooked **us** dinner.

infinitive An infinitive is a verb form, usually preceded by *to*, that is used as a noun, an adjective, or an adverb. (See page 70.)

EXAMPLES   Would you like **to dance**?

The casserole is ready **to go** into the oven.

infinitive phrase An infinitive phrase consists of an infinitive and any modifiers and complements it has. (See page 71.)

EXAMPLE   Aunt Usha, I would like **to introduce my fiancé.**

interjection An interjection expresses emotion and has no grammatical relation to the rest of the sentence. (See page 28.)

EXAMPLE   **Wow!** There goes another one!

interrogative sentence An interrogative sentence asks a question and is followed by a question mark. (See page 98.)

EXAMPLE   Are you Stephen Welch of Austin, Texas**?**

intransitive verb An intransitive verb is a verb that does not take an object. (See page 18.)

EXAMPLE   Arthur **called,** but no one **answered.**

irregular verb An irregular verb is a verb that forms its past and past participle in some way other than by adding *–d* or *–ed* to the base form. (See page 178. See also **regular verb.**)

Base Form	Present Participle	Past	Past Participle
arise	[is] arising	arose	[have] arisen
be	[is] being	was, were	[have] been
become	[is] becoming	became	[have] become
cost	[is] costing	cost	[have] cost
freeze	[is] freezing	froze	[have] frozen
lead	[is] leading	led	[have] led
meet	[is] meeting	met	[have] met
seek	[is] seeking	sought	[have] sought
spread	[is] spreading	spread	[have] spread

italics (See page 362.)

- **for titles**

    EXAMPLES   *A Portrait of the Artist as a Young Man* [book]

    People Weekly [periodical]

    Duke Ellington: Reminiscing in Tempo [film]

    Thor's Fight with the Giants [work of art]

    Pomp and Circumstance [long musical composition]

- **for words, letters, and symbols referred to as such and for foreign words**

    EXAMPLES   I had made two spelling errors in my report: I had added *i* after *l* in *similar* and had omitted *i* after *l* in *familiar.*

    Many epic poems begin *in medias res,* that is, "in the middle of the action."

its, it's (See page 413.)

EXAMPLES   **Its** [California's] nickname is the Golden State.
In land area **it's** [it is] the third-largest state in the Union.
It's [It has] been a state since 1850.

lie, lay (See page 194.)

EXAMPLES   As soon as he came home from school, Terence went to his room and **lay** down. [past tense of *lie*]

As soon as he came home from school, Terence **laid** his book bag down, took out his report card, and showed it to his father. [past tense of *lay*]

linking verb A linking verb connects its subject with a word that identifies or describes the subject. (See page 17.)

EXAMPLE   Brasilia **is** the capital of Brazil.

misplaced modifier A misplaced modifier is a word, phrase, or clause that seems to modify the wrong word or words in a sentence. (See page 250.)

MISPLACED   Written by Zeami Motokiyo, a videotaped performance of the Noh drama *Atsumori* inspired the drama club to write and produce a play in the style of the famous Japanese play-wright. [Was the performance written by Zeami Motokiyo?]

REVISED A videotaped performance of the Noh drama *Atsumori,* **written by Zeami Motokiyo,** inspired the drama club to write and produce a play in the style of the famous Japanese playwright.

modifier A modifier is a word or word group that makes the meaning of another word or word group more specific. (See page 228.)

EXAMPLE Forster **quickly** asked his **important** question.

mood Mood is the form a verb takes to indicate the attitude of the person using the verb. (See page 215. See also **imperative mood, indicative mood,** and **subjunctive mood.**)

nonessential clause/nonessential phrase A nonessential, or nonrestrictive, clause or phrase adds information not necessary to the main idea in the sentence and is set off by commas. (See page 338.)

EXAMPLES The lakeside hotel, **which was built in 1900,** is being renovated. [nonessential clause]

Juan and Howard, **the team's co-captains,** walked to the middle of the field. [nonessential phrase]

noun A noun names a person, place, thing, or idea. (See page 4.)

EXAMPLES The **study** of **subjects** such as **geography** and **chemistry** helps us to learn about the **world.**

Alsace is a **region** of **France.**

noun clause A noun clause is a subordinate clause used as a noun. (See page 87.)

EXAMPLE The main message of Ms. Pinckney's talk was **that we should always be punctual.**

number Number is the form a word takes to indicate whether the word is singular or plural. (See page 106.)

SINGULAR	chair	she	knife	child
PLURAL	chairs	they	knives	children

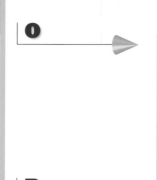

O

objective complement An objective complement is a word or word group that helps complete the meaning of a transitive verb by identifying or modifying the direct object. (See page 47.)

EXAMPLE   Sandy called her grandfather a **hero.**

object of a preposition An object of a preposition is the noun or pronoun that completes a prepositional phrase. (See page 60.)

EXAMPLE   He complained about **Minna.**

P

parallel structure Parallel structure is the use of the same grammatical forms or structures to balance related ideas in a sentence. (See page 475.)

NONPARALLEL   Each day, I reserve time for engaging in a forty-minute aerobic workout and to write in my journal.

PARALLEL   Each day, I reserve time **for engaging in a forty-minute aerobic workout** and **for writing in my journal.** [two prepositional phrases]

PARALLEL   Each day, I reserve time **to engage in a forty-minute aerobic workout** and **to write in my journal.** [two infinitive phrases]

parentheses (See page 384.)

EXAMPLES   The three small bones in the middle ear of a human (see diagram A) are the malleus (hammer), incus (anvil), and stapes (stirrup).

The three small bones in the middle ear of a human are the malleus (hammer), incus (anvil), and stapes (stirrup). (See diagram A.)

participial phrase A participial phrase consists of a participle and any complements and modifiers it has. (See page 65.)

EXAMPLE   The dog, **straining at the leash,** obviously wanted to go for a walk.

participle A participle is a verb form that can be used as an adjective. (See page 64.)

EXAMPLE   The painting depicts a calm landscape and **billowing** clouds.

passive voice The passive voice is the voice a verb is in when it expresses an action done to its subject. (See page 211. See also **voice.**)

EXAMPLE   Finally, Uncle Ed **was given** a promotion.

period (See **end marks.**)

phrase A phrase is a group of related words that does not contain both a verb and its subject and that is used as a single part of speech. (See page 59.)

EXAMPLES   Ahmed Nasr, **one of the Egyptian Embassy's attachés, will discuss** the excavations **in the Valley of the Kings.**
[*One of the Egyptian Embassy's attachés is an appositive phrase. Will discuss is a verb phrase. In the Valley of the Kings is a prepositional phrase.*]

Telling the truth is the best way **to stay out of trouble.**
[*Telling the truth is a gerund phrase. To stay out of trouble is an infinitive phrase.*]

Perching on a nearby branch, the bird sang a beautiful tune. [*Perching on a nearby branch is a participial phrase.*]

predicate The predicate is the part of a sentence that says something about the subject. (See page 39.)

EXAMPLE   **All his life,** he **wanted to walk along the Seine.**

predicate adjective A predicate adjective is an adjective that completes the meaning of a linking verb and modifies the subject of the verb. (See page 50.)

EXAMPLE   Grandma looked **rested** and **healthy.**

predicate nominative A predicate nominative is a noun or pronoun that completes the meaning of a linking verb and that identifies or refers to the subject of the verb. (See page 49.)

EXAMPLE   Joel is a **guitarist.**

prefix A prefix is a word part that is added before a base word or root. (See page 398.)

EXAMPLES   un + harmed = **un**harmed   im + proper = **im**proper mis + spoke = **mis**spoke   re + invest = **re**invest

mid + March = **mid**-March   ex + coach = **ex**-coach

self + addressed =   pre + Columbian =
    self-addressed   **pre**-Columbian

preposition A preposition shows the relationship of a noun or a pronoun to some other word in a sentence. (See page 23.)

EXAMPLE   *A Tale **of** Two Cities,* **by** Charles Dickens, is a novel **about** the French Revolution.

prepositional phrase A prepositional phrase includes a preposition, its object (a noun or a pronoun), and any modifiers of that object. (See page 60.)

EXAMPLE   **During class,** the teacher made us practice **for the exam.**

pronoun A pronoun is used in place of one or more nouns or pronouns. (See page 7.)

EXAMPLES   Paula left Mike alone, so as to give **him** more time.

                  Eric and Carla promised **they** would come to the party.

                  Everyone should get **himself** or **herself** a plate and a fork.

question mark (See **end marks.**)

quotation marks (See page 365.)

■ **for direct quotations**

EXAMPLE   **"**When using statistics in your writing,**"** said Mr. Torres, **"**you need to check more than one reliable source.**"**

■ **with other marks of punctuation** (See also preceding example.)

EXAMPLES   **"**In that year,**"** said Marlena, **"**the Commonwealth of Independent States was formed.**"**

            The teacher asked, **"**Which poem by Dylan Thomas ends **'**Rage, rage against the dying of the light**'?"**

■ **for titles**

EXAMPLES   **"**The Japanese Quince**"** [short story]

            "Do Not Go Gentle into That Good Night**"** [short poem]

            "Blowin' in the Wind**"** [song]

regular verb A regular verb is a verb that forms its past and past participle by adding *d* or *ed* to the base form. (See page 176. See also **irregular verb.**)

Base Form	Present Participle	Past	Past Participle
ask	[is] asking	asked	[have] asked
drown	[is] drowning	drowned	[have] drowned
perceive	[is] perceiving	perceived	[have] perceived
risk	[is] risking	risked	[have] risked
suppose	[is] supposing	supposed	[have] supposed
use	[is] using	used	[have] used

rise, raise (See page 196.)

EXAMPLES The price of a movie ticket is expected to **rise.**

The legislators are voting on whether to **raise** the minimum wage.

run-on sentence A run-on sentence is two or more complete sentences run together as one. (See page 483. See also **comma splice** and **fused sentence.**)

RUN-ON Frank Trilby and Benny O'Hara were a pair of Chicago detectives in the 1930s who specialized in tracking down those responsible for gangland executions, they made their name in a notorious case known as "The Navy Pier Slaying."

REVISED Frank Trilby and Benny O'Hara were a pair of Chicago detectives in the 1930s who specialized in tracking down those responsible for gangland executions; they made their name in a notorious case known as "The Navy Pier Slaying."

REVISED Frank Trilby and Benny O'Hara were a pair of Chicago detectives in the 1930s who specialized in tracking down those responsible for gangland executions. They made their name in a notorious case known as "The Navy Pier Slaying."

semicolon (See page 356.)

- **in compound sentences with no conjunction**

EXAMPLE The five-day forecast calls for unseasonably warm weather; daytime temperatures are expected to rise above seventy degrees Fahrenheit.

■ **in compound sentences with conjunctive adverbs or transitional expressions**

EXAMPLE   This story is written in the omniscient point of view**; that is,** the thoughts and actions of all of the characters are revealed to the reader by an all-knowing narrator who is not part of the story.

■ **between items in a series when the items contain commas**

EXAMPLE   The senior-class reading list includes *The Book of Songs,* an anthology of early Chinese poetry**;** *Panchatantra,* a collection of fables from India**;** and *Oedipus Rex,* a play by the Greek tragedian Sophocles.

sentence A sentence is a group of words that contains a subject and a verb and expresses a complete thought. (See page 36.)

                  S   **V**

EXAMPLE   **Rain falls** mostly on the central plains.

sentence fragment A sentence fragment is a group of words that is punctuated as if it were a complete sentence but that does not contain both a subject and a verb or that does not express a complete thought. (See page 36.)

FRAGMENT   Which is the growing of plants in solutions rather than in soils.

SENTENCE   The horticulturist explained the benefits of hydroponic gardening, which is the growing of plants in solutions rather than in soils.

FRAGMENT   Because she had left school early for her orthodontist appointment.

SENTENCE   Because she had left school early for her orthodontist appointment, Karen missed the pop quiz in her algebra class.

simple sentence A simple sentence has one independent clause and no subordinate clauses. (See page 94.)

EXAMPLES   May Francine and I have your mother's recipe for tabouli salad?

                  This magazine features an article about the Paiute writer and interpreter Thoc-me-tony, perhaps better known as Sarah Winnemucca.

sit, set (See page 195.)

EXAMPLES   Tamisha **sat** in the rocking chair, gently cradling her newly adopted Australian terrier puppy. [past tense of *sit*]

Emilia, who **set** this box of office supplies on the credenza? [past tense of *set*]

slow, slowly (See page 233.)

EXAMPLES   "**Slow** drivers can be as much of a menace on the road as fast drivers," said Erwin.

Dr. Emmet spoke very **slowly,** with a pronounced accent.

subject The subject tells whom or what a sentence is about. (See page 37.)

EXAMPLES   **Mr. Papastratos** proudly presided over the inauguration of his new restaurant.

Its **specialties** include moussaka, dolmades, and *keftedes*.

subject complement A subject complement is a word or word group that completes the meaning of a linking verb and identifies or describes the subject. (See page 49. See also **predicate nominative** and **predicate adjective.**)

EXAMPLES   Maurice's aunt is a college **administrator.**

The effect was **dramatic.**

subjunctive mood The subjunctive mood is used to express a suggestion, a necessity, a condition contrary to fact, or a wish. (See page 215.)

EXAMPLES   Ms. Chen recommended that Gloria **audition** for the leading role. [suggestion]

If I **were** you, I would have a skilled mechanic inspect the used car before I would consider buying it. [condition contrary to fact]

subordinate clause A subordinate, or dependent, clause does not express a complete thought and cannot stand alone as a sentence. (See page 83. See also **noun clause, adjective clause,** and **adverb clause.**)

EXAMPLE   **While we walk,** can we talk?

Grammar at a Glance   **595**

suffix A suffix is a word part that is added after a base word or root. (See page 399.)

EXAMPLES

habitual + ly = habitual**ly**　　easy + ly = easi**ly**

polite + ness = polite**ness**　　survey + or = survey**or**

believe + able = believ**able**　　manage + able = manage**able**

plan + ing = plann**ing**　　sugar + free = sugar-**free**

tense of verbs The tense of a verb indicates the time of the action or state of being expressed by the verb. (See page 198.)

Present Tense

I choose	we choose
you choose	you choose
he, she, it chooses	they choose

Past Tense

I chose	we chose
you chose	you chose
he, she, it chose	they chose

Future Tense

I will (shall) choose	we will (shall) choose
you will (shall) choose	you will (shall) choose
he, she, it will (shall) choose	they will (shall) choose

Present Perfect Tense

I have chosen	we have chosen
you have chosen	you have chosen
he, she, it has chosen	they have chosen

Past Perfect Tense

I had chosen	we had chosen
you had chosen	you had chosen
he, she, it had chosen	they had chosen

Future Perfect Tense

I will (shall) have chosen	we will (shall) have chosen
you will (shall) have chosen	you will (shall) have chosen
he, she, it will (shall) have chosen	they will (shall) have chosen

transitive verb A transitive verb is an action verb that takes an object. (See page 18.)

EXAMPLE   Jack, my poodle, **fetches** any ball as eagerly as a retriever would.

verb A verb expresses an action or a state of being. (See page 15.)

EXAMPLES   My cousin Ignacio **traveled** from the Arctic Circle to the Bay of Biscay.

            Where **is** the Bay of Biscay?

verbal A verbal is a form of a verb used as a noun, an adjective, or an adverb. (See page 64. See also **gerund, infinitive,** and **participle.**)

EXAMPLES   **Laughing** and **waving,** the president sat down. [participles]

            Hard work will help you **to succeed.** [infinitive]

            Make **saving** money a priority. [gerund]

verbal phrase A verbal phrase consists of a verbal and its modifiers and complements. (See page 64. See also **gerund phrase, infinitive phrase,** and **participial phrase.**)

EXAMPLES   **Schooled in ancient Celtic traditions,** the shanachie, or Irish storyteller, also sometimes learns **to sing folk songs.** [participial phrase/infinitive phrase]

            Brian will never forget **swimming in the ocean.** [gerund phrase]

verb phrase A verb phrase consists of a main verb and at least one helping verb. (See page 15.)

EXAMPLES   I **am sailing** across the bay.

            Have you ever **been** to Peru?

voice Voice is the form a transitive verb takes to indicate whether the subject of the verb performs or receives the action. (See page 211.)

ACTIVE VOICE   Percy Spencer **invented** the microwave oven in 1947.

PASSIVE VOICE   The microwave oven **was invented** by Percy Spencer in 1947.

RESOURCES

weak reference A weak reference is the incorrect use of a pronoun to refer to an antecedent that has not been expressed. (See page 167.)

WEAK Stephen King is a prolific writer; many of them have been made into films. [To what does *them* refer?]

REVISED Stephen King is a prolific writer; many of his **novels** have been made into films.

well (See *good, well.*)

who, whom (See page 152.)

EXAMPLES Family members, friends, and teachers are only a few of the people **who** play influential roles in our lives.

Advertisers, journalists, celebrities, and other people **whom** we have never met influence our lives every day, too.

wordiness Wordiness is the use of more words than necessary or of fancy words where simple ones will do. (See page 520.)

WORDY At the present time, I am currently reading a biography that chronicles the life of W.E.B. DuBois, who was an African American educator and writer who helped to cofound the National Association for the Advancement of Colored People (NAACP) in the year 1909.

REVISED Currently, I am reading a biography of W.E.B. DuBois, an African American educator and writer who cofounded the National Association for the Advancement of Colored People (NAACP) in 1909.

INDEX

documenting sources, 549–50
in-text citations, 549–50
legibility, 546, 547
margins, 548–49
MLA style model paper, 551–56
model research paper, 551–56
pagination, 548
paper and font style, 547
paraphrasing, 547, 549
parenthetical citations, 549–50
plagiarism, 547
preparing a manuscript, 546–47
quotations, 549–50, 553–55
spacing, 548–49
title page, 548
works cited page, 549, 556
Many, both, few, several, 126
Margins, manuscript form and, 548–49
Markham, Beryl, 368
"Mars Pathfinder Mission, The" (Golombek), 467
"Martín and Meditations on the South Valley" (Baca), 477
Match, **principal parts of,** 176
May, 218
"Meditation 17" (Donne), 356
Meet, **principal parts of,** 180
Middle English, 557, 559
Might, may, 218
Might of, 280
Miner, minor, 415
Misplaced modifiers, 250–51, 588–89
MLA Handbook for Writers of Research Papers, 547
MLA style model paper, 551–56
Modals, 16, 218–19
Model research paper, 551–56
Modern English, 557, 560
Modifiers. *See also* Adjective(s); Adverb(s).
clauses as, 229
comparison of, 236–42, 580
dangling modifiers, 252–53
definition of, 228, 589
diagramming sentences and, 532–33
double comparison of, 239
forms of, 228–29
fractions used as, 381
irregular comparison of, 237
linking verbs and, 230
misplaced modifiers, 250–51
one-word modifiers, 228
phrase modifiers, 516
phrases as, 229
regular comparison of, 236–37
single-word, 496
squinting modifiers, 250–51
troublesome modifiers, 232–33
two-way modifiers, 251

uses of, 230
varying sentence beginnings, 516
Momaday, N. Scott, 470
Mood of verbs
definition of, 589
imperative mood, 215
indicative mood, 215
subjunctive mood, 215–17
Moral, morale, 415
Multiple-choice questions, test-taking strategies and, 566–69
Must, 218
"Mustangs on the Move" (Mamatiuk), 504
Must of, 280
Myself, ourselves, 276

Nauseated, nauseous, 279
Negative, double negative, 286–87
Neuter pronouns, 139
Nguyen Thi Vinh, 373
Nightingale, Benedict, 500
1984 (Orwell), 503
Nominative case, 139–40. *See also* Predicate nominatives; Subjects.
Nonessential phrases and clauses, 86, 338–40, 344, 589
Nonsexist language, 288–89
Nonstandard English, 262, 564
Nor, or, 280
Not
as adverb, 20
Notorious, famous, 270
Noun(s)
abstract nouns, 4
collective nouns, 5
common nouns, 4
compound nouns, 5, 13
concrete nouns, 4
definition of, 4, 589
of direct address, 42
plurals of, 403–405
possessive nouns, 147, 374–77
preceding gerunds, 147
proper nouns, 4, 298–307
used as adjectives, 13
used as adverbs, 21
Noun clauses
combining sentences and, 506
definition of, 87, 589
diagramming sentences and, 540–41
introductory words for, 88
Nouns of direct address, diagramming sentences and, 530
Nowheres, 265

as integral part of sentence, 367
manuscript form and, 550
punctuation of, 327, 359, 365–69, 371–73, 385–86
reproducing exactly, 369
sic and, 369
within a quotation, 369

Raise, **principal parts of,** 196
Raise, rise, 196, 593
"Reach Your Peak" (Davidson), 470
Read, **principal parts of,** 188
Real, really, 233
Reason . . . because, 268
Reflexive pronouns, 8, 9, 150–51
Regional dialects, 563
Regular comparison of modifiers, 236–37
Regular verbs, 176–77, 593
Relative adverbs, 85–86
Relative pronouns
    functions of, 85
    list of, 9, 85
    pronoun-antecedent agreement, 130
    subject-verb agreement and, 120
    understood relative pronouns, 86, 88
    who, whom, 152–54
Remove, **principal parts of,** 176
Research paper. *See* Manuscript form.
Resolution
    capitalizing first word following *Resolved,* 296
Restrictive phrases. *See* Essential phrases and clauses.
Retained object, 211
Reverend, Honorable, 281
Ride, **principal parts of,** 184
Ring, **principal parts of,** 184
"Ring, The" (Dinesen), 373
Rise, **principal parts of,** 176, 184, 196
Rise, raise, 196, 593
"Rockpile, The" (Baldwin), 498
Run, **principal parts of,** 176, 184
Run-on sentences, 483–84
    definition of, 483, 593

Salutation of letter, punctuation of, 348, 360
Say, 281
    principal parts of, 180
Scarcely, 286
"Secret House, The" (Bodanis), 467
–sede, –cede, –ceed, 398
See, **principal parts of,** 184

Seek, **principal parts of,** 180
Sell, **principal parts of,** 180
Semicolons
    in compound sentences with conjunctive adverbs or transitional expressions, 594
    in compound sentences with no conjunction, 593
    between independent clauses, 356–57
    between items in series containing commas, 358, 594
    quotation marks and, 367
Send, **principal parts of,** 180
Sentence(s). *See also* headings beginning with Sentence.
    avoiding awkward combination, 476, 495, 499
    clarity in, 466–77
    classified by purpose, 97–98
    classified by structure, 94–96
    combining sentences for variety, 494–506
    complex sentences, 95–96
    compound-complex sentences, 96
    compound sentences, 41, 94–95, 336, 474, 503, 581
    coordinating ideas in, 466–68, 502–503
    declarative sentences, 97, 326
    definition of, 36, 594
    diagramming, 530–43
    end marks and, 326–27
    exclamatory sentences, 98
    faulty coordination in, 473–74
    fused sentences, 483
    imperative sentences, 97–98, 328, 586
    inserting prepositional phrases, 496
    inserting single-word modifiers, 496
    inserting words and phrases, 495–500
    interrogative sentences, 98, 326–27, 587
    obstacles to clarity in, 480–86
    parallel structure and, 475–77, 478
    reducing wordiness in, 520–24
    run-on sentences, 483–84
    sentence fragments, 36, 480–82, 594
    simple sentences, 41, 94, 95, 336, 594
    subordinating ideas in, 469–72, 504–506
    test-taking skills and, 566–70
    unnecessary shifts in, 485–86
    varying sentence beginnings, 515–17
    varying sentence length, 494–506
    varying sentence structure, 518–19
Sentence connectives, 467–68, 516–17
Sentence fragments. *See also* Sentence(s).
    accepted uses of, 37, 482
    definition of, 36, 480, 594
    revising sentences, 480–82
Sentence parts, 37–50
    complement, 44–50
    predicate, 37–41
    subject, 37–38, 40–42
Sentence structure
    complex sentences, 95–96
    compound-complex sentences, 96

ACKNOWLEDGMENTS

The permission to reprint copyrighted material, grateful acknowledgment is made to the following sources:

The Asia Society: "Thoughts of Hanoi" by Hguyen Thi Vinh, translated by Nguyen Ngoc Bich from *A Thousand Years of Vietnamese Poetry.* Copyright © 1975 by The Asia Society.

Anita Desai, c/o Rogers, Coleridge & White Ltd., 20 Powis Mews, London W11 1JN: From "Games at Twilight" from *Games at Twilight and Other Stories* by Anita Desai. Copyright © 1978 by Anita Desai. Published by William Heinemann.

Farrar, Straus & Giroux, LLC.: From "One Art" from *The Complete Poems 1927–1979* by Elizabeth Bishop. Copyright © 1979, 1983 by Alice Helen Methfessel.

Steve Faulkner: From "Common Water" by Steve Faulkner from *DoubleTake,* Winter 1998. Copyright © 1998 by Steve Faulkner.

George Lamming: From *In the Castle of My Skin* by George Lamming. Copyright © 1970 by Longman Group Limited. Published by Schocken Books Inc.

New Directions Publishing Corp.: From *Martín and Meditations on the South Valley* by Jimmy Santiago Baca. Copyright © 1987 by Jimmy Santiago Baca.

Newsweek, Inc.: From "www.Apply-Here.com" by T. Trent Gegax from *Newsweek,* October 19, 1998. Copyright © 1998 by Newsweek, Inc. All rights reserved.

North Point Press, a division of Farrar, Straus & Giroux, LLC.: From *West with the Night* by Beryl Markham. Copyright © 1942, 1983 by Beryl Markham.

University of Notre Dame Press: From *Barrio Boy* by Ernesto Galarza. Copyright © 1971 by University of Notre Dame Press.

SOURCES CITED
From a Mauritanian proverb from *African Proverbs,* compiled by Charlotte and Wolf Leslau. Published by Peter Pauper Press, Inc., White Plains, NY, 1985.

PHOTO/ILLUSTRATION CREDITS

Abbreviation used: (tl) top left, (tc) top center, (tr) top right, (l) left, (lc) left center, (c) center, (rc) right center, (r) right, (bl) bottom left, (bc) bottom center, (br) bottom right.

COVER: Kim Taylor/Bruce Coleman, Inc.

TABLE OF CONTENTS: Page iv, Photo Edit; v, Bill Aron/Photo Edit; vi, Tony Duffy/Allsport; viii, The Lowe Art Museum, The University of Miami/SuperStock; ix, Jeff Greenberg/David R. Frazier Photolibrary; xi, SuperStock; xiii, Royal Ontario Museum, Toronto Canada/HRW Photo Research Library; xiv, NASA; xv, Walter Bibikow/FPG International; xvii, Reuters/Dwight Andrews/Archive Photos; xxi, Sam Dudgeon/HRW; xxii, Sam Dudgeon/HRW; xxiii, HRW Photo Research Library.

CHAPTER 1: Page 6, AP/Wide World Photos; 15, FPG International; 20, Bill Aron/Photo Edit; 30, John Pinderhughes/The Stock Market.

CHAPTER 2: Page 43 (cl) (cr), The Lowe Art Museum, The University of Miami/SuperStock; 48, Michael Newman/PhotoEdit; 53 (tl) (tr), Bruno Barbey/Magnum Photos.

CHAPTER 3: Page 61, David Austen /Woodfin Camp & Associates; 63 (cr), Everett/CSU Archives; 68, Josef Armendariz/HRW Photo; 73, Sygma Paris; 75, Georgia Lowell/Photo Researchers, Inc.

CHAPTER 4: Page 84, British Museum, London/Art Resource, NY; 87, Corbis Images; 90, Courtesy of Dr. Athelstian Spilhaus; 92, Image Copyright © 2001 Photodisc, Inc.; 99, Corbis Images.

CHAPTER 5: Page 111, George Rinhart/Corbis-Bettmann; 114, SuperStock; 122, Walter Bibikow/FPG International; 123, Granitsas/The Image Works.

CHAPTER 6: Page 143, Tony Duffy/Allsport; 146, Baldwin H. Ward & Kathryn C. Ward/CORBIS.

CHAPTER 7: Page 166, Stock Montage, Inc.

CHAPTER 8: Page 182, Corbis Images; 185, Michel Garnier-Explorer/Photo Researchers, Inc.; 187, Fred Hirschmann; 193, The Avery Brundage Collection. Asian Art Museum of San Francisco.

CHAPTER 9: Page 232, Everett Collection; 235 (cr), Archive Photos; 244, The Kobal Collection.

CHAPTER 10: Page 255, The Granger Collection, New York.

CHAPTER 11: Page 267, Schomburg Center for Research in Black Culture. The New York Public Library; 273, The Granger Collection, New York; 285, Lawrence Migdale.

CHAPTER 12: Page 309, NASA; 315, Stan Byers.

CHAPTER 13: Page 338, Jeff Greenberg/David R. Frazier Photolibrary; 341, Photo Edit; 350, Mike Yamashita.

CHAPTER 14: Page 362, AP/Wide World Photos; 387, UPI/Corbis-Bettmann.

CHAPTER 15: Page 402, Photographs and Prints Division Schomburg Center for Research in Black Culture. The New York Public Library. Astor Lennox, and Tilden Foundations.; 403, Bob Strong/The Image Works; 409, Peter Van Steen/HRW Photo; 420, SuperStock.

CHAPTER 16: Page 429, HRW Photo Research Library; 430, Image Copyright © 2003 PhotoDisc, Inc.; 432, © 1997 Radlund & Associates for Artville; 437 (c), Planet Art; 438, Richard Weiss/HRW Photo Research Library; 451, Royal Ontario Museum, Toronto Canada/HRW Photo Research Library.

CHAPTER 17: Page 468, Culver Pictures, Inc.; 469, Bettmann/CORBIS; 474 (tr) (cl), Gary Retherford/Photo Researchers, Inc.; 479, Photofest; 481, Fred McConnaughey/Photo Researchers, Inc.; 487 (tl), Sinclair Stammers/Science Photo Library; 487 (br), The Gamma Liaison Network.

CHAPTER 18: Page 495, Ed Carlin/Archive Photos; 497, Larry West/FPG International; 499, Corbis/Bettmann-UPI; 502, NASA/Peter Arnold, Inc.; 507 (tr)(cr), Photofest; 508, Steve Vidler/Nawrocki Stock Photo.

CHAPTER 19: Page 516, Runk/Schoenberger/Grant Heilman Photography; 517, The Granger Collection, New York; 518, The Stock Market; 523, Reuters/Dwight Andrews/Archive Photos; 525, Photofest.

ART CREDITS: All art, unless otherwise noted, by Holt, Rinehart & Winston.

Page 63, Ortelius Design; 108, John Edwards; 191, Ortelius Design; 222, Rondi Collette; 256, MapQuest.com; 396, Leslie Kell; 526, Ortelius Design.